EUROPEAN CRIMINAL

EUROPEAN CRIMINAL LAW

An Integrative Approach

ANDRÉ KLIP

intersentia

Antwerp – Oxford – Portland

Distribution for the UK:
Hart Publishing Ltd.
16C Worcester Place
Oxford OX1 2JW
UK
Tel.: +44 1865 51 75 30
Fax: +44 1865 51 07 10

*Distribution for Switzerland and
Germany:*
Schulthess Verlag
Zwingliplatz 2
CH-8022 Zürich
Switzerland
Tel.: +41 1 251 93 36
Fax: +41 1 261 63 94

Distribution for the USA and Canada:
International Specialized Book Services
920 NE 58th Ave Suite 300
Portland, OR 97213
USA
Tel.: +1 800 944 6190 (toll free)
Tel.: +1 503 287 3093
Fax: +1 503 280 8832
Email: info@isbs.com

Distribution for other countries:
Intersentia Publishers
Groenstraat 31
BE-2640 Mortsel
Belgium
Tel.: +32 3 680 15 50
Fax: +32 3 658 71 21

European Criminal Law. An Integrative Approach
André Klip

Artwork on front and back cover: Titian, 'The Rape of Europe', 1559-1562, Isabella
Stuart Gardner Museum (Boston).

© 2009 Intersentia
   Antwerp – Oxford – Portland
   www.intersentia.com

ISBN 978-90-5095-772-4
D/2009/7849/7
NUR 824

PREFACE

What should the future of European criminal law be? Are we going to see further competences for the Union, while, at the same time, limiting national competences? I have raised these and similar questions every year since Treaty on European Union was concluded in Maastricht in 1992, when teaching courses on European Criminal Law. Students and practitioners alike were, by and large, consistent in their answers. They could, more or less, accept the developments to date at the time and were absolutely clear in stating that further European integration in the field of criminal law was undesirable. I found the consistency of this attitude over the years more and more fascinating, as it almost invariably remained unaffected by new treaties on further integration, new steps in case law of the Court, and enlargement with further Member States.

The idea for this book goes back to a common plan of Professor John Vervaele and myself made in 1999, when both of us worked at Utrecht University. I am most grateful to John for having introduced me to the law of the European Communities and its relevance for national criminal law in the early 1990s. However, the plan for the book had to be abandoned and impressive changes in circumstances made the 1999 outline into a historical document, which testified to the unbelievable changes that have taken place in the last decade. After the experience of having had to abandon my plan to write a book on European criminal law before, I realise how privileged I have been by the circumstances that allowed me to write this volume: I was able to take sabbatical leave in the academic year 2007–2008 due to a replacement subsidy of the *Nederlandse Organisatie voor Wetenschappelijk Onderzoek*, and my concentration on writing was further facilitated by the Department of Criminal Law and Criminology and by the Faculty of Law of Maastricht University which relieved me of my administrative obligations.

I am honoured with the comments on my drafts which I received from two panels. One panel consisted of colleagues and experts in the field. I owe many thanks to Dr. Pedro Caeiro (the University of Coimbra), Professor Michele Caianiello (the University of Bologna), Professor John Spencer (the University of Cambridge) and Professor John Vervaele (the University of Utrecht) for their willingness to comment on my drafts, whilst they were already overcommitted. The other panel that assisted me was an internal panel, consisting of colleagues of mine from the department at Maastricht University. I am most grateful to Jeroen Blomsma, Gerard de Jonge, Johannes Keiler, Maartje Krabbe, Anne-Sophie Massa, Christina Peristeridou and Martijn Zwiers. The assistance of this internal panel is also evidence that the research group on European criminal law has come into being. The comments of both panels have greatly improved the quality of the book.

Laura Bosch has provided me with most accurate help as a student-assistant. She enabled me to go through the approximately 750 Court cases in a structured manner. I am indebted to her for her patience in complying with my numerous requests for yet another document. I am also grateful to the assistance of Steffi Menz and of my secretary, Lydie Coenegrachts, who also protected me against those who might intrude upon the writing process. I thank Lucas van der Heijden for giving me shelter "far from the madding crowd". The co-operation with Chris Engert, who took care of editing the book, was one of the last, but also most pleasant, stages of writing this book.

I acknowledge once again the great co-operation with Hans Kluwer of Intersentia Publishers, who, after some eighteen volumes of *Annotated Leading Cases of International Criminal Tribunals* was willing to take the risk of publishing on an entirely different area of criminal law. Last, but not least, I thank all the students, practitioners and colleagues in court who shaped the structure of this book by raising persistent questions on European criminal law. The book has been written for students, practitioners and academics alike.

I would appreciate any comments and observations, and would be happy to try and answer any questions that any reader might have (andre.klip@strafr. unimaas.nl).

André Klip,
Maastricht, November 2008

TABLE OF CONTENTS

PART II.   CRIMINAL LAW IN THE EUROPEAN UNION

CHAPTER 4.
EUROPEAN SUBSTANTIVE CRIMINAL LAW

ANNEXES

LIST OF ABBREVIATIONS

CISA	Convention Implementing the Schengen Agreement
ECHR	European Convention of Human Rights
EComHR	European Commission of Human Rights
ECR	European Court Reports
ECtHR	European Court of Human Rights
ICC	International Criminal Court
OJ	Official Journal of the European Union
OLAF	Office de Coordination de la Lutte Anti-Fraude
par.	paragraph
SIS	Schengen Information System
TEC	Treaty establishing the European Community
TEU	Treaty on European Union
TFEU	Treaty on the Functioning of the European Union

CHAPTER 1.
INTRODUCTION

1. EUROPEAN CRIMINAL LAW

European criminal law deals with a multi-layered patchwork of legislation and case law in which both national and European courts, European and national legislatures, and other authorities and bodies play a role. It is a hybrid system, even though it does possess common notions and values, which justifies its classification as a separate field of law. European criminal law is also about the development of a criminal justice system for the European Union, which must be considered as a progressive task in act. Despite the fact that criminal law did not belong to the central areas of Community law in the first decades of the European Community, rules and principles which were applicable to criminal law gradually emerged. With the conclusion of the Treaty of Maastricht in 1992, criminal law was finally brought within the formal influence of Union law. Thus, the Maastricht Treaty started an ongoing process of the Europeanisation of national criminal law, a process whose final goals are still not within sight.

European criminal law is an evolving area of law, a field of law in transition which gradually changes its nature. In the past, competences in criminal law were exclusively the realm of the individual states. Reviewing the situation in the year 2009, many competences have been conferred to the European Union. However, most powers of the European Union in the field of criminal law are not exclusive, but are, instead, jointly executed with the Member States. One example is the prohibition of insider dealing by the European Union, which has to be enforced by the Member States via their own criminal law. The norms have been formulated at European level, but their implementation and enforcement takes place at national level. Another example is the mutual recognition of all kinds of documents throughout the European Union, sometimes on the basis of a specific Directive (for example, driving licences), or Framework Decision (for example, the European Arrest Warrant), sometimes on the basis of a general rule (no checks on goods already legally on the market). The aim of this book is to present a coherent picture of the influence of Union law in national criminal law and criminal procedure, and to sketch the contours of the emerging European criminal justice system within the Union.

European criminal law is defined as the multilevel field of law in which the European Union either has normative influence on substantive criminal law and criminal procedure or on the co-operation between the Member States. This is supplemented by the area in which the European Union directly enforces criminal law: namely, competition law and the European Public Prosecutor's Office. The first part thus deals with indirect enforcement of Union law by national authorities making use of national criminal law, while the second part deals with direct enforcement by bodies of the Union.

This definition of *European criminal law*, however, says more about the European Union character of the law, than of its criminal nature. What, then, should be regarded as *criminal* law? In this book, the definition that has been given to the criminal nature of a charge as defined in Article 6 of the European Convention of Human Rights (ECHR) will be followed. The European Court of Human Rights (ECtHR) defined *criminal* in the landmark case of *Öztürk* in 1984.[1] The ECtHR held that the criminal nature of the penalty can be deducted from the general character of the rule and the purpose of the penalty, which are deterrent and punitive. The use of this definition as such has been widely accepted as the definition which separates criminal law from other fields of law, and is confirmed by the ECtHR in consistent case law. The definition that national law attaches to a specific area of law is immaterial. One of the consequences of the use of the ECHR definition is that, in this book, competition law is regarded as criminal law.[2] As a result, and contrary to the message embodied in Article 23, paragraph 5 Regulation 1/2003 on competition law, which states that "Decisions taken pursuant to paragraph 1 and 2 shall not be of a criminal nature", competition law will be regarded as criminal law throughout this book. At this stage, it may be sufficient to mention that the Court itself uses all the principles that are guaranteed under the ECHR as principles relevant to the field of competition law.[3] Although a direct statement that competition law *is* criminal law is avoided by the Court,[4] it nonetheless *does* apply the principles relevant to criminal proceedings derived from the ECHR to competition law, and does, in practice, treat it *as* criminal law.

---

[1]   ECtHR, 21 February 1984, *Öztürk* v. *Germany*, Application 8544/79. See, further, Chapter 4, Section 2.

[2]   While, in the past, one of the arguments to consider competition law as falling out of the scope of criminal law related to the fact that it dealt with legal entities, and that imprisonment could not be imposed, this argument has lost considerable weight given the criminal liability of entities in the European Union. See Chapter 4, Section 3.6.

[3]   See, for instance, the reference to Article 7, paragraph 1, ECHR in 8 February 2007, Case C-3/06 P, *Groupe Danone* [2007] ECR I-1331, par. 88. See, also, Advocate General Léger: "It cannot be disputed (…) that, in the light of the case-law of the European Court of Human Rights and the Opinions of the European Commission of Human Rights, the present case involves a 'criminal charge'." Opinion of Advocate General Léger of 3 February 1998, Case C-185/95 P, *Baustahlgewebe GmbH* v. *Commission* [1998] ECR I-8417, point 31.

[4]   See, as an example, the Opinion of Advocate General Stix-Hackl of 26 September 2002, Case C-199/99P, *Corus UK Ltd* v. *Commission* [2003] ECR I-11177, point 150.

Later, the question of whether Union law itself defines criminal law will be discussed.[5]

2.   THE STRUCTURE OF THE BOOK

The existing works on Union law mainly deal with Union law in a top-down manner. They deal with the influence of Union law *in abstracto*, and not with its impact upon the national legal orders. The emphasis is almost exclusively focussed upon the European rule, and far less attention is dedicated to the relationship between Union law and national law. However, the application of Union law in the practice of national procedures does take place under the *mutual* influence of Union law *and* national criminal law. One should distinguish between clear and absolute cases of priority of Union law, and cases of relative priority. In cases of absolute priority, the freedoms that exist upon the basis of Union law may not be interfered with by national criminal law. In cases of relative priority of Union law, Union law narrows the discretion of states to a certain extent, while, at the same time, allowing for specific national regulation. The message is that the application of Union law or national law is not a straightforward black or white decision, but may, instead, include all kinds of grey zones. What are the procedural consequences when national law must be set aside because of overriding Union law: a decision of *non-lieu*, an acquittal, the dismissal of the charges, *etc.*? These are examples of the type of questions that will be dealt with in Chapter 5. Thus, this book combines a top-down approach (the perspective of the Union with a focus upon the obligations of the Member States) with a bottom-up approach (the perspective from the national criminal justice system, with a focus upon the position of the accused).

For the majority of situations, the application of *both* Union law *and* national criminal law cannot be reduced to a simple question of one having priority over the other. One may see situations in which principles of Union law may be overriding, but in which it may, at the same time, allow for further elaboration upon the basis of national law. It is here that the specific position of certain general principles of criminal law comes to the fore. Examples of this include the prohibition of retroactive force, the *nulla poena* rule, the principle that a suspect cannot be forced to incriminate himself, the *lex mitior* rule, the principle of proportionality, the principle of guilt, the *lex certa* principle, and the *ne bis in idem* principle. Under certain circumstances, these principles may override fundamental freedoms under Union law. It is important to identify when and under which circumstances this is the case. It is one of the aims of this book to

---

5   See Chapter 4, Section 2.

convey the understanding of European criminal law as a field of law in which there is, by definition, an overlap between Union law and national law.

This book also departs from the clear separation of the law into the law of the *internal market* and the law of the *area of freedom, security and justice*. Although these categorisations are still functional to a certain extent, there are various reasons to opt for another more integrative structure which recognises the convergence of the two areas as codified in the Treaties. However, this development had already started before the adoption of the Lisbon Treaty in December 2007. The institutional developments, as well as the case law of the Court of Justice, did not maintain the institutional distinction between the two areas as provided in the Treaty of Maastricht (or in pre-Lisbon terms: the First and the Third Pillar).

One important underlying assumption in this book is that a European criminal justice system is already in place. However, it is fragmentary and inconsistent in many aspects, but it is, gradually, taking shape. This approach has been chosen for two reasons. Firstly, it presents the European criminal justice system at the stage at which it presently exists. It demonstrates both its strengths and its weaknesses. It will provide those working in the field with a coherent picture with which to enable them to elaborate. For example, if one studies the interpretation of the principle of *ne bis in idem* in the context of criminal proceedings, this cannot be done without knowledge of the case law of the Court on *ne bis in idem* with regard to other topics. In other areas, such as mutual recognition, it is much more appropriate to look at the practice in civil law. If this book has one message to convey to criminal lawyers, it is that there is much more criminal law than one would assume from a mere national approach. The coherence of European criminal law can only be discovered by looking at all the relevant sources, including those not of a purely criminal nature.

The second reason to present European criminal law as a criminal justice system lies with its hybrid character. It is definitely incomplete as a separate system and does not intend to abolish the existing national criminal justice systems of the Member States. It provides an important role for the Member States. When European criminal law is presented in an integrative manner, it will be possible to identify the mutual influence of Union law and national law in criminal law. With this approach, it will be possible to delineate both the competences of the European Union and those of the Member States more precisely.

The book was written for both criminal lawyers as well as for European lawyers, for practitioners, and for academics as well as for students in European criminal law. It has the ambition that the mutual influence of Union law and criminal law is assessed in its proportions. Sometimes, Union law will prevail, and, occasionally, national criminal law will prevail over Union law. However, in the large area in between these extremes, both Union law and criminal law and criminal procedure influence the law in practice. Its case law orientated approach will clearly state what the law is on the relevant issues.

The book is divided into four parts and is composed of nine chapters.

In Part I, *The Legal Order of the Union*, consisting of Chapters 2 and 3, the general influence of Union law on national criminal justice systems is discussed. This part analyses the issues of a general institutional nature without which one cannot understand the functioning of the European Union in a criminal justice system. The issues selected are of particular importance for those who are more familiar with criminal law but less expert in European institutional law. Those trained in European (institutional) law will find themselves much more at ease in this part than those who have more experience in criminal law. With the growing importance of the Union for criminal law, students and practitioners of criminal law will find some background in the institutional foundations of the European Union and the constitutional principles of Union law indispensable. In other words, Part I can be described as what criminal lawyers need to know about European (institutional) law. As already stated, this is not a book on European institutional law. Users more interested in the latter will find, for instance, that the procedures on decision-making in the European Union and the democratic accountability and many other issues are only briefly mentioned. Despite its general importance, these are topics that do not directly relate to criminal litigation. In consequence, Part I concentrates on the obligations which Union law imposes upon Member States that may influence criminal law.

Chapter 2, *Institutional Foundations of the European Union*, is the least legally-technical chapter of the book. It deals with the coming into being of the European Union and the ideas that lie behind its legal initiatives. This is all described to the extent necessary to understand the context in which criminal justice systems now function in the European Union. It underlines the concept of European integration and the mechanisms that are applied to further its cause. The approach of this chapter is top-down, from the European origin to its implementation by the Member States.

In Chapter 3, *Constitutional Principles of Union Law*, the book starts to become more legally-technical. Again, the focus in this chapter is European. It concentrates on the legal instruments that the Union possesses and their meaning and influence. Despite the absence of a codified European Constitution, several principles and rules have obtained a status that justifies their classification as being constitutional in a broader sense. The common applicable principles on enforcement and implementation which have been developed in Union law play a role. What are the obligations that rest upon the Member States of the European Union? When answering this question, criminal law comes into the picture, but only as one of the fields to which these common principles and general issues apply. In Chapter 3 the individual citizen comes more to the fore. How does he profit from Union law? In this context, the chapter sets out the fundamental importance of the so-called five freedoms, and concludes with a large section on the interpretation of the law by the Court of Justice. On the one hand, this section explains the method by which the Court interprets the law. On the other, it forms a bridge to the second part of the book. In sketching its rules of interpretation, the Court also gives guidance to the courts and other authorities of the Member States on how to apply Union law. It is through the Court's supervision that the unity of the legal order is guaranteed. The approach of this chapter is mixed. It deals both with the demands of Union law, as with the ways in which Member States may meet these obligations and the discretion that they have in this process.

In Part II, *Criminal law in the European Union*, consisting of Chapters 4, 5 and 6, it will be shown that the European Union has legislated in the field of criminal law, but has left most of the implementation and enforcement of this law to the Member States. The perspective of Part II is the opposite to that of Part I. In this part, the influence of Union law on the criminal justice systems of the Member States is the angle from which issues of a substantive criminal legal nature or procedural nature are dealt with. The fact that these issues have a relation with Union law is secondary.

The Treaty on the Functioning of the European Union maintains the classical distinction between substantive criminal law, regulated in Article 83, and criminal procedure regulated in Article 82. As a corollary, Chapter 4, *European Substantive Criminal Law*, and Chapter 5, *European Criminal Procedure*, follow this distinction. In Chapter 5, in particular, attention is paid to the concerns of national courts, when they adjudicate in cases of European criminal law. Chapter 6, *European Sentencing and Penitentiary Law*, deals with the first steps in this area.

Where the angle of approach in Part II is from the viewpoint of the individual Member State and the parties involved in criminal proceedings, Part III changes the perspective again. In this part, *European Co-operation and European Enforcement*, a national perspective is abandoned, and a common European approach to combating crime emerges. The integrative approach can be summarised as follows: Part I deals with the influence of Union law on (mainly) indirect enforcement by the Member States; Part II covers the consequences of this for the national criminal justice systems of the Member States. A third dimension is chosen in Part III, which consists of Chapters 7 and 8, and deals with the interaction between the Member States in the field of criminal law. It will be demonstrated that the law applicable on co-operation between the Member States is of a common European origin. Unlike all other regional organisations, the European Union has created a system of co-operation of its own. Chapter 7, *Bilateral Co-Operation in Criminal Matters*, deals with all the forms of co-operation developed within the European Union as well as the use that is made of the framework created by the Council of Europe. It is shown that the Union has developed a model of its own: namely, mutual recognition. Chapter 8, *Multi-Lateral Co-Operation and Direct Enforcement*, discusses the various forms in which the Union has developed bodies of its own, which provide multilateral co-operation. Additionally, the European Union has taken steps to ensure the enforcement of Union law itself. In some fields, it can refer to the experience of some decades (competition law), while, in other fields, European enforcement is only now in the process of being started (the European Public Prosecutor's Office).

In Part IV, *The Challenges of European Criminal Law*, which consists of Chapter 9, *Rethinking European Criminal Law*, the challenges for European criminal law are sketched out and commented upon. In this part, an analysis is made of issues that deserve specific attention and need to be regulated. Where possible the author presents his recommendations. The book is supplemented with annexes. An index is included, as well as a Table of Case Law, a Table of Legislation, and a bibliography.

3.   THE TREATY OF LISBON AND THE USE OF TERMINOLOGY

Throughout the book, the new terminology, as applicable after the Treaty of Lisbon has taken effect, has been used. This means that the terminology used is exclusively the European Union or the *Union* and *Union Law*. However, the terminology which dates from the pre-Lisbon era, such as European Community, European Communities and Community law may appear in the quotations of case law and legislation. *Union law* is the term used to indicate the law of the European Union. It subsumes previous categorisations, such as *Community Law/ First Pillar law* and *EU Law/ Third Pillar Law*. With *Community Law*, which may still appear in quotations, and, occasionally, in the main text, in situations in which the author wishes to express a distinction, it refers to the body of law that resulted from the Treaty on the establishment of the European Community.

The currently applicable treaties are referred to in the following manner. With the entrance into force of the Lisbon Treaty, the existing Treaty on European Union (EU) has been amended and will be referred to as the *Treaty on European Union* (TEU). The Treaty establishing the European Community will be renamed as *Treaty on the Functioning of the European Union*. It will be abbreviated in this book as TFEU. The *Treaty on the Functioning of the European Union* and the *Treaty on European Union* constitute the Treaties on which the Union is founded. Together, they are referred to as *the Treaties*. The *Treaty establishing the European Community* (TEC) and the pre-Lisbon version of the Treaty on European Union

(EU) will be mentioned when it is necessary for the understanding of a specific topic. Throughout the text, the consistency of the old treaties to the new treaties has been expressed by referring to the previously applicable provisions (for example, Article 49 TFEU, formerly Article 43 TEC).

At the moment of the conclusion of the manuscript, it remains uncertain whether, and if so, when, the Treaty of Lisbon will enter into force. The only certainty is that it will not enter into force on 1 January 2009, the day provided in the Treaty of Lisbon. What are the practical consequences for using this book until the Treaty of Lisbon has formally entered into force? The references to the provisions of the Treaty on European Union (TEU) and to the Treaty on the Functioning of the European Union (TFEU) have their equivalents in the older treaties. In most cases, this reference has already been made in the main text. Where not, the reader is referred to the Tables of Equivalence.[6] Two other consequences of the Treaty of Lisbon not having yet entered into force must also be mentioned. These relate to the legal instruments that may be adopted by the Union,[7] and the competences of the Commission and the Court.[8] For the rest, the view is taken that the consequences are limited and that the main function of the Treaty of Lisbon is the codification of the Court's case law.

The last important topic in the context of criminal law is the confusing use of the vocabulary "fundamental rights" and "fundamental freedoms". This confusion might be greater for criminal lawyers than for specialists in European law. The practice of the Court which sharply distinguishes between the two concepts will be followed. *Fundamental rights* is the term reserved for the rights and freedoms guaranteed by the ECHR and other human rights treaties given to anyone within the jurisdiction of the state parties. *Fundamental freedoms* are the rights given to citizens by the TFEU within the Union: free movement of persons, goods, services and capital, as well as, more recently, free movement and residence, together also referred to as the five freedoms.

4. METHODOLOGY AND CHARACTERISATION OF THE LAW

As a consequence of the European approach, the book cannot deal with the particularities of each national criminal justice system of the Member States. It does not deal with national criminal law or national criminal procedure. Apart from the fact that this would require linguistic skills – which are not available for the study of all the national systems in their original language – it would extend

---

6   See Tables of Equivalence, Annexes.
7   It is referred to Chapter 3, Section 2.
8   See Chapter 2, Section 5; Chapter 3, Section 5.1.

the scope of the book beyond its European limits. However, the book tries to come as close as possible to the concrete relationship with national criminal justice systems. All chapters of Part II discuss the practical and legal consequences of various European obligations under national law. For instance, in Chapter 5, the consequences of a finding that a rule of national law cannot be applied is dealt with.

Another field of law, which, despite its European origin, has not been included extensively, is that of the Council of Europe. The focus of the book is one from the European Union perspective. European criminal law has been understood and defined as the law of the European Union. Although the law created by the Council of Europe does not play a central role in this book, to a certain extent, the *acquis* of the Council of Europe has been incorporated into the law of the Union. The two most relevant areas are given the attention that they merit: namely, the influence of the ECHR and the treaty network created by the Council of Europe in co-operation in criminal matters.

The method of writing this book was the following: the principles and rules relevant for European criminal law were filtered from primary sources: the legislation of the EU, as well as from the case law of the Court of Justice. All Conventions, Framework Decisions, Decisions and other relevant instruments adopted in the former Third Pillar have been incorporated. In addition, a representative selection was taken from Directives and Regulations. In referring to Directives and Regulations, is the author aimed to create awareness of certain influences and effects, not to give a complete overview of all existing Directives and Regulations that might have a possible influence on criminal law. Apart from the practical impossibility of performing such a task, this is justified by the fact that the influence of these legal instruments depends on the choice that individual Member States made with regard to the field of law for their implementation. A restriction with regard to the acts included in this book is found in the fact that only adopted legislation has been discussed. Occasionally, it is briefly referred to pending proposals.

With regard to the selection of cases, the following is worth noting. In principle, all cases relating to criminal proceedings, as well as cases in which issues of relevance to criminal law were discussed, have been studied. In addition, the case law of the Court on the general notions of Union law have been used. The result is that many more cases have been referred to than criminal cases alone. However, this is justified because of the fact that it has been established that the Court does not interpret Union law with a view to its implementation and influence in a specific (national) area of law. The fact that none of the various areas of law is immune to the influence of Union law justifies looking at a context much larger than that of criminal law alone.

Union law does not necessarily follow institutional divisions and may not draw upon writings of others, as may be found elsewhere. European criminal law was not designed following a master plan. It came into being as a consequence of an accumulation of entirely different and unrelated political and legal developments. The ambition aspired to in this book is to picture the fragments of an incomplete system into a regular criminal justice system. This not only makes it easier to understand its functioning, but also provides insight into its *lacunae*. It should enable the reader to recognise the character of European criminal law, independent of whether the political developments are favourable to the creation of direct criminal law enforcement by the European Union, or leave the enforcement of criminal law with the Member States, as is currently the case.

This finally brings us to the characterisation of European criminal law as a kind of *common law*. The main developments of the law take place under the influence of the Court. Revolutionary steps are often taken by decisions of the Court, not by amending the treaties, which often codify the developments in the case law of the Court. There are statutory elements of Union law, but they leave a relatively wide degree of discretion. European criminal law is definitively case law orientated. Legislation is instructive because it is dependent on implementation. The legal order of the Union has been codified incompletely. This both forces and allows the Court to make use of the discretion at its disposition to state the law. The Court has formulated rules of interpretation and recognised general principles of Union law. On the other hand, unlike the courts of common law jurisdictions, the Court does not refer to academic writings at all. However, Advocates General do refer to doctrine extensively.[9] To recognise the nature of Union law as being similar to common law may help the understanding of European criminal law, especially for those trained in continental jurisdictions.

5.   CONCLUSION OF THE MANUSCRIPT

The developments in legislation and case law are inclusive up to 1 November 2008.

---

[9]   The reader will notice the absence of any reference to literature in the text and footnotes. The main works consulted are referred to in the Selected Bibliography.

PART I.
THE LEGAL ORDER
OF THE UNION

The first part of this book deals with the general notions of Union law, which are of an institutional and constitutional character. What is Union law comprised of, and how can it be stated and interpreted? The general notions apply to all fields of law, including criminal law and criminal procedure. Part I focuses upon the balance between the freedoms to which Union citizens are entitled and the restrictions of these freedoms upon the basis of national (criminal) law. Due to its general approach, this part is mainly concerned with the obligations that Member States have in complying with the Treaties. It will be identified that one of these obligations is that individuals must have to possibility of directly invoking provisions of Union law. The notion that Union law creates rights and obligations for Member States as well as for individuals will be further elaborated on in Part II, in which the focus is narrowed down and limited to criminal law exclusively.

CHAPTER 2.
INSTITUTIONAL FOUNDATIONS
OF THE EUROPEAN UNION

1.   INTRODUCTION

Although the complex institutional framework of the European Union is not the central theme of this book, a basic knowledge of the historical developments, as well as the current and past institutional structure is absolutely indispensable to obtain a better understanding of the conglomerate of European criminal law. In addition, no lawyer who works in the field of criminal law may lack a basic knowledge of Union law, its binding effect and the legal remedies that it provides. Only then is one able to understand how Union law affects national criminal law and criminal procedure, as well as how the European Union is gradually creating a criminal justice system of its own.

2.   FROM THE EUROPEAN COAL AND STEEL COMMUNITY TO THE EUROPEAN UNION

The first step towards the Europe of today was taken back in 1951 when France, Germany, Italy, Belgium, the Netherlands and Luxembourg concluded the Treaty establishing the European Coal and Steel Community. This treaty was followed by the 1957 Treaty establishing the European Economic Community and the Treaty establishing the European Atomic Energy Community. In 1965, an agreement was reached (the so-called Merger Treaty) that all three communities would have one institutional framework.[10] Denmark, Ireland and the United Kingdom acceded to the European Communities in 1973, followed by Greece in 1981, and Spain and Portugal in 1986.

Although various attempts were made in the 1970s to give the European Communities competences in the domain of criminal law and to pave the way for the introduction of European criminal penalties, none of these proved successful. The Member States were in fundamental disagreement on this subject. In 1979, the Netherlands vetoed a proposal by French president Giscard d'Estaing for the

---

[10]   OJ 1967, No. 152/2.

creation of an *espace judiciaire*. The Member States still maintained the express desire to keep criminal law within the authority of the Member States themselves. Member States favoured further and more intensive co-operation in criminal matters, and it appeared that objections were focused against more powers for the Commission in the area of substantive criminal law. With the 1986 Single European Act, the three existing European Communities were united into one European Community.[11] The Treaty of Maastricht on European Union in 1992 created the present structure of European Union based upon a three pillar structure.[12] This treaty formally opened the way for the European Union to have competence in the field of criminal law. However, it was the Council, not the Commission, that was nominated to be the key figure in this area. Thus, the Member States maintained control over all initiatives with regard to criminal law. The Treaty on European Union was amended by the Treaty of Amsterdam in 1997 and by the Treaty of Nice in 2001.[13] The European Coal and Steel Community expired in 2002.

Further enlargement took place in 1995 when Finland, Austria and Sweden joined, and the European Union grew to an organisation of 15 Member States. No less then ten other European states became members in 2004: Cyprus, the Czech Republic, Estonia, Hungary, Latvia, Lithuania, Malta, Poland, Slovakia and Slovenia. The Constitution for Europe was also adopted in 2004.[14] This treaty created a common institutional framework for all fields of law. Although some Member States did ratify it, the Constitution never entered into force. It was rejected in the national referendums in France and the Netherlands in 2005. As a consequence of this, new negotiations took place. In the meantime, Bulgaria and Romania became Member States in 2007. On 13 December of that year, the Treaty of Lisbon was concluded,[15] which basically maintains the contents of the rejected constitutional treaty. However, some symbolic elements, such as the European flag and the European anthem, have been eliminated. The European Union is now mainly founded upon two new treaties: The Treaty on European Union (TEU) and the Treaty on the Functioning of the European Union (TFEU).[16] The TEU now regulates the institutional structure of the Union, and has abolished the pillar structure which was established under the Treaty of Maastricht. As a result, there is only one institutional structure for all the areas in which the Union is

---

[11]   OJ 1987, L 169/1.
[12]   OJ 1992, C 191/1.
[13]   OJ 1997, C 340/144 and OJ 2001, C 80/1.
[14]   OJ 2004, C 310/1.
[15]   Treaty of Lisbon, amending the Treaty on European Union and the Treaty establishing the European Community, OJ 2007, C 306/1.
[16]   Consolidated versions of these treaties have been published in OJ 2008, C 115/1. The 1957 Treaty establishing the European Atomic Energy Community remains in force.

competent.[17] Thus, the Union replaces and succeeds the European Community.[18] The Treaty on the Establishment of the European Communities has been renamed the *Treaty on the Functioning of the European Union*. Throughout the Treaties, the words "Community (law)" and "European Community" have been replaced by "Union (law)". Attached to the Treaty of Lisbon, a series of Protocols have been adopted, together with common Declarations and Declarations of individual Member States, which are part of the Union's law.

Apart from these developments within the institutional framework of the Communities and the European Union, some Member States took initiatives for further conventions, mainly in the field of co-operation in criminal matters. The first convention of this kind was the 1985 Schengen Agreement, which was soon followed by the 1990 Convention Implementing the Schengen Agreement (*CISA*). Although the 1997 Treaty of Amsterdam partly incorporated the *CISA* into the institutional framework of the European Union, it failed to bring an end to developments outside this structure. In 2005, the Treaty of Prüm on cross-border co-operation in criminal matters was concluded between a limited number of Member States.

3.   TWO CONVERGING AREAS: THE INTERNAL MARKET AND THE AREA OF FREEDOM, SECURITY AND JUSTICE

3.1.   A NEW LEGAL ORDER

At the foundation of the European Community in 1957, the Community set itself the goal of eliminating the internal borders and bringing about an Internal Market (then called the Common Market). Article 26 TFEU (formerly Article 2 TEC) states that the internal market is to comprise an area without internal frontiers in which the free movement of goods, persons, services and capital is ensured.[19] These so-called freedoms may not meet any obstacles. Thus, Union law creates a new legal order[20] that has become an integral part of the legal systems of the Member States, which their national courts are bound to apply,[21] independently of the various sub-areas of the law. As a practical consequence of this, it means

---

[17]   An exception has been made for the Common Foreign and Defence Policy, regulated in Articles 21–46 TEU. These will not be dealt with further.

[18]   Article 1, paragraph 3 TEU.

[19]   It refers to the common policies mentioned in Section 4.2 of this chapter.

[20]   13 November 1964, *Commission* v. *Luxembourg and Belgium*, Joined Cases 90/63 and 91/63 [1964] ECR 625.

[21]   5 February 1963, Case 26-62, *Van Gend en Loos* [1963] ECR 1 and 15 July 1964, Case 6/64, *Flaminio Costa* v. *E.N.E.L.* [1964] ECR 585.

that, for the interpretation of certain general principles of Union law, not only must the judgments of the Court in criminal cases be assessed, but also judgments in other fields of law. This is the approach that is followed in this book. Special attention is given to competition law, a field in which the Union has the power of direct enforcement. Union law is directly applicable and does not follow the rules of interpretation of other areas, such as international law or national law. The subjects of the new legal order comprise not only the Member States, but also their citizens. In *Internationale Handelsgesellschaft*, the Court held that the application of rules of national law would deprive the law stemming from the Treaties of its independent nature.[22]

3.2. SINCERE CO-OPERATION

According to the *principle of sincere co-operation*, previously called the *principle of loyalty* to the Community, also known as the *enforcement obligation*, Member States have a general obligation to enforce the law of the Union. Key Article 4, paragraph 3 TEU (formerly Article 10 TEC) carries this paramount obligation:

> "Pursuant to the principle of sincere cooperation, the Union and the Member States shall, in full mutual respect, assist each other in carrying out tasks which flow from the Treaties. The Member States shall take any appropriate measure, general or particular, to ensure fulfilment of the obligations arising out of the Treaties or resulting from the acts of the institutions of the Union. The Member States shall facilitate the achievement of the Union's tasks and refrain from any measure which could jeopardise the attainment of the Union's objectives."[23]

This obligation of compliance or enforcement rests upon all bodies of the Member States, and, in particular, upon the legislature and the judiciary. It creates the positive obligation to carry out all obligations as well as the negative obligation of refraining from doing anything that might be contrary to the objectives of the Union. This means, for instance, that, if it becomes clear from the Court's answer to a preliminary reference that national legislation is not in compliance with

---

22   17 December 1970, Case 11–70, *Internationale Handelsgesellschaft mbH* v. *Einfuhr- und Vorratsstelle für Getreide und Futtermittel* [1970] ECR 1125, par. 3.

23   Article 10 TEC (before renumbered by the Treaty of Amsterdam: Article 5 TEC) reads "Member States shall take all appropriate measures, whether general or particular, to ensure fulfilment of the obligations arising out of this Treaty or resulting from action taken by the institutions of the Community. They shall facilitate the achievement of the Community's tasks. They shall abstain from any measure which could jeopardise the attainment of the objectives of this Treaty".

Union law, the authorities of the Member State must take the necessary measures, be they general or specific.[24]

The obligation of Article 4, paragraph 3 TEU (formerly Article 10 TEC) can be characterised as an obligation to achieve a certain result, although it does not specifically tell the Member States how (by which mechanism) they should meet their obligations. Before the Treaty of Lisbon was adopted, it had long been assumed that Community law (TEC, Directives and Regulations) could not prescribe that Member States had to practice enforcement under criminal law, but that the power of Community law was limited to forcing Member States not to apply criminal law in certain areas because it would amount to a violation of the rules on the internal market. However, subsequent to decisions taken in 2005 and 2007, the Court opened the door for an obligation – under Community law – to use criminal law as the means to enforce.[25]

3.3. THE THREE PILLARS OF MAASTRICHT

Although the Treaty of Lisbon created one institutional framework for all policy fields, this has not always been the case. Both in legislation and in case law, the remains of the former pillar structure are visible. Consequently, a brief explanation is necessary. In addition, during the first five years after entry into force of the Treaty of Lisbon, the pillar structure remains to have some practical implications, although this will gradually fade away.[26]

The European Union was established by the Treaty of Maastricht,[27] which created a "pillar" structure, in which each pillar was distinguished by the different manner in which legislation was adopted, its binding effect and its compliance monitoring. In the First Pillar, Community law found a place, based upon the TEC. The Second Pillar was where a common defence and foreign policy took shape and was relevant with regard to sanctions and boycotts, and became even more important in the period following the attacks on the United States on 11 September 2001.

At the moment of its creation in 1992, the Third Pillar related to co-operation in the *areas of justice and home affairs*. Five years later, this title was replaced by the *area of freedom, security and justice*. While criminal law could be seen as a

---

[24]   21 June 2007, Joined Cases C-231/06 to 233/06, *National Pensions Office* v. *Emilienne Jonkman (C-231/06), Hélène Vercheval (C-232/06) and Noëlle Permesaen (C-233/06)* v. *National Pensions Office* [2007] ECR I-5149, par. 38.

[25]   13 September 2005, Case C-176/03, *Commission* v. *Council* [2005] ECR I-7879; 23 October 2007, Case C-440/05, *Commission* v. *Council* [2007] ECR I-9097. See, further, Chapter 3, Section 3.3.

[26]   See, further, Chapter 3, Section 5.1.

[27]   Treaty on European Union, 7 February 1992, consolidated version OJ 2002, C 325/1.

side issue in Community law (the main objective of the TEC was, of course, the creation of the internal market), this was not the case in the Third Pillar, in which criminal law is the main enforcement instrument. The objective that the Union formulated in this area was to:

"... maintain and develop the Union as an area of freedom, security and justice, in which the free movement of persons is assured in conjunction with appropriate measures with respect to external border controls, asylum, immigration and the prevention and combating of crime" (Article 2 EU).

Although the main objective of the Union bore some similarities to the objective of the Community, its final goals – freedom, security and justice – were far less concrete than those of the internal market without borders. To a certain extent, one could also say that the internal market prevailed over the area of freedom, security and justice: Article 47 EU stated that nothing in the Treaty on European Union was to affect the Treaties establishing the European Communities.

Whilst Community law had created its own legal order, Third Pillar law had preserved its international law character. It had no direct effect, and this meant that implementation into national law was always necessary. In addition, there was no obligation to enforce the law. However, somewhat ambiguously, the Court extended the enforcement obligation also to the Third Pillar. In *Pupino*, a reference by the judge in charge of the preliminary enquiries at the *Tribunale di Firenze* (Italy), the Court rejected the argument that the Treaty on European Union did not contain an obligation similar to that laid down in Article 10 TEC.[28] With reference to Article 1 EU and the ever closer union among the peoples of Europe, the Court held:

"It would be difficult for the European Union to carry out its task effectively if the principle of loyal cooperation, requiring, in particular, that Member States take all appropriate measures, (...) were not also binding in the area of police and judicial cooperation in criminal matters."[29]

With decisions such as that in *Pupino*, the Court made a strong contribution to the convergence of the pillars.

---

[28]   16 June 2005, Case C-105/03, *criminal proceedings against Maria Pupino* [2005] ECR I-5285, par. 39–40.
[29]   16 June 2005, Case C-105/03, *criminal proceedings against Maria Pupino* [2005] ECR I-5285, par. 42.

3.4. ONE LEGAL ORDER FOR THE UNION

Whilst differences in origin may occasionally remain visible, they will gradually disappear both as a result of the Court's case law and as a result of the Treaty of Lisbon, which creates one institutional framework which goes hand in hand with the complete merger of the internal market and the area of freedom, security and justice (Article 3, paragraphs 2 and 3 TEU). It results in the enforcement mechanism being applicable to all fields of law. As a result, the principle of sincere co-operation of Article 4, paragraph 3 TEU now governs all areas, including that of criminal law.

As is apparent from its title, the TFEU organises the functioning of the Union. In addition, it determines the areas of, the de-limitation of, and the arrangements for the exercising of its competences (Article 1, paragraph 1 TFEU). The Treaty on the Functioning of the European Union and the Treaty on European Union constitute the treaties upon which the Union is founded. Article 1, paragraph 2 TFEU even formally stipulates that it refers to these treaties as *the Treaties*. The Treaties have the same legal value.[30] The area of freedom, security and justice and the internal market have been slightly re-defined by the Treaty of Lisbon, and they now read as follows (Article 3, paragraphs 2 and 3 TEU):

"The Union shall offer its citizens an area of freedom, security and justice without internal frontiers, in which the free movement of persons is ensured in conjunction with appropriate measures with respect to external border controls, asylum, immigration and the prevention and combating of crime. The Union shall establish an internal market. It shall work for the sustainable development of Europe based on balanced economic growth and price stability, a highly competitive social market economy, aiming at full employment and social progress, and a high level of protection and improvement of the quality of the environment. It shall promote scientific and technological advance."

In Article 67, paragraph 1 TFEU, it is repeated in a slightly different way:

"The Union shall constitute an area of freedom, security and justice with respect for fundamental rights and the different legal systems and traditions of the Member States."

The guarantee of security, provided in Article 67, paragraph 1 TFEU is further specified in paragraph 3:

"The Union shall endeavour to ensure a high level of security through measures to prevent and combat crime, racism and xenophobia, and through measures for

---

[30] Article 1, paragraph 2 TFEU.

co-ordination and cooperation between police and judicial authorities and other competent authorities, as well as through the mutual recognition of judgments in criminal matters and, if necessary, through the approximation of criminal laws."

3.5. APPLICATION OF INTERNAL MARKET PRINCIPLES ON THE AREA OF FREEDOM, SECURITY AND JUSTICE

One consequence of the complete merger of the internal market and the area of freedom, security and justice is that all the principles that have been developed under Community law for the realisation of the internal market are now fully applicable to *all* fields of Union law, including former Third Pillar law. This process of adaptation had already been initiated by case law of the Court for quite some time and was subsequently codified in the Treaty of Lisbon.

The application of Union law in national criminal law gave rise to a form of indirect harmonisation. Most notions derived from Union law are not specifically geared towards criminal law, but apply to *all* legal areas.[31] The same applies to the normative influence that Union law exerts on coercive and investigatory measures in criminal law enforcement. If a Member State elects to enforce Union law through criminal law, then it must also use this means. The principle of sincere co-operation (formerly the enforcement obligation, Article 10 TEC)[32] and its enforceability (the Commission bringing an action against a Member State before the Court) have a harmonising effect on the national laws of the Member States.

The harmonising influence of Union law relating to the internal market goes beyond the scope of criminal law. The areas in which Union law strives for harmonisation are, in themselves, related, but the same cannot be said of their influence on criminal law. This is better described as coincidental, and is partly dictated by the Member State's choice of the realm of law (civil, administrative, disciplinary, criminal) in which it wishes to enforce this. The method of implementation is an individual choice left to the Member State (for example, Germany opts for the implementation of a Directive by civil law, Estonia by administrative law, and Malta by criminal law). Internal market issues where

---

[31]   There are, however, some notions specific to criminal law. The Court, for instance, does in some cases consider the sanction or the use of criminal law as such to be too severe as an enforcement instrument in proportion to the crime. See 29 February 1996, Case C-193/94, *criminal proceedings against Sofia Skanavi and Konstantin Chryssanthakopoulos* [1996] ECR I-929, par. 38: "a criminal conviction may have consequences for the exercise of a trade or profession by an employed or self-employed person, particularly with regard to access to certain activities or certain offices, which would constitute a further, lasting restriction on freedom of movement." See, further, Chapter 4, Section 2.

[32]   The enforcement obligation comprises the obligation to implement the standards as needed into the national legislation, and further, to comply with these standards. Violation of the standards must be sanctioned and cannot go unanswered.

there is effective harmonisation in the area of criminal law (because all Member States elect to implement Union law into criminal law) are individual themes or "single-issue harmonisation".[33] The fight against EU fraud, in particular, has led to an array of legal instruments in which criminal law is the main instrument of enforcement.[34]

The abolition of the internal borders created the internal market, and, at the same time, made the external borders even stronger. While within the European Union everything is free, movement from outside the Union into the Union is subject to severe restrictions (or at least checks). The importance of the external borders is also reflected in the asylum and aliens policy. In criminal law, the concept of external borders does not play a role. Criminal law is not oriented towards a specific area that must be defended against and by others, but on controlling *undesirable behaviour* of persons residing within and outside the area, regardless of whether they are allowed to reside there or not. The emphasis on combating unacceptable conduct, instead of defending a specific area, is also exemplified by Union law, which imposes upon Member States the obligation to extend their jurisdiction over crimes committed outside the area of freedom, security and justice.[35]

In the area of freedom, security and justice, the external border concept translates into the guarantee that, within the Union, this area is ensured for its citizens.[36] With this formulation, it is clear that the TEU shuts the door on non-EU citizens claiming the benefits of the area of freedom, security and justice. It raises the question as to whether there is a difference in treatment of EU citizens and others regarding the safeguards to which they are entitled. Generally speaking,

---

[33]   Examples include Directive 91/308/EEC on prevention of the use of the financial system for the purpose of money-laundering, OJ 1991, L 166/77. By means of a separate declaration after the adoption of this Directive, all Member States indicated their decision to opt for criminal law enforcement; see OJ 1991, L 166/83, Directive 91/308 is replaced by *Directive 2005/60 on Money Laundering*; Directive 89/592/EEC of 13 November 1989 coordinating regulations on insider dealing, OJ 1989, L 334/40; Regulation (EEC) No 3677/90 of 13 December 1990 laying down measures to be taken to discourage the diversion of certain substances to the illicit manufacture of narcotic drugs and psychotropic substances, OJ 1990, L 357/1.

[34]   Without being exhaustive: Regulation (EEC) No 595/91 of 4 March 1991 concerning irregularities and the recovery of sums wrongly paid in connection with the financing of the common agricultural policy and the organisation of an information system in this field and repealing Regulation (EEC) No 283/72, OJ 1991, L 67/11; Regulation (EEC) No 3508/92 of 27 November 1992 establishing an integrated administration and control system for certain Community aid schemes, OJ L 355/1; Convention of 26 July 1995 on the protection of the European Communities' financial interests, OJ 1995, C 316/49; Protocol to this convention of 27 September 1996, OJ 1996, C 313/2; *Regulation 2988/95 on Protection of the Financial Interests*; *Regulation 2185/96 Concerning on-the-spot Checks*.

[35]   See, further, Chapter 4, Section 3.2.

[36]   The formulation of Article 29 EU ("citizens") is somewhat weaker than that of Article 2 TEU ("its citizens").

however, criminal law does not make a distinction between perpetrators upon the basis of their nationality.

As each Member State applies its own substantive and procedural criminal law, whilst using diverging principles of geographical application, there are 29 criminal justice areas (or 29 national legal orders).[37] However, these 29 criminal justice areas partially overlap because the Member States have established both norms of substantive law as well as certain forms of criminal procedure that are applicable outside the territory of their own state. The Union legal order is, therefore, of a hybrid character. There is no criminal law "market" in which market participants compete. It would be hard to imagine any free movement of criminal law or of its "products". The most explicit way of using internal market principles in the criminal justice area is the development of the principle of mutual recognition and the principle of availability.[38] This literally means the introduction of the concept of free movement for both information and evidence. However, as is apparent from its formulation, the free movement is limited to police and judicial authorities. In this sense, another distinction with the internal market comes to the fore. While free movement – the abolition of internal borders – offers advantages to the European citizen, the free movement and abolition of internal borders in criminal law does not directly help the citizen, but does aid the (authorities of the) Member States.[39]

4.   EUROPEAN INTEGRATION

In this fourth section, the focus is on the origins of the law of the European Union. Where does its policy come from, what are the rationales behind it? Knowledge of these issues is essential to understand the meaning and importance of the various principles developed in the decades of Community law. If the European Union uses harmonisation or approximation as a tool of its policy in the area of freedom, security and justice, it might be wise to look at what several decades of harmonisation looked like in the former First Pillar.

4.1. EUROPEAN INTEGRATION

European integration can be defined as the progressive process of bringing European states, European peoples and their societies closer together. This never-

---

[37]   Please note that the United Kingdom consists of three separate jurisdictions; England and Wales, Scotland, and Northern Ireland.

[38]   See, further, Chapter 7, Section 3.

[39]   See, on the consequences, Chapter 9, Section 3-5.

ending process takes shape in a common foreign and defence policy and a common currency, the euro, but also in an array of exchange programmes for students, European research programmes, and a variety of other initiatives intended to bring Europeans closer together. Integration, as understood in the European Union, and harmonisation are understood as a linear process, or, in other words, as a one-way process. Integration need not necessarily take place in legal form. This is where the distinction with harmonisation lies, the latter has a legal connotation. The definition of harmonisation used here is: the convergence of the legal practice of the various legal systems based upon a common standard.[40] Harmonisation can be considered to be a legal means for achieving the political objective of integration. Harmonisation implies differences, otherwise there would be nothing to harmonise. Harmonisation constitutes an attempt to diminish these differences, but its ultimate goal is not to eliminate them. The elimination of all differences would correspond to the goal of unification. With the exception of competition law for which uniform standards apply, unification is not an issue in a criminal law context. The substantive rules of competition law are directly applicable and there is direct enforcement power for the Commission. The Commission may set fines itself, and may pursue its own policy.

Harmonisation distinguishes itself from *mutual recognition*, another concept of great importance in Union law. The mutual recognition of legal differences is, in fact, an acknowledgement of the Member States' right to be different and their desire not to change. A form is found to make these differences irrelevant. In the legal developments of the European Union, there is a clear relationship between ideas about harmonisation and mutual recognition. In some cases, the two concepts are considered to be alternatives to each other, while in others they are deemed to be instruments that can be used simultaneously. This may have to do with political considerations. If Member States cannot agree on the harmonisation of the law in a certain area, they may resort to mutual recognition. *Directive 91/439 on Driving Licences* is an example of the simultaneous use of harmonisation and mutual recognition. The directive harmonises the substantive criteria for issuing a licence, as well as its format. In addition, it obliges Member States mutually to recognise the harmonised licences.

The European Union essentially conducts a three-track long-term policy focused on harmonisation, mutual recognition, and integration. With harmonisation, the goal is to arrive at common rules, with mutual recognition the parties allow the differences to remain but ensure that they do not impede trade or co-operation, and, in the process of integration, something shared and

---

[40]   This is not to say that these are the only true definitions of these terms. However, it is important to adhere to explicit definitions. Using harmonisation and integration without making it explicit how one defines these terms, complicates the discussion about these phenomena enormously.

European is created. Because the objectives of the European Union are not always clearly formulated and the relationship between the various policy instruments is not always clarified, the picture of an unsteady course emerges. The guiding concepts: harmonisation, mutual recognition and integration are not defined. However, this may relate more to the necessity of achieving compromises in political decision-making.

Only one theme is precluded from integration and harmonisation: the legal language. All Union legislation and all case law is translated into all the languages of the European Union. The Union itself creates a major obstacle here by adhering to the position that all 23 European languages qualify as official language. If there is a means for bringing people closer together, then it is giving them access to a common language. In any event, it seems clear that harmonisation would benefit from a common legal language.[41]

Need for Integration and Harmonisation

It is striking how little the question of the need for the integration and harmonisation of criminal law comes up in the discussions in the Union. This is striking because, up until the advent of the Treaty of Maastricht in 1992, it was, in fact, a basic assumption that the Union and criminal law would have as little to do with each other as possible. Criminal law was the exclusive domain of the Member States. The fact that the need for the integration and harmonisation *of criminal law* is so marginalised as a theme may have something to do with the fact that the Member States are still not in agreement on the issue, as well as the fact that the objectives are formulated extremely vaguely. The integration offered is that the Union provides its citizens an area of freedom, security and justice. The impression that emerges is that the integrative component of the area of freedom, security and justice consists more of the establishment of common European offices and bodies (Europol, Eurojust and the European Public Prosecutor's Office) than of a normative influence.

Three Levels of Rationalisation of the Need

From the collective *acquis communautaire* of the Union, three different levels of motives for further integration can be deducted. There is the "macro-level". At this level, there is the great ideal: One Europe! Or: united we stand against terrorism. At the "meso-level", the argumentation revolves around the general purpose of fighting crime or improved co-operation. The arguments at the "micro-level" relate to solutions for all manner of practical problems.

---

41   See Chapter 3, Section 5.3, on the difficulties arising from having 23 authentic versions of the law for its interpretation.

Macro-Level

At macro-level, arguments in support of the need for harmonisation portray harmonisation as a sort of manifest destiny framed with rhetorical arguments (harmonisation as a goal in itself): in a united Europe, we simply cannot have someone being sentenced to 4 years in the Netherlands while that person would get 6 years in Spain for the same offence, or that something is prosecuted in Sweden while in Slovenia it is not a crime at all, can we?[42] There is no field of law which does not qualify for Europeanisation: why should we exclude criminal law if everything else is under European influence? Further integration is regarded as something that is self-evident. This explains the striking absence of any explanation. The impression is that integration and harmonisation as goals in themselves are extremely strong in the political process. It was a political decision to give the European Union powers in the field of criminal law in the 1992 Treaty of Maastricht. It was a political decision to come to one institutional framework in the Treaty of Lisbon. Thus, there is a clear political will to further European integration.

Meso-Level

The arguments that fighting crime is more effective if it happens in a harmonised way, or, a variation on this argument, that harmonisation leads to better law, is found at this level. The subsidiarity principle of Article 5 TEU stimulates this way of thinking in the sense that common European problems require a common European response. The argument that eliminating the differences among legal systems would remove the supposed advantage that the perpetrators of crimes may have is a purely rhetorical one. It is based upon the idea that good citizens and the criminal investigative system(s) are being impeded by the existence of borders, while "the criminals" have free rein.[43] The development of various framework decisions on co-operation, in which grounds for refusal are declared invalid, and which are based upon the concept of mutual recognition, is related to this.

---

[42]   See point 12 of the Resolution of the European Parliament of 18 September 1997 on the Convention relating to Extradition between the Member States of the European Union, OJ 1997, C 304/131. The rhetorical character lies in the incorrect supposition that "the same acts" are a common occurrence in criminal matters. However, a sentence does not only depend on the criminal act itself, but also the circumstances in which it is committed and the person of the accused.

[43]   It is difficult to understand this argument. It is based upon the assumption that one group of citizens, "the criminals", is very well-versed in all details of Union law, national and international criminal law and the comparison of criminal justice systems, and, based upon that evaluation, makes well-calculated choices when committing crimes, and that the other group of citizens, who show no interest in committing crimes at all, has its liberties severely curtailed by the different scopes of penal legislation in the various Member States.

Micro-Level

This level pertains to practical matters that must be regulated, and to practical needs which must be satisfied. On the whole, there are no big concepts behind this. Examples include setting up joint investigation teams, Eurojust, the European Judicial Network and the description of "good practices" in mutual legal assistance. It is regarded as both more practicable and more effective to join forces when confronted with common criminal problems.

Necessity-Obscuring Factors

A number of aspects interfere with the discussion on the necessity of harmonising criminal law in Europe. The first is a difference of opinion on the role that criminal law should play in European society. Across Europe, trust in the effectiveness of criminal law differs fundamentally. The Commission expects much from criminal law (and from the harmonisation of criminal law), and walks *Alice in Wonderland*-like through the garden of criminal law, wide-eyed in amazement at all the wonders that several centuries of modern criminal law have produced. Thus, many discussions that *seem* to be about harmonisation are, in essence, discussions upon the question of whether criminal law is the appropriate cure for the disease. The expectations seem to be that criminal law is an effective tool to influence European society. But the criminal law literature offers an entirely different perspective. Generally, very little can be found in the literature on the need for harmonisation and/or on the potentially positive effects of harmonisation. Indeed, the attitude in the literature is extremely defensive: the European Union must not meddle in what is national criminal law.

The second element that has obscured the discussion on the necessity of the harmonisation of criminal law is the struggle for power within the European Union. Sometimes, it appears as though this discussion runs parallel with the question of whether or not the European Union should be in charge of a certain area, or whether it should be left to the Member States. The Commission has tried for many years to obtain more competences in the area of criminal law, and would be most happy to see a European Public Prosecutor appointed immediately. The strengthening of the subsidiarity principle in the Treaty of Lisbon may contribute to a more context-based approach to the problems, because it will serve to remind the legislature of the question whether the problem to be legislated on is European or national.

4.2. COMMON POLICIES AND CO-ORDINATION

Starting with the foundation of the European Community in 1957, the goal was set to eliminate the internal borders and to create an internal market.[44] The creation of an internal market has resulted in protective measures, especially for goods coming from outside the European Union. The importation of non-EU goods into the European Union is subject to levies and other duties. On the other hand, the exportation of goods from the EU to the rest of the world is stimulated by subsidies. Article 3 TFEU stipulates the areas in which the Union is to have exclusive competence. Among other areas, it lists the customs union and competition rules. Article 4 TFEU deals with the areas in which the Union shares its competences with the Member States. It lists, among others, the internal market and the area of freedom, security and justice. The internal market policy further consists of a common agricultural and fisheries policy (Articles 38–44 TFEU, formerly Articles 32–38 TEC); common transport policy (Articles 90–100 TFEU, formerly Articles 70–80 TEC); common rules on competition and taxation (Articles 101–118 TFEU, formerly Articles 81–89 TEC). The economic and monetary policy is regulated in Articles 119–144 TFEU (formerly Articles 98–124 TEC). The policies on border checks, asylum and immigration (Articles 77–80 TFEU, formerly Articles 61–69 TEC) have been incorporated in the area of freedom, security and justice. Apart from judicial co-operation in criminal matters (Articles 82–86 TFEU) and police co-operation (Articles 87–89 TFEU), two other fields have been regulated in the area: the policies on border checks, asylum and immigration, mentioned already, as well as judicial co-operation in civil matters (Article 81 TFEU). With the exception of competition, these major policy areas as well as all the other areas regulated in the Treaties (Articles 145–221 TFEU) are not systematically dealt with in this book. The other (indirect) exception relates to subsidies. It is mainly in the area of subsidies that the financial interests of the Union lie. Fraud, such as inappropriate evasion of duties or unjustified grants or subsidies, is detrimental to the budget of the Union.

The economic and monetary policy is regulated in Articles 119–144 TFEU. In these areas, the Union stipulates a certain policy. For instance, in order to protect the environment, the economic interests of the fishermen, and the interests of the consumers, it has set rules on the amount of fish that may be caught. Another example is the transport sector, in which the Union has not only harmonised the rules on driving and rest hours of drivers, but has also harmonised driving licences and the roadworthiness of all motor vehicles. In these areas, a certain harmonisation of the law has taken place. Sometimes the focus is more on flanking measures in order to stimulate free movement, sometimes the emphasis is on the

---

[44]   Albeit named "common market" at the time.

creation of equal opportunities for all economic operators. Although the main emphasis of its approach is economically determined, other fields, such as public health, the environment or public policy, may also play a role as a corollary.

Gradually, a common approach to certain problems in the area of freedom, security and justice has been developed. The final goals are described in terms that are much more vague than those of the internal market, but this cannot be said of the short term goals set by the European Union. The European Council formulates new policy goals on a regular basis. An example of this can be found in the so-called Hague Programme,[45] in which various measures or points of interest are mentioned, such as the strengthening of the combating of terrorism, and the further facilitation of police co-operation, for example. The Programme reiterates the status of mutual recognition as a cornerstone of co-operation between the Member States of the European Union.

Pursuant to Article 119 TFEU, the Union is to adopt an economic policy that is, in part, based upon the close co-ordination of the economic policies of the Member States. The translation of this principle for the area of freedom, security and justice is that the Union is to endeavour to ensure a high level of security through measures designed to prevent and combat crime. The policy-based aspect is outlined particularly well in the conclusions of the presidency,[46] and a number of action plans,[47] which do not harmonise law directly, but serve to trigger further legislation or enforcement on a particular theme. For instance, if an action plan stipulates that the fight against terrorism must be intensified, it is most likely that legislative initiatives regarding terrorism will be taken and, at a certain moment, will be adopted. Other examples include centralised databases, which can be consulted by all Member States,[48] the phenomena of "best practices",[49] and the "scoreboard",[50] which sets out in a table what response follows which arrangements, and by whom (Member States, Council and/or Commission).

---

[45] Brussels European Council, 4 and 5 November 2004, Presidency Conclusions, The Hague Programme, Doc. 14292/04, 5 November 2004.

[46] See Document 15914/05 of 17 December 2005, European Council of Brussels, 15/16 December 2005.

[47] To name a few randomly selected examples: Council and Commission Action Plan of 3 December 1998 on how best to implement the provisions of the Treaty of Amsterdam on the creation of an area of freedom, security and justice; Council and Commission Action Plan to fight terrorism; Council and Commission Action Plan with a view to preventing and combating trafficking in human beings, 12402/3/05, Brussels, 18 November 2005.

[48] The Schengen Information System, the Customs Information System, the Visa Information System, the Europol systems.

[49] For example: Joint Action of 29 June 1998 on good practice in mutual legal assistance in criminal matters, OJ 1998, L 191/1; EU plan on best practices, standards and procedures for combating and preventing trafficking in human beings, OJ 2005, C 311/1.

[50] Report on the implementation of The Hague programme for 2006, Table 1 Institutional Scoreboard, Table 2, Implementation Scoreboard, 4 July 2007, Council Document 11516/07.

4.3. TOOLS

In essence, the European Union uses two legal tools to pursue its objectives, which can be referred to as "hard law" and "soft law". Hard law is legislation, and is the backbone of integration and harmonisation. "Soft law", in contrast, refers to those control instruments that are not legislation, which may, however, be based upon legislation. In the main, albeit not entirely, these terms go together with harmonisation and integration. All harmonisation and integration forms exhibit different accompanying principles. First and foremost, they are seen from the perspective of a process with varying speeds of enhanced co-operation. The very term "enhanced co-operation" was first used in the Schengen context, but it is now provided for in the Treaty of Lisbon. This means that, on certain issues, some Member States harmonise (or co-operate more intensively) somewhat faster than the other Member States of the European Union. Schengen is also an example of, and is considered to be, a forerunner of the EU, one that other states may join at some future point, when they are ready for it.

Hard Law: Form and Means

European legislation in the area of criminal law must be put into effect by means of implementation into the national legal system. Thus, European law creates layers of legislation (European and national) which are applicable in concrete cases. All legal instruments that have an influence on criminal law determine the period in which the Member States must meet the implementation obligations. In Directives, Regulations and Framework Decisions, such obligations can be found in one of the concluding articles of the instrument.[51] This period of implementation is two years, as a rule, and serves to provide the Member States with a reasonable term within which to meet their obligations. Draft implementing legislation must be submitted to the Commission for recommendations within this period.

Soft Law: Form and Means

The influence of the Union is extending ever further and is also making inroads into more policy-oriented areas ("soft law"), and, to a lesser degree, enforcement. In its legislative initiatives, the European Union makes choices on what it does and does not consider to be a criminal offence,[52] and on priorities in investigation

---

[51]   For example, Article 9 *Framework Decision 2004/757 on Illicit Drug Trafficking*, includes a term of 18 months. Most Framework Decisions, however, have a term of two years. See, for example, Article 12 *Framework Decision 2005/222 on Attacks against Information Systems*. Directives generally have a implementation term of two years; some have different terms. Regulations become effective a few days after publication. It is rather rare that a period of implementation is given to Member States regarding Regulations.

[52]   See, further, Chapter 4, Section 2 and 5.

and law enforcement.[53] This relates to both the criminal policy and to the prosecution policy. The constant insistence by both the Commission and the European Parliament that fraud against the financial interests of the Union is an extremely serious crime does seem to have had some effect. Such a prioritisation has led to initiatives in the legislative area, to enforcement and to the engagement of persons and means. In this case, the European Union does not determine what precisely the rules that must be formulated are, but it does determine that action must be taken on a particular theme. The objectives formulated in Article 67 TFEU give the Council and the Member States the legal standards by which to co-ordinate their operations. The higher the political priority, the more difficult it is for a Member State to avoid a common policy and follow its own course, because the legal instruments are drafted more forcefully and there is more political pressure. Member States rarely deviate from the common line on combating terrorism, but, with regard to combating drugs, they do allow themselves some room for differences.

European summits of heads of government often lead to the adoption of Action Plans or Programmes that act as guides for specific initiatives for the coming years.[54] Apart from these general Action Plans and Programmes, more concrete and detailed plans have also been developed and tabled on the European agenda. An example of this can be found in the Action Plan to combat organised crime,[55] which has announced and recommended numerous initiatives regarding legislative and practical measures with a view to combating organised crime. In addition to this, there have been times in which the Council has adopted Resolutions which called for similar initiatives.[56] Thus, at a certain point in time, it seems politically inevitable to group the obligations in the various soft law instruments and translate them into a hard law instrument.

---

[53]   What priorities are does shift over time. An example from the 1970s, 1980s and early 1990s was EC fraud. In the second half of the 1990s, drugs, trade in nuclear material, trafficking in women and child pornography rose as priorities. Since 2001, all of these have been superseded by terrorism.

[54]   In the field of criminal law it is referred to the 1998 Action Plan of the Council and the Commission on how to best implement the provisions of the Treaty of Amsterdam on an area of freedom, security and justice (OJ 1999, C/19/1). Presidency Conclusions of the Tampere European Council, 15 and 16 October 1999; Presidency Conclusions of the Brussels European Council, 4 and 5 November 2004, The Hague Programme, Doc. 14292/04, 5 November 2004.

[55]   OJ 1997, C 251/1.

[56]   Council Resolution of 21 December 1998 on the prevention of organised crime with reference to the establishment of a comprehensive strategy for combating it, OJ 1998, C 408/1.

4.4. HARMONISATION AND APPROXIMATION

The European Union does not practice one type of harmonisation. Traditionally, a distinction is made between positive and negative integration. *Positive integration* refers to areas in which the Union harmonises the substantive law in a certain field, and, as a consequence of this, the discretion of the Member States for other measures becomes more and more limited. Examples of areas in which positive integration has taken place include the introduction of the value added tax, and the introduction of roadworthiness tests for motor vehicles. Although the law in these areas may be harmonised, the degree to which this has actually taken place differs greatly. The other form of harmonisation is referred to as *negative integration*, by which Union law does not force Member States to implement specific legislation in order to harmonise the underlying norms. With negative integration, Union law simply states that certain actions may not meet any impediments. The five freedoms of the TFEU are examples of the freedoms which trigger negative integration. The consequences of negative integration are thus more determined by the situation existing in national law. Over the years, one can say that the influence of negative integration on national criminal law has been much greater than the measures of positive integration. This is logical, given the economic nature of most of these instruments. However, the exceptions here include the Tachograph Regulation (Regulation 3820/85) and the Money Laundering Directive (*Directive 2005/60 on Money Laundering*).

Minimum harmonisation, or *approximation*, as it is sometimes called, is a tried and trusted method deriving from Community law. With regard to the internal market, the legal basis for harmonisation can be found in Articles 114–118 TFEU. With regard to a given policy area, the Member States must respect the stated minimum obligations. They are, however, authorised to establish supplementary provisions. As required by the scope of the instrument, their supplementary provisions may be either more or less rigid. The minimum standards/provisions must be seen in the context of an alternative to full harmonisation in Union law. In some cases, minimum standards are also a first step towards the full harmonisation of a policy area. This can also be deducted from the case law on the disparities that exist in the legislation of Member States in a situation of partial harmonisation. If they compromise equal treatment, distort or impair the functioning of the market, "it is for the competent institutions to adopt the provisions needed to remedy such disparities".[57]

Both Articles 82 and 83 TFEU mention *minimum rules*. Article 82 does so in the context that these are to facilitate the mutual recognition of judgments and judicial decisions. Article 83 does so in respect of the need to combat serious

---

[57]   21 September 1983, Joined Cases 205 to 215/82, *Deutsche Milchkontor GmbH and others* v. *Germany* [1983] ECR 2633, par. 24.

crime on a common basis. Articles 82 and 83 TFEU delineate the areas in which approximation may take place. They concern:

- mutual admissibility of evidence between the Member States;
- the rights of individuals in criminal procedure;
- the rights of the victims of crime;
- any other specific aspects of criminal procedure added by decision of the Council;
- minimum rules concerning the definition of criminal offences and sanctions.

On evaluation, it seems fair to conclude that harmonisation is still reserved for areas of Union policy that previously belonged to the First Pillar.[58] Harmonisation provides a higher degree of integration and similarity than approximation. Approximation allows Member States more discretion in the choice of the means with which to comply with their Union obligations. However, neither the Treaties, nor the Court's case law are explicit about the dividing line between harmonisation and approximation.

Since the establishment of the Third Pillar, harmonisation and approximation have not always been used consistently. In one act, "harmonisation" appears as the appropriate term,[59] despite the fact that Article 82, paragraph 1 TFEU (formerly Articles 29, 31(e) and 34, paragraph 2 EU) refers to "approximation". Thus, the terminology is not always adjusted to the specific context of criminal law. An example of this can be found in Article 9 of the *Financial Interests Convention*: "No provision in this Convention shall prevent Member States from adopting internal legal provisions which go beyond the obligations deriving from this Convention." What is meant here? What is "beyond" and from which direction should one interpret this? Likewise, Article 82, paragraph 2 TFEU mentions that the adoption of minimum rules should not prevent Member States from maintaining or introducing a higher level of protection for individuals. What is a higher level? The *Framework Decision 2004/757 on Illicit Drug Trafficking* describes the conduct that must be made an offence as the minimum provision; Should this be interpreted as meaning that Member States can criminalise other forms of conduct and enforce more strictly? Based upon a standard-setting that prescribes a minimum of criminalisation and punishment, exceeding that minimum level can only mean sterner forms of punishment. On the one hand, this might satisfy the requirements that the area of freedom, justice and security sets with regard to the fight against crime, but, on the other, it may be in conflict

---

[58]   See, also, the reference to harmonisation measures in Article 83, paragraph 2 TFEU and the distinction made with approximation.

[59]   See preamble (9) of *Framework Decision 2004/757 on Illicit Drug Trafficking*.

with the above-mentioned freedom of movement of citizens. Checking everyone who crosses a border for drugs violations and imposing life sentences for drug offences might well make a significant contribution to suppressing this form of criminality, but would still seriously hinder the free movement of persons. Moreover, in this example, the principle of proportionality, which governs all Union legislation, is violated. The conclusion, therefore, must be that Member States must meet the implementation obligations of the instruments, regardless of whether they are labelled as "minimum provisions" or not.[60]

There are a few specific legal instruments that deal with approximation of criminal law. The most prominent example is *Joint Action 96/750 on Illegal Drug Trafficking*.[61] The usefulness of this specific instrument in specific criminal cases is rather small, as it merely postpones the real steps to be taken and is more of a programmatic character. Its value lies in the fact that it limits the discretion of the Member States to opt for non-criminal alternative-responses to drugs. It calls for a substantial number of measures of convergence, approximation and compatibility between the Member States.

4.5. THE PRINCIPLES OF CONFERRAL, SUBSIDIARITY AND PROPORTIONALITY

These three principles govern the legislative competences of the Union.

The Principle of Conferral

The competences of the European Union are conferred to it by the Member States in order to attain the objectives that they share (Article 1 TEU). Article 13, paragraph 2 TEU states that the principle of conferral is applicable to the individual institutions as well. Articles 4 and 5, paragraph 2 TEU, state that the competences not conferred upon the Union remain with the Member States.[62] In comparison to the previous treaties, more respect is being paid to the national identity of the Member States and to their responsibilities. The Union should, for instance, respect the national identities of the Member States, inherent in their fundamental structures, as well as their essential state functions, such as maintaining law and order (Article 4, paragraph 2 TEU). Article 5 TEU distinguishes between the limits of Union competences, which are governed by the principle of conferral and the use of Union competences. The use of Union competences is governed by the principles of subsidiarity and proportionality.

---

[60]　See, further, Chapter 4, Section 3.1.

[61]　OJ 1996, L 342/6.

[62]　An old example of this principle can be found in the Court's case law. 14 July 1976, Joined Cases 3, 4 and 6–76, *Cornelis Kramer and others* [1976] ECR 1279. See, further, Declaration 18 in relation to the delimitation of competences, attached to the Treaty of Lisbon.

The Treaties distinguish between exclusive competences for the Union and shared competences between the Union and the Member States. The scope and arrangements for exercising the competences is determined by the provisions of the Treaties relating to each specific area. The Union may use its exclusive competence in a specific area which has been conferred upon it by the Treaties to legislate and to adopt of binding acts (Article 2, paragraph 1 TFEU). In areas of exclusive competence, the Member States may only act if they have been empowered to do so or in order to implement the acts of the Union. In areas of shared competence, both the Union and the Member States may legislate and adopt legally-binding acts. Article 2, paragraph 2 TFEU further states:

> "The Member States shall exercise their competence to the extent that the Union has not exercised its competence. The Member States shall again exercise their competence to the extent that the Union has decided to cease exercising its competence."

The Principle of Subsidiarity

Article 5, paragraph 3 TEU reads as follows:

> "Under the principle of subsidiarity, in areas which do not fall within its exclusive competence, the Union shall act only if and in so far as the objectives of the proposed action cannot be sufficiently achieved by the Member States, either at central level or at regional and local level, but can rather, by reason of the scale or effects of the proposed action, be better achieved at Union level."[63]

What does this mean?

As is apparent from the Protocol on the Application of the Principles of Subsidiarity and Proportionality attached to the Treaty of Lisbon, the main influence should be in the legislative process. On the one hand, the principle distinguishes between areas in which the Union has exclusive competence. Here, one may refer to the areas of common policy mentioned earlier. On the other hand, there are areas in which such an exclusive competence does not exist. Here, the Union may be competent, depending on the application of an effectiveness criterion ("how action can be better achieved"). This may relate both to the scale and to the effects. However, in practice, it also seems that Member States look at the principle mainly because of its importance in protecting sovereignty. This may explain why the Protocol has entrusted national parliaments with the supervision of the compliance with this principle.

Article 69 TFEU stipulates that national parliaments are to ensure that proposals and legislative initiatives regarding judicial co-operation in criminal matters and police co-operation are in compliance with the principle of

---

[63]   Formerly Article 5 TEC.

subsidiarity.[64] Any national parliament may, within eight weeks of the date of transmission of a draft legislative act, send a reasoned opinion stating why it considers that the draft does not comply with the principle of subsidiarity (Article 6 Protocol No. 2). When a third of the national parliaments shares this view, the draft must be reviewed (Article 7 Protocol No. 2).

The Principle of Proportionality

Article 5, paragraph 4 TEU states that proportionality means that the content and form of Union action shall not exceed what is necessary to achieve the objectives of the Treaties. Similarly to the principle of subsidiarity, national parliaments may state reasoned opinions on compliance with this principle.[65]

4.6. FUNDAMENTAL ASPECTS OF THE CRIMINAL JUSTICE SYSTEM

Both Article 82, paragraph 3 and Article 83, paragraph 3 TFEU create the so-called emergency break procedure for a Member State that expresses serious concerns that a draft Directive would affect fundamental aspects of its criminal justice system. While Article 82 TFEU allows a Member State to have the draft referred to the European Council with regard to rules of criminal procedure and cooperation in criminal matters, Article 83 grants the same power with regard to the rules of substantive criminal law. The procedure was inserted after some Member States expressed their concern that the competences of the Union could force them to adopt rules that would be alien to the traditions of their criminal justice system. It remains to be seen what its use in practice will be. The sensitivity of issues relating to criminal law for the Member States is also expressed by the fact that this is the only area in which the initiatives for legislation may come from both the Commission and the Member States. Article 76 TFEU excludes criminal law from the regular procedure in which the initiatives for legislation come from the Commission.

From the formulation of Articles 82 and 83, it is clear that it is the Member State concerned that determines whether its criminal justice system is affected. At other instances, the Treaties refer to the respect to be paid to national identities and the diversity of Europe (Article 3 TEU, Article 67 TFEU). In addition, the principle of conferral, subsidiarity and proportionality may be influential to the finding that fundamental aspects of the criminal justice system are affected. Is

---

[64]   See, further, Protocol No. 1 on the Role of National Parliaments in the European Union and Protocol No. 2 on the Application of the Principles of Subsidiarity and Proportionality.

[65]   However, it seems that the review procedure of Article 6 and 7 of Protocol No. 2 is reserved for the principle of subsidiarity.

this assessment absolute or could the Court test whether the draft does or does not affect the fundamental aspects of the criminal justice system? This open question is most relevant. If it could, the Court would obtain a position similar to that of a constitutional court. If the Court cannot subject the use of the references to the European Council on the basis of paragraphs 3 of Articles 82 and 83 TFEU to a objective test, the mechanism results in a permanent veto of a Member State, blocking common Union legislation in the area.

The Treaty stipulates a suspension of the ordinary legislative procedure if a member of the Council uses this procedure. Subsequently, there is to be discussion in the European Council, and, in the event of consensus, the European Council is to refer the draft back to the Council. When the European Council reaches consensus, then matters can proceed as agreed. The second possibility, disagreement, raises more questions. Paragraphs 3 of Articles 82 and 83 TFEU state that, in cases of disagreement, and if at least nine Member States wish to establish enhanced co-operation on the basis of the draft directive, they can obtain authorisation to proceed. The result is that, in the most extreme situation in which one Member State opposes a directive that all the others Member States are in favour of, then that Member State will be able to block common decision-making on its own but cannot oppose the enhanced co-operation of the other Member States.

Subsidiarity Principle and Criminal Law: Something Special?

Could it be argued, in line with the recognition of the different legal systems and the different traditions of the Member States in Article 67, paragraph 1 TFEU, that the Union legislature should be reluctant to impose obligations that change the criminal justice systems of the Member States? The national criminal law and criminal procedure of all the individual Member States were developed in a process of centuries. A national criminal justice system symbolises both a national identity and its culture. It came about in a time in which law was understood as being of exclusively national origin. The fundamentally different natures of Union law and national criminal law call for consideration of the peculiarities of criminal law from a Union perspective. Awareness of these peculiarities can contribute to understanding the problems yet to be revealed between Union legal principles and those of national criminal law. Is criminal law more closely related to culture than other fields of law and thus less suitable for harmonisation? Does it differ according to whether it concerns substantive or procedural law? It is not easy to provide answers to the questions raised here.

In addition, there is also an element of effectiveness that would support maintaining the coherence of a national criminal justice system. Unlike private law, criminal law forms a closed system in the sense that neither individuals, nor the parties to a criminal trial, can develop their own criminal law. Because of this closed system character, it may prove more difficult to harmonise just a few aspects of criminal law, without affecting the system as a whole. There may, however, be the intention to harmonise one aspect of criminal law while leaving other aspects or fields unaltered. Can criminal law cope with this? The harmonisation of a specific definition of crime is influenced by the general part of criminal law. At the same level, harmonisation of the definition of a crime will have consequences in the procedural field – for instance, the application of coercive measures. Are the results desired or unwanted side-effects? Both extremes may be undesirable: the disturbance of the balance between repression and safeguards for the individual, and a situation in which effective law enforcement cannot take place. These examples show that the harmonisation of a specific element of criminal (procedural) law has contextual consequences, which will differ from state to state. A specific side-effect in one Member State may be completely absent in another. It may, therefore, force states to introduce changes in other fields of the law as well, despite the fact that such a change was neither required, nor intended by the drafters of the harmonising instrument.

4.7. THE EFFECTS OF HARMONISATION: A CRITICAL ASSESSMENT

Harmonisation of rules focuses on the implementation of the European rule into a national setting. This can be called as input-orientated harmonisation. However, it is also relevant to look at the actual output of harmonised rules. This is the law in practice, as it evolves from the actions of the executive and judicial powers. One may question whether the harmonisation of rules will lead to harmonisation of enforcement, in the event that enforcement mechanisms have not also been harmonised. This, of course, depends, to a certain extent, on the contents of the legal instruments that have been harmonised. This harmonising effect of clearly described legislation will be greater than when multi-interpretable terminology is used. Additionally, if the legal acts provide supervisory mechanisms, duties to report on implementation, or any other feedback on the effects of the rules, then the enforcement aspect has also been taken into consideration. An example of the inclusion of enforcement aspects can be found under Union law, where the Treaties, as well as secondary legislation, provide for supervision by the Commission and the Court.

Before the Treaty of Lisbon entered into force, such an enforcement or supervisory mechanism was not provided for under the Third Pillar. This resulted in very different treatment of First Pillar and Third Pillar law. The absence of both the enforcement obligations as the supervisory role of the Commission under the Third Pillar meant that there was no extra tool to stimulate harmonisation of the law in practice. The Court did not have jurisdiction to intervene on request of the Commission. The harmonising effect of Third Pillar law was, therefore, limited to a common norm, not to common enforcement.

One may question whether the method of harmonisation and approximation of criminal legislation does bring the criminal justice systems closer together. To date, the actual influence of the harmonisation and integration model has, with regard to Third Pillar law, been limited and well-below its potential. What causes can be identified to explain this? *Firstly*, it is related to the nature of compromise legislation. This bothers criminal lawyers, who prefer to have clarity on statutory or convention-based terms. In addition, criminal lawyers tend to see legislation as law, but European integration is, first and foremost, a political process. This may, in part, be an explanation not only for the vague and non-committal nature of European Union criminal legislation, but also for the criticism levelled against the Union from the legal field. This is one of the major problems for the application of the law. Union political decision-making is set out in a legal instrument, or, to put it another way, much more than national legislation, European legislation comprises an indicator of the direction of a political decision, and leaves a great deal of leeway for more specific national legislation.

An example of a relatively non-binding norm is taken from the definitions of offences. Article 2, paragraph 1, *Framework Decision 2005/222 on Attacks against Information Systems*, reads:

> "Each Member State shall take the necessary measures to ensure that the intentional access without right to the whole or any part of an information system is punishable as a criminal offence, at least for cases which are not minor."

The probability that Member States will significantly differ from each other is extremely high: what are the necessary measures, what is intentional, what is "without right", and which cases are not minor? Here, the approximating effect is practically non-existent. Article 7 of that same Framework Decision offers somewhat more of a controlling influence. Offences committed within the framework of a criminal organisation are defined as "aggravating circumstances for which a maximum penalty of 2–5 years is attached". Another example is *Framework Decision 2004/757 on Illicit Drug Trafficking*. This Framework Decision imposes the obligation to set, at least, a penalty of a given length as the maximum penalty for the offence.[66] The degree of freedom that a Member State has in

---

[66]   Article 4, paragraph 1, *Framework Decision 2004/757 on Illicit Drug Trafficking*: "Each Member State shall take the necessary measures to ensure that the offences referred to in Article 2 are punishable by criminal penalties of a maximum of at least between one and three years of imprisonment". See, further, Chapter 6, Section 2.

approaching this is great. It can opt to establish a longer penalty. If the Member State already has a longer penalty, it need do nothing.

The *second* reason for the meagre influence of integration and harmonisation is the use of the 23 legal languages. By definition, the use of various language versions leads to differences in some legal instruments.[67] In the European "Tower of Babel", every Member State interprets European law in its own language (legal language), and talks at cross purposes with other states.

The fact that implementation is inevitable in criminal law is the *third* reason for the divergent enforcement in the Member States. Common standards will be translated and incorporated into a national context. This is the cumulative effect of the first two factors observed: vague standard-setting in various languages is conducive to an interpretation that will change as little as possible in national law. National law enforcement officials will interpret the (new) rules with national eyes and as part of an entire national system. This could explain why some rules, which – on paper – ought to change standards in a specific country, may – in practice – not result in any noticeable change. Harmonisation which is limited to common European rules may, therefore, lead to formal harmonisation.[68] Additionally, a Member State that comes off the worst in the negotiation process can still retaliate afterwards by interpreting the implementation obligations in an extremely national manner.

The *fourth* reason is found in the incidental guidance provided by the Court. The actual role of the Court in the interpretation of Framework Decisions in preliminary questions is gradually taking on more shape, but still remains fragmented. The reason lies in the fact that not all Member States give the Court jurisdiction in the same way. There are countries that give all courts the competence for preliminary references, but there are other countries that restrict this to the highest court.[69] Additionally, national courts are rather reluctant to refer to the Court.

The *fifth* reason lies in the absence of a view on the role of criminal law in the Union. There is no grand design on the relationship of Union law and criminal law. This might even be the most important factor which creates the gap between the common instrument and the law in practice. Legislative initiatives are taken on single-issues without analysing the consequences for a broader context. One simple example of this is the minimum/maximum penalty. Even if all Member States were to adopt the exact same maximum penalty, this correspondence would only be superficial. The penalty provided in the Penal Code does not take into account all manner of other factors that go into determining the sentence (including, but not limited to, mitigating circumstances, conditional or early

---

[67]   See, further, Chapter 3, Section 5.3.
[68]   A more cynical comment would be that "window-dressing" takes place.
[69]   See, further, Chapter 3, Section 5.1.

release, detention system, pardon, *etc.*). It would be absolutely wrong to confuse nominal equivalence of the sentence as material equivalent of the penalty.

5. INSTITUTIONS, AGENCIES, BODIES AND OFFICES

Article 13 TEU mentions the seven institutions which have to carry out the tasks of the Union: the European Parliament, the European Council, the Council, the European Commission (hereinafter: the Commission), the Court of Justice of the European Union (hereinafter: the Court), the European Central Bank, and the Court of Auditors.[70] The competences of these institutions are further regulated in the TFEU. Apart from these formally recognised institutions, various agencies, bodies and offices have been established over the years.

INSTITUTIONS

The European Parliament[71]
The European Parliament represents the peoples of the European Union. It has its seat in Strasbourg, but certain sessions are held in Brussels and Luxembourg.[72] Article 14 TEU states that the Parliament is not to have more than 751 members, who are directly elected by the citizens of Europe. No Member State is to have less than six members, or have more than 96 seats. The TFEU distinguishes between the *ordinary legislative procedure* and the *special legislative procedure*. In the ordinary legislative procedure, the European Parliament will – jointly with the Council – adopt regulations, directives or decisions on proposals from the Commission (Articles 289 and 294 TFEU). The Treaties provide for specific cases in which acts are adopted by the European Parliament with the participation of the Council, or by the Council with participation by the European Parliament.

---

[70]   The European Council and the European Central Bank have been upgraded to institutions by the Treaty of Lisbon.

[71]   The TEU now mentions, for the first time, national parliaments in Article 12. They are to take part within the framework of the area of freedom, security and justice, in the evaluation mechanisms for the implementation of the Union policies in that area, in accordance with Article 70 TFEU, and through being involved in the political monitoring of Europol and the evaluation of Eurojust's activities with Articles 88 and 85 TFEU.

[72]   Protocol No. 6 on the location of the seats of the institutions and of certain bodies, offices, agencies and departments of the European Union.

The European Council

The European Council is the political body made up of the heads of state or government of the Member States, as well as the President of the European Council and the President of the Commission.[73] The European Council meets twice every six months. Article 15, paragraph 1 TEU states its political task clearly:

> "The European Council shall provide the Union with the necessary impetus for its development and shall define the general political direction and priorities thereof. It shall not exercise legislative functions."

The Council

The Treaties set aside an important role for the Council. Article 16 TEU states that the Council is, jointly with the European Parliament, to exercise the legislative and budgetary functions of the Union. It is to carry out the policy-making and co-ordinating functions. It has its seat in Brussels, but some meetings take place in Luxembourg. Pursuant to Article 16, paragraph 2 TEU, this institution consists of the representatives of the governments of the Member States. It decides by majority, unless a qualified-majority is provided in the Treaty.[74] The Council has delegated a lot of preparatory work to a committee of permanent representatives (Article 16, paragraph 6 TEU and Article 240 TFEU). The Council may request the Commission to submit proposals for legislation (Article 241 TFEU, formerly Article 208 TEC). The Council may conclude agreements with third states or international organisations (Article 218 TFEU, formerly Article 300 TEC). With the Treaty of Lisbon, the Union changed its system of decision-making from taking decisions by unanimity to majority-voting. The responsibilities of the Council were somewhat different in the previous Treaty on European Union, in which the Council adopted decisions unanimously (Article 34, paragraph 2, EU). Initiatives for legislation could be taken by any Member State and by the Commission. In practice, many initiatives were presented by the Member State holding the position of President of the Council.

The Commission

The Commission is the linchpin of Union law:

> "It shall promote the general interest of the Union and take appropriate initiatives to that end. It shall ensure the application of the Treaties, and of measures adopted by the institutions pursuant to them. It shall oversee the application of Union law under the

---

[73]   The Treaty of Lisbon changed the duration of the term of the President of the Council, which becomes two and a half years, under abolition of the rotation principle.

[74]   Article 238 TFEU provides for a new regime of decision-making to be applicable from 1 November 2014.

control of the Court of Justice of the European Union." (Article 17, paragraph 1 TEU).

The Commission ensures that the Treaty is applied and proposes legislation, which must be adopted by the Council and the European Parliament (Article 294 TFEU, formerly Article 251 TEC). In addition, the Commission supervises the uniform application of Union law at three different levels: it monitors implementing legislation (Member States inform the Commission of their draft implementing legislation); it monitors the enforcement of Union law by the Member States and it may institute infraction procedures against Member States that are not in compliance with Union law. The Commission also collects information itself, asks Member States to report, but may also receive complaints from individual citizens. If the Commission is of the opinion that a Member State does not comply with Union law, it may bring a case against that state before the Court (Article 258 TFEU, formerly Article 226 TEC).

Until 2014, the Commission is composed of 27 members. All nationalities have a member on the Commission. After 1 November 2014, a more limited number of members will be chosen (Article 244 TFEU). The commissioners are, however, not representatives of their Member States, but serve the general interest of the Union (Article 17, paragraph 2 TEU). The Commission is responsible to the European Parliament (Article 17, paragraph 8 TEU). It has its seat in Brussels. Before the Treaty of Lisbon, the Commission's position in the Third Pillar was considerably more modest than in the First Pillar. It could take legislative initiatives (Article 34, paragraph 2 EU), but had no a role in the decision-making, or in the supervision of compliance. It could not bring a Member State before the Court for non-compliance with Union law.

The Court of Justice

Article 19, paragraph 1 TEU states that "The Court of Justice shall include the Court of Justice, the General Court and specialised courts. It shall ensure that in the interpretation and application of the Treaties the law is observed." The Court sits in chambers or in the Grand Chamber (Article 254 TFEU), and is established to ensure the uniform interpretation of the Treaties. Article 19, paragraph 3 TEU, lists the three competences of the Court. It is:

- to rule on actions brought by a Member State, an institution or a natural or legal person;
- to give preliminary rulings, at the request of courts or tribunals of the Member States, on the interpretation of Union law or the validity of acts adopted by the institutions;
- to rule in other cases provided for in the Treaties.

The Commission may bring a case against a Member State that it considers to have failed to fulfil an obligation under the Treaties (Article 258 TFEU, formerly Article 226 TEC).[75] In such a case, the Court may determine whether or not the Member State has met its obligations (Article 260 TFEU, formerly Article 228 TEC). This procedure is used very frequently. A finding by the Court that a Member State has not fulfilled its obligations under the Treaties requires that Member State to take action in order to bring its national legislation into compliance with that of the Union.[76] If the Member State does not comply satisfactorily with the Court's judgment, the Commission may request the Court to impose a lump sum to be paid by that Member State (Article 260 TFEU, formerly Article 228 TEC). The Court may declare an act (legal instrument) of Union law as void on the application of a Member State, the European Parliament, the Council or the Commission (Articles 263 and 264 TFEU). Individuals, generally speaking, do not have access to the Court. However, Article 263 TFEU provides an exception. Natural and legal persons may institute proceedings against a Union act addressed to that person or which has direct effect and is of individual concern to them.[77]

An important manner in which cases may come to the Court is when a national court or tribunal requests the Court to interpret Union law, if it is involved in a pending dispute in which the interpretation of the law is relevant to the outcome of the matter (Article 267 TFEU, formerly Article 234 TEC). In this case, a national court refers for a *preliminary ruling* by the Court. References by national courts are also very frequently submitted to the Court.[78] In addition to former Article 234 TEC, a new sentence was inserted in Article 267 TFEU by the Treaty of Lisbon:

> "If such a question is raised in a case pending before a court or tribunal of a Member State with regard to a person in custody, the Court of Justice of the European Union shall act with the minimum of delay."

As a result of this, urgent proceedings have been created.[79] The preliminary questions must relate to the interpretation of Union law, but the ruling of the Court may have consequences for national implementing law (including criminal law). Over the years, the Court has used preliminary references for landmark

---

[75]   Every year, 180–220 direct actions are lodged with the Court by the Commission.

[76]   Such a judgment must be directly applied and does not depend on national implementing measures. See 13 July 1972, Case 48–71, *Commission v. Italy* [1972] ECR 527.

[77]   This mechanism has been successfully used by individuals listed on so-called terrorist lists with a view of confiscating their assets. See, further, Chapter 5, Section 6.

[78]   Every year, 200–250 references for a preliminary ruling are lodged with the Court by national courts. Article 227 further provides for complaints of a Member State against another Member State to be brought before the Court. This provision is not of any practical relevance.

[79]   See, further, Chapter 5, Section 8.6.

cases. The Court's position is made even stronger because of the fact that Union legislation is not always very clear as a result of political compromises. As a transitional measure for the first five years after the date of entry into force of the Treaty of Lisbon, the competence of the Court will not change with regard to acts adopted under the Third Pillar.[80] After this date, the Court will have the same competences with regard to legal acts within the area of freedom, security and justice as it currently has with regard to the internal market.[81] Thereafter the Court may assess whether or not a Member State has complied with a Framework Decision, a Convention or a Joint Action. The same goes for the powers of the Commission. Within five years after the entry into force of the Treaty of Lisbon, it will have the competence to bring a case against a Member State for violating a legal act of the area of freedom, security and justice on the basis of Article 258 TFEU.

The Court consists of one judge per Member State (Article 19, paragraph 2 TEU). It has its seat in Luxembourg. The Court reaches its judgment by a simple-majority, without expressing the votes in its decisions. Dissenting or Separate Opinions are not issued. All judgments and orders of the Court are available on-line and are published in the European Court Reports (ECR) in all the authentic languages of the European Union.[82]

The *General Court* (formerly, the *Court of First Instance*) is to include at least one judge per Member State (Article 19, paragraph 2 TEU). Article 256 TFEU (formerly Article 225 TEC) determines its jurisdiction precisely. In the field of criminal law, its role would seem to be limited to the review of the legality of certain legislative acts that affect individuals,[83] in contrast with the prominent role that it possesses in competition cases. Under certain circumstances, the Court of Justice may review decisions of the General Court. Article 257 TFEU creates the possibility of the establishment of special courts attached to the General Court.[84]

Article 252 TFEU (formerly Article 222 TEC) formally states that eight *Advocates General* assist the Court of Justice:[85]

"It shall be the duty of the Advocate General, acting with complete impartiality and independence to make, in open court, reasoned submissions on cases which, in accordance with the Statute of the Court of Justice require his involvement."

---

80   See, in more detail, Chapter 3, Section 5.1.

81   Article 10 of the Protocol on Transitional Provisions. The United Kingdom opted out.

82   See http://curia.eu.

83   For instance, individuals whose assets have been frozen, because they were listed as terrorists in *Common Position 2001/931 on Specific Measures to Combat Terrorism*.

84   The first specialised court to be established is the EU Civil Service Tribunal. See Annex 1 to Protocol 3 on the Statute of the Court of Justice of the European Union.

85   Following Declaration 38 on Article 252 of the Treaty on the Functioning of the European Union regarding the number of Advocates General in the Court of Justice, the number may be

Although the Opinions of the Advocate General are of an advisory nature, they will often be referred to in this book. Because of their advisory character, Advocates General use opinions with a fair degree of discretion with regard to the problems that arise in a specific case. The Advocate General is in a position to place cases in a larger context, and he may point to certain issues that relate to the pending matter, and he exercises, in most cases, a strong influence upon the arguments to be dealt with by the Court. Changes in the case law are often suggested first by the Advocate General. The Opinion of the Advocate General is issued before the Court takes a decision and is available on-line. Although there is no obligation to do so, in practice, the Court often follows the Opinion.

The European Central Bank

The European Central Bank was established on 1 July 1998 within the European System of Central Banks (Article 282 TFEU) and has its seat in Frankfort. Its primary objective is to maintain price stability (Article 127 TFEU, formerly Article 105 TEC). As of 1 January 2002, the European Central Bank is responsible for the euro and the monetary policy of the Union.

The Court of Auditors

Article 285 TFEU (formerly Article 246 TEC) simply states that the Court of Auditors is to carry out the audit. It examines the accounts of all revenue and expenditure of all bodies set up by the Union. It reports to the European Parliament and to the Council, in particular on any case of irregularities. The Court of Auditors may report cases of fraud to the *Office de Coordination de la Lutte Anti-Fraude* (OLAF),[86] and it is consulted on measures concerning the prevention and the fight against fraud affecting the financial interest of the Community (Article 325, paragraph 4 TFEU, formerly Article 280, paragraph. 4 TEC). It has its seat in Luxembourg.

AGENCIES

The European Ombudsman

The European Ombudsman may receive complaints from any citizen of the European Union concerning instances of mal-administration in the activities of institutions (Article 228 TFEU, formerly Article 195 TEC). However, the Ombudsman may not deal with complaints concerning the Court of Justice and

---

increased from eight to eleven. In that case Poland will, as is already the case for Germany, France, Italy, Spain and the United Kingdom have a permanent Advocate General.

[86] French acronym for *Office de Coordination de la Lutte Anti-Fraude* (Office for the co-ordination of the fight against fraud). See, further, Chapter 5, Section 5.3.

the General Court. He has a wide discretion to conduct inquiries, after the conclusion of which he sends a report to the European Parliament and to the institution concerned.

BODIES AND OFFICES IN THE FIELD OF CRIMINAL LAW

Since the Treaty of Maastricht of 1992 gave the European Union legislative authority in the area of criminal law, a number of agencies, bodies and offices have been established. 1993 saw the establishment of a European Police Office: *Europol*.[87] This office, based in The Hague, focuses on the exchange and analysis of information between the various European Union Member States.[88] It has no operational authority, it may not conduct investigations, make arrests or use any other coercive measures itself. It is dependent on the police forces of the Member States for obtaining its information. In 2002, *Eurojust* was established.[89] This is a network of public prosecutors of the Member States, who can support each other in obtaining mutual co-operation in criminal matters and can take joint-decisions on the most suitable place of prosecution. The *European Judicial Network* attempts to facilitate courts in obtaining mutual co-operation in criminal matters or information on foreign law.[90]

Article 86 TFEU allows for the establishment of a *European Public Prosecutor's Office* from *Eurojust* on the basis of regulations.[91] OLAF, already mentioned before, is a unit within the Commission which has been established and charged with the specific task of combating fraud.[92] Many of the investigations initiated by this unit ultimately lead to criminal law investigations.

By Regulation 168/2007, an Agency for fundamental rights has been established.[93] It aims to offer the institutions and agencies of the European Union help and expertise in the area of fundamental rights, although it does not have a judicial function.

---

[87]   The Commission mentioned Europol and Eurojust as agencies in the field of criminal law. Communication from the Commission to the European Parliament and the Council, European agencies – The way forward, 11.3.2008 COM (2008) 135 final.

[88]   *Europol Convention*. See, further, Chapter 8, Section 2.1.2.

[89]   *Eurojust Decision 2002/187*. See, further, Chapter 8, Section 2.2.

[90]   *Joint Action 98/428 on the European Judicial Network*. See, further, Chapter 8, Section 2.3.

[91]   See, further, Chapter 8, Section 3.2.

[92]   *OLAF Decision 1999/352*. See, further, on the collection of evidence by OLAF and possible prosecutions in national criminal justice systems, Chapter 5, Section 5.3.

[93]   Council Regulation (EC) 168/2007 of 15 February 2007 establishing a European Union Agency for Fundamental Rights, OJ 2007, L 53/1. The Agency's objective is, according to Article 2 of the Regulation "to provide the relevant institutions, bodies, offices and agencies of the Community and its Member States when implementing Community law with assistance an expertise when they take measures or formulate courses of action within their respective spheres of competence to fully respect fundamental rights".

CHAPTER 3.
CONSTITUTIONAL PRINCIPLES
OF UNION LAW

1. INTRODUCTION

Having introduced both the institutional structure of the European Union and the rationales of its policies in the previous chapter, it is now time to look at the legal implementation of its policy. The approach of this chapter is both top-down and bottom-up. It will deal both with the obligations imposed upon Member States, as well with their consequences under national law. Although criminal law is not the central issue of this chapter, more and more attention will increasingly be paid to it. The structure of the book is layered and brings us closer to the heart of our topic with each page.

Case law plays a prominent role in this chapter, the essence of which consists of an analysis of numerous cases of the Court. All the relevant case law will be examined. The principles of Union law collected in this chapter have obtained such a fundamental status that they can be classified as constitutional, and these constitutional principles consists of the enforcement obligation, direct effect, the *Greek maize* criteria, the five freedoms, the prohibition of discrimination on nationality, mutual recognition, general principles of law, and the interpretation in conformity. As expressed earlier, through the developments in the Court's case law and the perspectives of the Treaty of Lisbon, the former First and Third Pillars will be jointly dealt with throughout the book. Where appropriate, the book will point to the differences which are still in existence. The issue of how Union law should be interpreted is the topic of ample study in the fifth and final section of this chapter. In this last section, the general principles of law, as well as other criteria of interpretation of the law, will come to the fore.

2. LEGAL ACTS OF THE UNION

2.1. POST-LISBON LEGISLATION

The primary source of Union law consists of *the Treaties*. As mentioned before, the Treaties create the institutional framework and thus form the foundation of

Union law. The Treaties ensure a number of individual rights that have direct effect, notably the five freedoms. In addition to the Treaties, the Union is empowered to adopt secondary legislation. All legislation of the European Community and of the European Union has to be published in the Official Journal of the European Union.[94] Article 288 TFEU (formerly Article 249 TEC) states that "to exercise the Union's competences, the institutions shall adopt regulations, directives, decisions, recommendations and opinions". Pursuant to Article 288 TFEU, a Regulation has "general application. It shall be binding in its entirety and directly applicable in all Member States". Article 291 TFEU states, in a general manner, that Member States are to adopt all the measures of national law necessary to implement legally-binding acts. Pursuant to Article 288 TFEU, a Directive is "binding, as to the result to be achieved, upon each Member State to which it is addressed, but shall leave to the national authorities the choice of form and methods".[95] This means that Union law generally requires implementation into national law, but does not prescribe how the Member States must do this. The Member States may elect administrative enforcement, civil law or criminal law enforcement, or any other means. The obligation is one of results. This background explains again why, for a long time, criminal law played a subordinate role in the enforcement of Community law. The policy areas of the European Community were regarded as limited, and primarily of an economic bent. The remaining acts are the Decision, the Recommendation and the Opinion. A Decision is to be binding in its entirety. A decision which specifies those to whom it is addressed is to be binding only upon them. Recommendations and Opinions, in contrast, have no binding force.[96]

The Directive

The most influence on criminal law is exerted by the Directive.[97] In so far as the provisions of the Directive are described unconditionally and are sufficiently precise,[98] they leave the Member States no room for interpretation, and the Directive must be strictly complied with. In other words: if a Member State fails to implement Union law into its national law, Union law is nonetheless still effective, so long as its provisions are unconditional and sufficiently precise. It has been held in the case law of the Court that, for instance in *criminal proceedings*

---

[94]   The Official Journal has two series. The L series contains all legislative acts whose publication is obligatory under the Treaties, as well as other acts. The C series contain information and notices other than legislation.

[95]   Formerly Article 249 TEC and previously Article 189. Both the TEC and the EU were re-numbered before by the Treaty of Amsterdam (1997). This should be considered when interpreting case law dating from before these amendments were made.

[96]   Recommendations are adopted by the Council (Article 292 TFEU).

[97]   In the year 2007, 358 Directives were adopted.

[98]   19 January 1982, Case 8/81, *Ursula Becker* v. *Finanzamt Münster-Innenstadt* [1982] ECR 53.

against Società Agricola Industria Latte on preliminary reference of the *Pretura di Bari* (Italy), in national criminal proceedings, such provisions may be relied upon as a right that the accused and other parties can invoke.[99] The national court is obliged to interpret all implementing legislation as far as possible in the spirit of the Directive (interpretation in conformity).[100] A citizen may invoke rights under Union law at any time in any proceedings. Additionally, the Court has determined, in its case law, that criminal responsibility cannot be established directly upon the basis of a Directive which has not been implemented into national criminal law.[101] This means that the effect of Union law varies, because individual *obligations* under Union law cannot be directly applied against the citizen, even when they are formulated as being unconditional and sufficiently precise.[102] In contrast, the accused can invoke Union law if that law prescribes that a certain activity may not be prohibited even though that activity is an offence under the national criminal law.[103] Although Member States are under obligation to state the fact that Union law has been implemented when they change their legislation, they do not always do so, and this frustrates the possibilities of recognising the Union origin of national legislation.[104]

The Regulation

The significance to criminal law of the other main legal act of the Union, the Regulation,[105] is far more limited.[106] Under Article 288 TFEU (formerly 249 TEC), the Regulation is to have general application. It is to be binding in its entirety and to be directly applicable in all Member States.[107] Whilst implementing measures are not necessary to give a Regulation its direct effect, Member States have the competence to adopt criminal sanctions as an appropriate measure to

---

[99] 21 March 1972, Case 82-71, *criminal proceedings against Società Agricola Industria Latte* [1972] ECR 119; 5 April 1979, Case 148/78, *criminal proceedings against Tullio Ratti* [1979] ECR 1629.

[100] See, further, Chapter 5, Section 8.2.

[101] See, further, Chapter 4. Section 3.1.

[102] 8 October 1987, Case 80/86, *criminal proceedings against Kolpinghuis Nijmegen B.V.* [1987] ECR 3969; 3 May 2005, Case C-387/02, Case C-391/02 and Case C-403/02, *criminal proceedings against Silvio Berlusconi (C-387/02), Sergio Adelchi (C-391/02), Marcello Dell'Utri and others (C-403/02)* [2005] ECR I-3565.

[103] See, further, Chapter 5. Section 8.3.

[104] See, further, Chapter 4, Section 1 and Chapter 5, Section 1.

[105] In the year 2007, 2437 Regulations were adopted.

[106] An example of a Regulation that has been implemented in many Member States with the use of criminal law is Regulation 338/97 on the Protection of Species of Wild Fauna and Flora by Regulating Trade therein. See, also, 23 October 2003, Case C-154/02, *criminal proceedings against Jan Nilsson* [2003] ECR I-12733.

[107] The scope of a Regulation does not depend on the existence and content of national legislation. See 25 June 1992, Case C-116/91, *Licensing Authority South Eastern Traffic Area* v. *British Gas plc* [1992] ECR I-4071, par. 19.

enforce Regulations.[108] This means that implementing legislation at national level is not strictly necessary.[109] As a consequence, Regulations and criminal law only come into contact in the exceptional case in which a Member State uses the latter in support of the former.

The importance of a Regulation for criminal law will increase when the Union uses the competences received in the TFEU, which distinguishes between the changes that Union law may bring to national criminal law and criminal procedure on the one hand, and the establishment of European offices and accompanying law on the other. The approximation of both procedural and substantive criminal law will take place by means of Directives and will thus require implementation (Articles 82 and 83 TFEU). The establishment of Europol and of the European Public Prosecutor's Office will find its basis in a Regulation, as is stated in Articles 86 and 88 TFEU.

International Agreements of the European Union and Third Parties

The European Union (and previously the European Communities) has concluded (or acceded to) several agreements under international law. In the field of criminal law, one may refer to the EU as a party to a limited number of multilateral Conventions such as the United Nations Convention against Transnational Organized Crime of 2000, and its Protocol to Punish Trafficking in Persons, especially Women and Children.[110] More initiatives were taken to conclude a series of agreements on *partnership and co-operation,*[111] *association and stability*

---

[108]   2 February 1977, Case 50–76, *Amsterdam Bulb BV* v. *Produktschap voor Siergewassen* [1977] ECR 137.

[109]   17 May 1972, Case 93–71, *Orsolina Leonesio* v. *Ministero dell'agricultura e foreste* [1972] ECR 287, par. 22; 7 February 1973, Case 39–72, *Commission* v. *Italy* [1973] ECR 101; 10 October 1973, Case 34–73, *Fratelli Variola S.p.A.* v. *Amministrazione italiana delle Finanze* [1973] ECR 981.

[110]   OJ 2001, L 30/44; United Nations Protocol on the illicit manufacturing of and trafficking in firearms, their parts, components and ammunition, annexed to the Convention against transnational organised crime, OJ 2001, L 280/5; United Nations Convention against Illicit Traffic in Narcotic Drugs and Psychotropic Substances, OJ 1990, L 326/57; Decision 2008/801 of 25 September 2008 on the conclusion, on behalf of the European Community, of the United Nations Convention against Corruption, OJ 2008, L 287/1.

[111]   For instance Article 11 Co-operation Agreement between the European Community and the Republic of Yemen, OJ 1998, L 72/17.

agreements,[112] *Euro-mediterreanean agreements,*[113] as well as *agreements on trade, economic partnership and development.*[114] Finally, bilateral agreements regarding

---

[112] Agreement on partnership and cooperation establishing a partnership between the European Communities and their Member States, of one part, and the Russian Federation of the other part, OJ 1997, L 327/3; Partnership and Co-operation Agreement between the European Communities and their Member States, and Ukraine, OJ 1998, L 49/3; Partnership and Co-operation Agreement between the European Communities and their Member States and the Republic of Moldova, OJ 1998, L 181/3; Partnership and Cooperation Agreement between the European Communities and their Member States and the Republic of Kazakhstan, OJ 1999, L 196/3; Partnership and Co-operation Agreement establishing a partnership between the European Communities and their Member States, of the one part, and the Kyrgyz Republic, of the other part, OJ 1999, L 196/48; Partnership and Co-operation Agreement between the European Communities and their Member States, of the one part, and Georgia, of the other part, OJ 1999/ L 205/3; Partnership and Co-operation Agreement establishing a partnership between the European Communities and their Member States, of the one part, and the Republic of Uzbekistan, of the other part, OJ 1999, L 229/3; Partnership and Co-operation Agreement between the European Communities and their Member States, of the one part, and the Republic of Armenia, of the other part, OJ 1999, L 239/3; Partnership and Co-operation Agreement between the European Communities and their Member States, of the one part, and the Republic of Azerbaijan, of the other part OJ 1999, L 246/3; Stabilisation and Association Agreement between the European Communities and their Member States, of the one part, and the former Yugoslav Republic of Macedonia, of the other part, OJ 2004, L 84/1; Stabilisation and Association Agreement between the European Communities and their Member States, of the one part, and the Republic of Croatia, of the other part, OJ 2005, L 26/3.

[113] Euro-Mediterranean Agreement establishing an association between the European Communities and their Member States, of the one part, and the Kingdom of Morocco, of the other part, OJ 2000, L 70/2; Euro-Mediterranean Agreement establishing an association between the European Communities and their Member States, of the one part, and the State of Israel, of the other part, OJ 2000, L 147/3; Euro-Mediterranean Agreement establishing an Association between the European Communities and their Member States, of the one part, and the Hashemite Kingdom of Jordan, of the other part, OJ 2002, L 129/3; Euro-Mediterranean Agreement establishing an Association between the European Communities and their Member States, of the one part, and the Arab Republic of Egypt, of the other part, OJ 2004, L 304/39; Euro-Mediterranean Agreement establishing an Association between the European Community and its Member States, of the one part, and the People's Democratic Republic of Algeria, of the other part, OJ 2005, L 265/2; Euro-Mediterranean Agreement establishing an association between the European Communities and their Member States, of the one part, and the Republic of Tunisia, of the other, OJ 2005, L 278/9; Euro-Mediterranean Agreement establishing an Association between the European Community and its Member States, of the one part, and the Republic of Lebanon, of the other part, OJ 2006, L 143/2.

[114] Agreement on Trade, Development and Co-operation between the European Community and its Member States, of the one part, and the Republic of South Africa, of the other part, OJ 1999, L 311/3; Economic Partnership, Political Co-ordination and Co-operation Agreement between the European Community and its Member States, of the one part, and the United Mexican States, of the other part, OJ 2000, L 276/44; Interim Agreement on trade and trade-related matters between the European Community, of the one part, and the Republic of Albania, of the other part, OJ 2006, L 239/2; Interim Agreement on trade and trade-related matters between the European Community, of the one part, and the Republic of Montenegro, of the other part, OJ 2007, L 345/2; Interim Agreement on trade and trade-related matters between the European community and the European Atomic Energy Community, of the one part, and the Republic of Tajikistan, of the other part, OJ 2004, L 340/2.

precursors for psychotropic substances were concluded.[115] The relevance of these agreements for criminal law differs from treaty to treaty. Some contain provisions that facilitate co-operation in criminal matters, other carry obligations to criminalise certain conduct, to fight corruption and to help the non-Member State to build a fair administration of justice.

To date, treaties negotiated by the Union dealing exclusively with criminal law are rare. Prominent examples of the latter are the treaties with the United States of America on extradition and on mutual legal assistance. Article 216, paragraph 1 TFEU gives a mandate to the Union to conclude agreements with one or more third countries:

> "where the Treaties so provide or where the conclusion of an agreement is necessary in order to achieve, within the framework of the Union's policies, one of the objectives referred to in the Treaties, or is provided for in a legally binding Union act or is likely to affect common rules or alter their scope."

What are the effects of these kinds of treaties concluded by the European Union? Paragraph 2 of Article 216 TFEU states that such agreements are binding upon the institutions and upon its Member States. The Court has held (with regard to a free trade agreement between the Community and a third state) that such an agreement forms an integral part of the Community legal system:

> "The effects within the Community of such provisions of an agreement concluded by the Community with a non-member country may not be determined without taking into account of the international origin of the provisions in question."[116]

2.2. PRE-LISBON LEGISLATION

Because of the fact that there are a fair number acts adopted under the Treaty on European Union before the Treaty of Lisbon entered into force, it is necessary to look at the different set of legal instruments that were available in the third pillar. Firstly, there was the Treaty on European Union, and in addition there are Common Positions, Framework Decisions, Decisions and Conventions, adopted upon the basis of Article 34 EU. The significance of the Treaty on European Union (in the version before the Treaty of Lisbon amended it) on criminal law, and, in

---

[115]   See, for instance, the Agreements between the European Community and several states on precursors and chemical substances frequently used in the illicit manufacture of narcotics drugs or psychotropic substances. Bolivia, OJ 1995, L 234/1; Colombia, OJ 1995, L 234/10; Ecuador, OJ 1995, L 324/18; Peru, OJ 1995, L 324/26; Chile, OJ 1998, L 336/46; Turkey, OJ 2003, L 64/28.

[116]   26 October 1982, Case 104/81, *Hauptzollamt Mainz* v. *C.A. Kupferberg & Cie KGa.A.* [1982] ECR 3641, par. 13.

particular, the objective of "creating an ever closer union among the peoples of Europe",[117] and the creation of an area of freedom, security and justice (Article 29 EU), seems to be limited to referring to a very distant ideal, as well as to providing a legal basis for the four legal instruments.[118] In other words, it does not directly grant citizens rights which they may invoke before a national court.

Despite the fact that previous versions of the Treaty on European Union were less specific with regard to the definition of the legal acts than the current Treaties, a few additional observations are appropriate. *Common Positions* define the Union's approach with regard to a particular matter.[119] *Framework Decisions* are drafted for the approximation of the laws and regulations of the Member States. They are binding, as to the result to be achieved, upon each Member State, but the choice of form and methods is left to the national institutions. Moreover, they do not have direct effect. Although the similarity with the definition of the Directive is striking,[120] the difference lies in the last sentence of the definition of the Framework Decision in paragraph 2 sub c of Article 34 EU: "They shall not entail direct effect." Despite this indication that Framework Decisions do not have a power of their own, the Court has held that national courts must interpret implementing legislation in conformity with the Framework Decisions in order to give a Framework Decision its useful effect.[121] The topic of approximation of the laws and regulations by the adoption of Framework Decisions is not limited to the Member States' rules of criminal law.[122] In the words of Article 34, paragraph 2, EU, *Decisions* concern any other purpose that is consistent with the objectives of the Third Pillar, excluding the approximation of the laws and regulations of the

---

[117] "Ever closer" does not imply any moment of completion: European integration is a never-ending process.

[118] On the one hand, the term "area" can imply something with no internal boundaries, while, at the same time, it can be a catch-all term that can be attached to anything with a political will behind it.

[119] Examples are the Common Position 97/661 of 6 October 1997 on negotiations in the Council of Europe and the OECD relating to corruption, OJ 1997, L 297/1; Second Common Position 97/783 of 13 November 1997 on negotiations in the Council of Europe and the OECD relating to corruption, OJ 1997, L 320/1; Joint Position 1999/235 of 29 March 1999 on the proposed United Nations conventions against organised crime, OJ 1999, L 87/1; Common Position 1999/364 of 27 May 1999, on negotiations relating to the Draft Convention on Cyber Crime held within the Council of Europe, OJ 1999, L 142/1; Common Position 2000/130 of 31 January 2000 on the proposed Protocol against the illicit manufacturing of and trafficking in firearms, their parts and components and ammunition, supplementing the United Nations Convention against Transnational organised crime, OJ 2000, L 37/1.

[120] In general, such as Directives, Framework Decisions give Member States a period of two years to implement the obligations deriving from the instrument. An example of a much shorter period of implementation is *Framework Decision 2002/475 on Combating Terrorism* of 13 June 2002, which, according to its Article 11, had to be implemented by 31 December 2002.

[121] 16 June 2005, Case C-105/03, *criminal proceedings against Maria Pupino* [2005] ECR I-5285. See, further, Chapter 5, Section 8.

[122] 3 May 2007, Case C-303/05, *Advocaten voor de Wereld VZW v. Leden van de Ministerraad* [2007] ECR I-3633, par. 32.

Member States.[123] Decisions are binding, but do not have direct effect. The *Conventions* mentioned in Article 34 EU are Conventions in the international law sense. Unlike all the other instruments, Conventions must be ratified by the national parliaments in order to enter into force.

The Treaty of Maastricht (1992) had three kinds of legal acts: *Joint Positions*,[124] *Joint Actions* and *Conventions*. The Treaty of Amsterdam (1997) abolished the Joint Action and introduced the *Framework Decisions* and *Decisions*. The Treaty of Nice (2001) left all four acts untouched. There are still a few *Joint Actions* remaining from the time of the Treaty of Maastricht, which will fall under the same transition rules as the other four acts.[125] It is assumed that those Joint Actions also do not have direct effect and that they require implementation into national law, as the Treaty of Maastricht introduced this legal instrument, without further describing it in its Article K.3. While the Treaty of Amsterdam did not clarify the relationship between the new legal instruments and the older ones that were enacted under the Maastricht regime, the Treaty of Lisbon provides a clear transition scheme.

The legal instruments of the Treaty on European Union (Common Positions, Framework Decisions, Decisions and Conventions) will not be continued under the new regime. What will happen to these legal acts? Article 9 of the Protocol on Transitional Provisions provides that all acts and agreements will be preserved until these acts are repealed, annulled or amended. The same applies to agreements concluded between Member States upon the basis of the Treaty on European Union. Article 10 of the Protocol on Transitional Provisions deals with the transitional measures regarding "acts of the Union in the field of police co-operation and judicial co-operation in criminal matters which have been adopted before the entry into force of the Treaty of Lisbon". With regard to these acts, the Commission cannot make use of its powers under Article 258 TFEU. This means that the Commission cannot bring a case against a Member State to the Court because of non-compliance. Similarly, the powers of the Court remain the same as before the Treaty of Lisbon entered into force. Should an act of the pre-Lisbon period be amended after the entry into force of the Treaty of Lisbon, it will automatically fall within the new supervisory regime in which both the Commission and the Court are fully competent.[126]

---

[123] An example is the Decision of 6 December 2001 extending Europol's mandate to deal with the serious forms of international crime listed in the Annex to the *Europol Convention*, OJ 2001, C 362/1.

[124] The Treaty on European Union in the version of Maastricht 1992 referred to Joint Position. The Joint Position was replaced by the Treaty of Amsterdam for the Common Position.

[125] Without being exhaustive: Joint Action 98/427 on good practice in mutual legal assistance in criminal matters; *Joint Action 98/428 on the European Judicial Network; Joint Action 98/733 on Participation in a Criminal Organisation.*

[126] Declaration No. 50 concerning Article 10 of the Protocol on transitional provisions: The Conference invites the European Parliament, the Council and the Commission, within their

The same will happen to all the remaining acts of the pre-Lisbon period, 5 years after the Treaty of Lisbon has entered into force. However, Article 10, paragraphs 4 and 5 of Protocol 36 on Transitional Provisions make an exception for the United Kingdom. Six months before the expiry of the transitional period, the United Kingdom may notify that it does not accept the supervising powers of the Commission and the Court in the area of co-operation in criminal matters. In this case, all acts adopted under the Treaty on European Union (the version before the Treaty of Lisbon) will cease to apply.[127]

Overview of the development of the law under the various treaties

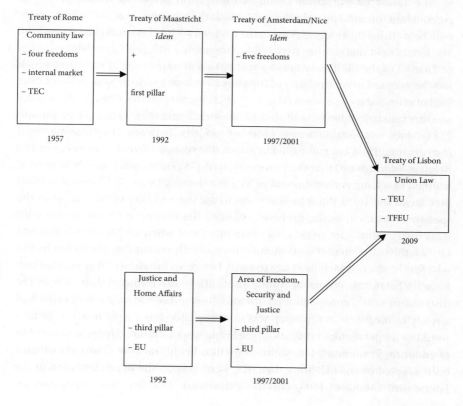

respective powers, to seek to adopt, in appropriate cases and as far as possible within the five-year period referred to in Article 10(3) of the Protocol on transitional provisions, legal acts amending or replacing the acts referred to in Article 10(1) of that Protocol.

[127]   The Protocol of the Schengen *acquis* integrated into the framework of the European Union regulates its continuing application. See, further, on Schengen, Sections 2.4 and 5.1 in this Chapter.

2.3. CHOICE OF THE UNION ACT

The reduction of the number of acts of the Union and the indication of the particular act with which the Union should legislate in each policy area, make the choice of the acts much clearer. Consequently, it is hoped that discussions on the question of whether the appropriate legal instrument was used will now belong to the past. In the past, the Commission and the Council fought their battles on the question of whether certain policy fields should be regulated in a Directive or in a Framework Decision.[128]

The Treaty on European Union in the version before the Treaty of Lisbon entered into force did not stipulate which was the appropriate act of legislation for each field. Third Pillar legislation left the Council with a certain degree of freedom. The Court held that neither Article 34, paragraph 2 EU, nor any other provision of Title VI of the EU Treaty draws a distinction as to the type of measures which may be adopted upon the basis of the subject-matter to which joint action in the field of criminal co-operation relates.[129] There are no precise criteria to determine whether legislation should take place in one form or another. Article 34, paragraph 2 EU does not establish any order of priority between the different legal instruments. The Court admitted in *Advocaten voor de Wereld* (a reference by the Belgian *Arbitragehof*) that the European Arrest Warrant could equally have been adopted as a Convention, instead of as a Framework Decision.[130] The legislative practice in the Third Pillar basically was to use the necessity of ratification of the specific instrument as the decisive criterion. The European Union started with legal instruments that could only enter into force when all Member States had ratified the instrument (Convention). This basically meant that the Union had to wait for the slowest Member State to ratify before an instrument would enter into force.[131] Later, the system of rolling ratification was introduced, by which the instrument would enter into force for and among those Member States that had already ratified it.[132] A final step was taken by choosing a legal instrument that would no longer require ratification: the Framework Decision. Since the possibility of adopting Framework Decisions came into being, no new Conventions have been adopted by the EU. Since then, the focus is upon the implementation of the Framework Decision. However, the Framework Decision has not solved all

---

[128]   See 13 September 2005, Case C-176/03, *Commission* v. *Council* [2005] ECR I-7879; 23 October 2007, 440/05, *Commission* v. *Council* [2007] ECR I-9097.
[129]   3 May 2007, Case C-303/05, *Advocaten voor de Wereld VZW* v. *Leden van de Ministerraad* [2007] ECR I-3633, par. 37.
[130]   3 May 2007, Case C-303/05, *Advocaten voor de Wereld VZW* v. *Leden van de Ministerraad* [2007] ECR I-3633, par. 41.
[131]   There is a number of Conventions dating from the 1980s and 1990s that never entered into force.
[132]   See, also, Article 34, paragraph 2, last two sentences, EU.

problems, either. Since a Framework Decision requires implementation into national law, the problem has been merely shifted to the question of whether a Member State has implemented (in time). In this sense, the legal questions relating to Framework Decisions, as well as their answers, are increasingly similar to those regarding Directives.

2.4. VARIABLE GEOMETRY: DIVERGING APPLICATION OF THE LAW[133]

In principle, all European legislation is, without distinction, applicable throughout the entire Union.[134] However, there are some exceptions to this, which are especially relevant in the field of criminal law.[135] The United Kingdom and Ireland have obtained a special position with regard to the area of freedom, security and justice,[136] and do not take part in the adoption of measures in this area.[137] However, Article 3 of the Protocol allows both countries *to opt in* and to take part with regard to a specific proposed measure.[138] The Protocol on the Position of Denmark contains a different rule for Denmark, too.[139] Denmark may decide to

---

[133]   The Europa glossary defines variable geometry as the term used to describe the idea of a method of differentiated integration which acknowledges that there are irreconcilable differences within the integration structure and therefore allows for a permanent separation between a group of Member States and a number of less developed countries. See http://europa. eu/scadplus/glossary/variable_geometry_europe_en.htm, last accessed on 21 August 2008.

[134]   A good overview of the special position of some Member States is given by Advocate General Trstenjak in his Opinion of 10 July 2007 in Case C-77/05, *United Kingdom v. Council* [2007] ECR I-11459, par. 90–128.

[135]   But not only here. See, for instance, *Regulation 44/2001 on Jurisdiction and Recognition of Civil Judgments*, which does not apply to Denmark.

[136]   Protocol No. 21 on the position of the United Kingdom and Ireland in respect of the area of freedom, security and justice.

[137]   Article 2 of Protocol No. 21 states that, in consequence of this, "no measure adopted pursuant to that Title, no provision of any international agreement concluded by the Union pursuant to that Title, and no decision of the Court of Justice interpreting any such provision or measure shall be binding upon or applicable in the United Kingdom or Ireland; and no such provision, measure or decision shall in any way affect the competences, rights and obligations of those States; and no such provision, measure or decision shall in any way affect the Community or Union acquis nor form part of Union law as they apply to the United Kingdom or Ireland".

[138]   Ireland declared that it will do so to the maximum extent it deems possible. See Declaration 56 by Ireland on Article 3 of the Protocol No. 21 on the position of the United Kingdom and Ireland in respect of the area of freedom, security and justice.

[139]   Article 2 Protocol No. 22 reads: "None of the provisions of Title V of Part Three of the Treaty on the Functioning of the European Union, no measure adopted pursuant to that Title, no provision of any international agreement concluded by the Union pursuant to that Title, and no decision of the Court of Justice of the European Union interpreting any such provision or measure or any measure amended or amendable pursuant to that Title shall be binding upon or applicable in Denmark; and no such provision, measure or decision shall in any way affect the competences, rights and obligations of Denmark; and no such provision, measure or

implement a measure adopted by the Council building upon the Schengen *acquis* (Article 4 Protocol No. 22). If it decides to do so, this measure will create an obligation under international law between Denmark and the other Member States bound by the measure. Furthermore, at any time, Denmark may notify the other Member States that it wishes to be bound by the different opt-in regime applicable to the United Kingdom and Ireland (Article 8 Protocol No. 22).[140]

Whilst Article 6, paragraph 1 TEU recognises the Charter of Fundamental Rights of the European Union of 7 December 2000 as having the same legal value as the Treaties, Protocol No. 30 attached to the Treaties, excludes the application of the Charter to Poland and the United Kingdom.[141] Additionally, Poland declared that the Charter does not affect, in any way, the right of Member States to legislate in the sphere of public morality, family law, the protection of human dignity, and respect for human physical and moral integrity.[142] The Czech Republic attached a Declaration to the Treaty of Lisbon declaring that the Charter is addressed to the institutions and bodies of the European Union and to Member States only when they are implementing Union law.[143]

When integrating the Schengen *acquis* into the framework of the European Union in 1999, two decisions were taken by the Council. One defined the Schengen *acquis*,[144] the other determined the legal basis of each and every individual

---

decision shall in any way affect the Community or Union acquis nor form part of Union law as they apply to Denmark. In particular, acts of the Union in the field of police cooperation and judicial cooperation in criminal matters adopted before the entry into force of the Treaty of Lisbon which are amended shall continue to be binding upon and applicable to Denmark unchanged".

[140]   Switzerland is also associated. See Agreement between the European Union, the European Community and the Swiss Confederation's association with the implementation, application and development of the Schengen *acquis*.

[141]   Protocol No. 30 on the Application of the Charter of Fundamental Rights of the European Union to Poland and the United Kingdom. Article 1 of Protocol 30 reads: "1. The Charter does not extend the ability of the Court of Justice of the European Union, or any court or tribunal of Poland or of the United Kingdom, to find that the laws, regulations or administrative provisions, practices or action of Poland or of the United Kingdom are inconsistent with the fundamental rights, freedoms and principles that it re-affirms. 2. In particular, and for the avoidance of doubt, nothing in Title IV of the Charter creates justiciable rights applicable to Poland or the United Kingdom except in so far as Poland or the United Kingdom has provided for such rights in its national law".

[142]   Declaration 61 by the Republic of Poland on the Charter of Fundamental Rights of the European Union.

[143]   Declaration 53 by the Czech Republic on the Charter of Fundamental Rights of the European Union.

[144]   Decision 1999/435 of 20 May 1999 concerning the definition of the Schengen *acquis* for the purpose of determining, in conformity with the relevant provisions of the Treaty establishing the European Community and the Treaty on European Union, the legal basis for each of the provisions or decisions which constitute the *acquis*, OJ 1999, L 176/1.

provision of the *acquis*.[145] While the majority of Member States is a party to the Schengen *acquis, some Member States have accepted only part of this legislation.* As we have seen, Ireland, the United Kingdom and Denmark obtained a special position.[146] This specific position has been maintained and made even stronger (some will say: worse) under the Treaty of Lisbon.[147] The provisions in which the United Kingdom and Ireland do not take part may be further developed by the other Member States, using the framework of the European Union. At any time, Ireland and the United Kingdom may request to take part in some, or all, of the provisions of the Schengen *acquis*.[148] The United Kingdom may not participate on choosing a specific measure, but must first accept the area of the *acquis* to which that measure is based.[149] Outside the framework of the Union, some Member States have adopted the Treaty of Prüm of 27 May 2005 on the stepping up of cross-border co-operation, particularly for combating terrorism, cross-border crime and illegal immigration.[150]

In addition, the Convention Implementing the Schengen Agreement,[151] and the Convention on Mutual Assistance in Criminal Matters between the Member States of the European Union have accepted two non-Member States, Norway and

---

[145]   Decision 1999/436 of 20 May 1999 determining, in conformity with the relevant provisions of the Treaty establishing the European Community and the Treaty on European Union, the legal basis for each of the provisions or decisions which constitute the *acquis*, OJ 1999, L 176/17.

[146]   Agreement of 28 June 1999 concluded by the Council of the European Union and the Republic of Iceland and the Kingdom of Norway on the establishment of rights and obligations between Ireland and the United Kingdom of Great Britain and Northern Ireland, on the one hand, and the Republic of Iceland and the Kingdom of Norway on the other, in areas of the Schengen *acquis* which apply to these States, OJ 2000, L 15/2; Council Decision of 29 May 2000 concerning the request of the United Kingdom of Great Britain and Northern Ireland to take part in some of the provisions of the Schengen *acquis*, OJ 2000, L 131/43; Decision 2002/192 of 28 February 2002 concerning Ireland's request to take part in some of the provisions of the Schengen *acquis*, OJ 2002, L 64/20.

[147]   Protocol No. 19 on the Schengen *acquis* integrated into the framework of the European Union.

[148]   Article 4 Protocol No. 19 on the Schengen *acquis* integrated into the framework of the European Union. See, further, Declarations 44–47 attached to the Treaties.

[149]   18 December 2007, Case C-77/05, *United Kingdom* v. *Council* [2007] ECR I-11459, par. 62–63.

[150]   Concluded between Austria, Belgium, France, Germany, Luxembourg, the Netherlands and Spain.

[151]   Agreement by the Council of the European Union and the Republic of Iceland and the Kingdom of Norway concerning the latter's association with the implementation, application and development of the Schengen *acquis*, OJ 1999, L 176/36. The agreement has been implemented by Decision 1999/437 of 17 May 1999 on certain arrangements for the application of the Agreement concluded by the Council of the European Union and the Republic of Iceland and the Kingdom of Norway concerning the association of those two States with the implementation, application and development of the Schengen *acquis*, OJ 1999, L 176/31; Agreement in the form of Exchanges of Letters between the Council of the European Union and the Republic of Iceland and the Kingdom of Norway concerning committees which assist the European Commission in the exercise of its powers, OJ 1999, L 176/53.

Iceland as parties.[152] While the accession of Iceland and Norway to these instruments under international law is already far reaching, this is even more the case with the specific surrender procedures that have been agreed upon with these two countries.[153]

Enhanced Co-Operation

The Treaties allow for *enhanced co-operation*, subject to certain conditions (Article 20 TEU and Articles 326–334 TFEU). This gives a smaller group of Member States the possibility of dealing with issues that are of particular concern to them but not to other Member States, as well as the possibility of developing forms of co-operation with like minded states, which are unacceptable to others. The aim of enhanced co-operation is to further the objectives of the Union, to protect its interests, and to reinforce its integration process. The procedures to be followed to establish enhanced co-operation are mentioned in Articles 329–331 TFEU. When the enhanced co-operation is established, it will also be open to other Member States, which are not yet participating. Although Member States can thus always join enhanced co-operation mechanisms at a later stage, they have to take it or leave it as it is then, and cannot re-open negotiations again.

The Treaties provide for the mechanism of enhanced co-operation in all areas relevant for criminal law. It is foreseen both in Articles 82 and 83 TFEU, and may thus relate to substantive criminal law, criminal procedure and international co-operation between the Member States. In addition, the European Public Prosecutor's Office may be established by enhanced co-operation (Article 86 TFEU). Similarly, measures of police co-operation can be taken on the basis of this mechanism (Article 87 TFEU). Enhanced co-operation is not provided for regarding Europol (Article 88 TFEU).

Furthermore, Article 20, paragraph 2 TEU contains new elements when compared with the closer co-operation that existed before. The decision authorising enhanced cooperation is to be adopted only "as a last resort, when it has established that the objectives of such co-operation cannot be attained within a reasonable period by the Union as a whole". Article 20, paragraph 4 stipulates that acts adopted in the framework of enhanced co-operation only bind the participating Member States. It further states that the *acquis* of enhanced co-operation is not to be regarded as part of the *acquis* which has to be accepted

---

152 Article 29 of the Convention and Article 15 of the Protocol to the Mutual Assistance Convention. See the Agreement between the European Union and the Republic of Iceland and the Kingdom of Norway on the application of certain provisions of the Convention of 29 May 2000 on Mutual Assistance in Criminal Matters between the Member States of the European Union and the 2001 Protocol thereto, OJ 2004, L 26/3.

153 Agreement of 28 June 2006 between the European Union and the Republic of Iceland and the Kingdom of Norway on the surrender procedure between the Member States of the European Union and Iceland and Norway, OJ 2006, L 292/2. See, further, Chapter 7, Section 3.2 and 4.4.

by candidate states for accession. The importance of this sentence lies more with the interests of the Member States *not participating* in the enhanced co-operation. The fact that candidate states do not have to accept the enhanced co-operation *acquis* does not change the balance in decision-making. Otherwise, it would be very difficult for an old Member State to avoid the enhanced co-operation in the long term. Article 20, paragraph 4 also raises the question of how much weight the Court is to give to provisions of this kind which undermine the uniformity in the application of Union law.

The fact that a Member State may or may not accept certain legislation can lead to rather confusing situations. In *Kretzinger*, the question came up as to whether *Framework Decision 2002/584 on the European Arrest Warrant* could have implications for the principle of *ne bis in idem* of Article 54 *CISA*. Although the Court correctly pointed out, upon the basis of the distinct meaning of the two instruments, that it could not have such an impact, it raises a much more interesting issue. What is the influence of a legal instrument that is binding for all Member States on an instrument that is binding for a limited number of Member States only (or *vice versa*)? Advocate General Sharpston briefly touched upon this issue in her Opinion:

> "Thus, it is clear from the Framework Decision itself that the actual issue of a European arrest warrant, let alone the mere possibility that it might be issued in the future, has no implications for the principle of *ne bis in idem*. On the contrary, as Article 3(2) shows, the principle of *ne bis in idem* governs whether a European arrest warrant issued under the Framework Decision will, or will not, be executed. (...) That conclusion is further warranted by the fact that, as noted by Austria in its observations, the parties to the Schengen Agreement are not the same as those subject to the Framework Decision. If the application of the *ne bis in idem* principle in Article 54 of the CISA were dependent on the provisions of the Framework Decision, the result would be legal uncertainty."[154]

The various and diverging regimes of application described above increase these kind of problems. Inevitably, measures adopted within mechanisms of enhanced co-operation, the continuation of the Schengen *acquis* and the opt-out possibilities for the United Kingdom, Ireland, Denmark and Poland, will also deal with rules and principles that relate to more general issues of Union law. The Court will have to perform its task of ensuring the uniform interpretation of Union attentively. It cannot be that the effect of a Directive under enhanced co-operation is different from the effect of a Directive applicable to all Member States.

---

[154]   Opinion of Advocate General Sharpston of 5 December 2006, Case C-288/05, *criminal proceedings against Jürgen Kretzinger* [2007] ECR I-6441, points 89–90, footnotes omitted.

3. RULES ON THE ENFORCEMENT OF UNION LAW

This section deals with the rules that regulate the enforcement of Union law, which must be regarded as a form of indirect enforcement. Although the Union creates the law, the common norms, it does (apart from competition law) not implement it itself, but depends on the Member States. It is for them to implement Union law correctly, albeit under the supervision of the institutions of the Union. The angle of approach of this section is to deal with the general requirements of Union law regarding the enforcement of Union law by the Member States. In Sections 4 and 5, specific individual rights as well as the interpretation of the law will be discussed. These sections will analyse the position of the individual, and more and more often that individual will be the accused in criminal proceedings.

3.1. UNION LAW CREATES ITS "OWN LEGAL SYSTEM"

In *Costa* v. *E.N.E.L*, the Court held that Union legislation has direct effect and has supremacy over national law:[155]

> "By creating a Community of unlimited duration, having its own institutions, its own personality, its own legal capacity and capacity of representation on the international plane and, more particularly, real powers stemming from a limitation of sovereignty or a transfer of powers from the States to the Community, the Member States have limited their sovereign rights, albeit within limited fields, and have thus created a body of law which binds both nationals and themselves."[156]

Declaration 17 attached to the Treaty of Lisbon confirms the settled case law of the Court in which Union law has primacy over the law of the Member States, under the conditions laid down by the said case law.

Union law is directly applicable. National courts cannot hold themselves bound by a provision of national law which purports to exclude all judicial review of the implementation of Union legislation.[157] National procedural rules that preclude the direct application of *unconditional and sufficiently clear* provisions must be set aside by national courts:

---

[155] Throughout the book Community has been replaced by Union in the main text, but kept in the quotations. See Chapter 1, Section 3.

[156] 15 July 1964, Case 6/64, *Flaminio Costa* v. *E.N.E.L.* [1964] ECR 585.

[157] 2 February 1977, Case 50–76, *Amsterdam Bulb BV* v. *Produktschap voor Siergewassen* [1977] ECR 137, par. 7; Opinion of Advocate General Darmon of 28 January 1986, Case 222/84, *Marguerite Johnston* v. *Chief Constable of the Royal Ulster Constabulary* [1986] ECR 1651, point 4.

"the derogation from the principle of equal treatment which, as stated above, is allowed by Article 2(2) constitutes only an option for the Member States. It is for the competent national court to see whether that option has been exercised in provisions of national law and to construe the content of those provisions. The question whether an individual may rely upon a provision of the directive in order to have a derogation laid down by national legislation set aside arises only if that derogation went beyond the limits of the exceptions permitted by Article 2(2) of the Directive. In this context it should be observed first of all that, as the Court has already stated in its judgments of 10 April 1984 (Case 14/83 *Von Colson and Kamann* v, *Land Nordrhein-westfalen* (1984) ECR 1891 and Case 79/83 *Harz* v. *Deutsche Tradax GmbH* (1984) ECR 1921) the Member States' obligation under a Directive to achieve the result envisaged by that Directive and their duty under Article 5 of the Treaty to take all appropriate measures, whether general or particular, to ensure the fulfilment of that obligation, is binding on all the authorities of Member States including, for matters within their jurisdiction, the courts. It follows that, in applying national law, and in particular the provisions of national legislation specifically introduced in order to implement Directive no 76/207, national courts are required to interpret their national law in the light of the wording and the purpose of the Directive in order to achieve the result referred to in the third paragraph of Article 189 of the EEC Treaty. It is therefore for the industrial tribunal to interpret the provisions of the sex discrimination order, and in particular Article 53(1) thereof, in the light of the provisions of the Directive, as interpreted above, in order to give it its full effect."[158]

The principle of the precedence of Union law renders any national law in conflict with Union law automatically inapplicable. In *Simmenthal*, the Court specifically addressed the important role of national courts in this respect:

"Every national court must in a case within its jurisdiction, apply Community law in its entirety and protect rights which the latter confers on individuals and must accordingly set aside any provision of national law which may conflict with it, whether prior or subsequent to the community rule. Accordingly any provision of a national legal system and any legislative, administrative or judicial practice which might impair the effectiveness of community law by withholding from the national court having jurisdiction to apply such law the power to do everything necessary at the moment of its application to set aside national legislative provisions which might prevent community rules from having full force and effect are incompatible with those requirements which are the very essence of community law. This would be the case in the event of a conflict between a provision of community law and a subsequent national law if the solution of the conflict were to be reserved for an authority with a discretion of its own, other than the court called."[159]

---

[158]   15 May 1986, Case 222/84, *Marguerite Johnston* v. *Chief Constable of the Royal Ulster Constabulary* [1986] ECR 1651, par. 52–53.

[159]   9 March 1978, Case 106/77, *Amministrazione delle Finanze dello Stato* v. *Simmenthal SpA* [1978] ECR 629, par. 21–23.

The requirement of judicial control reflects a general principle of law which underlies the constitutional traditions common to the Member States.[160]

The Court held in *van Schijndel* that binding rules are:

"directly applicable in the national legal order. Where, by virtue of domestic law, courts or tribunals must raise of their own motion points of law based on binding domestic rules which have not been raised by the parties, such an obligation also exists where binding Community rules are concerned. The position is the same if domestic law confers on courts and tribunals a discretion to apply of their own motion binding rules of law. Indeed, pursuant to the principle of cooperation laid down in Article 5 of the Treaty, it is for the national courts to ensure the legal protection which persons derive from the direct effect of provisions of Community law."[161]

Advocate General Jacobs vehemently, albeit unsuccessfully, opposed this interpretation. In his view, it would infringe the principle of subsidiarity:

"It would also give rise to widespread anomalies, since the effect would be to afford greater protection to rights which are not, by virtue of being Community rights, inherently of greater importance than rights recognised by national law."[162]

However, the Court did not follow the Advocate General. To the contrary, it also held that if the objectives of the specific Union act can only be met by the national court raising Union rules on its own motion, the national court may do so.[163]

The characterisation of the European Union's own legal order is best expressed by the fact that, despite the failure of a Member State to implement the obligations that are imposed, a citizen may invoke the relevant provisions of a Directive.[164] The Court has repeatedly held that:

---

[160]   15 May 1986, Case 222/84, *Marguerite Johnston* v. *Chief Constable of the Royal Ulster Constabulary* [1986] ECR 1651, par. 18.

[161]   14 December 1995, Joined Cases C-430/93 and Case C-431/93, *Jeroen van Schijndel and Johannes Nicolaas Cornelis van Veen* v. *Stichting Pensioenfonds voor fysiotherapeuten* [1995] ECR I-4705, par. 13 and 14, references omitted. 7 June 2007, Joined Cases C-222/05 to C-225/05, *J. van der Weerd, Maatschap Van der Bijl, J.W. Schoonhoven (C-222/05), H. de Rooy, sen., H. de Rooy, jun. (C-223/05), Maatschap H. en J. van 't Oever, Maatschap F. van 't Oever en W. Fien, B. van 't Oever, Maatschap A. en J. Fien, Maatschap K. Koers en J. Stellingwerf, H. Koers, Maatschap K. en G. Polinder, G. van Wijhe (C-224/05), B.J. van Middendorp (C-225/05),* v. *Minister van Landbouw, Natuur en Voedselkwaliteit* [2007] ECR I-4233.

[162]   Opinion of Advocate General Jacobs of 15 June 1995, Joined Cases C-430/93 and C-431/93, *Jeroen van Schijndel and Johannes Nicolaas Cornelis van Veen* v. *Stichting Pensioenfonds voor fysiotherapeuten* [1995] ECR I-4705, point 27.

[163]   4 October 2007, Case C-429/05, *Max Rampion, Marie-Jeanne Rampion, née Godard* v. *Franfinance SA, K par K SAS* [2007] ECR I-8017.

[164]   The obligation to implement rests upon each individual Member State. A failure to do so cannot be justified by referring to the failures of other Member States. See 26 February 1976, Case 52–75, *Commission* v. *Italy* [1976] ECR 277, par. 11.

"wherever the provisions of a Directive appear, so far as their subject-matter is concerned, to be unconditional and sufficiently precise, they may be relied upon before national courts by an individual against the State where that State has failed to implement the Directive in national law by the end of the period prescribed or where it has failed to implement the Directive correctly."[165]

This power is also given to national courts, and, even in situations in which the individual did not rely on a Directive, the national court may examine – on its own motion – whether the national rules are in conformity.[166] Union law is applicable from the moment of accession of a new Member State and must be applied even when the facts of the main proceedings date from before the accession, so the Court held on reference of the Czech *Obvodní soud pro Prahu 3*.[167]

In *Pupino*, the Court more or less transposed the direct application rules of Community law to Third Pillar law, more specifically on Framework Decisions. With reference to the "ever closing union among the peoples of Europe" and the necessity "to contribute effectively to the pursuit of the Union's objectives",[168] it held that its jurisdiction "would be deprived of most of its useful effect if individuals were not entitled to invoke Framework Decisions in order to obtain a conforming interpretation of national law before the courts in the Member States".[169] However, it must be noted here that the Court circumvented the question of direct effect, which is understandable given the clear language of Article 34, paragraph 2, EU: "They shall not entail direct effect." This basically means that the Court could not formally attach direct effect to Framework Decisions. However, it attached material effects to Framework Decisions which are similar to those of Directives. In following this method, the Court behaved exactly as it had done some 25 years earlier in the *Ratti* case.[170] In 1979, the Court held that a person who has complied with the provisions of a Directive may invoke that Union act directly when prosecuted upon the basis of having violated a national criminal provision which had not yet been adopted in compliance with the Directive.

---

[165]   1 June 1999, Case C-319/97, *criminal proceedings against Antoine Kortas* [1999] ECR I-3143, par. 21.

[166]   11 July 1991, Joined Cases C-87/90, C-88/90 and C-89/90, *A. Verholen and others* v. *Sociale Verzekeringsbank Amsterdam* [1991] ECR I- 3757, par. 16.

[167]   14 June 2007, Case C-64/06, *Telefónica O2 Czech Republic as* v. *Czech On Line as* [2007] ECR I-4887.

[168]   16 June 2005, Case C-105/03, *criminal proceedings against Maria Pupino* [2005] ECR I-5285, par. 36–42.

[169]   16 June 2005, Case C-105/03, *criminal proceedings against Maria Pupino* [2005] ECR I-5285, par. 38.

[170]   5 April 1979, Case 148/78, *criminal proceedings against Tullio Ratti* [1979] ECR 1629, par. 18–24.

What is the (direct) effect of other instruments? The Court has held that "whilst under Article 189 Regulations are directly applicable and, consequently, by their nature capable of producing direct effects, that does not mean that other measures covered by that article can never produce similar effects".[171] As a consequence, the Court not only looks at the formal aspects of the legislation, but also at its nature: "Since it follows from the settled case-law of the Court that the choice of form cannot alter the nature of a measure, it must nevertheless be ascertained whether the content of a measure is wholly consistent with the form attributed to it."[172] In the *Grimaldi* case, the Court considered that the measures were not intended to produce binding effects and added:

> "The national courts are bound to take recommendations into consideration in order to decide disputes submitted to them, in particular where they cast light on the interpretation of national measures adopted in order to implement them or where they are designed to supplement binding Community provisions."[173]

The first threshold is, therefore, that it must be established that the relevant provision is unconditional and insufficiently precise. In *Cooperativa Agricola*, the Court further defined those criteria:

> "A community provision is unconditional where it sets forth an obligation which is not qualified by any condition, or subject, in its implementation or effects, to the taking of any measure either by the Community institutions or by the Member States. Moreover, a provision is sufficiently precise to be relied on by an individual and applied by a national court whether it sets out an obligation in unequivocal terms."[174]

Depending upon the legal basis, some Directives allow Member States to apply to the Commission for a derogation from full implementation if they consider this necessary. Article 114 TFEU (formerly Article 95 TEC) is an example of this. The fact that the Commission does not respond to such an application by the Member State does not delay the entry into effect of the Directive. If the Member State considers the Commission in breach of its obligations, it should bring proceedings

---

[171] 13 December 1989, Case C-322/88, *Salvatore Grimaldi v. Fonds des maladies professionnelles* [1989] ECR 4407, par. 11.

[172] 13 December 1989, Case C-322/88, *Salvatore Grimaldi v. Fonds des maladies professionnelles* [1989] ECR 4407, par. 14 (references omitted).

[173] 13 December 1989, Case C-322/88, *Salvatore Grimaldi v. Fonds des maladies professionnelles* [1989] ECR 4407, par. 18.

[174] 17 September 1996, Joined Cases C-246/94, C-247/94, C-248/94 and C-249/94, *Cooperativa Agricola Zootecnica S. Antonio and Others v. Amministrazione delle finanze dello Stato* [1996] ECR I-4373, par. 18 and 19, references omitted.

before the Court in compliance with Article 265 TFEU (formerly Article 232 TEC).[175]

3.2. THE PRINCIPLE OF SINCERE CO-OPERATION

One of the most important obligations of Union law is the obligation for the Member States to be loyal to the objectives of the Union and to enforce its legislation. This has been formulated as the so-called principle of *sincere co-operation* in Article 4, paragraph 3 TEU (formerly Article 10 TEC):

> "Pursuant to the principle of sincere co-operation, the Union and the Member States shall, in full mutual respect, assist each other in carrying out tasks which flow from the Treaties. The Member States shall take any appropriate measure, general or particular, to ensure fulfilment of the obligations arising out of the Treaties or resulting from the acts of the institutions of the Union. The Member States shall facilitate the achievement of the Union's tasks and refrain from any measure which could jeopardise the attainment of the Union's objectives."

The presumption under Union law that Member States have to enforce it loyally and correctly also has consequences for the relationship between Member States: Member States must trust that other Member States will be loyal to their obligations.[176]

Through this obligation, the compliance of which can be tested before the Court, the effectiveness of Union law is secured in all aspects: the implementation of Union measures into national law, the enforcement of Union legislation, co-operation with the Commission, and co-operation with law enforcement authorities of other Member States. Under the Treaties, the obligation to comply with the demands of Union law rests with the Member States. However, Member States act through various organs. The obligation of sincere co-operation rests with all the authorities of the Member States, independent of whether they have a judicial task or not. When applying national law, whether adopted before or after the Directive, the national court must interpret it, as far as possible, in the light of the wording and the purpose of the Directive so as to achieve the result pursued by the Directive.[177]

---

[175] 1 June 1999, Case C-319/97, *criminal proceedings against Antoine Kortas* [1999] ECR I-3143, par. 37.

[176] 14 January 1997, Case C-124/95, *The Queen, ex parte Centro-Com Srl v. HM Treasury and Bank of England* [1997] ECR I-81, par. 49.

[177] 13 November 1990, Case C-106/89, *Marleasing SA* v. *La Comercial Internacional de Alimentacion SA* [1991] ECR I-4135, par. 8; 27 June 2000, Joined Cases C-240/98 to C-244/98, *Océano Grupo Editorial SA and Rocío Marciano Quintero and others* [2000] ECR I-4941, par. 30.

In the case of Directives, sincere co-operation generally requires that implementing legislation be enacted, a change of the administrative practice is insufficient.[178] Even in a situation in which the courts of the Member State did not apply a provision of national law that was not in compliance with Union law, the Court held that:

> "the contested provision is still part of national law. As the Court has held on a number of occasions, the primary and direct effect of the provisions of community law do not release Member States from their obligation to remove from their domestic legal order any provisions incompatible with community law, since the maintenance of such provisions gives rise to an ambiguous state of affairs in so far as it leaves persons concerned in a state of uncertainty as to the possibilities available to them of relying on community law."[179]

Member States are only relieved of the obligation to implement legislation if the national law is already in compliance with the Directive.[180]

Many cases before the Court have dealt with the enforcement criteria that can be deduced from Article 4, paragraph 3 TFEU. However, one case must be singled out as the most important case with regard to enforcement obligations in general, and with regard to the requirements of Union law *vis-à-vis* criminal law in particular.[181] The facts of this case, formally known as the *Commission* v. *Greece*, but in practice often referred to as the *Greek maize case*, are the following. The Commission had brought proceedings against Greece for failing to establish and pay to the Community resources that were fraudently being withheld from the Community budget.[182] This related to maize imported from the non-Member State Yugoslavia to Greece without a levy being collected, subsequently declaring the maize to be of Greek origin and then transporting it to another Member State, Belgium. This incident had its origin in allegations of fraud (false declarations) and corruption (bribery and the frustration of investigations and prosecution).

---

[178] 6 May 1980, Case 102/79, *Commission* v. *Belgium* [1980] ECR 1473, par. 10. In his Opinion of 27 March 1980 on this case, Advocate General Reischl points to another reason to require legislation: "If Member States were permitted to avoid their obligations under the Treaty by relying on the direct effect of the directives and on the precedence of Community law, directives would, contrary to the scheme of the Treaty, become the same as regulations which are of general application." The necessary amendment of national rules cannot be compensated by issuing a ministerial circular to set the provisions violating Union law aside. See 2 December 1986, Case 239/85, *Commission* v. *Belgium* [1986] ECR 3645.

[179] 24 March 1988, Case 104/86, *Commission* v. *Italy* [1988] ECR 1799, par. 12.

[180] 23 May 1985, Case 29/84, *Commission* v. *Germany* [1985] ECR 1661.

[181] NB: Tip for students: if there is one case that deserves extra study, it is Case 68/88.

[182] If the real origin of the maize had been stated, levies would have to be paid to the Community.

After an investigation, the Commission informed the Greek government of its conclusions and called on it to take the following measures:

- the payment to the Commission of the agricultural levies on the imports of Yugoslav maize, together with default interest;
- the recovery of all unpaid sums from the authors of the fraud;
- the institution of criminal or disciplinary proceedings against the authors of the fraud and their accomplices;
- an investigation into certain import, export and transit operations involving cereals carried out since the beginning of 1985.

The Greek authorities replied, as appears from the factual description in the judgment, "that an administrative inquiry had been ordered and that the matter had been placed in the hands of an examining magistrate, and that it was necessary to await the conclusions of the judicial authorities before taking the measures indicated by the Commission".[183] After further correspondence failed to produce a positive outcome, the Commission brought a case against Greece. In this extraordinary case before the Court, the Greek government did not submit any pleadings on its own behalf.[184]

The relevant considerations of the Court read as follows:

"22. According to the Commission, the Member States are required by virtue of Article 5 of the EEC Treaty to penalize any persons who infringe Community law in the same way as they penalize those who infringe national law. The Hellenic Republic failed to fulfil those obligations by omitting to initiate all the criminal or disciplinary proceedings provided for by national law against the perpetrators of the fraud and all those who collaborated in the commission and concealment of it.

23. It should be observed that where Community legislation does not specifically provide any penalty for an infringement or refers for that purpose to national laws, regulations and administrative provisions, Article 5 of the Treaty requires the Member States to take all measures necessary to guarantee the application and effectiveness of Community law.

24. For that purpose, whilst the choice of penalties remains within their discretion, they must ensure in particular that infringements of Community law are penalized under conditions, both procedural and substantive, which are analogous to those applicable to infringements of national law of a similar nature and importance and which, in any event, make the penalty effective, proportionate and dissuasive.

---

[183] 21 September 1989, Case 68/88, *Commission* v. *Greece* [1989] ECR 2965, par. 4.
[184] AG Tesauro underlines the historic dimension of that element: "For the second time the Court of Justice is called upon to give judgment by default." Opinion of Advocate General Tesauro of 30 June 1989, Case 68/88, *Commission* v. *Greece* [1989] ECR 2965, point 1.

25. Moreover, the national authorities must proceed, with respect to infringements of Community law, with the same diligence as that which they bring to bear in implementing corresponding national laws.

26. In the present case, it does not appear from the file on the case that the Greek authorities have instituted criminal or disciplinary proceedings against the persons who took part in the commission and concealment of the fraud denounced by the Commission or that there was any impediment to the institution of such proceedings.

27. In the pre-litigation phase, the Greek Government contended that the matter had been placed in the hands of the national judicial authorities and that it was necessary to await the outcome of the judicial inquiries. However, the Commission quite properly refutes that argument, observing that, according to the information in its possession, the legal proceedings in question, which in fact were commenced not by the national authorities but by a competitor of ITCO, relate only to the fraud connected with the consignment carried by the vessel Alfonsina.

28. In those circumstances, the Commission's submission must be upheld."[185]

As a consequence of which, the Court found that Greece had violated its obligations under the Treaties.

Looking at the rather short Opinion of Advocate General Tesauro which preceded this judgment, one would certainly not have anticipated that the Court would use this case to introduce the criteria for the enforcement of Union law that would build the standard by which the efforts of all the Member States would be measured. Maybe, this was, to a large extent, caused by the obstruction and lack of co-operation from the Greek authorities in almost every aspect, up to and including the proceedings before the Court.

The following principles to assess the activity of Member States have been deduced from the judgment. The *assimilation principle*, which requires implementation "under conditions, both procedural and substantive, which are analogous to those applicable to infringements of national law of a similar nature and importance". Penalties must be *effective, proportionate* and *dissuasive*. The expected attitude of the local authorities in dealing with the matter is one of *same diligence*. These five criteria will be analysed more in detail below. They are to be applied cumulatively. While the *assimilation* principle relates more to legislation, the other (*effective, proportionate* and *dissuasive*) criteria stipulated in *Commission v. Greece* relate to both legislation and to practical enforcement. The last criterion (*same diligence*) relates to enforcement in practice only.

---

[185]   21 September 1989, Case 68/88, *Commission v. Greece* [1989] ECR 2965, par. 22–28.

Assimilation

The obligation to pay respect to the assimilation principle requires Member States to use the same or similar means of legislation that they (would) use with regard to similar violations of national law ("analogous procedural and substantive conditions"). It is related to the same diligence requirement, although "assimilation" relates to legislation and "same diligence" to what states do with the legislation which they have in place. In a situation in which the national penal law of a Member State has criminalised subsidy fraud as a serious crime that may result in imprisonment of 6 years and a maximum fine of € 1,000,000, the assimilation principle would require a Member State to criminalise EU fraud under more or less the same conditions. It would prevent a Member State from making EU fraud an administrative offence. This would make the gap between the national fraud provision and the provision on EU fraud too large. However, a Member State under whose national system subsidy fraud is an administrative offence, *i.e.*, it may lead to an administrative fine of € 200, is free to do the same with EU fraud in order to comply with the demands of the assimilation principle.[186] The application of the assimilation principle may be problematical when it concerns the determination of whether the infringements are of a similar nature. What is similar? There is not much case law on this issue, yet.[187]

The "same conditions" may refer to situations under which there is a procedural condition of a formal complaint by the institution that gave the subsidy before prosecution may take place. Under the assimilation principle, a Member State may not introduce such a condition for EC subsidy fraud, while it continues not to have it for fraud in relation to national subsidies.

Effective

It is not easy to define the meaning of "effective" in the field of measures to enforce Union law. Since it ought to distinguish itself from "dissuasive", it seems that "effective" relates to the fact that, if violations occur, the system is capable of responding to it. The system is not rendered lame, but can react to violations of Union law. "Effective" means, according to Advocate General van Gerven, "amongst other things, that the Member States must endeavour to attain and implement the objectives of the relevant provisions of Community law".[188] Advocate General Kokott stated that, "Rules laying down penalties are effective where they are framed in such a way that they do not make it practically impossible

---

[186]   Clearly, this may run contrary to the requirements of proportionality and dissuasiveness.
[187]   18 October 2001, Case C-354/99, *Commission* v. *Ireland* [2001] ECR I-7657.
[188]   Opinion of Advocate General van Gerven of 5 December 1989, Case C-326/88, *Anklagemyndigheden* v. *Hansen and Søn I/S* [1990] ECR I-2911, point 8.

or excessively difficult to impose the penalty provided for".[189] The Court held that effective measures "may include criminal penalties even where the Community legislation only provides for civil ones".[190]

Proportionate

The necessity of respecting the principle of proportionality was not pronounced for the first time in *Commission* v. *Greece*, but was already recognised as a general principle. The Court gave various hints on how to interpret it.[191] "Proportionality" should be interpreted as the relationship between the gravity of the offence and the sanction provided. Advocate General van Gerven took proportionality and dissuasiveness to be one criterion, to mean "that the penalties must be sufficiently, though not excessively strict, regard being had to the objectives pursued".[192] Advocate General Kokott defined proportionate as follows:

> "A penalty is proportionate where it is appropriate (that is to say, in particular, effective and dissuasive) for attaining the legitimate objectives pursued by it, and also necessary. Where there is a choice between several (equally) appropriate penalties, recourse must be had to the least onerous. Moreover, the effects of the penalty on the person concerned must be proportionate to the aims pursued."[193]

Dissuasive

Seen from the way in which Advocate General van Gerven establishes the dissuasiveness of a measure, it appears that he refers to a certain expectation of the effects of the measure on the conduct of the persons to whom the norm is addressed. The measure must have the potential to deter persons from conducting themselves in the undesired manner. Advocate General Kokott uses similar wording and regards a penalty as dissuasive when it prevents an individual from infringing the objective pursued and rules laid down by Union law.[194]

A critical comment on this criterion would be that a measure that did not prevent an individual from committing the offence was insufficiently dissuasive,

---

[189]   Opinion of Advocate General Kokott of 14 October 2004, C-387/02, C-391/02 and C-403/02, *criminal proceedings against Silvio Berlusconi (C-387/02), Sergio Adelchi (C-391/02), Marcello Dell'Utri and others (C-403/02)* [2005] ECR I-3565, point 88.

[190]   8 July 1999, Case C-186/98, *criminal proceedings against Maria Amélia Nunes and Evangelina de Matos* [1999] ECR I-4883, par. 14.

[191]   See Chapter 6, Section 3.

[192]   Opinion of Advocate General van Gerven of 5 December 1989, Case C-326/88, *Anklagemyndigheden v. Hansen and Søn I/S* [1990] ECR I-2911, point 8.

[193]   Opinion of Advocate General Kokott of 14 October 2004, C-387/02, C-391/02 and C-403/02, *criminal proceedings against Silvio Berlusconi (C-387/02), Sergio Adelchi (C-391/02), Marcello Dell'Utri and others (C-403/02)* [2005] ECR I-3565, point 90.

[194]   Opinion of Advocate General Kokott of 14 October 2004, C-387/02, C-391/02 and C-403/02, *criminal proceedings against Silvio Berlusconi (C-387/02), Sergio Adelchi (C-391/02), Marcello Dell'Utri and others (C-403/02)* [2005] ECR I-3565, point 89.

the violation being proof of the fact that it was not. To argue in this manner would set an extremely high standard for the judging of legislation and would require Member States to make it theoretically impossible for infringements to occur. Since all criteria must be taken together, the proportionality requirement will prevent such extremist positions.

Same Diligence

This requirement means that the authorities of a Member State may not, on the one hand, categorically turn a blind eye to violations of Union law, and, on the other, spend a fair deal of time and resources on cases in which infringements of purely national rules are concerned. "Same diligence" requires Member States to make the same effort, not more, not less. Given the nature of some criminal justice systems, the question arises as to whether a prosecutor may stop an investigation on grounds of common interest. This is especially relevant for Member States that apply the so-called *opportunity principle*, as opposed to the *legality principle*, when making decisions on prosecution.[195] Does the enforcement obligation allow a decision not to prosecute to be taken, in spite of the fact that the prosecution might be convinced that an offence has been committed? The answer is not a black or white one. It depends on the circumstances of the case. If it concerned a matter in which the prosecution had made a considerable effort to obtain more evidence that would support the allegations, but had been unsuccessful, and subsequently were to find that it was impossible to obtain a conviction, such a decision to end proceedings would be acceptable under Union law. However, if the prosecution did not invest in further investigations, because of the fact that it required difficult and complicated international investigations, then the question of whether this is in compliance with the same diligence requirement does, indeed, arise.[196]

Codification of the Greek Maize Criteria

The enforcement principles of effectiveness, proportionality and dissuasiveness, as well as the assimilation principle, developed in the case law of the Court in the matter of the *Commission* v. *Greece*, are codified in various Third Pillar instruments.[197] It is for the Member States to combat fraud effectively, "where a Community regulation does not specifically provide any penalty for an infringement or refers for that purpose to national laws, regulations and administrative provisions, Article 5 of the Treaty requires the Member States to take all measures necessary to guarantee the application and effectiveness of

---

[195]   See, on these principles, Chapter 5, Section 4.
[196]   See, further, Chapter 5, Section 4.
[197]   *Framework Decision 2004/757 on Illicit Drug Trafficking*; Article 2 *Financial Interests Convention*; Article 2 *Joint Action 98/733 on Participation in a Criminal Organisation*.

Community law".[198] Case law after the *Greek maize* case does not always refer to the same diligence principle. Also, in codification of the criteria, this principle is (often) absent.

Three different steps of enforcement of Union law are thus discovered: 1) the implementation into national legislation; 2) the creation of the possibility to invoke Union law in proceedings; and 3) the active response to violations of Union rules. Finally, there is one overall enforcement aspect that can be ascertained within the legislation, although it is somewhat more weakly developed. Many legal acts impose the obligation that the Member States report to the Commission on how they implemented. Often, this obligation is limited to the formal requirement to send the text of the implementing legislation to the Commission,[199] but, in some cases, more materially detailed reporting obligations appear separately. The risk with this method is that it may serve to confirm formal harmonisation. If the reporting request consists of a Member State having to report on the method in which it has met the obligations of the instrument, there is a significant chance that the report will conclude that this has happened ("five-year plan effect" or desired answer).[200] This self-affirming effect will be even stronger if the evaluation is performed by the institution (or official of that institution) responsible for the implementing legislation.

Due to the absence of the Commission as the institution supervising compliance with the law, the Third Pillar potential towards integration and common enforcement was more modest than under Community law. However, even without a common institutional framework, various tendencies were pushing towards common enforcement. In the area of investigation and analysis of offences, Europol was established. OLAF obtained a major role specifically in the area of EC fraud. With the foundation of Eurojust and the joint investigation teams, the way is paved for operations by units that are of multinational composition. While the other developments discussed so far may lead to the harmonisation of legislation, decisions by Eurojust actually have an impact on individual criminal proceedings. The consequences of these decisions, however,

---

[198]   14 July 1994, Case C-352/92, *Milchwerke Köln/ Wuppertal eG* v. *Hauptzollamt Köln-Rheinau* [1994] ECR I-3385, par. 23.

[199]   See, for example, Article 9, paragraph 2, *Framework Decision 2004/757 on Illicit Drug Trafficking*: "By the deadline referred to in paragraph 1, Member States shall transmit to the General Secretariat of the Council and to the Commission the text of the provisions transposing into their national law the obligations imposed on them under this Framework Decision".

[200]   Here, the Commission has been given a task. The article referenced in the preceding footnote goes on to state: "The Commission shall, by 12 May 2009, submit a report to the European Parliament and to the Council on the functioning of the implementation of the Framework Decision, including its effects on judicial co-operation in the field of illicit drug trafficking." The Council also conducts informal evaluations. See, for example, the Third round of Mutual Evaluations "Exchange of information and intelligence between Europol and the Member States and among the Member States respectively", 7917/2/05 REV 2, Brussels, 21 June 2005.

go further than that: they can take a position in determining crime policy. What offences should be given priority in law enforcement? What resources should be deployed to this end? These are issues which will be dealt with at a later stage.[201]

3.3. FREEDOM OF CHOICE OF MEANS

Traditionally, Member States were free in their choice of the means of enforcement of Directives (and Framework Decisions). The Court held in *von Colson* and *Kamann*:

> "Although that provision leaves Member States to choose the ways and means of ensuring that the Directive is implemented, that freedom does not affect the obligation imposed on all the Member States to which the Directive is addressed, to adopt, in their national legal systems, all the measures necessary to ensure that the Directive is fully effective, in accordance with the objective it pursues."[202]

In the early days of the Union, it was regarded as much more important to reach the results that were aimed at, than to prescribe the way to achieve them. The enforcement obligations of Article 4, paragraph 3 TEU may, in this sense, be characterised as obligations towards a result. By leaving the Member States with the freedom to choose the means by which to arrive at the desired result, it was guaranteed that states could select the most appropriate means to achieve that result. In addition, it gave the Member State the possibility of selecting which areas of law that it would use for the enforcement of Union law, and which areas would not be "affected" by it. The freedom that was given to Member States to choose the means of enforcement has – for a long time – also been read as an indication that the Union did not have the competence to prescribe the means of enforcement: notably criminal law.

If a Member State considers the imposition of criminal penalties "to be the most appropriate way of ensuring their effectiveness, provided that the penalties laid down are analogous to those applicable to infringements of national law of a similar nature and importance and are effective, proportionate and dissuasive",[203] then, it is free to criminalise. As a result, it follows that where a Directive does not impose any specific obligations with regard to the system of penalties, Member

---

[201]   See, further, Chapter 5, Section 4.

[202]   10 April 1984, Case 14/83, *Sabine von Colson and Elisabeth Kamann v. Land Nordrhein-Westfalen* [1984] ECR 1891, par. 15.

[203]   12 September 1996, Joined Cases C-58/95, C-75/95, C-112/95, C-119/95, C-123/95, C-135/95, C-140/95, C-141/95, C-154/95 and C-157/95, *criminal proceedings against Sandro Gallotti, Roberto Censi, Giuseppe Salmaggi, Salvatore Pasquire, Massimo Zappone, Francesco Segna and others, Cesare Cervetti, Mario Gasbarri, Isodoro Narducci and Fulvio Smaldone* [1996] ECR I-4345, par. 15.

States may provide criminal penalties, as long as these are in compliance with the assimilation principle.[204] Likewise, in *Hansen and Søn*, the Court stated that the manner in which liability is attributed to individuals or to undertakings also falls within the discretion of the Member States: strict criminal liability is acceptable, as long as the Member State complies with the enforcement criteria of the *Greek maize* case.[205] However, a criminal penalty occasionally becomes imperative because it is the only sanction that would fulfil the requirements of the case in question.[206] On the other hand, the Court has indicated in other situations that, in view of the limited gravity of the crime, specific penalties,[207] notably imprisonment would be disproportional.[208] Then, the penalties may become an obstacle to the freedoms enshrined in the Treaties.[209]

In X, the Court recognised the particular problem that arises when the principle of interpretation in conformity is applied in criminal matters,[210] and subsequently deviates from the general rule that Regulations do not require any national implementing measures. If the Member State on top of the directly applicable Regulation has additionally opted for criminal legislation, the legality principle requires that criminal prosecution finds its basis in national criminal law, not in the Regulation. The statement of the Court in *Grøngaard and Barg* (reference for a preliminary ruling from the *København Byret*, Denmark), that the scope of a Directive cannot be dependent on the nature of the national proceedings, must be understood in the distinction which has been made between the obligations of the *Member States* under Union law and those of the *individual*

---

[204] 8 September 2005, Case C-40/04, *criminal proceedings against Syuichi Yonemoto* [2005] ECR I-7755, par. 60.

[205] 10 July 1990, Case C-326/88, *Anklagemyndigheden* v. *Hansen and Søn I/S* [1990] ECR I-2911, par. 11–17.

[206] Opinion of Advocate General Ruiz-Jarabo Colomer of 26 May 2005, Case C-176/03, *Commission* v. *Council* [2005] ECR I-7879, par. 43.

[207] 6 November 2003, Case C-243/01, *criminal proceedings against Piergiorgio Gambelli and others* [2003] ECR I-13031, par. 72.

[208] 12 December 1989, Case C-265/88, *criminal proceedings against Lothar Messner* [1989] ECR 4209, par. 14. See, also, 26 October 1989, Case 212/88, *criminal proceedings against F. Levy* [1989] ECR 3511, par. 14. See, also, 29 February 1996, Case C-193/94, *criminal proceedings against Sofia Skanavi and Konstantin Chryssanthakopoulos* [1996] ECR I-929, par. 36; 2 October 2003, Case C-12/02, *criminal proceedings against Marco Grilli* [2003] ECR I-11585, par. 49. In *Grilli*, the Court replied to the question of the proportionality of criminal sanctions in a situation where the accused was prosecuted for using Italian temporary number plates where German plates were required, the Court simply held: Either the German rules are not contrary to the TEC, then the question of proportionality does not arise. Or, the German rules are contrary to the TEC and then penalties are totally inapplicable.

[209] 5 July 2007, Case C-430/05, *Ntionik Anonymi Etaireia Emporias H/Y, Logismikou kai Paroxis Ypiresion Michanografisis and Ioannis Michail Pikoulas* v. *Epitropi Kefalaiagoras* [2007] ECR I-5853, par. 54.

[210] 7 January 2004, Case C-60/02, *criminal proceedings against X* [2004] ECR I-651, par. 61.

under Union law.[211] While the Member State is always obliged to implement a Directive, independently of whether it uses administrative law, civil law or criminal law, the choice of the actual means of implementation has repercussions for individuals. While the use of criminal law is, due to the legality principle, dependent on the written codification of the criminal offence, other fields of law might allow for direct application of a Directive without a specific national provision.

4. SUBSTANTIVE RULES OF UNION LAW: THE FIVE FREEDOMS

4.1. INTRODUCTION

Traditionally, the substantive rules of Union law relate to the four freedoms as recognised under the Treaties: free movement of goods, persons, services and capital. The TFEU stipulates that these fundamental freedoms may not meet with any restriction.[212] In this section, what exactly is to be understood as falling under each of these four freedoms will be identified. Thus, it will be established that only certain activities fall within the scope of the Treaties. Only relevant activities may profit from the rights given under the Treaties. In order to understand the meaning of the rights fully, it will be necessary to analyse what precisely amounts to quantitative restrictions, which are, as such, forbidden. Despite their "fundamental" nature, even the freedoms do not entail an absolute character. Some restrictions of the free movement rights are allowed. What are the exceptions provided and, under which circumstances do they apply? This will bring us to the discretion that Member States avail of in both preventing and prosecuting crime. With the introduction of a right to free movement and residence for EU nationals, a fifth freedom has emerged. As will gradually be demonstrated, this fifth freedom has great relevance for criminal law.

The relationship between the fundamental freedoms of the TFEU and the rights ensured in specific Union legislation (secondary Union law: for example, Directives, Regulations and Framework Decisions) will be discussed. This paragraph will further deal with the influence of mutual recognition in the context of the substantive rights and the possible exceptions to free movement. Special attention is paid to the question of whether Union law provides for goods and services which are illegal by nature, and, as a consequence of this, cannot

---

[211]   22 November 2005, Case C-384/02, *criminal proceedings against Knud Grøngaard and Allan Barg* [2005] ECR I-9939, par. 28.

[212]   See, on the differences between fundamental freedoms and fundamental rights, Chapter 1, Section 3.

enjoy any rights under the Treaties. This section predominantly deals with internal market issues and relates to the fact that the fundamental freedoms are given to citizens. The provisions of the area of freedom, security and justice and its secondary legislation do not offer any comparable rights. To the contrary, the area of freedom, security and justice creates rights and forms of co-operation for Member States. Citizens cannot profit directly from what has been regulated in the area of freedom, security and justice.

4.2. FREE MOVEMENT

Since the original goal of the realisation of the internal market was the creation of a legal order without national barriers, the focus was and still is on removing transnational problems. The Treaty, therefore, does not, in principle, deal with activities that have no relation with transnational movements. In other words, if all activity takes place within the borders of one state and relates to the workers of that state or to goods, services or capital in and from that state, then that activity does not come within the scope of the Treaties. The first test in assessing the law applicable to a specific activity is, therefore, always whether the conduct falls within the scope of the Treaties.

It is therefore useful, as a first step, to establish what falls within the definition of goods, persons, services and capital. For these four categories, it is relevant that there be some *economic activity*.[213] The High Court of Ireland referred for a preliminary ruling the case of the Irish student associations which distributed specific information on where abortion in England could be performed. Abortion, as well as any activity related to it, is criminalised in Ireland. The students circulated the information for political reasons, without being paid by the English abortion clinics. Although the Court had qualified abortion as an economic activity, this was not the case for what the students did. The students did not distribute information on behalf of the clinics, were not paid by them. Thus, the distribution of information with no link to economic activity did not fall within the sphere of the Treaty.[214]

---

[213] The Court does not require the completion of all kinds of formal procedures to recognise an activity as economic. See, for instance, 5 February 1991, Case C-363/89, *Danielle Roux* v. *Belgium* [1991] ECR I-273.

[214] 4 October 1991, Case C-159/90, *The Society for the Protection of the Unborn Children Ireland Ltd* v. *Stephen Grogan and others* [1991] ECR 4685, par. 26. Payment is not always decisive. See 5 October 1988, Case 196/87, *Udo Steymann* v. *Staatssecretaris van Justitie* [1988] ECR 6159, par. 11–12, in which non-paid work as a member for the Bhagwan Community was regarded as being aimed to ensure a measure of self-sufficiency.

Freedom of Goods (Articles 28–37 TFEU, formerly Articles 23–31 TEC)

Article 28 TFEU prohibits all customs duties on imports and exports, as well as other charges which have an equivalent effect between the Member States. Products coming from a third country are considered to be in *free circulation* if the importation formalities have been complied with in a specific Member State (Article 29 TFEU, formerly Article 24 TEC).[215] The principle of freedom of goods is applicable regardless of whether it concerns very costly restrictions or minor hindrances. The Court held that the relatively-limited economic significance of a hindrance cannot be accepted as an exception: "all trading rules of Member States which are capable of hindering, directly or indirectly, actually or potentially, intra-community trade must be regarded as measures having an effect equivalent to a quantitative restriction on imports."[216] Freedom of goods does not mean that there are no exceptions at all. The Court accepted that a Member State may require, even on pain of criminal sanctions,[217] that goods carry a declaration of their real origin.[218] In the public interest of consumer protection, a Member State may also require that the original label contains certain content information on the product.[219] In addition, Member States remain free to criminalise the use of goods that are not yet in compliance with the appropriate tax rules,[220] even though it appears that such goods are not in free circulation yet.

---

[215]   Requiring a certificate of authenticity for a product that was put into free circulation constitutes a measure having an effect equivalent to a quantative restriction. See 11 July 1974, Case 8–74, *Procureur du Roi* v. *Benoît and Gustave Dassonville* [1974] ECR 837, par. 9; 15 December 1976, Case 41–76, *Suzanne Criel, née Donckerwolcke and Henri Schou* v. *Procureur de la Republique au tribunal de grande instance de Lille and Director General of Customs* [1976] ECR 1921.

[216]   5 June 1986, Case 103/84, *Commission* v. *Italy* [1986] ECR 1759, par. 18.

[217]   However, these measures may not go beyond what is strictly necessary for the purpose of enabling the importing Member State to know the origin of goods. See 30 November 1977, Case 52–77, *Leonce Cayrol* v. *Giovanni Rivoira & Figli* [1977] ECR 2261.

[218]   15 December 1976, Case 41–76, *Suzanne Criel, née Donckerwolcke and Henri Schou v. Procureur de la Republique au tribunal de grande instance de Lille and Director General of Customs* [1976] ECR 1921, par. 35–38; 11 May 1989, Case 25/88, *criminal proceedings against Esther Renée Bouchara, née Wurmser, and Norlaine SA* [1989] ECR 1105, par. 18; 26 October 1989, Case 212/88, *criminal proceedings against F. Levy* [1989] ECR 3511, par. 14–15. It is important noting that, in *Bouchara*, one of the reasons for the Court allowing for certain verifications when placing a good on the market for the first time consisted in the absence of the possibility of enforcing criminal judgements in another state (see par. 14–15). With the emergence of instruments on mutual recognition of penalties, this argument loses weight.

[219]   16 December 1980, Case 27/80, *criminal proceedings against Anton Adriaan Fietje* [1980] ECR 3839, par. 10; Opinion of Advocate General Bot of 14 October 2008, Case C-42/07, *Liga Portuguesa de Futebol Profissional (CA/LPFP) Baw International Ltd v Departamento de Jogos da Santa Casa da Misericórdia de Lisboa* ECR not yet reported.

[220]   9 October 1980, Case 823/79, *criminal proceedings against Giovanni Carciati* [1980] ECR 2773. Article 110 TFEU (formerly Article 90 TEC) supports the free movement of goods in the field of taxation. No distinctions between domestic and foreign products may be made. The Court has held that the same goes for penalties provided for tax evasion in relation to such goods. The evasion of VAT regarding products coming from another Member State may not meet higher

The TFEU provides for a clear prevailing rule of full freedom of movement of goods in Articles 34 and 35.[221] The exceptions to full freedom that may be justified are found in Article 36.[222] As will be seen later, these exceptions must be interpreted narrowly.[223] Restrictions may also find a place in harmonising legislation, because of the nature of the goods, such as firearms and drug precursors.[224]

Having established that the case deals with intra-community trade of goods, it is relevant to determine what amounts to a quantitative restriction. Over the years, the Court has been able to render a great deal of case law on this issue. In the *Casati* case, the Court dealt with impediments to free movement which found their origin in the application of criminal law:

> "In principle, criminal legislation and the rules of criminal procedure are matters for which the Member States are still responsible. However, it is clear from a consistent line of cases decided by the Court, that Community law also sets certain limits in that area as regards the control measures which it permits the Member States to maintain in connection with the free movement of goods and persons. The administrative measures or penalties must not go beyond what is strictly necessary, the control procedures must not be conceived in such a way as to restrict the freedom required by

---

penalties than the evasion of VAT to domestic products. See 2 August 1993, Case C-276/91, *Commission* v. *France* [1993] ECR I-4413.

221   Article 34 TFEU (formerly Art. 28 TEC) reads: "Quantative restrictions on imports and all measures having equivalent effect shall be prohibited between Member States".
Article 35 TFEU (formerly Article 29 EC) reads: "Quantative restrictions on exports and all measures having equivalent effect, shall be prohibited between Member States".

222   Article 36 TFEU (formerly Art. 30 EC) reads: "The provisions of Articles 34 and 35 shall not preclude prohibitions or restrictions on imports, exports or goods in transit justified on grounds of public morality, public policy or public security; the protection of health and life of humans, animals or plants; the protection of national treasures possessing artistic, historic or archaeological value; or the protection of industrial and commercial property. Such prohibitions or restrictions shall not, however, constitute a means of arbitrary discrimination or a disguised restriction on trade between Member States".

223   7 March 1990, Case C-362/88, *GB-INNO-BM* v. *Confédération du commerce luxembourgeois* [1990] ECR I-667, par. 10. See, further, Section 4.6.1 in this Chapter.

224   E.g. Directive 91/477/EEC of 18 June 1991 on control of the acquisition and possession of weapons, OJ 1991, L 256/51. The Directive creates unionwide four categories of weapons: prohibited firearms; firearms subject to authorisation; firearms subject to declaration; other firearms. Directive 92/12 on the General Arrangements for Products subject to Excise Duty and on the Holding, Movement and Monitoring of such Products, OJ 1992, L 76/1. Directive 92/12 contains an exemption from the general freedom of goods for transporting mineral oil. See, further, on this Directive 15 November 2007, C-330/05, *criminal proceedings against Fredrik Granberg* [2007] ECR I-9871. Similar arrangements have been made in Regulation 273/2004 of the European Parliament and of the Council of 11 February 2004 on drug precursors, OJ 2004, L 47/1. For trading in some substances, a licence is required, for others, registration. Means of payment are not regarded as goods in the meaning of the Treaty. 23 February 1995, Joined Cases C-358/93 and C-416/93, *criminal proceedings against Aldo Bordessa and Vicente Marí Mellado and Concepción Barbero Mestre* [1995] ECR I-361, par. 12.

---

the Treaty and they must not be accompanied by a penalty which is so disproportionate to the gravity of the infringement that it becomes an obstacle to the exercise of that freedom."[225]

In other words, the application of criminal law itself may amount to a restriction.[226]

The fact that national rules require prior authorisation for itinerant sales may reduce the volume of the sales of goods from other Member States.[227] It will be for the national court to decide as to whether the measure affects the marketing of products originating from other Member States more than it affects local products. If this is the effect, then there is a clear violation.[228] Article 35 TFEU (formerly Article 29 TEC) specifically protects exportation to another Member State. National legislation may also not treat products destined for exportation differently from products sold within the Member State. If a national provision restricting or prohibiting certain selling arrangements applies to all the relevant traders operating within the national territory and affects them in the same manner, in law and in the fact, then marketing of both domestic products and those from other Member States is not such as to hinder trade between the Member States either directly or indirectly.[229]

Free Movement of Persons (Articles 45–55 TFEU)

The provisions on the free movement of persons make a distinction between the *freedom of movement of workers* (Article 45 TFEU, formerly Article 39 TEC) and the *right of establishment* (Article 49 TFEU, formerly Article 43 TEC). Article 45, paragraph 1 TFEU states that the freedom of movement for workers is to be secured within the Union. Unlike the rules on the free movement of goods, Article 45, paragraph 3 TFEU provides for three general exceptions only: public policy, public security and public health.[230] Decades after the introduction of the internal market, direct restrictions on foreign workers no longer appear very often in the law of the Member States. The case law is now sensitive to the conditions for workers, which may – indirectly – be restrictive to them. A Member State of

---

[225] 11 November 1981, Case 203/80, *criminal proceedings against Guerrino Casati* [1981] ECR 2595, par. 27.

[226] 30 October 1974, Case 190–73, *Officier van Justitie* v. *J.W.J. van Haaster* [1974] ECR 1123, concerning the prosecution for producing a product without the applicable licence.

[227] 26 May 2005, Case C-20/03, *criminal proceedings against Marcel Burmanjer, René Alexander van der Linden, Anthony de Jong* [2005] ECR I-4133, par. 30.

[228] 24 January 1978, Case 82/77, *criminal proceedings against Jacobus Philippus van Tiggele* [1978] ECR 25.

[229] 26 May 2005, Case C-20/03, *criminal proceedings against Marcel Burmanjer, René Alexander van der Linden, Anthony de Jong* [2005] ECR I-4133, par. 24; 23 February 2006, Case C-441/04, *A-Punkt Schmuckhandels GmbH* v. *Claudia Schmidt* [2006] ECR I-2093, par. 15.

[230] There is, however, a specific exception which relates to employment in the public service.

residence may not criminalise a worker working in another Member State for using, on its territory, a vehicle registered to a leasing company established in the Member State in which he works and made available to the worker by his employer who is also established in that same Member State.[231] In this case, it was argued that the obligation to register vehicles under the national rules was necessary to ensure road safety and to combat the erosion of the tax base. The Court passed this argument by observing that, since the Dutch vehicle could not be registered in Belgium, the objectives for registration could not be achieved.[232]

EU nationals who establish themselves in another Member State must be able to do so freely and may not meet any impediments. The right to acquire, use or dispose of immovable property is corollary of freedom of establishment.[233] Article 52, paragraph 1 TFEU provides for three general exceptions only: public policy, public security and public health. Establishment which is subject to a licence or authorisation on pain of criminal penalties is a violation of Articles 49 TFEU (formerly Article 43 TEC) and 56 TFEU (formerly Article 49 TEC), if there is no acceptable justification for it.[234]

Freedom to Provide Services

Article 56 TFEU (formerly Article 49 TEC) provides:

> "Within the framework of the provisions set out below, restrictions on freedom to provide services within the Union shall be prohibited in respect of nationals of Member States who are established in a Member State other than that of the person for whom the services are intended. The European Parliament and the Council, acting in accordance with the ordinary legislative procedure, may extend the provisions of the Chapter to nationals of a third country who provide services and who are established within the Union."

Article 57 TFEU further specifies what are to be considered as services within the meaning of the Treaty. In principle, any measure that makes it more difficult to provide services across borders is prohibited.[235] However, restrictions may be justified on grounds of public policy, public security or public health (Articles 62

---

[231] 2 October 2003, Case C-232/01, *criminal proceedings against Hans van Lent* [2003] ECR I-11525.

[232] 2 October 2003, Case C-232/01, *criminal proceedings against Hans van Lent* [2003] ECR I-11525, par. 23 and 24.

[233] 25 January 2007, Case C-370/05, *criminal proceedings against Uwe Kay Festersen* [2007] ECR I-1129, par. 22. Please note Protocol No. 32 on the Acquisition of Property in Denmark, which allows Denmark to maintain the existing legislation on the acquisition of second homes.

[234] 6 March 2007, Joined Cases C-338/04, C-359/04 and C-360/04, *criminal proceedings against Placanica, Palazzese and Sorrichio* [2007] ECR I-1891.

[235] For example, 6 November 2003, Case C-243/01, *criminal proceedings against Piergiorgio Gambelli and others* [2003] ECR I-13031.

and 52 TFEU).[236] In a case in which Italian law required, *inter alia*, a declaration of "good conduct" before a licence to provide extrajudicial debt recovery, the requirement of the declaration as such is justified by reasons relating to the public interest.[237] However, to require that such a licence must be applied for in each of the 103 Italian provinces and that the applicant must have premises in each province, is clearly in violation of the right. The Court held that "any system of prior authorisation must be based on objective criteria which are non-discriminatory and known in advance".

Free Movement of Capital

Article 63 TFEU (formerly Article 56 TEC) reads:

> "1. Within the framework of the provisions set out in this Chapter, all restrictions on the movement of capital between the Member States and between Member States and third countries shall be prohibited. 2. Within the framework of the provisions set out in this Chapter, all restrictions on payments between the Member States and between Member States and third countries shall be prohibited."

It must be noted that Article 63, unlike the other freedoms, also creates free movement of capital and payment between Member States and third countries. Restrictions of Article 63 may be permitted if justified on grounds of public policy and public security (Article 65 TFEU),[238] and if they are applied in a non-discriminatory way which respects the principle of proportionality.[239] In judging whether the national legislation is in compliance with these principles, the Court looks at the objectives of that legislation.[240] If the objective can also be pursued with measures that do not restrict fundamental freedoms, the measures are not regarded as being proportional. One example of this is the requirement of prior authorisation for the transfer of capital. The interest that a Member State wants (and is entitled) to protect by such a requirement (fiscal supervision, prevention of tax evasion, money-laundering, drug trafficking or terrorism) can also be served by alternatives, such as a prior declaration. This declaration should be distinguished from a prior authorisation which would cause the exercise of free movement of

---

[236]   The fact that the Member States would see a severe reduction of tax income does not count as a justification. See 6 November 2003, Case C-243/01, *criminal proceedings against Piergiorgio Gambelli and others* [2003] ECR I-13031, par. 61.

[237]   18 July 2007, Case C-134/05, *Commission* v. *Italian Republic* [2007] ECR I-6251.

[238]   See, for instance, the reporting obligations that follow from *Directive 2005/60 on Money Laundering.*

[239]   25 January 2007, Case C-370/05, *criminal proceedings against Uwe Kay Festersen* [2007] ECR I-1129, par. 26.

[240]   31 January 1984, Case 286/82 and 26/83, *Graziana Luisi and Giuseppe Carbone* v. *Ministero del Tesero* [1984] ECR 377.

capital to be subject to the discretion of administrative authorities and would thus be such as to render this freedom illusory.[241]

Free Movement and Residence

In addition to the nationality of a Member State, Article 9 TEU and Article 20 TFEU (formerly 17 TEC) establish citizenship of the Union. Article 21, paragraph 2 TEU (formerly Article 18, paragraph 1 TEC), gives every citizen of the Union who does not enjoy a right of residence as a result of other provisions of the Treaties, the right to move and reside freely within the territory of the Member States. This is a fundamental freedom,[242] although it is not, however, unconditional.[243] The right of free movement and residence entitles every EU citizen to move and reside freely for a period of three months without being subject to any specific conditions.[244] After these three months, EU citizens must either be employed or self-employed.[245] The independence of this right from any of the other four freedoms and from conducting an economic activity justifies its recognition as *the fifth freedom*. Being a EU national is sufficient to claim the benefits of this right. As will gradually become clear, it is the freedom of movement which will have an enormous impact on criminal law and procedural law. The Court held in *Schwarz*:

> "In as much as a citizen of the Union must be granted in all Member States the same treatment in law as that accorded to nationals of those Member States who find themselves in the same situation, it would be incompatible with the right to freedom of movement were a citizen to receive in the Member State of which he is a national

---

[241]   23 February 1995, Joined Cases C-358/93 and C-416/93, *criminal proceedings against Aldo Bordessa and Vicente Marí Mellado and Concepción Barbero Mestre* [1995] ECR I-361, par. 19 and 25; 14 December 1995, Joined Cases C-163/94, C-165/94 and C-250/94, *criminal proceedings against Lucas Emilio Sanz de Lera, Raimundo Díaz Jiménez and Figen Kapanoglu* [1995] ECR I-4821. It is interesting to see that the Court in Sanz de Lera describes in detail a possible alternative which would not meet the objections of prior authorization. In Scientology, the Court added that "it has not held that a system of prior authorisation can never be justified, particularly where such authorisation is in fact necessary for the protection of public policy or public security". 14 March 2000, Case C-54/99, *Association Église de scientologie de Paris and Scientology International Reserves Trust,* v. *The Prime Minister* [2000] ECR I-1335, par. 19. The Court refers here to 1 June 1999, Case C-302/97, *Konle* v. *Austria* [1999] ECR I-3099, par. 45–46.

[242]   11 September 2007, C-76/05, *Herbert Schwarz, Marga Gootjes Schwarz* v. *Finanzamt Bergisch Gladbach* [2007] ECR I-6849, par. 87.

[243]   The preamble of the TEU states that the Member States are "resolved to facilitate the free movement of persons, while ensuring the safety and security of their peoples by establishing an area of freedom, security and justice".

[244]   Article 6 *Directive 2004/38 on Free Movement*.

[245]   Article 7 *Directive 2004/38 on Free Movement*.

treatment less favourable than he would enjoy if he had not availed himself of the opportunities offered by the EC Treaty in relation to freedom of movement."[246]

Article 67, paragraph 2 and Article 77 TFEU state that the Union is to ensure the absence of internal border controls for persons. In the criminal proceedings against *Wijsenbeek*, the question was raised as to whether Articles 7A and 8A TEC, which were applicable at the time (now Articles 21 and 26 TFEU), actually have direct effect. *Wijsenbeek* was prosecuted for having refused to identify himself when entering the Netherlands via a plane from another Member State. The Court held, "that in the absence of Community rules governing the matter, the Member States remain competent to impose penalties for such an obligation", subject to the assimilation and proportionality principle.[247] In practice, border controls have been maintained in air traffic for security reasons. Formally, this is not related to border checks, because the obligation to carry an identity card is also applicable to internal flights.

Like the other four freedoms, the principle of free movement is not absolute. However, the applicability of the public-policy exception is a derogation that must be interpreted strictly and whose scope cannot be determined unilaterally by the Member State.[248] As a consequence, derogations to this fundamental freedom are not easily accepted. This became clear in a case in which the Commission lodged a complaint against the Netherlands.[249] The Court held that a systematic and automatic connection between a criminal conviction and a measure ordering expulsion was in violation of *Directive 64/221 on Movement and Residence of Foreign Nationals* (applicable to the facts of the case before the Court) on the co-ordination of special measures concerning the movement and residence of foreign nationals, which are justified on ground of public policy.[250] A decision of expulsion must be based upon personal conduct and may not be justified merely on previous convictions.[251] There must be a genuine and sufficiently serious threat to one of the fundamental interests of society. Expulsion as a measure of a general

---

[246]   11 September 2007, C-76/05, *Herbert Schwarz, Marga Gootjes Schwarz* v. *Finanzamt Bergisch Gladbach* [2007] ECR I-6849, par. 88.

[247]   21 September 1989, Case C-378/97, *criminal proceedings against Floris Ariël Wijsenbeek* [1999] ECR I-6207, par. 44.

[248]   27 April 2006, Case C-441/02, *Commission* v. *Germany* [2006] ECR I-3449, par. 34.

[249]   7 June 2007, Case C-50/06, *Commission* v. *The Netherlands* [2007] ECR I-4383.

[250]   *Directive 64/221 on Movement and Residence of Foreign Nationals* was replaced by *Directive 2004/38 on Free Movement* on 30 April 2006.

[251]   The existence of a previous criminal conviction can only be taken into account for an expulsion order in so far as the circumstances which gave rise to that conviction are evidence of personal conduct constituting a present threat to the requirements of public policy. See 27 October 1977, Case 30–77, *Regina* v. *Pierre Bouchereau* [1977] ECR 1999, par. 28.

preventive nature is precluded.[252] In a preliminary ruling on a reference from the Greek *Areios Pagos*, the Court demonstrated, that it is not easily inclined to accept an expulsion of an EU national. Although it is accepted that the use of drugs may constitute a danger for society, such as to justify special measures against Union nationals in order to maintain public order, it must comply with the demands of the right to free movement; the expulsion for life is the very negation of this freedom.[253] Occasionally, one sees that the Court allows for measures of a different character: for example, the limitation of the free movement to part of the territory.[254]

The Court obliges the authorities to assess both the personal conduct of the offender and whether it constitutes a present, genuine and sufficiently serious threat to public order and security.[255] It underlines the fact that it may not be an automatic consequence of the mere commission of an offence. The principle of proportionality must be observed and the authority taking the measure must indicate the specific risk of new and serious prejudice to the requirements of public policy. On 7 November 2007, as a response to several violent crimes which were allegedly committed by Romanian nationals in the year 2007, the Italian government took the decision to expel collectively large numbers of Romanians.[256] This decision was, surprisingly, approved or tolerated by the Commission. This was a clear violation of the rule that there must be an individual assessment of the threat to society of the individual EU citizen and that measures of general or special prevention are not acceptable.[257] In 1975, the Court had already held, with

---

[252] 29 April 2004, Case C-482/01 and Case C-493/01, *proceedings related to Georgios Orfanopoulou and Raffaele Oliveri* [2004] ECR I-5257, par. 66 and 68. This is not different when it concerns third nationals who are spouse of an EU national and who are also protected by *Directive 64/221 on Movement and Residence of Foreign Nationals* (replaced by *Directive 2004/38 on Free Movement* as of 30 April 2006). If there is an automatic alert in the SIS for the purposes of refusing entry and the entry into SIS does not provide the Member State with sufficient information to assess the threat of this person to society, it must verify this with the Member State that provided the information. See 31 January 2006, Case C-503/03, *Commission v. Spain* [2006] ECR I-1097.

[253] 19 January 1999, Case C-348/96, *criminal proceedings against Donatella Calfa* [1999] ECR I-11, par. 18 and 22.

[254] 26 November 2002, Case C-100/01, *Ministre de l'Intérieur* v. *Autor Oteiza Olazabal* [2002] ECR I-10981. Restriction of the right of residence to an EU national to part of the national territory would be more or less equal to punitive measures or other genuine and effective measures designed to combat certain conduct.

[255] 18 July 2007, Case C-325/05, *Ismail Derin* v. *Landkreis Darmstadt-Dieburg* [2007] ECR I-6495. See, on the necessity to assess personal conduct, 28 October 1975, Case 36–75, *Roland Rutili* v. *Ministre de l'intérieur* [1975] ECR 1219.

[256] Article 347 TFEU, formerly 297 TEC, does allow for certain restrictions as a result of measures "in the event of serious internal disturbances affecting the maintenance of law and order, in the event of war, serious international tension constituting a threat of war, or in order to carry out obligations it has accepted for the purpose of maintaining peace and internal security".

[257] The European Parliament condemned the Italian measure as being contrary to *Directive 2004/38 on Free Movement*. See European Parliament Resolution of 15 November 2007 on

reference to the Community law applicable at the time, that the law "prevents the deportation of a national of a Member State if such deportation is ordered for the purpose of deterring other aliens".[258] Similar considerations apply for the maintenance of banning orders decades after a crime has been committed. Banning an EU national for life cannot easily be justified.[259] This should bring an end, for instance, to the Italian banning orders on political activists for the separation of German-speaking Südtirol/Alto Adige from Italy, a matter that still troubles the relationship between the provincial government and the central Italian government.[260]

4.3. WITHIN THE SCOPE OF THE TREATIES

At first sight, the provisions of the TFEU do not give any rights to the nationals of Member States *vis-à-vis* their own state.[261] To put it in a very simple but not very precise way, the TFEU gives rights to foreign workers, foreign goods, foreign services, foreign capital and foreign EU nationals. It does not say anything with regard to purely internal situations.[262] Nationals of the state,[263]

---

application of Directive 2004/38/EC on the right of EU citizens and their family members to move and reside freely within the territory of the Member States.

[258]   26 February 1975, Case 67–74, *Carmelo Angelo Bonsignore* v. *Oberstadtdirektor der Stadt Köln* [1975] ECR 297, par. 7.

[259]   19 January 1999, Case C-348/96, *criminal proceedings against Donatella Calfa* [1999] ECR I-11.

[260]   Http://www.provinz.bz.it/land/landesregierung/durnwalder/aktuelles-durnwalder.asp?redas =yes&rCSS=alternate_01&aktuelles_action=4&aktuelles_article_id=214328 last accessed on 22 August 2008.

[261]   To restrict the freedom of movement of a worker who is a national of that Member State to a part of the territory of that Member State as a penal measure is a wholly domestic situation. See 28 March 1979, Case 175/78, *Regina* v. *Vera Ann Saunders* [1979] ECR 1129. The conviction of an Austrian national in Austria for violation of the Austrian Penal Code not being implementation legislation of Community law obviously does not fall within the scope of application of the Treaty. See 29 May 1997, Case C-299/95, *Friedrich Kremzow* v. *Republik Österreich* [1997] ECR I-2629.

[262]   While, in a number of cases, the Court was quite willing to assume that the facts of the case fell within the scope of the Treaty, it did not so in 24 November 1993, Joined Cases C-267/91 and C-268/91, *criminal proceedings against Bernard Keck and Daniel Mithouard* [1993] ECR I-6097. In this case, it held that a general prohibition on resale at a loss is not designed to regulate trade in goods between Member States. The Court deviated from a position taken earlier in *Dassonville*, because the measures in *Keck* affect domestic products in the same manner as products from another Member State.

[263]   For instance, the prosecution of French nationals and residents, for operating hairdressing salons in France without a hairdressing diploma, does not come within the scope of the Treaty. See 16 February 1995, Joined Cases C-29/94, C-30/94, C-31/94, C-32/94, C-33/94, C-34/94, C-35/94, *criminal proceedings against Jean-Louis Aubertin, Bernard Collignon, Guy Creusot, Isabelle Diblanc, Gilles Josse, Jacqueline Martin and Claudie Normand* [1995] ECR I-301. With

national goods,[264] national services,[265] and national capital can thus not profit from the fundamental freedoms, because of their national status. However, the Court has held that the fundamental freedoms may be relied upon by nationals in and against their own Member State if they relate to the fundamental freedoms of others. An example of such a case is the prosecution of the Austrian national *Erich Ciola*, operator of a boat harbour in Austria, who rented more than the specific quota of moorings permitted under the applicable Austrian law to boat-owners who are resident in another Member State. The freedom to provide services "includes the freedom for recipients of services to go to another Member State in order to receive a service there, without being obstructed by restrictions".[266] Likewise, provisions which preclude or deter a national of a Member State from leaving his country of origin in order to exercise his free movement rights constitutes an infringement.[267] It demonstrates that the Court examines the restricting potential of a rule. For example, even if the national law in practice is not applied to imported products, it does not exclude the possibility of it having effects that hinder intra-Community trade.[268] However, only real situations count. The Court has held that the mere theoretical possibility of transnational situations is insufficient to establish the link required for the purpose of applying the Treaty.[269]

The fact that the Austrian national *Ciola* could rely on Union law *vis-à-vis* his own state finds its basis in the Court's interpretation of the freedom to free movement of services. Consistent case law has interpreted this as protecting both offering and receiving services. Individuals who are not entitled to Union

---

regard to freedom of establishment, see, 8 December 1987, Case 20/87, *Ministère public* v. *André Gauchard* [1987] ECR 4879.

[264]   Certain restrictions based on public health considerations may be accepted for products produced in the Member State. However, such a restriction may not be upheld for a product imported from another Member State, where it was legally brought on the market. See 13 December 1990, Case C-42/90, *criminal proceedings against Jean-Claude Bellin* [1990] ECR I-4863.

[265]   For instance, the fact that the treatment of horses' teeth by persons who are not veterinarians is allowed in other Member States, does not help an individual who performs such activity in a Member State in which this is forbidden. See 16 November 1995, Case C-152/94, *criminal proceedings against Geert van Buynder* [1995] ECR I-3981.

[266]   29 April 1999, Case C-224/97, *Erich Ciola* v. *Land Vorarlberg* [1999] ECR I-2517, par. 11.

[267]   12 December 2000, Case C-385/00, *F.W.L. de Groot* v. *Staatssecretaris van Financiën* [2002] ECR I-11819, par. 78. See, also, 15 December 1995, Case C-415/93, *Union royale belge des société de football association ASBL* v. *Jean-Marc Bosman, Royal club liégeois SA* v. *Jean-Marc Bosman and others and Union des associations européennes de football (UEFA)* v. *Jean-Marc Bosman* [1995] ECR I-4921, par. 94–97.

[268]   5 December 2000, Case C-448/98, *criminal proceedings against Jean-Pierre Guimont* [2000] ECR I-10663, par. 17.

[269]   23 April 1991, Case C-41/90, *Klaus Höfner and Fritz Elser* v. *Macotron GmbH* [1991] ECR I-1979, par. 39; 17 June 1997, Case C-70/95, *Sodemar SA, Anni Azzurri Holding SpA and Anni Azzurri Rezzato Srl* v. *Regione Lombardia* [1997] ECR I-3395.

freedoms themselves may thus "profit" from the freedoms of others. It appears from the case law that the link with Union law does not necessarily need to be very strong. A case in point here is the case of *Mary Carpenter*, which was referred to the Court by the Immigration Appeal Tribunal in the United Kingdom. Mary Carpenter was a Philippine national, married to a United Kingdom husband who provided services to both the United Kingdom and other Member States. The couple lived in the United Kingdom. When the United Kingdom authorities issued a deportation order against Mrs Carpenter for violation of the immigration law, she invoked the fundamental freedoms of her husband on the basis of the Treaty. The Court followed her reasoning in the following manner: it held that the activities of Mr Carpenter fall within the scope of the Treaties, given that Union law has recognised the importance of ensuring the protection of family life in order to eliminate obstacles to the exercise of the fundamental freedoms. Since it is clear that the separation of Mr and Mrs Carpenter would be detrimental to their family life, the conditions to exercise his fundamental freedoms would not be fully effective.[270] Another example is the case of *Vander Elst*, who performed various jobs both in Belgium, where his undertaking was located, and in France, together with his Belgian and Moroccan workers. The Moroccans had Belgian working permits. When working with his team in France, the latter initiated a prosecution because Vander Elst had employed third state nationals who did not possess French working permits. The Court held that such an requirement restricted the freedom of service to which Vander Elst was entitled.[271]

A national may also rely on his free movement rights against his own state if the latter prohibits him from travelling to another Member State. The case of *Gheorghe Jipa* dealt with a Romanian national who was prohibited by Romania from travelling to Belgium after he had been repatriated from that country on account of his illegal residence there. On reference for a preliminary ruling from the *Tribunalul Dâmbovita* of Romania, the Court decided that, that a national decision to restrict the free movement of a national to other Member States could be taken, provided that his personal conduct with regard to the risks to public order have been taken into account.[272]

---

[270] 11 July 2002, Case C-60/00, *Mary Carpenter* v. *Secretary of State for the Home Department* [2002] ECR I-6279, par. 37–39. Similarly 7 July 1992, Case C-370/90, *The Queen* v. *Immigration Appeal Tribunal and Surinder Singh, ex parte Secretary of State for Home Department* [1992] ECR I-4265.

[271] 9 August 1994, Case C-43/93, *Raymond Vander Elst* v. *Office des Migrations Internationales* [1994] ECR I-3803.

[272] 10 July 2008, C-33/07, *Ministerul Administraţiei şi Internelor – Direcţia Generală de Paşapoarte Bucureşti* v. *Gheorghe Jipa* [2008] ECR not yet reported.

4.4. NO DISCRIMINATION UPON THE BASIS OF NATIONALITY

Article 18, first sentence, TFEU (formerly Article 12 TEC) states: "Within the scope of application of the Treaties, and without prejudice to any special provisions contained therein, any discrimination on grounds of nationality shall be prohibited."[273] Unlike the five freedoms, the prohibition of discrimination on the basis of nationality is not an independent right. Its dependency is expressed by the requirement "within the scope of the treaties". A link must, therefore, be established with one of the five freedoms. The fifth freedom, in particular, free movement of EU nationals, will make it easy to bring situations of discrimination within the scope of the treaties.

Article 18 TFEU protects EU nationals against both overt and covert discrimination.[274] Later, it will be seen that the prohibition to discriminate on nationality influences the entire criminal justice system (Articles 18 and 21 TFEU, formerly Articles 12 and 18 TEC).[275] Discrimination can arise through the application of different rules to comparable situations, or by the application of the same rule to different situations.[276] Cases of covert discrimination exist if the applicable criterion does not directly relate to nationality, but does have such an effect. This is, for instance, the case if the Italian criminal law regarding traffic offences requires offenders driving a vehicle registered in other Member States than Italy to pay the minimum amount of the fine immediately or to provide security of twice that amount, on pain of having their licence confiscated or their vehicle impounded.[277] Clearly, the great majority of offenders in possession of a vehicle registered in another Member State are not Italian nationals, while the great majority of offenders in possession of a vehicle registered in Italy are Italian

---

[273]   Article 21, paragraph 1 Charter prohibits discrimination on any ground, without requiring a link with the scope of the Treaty. Article 45, paragraph 2 TFEU specifically stipulates the abolition of discrimination for workers.

[274]   14 February 1995, Case C-279/93, *Finanzamt Köln-Altstadt* v. *Roland Schumacker* [1995] ECR I-225, par. 26.

[275]   The prohibition is further specified in *Directive 2004/38 on Free Movement*. See, further, in Chapters 4, Section 1 and 6, Section 2.

[276]   14 February 1995, Case C-279/93, *Finanzamt Köln-Altstadt* v. *Roland Schumacker* [1995] ECR I-225, par. 30.

[277]   19 March 2002, Case C-224/00, *Commission* v. *Italy* [2002] ECR I-2965. For an older similar case, 23 January 1997, Case C-29/95, *Eckehard Pastoors and TransCap GmbH* v. *Belgium* [1997] ECR I-285. In *Pastoors*, Belgian law provided for non-residents either the immediate payment of the prescribed fine, or in the event that they opted for criminal proceedings, the deposit of security in respect of each offence, to wit, a fixed sum higher than that provided for in the case of immediate payment, in default of which their vehicle is impounded. Although the Court did not mention it, Advocate General Tesauro pointed to the fact that the Belgian rules ultimately limit access to the courts for non-resident citizens. See Opinion of Advocate General Tesauro of 3 October 1996, point 20.

nationals. However, the difference in treatment in this Italian case could be justified if there is, in the absence of international or Union instruments to ensure that an eventual penalty is enforced,[278] the risk that the penalty will not be paid or collected.[279] Where different treatment as such is acceptable, the concrete treatment does not pass the proportionality test on the combinations of three factors: a) immediate payment is required; b) the fine is twice the minimum prescribed; c) payment implies a waiver of rights.[280]

One of the most important examples of the prohibition of discrimination relates to the freedom to enjoy services. Ian Cowan, a British citizen, was assaulted and injured in Paris, when he visited the city as a tourist. When he applied for compensation as a victim of violence, his request was denied because he did not have French nationality. Compensation was granted to residents in France – irrespective of their nationality – and to French nationals residing abroad. The Court held, in a preliminary ruling on reference of the *Tribunal de Grande Instance de Paris* (France), that this was a matter, within the scope of the Treaties, which created less favourable conditions for tourists who must be regarded as recipients of services "as regards protection against the risk of assault and the right to obtain financial compensation provided for by national law when that risk materialises".[281] Other examples of indirect discrimination relate to distinctions made on residence.[282] Even the risk that local owners may not be able to pay higher rental charges does not justify more favourable treatment, as economic aims cannot justify grounds of public policy.[283]

Disfavourable Treatment of Nationals

The application of Union law in the national legal order may lead to situations in which non-nationals can rely on these rights, whereas nationals cannot. An example here is the situation with regard to the validity of driving licences in the Netherlands. The validity of Dutch driving licences expires after 10 years. The

---

[278]   Nowadays with the existence of *Framework Decision 2005/214 on Financial Penalties*, such a justification will no longer be acceptable. Advocate General Stix-Hackl, Opinion of 6 December 2001, Case C-224/00, *Commission* v. *Italy* [2002] ECR I-2965, point 8 referred to that already.

[279]   In a civil case, the Court held that national law that creates possibilities for interim seizure only because of the fact that the enforcement of the final judgment should take place abroad violates the principle of non-discrimination on the basis of nationality. 10 February 1994, Case C-398/92, *Mund & Fester* v. *Hatrex Internationaal Transport* [1994] ECR I-467, par. 16.

[280]   19 March 2002, Case C-224/00, *Commission* v. *Italy* [2002] ECR I-2965, par. 25.

[281]   2 February 1989, Case 186/87, *Ian William Cowan* v. *Trésor Public* [1989] ECR 195, par. 17.

[282]   7 May 1998, Case C-350/96, *Clean Car Autoservice GesmbH* v. *Landeshauptmann von Wien* [1998] ECR I-2521. More recent examples related to a residence requirement, see 22 May 2008, Case C-499/06, *Halina Nerkowska* v. *Zakład Ubezpieczeń Społecznych Oddział w Koszalinie* [2008] ECR not yet reported, and to a nationality requirement. See 5 June 2008, Case C-164/07, *James Wood* v. *Fonds de garantie des victimes des actes de terrorisme et d'autres infractions* [2008] ECR not yet reported.

[283]   29 April 1999, Case C-224/97, *Erich Ciola* v. *Land Vorarlberg* [1999] ECR I-2517, par. 16.

Netherlands government argued that it could not recognise longer validity periods stipulated by other Member States because this would constitute discrimination against the holders of Dutch driving licences, who are required to renew this document every 10 years. Does Union law also protect against such discrimination of nationals? The answer of the Court to the questions of the *Arrondissementsrechtbank te Rotterdam* (the Netherlands) is consistent and clear:

> "Any discrimination which nationals of a Member State may suffer under the law of that State fall within the scope of that law and must therefore be dealt with within the framework of the internal system of that State."[284]

The prohibition of discrimination on the basis of nationality does not require all disparities in treatment resulting from differences existing between the laws of the various Member States to be eliminated.[285] The mere fact that a national of a Member State may be subjected to criminal jurisdiction for offences committed abroad where non-nationals cannot be prosecuted does not amount to discrimination on the basis of nationality.[286] Likewise, the fact that Danish undertakings (unlike non-Danish undertakings) are subject to strict criminal liability does not, in itself, involve a distortion of the conditions of competition.[287] It is, however, apparent that the Court does not want to give full discretion to the Member States. This is expressed by the words "in itself" in paragraph 15 in the case of *Hansen and Søn*. Additionally, the Court held that the economic consequences of the Regulation not only vary according to the system of criminal liability, but also according to the level of the fine imposed and the degree of effectiveness of the checks carried out.

Dual Nationality

Individuals that have both the nationality of the host state and of another Member State may invoke the nationality of the other Member State with regard to the rights under the Treaty.[288]

---

[284] 29 January 2004, Case C-253/01, *S.A. Krüger* v. *Directie van de rechtspersoonlijkheid bezittende Dienst Wegverkeer* [2004] ECR I-1191, par. 36.

[285] The principle does not preclude requiring a victim of a criminal offence who wishes to bring a suit as the civil party in criminal proceedings to grant his representative special power of attorney, even when the law of the Member State of which the victim is a national does not lay down such a formality. See 1 February 1996, Case C-177/94, *criminal proceedings against Gianfranco Perfili* [1996] ECR I-161.

[286] 14 July 1994, Case C-379/92, *criminal proceedings against Matteo Peralta* [1994] ECR I-3453.

[287] 10 July 1990, Case C-326/88, *Anklagemyndigheden* v. *Hansen and Søn I/S* [1990] ECR I-2911, par. 15.

[288] 19 January 1988, Case 292/86, *Claude Gullung* v. *Conseil de l'ordre des avocats du barreau de Colmar et de Saverne* [1988] ECR 111, par. 12–13.

4.5. MUTUAL RECOGNITION AND MUTUAL TRUST

Member States must trust each other, so that, when goods are placed on the market in one Member State, the other Member States must trust that the verifications to check compliance with Union law have been genuinely executed by that Member State.[289] If goods are legally placed on the market in one Member State, other Member States may not subject those goods to further checks or formalities.[290] This concept endeavours to make the differences arising from the requirements set on products, services or diplomas irrelevant for the purposes of their recognition in another Member State. In Union law, this means that, if a beer brewed in the Netherlands meets the requirements set for beer in the Netherlands, this beer should also be able to be marketed on the German market, even if the Dutch beer does not meet the requirements placed on beer brewed in Germany under German law.[291] The consequence is that Germany may not set further requirements on admission to the German market.[292]

A prominent place for the understanding of the principle of mutual recognition exists for driving licences. Two Directives regulate the matter in a way that should facilitate the use that citizens make of their fundamental freedoms. The driving licence cases are of utmost importance, as will be seen later, to the development of mutual recognition in the area of freedom, security and justice. They can be regarded as the laboratory for mutual recognition of all kinds of criminal law "products". As a corollary of the freedom for workers and establishment, these cases build the bridge to mutual recognition without a nexus with free movement rights.

In various cases, the Court has decided that *Directive 91/439 on Driving Licences* confers exclusive competence on the Member State which issues a licence in order to ensure that the holder complies with all the relevant requirements.[293] If another Member State doubts the validity, it must inform the issuing Member State of this. Systematic checks in the receiving Member State to verify whether the conditions for issuance are being fulfilled are precluded. It is for the issuing Member State to take action. The Directive imposes on all other Member States "a clear and precise obligation, which leaves no room for discretion as to the measures

---

[289]   11 May 1989, Case 25/88, *criminal proceedings against Esther Renée Bouchara, née Wurmser, and Norlaine SA* [1989] ECR 1105.

[290]   8 July 1975, Case 4–75, *Rewe-Zentralfinanz eGmbH* v. *Landwirtschaftskammer* [1975] ECR 843; 22 September 1988, Case 286/86, *Ministère public* v. *Gérard Deserbais* [1988] ECR 4907.

[291]   Especially the *Reinheitsgebot*, dating from 1516 still applicable and providing that bottom-fermented beers may be manufactured only from malted barley, hops, yeast and water.

[292]   12 March 1987, Case 178/84, *Commission* v. *Germany* [1987] ECR 1227.

[293]   29 April 2004, Case C-476/01, *criminal proceedings against Felix Kapper* [2004] ECR I-5205, par. 48. In his Opinion of 16 October 2003, Advocate General Léger emphasises the exclusive power of the issuing Member State. See point 39.

to be adopted in order to comply with it".[294] There is no margin of discretion.[295] This means that obligatory registration of licences, as well as the obligation, under certain circumstances, to exchange a driving licence for one of the Member State of residence is inadmissible.[296] Only if it is apparent from entries on the second driving licence itself that the holder did not comply with the conditions for a new driving licence, can the Court exceptionally see room for non-recognition.[297]

In the *Kapper* case, the accused was prosecuted for driving without a driving licence in Germany. However, *Kapper*, whose German licence had been revoked by criminal order in 1998, had obtained a new Dutch driving licence in 1999, after the German temporary ban on applying to the competent authorities for the issue of a new licence had expired. Under these circumstances, the German authorities simply had to recognise the new Dutch licence. The *Kapper* case is much more relevant for situations that do not relate to the facts of this specific case itself. A logical consequence of the Court's decision in *Kapper* is that, if the German ban had still been applicable at the moment of issuing the Dutch licence, the German authorities would not have been obliged to recognise the new licence. Does this also mean that the Germans might be entitled to withdraw the Dutch licence if the holder took up residence again (or only drove) in Germany?[298] What, then, are the consequences for the Dutch authorities, who will not have been aware of the German ban at the time of issuance? Should they, if they had learned the German ban, have cancelled the Dutch licence? The question that evolves here is, how the principle of mutual recognition deals with competing decisions of the Member States. Who has to recognise whom? Here, one can see that mutual recognition is more difficult to deal with than with the once-and-for-all legal placement of goods on the market in another Member State. At the end of this section, it seems safe to conclude that an absolute obligation to mutual recognition

---

[294] 29 April 2004, Case C-476/01, *criminal proceedings against Felix Kapper* [2004] ECR I-5205, par. 45.

[295] 10 July 2003, Case C-246/00, *Commission v. the Netherlands* [2003] ECR I-7485, par. 61. Such a margin did exist before *Directive 91/439 on Driving Licences* entered into force. However, requirements relating to the exchange of a driving licence of another Member State into a driving licence of the Member State of residence may not be disproportional to the requirements of road safety. See 28 November 1978, Case 16/78, *criminal proceedings against Michel Choquet* [1978] ECR 2293, par. 8–9.

[296] 10 July 2003, Case C-246/00, *Commission v. the Netherlands* [2003] ECR I-7485, par. 67. 29 January 2004, Case C-253/01, *S.A. Krüger* v. *Directie van de rechtspersoonlijkheid bezittende Dienst Wegverkeer* [2004] ECR I-1191, par. 32 and 33.

[297] 26 June 2008, Joined Cases C-329/06 and C-343/06, *Arthur Wiedemann (C-329/06)* v. *Land Baden-Württemberg and Peter Funk (C-334/06)* v. *Stadt Chemnitz* ECR not yet reported; 26 June 2008, Joined Cases C-334/06 to C-336/06, *Matthias Zerche (C-334/06), Manfred Seuke (C-336/06)* v. *Landkreis Mittweida and Steffen Schubert (C-335/06)* v. *Landkreis Mittlerer Erzgebirgskreis* ECR not yet reported. See, further, Chapter 7, Section 3.2.

[298] AG Léger seems to suggest this. See Opinion of 21 November 2002, Case C-246/00, *Commission* v. *the Netherlands* [2003] ECR I-7485, point 67.

exists in situations of full harmonisation. In cases of partial harmonisation, mutual recognition will be the rule, but limited exceptions are possible. The issue of irreconcilable decisions will be dealt with more extensively in Chapter 7.

4.6. JUSTIFIED RESTRICTIONS ON FREE MOVEMENT

When dealing with the question of whether a certain fundamental freedom under the Treaty had been restricted or not, the fact that a number of restrictions might be justified under Union law was brought to light. The five freedoms are not of an absolute character. In this section, a more detailed analysis is given concerning what kind of exceptions to these freedoms of a fundamental nature are allowed.

Union law provides two categories of justifications of restrictions. The first category of restrictions which are accepted concerns areas in which a certain harmonisation has taken place. This will relate to specific common policies or to a common organisation of the market.[299] In situations in which there is specific harmonised legislation at Union level, then, that Directive or Regulation is the tool by which to assess compliance with Union law, and not the general provisions on free movement.[300] However, the Court held that, only when full harmonisation is provided by Union legislation, are the general provisions of fundamental freedoms to be excluded.[301] In other words, in cases of minimum harmonisation, the freedoms continue to play a role and the secondary legislation must be interpreted in the light of the fundamental freedoms.

The second category of restrictions deals with exceptions provided in the Treaty for each of the specific freedoms. These are justifications such as public policy, public security and public health. The TFEU gives Member States some discretion to make exceptions, but Union law supervises whether such justifications fall within the terms of the Treaty. A great deal of these exceptions find their basis in national criminal law. Article 67, paragraph 3 TFEU (formerly Article 61 sub a TEC) allows, rather generally, for certain measures to prevent and combat crime that could have consequences for the right of free movement. Finally, a more limited number of still existing state monopolies may be justified.

---

[299] Examples are Regulation 3796/81 of 29 December 1981 on the common organisation of the market in fishery products, OJ 1981, L379/1 and Regulation 1493/1999 of 17 May 1999 on the common organisation of the market in wine, OJ 1999, L 179/1.

[300] 12 October 1993, Case C-37/92, *criminal proceedings against José Vanacker and André Lesage and SA Baudoux combustibles* [1993] ECR I-4947, par. 9.

[301] 10 December 1985, Case 247/84, *criminal proceedings against Léon Motte* [1985] ECR 3887, par. 16.

4.6.1. Justifications

The TFEU provides for the following categories of justifications of restrictions: public morality (Article 36); public policy (Articles 36, 45, 52, 65); public security (Articles 36, 45, 52, 65); public health (Articles 36, 45, 52); the protection of national treasures possessing artistic, historic or archeological value (Article 36); and the protection of industrial and commercial property (Article 36). These justifications are dealt with individually below.

General Aspects Regarding Justifications

With regard to the exceptions to free movement, the Court held in the *Schreiber* case, that justifications must be examined on the basis of the following four points: "(i) whether there is a restriction within the meaning of Article 28 EC; (ii) whether there are Community harmonising measures on the matter; (iii) whether the system of prior authorisation at issue in the main proceedings may be justified on the basis of Article 30 EC, and (iv) whether that system is proportionate."[302] However, many alleged justifications fall down on the proportionality requirement. In *Commission* v. *France*,[303] France had prohibited advertising for certain alcoholic beverages and argued before the Court that this was justified in the interest of protecting public health. Although the Court acknowledged that this measure could, in principle, produce the result of protecting public health, it did not fulfil the test, because it was applied on some alcoholic beverages and not on others.

In the *Association Église de scientologie de Paris* and the *Scientology International Reserves Trust*, the Court held:

> "that while Member States are still, in principle, free to determine the requirements of public policy and public security in the light of their national needs, those grounds must, in the Community context and, in particular, as derogations from the fundamental principle of free movement of capital, be interpreted strictly, so that their scope cannot be determined unilaterally by each Member State without any control by the Community institutions. Thus, public policy and public security may be relied on only if there is a genuine and sufficiently serious threat to a fundamental interest of society. Moreover, those derogations must not be misapplied so as, in fact, to serve purely economic ends. Further, any person affected by a restrictive measure based on such a derogation must have access to legal redress."[304]

---

[302] 15 July 2004, Case C-443/02, *criminal proceedings against Nicolas Schreiber* [2004] ECR I-7275, par. 44.

[303] 10 July 1980, Case 152/78, *Commission* v. *France* [1980] ECR 2299.

[304] 14 March 2000, Case C-54/99, *Association Église de scientologie de Paris and Scientology International Reserves Trust* v. *The Prime Minister* [2000] ECR I-1335, par. 17 (references omitted).

The mere fact that a Member State has chosen a system of protection which is different from that adopted by another Member State cannot affect the appraisal as to the need for and the proportionality of the provisions adopted, so the Court held in a preliminary ruling on a reference from the *Tribunal Cível da Comarca de Lisboa*, Portugal.[305] Thus, Member States enjoy an area of discretion.[306] Justifications must be interpreted in the light of the general principles of law and, in particular, of fundamental rights.[307] However, if the national legislation is incompatible with a provision of the ECHR, then it is incapable of satisfying the requirement of proportionality.[308] If the measure additionally violates a right recognised under the ECHR, it is most unlikely that the Court will subsume the measures as a justified restriction of Article 63 TFEU.[309] In other words, restrictions to the freedoms which are violations of the ECHR cannot be justified. General principles regarding the restrictions on the right of entry and the right of residence on grounds of public policy, public security and public health have been stipulated in Article 27 of *Directive 2004/38 on Free Movement*.

Public Morality

This justification is formulated in Article 36 TFEU with regard to goods only. The Court has held, with regard to pornographic material, that it is for each Member State to determine in accordance with its own scale of values and in the form selected by it, the requirements of public morality on its territory.[310] However, a Member State cannot prohibit the importation of certain goods on the grounds that they are indecent or obscene, where it does not prohibit the manufacturing and marketing such products on its own territory.[311]

Public Policy

Public policy is one of the most important justifications found in the Treaty with regard to goods (Articles 36), workers (Article 45), establishment (Article 52), services (Article 62), and capital (Article 65). How must public policy be interpreted? The case law of the Court provides numerous examples of cases in

---

[305]   11 September 2003, Case C-6/01, *Associação Nacional de Operadores de Máquinas Recreativeas (Anomar) and others* v. *Estado Português* [2003] ECR I-8621, par. 80.

[306]   4 December 1974, Case 41–74, *Yvonne van Duyn* v. *Home Office* [1974] ECR 1337, par. 18.

[307]   26 June 1997, Case C-368/95, *Vereinigte Familiapress Zeitungsverlags- und vertriebs GmbH* v. *Heinrich Bauer Verlag* [1997] ECR I-3689, par. 24.

[308]   20 May 2003, Joined Cases C-465/00, C-138/01 and C-139/01, *Rechnungshof* v. *Österreichischer Rundfunk and Others and Christa Neukomm and Joseph Lauermann* v. *Österreichischer Rundfunk* [2003] ECR I-4989, par. 91.

[309]   25 January 2007, Case C-370/05, *criminal proceedings against Uwe Kay Festersen* [2007] ECR I-1129, par. 35.

[310]   14 December 1979, Case 34/79, *Regina* v. *Maurice Donald Henn and John Frederick Ernest Darby* [1979] ECR 3795, par. 15–16.

[311]   11 March 1986, Case 121/85, *Conegate Limited* v. *HM Customs & Excise* [1986] ECR 17, in which it concerned inflatable life-size dolls of a clearly sexual nature.

which public policy has, or has not, been accepted. In the case law, the justification of public policy is also referred to as *public interest*, and any restrictions must be justified in the general interest, be suitable for achieving the objectives which they pursue, and not go beyond what is necessary. The Court held that maintaining the good reputation of the national financial sector may, therefore, constitute an imperative reason of public interest sufficient to justify restrictions on the freedom to provide financial services.[312] The mere fact that national legislation carries penal sanctions cannot, as such, justify the exception on the basis of public policy.[313] Penal sanctions must be applied without discrimination.[314] Regard must be paid to the nature of the impediment and its justification. The specific circumstances which may justify recourse to the concept of public policy may vary from one state to another.[315] This also means that the application of the public policy exception does not depend on a common conception shared by all Member States.[316] In *Omega Spielhallen*, German law punished the opening of a "laserdrome" on the grounds that it would violate human dignity and glorify the killing of human beings. The Court allowed for a certain discretion, even in view of the fact that the concept was legally brought on the market of another Member State.[317]

Comparable considerations were voiced by the Court in cases that dealt with gambling. Moral, religious and cultural factors, as well as the morally and financially harmful consequences for both the individual and all society associated with gaming and betting, could serve to justify the existence on the part of the national authorities of a margin of appreciation sufficient to enable them to determine what consumer protection and the preservation of public order require.[318] Various factors contribute to a wide discretion for Member States to determine what is required to protect the players:

---

[312]   10 May 1995, Case C-384/93, *Alpine Investments BV* v. *Minister van Financiën* [1995] ECR I-1141, par. 44.

[313]   13 March 1984, Case 16/83, *criminal proceedings against Karl Prantl* [1984] ECR 1299, par. 36.

[314]   6 November 2003, Case C-243/01, *criminal proceedings against Piergiorgio Gambelli and others* [2003] ECR I-13031, par. 63 and 65. If a Member State expels foreign prostitutes, but does not prosecute its own nationals performing similar conduct, it cannot rely on the public policy justification. See 18 May 1982, Joined Cases 115 and 116/81, *Rezguia Adoui* v. *Belgium and City of Liège; Dominique Cornuaille* v. *Belgium* [1982] ECR 1665.

[315]   14 October 2004, Case C-36/02, *Omega Spielhallen- und Automatenaufstellungs-GmbH* v. *Oberbürgermeisterin der Stadt Bonn* [2004] ECR I-9609, par. 31.

[316]   14 October 2004, Case C-36/02, *Omega Spielhallen- und Automatenaufstellungs-GmbH* v. *Oberbürgermeisterin der Stadt Bonn* [2004] ECR I-9609, par. 37.

[317]   Similarly, the requirement that certain video cartoons could only be admitted on the market after having been examined and classified for the purposes of protecting young persons is acceptable in the public interest. 14 February 2008, Case C-244/06, *Dynamic Medien Vertriebs GmbH* v. *Avides Media AG* [2008] ECR not yet reported.

[318]   In 21 October 1999, Case C-67/98, *Questore di Verona* v. *Diego Zenatti* [1999] ECR I-7289, the Court accepted that the avoidance of risks of crime and fraud could justify restrictions on taking bets.

"First of all, it is not possible to disregard the moral, religious or cultural aspects of lotteries, like other types of gambling, in all the Member States. The general tendency of the Member States is to restrict, or even prohibit, the practice of gambling and to prevent it from being a source of private profit. Secondly, lotteries involve a high risk of crime or fraud, given the size of the amounts which can be staked and of the winnings which can hold out to the players, particularly when they are operated on a large scale. Thirdly, they are an incitement to spend which may have damaging individual and social consequences. A final ground which is not without relevance, although it cannot in itself be regarded as an objective justification, is that lotteries may make a significant contribution to the financing of benevolent or public interest activities such as social works, chartable works, sport or culture."[319]

Under Finnish law, the importation of undenatured ethyl alcohol of over 80% is subject to a licence, and the importation of strong spirits without a licence is a criminal offence for which imprisonment is provided. On reference from the *Korkein oikeus*, Finland, the Court, however, regards this as a formality that hinders intra-Community trade and impedes access to the market for goods from other Member States.[320] Is this a system that could be justified under Article 36 TFEU, which allows for restrictions of the freedom of goods if they find their basis in public health and public policy concerns?[321] Moreover, case law has established that the exceptions to the fundamental principle of free movement must be strictly formulated.

With regard to free movement of EU citizens, Article 27, paragraph 2 *Directive 2004/38 on Free Movement* on the rights of citizens stipulates that "previous criminal convictions shall not in themselves constitute" grounds of public policy to take restrictive measures. In addition, the Member State must demonstrate that the measure at issue is appropriate to the aim pursued (the suitability test) and that it does not go beyond what is necessary (the necessity test) to achieve that aim (the proportionality test). In addition, the measure may not constitute a means of arbitrary discrimination. The burden of proof that the exception is justified lies with the state concerned.

---

[319]   24 March 1994, Case C-275/92, *Her Majesty's Customs and Excise* v. *Gerhart Schindler and Jörg Schindler* [1994] ECR I-1039, par. 60.

[320]   28 September 2006, Case C-434/04, *criminal proceedings against Ahokainen and Leppik* [2006] ECR I-9171.

[321]   However, it may not amount to considerations of consumer protection, because there is secondary legislation on that topic. The Court has categorically ruled out that consumer protection could be included on public policy. See 6 November 1984, Case 177/83, *Th. Kohl KG* v. *Ringelhan & Rennett SA and Ringelhan Einrichtungs GmbH* [1984] ECR 3651, par. 19. Despite this, in *Buet*, the Court considered the need to protect consumers against canvassing at private dwellings to be a sufficient justification to allow prosecution. See 16 May 1989, Case 382/87, *R. Buet and Educational Business Services (EBS)* v. *Ministère Public* [1989] ECR 1235, par. 13, at which the Court looked at the vulnerability of the potential purchasers and the numerous documented complaints.

In the Finnish alcohol case, it was obvious that, given the general policy on alcohol, the element of discrimination of foreign alcohol in favour of Finnish alcoholic products was absent. The Court left it to the national court to decide whether the measures adopted were such that they effectively combatted abuse arising from the consumption of spirits as a drink, or whether less restrictive measures could ensure a similar result.[322] Years earlier, in *van Duyn*, the Court held that the United Kingdom could refuse entry of an EU national who wanted to take up employment as a secretary of the Church of Scientology on grounds of public policy, even when the United Kingdom neither prohibited the organisation, nor impeded its own nationals from working for Scientology.[323] Does the Court leave some discretion here, because it knows how sensitive the issue is to the relevant Member State?

Member States have a fair degree of discretion for making exceptions to the five freedoms. The mere fact that a Member State has opted for a system of protection which differs from that adopted by another Member State is, as such, irrelevant.[324] The application of justifications does not require a common European view, and, thus, disparity between the Member States is possible. The fact that the games at issue in *Läärä* were not totally prohibited (but exclusively given to a state-owned company) was not sufficient to show that the national legislation was not, in reality, intended to achieve the public interest objectives at which it was purportedly aimed.[325] The Court recognised that limited authorisation of gambling on an exclusive basis could serve public interest objectives, such as preventing the risk of fraud or crime in the context of such exploitation. It then left it to the discretion of the Member State to decide whether the objectives could also be served by imposing the necessary code of conduct on operators concerned:

"However, the obligation imposed on the licensed public body, requiring it to pay over the proceeds of its operations, constitutes a measure which, given the risk of crime and

---

[322]   28 September 2006, Case C-434/04, *criminal proceedings against Ahokainen and Leppik* [2006] ECR I-9171, par. 38. In 5 June 2007, C-170/04, *Klas Rosengren, Bengt Morelli, Hans Särman, Mats Åkerström, Åke Kempe, Anders Kempe, Mats Kempe, Björn Rosengren, Martin Lindberg, Jon Pierre, Tony Staf v. Riksåklagaren* [2007] ECR I-4071, the Court considered the prohibition of ordering alcohol by mail to Sweden from another Member State. The Court could only see a justification in protecting the health of the youth. However, a general prohibition does not make a distinction on the age of the possible customers and cannot therefore be accepted.

[323]   4 December 1974, Case 41–74, *Yvonne van Duyn* v. *Home Office* [1974] ECR 1337, par. 23.

[324]   See, for instance, 21 September 1999, Case C-124/97, *Markku Juhari Läärä, Cotswold Microsystems Ltd and Oy Transatlantic Software Ltd* v. *Kihlakunnansyyttäjä (Jyväskylä) and Suomen valtio* [1999] ECR I-6067, par. 36.

[325]   21 September 1999, Case C-124/97, *Markku Juhari Läärä, Cotswold Microsystems Ltd and Oy Transatlantic Software Ltd* v. *Kihlakunnansyyttäjä (Jyväskylä) and Suomen valtio* [1999] ECR I-6067, par. 37.

fraud, is certainly more effective in ensuring that strict limits are set to the lucrative nature of such activities."[326]

Public Security

Public security also finds its place in Articles 36, 45, 52 and 65 TFEU. Both Articles 346 and 347 TFEU (formerly Articles 296 and 297 TEC) allow for certain restrictions for security concerns. Article 346, paragraph 2 TFEU refers to a (never published) and, apparently, never amended list of 15 April 1958 to which the provisions apply.[327] The Court has held that the importation, exportation and transit of (military) goods capable of being used for strategic purposes may affect the public security of a Member State.[328]

Article 207 TFEU (former Article 133 TEC) has been used in the past as the legal basis for Regulations which limit or prohibit certain goods and services from being delivered. Such Regulations are especially relevant with regard to dual use products which have both a civil and a military purpose. Or, in the case of drug precursors, substances which may also be used for purposes not related to the production of drugs. Complementary to a Regulation based upon Article 133 TEC, a Member State may implement national restrictive measures (also of a criminal nature) for the purpose of protecting internal and external security.[329] Although rules restricting exports of dual use goods to non-member countries are in principle of exclusive competence for the Union,[330] Member States have some discretion, where specific authorisation is granted,[331] this is especially so with regard to goods that are capable of being used for military purposes to a country at war. Thus, following a United Nations Security Council Resolution, the Council took a Common Position by which it prohibited the sale of weapons to Sierra Leone.[332]

---

[326]   21 September 1999, Case C-124/97, *Markku Juhari Läärä, Cotswold Microsystems Ltd and Oy Transatlantic Software Ltd v. Kihlakunnansyyttäjä (Jyväskylä) and Suomen valtio* [1999] ECR I-6067, par. 41.

[327]   It was never published according to Advocate General Jacobs in his Opinion of 18 May 1998, Cases C-70/94 and C-83/94, *Werner v. Germany* [1998] ECR I-3231, and Case C-83/94, *criminal proceedings against Peter Leifer, Reinhold Otto Krauskopf and Otto Holzer* [1995] ECR point 20. I have not been able to trace the text of either.

[328]   4 October 1991, Case C-367/89, *criminal proceedings against Aimé Richardt and Les Accessoires Scientifiques SNC* [1991] ECR I-4621, par. 22.

[329]   17 October 1995, Case C-70/94, *Fritz Werner Industrie-Ausrüstungen GmbH v. Germany* [1995] ECR I-3189.

[330]   14 January 1997, Case C-124/95, *The Queen, ex parte Centro-Com Srl v. HM Treasury and Bank of England* [1997] ECR I-81.

[331]   17 October 1995, Case C-83/94, *criminal proceedings against Peter Leifer, Reinhold Otto Krauskopf and Otto Holzer* [1995] ECR I-3231, par. 13 and 29.

[332]   Common Position 98/409/CFSP of 29 June 1998 concerning Sierra Leone, OJ 1998, L 187/1.

Public Health

While Article 36 allows for justification on grounds of "the protection of health and life of humans, animals or plants", Articles 45 and 52 briefly refer to "public health". It is assumed that this difference in formulation does not lead to a difference of interpretation. From the case law it is clear, as with other justifications, that States enjoy a certain discretion to follow their own public health policy. However, restrictions may not be of a general character. If a Member State systematically carries out health inspection checks on certain goods when they cross the frontier, this cannot be justified on grounds of public health.[333] In *Schwarz*, a reference from the *Unabhängiger Verwaltungssenat Salzburg*, Austria, Austrian legislation prohibited unwrapped sugar confectionary (chewing gum) being offered for sale from vending machines. In the absence of secondary Union legislation on the packaging of such products, the national measures must be assessed against the yardstick of the free movement of goods.[334] The Austrian government argued that only wrapping could protect these products from moisture and ants. In addition, the goods might be contaminated in the delivery tray. In this chewing gum case, the Court also noted that other Member States allowed the same product to be sold unwrapped. However, in the absence of specific Union legislation on the topic, the Member States keep their discretion and may maintain more severe rules than other Member States.

As with the other justifications, the Court does not require a common European view on public health. The Court has held that the assessment of the risk connected with the consumption of certain products depends upon several factors of a variable nature, in particular, the dietary habits of each country.[335] The result is that products might be prohibited for reasons of public health in one Member State and not meet any obstacles of this kind in another. In the *Schreiber* case, Italy required an authorisation, on the grounds of the protection of public health, before placing blocks of cedar wood on the market. The Court has allowed this even in situations in which the product was imported from a Member State in which it was lawfully placed on the market without the requirement of authorisation.[336]

Another question is whether a Member State may prohibit the marketing of a new product for reasons of public health because of alleged uncertainties regarding

---

[333]   20 September 1988, Case 190/87, *Oberkreisdirektor des Kreises Borken and Vertreter des öffentlichen Interesses beim Oberverwaltungsgericht für das Land Nordrhein Westfalen* v. *Handelsonderneming Moormann BV* [1988] ECR 4689. In this case, it is also relevant that there is a Directive applicable that introduces a harmonised system of health inspections in the exporting state.

[334]   24 November 2005, Case C-366/04, *proceedings against Schwarz* [2005] ECR I-10139.

[335]   5 February 1981, Case 53/80, *Officier van justitie* v. *Koninklijke Kaasfabriek Eyssen BV* [1981] ECR 409.

[336]   15 July 2004, Case C-443/02, *criminal proceedings against Nicolas Schreiber* [2004] ECR I-7275.

the exact dangers of the product. The Court held that Member States, "in the absence of harmonisation and to the extent that there is still uncertainty in the current state of scientific research", retain a certain discretion, subject to the principle of proportionality.[337] The Court refers to this as the *precautionary principle*,[338] which allows the Member States to protect real[339] (not purely hypothetical) risks to public health "on the basis of the latest scientific data available at the date of the adoption of such decision".[340] The existence of objective data on the health risks of certain products reduces the discretion of the Member States.

With regard to the food and feed, the Court held that:

> "the use of a specific additive which is authorised in another Member State must be authorized in the case of a product imported from that Member State where, in view, on the one hand, of the findings of international scientific research, and in particular of the work of the Community's Scientific Committee for Food, the Codex alimentarious Committee of the Food and Agriculture Organization of the United Nations (FAO) and the World Health Organization, and, on the other hand, of the eating habits prevailing in the importing Member State, the additive in question does not present a risk to public health and meets a real need, especially a technological one."[341]

Article 36 may justify a national prohibition on the sale of medicinal products by mail order in so far as the prohibition covers medicinal products subject to prescription. Such a justification cannot be found for an absolute prohibition of the mail order sale of medicinal products which are not subject to prescription in the Member State concerned.[342] Although Article 36 may allow Member States to

---

[337] 14 July 1983, Case 174/82, *criminal proceedings against Sandoz BV* [1983] ECR 2445, par. 16–18; 5 February 2004, Case C-95/01, *criminal proceedings against John Greenham and Léonard Abel* [2004] ECR I-1333, par. 37–39.

[338] The precautionary principle is formulated in Article 7 Regulation 178/2002 laying down the general principles and requirements of food law, establishing the European Food Safety Authority and laying down procedures in matters of food safety.

[339] 6 May 1986, Case 304/84, *criminal proceedings against Claude Muller and others* [1986] ECR 1511.

[340] 5 February 2004, Case C-95/01, *criminal proceedings against John Greenham and Léonard Abel* [2004] ECR I-1333, par. 42–43. See, also, 24 October 2002, Case C-121/00, *criminal proceedings against Walter Hahn* [2002] ECR I-9193, in which the Court thoroughly investigates the current state of scientific research, which does not make it possible to determine with any certainty the precise concentration of certain micro-organisms that pose a threat to human health.

[341] 13 December 1990, Case C-42/90, *criminal proceedings against Jean-Claude Bellin* [1990] ECR I-4863, par. 14; 10 December 1985, Case 247/84, *criminal proceedings against Léon Motte* [1985] ECR 3887.

[342] 11 December 2003, Case C-322/01, *Deutscher Apothekerverband eV* v. *0800DocMorris NV and Jacques Waterval* [2003] ECR I-14887.

maintain restrictions on the free movement of goods, the use of this provision is, nevertheless, precluded where Directives provide for the harmonisation of the measures necessary to achieve the specific objective of Article 42 TFEU (aid scheme).[343]

The last two categories provided in Article 36, namely, "the protection of national treasures possessing artistic, historic or archaelogical value" and "the protection of industrial and commercial property", do not seem to have led to any case law from the Court.[344]

The Competition of Freedoms and the Abuse of Freedoms

The Court has held that, where a measure affects both the freedom to provide services and the free movement of goods, the Court will, in principle, examine it in relation to only one of the two fundamental freedoms if it is clear that, in the circumstances of the case, one of the freedoms is entirely secondary in relation to the other and may be attached to it.[345] This seems to be more a matter of judicial economy, than of principle. An example can be given by reference to the case of *van Schaik*, in which the servicing of a motor vehicle took place in another Member State. Although the servicing, as such, may involve the supplying of goods (spare parts, oil, *etc.*), this is not an end in itself, but is incidental to the general provision of services.[346]

The Court has held that "a Member State is entitled to take measures designed to prevent certain of its nationals from attempting, under cover of the rights created by the Treaty, improperly to circumvent their national legislation or to prevent individuals from improperly or fraudulently taking advantage of provisions of Community law".[347] Although the Court did not rule out that combating fraud could justify restrictive measures, concrete measures (such as the general practice of refusing to register a branch of a company which has its registered office in another Member State) do not qualify, because there are less intrusive alternatives. Union law cannot be relied on for abusive or fraudulent ends.[348] As such, the prevention of tax evasion and fraud may justify certain

---

[343] 24 October 2002, Case C-99/01, *criminal proceedings against Gottfried Linkart and Hans Biffl* [2002] ECR I-9375, par. 25.

[344] This can be explained by the fact that the discretion for Member States to apply this justification is rather limited. In an Annex to Directive 93/7 on the Return of Cultural Objects Unlawfully Removed from the Territory of a Member State, national treasures have been defined in an exhaustive list.

[345] 14 October 2004, Case C-36/02, *Omega Spielhallen- und Automatenaufstellungs-GmbH* v. *Oberbürgermeisterin der Stadt Bonn* [2004] ECR I-9609, par. 26.

[346] 5 October 1994, Case C-55/93, *criminal proceedings against Johannes Gerrit Cornelis van Schaik* [1994] ECR I-4837, par. 14.

[347] 9 March 1999, Case C-212/97, *Centros Ltd* v. *Erhvervs – og Selskabsstyrelsen* [1999] ECR I-1459, par. 24.

[348] 21 February 2006, Case C-255/02, *Halifax plc, Leeds Permanent Development Services Ltd, County Wide Property Investments Ltd* v. *Commissioners of Customs and Excise* [2006] ECR

limitations to free movement. However, the mere risk of abuse or fraud cannot justify a general restriction, which would prevent the *bona fide* exercise of Union rights.[349]

Monopolies

The last category of exceptions is found in Article 37 TFEU, which deals with state monopolies. Clearly, the internal market brought a general end to state monopolies, for a legal order without borders cannot allow monopolies to exist. However, Article 37 TFEU does not completely rule out state monopolies of a commercial character. It gives Member States the task of adjusting these remaining monopolies in order "to ensure that no discrimination regarding the conditions under which goods are procured and marketed exists between the Member States".[350] Thus, it plainly establishes a link with Article 34 TFEU. In the criminal proceedings against *Hanner*, the Court formulates the three relevant criteria before a state monopoly passes the test: 1) the criteria for the selection of a sales monopoly must be independent from the origin of the products; 2) the retail network must be organised in a way that guarantees consumer access; and 3) all marketing and advertising must be impartial and independent of the origin.[351]

What does this mean for the *Stockholms tingsrätt*, dealing with the prosecution of *Hanner*, for having marketed packages of Nicolette patches and of Nicorette chewing gum, despite a Swedish monopoly? The Court's reply to the national court was rather brief: "Article 31(1) EC precludes a sales regime which grants an exclusive retail right and is arranged in the same way as the sales regime at issue in the main proceedings."[352] The Court did not directly tell the national court whether it should convict, acquit or set aside the national penal provision. Instead, its reply relates to the contextual system in force in Sweden. It is clear that the applicable national system violates Union law. However, a system that complies with the criteria which the Court stipulates is not impossible. In such a system, any marketing outside the monopoly may be prosecuted. Since the accused operated under a system that was not in compliance with Union law, the national penal provision could not be applied.

I-1609, par. 68–69.

[349] 15 December 2005, Joined Cases C-151/04 and C-152/04, *criminal proceedings against Claude Nadin, Nadin-Lux SA and Jean-Pascal Durré* [2005] ECR I-11203, par. 45–46.

[350] 3 February 1976, Case 59–75, *Pubblico Ministero v. Flavia Manghera and others* [1976] ECR 91.

[351] 31 May 2005, Case C-438/02, *criminal proceedings against Krister Hanner* [2005] ECR I-4551, par. 49. See, also, 23 October 1997, Case C-189/95, *criminal proceedings against Harry Franzén* [1997] ECR I-5909.

[352] 31 May 2005, Case C-438/02, *criminal proceedings against Krister Hanner* [2005] ECR I-4551, par. 49.

4.6.2. Substantive Rights in Secondary Legislation and Under the Area

In order to assess whether there is a violation of Union law or not, the Court always investigates first whether there is specific Union legislation (Directive, Regulation, Framework Decision, Convention) on the matter. In the absence of any harmonising instrument, Member States alone are competent to determine the rules, and may also decide to apply penalties when the conditions are breached. However, this national discretion may not, of course, infringe upon the fundamental freedoms provided for in the TFEU.[353]

Union law, for instance, provides for specific measures taken in the context of a Common Agricultural Policy. This takes precedence over the general provisions of the Treaty (Article 38 TFEU, formerly Article 32 TEC).[354] If the relevant regulation governs the matter completely, there is no need to look at the general provisions of Articles 34 and 36 TFEU. The general prohibition in Sweden of the cultivation and possession of industrial hemp undermines the common organisation of the market in flax and hemp regulated in a regulation.[355] In summary, where a matter is regulated in a harmonised manner at Union level, any measure relating to it must be assessed in the light of the provisions of that harmonising measure and not on the basis of Articles 36 and 42 TFEU.[356]

In *Yonemoto*, the Court elaborated on the rules established in *Wurmser*,[357] regarding the liability of importers when importing defective goods from another Member State. Wurmser was prosecuted for marketing a textile product which bore false information with regard to its composition. The Court held, at the time, that the importer could rely on certificates issued by the authorities of the producing Member State. However, contrary to *Wurmser*, a Directive was applicable in *Yonemoto*. In this Finnish case, the accused had imported a machine manufactured in France. Despite the use of the emergency stop, an employee lost eight fingers while changing the blades of the machine. Yonemoto was prosecuted

---

[353] 2 October 2003, Case C-12/02, *criminal proceedings against Marco Grilli* [2003] ECR I-11585, par. 39–40.

[354] 16 January 2003, Case C-462/01, *criminal proceedings against Ulf Hammarsten* [2003] ECR I-781, par. 24.

[355] 16 January 2003, Case C-462/01, *criminal proceedings against Ulf Hammarsten* [2003] ECR I-781, par. 30. Similarly, the question of whether in the context of a common organisation of the market, there is still room for national legislation, must be answered on the basis of the relevant Regulation. See 16 January 2003, Case C-265/01, *criminal proceedings against Annie Pansard and others* [2003] ECR I-683.

[356] 23 May 1990, Case C-169/89, *criminal proceedings against Gourmetterie van den Burg* [1990] ECR I-2143, par. 9; 24 October 2002, Case C-99/01, *criminal proceedings against Gottfried Linkart and Hans Biffl* [2002] ECR I-9375, par. 18; 23 January 2003, C-421/00, C-426/00 and C-16/01, *criminal proceedings against Renate Sterbenz and Paul Dieter Haug* [2003] ECR I-6445, par. 24.

[357] 11 May 1989, Case 25/88, *criminal proceedings against Esther Renée Bouchara, née Wurmser, and Norlaine SA* [1989] ECR 1105.

in Finland for having imported an object that increased the risk of accident or sickness, to which he argued that he could not be obliged to check whether the machine was in compliance with all the safety regulations.

This is a case that serves very well to explain the relationship between the TFEU and secondary legislation. The machine imported in this case was subject to the rules of Directive 98/37 on the Approximation of the Laws of the Member States relating to machinery. This is a Directive that harmonises the various rules relating to machinery, including rules relating to safety. It provides for a EC Declaration of Conformity. The machine imported by Yonemoto was provided with such a EC Declaration of Conformity issued by the authorities of another Member State. The Court held that, under these circumstances, there was no obligation on the importer to verify for himself that the machine was in compliance with all the requirements of the Directive.[358] In essence, the specific rules of the Directive determine the exceptions to the prohibition of quantitative restrictions on imports, as a result of which, it was established that the only obligation with which Yonemoto had not complied was that he had not provided the machine with user instructions in the language of the importing Member State. The Court added that "if it transpires that that machinery poses risks to safety or health", the importer may be obliged to give all appropriate information and co-operation to the national inspection authorities.[359] In summary, in principle, there is no possibility (no obligation and no right) for importers such as Yonemoto to check the compliance with safety rules. They must take the Declaration of Conformity of the Exporter or of other Member States for granted. However, if the importer possesses information which is in contradiction with the compliance with the safety requirements, he may not close his eyes to this and must take action.

Can Regulations, Directives and Framework Decisions infringe upon fundamental freedoms? Does the fact that the obligations imposed on undertakings by a Regulation constitute a measure which has the equivalent effect of a quantitative restriction prohibited by the Treaty lead to invalidity of the Regulation? These, in essence, were the questions raised by the *Tribunal de police*, Luxembourg, in the criminal proceedings against *Kieffer and Thill* on charges of failing to provide declarations regarding the statistical information required under the regulation.[360] Although the Court admitted that the Regulation had restrictive effects with regard to the free movement of goods, it regarded these as proportional in the light of the objectives of the Regulation. A restriction to the free movement of goods may also find its basis in a Directive. If it appears that the

---

[358]   8 September 2005, Case C-40/04, *criminal proceedings against Syuichi Yonemoto* [2005] ECR I-7755, par. 53.

[359]   8 September 2005, Case C-40/04, *criminal proceedings against Syuichi Yonemoto* [2005] ECR I-7755, par. 61.

[360]   25 June 1997, Case C-114/96, *criminal proceedings against René Kieffer and Romain Thill* [1997] ECR I-3629.

objective of the Directive is the protection of public health, then it follows that the prohibition laid down by the Directive must be interpreted widely and the exception must be interpreted narrowly.[361] Even if it can be established that the prohibition protects the interest covered by the Directive, the restriction may not make all international transit impossible.[362] Secondary legal instruments may, therefore, limit fundamental freedoms. Only disproportional infringements may lead to the invalidity of the legal instruments.

The *van Schaik* case also provides an excellent example of the consequences of the application of a Directive partially harmonising the relevant area. Van Schaik, a Dutch national living in the Netherlands (close to both the German and the Belgian border) and the owner of a motor vehicle registered in the Netherlands, was prosecuted there for driving a motor vehicle without a valid test certificate of roadworthiness. The Dutch act imposing this obligation forms the implementation of Directive 77/143 on the Approximation of the Laws of the Member States relating to roadworthiness tests for motor vehicles and their trailers. Van Schaik had the servicing and testing of his car done in Germany. However, the garage in Germany could not provide him with a German roadworthiness certificate, because his car was not registered there. Van Schaik argued that his freedom to make use of services in another Member State had been infringed because he was not allowed to choose German or Belgian garages, but had a limited choice of Dutch garages only. Although the Court admitted that this was an infringement of the freedom of services, it regarded it as an acceptable situation given the fact that the Directive created an incomplete harmonisation of the criteria for testing and the fact that the Directive stipulated that supervision of the roadworthiness tests should be performed by the authorities of the Member State in which the vehicle is registered.[363]

Substantive Rights of the Area of Freedom, Security and Justice?

Article 67 TFEU states that "The Union shall constitute an area of freedom, security and justice with respect for fundamental rights and the different legal systems and traditions of the Member States". Does this mean that the rights mentioned in this provision should be placed on the same footing as the five freedoms? Is there, for instance, direct effect of the right to freedom, the right to security, and the right to justice? This cannot be read from the Treaties. In comparison to the freedoms given under the internal market, the rights of the area are not defined so precisely. More importantly, the rights given in the area

---

[361]   16 September 2004, Case C-404/03, *criminal proceedings against Olivier Dupuy and Hervé Rouvre* [2004] ECR I-8557.

[362]   11 May 1999, Case C-350/97, *Wilfried Monsees* v. *Unabhängiger Verwaltungssenat für Kärnten* [1999] ECR I-2921.

[363]   5 October 1994, Case C-55/93, *criminal proceedings against Johannes Gerrit Cornelis van Schaik* [1994] ECR I-4837, par. 18–22.

are more favourable to the authorities of the Member States than to their citizens. Suspected, accused and convicted citizens cannot profit from the area, but suffer from it. Citizens, in general (including those mentioned before), can only profit indirectly from the area, as a consequence of the fact that combating crime will contribute to more freedom, security and justice for society as a whole. It is rather strange that Union law considers fundamental rights (human rights) to be general principles of law, *only* in the economic setting of the internal market. Given the nature of the changes brought about by the Treaty of Lisbon, there is quite a challenge to develop a fundamental rights component of Union law.[364]

4.7. THE STAND ALONE STATUS OF SECONDARY LEGISLATION

So far, the freedoms that find their basis in the primary law of the Union have been discussed: the five freedoms recognised in the TFEU. Whilst most secondary Union law further elaborates on these freedoms within the context of the internal market, situations may arise in which secondary legislation (Directive, Regulations, Framework Decision) stipulates rights or claims for individuals with no link to the fundamental freedoms. Union law allows for two categories of individuals who are excluded from invoking the fundamental freedoms, to rely on the provisions of a Directive.[365] The first category consist of nationals against their own state,[366] the second consists of non-EU nationals. Despite the fact that a person who falls within the above-mentioned two categories is not entitled to the fundamental freedoms under Union law, circumstances exist in which he can invoke a Directive. A case in point here is the prosecution of *Ibiyinka Awoyemi*, a Nigerian national working and living in Belgium. He was prosecuted in Belgium for driving without a valid driving licence, despite the fact that he possessed a valid Community-model driving licence issued by the UK authorities. The provisions of the Directive apply to anyone holding a European driving licence, regardless of the nationality of the holder.[367] Likewise, a national of a Member State may invoke his rights, under a Directive, concerning mutual recognition of diplomas and certificates against his own state, if he has obtained qualifications

---

[364] See Chapter 9.

[365] In this subparagraph the direct reliance of nationals and third state nationals on secondary legislation is discussed. This should be distinguished from the indirect reliance on primary Union law discussed in Section 4.3.

[366] Clearly, the situation must fall under the Directive. When this is not the case, national criminal proceedings are not precluded. See 16 February 1982, Case 204/80, *Procureur de la République and others* v. *Guy Vedel and others* [1982] ECR 465.

[367] 29 October 1998, Case C-230/97, *criminal proceedings against Ibiyinka Awoyemi* [1998] ECR I-6781, par. 22.

in another Member State.[368] However, the situation of these two categories of persons does not bring them within the scope of the Treaties, which explains why third country nationals cannot profit from the fundamental freedoms, even if the protection thereof is the purpose of the Directive in question.[369]

In the *Bodil Lindqvist* case (a Swedish national in Sweden), the question was raised as to whether the application of a Directive always pre-supposes the existence of an actual link with free movement. Lindqvist was prosecuted because she had processed personal data of herself and colleagues on the website of the local parish of the Swedish church. She was prosecuted for violating the Swedish national act that implemented *Directive 95/46 on Data Protection*. Since the Directive was based upon Article 114 TFEU (formerly Article 95 TEC), it did not pre-suppose the existence of an actual link with free movement between Member States in every situation referred to by the measure.[370] In addition, the Directive explicitly excluded the activities provided for by Titles V (Common Foreign and Security Policy) and VI (Police and Judicial Co-Operation in Criminal Matters) EU from application. The Court therefore held that the exception only applied to the activities expressly listed.[371] It also stipulated that Member States could extend the scope of national legislation implementing the Directive to areas not included in the scope, provided that no other provision of Union law precluded it.[372]

The question of whether the application of a Directive requires a link with free movement in every situation may depend on the legal basis of the instrument. Article 114 TFEU (formerly Article 95 TEC), for instance, was intended to harmonise certain provisions of national legislation in order to facilitate free movement. However, to require a link with free movement in every situation could, as the Court held,

> "make the limits in the field of application of the Directive particularly unsure and uncertain, which would be contrary to its essential objective of approximating the laws, regulations and administrative provisions of the Member States in order to eliminate obstacles to the functioning of the internal market deriving precisely from disparities between national legislations."[373]

---

[368] 22 September 1983, Case 271/82, *Vincent Rodolphe Auer* v. *Ministère public* [1983] ECR 2727.

[369] 29 October 1998, Case C-230/97, *criminal proceedings against Ibiyinka Awoyemi* [1998] ECR I-67, par. 27 and 29.

[370] 6 November 2003, Case C-101/01, *criminal proceedings against Bodil Lindqvist* [2003] ECR I-12971, par. 40.

[371] 6 November 2003, Case C-101/01, *criminal proceedings against Bodil Lindqvist* [2003] ECR I-12971, par. 44.

[372] 6 November 2003, Case C-101/01, *criminal proceedings against Bodil Lindqvist* [2003] ECR I-12971, par. 99.

[373] 20 May 2003, Joined Cases C-465/00, C-138/01 and C-139/01, *Rechnungshof* v. *Österreichischer Rundfunk and Others and Christa Neukomm and Joseph Lauermann* v. *Österreichischer Rundfunk* [2003] ECR I-4989, par. 42.

4.8. OUT OF THE SCOPE OF THE TREATIES?

The existence of products that are prohibited, as well as the appearance of conduct that has been criminalised, raises the question of what the consequences are for these categories under Union law. This includes goods that are prohibited because of their inherent character, such as narcotic drugs, counterfeit products and child pornography. What is their status under Union law? Can a Member State impose VAT or income tax on the selling of these goods? Or is it precluded by Union law? The same questions are raised with regard to illegal workers, individuals who are not allowed to work within the Union. What about illegal services, such as illegal abortion, slavery and forced prostitution? And what should be done with illegal capital, the proceeds from crime or from tax evasion? Are all of these to be considered as goods, workers, services and capital that may profit from the guarantees under the Treaties, or are they outside the scope of the Treaty so that Union rules do not apply to them? Can an undertaking profit from the freedom to provide services if it makes use of illegal third-country nationals or forced prostitution for its sexual services? Does the fact that goods, workers, services and capital may not legally exist under (inter)national criminal law bear the consequence that they cannot profit from any of the provisions under the Treaties? To what extent is this different when the criminalisation exists in one Member State, but not in another? These questions all relate to the discretion that the Member States have in the determination of exceptions, especially in the field of combating crime.

In an attempt to try to answer these questions, we should first examine whether there is a Union view on illegal products and services. Does a "European Union" view on morality, which has consequences for the answer to the question of whether an activity falls within or outside of the scope of the Treaty, exist? At first sight, upon the basis of the Court's case law, it seems that prohibitions are divided into two categories. The first category consists of products, substances or conduct that are completely prohibited under Union law or international law. The second is the category of products and services that are illegal and criminalised in one Member State but not in another. With the latter, the rule is that, as long as the national prohibition can be brought under one of the justifications of the Treaty, Member States maintain their discretion in criminalising what other Member States do not criminalise.[374]

The first category (goods completely prohibited) has led to a great deal of case law in the field of VAT and customs duties. The Court has consistently held that the importation of drugs cannot give rise to a customs duty since these drugs

---

[374] See, further, Section 4.6 in this chapter.

must be seized and destroyed immediately.[375] With regard to tax law, the Court has, however, stipulated a "principle of fiscal neutrality". This prevents there being any general distinction in the levying of VAT between lawful and unlawful transactions:

> "However, that is not true in the case of the supply of products such as narcotic drugs which have special characteristics, in as much as, because of their very nature, they are subject to a total prohibition on marketing in all the Member States."[376]

The exception to fiscal neutrality is without prejudice to the powers of the Member State to impose criminal sanctions.[377] The only two products recognised as an exception to this rule of fiscal neutrality are narcotic drugs and counterfeit money.[378] The relevance of this discussion on VAT lies in the fact that the introduction of VAT was a result of Union legislation. Given the fact that Union law is applied to illegal products and services, the question arises as to whether other rules of Union law also apply.

In *Coffeeshop Siberië*, the question came up as to whether the principle of fiscal neutrality precluded the renting of a table upon which soft drugs were sold being subject to VAT. The Court held that:

> "Renting out a place intended for commercial activities is, in principle, an economic activity and therefore falls within the scope of the Sixth Directive.[379] The fact that the activities pursued there constitute a criminal offence, which may make the renting unlawful, does not alter the economic character of the renting and does not prevent competition in the sector, including that between lawful and unlawful activities."[380]

---

[375] 5 February 1981, Case 50/80, *Joszef Horvath* v. *Hauptzollamt Hamburg-Jonas* [1981] ECR 385, par. 10; 26 October 1982, Case 221/81, *Wilfried Wolf* v. *Hauptzollamt Düsseldorf* [1982] ECR 3681, par. 13–14 and 26 October 1982, Case 240/81, *Senta Einberger* v. *Hauptzollamt Freiburg* [1982] ECR 3699, par. 13–14.

[376] 29 June 1999, Case C-158/98, *Staatssecretaris van Financiën* v. *Coffeeshop Siberië vof* [1999] ECR I-3971, par. 14. See, also, 5 July 1988, Case 269/86, *W.J.R. Mol* v. *Inspecteur der Invoerrechten en Accijnzen* [1988] ECR 3627, par. 18; 5 July 1988, Case 289/86, *Vereniging Happy Family Rustenburgerstraat* v. *Inspecteur der Omzetbelasting* [1988] ECR 3655, par. 20.

[377] 28 February 1984, Case 294/82, *Senta Einberger* v. *Hauptzollamt Freiburg* [1984] ECR 1177.

[378] 6 December 1990, Case C-343/89, *Max Witzemann* v. *Hauptzollamt München-Mitte* [1990] ECR I-4477, par. 14–16. In a similar way 2 August 1993, Case C-111/92, *Wilfried Lange* v. *Finanzamt Fürstenfeldbruck* [1993] ECR I-4677, par. 12–13.

[379] The Sixth Directive is Directive 77/388 on the harmonisation of the laws of the Member States relating to turnover taxes. Article 2, paragraph 1, of this Directive provides that "the supply of goods or services effected for consideration within the territory of the country by a taxable person acting as such shall be subject to VAT".

[380] 29 June 1999, Case C-158/98, *Staatssecretaris van Financiën* v. *Coffeeshop Siberië vof* [1999] ECR I-3971, par. 22.

The fact that the activity (renting out the table) is linked to pure criminal activity (selling drugs) does not alter the fact that this is a legal activity. The mere fact that conduct amounts to an offence is not sufficient to justify exemption from VAT.[381]

The Court has a great struggle with the qualification of soft drugs.[382] In contrast to the most interesting Opinion of Advocate General Fennelly, the Court does not make any statement on the sensitive issue of drugs policy in the Member States.[383] Whereas the *Hoge Raad* of the Netherlands referred to the Court because it wanted to know if the evolution of society's view on the illegal nature of conduct relating to the supply of soft drugs would lead to a different view of the Court, the Court circumvented the question, as the Advocate General had recommended.[384] Advocate General Fennelly deduced the following key elements from this case law:

"… firstly, the generally recognised harmfulness of narcotic drugs, as confirmed by the Single Convention; secondly, the existence of a total prohibition in all the Member States on their entry into normal economic channels; thirdly, the fact that they can give rise only to criminal penalties."[385]

He further stated that the distinction of hard and soft drugs finds no basis in Union law or in international law. With reference to the Joint Action 96/750 on Illegal Drug Trafficking, the Advocate General states that the EU did not take a position as to the discretion of Member States. However, Advocate General Fennelly recognised a "*de facto* decriminalisation of the sale of cannabis in coffeeshops in the Netherlands, consequently, as a commercial activity that is in potential but direct competition with taxable persons operating similar but ordinary bars or coffee-houses in the Netherlands".[386] The Court ruled in *Goodwin and Unstead* that the trade in counterfeit perfume products is also subject to VAT:

---

[381] 29 June 1999, Case C-158/98, *Staatssecretaris van Financiën* v. *Coffeeshop Siberië vof* [1999] ECR I-3971, par. 21.

[382] 5 July 1988, Case 289/86, *Vereniging Happy Family Rustenburgerstraat* v. *Inspecteur der Omzetbelasting* [1988] ECR 3655, par. 25.

[383] Opinion of Advocate General Fennelly of 11 March 1999, 29 June 1999, Case C-158/98, *Staatssecretaris van Financiën* v. *Coffeeshop Siberië vof* [1999] ECR I-3971.

[384] Opinion of Advocate General Fennelly of 11 March 1999, 29 June 1999, Case C-158/98, *Staatssecretaris van Financiën* v. *Coffeeshop Siberië vof* [1999] ECR I-3971, point 19.

[385] Opinion of Advocate General Fennelly of 11 March 1999, 29 June 1999, Case C-158/98, *Staatssecretaris van Financiën* v. *Coffeeshop Siberië vof* [1999] ECR I-3971, point 15.

[386] Opinion of Advocate General Fennelly of 11 March 1999, 29 June 1999, Case C-158/98, *Staatssecretaris van Financiën* v. *Coffeeshop Siberië vof* [1999] ECR I-3971, point 35. The unique character of coffeeshops raises the question with which "ordinary" bars or coffee-houses that competition would take place.

"Although transactions involving counterfeit products infringe intellectual property rights, any consequential prohibition is not linked to the nature or essential characteristics of such products, but to their detrimental impact on the rights of third parties."[387]

The other relevant criterion is that the illegal trade in counterfeit perfume products may compete with the legal trade.[388]

In *Witzemann*, Advocate General Jacobs proposed that a dividing line be drawn between "on the one hand, transactions that lie so clearly outside the sphere of legitimate economic activity that, instead of being taxed, they can only be the subject of criminal prosecution and, on the other hand, transactions which, though unlawful, must none the less be taxed, if only for the sake of ensuring, in the name of fiscal neutrality, that the criminal is not treated more favourably than the legitimate trader".[389] Advocate General Jacobs further raised the question of what the origin of the rule that no taxation was possible on drugs and counterfeit currency actually was. He argued that it does not derive directly from the TEC, or from some general principle of law, and concluded that the basis for this rule was "somewhat obscure".[390] It also seems that for Advocate General Jacobs the different treatment of counterfeit money and narcotics drugs find their basis in the existence of international conventions to which all the Member States are parties.[391] But this would require an interpretation by the Court as to the scope of the obligation deriving from those conventions. A further question that arises here is whether similar criteria are applicable when the common instrument outlawing a certain good, is of EU origin, such as a Joint Action or a Framework Decision.

---

[387] 28 May 1998, Case C-3/97, *criminal proceedings against John Charles Goodwin and Edward Thomas Unstead* [1998] ECR I-3257, par. 14.

[388] The competition argument is also found in 11 June 1998, Case C-283/95, *Karlheinz Fischer* v. *Finanzamt Donaueschingen* [1998] ECR I-3369, par. 22.

[389] Opinion of Advocate General Jacobs of 25 October 1990, Case C-343/89, *Max Witzemann* v. *Hauptzollamt München-Mitte* [1990] ECR I-4477, point 10.

[390] Opinion of Advocate General Jacobs of 25 October 1990, Case C-343/89, *Max Witzemann* v. *Hauptzollamt München-Mitte* [1990] ECR I-4477, point 20.

[391] It was not the first time that an Advocate General raised the question what the justification was for the different treatment. Advocate General Capotorti in his Opinion of 30 June 1982, Case 221/81, *Wilfried Wolf* v. *Hauptzollamt Düsseldorf* [1982] ECR 3681, point 6 stated: "In my opinion, the justification may lie in the fact that, in contrast to other goods, nearly all traffic in drugs is contraband and is intended for an unlawful use, so that for them to be put into commercial circulation may be regarded as an exceptional event of minor importance. Moreover, once smuggled drugs are discovered and seized it is normal for them to be destroyed. (…) In any case, the interpretation of the customs rules given by the Court with reference to drugs is specific in character and must not be extended to other products which may also be imported and released for consumption only within the framework of a system of authorizations and checks".

The Court, for its part, relied heavily on the fact that the goods are formally criminalised under national law:

> "It must be observed first that the total prohibition on the marketing of narcotic drugs is not affected by the mere fact that, in view of their – obviously limited – manpower and means and in order to use the available resources for combating narcotic drugs in a concentrated manner, the national authorities responsible for implementing that prohibition give lower priority to bringing proceedings against a certain type of trade in drugs, because they consider other types to be more dangerous. Above all, such an approach cannot put illegal drugs dealing on the same footing as economic channels which are strictly controlled by the competent authorities in the medical and scientific field. The latter trade is actually legalized whereas prohibited dealings, albeit tolerated within certain limits, remain illegal and may at any time be the subject of police action when the competent authorities consider such action to be appropriate."[392]

On the issue of abortion, the Court had a chance to answer the question of whether there is such a thing as an illegal service, when one of the parties in the main proceedings argued that abortion cannot be regarded as a service, on the grounds that it is grossly immoral and involves the destruction of the life of a human being. The Court referred back to national law:

> "Whatever the merits of those arguments on the moral plane, they cannot influence the answer to the national court's first question. It is not for the Court to substitute its assessment for that of the legislature in those Member States where the activities in question are practised legally."[393]

A similar reasoning can be found with regard to the status of lotteries:

> "Even if the morality of lotteries is at least questionable, it is not for the Court to substitute its assessment for that of the legislatures of the Member States where that activity is practised legally."[394]

In connection with the discretion that Member States have in criminalising conduct, this raises the question of whether Union law acknowledges moral values at all. Article 57 TFEU gives a very clear and broad definition of "services" within the meaning of the Treaty, the decisive element being that it is something for which renumeration is provided. Could it be argued that, since the TFEU applies

---

[392]   5 July 1988, Case 289/86, *Vereniging Happy Family Rustenburgerstraat* v. *Inspecteur der Omzetbelasting* [1988] ECR 3655, par. 29.

[393]   4 October 1991, Case C-159/90, *The Society for the Protection of the Unborn Children Ireland Ltd* v. *Stephen Grogan and others* [1991] ECR 4685, par. 20.

[394]   24 March 1994, Case C-275/92, *Her Majesty's Customs and Excise* v. *Gerhart Schindler and Jörg Schindler* [1994] ECR I-1039, par. 32.

to economic activities relating to the objectives of the Treaty, and that, as a consequence of this, some activities fall outside the scope of the Treaty? The Court is reluctant to go along with this reasoning.[395]

What are the rules that can be deduced from this case law? First, there are goods which are completely prohibited. On reflection, they may be divided in three sub-categories. Subcategory A consists of narcotic drugs and counterfeit money. Member States may not impose customs duties or VAT on these goods, because they can only be subject to seizure followed by destruction. Sub-category B consists of a group of products which is, as such, also completely prohibited (for example, counterfeit perfume products) but on which the principle of fiscal neutrality (no distinction between lawful and unlawful products and services) is applied, because illegal trade would otherwise have an advantage over legal trade. Finally, as previously stated, there is the category of goods and services which are criminalised in one Member State, but not in another, subcategory C. This is left to the discretion of the Member States. Union law, as such, does not have any moral views on goods and services.

The absence of a Union law perspective on the morality of certain goods and services is problematical. Both the criteria applied (essential characteristics and competition with legal trade) are not particularly convincing or sound. This becomes especially clear when the positions of narcotic drugs and counterfeit perfume products are compared. While, on the one hand, narcotic drugs are not inherently illegal, given the fact that international conventions, which prohibit production, use and possession of psychotropic substances, make an exception for medical purposes,[396] there is no legal use for counterfeit perfume products. In other words, for narcotics, it is the purpose that matters, whereas, for counterfeit perfume products, the purpose is irrelevant.

Furthermore, the other criterion used, the disadvantage to the legitimate trader, which should lead to fiscal neutrality, does not meet the standards of logical reasoning. For every illegal product or service, there will be an (albeit illegal) market, as a consequence of which these activities will compete with the legal market. A more principled approach is, therefore, needed, which will take

---

[395]   See 24 March 1994, Case C-275/92, *Her Majesty's Customs and Excise* v. *Gerhart Schindler and Jörg Schindler* [1994] ECR I-1039, par. 19. See, also, 28 March 1995, Case C-324/93, *The Queen* v. *Secretary of State for Home Department, ex parte Evans Medical Ltd and Macfarlan Smith Ltd* [1995] ECR I-563, par. 20, in which the Court held that: "goods taken across a frontier for the purposes of commercial transactions are subject to Article 30 of the Treaty, whatever the nature of those transactions. Since they have those characteristics, the drugs covered by the Convention and marketable under it are subject to Article 30." (reference omitted).

[396]   Article 4 Single Convention on Narcotic Drugs 1961.

into consideration the existence of three categories of goods, services and capital:

- absolutely prohibited under international law or Union law (for example, child pornography, slavery, counterfeit products and counterfeit money);
- relatively prohibited under international law or Union law (for example, narcotics, forced prostitution, money-laundering). The prohibition is relative because it depends on the circumstances and is not inherent to the good, service or capital itself;
- prohibitions under national criminal law of one Member State, which are legal under the law of another Member State (soft drugs, providing abortion, provide banking services without a national licence, *etc.*).

Disfavourable Treatment of Foreigners?

Above, the position of goods and services with diverging regimes among the Member States was discussed. One of the conclusions was that the fact that the goods and services were not prohibited in one Member State does not preclude another Member State from criminalisation. The Court's case law does not require an identical application of the justifications for restrictions among the Member States. The specific policy on soft drugs in the Netherlands in general, as well as the coffeeshop policy of the mayor of the city of Maastricht in particular, raise questions relating to the consequences of partial or *de facto* de-criminalisation. As is well known, although it formally remains a criminal offence under Dutch law,[397] the possession of marihuana and other soft drugs in a quantity for personal use is not prosecuted. What are the consequences for *de facto* de-criminalisation with regard to the freedom for non-nationals and non-residents to buy these goods? This question came to the fore when the mayor of Maastricht issued local legislation that prohibited on pain of criminal prosecution the selling of soft drugs to non-residents.[398] The background to this decision was that drug tourists are regarded as a great nuisance to this border city. One immediately recognises the covert discriminatory element here. It is a rule that clearly discriminates non-Dutch nationals in their access to soft drugs. Could they invoke Union law with regard to their unrestricted access to the service of being able to buy soft drugs under the same conditions as nationals? The first inclination might be to argue that, if the national law allows a product on the market in practice, then the conditions for its availability should not discriminate between nationals.

---

[397] As the Court correctly recognised in *Happy Family* by emphasising the formal criminalisation instead of the material de-criminalisation. However, it circumvented the question of principle.

[398] *Http://www.maastricht.nl/maastricht/show/id=179675/framenoid=39732*, last accessed 22 August 2008.

However, upon reflection, other solutions are possible. Earlier on, it was established that the Court does not regard narcotics as taxable goods for the VAT Directive. If the conclusion from this case law must be that narcotics are not goods at all in the meaning of Articles 28–37 TFEU, it would give the Member States more discretion regarding such substances. Additionally, the *van Duyn* case offers grounds to argue that a Member State may distinguish between nationals and non-nationals on the grounds of public interest. It may prohibit the conduct that is allowed to nationals.[399] More recently, with reference to *van Duyn*, the Court held that:

> "the reservations contained in Articles 39 EC and 46 EC permit Member States to adopt, with respect to nationals of other Member States, and, in particular on grounds of public policy, measures which they cannot apply to their own nationals, inasmuch as they have no authority to expel the latter from the territory or to deny them access thereto."[400]

A justification can be found in various legal instruments that require Member States to combat drug tourism. In addition, other Member States are concerned that their nationals will bring drugs legally obtained in the Netherlands into their countries, which is a criminal offence under the criminal law of the latter Member States which they may prevent from being committed. A measure that would preclude buying goods legally in the Netherlands which are illegal in another Member State would certainly reduce the importation of illegal goods in those states. In short, the criminalisation of conduct under the law of one Member State would then be taken as a criterion for prohibiting that conduct in another Member State by the nationals or residents of the first Member State, despite the fact that the same conduct remains legal for the nationals and residents of the latter Member State.

The necessity to maintain order in society in the general interest might allow clearly discriminating measures. As is apparent from the general acceptance of the disparities in national legislation of the Member States and the leniency with which the Court has tolerated Scandinavian restrictive legislation on access to alcohol and gambling, there is some discretion for the Member States to pursue their own policy. Additionally, the Court occasionally evades the real question itself, and stipulates that it is for the national authorities to assess whether the restriction is proportional.[401] In summary, discrimination, as provided under

---

[399] 4 December 1974, Case 41–74, *Yvonne van Duyn* v. *Home Office* [1974] ECR 1337.

[400] 4 October 2007, Case C-349/06, *Murat Polat* v. *Stadt Rüsselsheim* [2007] ECR I-8167, par. 38 (references omitted).

[401] 21 September 1999, Case C-124/97, *Markku Juhari Läärä, Cotswold Microsystems Ltd and Oy Transatlantic Software Ltd* v. *Kihlakunnansyyttäjä (Jyväskylä) and Suomen valtio* [1999] ECR I-6067, par. 35.

local Maastricht law, is acceptable under Union law if narcotics generally do not fall within the definition of goods under the Treaty. Only if narcotics must be regarded as goods, can the rules on discrimination and the possible justifications thereof apply.

5. THE INTERPRETATION OF UNION LAW

5.1. COMPETENCE OF THE COURT

Earlier, it was discussed how the Court may be called upon to give judgment, what its jurisdiction is, and what the effects of its judgments are.[402] It is the Court's task to ensure the uniform interpretation of Union law. It was established that there are basically two ways in which the Court may be called to interpret the law. The first being a case brought against a Member State by the Commission for its failure to respect its obligations under the Treaty. Such a procedure may result in a finding by the Court that the Member State violated Union law, or even more specific, the Court may say that a specific national law is contrary to European law. The second manner in which the Court can be asked to give its interpretation of Union law is by reference for a *preliminary ruling*.

In answering questions for preliminary rulings, the Court will not rule on the compatibility of the provisions of a national law with the Treaty. It regards its jurisdiction as limited to providing the national court with all the criteria of interpretation relating to Union law which may enable it to assess such compatibility.[403] It will limit itself to giving an interpretation of Union law on the facts supplied by the national court. The interpretation which the Court "gives to a rule of Union law clarifies and defines where necessary the meaning and scope of that rule *as it must be or ought to have been understood and applied from the time of its coming into force*".[404] The interpretation given by the Court will enable the national court to apply Union law correctly. In so doing, it is foreseen that the Member State itself may provide corrections to national legislation which is not in compliance with Union law. If the Court pronounces judgment on a reference for a preliminary ruling by stating that a legal instrument is null and void, this is

---

[402] See Chapter 2, Section 5.

[403] 28 November 1991, Case C-186/90, *Giacomo Durighello* v. *Istituto Nazionale Della Providenza Sociale* [1991] ECR I-5773, par. 10.

[404] 27 March 1980, Case 61/79, *Amministrazione delle finanze dello Stato* v. *Denkavit italiana Srl* [1980] ECR 1205, par. 16; 13 February 1996, Joined Cases C-197/94 and C-252/94, *Société Bautiaa* v. *Directeur des Services Fiscaux des Landes et Société Française Maritime* v. *Directeur des Service Fiscaux du Finistère* [1996] ECR I-505, par. 47.

sufficient reason for any other national court to regard the legal instrument in question as being nullified.[405]

The Court uses the term "judicial or close co-operation" – based upon the assignment both to national courts and to the Court of different functions – to refer to the help, in the interpretation of Union law, which it gives to national courts upon the basis of Article 267 TFEU (formerly Article 234 TEC).[406] In the context of criminal law, this terminology becomes confused with the meaning of the traditional terminology of judicial co-operation in criminal matters, which has an entirely different connotation. Traditionally, judicial co-operation in criminal matters is understood as the assistance offered between the judicial authorities of different states when they are in need of, for instance, an accused person or of evidence to be found on the territory of the other state.

5.1.1. The Lisbon Competence

In Section 5 of Chapter 2, the jurisdiction of the Court concerning the legal acts adopted before and after the Treaty of Lisbon entered into force was discussed. Articles 267 and 276 TFEU, which clarify the competence of the Court for all new legal acts as well as the *acquis* of the Community, were referred to.[407] It provides no role for the Court in the field of Common Foreign and Security Policy (Article 24, paragraph 1 TEU).[408] In this area, legislative acts may not be adopted. Article 267 TFEU (formerly Article 234 TEC) provides for a general competence of the

---

405   13 May 1981, Case 66/80, *SpA International Chemical Corporation* v. *Amministrazione delle finanze dello Stato* [1981] ECR 1191, par. 9–18.

406   For example 21 April 1988, Case 338/85, *Fratelli Pardini SpA* v. *Ministero del Commercio con l'Estero and Banca Toscana (Lucca Branch)* [1988] ERC 2041, par. 8.

407   Article 267 TFEU (formerly Article 234 TEC) reads: "The Court of Justice of the European Union shall have jurisdiction to give preliminary rulings concerning: (a) the interpretation of the Treaties;
(b) the validity and interpretation of acts of the institutions, bodies, offices or agencies of the Union;
Where such a question is raised before any court or tribunal of a Member State, that court or tribunal may, if it considers that a decision on the question is necessary to enable it to give judgment, request the Court to give a ruling thereon. Where any such question is raised in a case pending before a court or tribunal of a Member State against whose decisions there is no judicial remedy under national law, that court or tribunal shall bring the matter before the Court. If such a question is raised in a case pending before a court or tribunal of a Member State with regard to a person in custody, the Court of Justice of the European Union shall act with the minimum of delay.
Article 276 TFEU reads: In exercising its powers regarding the provisions of Chapters 4 and 5 of Title V of Part Three relating to the area of freedom, security and justice, the Court of Justice of the European Union shall have no jurisdiction to review the validity or proportionality of operations carried out by the police or other law-enforcement services of a Member State or the exercise of the responsibilities incumbent upon Member States with regard to the maintenance of law and order and the safeguarding of internal security".

408   Exceptions provided in Articles 40 TEU and 275 TFEU.

Court for questions of interpretation of the Treaty. Each national court or tribunal may request the Court to give a ruling if it considers it necessary to enable it to pronounce judgment in a national case. Courts against whose decisions there is no judicial remedy have less discretion.[409] Article 267 stipulates in its last sentence that, where any such question is raised, the supreme courts are to bring the matter before the Court.

5.1.2. The Transition Period: The First Five Years

The jurisdiction of the Court, in the first five years following the adoption of the Treaty of Lisbon regarding all the acts that were adopted in the field of police co-operation and judicial co-operation in criminal matters are to be those under Title VI of the Treaty on European Union in the version in force before the entry into force of the Treaty of Lisbon. Article 35 EU in the version before the Treaty of Lisbon entered into force continues to determine the jurisdiction of the Court regarding those acts.[410]

---

[409] See, further, Chapter 5, Section 8.

[410] Article 35 EU reads: "1. The Court of Justice of the European Communities shall have jurisdiction, subject to the conditions laid down in this article, to give preliminary rulings on the validity and interpretation of framework decisions and decisions, on the interpretation of conventions established under this title and on the validity and interpretation of the measures implementing them. 2. By a declaration made at the time of signature of the Treaty of Amsterdam or at any time thereafter, any Member State shall be able to accept the jurisdiction of the Court of Justice to give preliminary rulings as specified in paragraph 1. 3. A Member State making a declaration pursuant to paragraph 2 shall specify that either: (a) any court or tribunal of that State against whose decisions there is no judicial remedy under national law may request the Court of Justice to give a preliminary ruling on a question raised in a case pending before it and concerning the validity or interpretation of an act referred to in paragraph 1 if that court or tribunal considers that a decision on the question is necessary to enable it to give judgment; or (b) any court or tribunal of that State may request the Court of Justice to give a preliminary ruling on a question raised in a case pending before it and concerning the validity or interpretation of an act referred to in paragraph 1 if that court or tribunal considers that a decision on the question is necessary to enable it to give judgment. 4. Any Member State, whether or not it has made a declaration pursuant to paragraph 2, shall be entitled to submit statements of case or written observations to the Court in cases which arise under paragraph 1. 5. The Court of Justice shall have no jurisdiction to review the validity or proportionality of operations carried out by the police or other law enforcement services of a Member State or the exercise of the responsibilities incumbent upon Member States with regard to the maintenance of law and order and the safeguarding of internal security. 6. The Court of Justice shall have jurisdiction to review the legality of framework decisions and decisions in actions brought by a Member State or the Commission on grounds of lack of competence, infringement of an essential procedural requirement, infringement of this Treaty or of any rule of law relating to its application, or misuse of powers. The proceedings provided for in this paragraph shall be instituted within two months of the publication of the measure. 7. The Court of Justice shall have jurisdiction to rule on any dispute between Member States regarding the interpretation or the application of acts adopted under Article 34(2) whenever such dispute cannot be settled by the Council within six months of its being referred to the Council by one of its members. The Court shall also have jurisdiction to rule on any dispute

In the old Third Pillar, the jurisdiction of the Court may differ from Member State to Member State. Article 35 EU gives the Court jurisdiction to make preliminary rulings on the interpretation of Third Pillar legal instruments.[411] However, there is a wide variety of conditions under which Member States have or have not made the Court competent in cases related to Third Pillar issues. Article 35, paragraphs 2 and 3 allow the Member States to make a declaration to this extent. The result is three different regimes among the Member States: 1) full competence with regard to some Member States; 2) no competence at all with regard to other Member States; and 3) limited competence with regard to another group as provided for in Article 35, paragraph 3.

Neither the Commission nor a Member State may bring a case against another Member State for violation of a legal instrument of the Third Pillar.[412] The Court can rule on the validity and interpretation of Framework Decisions and Decisions, and on the interpretation of Conventions (Article 35, paragraph 1, EU). The first decision of this nature was taken in 2003,[413] and since then, more have followed, and so many have been made pending that it can be assumed that the significance of the case law of the Court will be just as groundbreaking in Union law as it is in Community law. The Court can only review the legality of Framework Decisions and Decisions on action taken by a Member State or the Commission (Article 35, paragraph 6 EU).[414] There is no indication that the Court takes the fact that some Member States are not bound by specific legal instruments, or have not accepted the Court's jurisdiction with regard to specified legal instruments, into consideration. To the contrary, the Court has held that it had jurisdiction on an application for the annulment of a Joint Action, despite the fact that some states had not individually recognised the Court's competence.[415]

---

between Member States and the Commission regarding the interpretation or the application of conventions established under Article 34(2)(d)".

[411]   28 June 2007, Case C-467/05, *criminal proceedings against Giovanni Dell'Orto* [2007] ECR I-5557, par. 34. The fact that the order for reference does not mention Article 35 EU cannot, of itself, make the reference for preliminary ruling inadmissible (par. 36). If the questions fall outside the Court's competence, it has no jurisdiction: 7 April 1995, Case C-167/94, *criminal proceedings against Juan Carlos Grau Gomis* [1995] ECR I-1023. The *Gomis* case related to a question of interpretation of the Treaty of Maastricht before the Court had been declared competent by the Treaty of Amsterdam.

[412]   However, paragraph 7 of Article 35 EU gives the Court jurisdiction to rule on any dispute between Member States as to the interpretation or the application of acts adopted under Article 34, paragraph 2 EU. So far, this provision has never been used.

[413]   11 February 2003, Case C-187/01 and Case C-385/01, *criminal proceedings against Hüseyin Gözütok (C-187/01) and Klaus Brügge (C-385/01)* [2003] ECR I-1345.

[414]   The Commission was succesful twice in an application for annulment a Framework Decision. See 13 September 2005, Case C-176/03, *Commission v. Council* [2005] ECR I-7879; 23 October 2007, Case C-440/05, *Commission v. Council* [2007] ECR I-9097.

[415]   12 May 1998, Case C-170/96, *Commission v. Council* [1998] ECR I-2763.

The fact that some states have not recognised the Court's competence and others have, is not regarded by the Court as an impediment to give its interpretation of the law. However, it raises the question of whether the Member States that did not recognise the Court are bound by its judgment in such a matter.[416] The Protocols providing a special position for the United Kingdom, Ireland and Denmark in the area of freedom, security and justice stipulate that these Member States will not be bound by decisions of the Court.[417] With regard to the Conventions dating from the period before the competence of the Court was generally regulated in the Treaty of Amsterdam, Protocols annexed to the Convention determine the competence of the Court for each individual convention.[418] The Protocol integrating the Schengen *acquis* into the framework of the Treaties does not contain any provision regarding the jurisdiction of the Court for the United Kingdom and Ireland.

Article 35, paragraph 5 EU, which re-appeared identically in Article 276 TFEU, is of specific interest to criminal law. It rules out that the Court has jurisdiction over the legality of operative acts of the authorities of the Member States:

> "The Court of Justice shall have no jurisdiction to review the validity or proportionality of operations carried out by the police or other law enforcement services of a Member State or the exercise of the responsibilities incumbent upon the Member States with regard to the maintenance of law and order and the safeguarding of internal security."[419]

In a schematic reproduction, the foregoing can be summarized and visualised for all Member States, except the United Kingdom in Scheme 2 and for the United Kingdom in Scheme 3.

---

[416]   16 June 2005, Case C-105/03, *criminal proceedings against Maria Pupino* [2005] ECR I-5285 par. 36.

[417]   See, further, Section 2.4 of this chapter.

[418]   See Protocol of 23 July 1996 on the interpretation, by way of preliminary rulings, by the Court of Justice of the European Communities of the Convention on the establishment of a European Police Office, OJ 1996, C 299/2; Protocol of 29 November 1996 on the interpretation, by way of preliminary rulings, by the Court of Justice of the European Communities of the Convention on the Protection of the European Communities' financial interests, OJ 1997, C 151/1; Protocol of 29 November 1996 on the interpretation, by way of preliminary rulings, by the Court of Justice of the European Communities of the Convention on the use of information technology for customs purposes, OJ 1997, C 151/15; After this practice became usual, the provision was incorporated in the convention itself. See Article 26 *Convention on Mutual Assistance between Customs Administrations.* The Treaty of Amsterdam inserted the provision on the opt-in competence of the Court in the Treaty on European Union.

[419]   Article 72 TFEU also excludes this from Union law by giving Member States a certain margin of discretion.

Table for all Member States except the UK

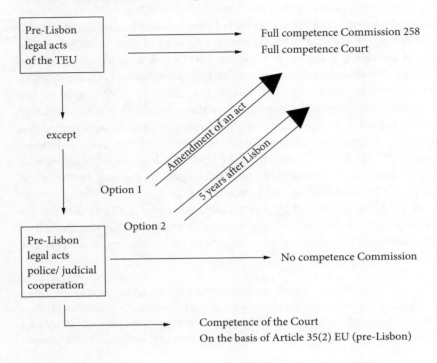

Pre-Lisbon legal acts of the TEU → Full competence Commission 258
→ Full competence Court

except

Option 1 — Amendment of an act

Option 2 — 5 years after Lisbon

Pre-Lisbon legal acts police/ judicial cooperation → No competence Commission

→ Competence of the Court
On the basis of Article 35(2) EU (pre-Lisbon)

Table for the UK

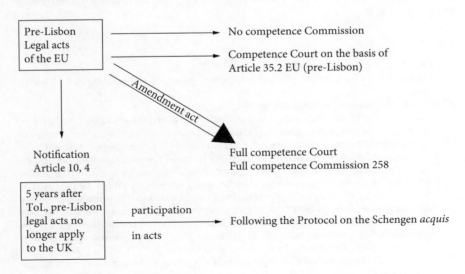

Pre-Lisbon Legal acts of the EU → No competence Commission
→ Competence Court on the basis of Article 35.2 EU (pre-Lisbon)

Amendment act → Full competence Court
Full competence Commission 258

Notification Article 10, 4

5 years after ToL, pre-Lisbon legal acts no longer apply to the UK — participation in acts → Following the Protocol on the Schengen *acquis*

5.2. ADMISSIBILITY OF THE REFERENCE

Before the Court may interpret Union law, first the admissibility of the reference by the national court must be determined.[420] The case law of the Court on admissibility under Article 267 TFEU (formerly Article 234 TEC)[421] is also applied to references upon the basis of Article 35 EU.[422] This sub-section will subsequently deal with the question of which national courts may refer, discuss whether and when a question must be referred, what information must be supplied, and what questions are admissible and what the answer of the Court may be.

Which Courts May Be Admissible?

Article 267 TFEU (formerly Article 234 TEC) states which national courts may refer questions to the Court. As mentioned before, with regard to Third Pillar legislation, the construction of Article 35 EU has resulted in a patchwork of different competences for each individual Member State, which has been addressed in the previous section. In these cases, the competence of the national courts or tribunals is determined by national law.

The more general applicable rules are the following. Not only do courts and tribunals have the competence to refer, but also judges investigating a criminal matter or investigating magistrates qualify. The following authorities were accepted in case law:

- *Giudice per le indagini preliminari* (the Italian judge responsible for preliminary inquiries);[423]
- *Pretura circondariale* (circuit magistrate's court);[424]
- *Pretore* (magistrate);[425]
- *rechter-commissaris bij de arrondissementsrechtbank* (examining magistrate);[426]

---

[420] This paragraph is limited to the admissibility of references by national courts or tribunals only and does not discuss the admissibility of other actions to the Court (by the Commission or by a Member State).

[421] Cases before the Treaty of Maastricht entered into force refer to its predecessor Article 177. The substance of the provision has never been amended.

[422] 16 June 2005, Case C-105/03, *criminal proceedings against Maria Pupino* [2005] ECR I-5285 par. 29; 9 October 2008, Case C-404/07, *criminal proceedings György Katz* v. *István Roland Sós* [2008] ECR not yet reported, par. 30.

[423] 15 January 2004, Case C-235/02, *criminal proceedings against Marco Antonio Saetti and Andrea Frediani* [2004] ECR I-1005, par. 23.

[424] 12 December 1996, Joined Cases C-74/95 and C-129/95, *criminal proceedings against X* [1996] ECR I-6609. Since 1998, Italian law abolished the Pretura.

[425] 11 June 1987, Case 14/86, *Pretore di Salò* v. *Persons unknown* [1987] ECR 3969.

[426] 13 July 1990 and 6 December 1990, Case C-2/88 Imm., *J.J. Zwartveld and others* [1990] ECR I-4405.

- *Consiglio Nazionale Forense* (National Council of the Bar);[427]
- *Fonds de garantie des victimes des actes de terrorisme et d'autres infractions* (Victim Compensation Fund).[428]

The Court did not regard the following organs, as tribunals or courts in the sense of Article 267 TFEU (formerly Article 234 TEC):

- *Directeur des Contributions Directes et des Accises* (Director of the Revenue Services);[429]
- a representative of the Public Prosecutor's Office who was acting as a party to the proceedings;[430]
- *Epitropi Antagonismon* (the Greek Competition Commission).[431]

In 1972, the Court already held that the nature of the national proceedings does not have any influence on the admissibility of the order for reference:

"Article 177, which is worded in general terms, draws no distinction according to the nature, criminal or otherwise, of the national proceedings within the framework of which the preliminary questions have been formulated. The effectiveness of Community law cannot vary according to the various branches of national law which it may affect."[432]

The Court only has jurisdiction if the question relates to a pending dispute and if the national court or tribunal "is called upon to give a decision capable of taking into account the preliminary ruling".[433] The general view is that public prosecutors are not admissible when referring to the Court. However, in one of the first criminal cases to be decided by the Court, it declared the *Pretore di Salò* admissible.

---

[427]   30 November 1995, Case C-55/94, *Reinhard Gebhard* v. *Consiglio dell'Ordine degli Avvocati e Procuratori di Milano* [1995] ECR I-4165.

[428]   See 5 June 2008, Case C-164/07, *James Wood* v. *Fonds de garantie des victimes des actes de terrorisme et d'autres infractions* [2008] ECR not yet reported.

[429]   30 March 1993, Case C-24/92, *Pierre Corbiau* v. *Administration des Contributions* [1993] ECR I-1277.

[430]   12 December 1996, Joined Cases C-74/95 and C-129/95, *criminal proceedings against X* [1996] ECR I-6609.

[431]   31 May 2005, Case C-53/03, *Synetairismos Farmakopoion Aitolias & Akarnanias (Syfait) and Others* v. *GlaxoSmithKline plc and GlaxoSmithKline AEVE, formerly Glaxowellcome AEVE* [2005] ECR I-4609. One of the reasons for the Court not to regard the Greek Competition Commission as a court or tribunal in the sense of Article 234 TEC is that it may be relieved of its competence by a decision of the Commission pursuant to Article 11, paragraph 16 Regulation 1/2003. See judgment par. 34.

[432]   21 March 1972, Case 82–71, *criminal proceedings against Società Agricola Industria Latte* [1972] ECR 119, par. 5.

[433]   21 April 1988, Case 338/85, *Fratelli Pardini SpA* v. *Ministero del Commercio con l'Estero and Banca Toscana (Lucca Branch)* [1988] ERC 2041, par. 11.

It observed that, in the pending proceedings, the *Pretore* combined the functions of a public prosecutor and those of an examining magistrate. What mattered was that the "request emanates from a court or tribunal which has acted in the general framework of its task of judging, independently and in accordance with the law, cases coming within the jurisdiction conferred on it by law, even though certain functions of that court or tribunal in the proceedings which gave rise to the reference for a preliminary ruling are not, strictly speaking, of a judicial nature".[434]

With reference to *Pretore di Salò*, Advocate General Ruiz-Jarabo Colomer stated that all kinds of preliminary investigations could qualify:

> "The investigation could have resulted in an order that no further action be taken, in a summons to appear, or in an acquittal, but it could not, under any circumstances, create an irreversible procedural situation, nor did it constitute, for the purposes of national law, a judicial act subject to the fundamental safeguards."[435]

In the light of the development of the case law of the Court on *ne bis in idem* and out-of-court-settlements by the Prosecutor,[436] the question arises as to whether a request by the prosecution should remain inadmissible. In a most interesting Opinion, Advocate General Ruiz-Jarabo Colomer pointed to the fact that, at the material time of the case of *Pretore di Salò*, the functions of the Pretore under Italian law were both those of a public prosecutor and those of an examining magistrate.[437] If the Court in *Gözütok* attached much weight to the fact that an out-of-court-settlement has the same value as a court decision, then an investigation by the prosecution might qualify for a reference. The prosecution in *Gözütok* complied with the criteria formulated in *Pretore di Salò*:

> "... following such a procedure, further prosecution is definitively barred, the person must be regarded as someone whose case has been finally disposed of for the purposes of Article 54 of the CISA in relation to the acts which he is alleged to have committed. In addition, once the accused has completed with his obligations, the penalty is entailed in the procedure whereby further prosecution is barred must be regarded as having been enforced for the purposes of Article 54."[438]

---

[434] 11 June 1987, Case 14/86, *Pretore di Salò* v. *Persons unknown* [1987] ECR 3969, par. 7. See, also, the analysis of the functions of the Pretore in the Opinion of Advocate General Mancini of 17 March 1987, point 4.

[435] Opinion of Advocate General Ruiz-Jarabo Colomer of 25 June 2003, Case C-60/02, *criminal proceedings against X* [2004] ECR I-651, point 22.

[436] See Chapter 5, Section 4.

[437] Opinion of Advocate General Ruiz-Jarabo Colomer of 18 June 1996, Joined Cases C-74/95 and C-129/95, *criminal proceedings against X* [1996] ECR I-6609, points 5–9 and endnote 2 thereof. Since 1989, the Pretore no longer performs the task of a public prosecutor.

[438] See 11 February 2003, Case C-187/01 and Case C-385/01, *criminal proceedings against Hüseyin Gözütok (C-187/01) and Klaus Brügge (C-385/01)* [2003] ECR I-1345, par. 30.

Who Determines Whether a Question Must Be Raised and When?[439]

It is the national court that determines whether the questions are necessary in order to pronounce judgment.[440] The presumption of relevance attached to questions referred by national courts may be rebutted only in exceptional circumstances.[441] As a general rule, the referring national court determines whether the reference is necessary for solving the dispute in the case that is pending before it. It is this court that has direct knowledge of the facts of the case and is in the best position to assess whether a preliminary ruling is necessary to enable it to pronounce judgment. If the questions concern the interpretation of Union law, the Court is, in principle, bound to give a ruling, so the Court held on a reference from the *Tribunal Fiscal Aduaneiro do Porto*, Portugal.[442] If the national court refers for the sole purpose of determining whether Treaty provisions are capable of having any bearing on the application of the relevant national rules, such a reference is admissible.[443] However, the Court has not given national courts absolute discretion in this respect.[444] When the question does not seem to relate to the facts of the case before the national court, the Court will not answer it.

In any stage of the national proceedings, it must be possible to raise questions for reference. A rule of national law precluding this must be set aside.[445] The fact that the referring court simply replicated the questions sent to it by the counsel for the accused and forwarded them to the Court, does not make the reference inadmissible.[446] The fact that the relevant events took place before the entry into force of the Directive is not a ground for the inadmissibility of the reference for a preliminary ruling. The fact that investigations are still pending and that the suspects are still unknown is, as such, not an impediment to admissibility.[447]

---

[439]   See, also, Section 8 in Chapter 5.

[440]   12 January 2006, Case C-246/04, *Turn- und Sportunion Waldburg* v. *Finanzlandesdirektion für Oberösterreich* [2006] ECR I-589, par. 20–21.

[441]   16 June 2005, Case C-105/03, *criminal proceedings against Maria Pupino* [2005] ECR I-5285 par. 30. The Court has transposed this case law on Article 234 EC to references on the basis of Article 35 EU. See, also, 28 June 2007, Case C-467/05, *criminal proceedings against Giovanni Dell'Orto* [2007] ECR I-5557, par. 39.

[442]   16 July 1992, Case C-343/90, *Manuel José Lourenço Dias* v. *Director da Alfândega do Porto* [1992] ECR I-4673, par. 15–16.

[443]   11 September 2003, Case C-6/01, *Associação Nacional de Operadores de Máquinas Recreativeas (Anomar) and others* v. *Estado Português* [2003] ECR I-8621, par. 38.

[444]   21 March 2002, Case C-451/99, *Cura Anlagen GmbH* v. *Auto Service Leasing GmbH (ASL)* [2002] ECR I-3193.

[445]   14 December 1995, Case C-312/93, *Peterbroeck, Van Campenhout & Cie SCS* v. *Belgian State* [1995] ECR I-4599, par. 21; 14 December 1995, Joined Cases C-430/93 and C-431/93, *Jeroen van Schijndel and Johannes Nicolaas Cornelis van Veen* v. *Stichting Pensioenfonds voor fysiotherapeuten* [1995] ECR I-4705, par. 18.

[446]   7 December 1995, Case C-17/94, *criminal proceedings against Denis Gervais, Jean-Louis Nougaillon, Christian Carrard and Bernard Horgue* [1995] ECR I-4353.

[447]   11 June 1987, Case 14/86, *Pretore di Salò* v. *Persons unknown* [1987] ECR 3969, par. 10–12.

Where the accused are identified after the reference for a preliminary ruling, a new question may be referred if necessary. This is especially so in criminal proceedings in which the least harsh provisions must be applied.[448] The Court has no jurisdiction when the procedure before the referring court has already been terminated,[449] nor when there is no case pending.[450]

What Information Must Be Supplied with the Order for Reference?

In the case of *Placanica*, the Court gave a checklist of what a referring court should submit:

> "Concerning the information that must be provided to the Court in the context of a reference for a preliminary ruling, it should be noted that that information does not serve only to enable the Court to provide answers which will be of use to the national court; it must also enable the Governments of the Member States, and other interested parties, to submit observations in accordance with Article 23 of the Statute of the Court of Justice. For those purposes, according to settled case-law, it is firstly necessary that the national court should define the factual and legislative context of the questions it is asking or, at the very least, explain the factual circumstances on which those questions are based. Secondly, the referring court must set out the precise reasons why it was unsure as to the interpretation of Community law and why it considered it necessary to refer questions to the Court for a preliminary ruling. In consequence, it is essential that the referring court provide at the very least some explanation of the reasons for the choice of the Community provisions which it requires to be interpreted and of the link it establishes between those provisions and the national legislation applicable to the dispute in the main proceedings."[451]

If the referring court has failed to provide the Court with any evidence to support the view that the court hearing the case may be required to apply provisions intended to ensure compliance with the rules of Union law, the Court will declare that it has no jurisdiction.[452]

For the use of national courts, but also with the aim of reducing the number of references, the Court issued guidelines.[453] If the national court supplies

---

[448]   1 June 1999, Case C-319/97, *criminal proceedings against Antoine Kortas* [1999] ECR I-3143, par. 17.

[449]   21 April 1988, Case 338/85, *Fratelli Pardini SpA* v. *Ministero del Commercio con l'Estero and Banca Toscana (Lucca Branch)* [1988] ERC 2041, par. 11.

[450]   18 June 1980, Case 138/80, *Jules Borker* [1980] ECR 1975.

[451]   6 March 2007, Joined Cases C-338/04, C-359/04 and C-360/04, *criminal proceedings against Placanica, Palazzese and Sorrichio* [2007] ECR I-1891, par. 34 (references omitted).

[452]   9 October 1997, Case C-291/96, *criminal proceedings against Martino Grado and Shahid Bashir* [1997] ECR I-5531; 30 April 1998, Joined Cases C-128/97 and C-137/97, *criminal proceedings against Italia Testa and Mario Modesti* [1998] ECR I-2181.

[453]   Information Note on References from National Courts for Preliminary Rulings 2005, OJ 2005, C 143/1.

insufficient information on the facts of the case to answer the questions raised, the reference will be declared inadmissible.[454] The obligation to provide information in the order for reference not only serves to enable the Court to give a helpful answer, but also to enable the Member States and other interested parties to submit observations.[455] The fact that the Court declared the reference inadmissible does not prevent the national court from raising questions again, on condition that sufficient information is provided this time.[456]

Which Kind of Questions Are Admissible?

Article 267 TFEU stipulates that the Court's task will be to interpret the Treaties and the acts that were adopted on the basis of the Treaties. A national court may raise the question of whether Union measures are valid.[457] Questions referred by the national court should, therefore, ask the Court to give an interpretation of a specific aspect of Union law. Since *Foto-Frost*, it is clear that national courts have no jurisdiction themselves to declare that acts of Union institutions are invalid.[458] Should a national court doubt the validity of a Union legal instrument, it should refer to the Court, which held in *Foto-Frost* that:

> "Divergences between courts in the Member States as to the validity of community acts would be liable to place in jeopardy the very unity of the community legal order and detract from the fundamental requirement of legal certainty."[459]

This main argument, also put forward by Advocate General Mancini,[460] might be looked at differently in the European Union context of today, which already offers quite a patchwork with regard to the jurisdiction of the Court. In a very interesting

---

454   23 March 1995, Case C-458/93, *criminal proceedings against Mostafa Saddik* [1995] ECR I-511; 20 March 1996, Case C-2/96, *criminal proceedings against Carlo Sunino and Giancarlo Data* [1996] ECR I-1543; 25 June 1996, Case C-101/96, *criminal proceedings against Italia Testa* [1996] I-3081; 19 July 1996, Case C-191/96, *criminal proceedings against Mario Modesti* [1996] ECR I-3937.

455   12 September 1996, Joined Cases C-58/95, C-75/95, C-112/95, C-119/95, C-123/95, C-135/95, C-140/95, C-141/95, C-154/95 and C-157/95, *criminal proceedings against Sandro Gallotti, Roberto Censi, Giuseppe Salmaggi, Salvatore Pasquire, Massimo Zappone, Francesco Segna and others, Cesare Cervetti, Mario Gasbarri, Isodoru Narducci and Fulvio Smaldone* [1996] ECR I-4345, par. 8.

456   An example is 14 December 1995, Case C-387/93, *criminal proceedings against Giorgio Domingo Banchero* [1995] ECR I-4663.

457   1 December 1965, Case 16–65, *Firma G. Schwarze* v. *Einfuhr- und Vorratsstelle für Getreide und Futtermittel* [1965] ECR English Special Edition 877.

458   22 October 1987, Case 314/85, *Foto-Frost* v. *Hauptzollamt Lübeck-Ost* [1987] ECR 4199, par. 12–16.

459   22 October 1987, Case 314/85, *Foto-Frost* v. *Hauptzollamt Lübeck-Ost* [1987] ECR 4199, par. 15.

460   Opinion of Advocate General Mancini of 19 May 1987, Case 314/85, *Foto-Frost* v. *Hauptzollamt Lübeck-Ost* [1987] ECR 4199, point 5.

Opinion, Advocate General Mengozzi took the view that national courts were entitled to give their own judgments on the validity of any Framework Decisions and Decisions before them.[461] With reference to the *Pupino* case, he argues that national courts are entitled to do this, because Union law does not constitute a complete system of legal remedies. In addition, the fact that the competence of the Court differs from state to state does not guarantee uniform application of Union law in the context of the Third Pillar.

The fact that an answer by the Court would inevitably lead to an interpretation of the provisions of primary law does not mean that the Court does not have jurisdiction. If the national court hesitates on the question of whether Union rules apply to the situation, the question is admissible because the purpose of the question is the interpretation of the Treaties.[462] This applies, of course, independently of the result of the interpretation. In other words, even if the Court held that no Union rules applied to the situation, it would still give an interpretation of Union law.

The fact that the Court has already ruled in a specific way in other cases does not, as such, lead to inadmissibility. However, in situations in which references for a preliminary ruling relate to questions that have already been answered by the Court, the Court may, upon the basis of Article 104, paragraph 3 of the Rules of Procedure, issue an order instead of rendering a judgment.[463] When the national court encounters difficulties in understanding the Court's judgment, it may refer to the Court, which could lead to a different answer than to a question submitted earlier.[464]

It is settled case law that the Court in proceedings for a preliminary ruling has no jurisdiction to decide whether a national provision is compatible with Union law.[465] However, in some situations, the Court has reformulated the question referred to in order to extract the aspects relating to the interpretation of Union

---

[461] Opinion of Advocate General Mengozzi of 26 October 2006, Case C-354/04 P, *Gestoras Pro Amnistiá and others* [2007] ECR I-1579, par. 121–130.

[462] 5 March 2002, Joined Cases C-515/99 and C-527/99 to C-540/99, *Hans Reisch and others* v. *Bürgermeister der Landeshauptstadt Salzburg and Grundverkehrsbeauftragter des Landes Salzburg* and Joined Cases C-519/99 and C-524/99 to C-526/99, *Anton Lassacher and others* v. *Grundverkehrsbeauftragter des Landes Salzburg and Grundverkehrslandeskommission des Landes Salzburg* [2002] ECR I-2157, par. 23 and 26.

[463] See, for instance, 6 March 2007, Case C-191/06, *criminal proceedings against Gallo and Damonte* [2007] ECR I-30, which dealt with questions similar to those answered in the judgment of 6 March 2007, Joined Cases C-338/04, C-359/04 and C-360/04, *criminal proceedings against Placanica, Palazzese and Sorrichio* [2007] ECR I-1891.

[464] 5 March 1986, Case 69/85, *Wünsche Handelsgesellschaft GmbH & Co.* v. *Germany* [1986] ECR 947, par. 15. This does not affect the validity of a previously delivered judgment.

[465] 7 April 1995, Case C-167/94, *criminal proceedings against Juan Carlos Grau Gomis* [1995] ECR I-1023.

law,[466] even in cases in which the question was formulated extremely broadly: "is (the applicable national legislation) compatible with the provisions of the Treaty of Rome and the directives of the EEC?"[467] This leniency of the Court may be attributed to the "spirit of co-operation which must prevail in the preliminary ruling procedure".[468]

Clearly hypothetical problems will not be dealt with.[469] The Court does not give an advisory opinion, its task is to assist in the administration of justice in the Member States.[470] If it is obvious that the interpretation of Union law sought bears no relation to the facts of the case, the Court may refuse to rule.[471] However, the Court is occasionally lenient:

> "... even if some of the information on the file might give rise to a suspicion that the situation underlying the main proceedings was contrived with a view to obtaining a decision from the Court of Justice on a question of Community law of general interest, it cannot be denied that there is a genuine contract the performance or annulment of which undeniably depends on a question of Community law."[472]

The Court also accepted jurisdiction in which a provision of Union law has been made applicable under national law, although there was no obligation to do so.[473] Even in a case in which the Court mentioned that it was too difficult to see how the answer related to questions of Union law could influence the case, the Court accepted jurisdiction.[474]

The Court regarded the questions referred to in the case of *der Weduwe*, a Dutch national living in Luxembourg, as hypothetical. The accused *der Weduwe*,

---

[466]   29 November 1978, Case 83/78, *Pigs Marketing Board* v. *Raymond Redmond* [1978] ECR 2347; 22 September 1988, Case 228/87, *Pretura unificata di Torino* v. *X* [1988] ECR 5099; 26 September 1996, Case C-168/95, *criminal proceedings against Luciano Arcaro* [1996] ECR I-4705.

[467]   8 December 1987, Case 20/87, *Ministère public* v. *André Gauchard* [1987] ECR 4879. See, also, 1 April 1982, Joined Cases 141 to 143/81, *Gerrit Holdijk and others* [1982] ECR 1299.

[468]   16 July 1992, Case C-343/90, *Manuel José Lourenço Dias* v. *Director da Alfândega do Porto* [1992] ECR I-4673, par. 17.

[469]   28 September 2006, Case C-467/04, *criminal proceedings against Gasparini and others* [2006] ECR I-9199, par. 45. If parties construct a dispute on Community law for use in other than the pending proceedings, the Court will not have jurisdiction upon the matter. See 11 March 1980, Case 104/79, *Pasquale Foglia* v. *Mariella Novello* [1980] ECR 745.

[470]   16 July 1992, Case C-83/91, *Wienand Meilicke* v. *ADV/ORGA F.A. Meyer AG* [1992] ECR I-4871, par. 25.

[471]   22 January 2002, Case C-390/99, *Canal Satélite Digital SL* v. *Administración General del Estado* [1999] ECR I-607.

[472]   21 March 2002, Case C-451/99, *Cura Anlagen GmbH* v. *Auto Service Leasing GmbH (ASL)* [2002] ECR I-3193, par. 27.

[473]   8 November 1990, Case C-231/89, *Krystyna Gmurzynska-Bscher* v. *Oberfinanzdirektion Köln* [1990] ECR I-4003; 18 October 1990, Joined Cases C-297/88 and C-197/89, *Massam Dzodzi* v. *Belgium* [1990] ECR I-3763, par. 36–39.

[474]   12 June 1986, Joined Cases 98, 162 and 128/85, *Michele Bertini and Giuseppe Bisignani and others* v. *Regione Lazio and Unità sanitare locali* [1986] ECR 1885.

during investigations against him in Belgium, refused to answer the questions put to him by invoking the obligation of professional secrecy imposed upon him by Luxembourg banking legislation. The Belgian national court referred to the Court in order to learn whether the relevant Luxembourg legislation was in violation of the freedom to provide services. The inadmissibility of the reference found its basis in the fact that the Belgian court took one interpretation of the Luxembourg legislation as the only possible interpretation. In view of the fact that Luxembourg courts did not rule on the matter, as well as the fact that the Luxembourg government challenged that interpretation when making its observations before Court, the reference was hypothetical.[475] However, by stating that the question formulated was hypothetical at this stage of the proceedings, the Court had still given the national court an answer to its concerns on the compliance with Union law.

The Court may examine whether a Framework Decision has been properly adopted.[476] Following the *Pupino* case, the possibility of an interpretation of national law in conformity with the Framework Decision is a requirement for admissibility.[477] As with questions related to Directives, they must relate to the actual facts of the case, or to its purpose, and the problem may not be of a purely hypothetical nature. Only if it is quite obvious that the interpretation of Union law or the examination of the validity of a rule of Union law bears no relation to the actual nature of the case may the Court reject a reference.[478] If the question bears no relation to Union law, but the referring tribunal is in doubt "only as to the possible psychological reactions of certain Italian judges as a result of the enactment of the Italian law of 13 April 1988", the Court will not assume jurisdiction.[479]

Quite often, a national court refers to the Court because it needs clarification of certain terminology in a Union instrument. One example out of many others is what "acquire" means under Regulation 338/97 on the protection of species of wild fauna and flora by regulating trade therein or whether the person who acquired a specimen as listed in Regulation 338/97 more than 50 years previously must be the present owner?[480] What does "labelling" in Regulation 2392/89 laying

---

[475] 10 December 2002, Case C-153/00, *criminal proceedings against Paul der Weduwe* [2002] ECR I-11319, par. 37.

[476] 3 May 2007, Case C-303/05, *Advocaten voor de Wereld VZW v. Leden van de Ministerraad* [2007] ECR I-3633, par. 18.

[477] 28 June 2007, Case C-467/05, *criminal proceedings against Giovanni Dell'Orto* [2007] ECR I-5557, par. 44.

[478] 11 July 1991, Case C-368/89, *Antonio Crispoltoni v. Fattoria autonoma tabacchi di Città di Castelo* [1991] ECR I-3695, par. 11.

[479] 26 January 1990, Case C-286/88, *Falciola Angelo SpA v. Comune di Pavia* [1990] ECR I-191, par. 9.

[480] 23 October 2003, Case C-154/02, *criminal proceedings against Jan Nilsson* [2003] ECR I-12733.

down General Rules for the Description and Presentation of Wines and Grape Musts mean? The Court answered that it covers decoration or advertising which is unconnected with the wine concerned.[481] Some questions raised in criminal proceedings require scientific knowledge of an entirely different field.[482] The bird cases gives a good example of questions of interpretation which belong to the task of the Court and those which are of a nature that fall outside the scope of jurisdiction of the Court. The question of whether the bird sold was a dwarf Canada goose, or *Branta canadensis minima*, is one of the matters of fact which falls within the competence of the national court, and not one for the Court. However, the question of whether a dwarf Canada goose, or *Branta canadensis minima*, is listed on the Annexes to Directive 79/409 on the conservation of wild birds, is a question that deals with the interpretation of Union law, for which the Court is competent.[483]

What Kind of Answer Will the Court Give?

The Court regards its own task as "to provide the national court with guidance on the scope of the rules of Community law so as to enable that court to apply the rules correctly to the facts in the case before it and it is not for the Court of Justice to apply those rules itself, a fortiori since it does not necessarily have available to it all the information that is essential for that purpose."[484] This is a preliminary statement the Court often gives in order to make it clear that it will limit itself to the interpretation of Union law. It will neither apply Union law to the facts nor interpret national law.[485] Both are tasks to be performed by the national court. Clearly, the answer of the Court might often imply that national law is incompatible. However, Union law leaves it to the Member States to repair this.

The Court will not answer the question of what a lower national court should do with an interpretation of the supreme court, which it considers to be in violation of Union law.[486] The Court will also not state whether or not its ruling is binding on the national court in the same way that a court is bound by a point of

---

[481] 5 July 1995, Case C-46/94, *criminal proceedings against Michèle Voisine* [1995] ECR I-1859.

[482] "Does Directive 79/409 on the conservation of wild birds apply to bird sub-species which occur naturally in the wild only outside the European territory of the Member States, where the species to which they belong or other subspecies of that species do occur naturally in the wild state within the territory in question." This led to a long discussion, in which bird experts were involved on the distinction of species and sub-species in light of the purposes of the Directive. See 8 February 1996, Case C-202/94, *criminal proceedings against Godefridus van der Feesten* [1996] ECR I-355.

[483] 8 February 1996, Case C-149/94, *criminal proceedings against Didier Vergy* [1996] ECR I-299.

[484] 21 June 2007, Case C-259/05, *criminal proceedings against Omni Metal Service* [2007] ECR I-4945, par. 15.

[485] 30 June 1966, Case 61–65, *G. Vaasse-Göbbels* v. *Management of the Beambtenfonds voor het Mijnbedrijf* [1966] ECR English special edition 261.

[486] 6 March 2007, Joined Cases C-338/04, C-359/04 and C-360/04, *criminal proceedings against Placanica, Palazzese and Sorrichio* [2007] ECR I-1891, par. 38.

law laid down by the national Court of Cassation.[487] It follows from Union law that, if national law obliges lower courts to follow the decision of the supreme court, then national law must provide an answer to the problem.[488]

5.3. SOURCES AND TECHNIQUES OF INTERPRETATION

As with all law, Union law must also be interpreted. It is consistent case law of the Court from the days of Community law that it requires a uniform interpretation throughout the European Union. Due to vague terminology and the use of various authentic languages, questions of interpretation may arise. Although it is the task for all courts to interpret and apply Union law, the Court is the supreme court in these matters. It is, therefore, relevant to identify the rules of interpretation followed by the Court, because they should be followed by national courts as well.

Literal and Contextual Interpretation

The predominant interpretation performed by the Court is the literal interpretation.[489] The interpretation of the letter of the text in question may be difficult as a result of contradictory interpretations in the various authentic versions of the legal instrument.[490] In these circumstances, the Court will resort to a contextual interpretation.[491] The Court seems to rely occasionally on a quantitative approach: "most of the language versions."[492] Settled case law has established that a provision cannot be considered in isolation, but that it is

---

[487] 3 February 1977, Case 52–76, *Luigi Benedetti* v. *Munari F.lli s.a.s.* [1977] ECR 163.

[488] See, also, Opinion of Advocate General Ruiz-Jarabo Colomer of 16 May 2006, Joined Cases C-338/04, C-359/04 and C-360/04, *criminal proceedings against Placanica, Palazzese and Sorrichio* [2007] ECR I-1891, points 76–90.

[489] 28 June 2007, Case C-467/05, *criminal proceedings against Giovanni Dell'Orto* [2007] ECR I-5557, par. 54.

[490] Occassionally, the Court may even find that the version in a specific language contains a substantive error. See 27 February 1997, Case C-177/95, *Ebony Maritime SA and Loten Navigator Co. Ltd* v. *Prefetto della Provincia di Brindisi and others* [1997] ECR I-1111, par. 31 and 17 October 1996, Case C-64/95, *Konservenfabrik Lubella Friedrich Büker GmbH & Co. KG* v. *Hauptzollamt Cottbus* [1996] ECR I-515, in which the German version of a Regulation contained a material error, using *Süßkirschen* instead of *Sauerkirschen*.

[491] For instance 19 November 1998, Case C-210/97, *Haydar Akman* v. *Oberkreisdirektor des Rheinisch-Bergischen-Kreises* [1998] ECR I-7519, par. 30–32; 28 June 2007, Case C-467/05, *criminal proceedings against Giovanni Dell'Orto* [2007] ECR I-5557, par. 55–57.

[492] 21 January 2003, Case C-378/00, *Commission* v. *European Parliament and Council* [2003] ECR I-937, par. 45. However, the Court had rejected such a quantitative approach already in 2 April 1998, Case C-296/95, *The Queen* v. *Commissioners of Customs and Excise, ex parte EMU Tabac SARL, The Man in Black Ltd, John Cunningham* [1998] ECR I-1605, par. 36: "All the language versions must, in principle, be recognised as being the same weight and this cannot vary according to the size of the population of the Member States using the language in question".

required that it be interpreted and applied in the light of other official versions.[493] In the case of divergence between the language versions, the provision must be interpreted by reference to the purpose and general scheme of the rules of which it forms a part.[494] The Court has consistently held that the wording of secondary legislation is open to more than one interpretation, "preference should be given to the interpretation which renders the provision consistent with the TEC, rather than to the interpretation which leads to its being incompatible with the Treaty".[495] The Court stresses that words in the legal instruments have their own independent meaning in Union law. Advocate General Ruiz-Jarabo Colomer added that "the term should not have attributed to it a meaning deriving from domestic law where that would lead to disparate interpretations".[496] The autonomous interpretation (not relying on notions from a national system) is more or less the interpretation that will give the rule its *useful effect*. One will also find this in other words, such as "the effectiveness of the rule". Very often formulated in the following manner: "such an interpretation would compromise the useful effect of provision xy." The corollary of the literal interpretation by the Court is the task of the national court to interpret national implementing legislation in conformity with the act of the Union.[497]

The Influence of International Law

The Court does not use other treaties to interpret the wording of a legal instrument: "the mere similarity between the wording of a provision of one of the Treaties establishing the Communities and of an international agreement between the

---

[493] 5 December 1967, Case 19-67, *Bestuur der Sociale Verzekeringsbank* v. *J.H. van der Vecht* [1967] ECR English Special Edition p. 345; 17 June 1998, Case C-321/96, *Wilhelm Mecklenburg* v. *Kreis Pinneberg – Der Landrat* [1998] ECR I-3809, par. 29; 26 May 2005, Case C-498/03, *Kingscrest Associates Ltd, Montecello Ltd* v. *Commissioners of Customs and Excise* [2005] ECR I-4427, par. 26 and 27.

[494] 27 March 1990, Case C-372/88, *Milk Marketing Board of England and Wales* v. *Cricket St. Thomas Estate* [1990] ECR I-1345, par. 19; 27 February 1986, Case 238/84, *criminal proceedings against Hans Röser* [1986] ECR 795, par. 22; 24 October 1996, Case C-72/95, *Aannemersbedrijf P.K. Kraaijeveld B.V. e.a.* v. *Gedeputeerde Staten van Zuid-Holland* [1996] ECR I-5403; 19 April 2007, Case C-455/05, *Velvet & Steel Immobilien und Handels GmbH* v. *Finanzamt Hamburg-Eimsbüttel* [2007] ECR I-3225, par. 18–20. Occasionally, the wording of the different language versions is so confusing that the Court simply takes one interpretation to make an end to the ambiguity. See 25 January 1994, Case C-212/91, *Angelopharm GmbH* v. *Freie Hansestadt Hamburg* [1994] ECR I-171.

[495] For instance 26 June 2007, Case C-305/05, *Ordre des barreaux francophones et germanophone, Ordre français des avocats du barreau de Bruxelles, Ordre des barreaux flamands, Ordre néerlandais des avocats du barreau de Bruxelles* v. *Conseil des Ministres* [2007] ECR I-535, par. 28.

[496] See Opinion of Advocate General Ruiz-Jarabo Colomer of 22 February 2005, Case C-498/03, *Kingscrest Associates Ltd, Montecello Ltd* v. *Commissioners of Customs and Excise* [2005] ECR I-4427, point 23.

[497] See, further, on the task of the national court, Chapter 5, Section 8.

Communities and a non-member country does not suffice for the same meaning to be ascribed to the terms of that agreement as they bear in the Treaties."[498] Advocate General Cosmas explicitly denied the applicability of the rules on interpretation that are stipulated in the 1969 Vienna Convention on the Law of Treaties.[499] Because of the *sui generis* character of the legal order of the Union the rules of public international law do not apply: "Once provisions of primary Community law have been inserted into the text of the Treaty and made applicable in the community legal order, *they acquire autonomous value in relation to the will of their authors*."[500] In *Metalsa*, the Court had to interpret an Agreement between the EEC and a third state. In this situation, it specifically deviated from the regular rules of interpretation under Union law:

> "An international treaty must not be interpreted solely by reference to the terms in which it is worded but also in light of its objectives. Article 31 of the Vienna Convention of 23 May 1969 on the law of treaties stipulates in that respect that a treaty is to be interpreted in good faith in accordance with the ordinary meaning to be given to its terms in their context and in the light of its object and purpose (Opinion 1/91 [1991] ECR I-6079, paragraph 14)."[501]

As a consequence of it, the Court did not transplant the interpretation of wording of the Treaty to identical wording in an international agreement.

A slightly different issue was raised in the *Racke* case. Racke disputed the validity of a Regulation on the grounds that the Regulation had suspended the Co-operation Agreement with Yugoslavia in violation of the Vienna Convention on the Law of Treaties.[502] The Court held that the rules of customary international law concerning the termination and the suspension of treaty obligations by reason of a fundamental change of circumstances (in this case, war in Yugoslavia) were

---

[498] 23 October 2003, Case C-115/02, *Administration des douanes et droits indirects* v. *Rioglass SA and Transremar SL* [2003] ECR I-12705, par. 13; 26 October 1982, Case 104/81, *Hauptzollamt Mainz* v. *C.A. Kupferberg & Cie KGa.A.* [1982] ECR 3641, par. 29–31;1 July 1993, Case C-312/91, *Procedural issue relating to a seizure of goods belonging to Metalsa Srl.* [1993] ECR I-3751, par. 11–12; 27 September 2001, Case C-63/99, *The Queen and Secretary of State for the Home Department* v. *Wieslaw Gloszczuk and Elzbieta Gloszczuk* [2001] ECR I-9565, par. 48. The same goes for an interpretation that derives from a specific national system: "the Community legal order does not, in principle, aim to define concepts on the basis of one or more national legal systems unless there is express provision to that effect." See 2 April 1998, Case C-296/95, *The Queen* v. *Commissioners of Customs and Excise, ex parte EMU Tabac SARL, The Man in Black Ltd, John Cunningham* [1998] ECR I-1605, par. 30.

[499] Opinion of 16 March 1999, Case C-378/97, *criminal proceedings against Floris Ariël Wijsenbeek* [1999] ECR I-6207, points 50–54.

[500] Opinion of 16 March 1999, Case C-378/97, *criminal proceedings against Floris Ariël Wijsenbeek* [1999] ECR I-6207, point 54.

[501] Case C-312/91, *Procedural issue relating to a seizure of goods belonging to Metalsa Srl.* [1993] ECR I-3751, par. 12.

[502] 16 June 1998, Case C-162/96, *A.Racke GmbH & Co* v. *Hauptzollamt Mainz* [1998] ECR I-3655.

binding upon the Union institutions and form part of the Union legal order.[503] An individual relying on rights deriving from the suspended agreement may challenge the validity of the Regulation suspending the agreement. Is the decisive criterion on whether the Court will use an international treaty as a source of interpretation the fact that the Union is a party to it?[504] The fact that the Union is a party to a Convention obliges the Court to regard such a Convention as part of the *acquis communautaire*.[505] The situation in which the Union is a party to an international agreement should be distinguished from one in which all Member States, but not the Union, are parties to an international Convention. In the latter case, the international Convention cannot be the standard for assessing the validity of a Union act.[506]

Different Interpretation of Third Pillar Law?

In an interesting Opinion, Advocate General Kokott discussed the issue of whether the terms of legislation adopted under the First Pillar should have identical meaning in the Third. Whilst she supports coherent interpretation, "the differences laid down in the treaties between supranational Community law and Union law, which is based more heavily on traditional international law, should not be confused".[507] With reference to Article 6 EU, her colleague Sharpston argued that the principle of *ne bis in idem* should be the same in all areas of EU law.[508]

The Court does not specifically exclude that a Directive is capable of having any effect on the interpretation of provisions of a Framework Decision.[509] However, since it uses the Directive in order to justify its reasoning, it seems safe to conclude that other acts may be used in order to interpret a specific legal instrument. Advocate General Kokott stated in a very clear manner: "Regulatory techniques, approaches to problems and concepts which have proven themselves

---

503 16 June 1998, Case C-162/96, *A.Racke GmbH & Co v. Hauptzollamt Mainz* [1998] ECR I-3655, par. 46.

504 That impression arises from the Peralta case. 14 July 1994, Case C-379/92, *criminal proceedings against Matteo Peralta* [1994] ECR I-3453, where the Court refuses to interpret the Marpol Convention, because the Community is not a party to that convention.

505 See Chapter 3, Section 2.

506 3 June 2008, Case C-308/06, *The Queen on the application of: International Association of Independent Tanker Owners (Intertanko), International Association of Dry Cargo Shipowners (Intercargo), Greek Shipping Co-operation Committee, Lloyd's Register, International Salvage Union, v. Secretary of State for Transport* [2008] ECR, not yet reported, par. 49–52.

507 Opinion of Advocate General Kokott, 8 March 2007, Case C-467/05, *criminal proceedings against Giovanni Dell'Orto* [2007] ECR I-5557, par. 46.

508 Opinion of Advocate General Sharpston, 15 June 2006, Case C-467/04, *criminal proceedings against Gasparini and others* [2006] ECR I-9199, par. 101.

509 28 June 2007, Case C-467/05, *criminal proceedings against Giovanni Dell'Orto* [2007] ECR I-5557, par. 58.

in Community secondary law can also be used for Union legislation."[510] With regard to the Schengen *acquis*, the Court has stated, on a number of occasions, that it regards it as part of Community law, because of Article 1 of the Protocol integrating the Schengen *acquis* into the framework of the European Union.[511] Occasionally, the Court discusses First and Third Pillar legislation under the common heading of "Community law".[512] From this, it may be concluded that the use of terminology in the (former) First and Third Pillar is interchangeable.

No Historical Interpretation

The Court definitely does not rely on an historical interpretation.[513] The most prominent example of the irrelevance of the historical interpretation in the field of criminal law is the interpretation of Article 54 *CISA*.[514] In the light of the history of the negotiations of the *CISA*, the irrelevance, as the Court stated it, of the fact that no court is involved in such a procedure,[515] is astonishing.[516] The inclusion of settlements by the prosecution was proposed by the Netherlands but rejected by the other negotiating Member States, as a result of which, it was not

---

[510]   Opinion of Advocate General Kokott, 8 March 2007, Case C-467/05, *criminal proceedings against Giovanni Dell'Orto* [2007] ECR I-5557, par. 45.

[511]   18 July 2007, Case C-367/05, *criminal proceedings against Norma Kraaijenbrink* [2007] ECR I-6619, par. 3.

[512]   28 September 2006, Case C-467/04, *criminal proceedings against Gasparini and others* [2006] ECR I-9199; 18 January 2007, Case C-229/05, *Osman Öcalan (PKK) and Serif Valy (KNK) appellants, Council, defendant* [2007] ECR I-439; 28 September 2006, Case C-150/05, *van Straaten* v. *the Netherlands and Italy* [2006] ECR I-9327, par. 3–15. See, also, Advocate General D. Ruiz-Jarabo Colomer, Opinion of 8 June 2006, Case C-150/05, *van Straaten* v. *the Netherlands and Italy* [2006] ECR I-9327, par. 45. However, the same Advocate General referred to it as "law of the European Union" in his Opinion of 20 October 2005, Case C-436/04, *criminal proceedings against van Esbroeck* [2006] ECR I-2333.

[513]   There are a few exceptions to be found in the case law. See 26 May 1981, Case C-157/80, *criminal proceedings against Siegfried Ewald Rinkau* [1981] ECR 1395, interpreting provisions of the Protocol annexed to the Convention of 27 September 1968 on jurisdiction and the enforcement of judgments in civil and commercial matters. In 17 June 1998, Case C-321/96, *Wilhelm Mecklenburg* v. *Kreis Pinneberg – Der Landrat* [1998] ECR I-3809, par. 28, the Court did take the history of the Directive into consideration. 18 October 1990, Joined Cases C-297/88 and C-197/89, *Massam Dzodzi* v. *Belgium* [1990] ECR I-3763, par. 36, where the Court refers to "the intention of the authors of the Treaty".

[514]   See, further, Chapter 5, Section 3.2.

[515]   Although such a provision is not completely new in European law. See one of the preambular recitals of *Regulation 2988/95 on Protection of the Financial Interests*: "Whereas for the purposes of applying this Regulation, criminal proceedings may be regarded as having been completed where the competent national authority and the person concerned come to an arrangement".

[516]   "The fact that no court is involved in such a procedure and that the decision in which the procedure culminates does not take the form of a judicial decision does not cast doubt on that interpretation, since such matters of procedure and form do not impinge on the effects of the procedure." 11 February 2003, Case C-187/01 and Case C-385/01, *criminal proceedings against Hüseyin Gözütok (C-187/01) and Klaus Brügge (C-385/01)* [2003] ECR I-1345, par. 31.

included. This also explains that it was unnecessary to state the opposite, as the Court requires: "in the absence of an express indication to the contrary."[517] As a miracle formula, the Court uses the area of Freedom, Security and Justice (which was established by a later treaty) in order to interpret the provisions of the *CISA*. It establishes a relationship with the freedom of movement, which would be restricted by non-recognition. It uses an argument based upon equal treatment (not only protection for those who commit serious offences, but also for those who commit minor offences) and therefore extended the recognition to out-of-court-settlements. In addition, the reference to "most of the language versions" (paragraph 44) is not very convincing in a historical interpretation. The three language versions existing at the time of concluding the Convention (German/French/Dutch) point in another direction. The Court simply declares the intention of the Contracting Parties irrelevant to the interpretation of a provision.[518] It is clear that the Court followed an autonomous interpretation.[519]

The fact that the Court does not look at the history of the legal instrument may be rather strange to those trained in (international) criminal law. However, in its judgment in *Gözütok*, the Court followed the consistent case law: the (con)text of the provision and nothing else is relevant for its interpretation. An example of this case law is *VAG Sverige AB*, in which the Court held that:

> "Declarations recorded in minutes are of limited value, since they cannot be used for the purposes of interpreting a provision of Community law where no reference is made to the content of the declaration in the wording of the provision in question and the declaration therefore has no legal significance."[520]

In *Grøngaard and Barg*, the prosecution relied on the preparatory documents to the Directive, which supported the argument that the behaviour of the suspects

---

[517]   As a rule of interpretation, this raises the question of whether everything that is not specifically excluded is included. A general application of such a rule would violate the principle of legitimate expectation and the rule of law.

[518]   See, also, the Opinion of Advocate General Ruiz-Jarabo Colomer of 19 September 2002, Case C-187/01 and Case C-385/01, *criminal proceedings against Hüseyin Gözütok (C-187/01) and Klaus Brügge (C-385/01)* [2003] ECR I-1345, point 117: "irrelevant because the Member States disagree".

[519]   As suggested by the Commission. See, also, the Opinion of Advocate General Ruiz-Jarabo Colomer of 19 September 2002, C-187/01 and C-385/01, *criminal proceedings against Hüseyin Gözütok (C-187/01) and Klaus Brügge (C-385/01)* [2003] ECR I-1345, point 42.

[520]   29 May 1997, Case C-329/95, *Administrative proceedings brought by VAG Sverige AB* [1997] ECR I-2675, par. 23; See, also, 13 February 1996, Joined Cases C-197/94 and C-252/94, *Société Bautiaa v. Directeur des Services Fiscaux des Landes and Société Française Maritime v. Directeur des Service Fiscaux du Finistère* [1996] ECR I-505, par. 51. In older case law, the Court did use the recorded minutes of the meeting of the Council during which the instrument was adopted. See 7 February 1979, Case 136/78, *criminal proceedings against Vincent Auer* [1979] ECR 437, par. 25.

fell under the prohibition. The accused, of course, held the opposite view. Advocate General Poiares Maduro said:

> "It is true that no general standard can be deduced from preparatory works, since they can only add to the literal meaning of the provision in question. It may also be added that, in the present instance, the preparatory documents cited have not been published, which militates against their use in interpreting the Directive. The word 'normal' will in fact be interpreted by reference to the national context. The preparatory works none the less reinforce the appropriateness of a restrictive interpretation of the exception to the prohibition of disclosure."[521]

The Court did not feel tempted to deal with the preparatory works when interpreting the provision. It briefly held: "having regard to the terms used."[522]

General Principles of the Union's Law

Over the years, the Court has formulated "general principles of Community law, which must be applied when interpreting the law".[523] General principles of Union law prevail over the obligations found in primary and secondary European Union legislation.[524] The general principles have been codified by general reference in Article 6 TEU:

> "1. The Union recognises the rights, freedoms and principles set out in the Charter of Fundamental Rights of the European Union of 7 December 2000, as adapted at Strasbourg, on 12 December 2007, which shall have the same legal value as the Treaties. (...) 3. Fundamental rights, as guaranteed by the European Convention for the Protection of Human Rights and Fundamental Freedoms and as they result from the constitutional traditions common to the Member States, shall constitute general principles of the Union's law."

Despite the symbolic recognition of the general principles of law through its codification, it is necessary to turn to the case law of the Court in order to shed more light on what the general principles of law are. On the basis of the case law, an attempt is made to find answers to the following questions. What are general

---

[521]   Opinion of Advocate General Poiares Maduro of 24 May 2004, Case C-384/02, *criminal proceedings against Knud Grøngaard and Allan Barg* [2005] ECR I-9939, point 33.

[522]   22 November 2005, Case C-384/02, *criminal proceedings against Knud Grøngaard and Allan Barg* [2005] ECR I-9939, par. 27.

[523]   General principles cannot, as other rules of Union law, set aside obligations under earlier Conventions. See, with regard to the principle of equal treatment, 2 August 1993, Case C-158/91, *criminal proceedings against Jean-Claude Levy* [1993] ECR I-4287.

[524]   21 September 1989, Joined Cases 46/87 and 227/88, *Hoechst AG* v. *Commission* [1989] ECR 2859, par. 12; 17 October 1989, Case 85/87, *Dow Benelux NV* v. *Commission* [1989] ECR 3137, par. 23.

principles of law? How does the Court find these principles? What is the influence of the law of the Member States?

Various criminal law principles from the national criminal justice systems have been recognised as general principles of Union law in the case law of the Court. Both in the Preamble and in Article 2 TEU, the rule of law is mentioned. Further examples include the prohibition of retroactive effect,[525] the nulla poena rule,[526] *nulla poena sine culpa*,[527] the principle that a suspect cannot be forced to incriminate himself,[528] the lex mitior rule,[529] the principle of proportionality,[530] the principle of legal certainty,[531] the principle of *res judicata*,[532] the principle of legitimate expectations,[533] the principle of guilt,[534] the right to property,[535] the lex certa principle,[536] the principle of equal treatment,[537] the rights of the defence,[538]

---

[525]   10 July 1984, Case 63/83, *Regina v. Kent Kirk* [1984] ECR 2689, par. 21–23; 13 November 1990, Case C-331/88, *The Queen v. Minister of Agriculture, Fisheries and Food and Secretary of State for Health, ex parte: Fedesa and others* [1990] ECR I-4023; 14 July 1994, Case C-352/92, *Milchwerke Köln/ Wuppertal eG v. Hauptzollamt Köln-Rheinau* [1994] ECR I-3385.

[526]   8 October 1987, Case 80/86, *criminal proceedings against Kolpinghuis Nijmegen B.V.* [1987] ECR 3969; 3 May 2005, C-387/02, C-391/02 and C-403/02, *criminal proceedings against Silvio Berlusconi (C-387/02), Sergio Adelchi (C-391/02), Marcello Dell'Utri and others (C-403/02)* [2005] ECR I-3565. *Nulla poena* also carries the element that the penalty must be foreseeable. That was stipulated in competition cases. See, for instance, 8 February 2007, Case C-3/06 P, *Groupe Danone* [2007] ECR I-1331, par. 90–92.

[527]   10 July 1990, Case C-326/88, *Anklagemyndigheden v. Hansen and Søn I/S* [1990] ECR I-2911.

[528]   18 October 1989, *Orkem v. Commission*, Case C-374/87, ECR 1989, 3283, par. 28–35.

[529]   1 June 1999, Case C-319/97, *criminal proceedings against Antoine Kortas* [1999] ECR I-3143, par. 16. See 29 October 1998, Case C-230/97, *criminal proceedings against Ibiyinka Awoyemi* [1998] ECR I-67, par. 38: "Community law does not prevent the national court from taking into account, in accordance with a principle of its criminal law, of the more favourable provisions of Directive 91/439 for the purposes of the application of national law, even though, as the Commission has pointed out in its written observations, Community law imposes no obligation to that effect." 1 July 2004, Case C-295/02, *Gisela Gerken v. Amt für Agrarstruktur Verden* [2004] ECR I-6369, par. 57.

[530]   5 March, 1980, Case C-265/78, *H. Ferwerda BV v. Produktschap voor Vee en Vlees* [1980] ECR 617; 13 December 1979, Case C-44/79, *Liselotte Hauer v. Land Rheinland-Pfalz* [1979] ECR 3727.

[531]   5 March, 1980, Case C-265/78, *H. Ferwerda BV v. Produktschap voor Vee en Vlees* [1980] ECR 617; 8 February 2007, Case C-3/06 P, *Groupe Danone* [2007] ECR I-1331, par. 23.

[532]   16 March 2006, Case C-234/04, *Rosemarie Kapferer v. Schlank & Schick GmbH* [2006] ECR I-2585, par. 21.

[533]   12 November 1981, Joined Cases 212 to 217/80, *Amministrazione delle finanze dello Stato v. Srl Meridionale Industria Salumi and others; Ditta Italo Orlandi & Figlio and Ditta Vincenzo Divella v. Amministrazione delle finanze dello Stato* [1981] ECR 2735, par. 10.

[534]   26 May 1981, Case C-157/80, *criminal proceedings against Siegfried Ewald Rinkau* [1981] ECR 1395.

[535]   13 December 1979, Case C-44/79, *Liselotte Hauer v. Land Rheinland-Pfalz* [1979] ECR 3727.

[536]   12 December 1996, Joined Cases C-74/95 and C-129/95, *criminal proceedings against X* [1996] ECR I-6609; 7 January 2004, Case C-60/02, *criminal proceedings against X* [2004] ECR I-651.

[537]   13 July 2000, Case C-36/99, *Idéal Tourisme SA v. Belgium* [2000] ECR I-649, par. 35.

[538]   21 September 1989, Joined Cases 46/87 and 227/88, *Hoechst AG v. Commission* [1989] ECR 2859; 17 October 1989, Case 85/87, *Dow Benelux NV v. Commission* [1989] ECR 3137.

the right to an effective remedy,[539] and the ne bis in idem principle.[540] These are principles either common to substantive or procedural criminal law in all Member States, or principles derived from human rights conventions.[541]

How Does the Court Find these General Principles?

The Union is founded on the values of respect for the rule of law and respect for human rights. These fundamental rights form an integral part of the general principles of law. Despite the fact that human rights treaties do not have direct effect in the Union legal order, the case law "regards those treaties, together with the constitutional traditions common to the Member States, as helping to determine the content of the general principles of Community law".[542]

The ECHR is of "special significance".[543] It follows that the Union cannot accept measures which are incompatible with the observance of the human rights, thus recognised and guaranteed.[544] The Court further refers to the fact that these principles have been re-stated in Article 6, paragraph 2 TEU.[545] The Court explicitly refers to the case law of the ECHR and uses it,[546] and will interpret the

---

[539]   15 May 1986, Case 222/84, *Marguerite Johnston* v. *Chief Constable of the Royal Ulster Constabulary* [1986] ECR 1651, par. 18, adding "That principle is also laid down in Articles 6 and 13" ECHR.

[540]   13 February 1969, Case 14–68, *Wilhelm* [1969] ECR 1. With regard to Articles 55 and 56 *CISA*, there is a general principle of set-off. See Advocate General Sharpston in her Opinion of 5 December 2006, Case C-367/05, *criminal proceedings against Norma Kraaijenbrink* [2007] ECR I-6619, points 58–60, who submits that the Court has rendered contradictory judgments on the principle of set-off.

[541]   The fundamental rights from the ECHR by definition fall under the general principles of Union law. See 4 October 1991, Case C-159/90, *The Society for the Protection of the Unborn Children Ireland Ltd* v. *Stephen Grogan and others* [1991] ECR 4685. See, also, 14 May 1974, Case 4–73, *J. Nold, Kohlen- und Baustoffgroßhandlung* v. *Commission* [1974] ECR 491; 21 September 1989, Joined Cases 46/87 and 227/88, *Hoechst AG* v. *Commission* [1989] ECR 2859.

[542]   Opinion of Advocate General van Gerven of 11 June 1991, Case C-159/90, *The Society for the Protection of the Unborn Children Ireland Ltd* v. *Stephen Grogan and others* [1991] ECR 4685, point 30.

[543]   26 June 2007, Case C-305/05, *Ordre des barreaux francophones et germanophone, Ordre français des avocats du barreau de Bruxelles, Ordre des barreaux flamands, Ordre néerlandais des avocats du barreau de Bruxelles* v. *Conseil des Ministres* [2007] ECR I-535, par. 29. Other human rights obligations apparently do not have the special status given to the ECHR. The International Covenant on Civil and Political Rights belongs to the legal instruments that are taken into account in the application of general principles of Union law. 27 June 2006, Case C-540/03, *European Parliament* v. *Council* [2006] ECR I-5769, par. 37.

[544]   13 July 1989, Case 5/88, *Hubert Wachauf* v. *Bundesamt für Ernährung und Forstwirtschaft* [1989] ECR 2609, par. 17.

[545]   6 March 2001, Case C-274/99 P, *Bernard Connolly* v. *Commission* [2001] ECR I-1611, par. 38.

[546]   26 June 2007, Case C-305/05, *Ordre des barreaux francophones et germanophone, Ordre français des avocats du barreau de Bruxelles, Ordre des barreaux flamands, Ordre néerlandais des avocats du barreau de Bruxelles* v. *Conseil des Ministres* [2007] ECR I-535, par. 30–32.

ECHR when the situation it has to interpret falls within the scope of Union law.[547] Although the ECHR is often used as a source of interpretation, the Court has been rather reluctant to state explicitly that there has been a violation of the ECHR.[548] More recently, the Charter has been recognised as part of the general principles of law.[549]

The picture is thus that the general principles first consist of the fundamental rights, as embodied in human rights treaties, of which the ECHR is of "special significance". Second, fundamental rights may also result from the constitutional traditions common to the Member States.[550] But how then, it must again be asked, does the Court arrive at these general principles? In *Internationale Handelsgesellschaft*, the Court held that:

> "… fundamental rights form an integral part of the general principles of law protected by the Court of Justice. The protection of such rights, whilst inspired by the constitutional traditions common to the Member States, must be ensured within the framework of the structure and objectives of the Community".[551]

However, what is undisputed is that the Court does not transform the constitutional principles or traditions which can be found in only one Member State to general

---

547 See, for instance, 30 September 1987, Case 12/86, *Meryem Demirel* v. *Stadt Schwäbisch Gmünd* [1987] ECR 3719, par. 28; 18 June 1991, Case C-260/89, *Elliniki Radiophonia Tiléorassi AE and Panellinia Omospondia Syllogon Prossopikou* v. *Dimotiki Etairia Pliroforissis and Sotirios Kouvelas and Nicolaos Avdellas and others* [1991] ECR I-2925, par. 43–45; 4 October 1991, Case C-159/90, *The Society for the Protection of the Unborn Children Ireland Ltd* v. *Stephen Grogan and others* [1991] ECR 4685, par. 31.

548 25 January 2007, Case C-370/05, *criminal proceedings against Uwe Kay Festersen* [2007] ECR I-1129, par. 35. The Court does not say that the measures violate a convention right. It merely states that the requirement restricts a right under the ECHR. Although the Court structures the arguments to conclude that a specific situation violates the ECHR, it leaves that final conclusion to the national court. See 20 May 2003, Joined Cases C-465/00, C-138/01 and C-139/01, *Rechnungshof* v. *Österreichischer Rundfunk and Others and Christa Neukomm and Joseph Lauermann* v. *Österreichischer Rundfunk* [2003] ECR I-4989, par. 91.

549 3 May 2007, Case C-303/05, *Advocaten voor de Wereld VZW* v. *Leden van de Ministerraad* [2007] ECR I-3633, par. 46.

550 Declaration 1 attached to the Treaties states that The Charter of Fundamental Rights of the European Union, which has legally binding force, confirms the fundamental rights guaranteed by the European Convention for the Protection of Human Rights and Fundamental Freedoms and *as they result from the constitutional traditions common to the Member States*. The Czech Republic declared (Declaration 53) that fundamental rights and principles as they result from the constitutional traditions common to the Member States, are to be interpreted in harmony with those traditions.

551 17 December 1970, Case 11–70, *Internationale Handelsgesellschaft mbH* v. *Einfuhr- und Vorratsstelle für Getreide und Futtermittel* [1970] ECR 1125, par. 4; 14 May 1974, Case 4–73, *J. Nold, Kohlen- und Baustoffgroßhandlung* v. *Commission* [1974] ECR 491; 13 December 1979, Case C-44/79, *Liselotte Hauer* v. *Land Rheinland-Pfalz* [1979] ECR 3727, par. 15; 18 June 1991, Case C-260/89, *Elliniki Radiophonia Tiléorassi AE and Panellinia Omospondia Syllogon Prossopikou* v. *Dimotiki Etairia Pliroforissis and Sotirios Kouvelas and Nicolaos Avdellas and others* [1991] ECR I-2925, par. 41.

principles of the Union's law. Again in *Internationale Handelsgesellschaft*, the Court stated:

> "the validity of a Community measure or its effect within a Member State cannot be affected by allegations that it runs counter to either fundamental rights as formulated by the Constitution of that state or the principles of a national constitutional structure."[552]

In *Orkem*, the Court followed the following method: it first looked at the situation in the legal systems of the Member States, then, at the ECHR, and, lastly, at the International Covenant of Civil and Political Rights. Despite the fact that the Court recognised the right not to give evidence against oneself as part of the rights of the defence, this led to the conclusion that this right was not recognised in these sources.[553] How does the Court arrive at the "constitutional traditions of the Member States"? This is done on the basis of a comparative research.[554] In older cases, the Court mentioned the result of this research itself in the judgment,[555] but in more recent cases, it relies on the Opinion of the Advocate General. Analysing the case law, it is difficult to discern a specific constitutional dimension of the principles. It seems that it is much more important that a principle is common to the national systems than that one can refer to a provision in the written Constitution of a Member State. Occasionally, without further explanation, the Court states what it does not recognise as a general principle: for example, the Court does not recognise the principle that Union law may not be applied if it causes unintended hardship,[556] nor does the need to ensure animal welfare belong to the general principles.[557]

---

[552]   17 December 1970, Case 11–70, *Internationale Handelsgesellschaft mbH* v. *Einfuhr- und Vorratsstelle für Getreide und Futtermittel* [1970] ECR 1125, par. 3.

[553]   18 October 1989, Case C-374/87, *Orkem v. Commission* [1989] ECR 3283, par. 28–35. See, also, the comparative research conducted by Advocate General Darmon in his Opinion of 18 May 1989, points 84–152.

[554]   13 December 1979, Case C-44/79, *Liselotte Hauer* v. *Land Rheinland-Pfalz* [1979] ECR 3727, par. 20; See, for instance, Advocate General Mischo, Joined Opinions of 21 February 1989, Joined Cases 46/87 and 227/88, *Hoechst AG* v. *Commission* [1989] ECR 2859 and Case 85/87, *Dow Benelux NV* v. *Commission* [1989] ECR 3137, points 48–120. Advocate General Léger in his Opinion of 10 July 2001, Case C-353/99 P, *Council* v. *Heidi Hautala* [2001] ECR I-9565, point 57: "Thirteen of the fifteen Member States have a general rule that the public has a right of access to documents held by the administration. In nine of those thirteen States, the right of access is a fundamental rights, a principle of a constitutional nature or a right founded in the constitution but of a legislative nature. In the four other Member States, the right derives from one or more laws".

[555]   13 December 1979, Case C-44/79, *Liselotte Hauer* v. *Land Rheinland-Pfalz* [1979] ECR 3727, par. 20.

[556]   28 June 1990, Case C-174/89, *Hoche GmbH* v. *Bundesanstalt für Landwirtschaftliche Marktordnung* [1990] ECR I-2681, par. 31.

[557]   12 July 2001, Case C-189/01, *H. Jippes, Afdeling Groningen van de Nederlandse Vereniging tot Bescherming van Dieren and Afdeling Assen van de Nederlandse Vereniging tot Bescherming*

As a system subject to the rule of law, the Court has stated that the interpretation of the fundamental freedoms must be reconcilable with the interpretation of fundamental rights. In *Omega Spielhallen*, Advocate General Stix-Hackl raised the question of whether there is a hierarchy between the fundamental rights applicable as general principles and the fundamental freedoms enshrined in the Treaty.[558] From her perspective, fundamental rights rank at the same level as other primary legislation, particularly, the fundamental freedoms. She also raised the question of the relationship between fundamental freedoms and fundamental rights:

> "However, fundamental freedoms themselves can also perfectly well be materially categorised as fundamental rights – at least in certain respects: in so far as they lay down prohibitions on discrimination, for example, they are to be considered a specific means of expression of the general principle of equality before the law. In this respect, a conflict between fundamental freedoms enshrined in the Treaty and fundamental and human rights can also, at least in many cases, represent a conflict between fundamental rights."[559]

The reconciliation between freedoms and rights may be helpful at a later stage, when the impact of freedoms and rights in the area of freedom, security and justice is discussed.[560]

Visualisation of the origins of general principles of law

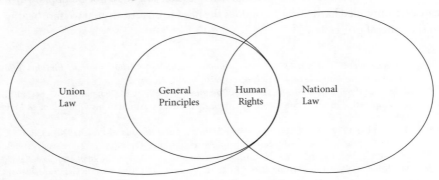

---

van Dieren v. *Minister van Landbouw, Natuurbeheer en Visserij* [2001] ECR I-5689, par. 76.

[558]   Opinion of Advocate General Stix-Hackl of 18 March 2004, Case C-36/02, *Omega Spielhallen-und Automatenaufstellungs-GmbH* v. *Oberbürgermeisterin der Stadt Bonn* [2004] ECR I-9609, the most relevant parts are points 49, 50, 53, 62, 71 and 72.

[559]   Opinion of Advocate General Stix-Hackl of 18 March 2004, Case C-36/02, *Omega Spielhallen-und Automatenaufstellungs-GmbH* v. *Oberbürgermeisterin der Stadt Bonn* [2004] ECR I-9609, point 50.

[560]   See Chapter 9.

The Influence of Implementing Practice in the Member States
As is apparent from the case law, the general principles of law derive from the constitutional traditions common to the Member States. In this sense, national law contributes to the development of Union law. This raises the question of to what extent national law is important in the interpretation of Union law. This question will be dealt with by looking at the requirements of harmonisation.

The harmonisation of law gives rise to certain expectations. One might expect the differences to be virtually absent between various states. The expectation of the citizen might be that, what constitutes a crime in one Member State cannot remain an individual liberty in the other. Or the exact opposite, that one Member State will not prosecute where another Member State will leave the matter unpunished. The presumption of harmonisation and approximation is that the law in the Member States will be more or less the same. Could an individual invoke a Member State's interpretation of the harmonised norm (or is there only one interpretation: the Court's judgment?). Could a suspect in criminal proceedings invoke a certain interpretation because that interpretation specifically goes the furthest towards the intended harmonising effect?

These questions appear to revolve around the aspect of harmonisation and not of implementation in general. Although harmonisation should bring the different legal systems closer together, the control mechanisms steer towards an effect that brings an individual legal system closer to the common instrument. The element that this should be placed in the light of how other Member States deal with the same standard is missing. The Court does not do this, it assumes an established European standard and only reviews the extent to which the Member State in question addresses this standard. The way in which Member States interpret this standard does not influence the Court's interpretation.[561] This is logical, because, if the Court were to take national implementation as a source of interpretation, the discussion would then not be limited to whether a Member State has implemented Union law correctly, but on what, in practice, the Member States have developed as the European norm in their respective national criminal justice systems.[562]

---

[561] An old case in which the Court did refer to national legal provisions of the Member States has not been followed in later decisions. See 21 February 1973, Case 6–72, *Europemballage Corporation and Continental Can Company Inc. v. Commission* [1973] ECR 215, par. 19.

[562] Cases in which it was relied on the fact that other Member States have also failed to perform their obligations have been unsuccesful. See, for instance, 11 January 1990, Case C-38/89, *Ministère public v. Guy Blanguernon* [1990] ECR I-83.

PART II.
CRIMINAL LAW IN THE
EUROPEAN UNION

In Part I, the balance in the relationship between fundamental freedoms and national law was the central focus. The fact that criminal law played a role was corollary, and not of primary importance. As a consequence of their general nature, the notions dealt with in Part I are *also* relevant for criminal law, criminal procedure, as well as for sentencing. While Part I predominantly dealt with the obligations of the Member States, the perspective in Part II is different. Here, the focus is on the criminalisation of conduct, as well as on criminal procedure and sentencing. Thus, it is not the freedoms created by the European Union for its citizens, but the *restrictions* of their freedom by both the Member States and the European Union that will be looked at. Although this will mainly take place in a national criminal justice system, we must ask ourselves what the consequences of the overlap of Union law and national criminal law are in criminal proceedings for the accused, the prosecution, victims and national courts? In addition, Part II also serves as a picture which reveals the European criminal justice system which emerges from the fragments of Union law that relate to criminal law. This will build the bridge towards Part III, in which more common European approaches to crime are the focus.

CHAPTER 4.
EUROPEAN SUBSTANTIVE
CRIMINAL LAW

1. INTRODUCTION

THE MULTI-LEVEL SOURCES OF EUROPEAN CRIMINAL LAW

This chapter deals with the notions of European substantive criminal law as they emerge from multi-layered European criminal law. It will first be shown that one of the characteristics of European criminal law is that it derives from multi-level sources. There is Union law, which constitutes statutory law and the general principles of law; and there is national law and there are human rights obligations, which are both part of national law and of the general principles of law. As a consequence, the application of Union law in a national criminal setting can be rather complicated. Union law and national law mutually influence each other. Since the Treaty of Maastricht, the general principles have been codified (now in Article 6, paragraph 3 TEU), and the relevance of the legal traditions of the Member States has been specifically referred to in Article 4, paragraph 3 TEU.

In Section 2, the legislative competences and influences of the European Union in substantive criminal law will be dealt with. What powers does the Union have in criminal law? How does it shape criminal law in practice? The existing fragments of European substantive criminal law will be presented in a form which corresponds to a regular criminal justice system. Thus, Section 3 will present the general part of European criminal law, and Section 4 its special part. The value of sketching fragments of a system lies in identifying the specific way in which legal developments take place in the European Union. The practical relevance of this chapter is twofold. On the one hand, it provides guidance for the relationship of national criminal law and Union law. On the other, it serves to illustrate the development of a general part of European criminal law, which will come into being with the establishment of the European Public Prosecutor's Office. In Section 5, some distance is taken and an analysis is made of the picture which emerged in terms of what kind of criminal policy specific to the Union is visible from its law. The chapter concludes with a discussion of the substantive criminal law issues which relate to the implementation of Union law into the national law of the Member States.

The use of terminology here is a matter that deserves specific attention. Union law may use terminology that is also used in national criminal justice systems. For instance, the use of *intent* or *participation* in a Framework Decision will immediately lead to connotations with the identical or similar word in the national criminal justice system. This inclination is further enhanced by the fact that both Union legislation and case law are available in the national language. However, it is important to bear in mind that Union law must be interpreted in an autonomous way,[563] and that the national meaning is not decisive. The explanation being that if national definitions were decisive, a uniform interpretation could no longer be guaranteed. These remarks count for the whole Part II. The same phenomenon also arises with procedural terminology. Member States differ greatly with regard to what the terms *hearing of witnesses, acquittal* or *imprisonment* actually mean.

The Limitations of National Law

Although this chapter focuses on the principles and elements of substantive criminal law, the substantive norms of Union law discussed in Part I must be applied as well. As a result, the fundamental freedoms that shape the internal market must be respected when enforcing national criminal law.[564] Additionally, the *Greek maize* criteria apply. This may lead to national law being set aside *and* to national criminal law not being applied. When it comes to the enforcement of Union law via criminal law, the Member States remain under the obligation of sincere co-operation. The discretion that Member States have is very well described by the Court in the *Cowan* case, where it held that:

> "Although, in principle, criminal legislation and the rules of criminal procedure, among which the national provision in issue is to be found, are matters for which the Member States are responsible, the Court has consistently held that Community law sets certain limits to their power. Such legislative powers may not discriminate against persons to whom Community law gives the right to equal treatment or restrict the fundamental freedoms guaranteed by Community law."[565]

In addition, the prohibition of discrimination of nationality may influence national law. However, where prohibitions do not have detrimental effects with regard to nationality or origin Member States are free.[566] Likewise, criminal

---

[563] See Chapter 3, Section 5.3.
[564] 6 March 2007, Joined Cases C-338/04, C-359/04 and C-360/04, *criminal proceedings against Placanica, Palazzese and Sorrichio* [2007] ECR I-1891, par. 68.
[565] 2 February 1989, Case 186/87, *Ian William Cowan* v. *Trésor Public* [1989] ECR 195, par. 19.
[566] 18 March 1980, Case 52/79, *Procureur du Roi* v. *Marc J.V.C. Debauve and others* [1980] ECR 833.

offences for foreigners, which do not exist for nationals, may be upheld if there is no standard of comparison.[567]

Under some circumstances, the Court has held that, although Member States should prevent certain infringements of Union law, the use of criminal law in a specific case is disproportionate.[568] Criminal sanctions, in general, and imprisonment, in particular, have been regarded as disproportional in situations in which the violations are merely of an administrative nature. This may appear paradoxical. On the one hand, Union law requires the Member States to enforce Union law. On the other, it excludes criminal law as the appropriate mechanism to do so. Consequently, it is up to the Member States to find the right balance here. Union law may influence the application, the discretion and the extent to which Member States apply their national criminal law. A Member State may not apply a criminal penalty for the failure to complete an administrative formality where such completion has been refused or rendered impossible by the Member State concerned in infringement of Union law.[569] In areas that have not been harmonised, the Member States remain completely free to criminalise conduct,[570] upon the basis of national principles.[571]

Full discretion for national law

NATIONAL LAW	Full discretion for the Member States in areas that do not come within the scope of the Treaties

A case in point which highlights the diverging influence of Union law on national criminal law is the prosecution of *Michelangelo Rivoira and others* for having made false declarations with regard to the origin of table grapes imported from

---

[567]   14 July 1977, Case 8–77, *Concetta Sagulo, Gennaro Brenca and Addelmadjid Bakhouche* [1977] ECR 1495, par. 12.

[568]   7 July 1976, Case 118–75, *Lynne Watson and Alessandro Bellmann* [1976] ECR 1185, par. 21; 15 December 1976, Case 41–76, *Suzanne Criel, née Donckerwolcke and Henri Schou* v. *Procureur de la Republique au tribunal de grande instance de Lille and Director General of Customs* [1976] ECR 1921; 29 February 1996, Case C-193/94, *criminal proceedings against Sofia Skanavi and Konstantin Chryssanthakopoulos* [1996] ECR I-929.

[569]   6 March 2007, Joined Cases C-338/04, C-359/04 and C-360/04, *criminal proceedings against Placanica, Palazzese and Sorrichio* [2007] ECR I-1891, par. 69. See, further, in Chapter 5, Section 8.3 on the procedural implications of a finding that a provision of national criminal law may not be applied.

[570]   Even if there is a Directive in a related area. See 5 February 1981, Case 108/80, *criminal proceedings against René Joseph Kugelmann* [1981] ECR 433.

[571]   They may for instance apply the more favourable new criminal legislation to old facts. See 26 September 1996, Case C-341/94, *criminal proceedings against André Allain and Steel Trading France SARL, as a party liable at civil law* [1996] ECR I-4631, par. 28–30.

Spain (reference from the *Tribunal de grande instance de Montpellier*, France).[572] Rivoira and his partners declared that the grapes came from Italy. The French custom authorities checked the importation and discovered the false declaration of origin. However, upon the basis of an Agreement between the EEC and Spain (which, at the time, was not a Member State), Spanish grapes, at the time of the importation in question, were not subject to any prohibition. Additionally, whilst France was therefore not allowed to prevent the importation, it did have the competence to require declarations of origin and to perform checks. The Court demonstrated where the limits of national criminal law lay:

> "Although the fact that Spanish grapes imported into France from Italy have been declared as being of Italian origin may, in appropriate cases, give grounds for the application of the criminal penalties provided against false declarations, it would be disproportionate to apply, without distinction, the criminal penalties provided in respect of false declarations made in order to effect prohibited imports."[573]

In other words, the French were allowed to check and were entitled to prosecute Rivoira for making false declarations. However, the assessment of the seriousness of the false declarations may not be linked to prohibited imports.[574]

Apart from its influence on existing law, Union law also imposes obligations to legislate in the field of criminal law. The way the obligation to criminalise has been shaped raises the question of whether the obligations to criminalise should be regarded as *minimum criminalisation*. The use of "at least" to cover certain conduct (for example, Articles 2 and 3 *Joint Action 98/742 on Corruption in the Private Sector*) points in this direction. Although it does give some discretion to Member States, it cannot be seen as a *carte blanche* to create an extremely repressive system that will also limit the four freedoms.

How the term "minimum" must be interpreted depends therefore on the objective (or spirit) of the instrument and the broader context of the internal market. This "spirit" must show what the intended direction is. Acting contrary to this spirit is therefore not permitted. *Framework Decision 2004/757 on Illicit*

---

[572] 28 March 1979, Case 179/78, *Procureur de la Republique, Michelangelo Rivoira and others* [1979] ECR 1147.

[573] 28 March 1979, Case 179/78, *Procureur de la Republique, Michelangelo Rivoira and others* [1979] ECR 1147, par. 20.

[574] In the course of the implementation of measures following Directive 2001/37 of 5 June 2001 on the approximation of the laws, regulations and administrative provisions of the Member States concerning the manufacture, presentation and sale of tobacco products, OJ 2001, L 194/26 and Council Recommendation of 2 December 2002 on the Prevention of Smoking and on Initiatives to Improve Tobacco Control, OJ 2003, L 22/31, the Netherlands outlawed the smoking of tobacco products in all places accessible to the public, as of 1 July 2008. The somewhat somewhat bizarre consequence of this is that, in "coffeeshops", soft drugs, such as marihuana, may be consumed, but regular cigarettes are no longer allowed.

Drug Trafficking stipulates the "adopt[ion of] minimum rules relating to the constituent elements of the offences....". How should "minimum" be interpreted here? If this means that the national penal code must contain at least the constituent elements summarised in the Framework Decision, but may additionally contain more constituent elements, this would appear to be contrary to the more repressive spirit of the Framework Decision. Clearly, the more the constituent elements, the stricter the proof and the more difficult the position of the Public Prosecutor will be. It seems to be in line with the spirit of the legislation to conclude that this simply means that the conduct described must be criminalised.

The lower margin of the implementation into national criminal law requires that the national offence must be as severe as the specific legal instruments require.[575] The quest for the minimum threshold of criminalisation is further facilitated by the application of the enforcement criteria. Third Pillar legal instruments contain a codification of the enforcement obligation as defined by the Court in the *Greek maize* case. The *Greek maize* criteria appear in various legal instruments.[576] Should this be regarded as an incentive to criminalise as much conduct as possible and with the highest penalties as possible?[577] The answer to this question can be found in the criteria itself. Apart from *dissuasive* and *effective* measures, which would support more repression, measures should also be *proportional.* Furthermore, the assimilation principle applies. National legislation on subsidy fraud in the European Union may not be more stringent than national law on comparable subsidies.[578] As a rule, the upper margin of the criminalisation of conduct is determined by proportionality in general, and, more in particular, by the requirement that the definition of criminal conduct may not restrict the freedoms of citizens in a manner that cannot be justified.[579]

---

[575]   See, further, Sections 3 and 4 of this chapter.

[576]   *Framework Decision 2002/475 on Combating Terrorism; Framework Decision 2002/629 on Combating Trafficking in Human Beings; Framework Decision 2004/757 on Illicit Drug Trafficking.*

[577]   In a rare case on the question of whether the definition of the offence and the penalty provided were in compliance with the enforcement criteria, the Court held, without substantiating it, that the national legislation did not meet the criteria. 18 October 2001, Case C-354/99, *Commission* v. *Ireland* [2001] ECR I-7657. The Commission argued in this case that the penalty should be at least 1,000 Irish Pounds, where 5 to 100 Pounds were provided in the law.

[578]   6 May 1982, Case 54/81, *Firma Wilhelm Fromme* v. *Bundesanstalt für landwirtschaftliche Marktordnung* [1982] ECR 1449, par. 7.

[579]   See, for acceptable justifications, Chapter 3, Section 4, especially Section 4.6.

Mutual influence of Union law and national law

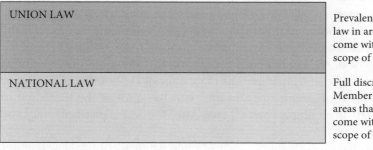

UNION LAW	Prevalence of Union law in areas that do come within the scope of the Treaties
NATIONAL LAW	Full discretion for the Member States in areas that do not come within the scope of the Treaties

The Limitations of Union Law

The principles of conferral, subsidiarity and proportionality limit the possible influence of Union law.[580] These are principles that are very influential in the legislative process. The assessment by a Member State that a draft Directive would affect fundamental aspects of its criminal justice system is also of great relevance in the legislative process.[581] This rule has now been codified in Article 83 TFEU.[582] However, it was already provided in various legal instruments which were adopted under the Third Pillar. The general tenor is that Union legislation should not have the effect of changing the legal system of the Member State. This can be concluded from phrases such as Article 2 of *Joint Action 98/733 on Participation in a Criminal Organisation*, which states that the criminalisation of preparatory offences is "subject to the general principles of the criminal law of the Member State concerned". Point B Title I *Joint Action 97/154 on Trafficking in Human Beings* refers to "respecting the constitutional rules and legal traditions of each Member State". Even more explicit is Article 1, paragraph 4 of *Framework Decision 2002/946 on Unauthorised Entry*: "If imperative to preserve the coherence of the national penalty system, the actions defined in paragraph 3 shall be punishable by custodial sentences with a maximum sentence of not less than six years, provided that it is among the most severe maximum sentences available for crimes of comparable gravity."

Article 4 of the *First Protocol Financial Interests Convention* stipulates the application of the assimilation principle. A Member State must "ensure that, in its criminal law, the descriptions of the offence (...) apply similarly in case where such offences are committed by Community officials".[583] *Framework Decision 2003/568 on Corruption in the Private Sector* refers to the context under national

---

580   See Chapter 2, Section 4.5.
581   See, also, Protocol No. 35 which prevents Ireland from having to accept any rule which goes against Article 40.3.3. of the Constitution of Ireland. This provision protects the right to life and prohibits abortion.
582   See Chapter 2, Section 4.6.
583   Article 4 *Corruption Convention*.

criminal law twice. Article 1 stipulates that breach of duty is to be understood in accordance with national law and Article 4, paragraph 3 refers to "necessary measures in accordance with its constitutional rules and principles". The reference to the assimilation principle in specific legal instruments as well as its general applicability in situations in which Member States are free to make their own choices of the mechanism to implement and enforce Union law, is conclusive to an interpretation that Union law obligations in criminal law should not go against the fundamental principles of the existing criminal justice systems.[584]

Upon the basis of the sources just given, as well as on the reluctance of Member States to accept systematic changes to their national criminal justice systems, it is evident that Union law does not require Member States to alter the fundamental characteristics of their criminal law, when implementing Union law. In this sense, national criminal law influences Union law. An exception to this general rule is the explicit changes that result from specific legal instruments, the most prominent example in substantive criminal law being the introduction of the criminal liability for legal entities.

General principles are part of Union law and national law

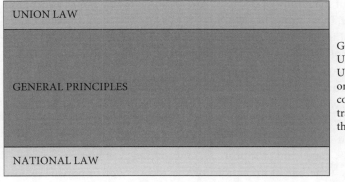

UNION LAW

GENERAL PRINCIPLES

General principles of Union law apply in Union law and originate from the constitutional traditions common to the Member States

NATIONAL LAW

2.   LEGISLATIVE COMPETENCES OF THE UNION IN CRIMINAL LAW

Article 83, paragraph 1 TFEU states that the Union may, by means of Directives, establish minimum rules concerning the definition of criminal offences and sanctions in the area of particularly serious crime with a cross-border dimension resulting from the nature or impact of such offences or from a special need to

---

[584]   The Joint Action 97/396 of 16 June 1997 concerning the information exchange, risk assessment and the control of new synthetic drugs, OJ 1997, L 167/1 is concerned with exchanging information regarding the risks of new drugs as soon as possible, which will enable Member States to list them as illegal.

combat them on a common basis. These areas of crime are the following: terrorism, trafficking in human beings and sexual exploitation of women and children, illicit drug trafficking, illicit arms trafficking, money laundering, corruption, counterfeiting of means of payment, computer crime and organised crime. Additionally, Decisions may be taken to add other crimes to the list. Article 83, paragraph 1 and 2 TFEU gives three reasons for the approximation of the criminal laws and regulations of the Member States, the first being the nature or impact of the offences, the second, the special need to combat the offences upon a common basis, the third being that approximation is essential to ensure the effective implementation of a Union policy in an area which has been subject to harmonisation measures. The latter category, expressed in Article 83, paragraph 2, constitutes what was previously called the First Pillar.

What Are Criminal Sanctions? What Is Criminal Law?

Because of the fact that the Union has competence to legislate in the field of criminal law, it is relevant to determine what the Union's definition of criminal law is. Is there a Union definition of *criminal law*?[585] Advocate General Mazák raised this issue in his opinion in Case C-440/05.[586] He identified that there is no uniform concept of the notion of criminal law, and took the ECHR as a common point of departure. In so doing, he referred to the case law of the European Court of Human Rights, in which the notion of a criminal charge has been given an autonomous interpretation. An important element of this definition is that a punitive element must be attached to the sanction.[587]

To date, the Court itself has not explicitly spoken on the issue, although there have been cases in which the criminal nature of proceedings was relevant. A case in point here is the *Meico-Fell* case.[588] This case dealt with the meaning of the words "an act that could give rise to criminal court proceedings" in Article 3 Regulation 1697/79, concerning the post-clearance recovery of import duties and export duties. The time-bar of an action for the recovery of import or export duties is excluded when it concerns "an act that could give rise to criminal court proceedings". The Court, therefore, had to answer the question of what the character of the underlying act actually was. Unlike Advocate General van

---

585   Advocate General Jacobs gave the following definition in his Opinion of 3 June 1992, Case C-240/90, *Germany* v. *Commission* [1992] ECR I-5383, point 11: "Typically, the purpose of a criminal sanction exceeds that of simple deterrence, and will normally involve such matters as the stigma of social disapproval or the attribution of moral blame. Thus, the amount of the penalty, in a criminal case, will often reflect the extent of society's disapproval of the conduct in question, rather than any more pragmatic consideration".

586   Opinion of Advocate General Mazák, 28 June 2007, Case C-440/05, *Commission* v. *Council* [2007] ECR I-9097, points 69–71.

587   See Chapter 1, Section 1, where it is explained that this book follows the ECtHR case law on the definition of criminal charge.

588   27 November 1991, Case C-273/90, *Meico-Fell* v. *Hauptzollamt Darmstadt* [1991] ECR I-5569.

Gerven, the Court circumvented the matter by referring to national criminal law:

> "It appears from the context in which that provision was adopted that the expression 'an act that could give rise to criminal court proceedings' means acts which, under the legal system of the Member State whose competent authorities are seeking post-clearance recovery of duties, may be classified as offence under national criminal law."[589]

The Court is aware of the fact that this may lead to different results among the Member States, but this is the consequence of the fact that "the classification of certain kinds of conduct for the purposes of criminal law is not harmonised and is, therefore, governed by national law".[590]

Advocate General van Gerven proposed in *Meico-Fell* that a Community definition of the term "criminal proceedings" be found.[591] His proposal was to implement the criteria formulated by the ECtHR in regard of the term "criminal charge" in Article 6 ECHR fully. This was not surprising, given the fact that the case in point concerned a German "*Ordnungswidrigkeit*", an administrative irregularity, a situation similar to the ECtHR landmark case of *Öztürk*. Van Gerven stated:

> "It is not the formal classification of the sanction which matters, or is of prime importance at least, but its nature and degree of gravity. (…) What does this mean specifically as far as the present case is concerned? In my view, the referring court may conclude that 'an act that could give rise to criminal court proceedings' exist first of all where the act in question is one which, under the applicable national law, is punished with a criminal sanction in the strict sense; and, secondly, where the act is one which infringes a general provision and under the applicable national law is punished with a sanction which is of such a deterrent or punitive character and/or characterised by such a degree of gravity that it must be regarded as being equivalent to a criminal penalty in the strict sense."[592]

---

[589] 27 November 1991, Case C-273/90, *Meico-Fell* v. *Hauptzollamt Darmstadt* [1991] ECR I-5569, par. 9. More recently, 18 December 2007, Case C-62/06, *Fazenda Pública – Director Geral das Alfândegas* v. *ZF Zefeser – Importação e Exportação de Produtos Alimentares Lda* [2007] ECR I-11995, par. 25–26.

[590] 27 November 1991, Case C-273/90, *Meico-Fell* v. *Hauptzollamt Darmstadt* [1991] ECR I-5569, par. 12.

[591] Opinion of Advocate General van Gerven of 26 September 1991, Case C-273/90, *Meico-Fell* v. *Hauptzollamt Darmstadt* [1991] ECR I-5569. The Opinion also sheds more light on the arguments brought forward by Meico-Fell and the Commission. The approach of van Gerven was followed 16 years later by Advocate General Trstenjak in an Opinion of 3 May 2007, Case C-62/06, *Fazenda Pública – Director Geral das Alfândegas* v. *ZF Zefeser – Importação e Exportação de Produtos Alimentares Lda* [2007] ECR I-11995, points 35–36 and 57.

[592] Opinion of Advocate General van Gerven of 26 September 1991, Case C-273/90, *Meico-Fell* v. *Hauptzollamt Darmstadt* [1991] ECR I-5569, point 10.

With both the new legislative competences of the Union and the supervisory mechanisms for Commission and Court in mind, it will, after the Treaty of Lisbon enters into force, no longer be possible to circumvent this question. If the obligation that derives from a Directive is to implement certain "criminal offences" and "criminal sanctions", then the criminal nature of these offences and sanctions are subject to the Court's assessment of whether a Member State has complied with its obligations under the Treaties. The accession of the European Union to the ECHR will entail the application of the *Öztürk* criteria. This could mean that some cases will be decided differently in the future than they were in the past. In the terrorist cases, the Court of First Instance held that the freezing of assets took place "as a precautionary measure", and that such "measures do not constitute criminal sanctions and do not, moreover, imply any accusation of a criminal nature".[593] In other cases, too, the Court held that the forfeiture of a deposit or security provided voluntarily by traders was not regarded as being of a criminal nature.[594] The accession of the Union may, in the future, have to lead to a revision of this case law. The Court and Court of First Instance (now renamed the General Court) have consistently applied the human rights enacted under the ECHR not only to the accused in criminal proceedings but also to defendant undertakings in competition proceedings.[595] The combination of the application of the ECHR criteria, the fact that the Union is bound by the ECHR, and the fact that Articles 82 and 83 TFEU force the Union legislature to be specific about what it considers to be "criminal law", will lead to the formal inclusion of competition law as criminal law.

Pre-Lisbon Competences

Despite the fact that the Treaty of Lisbon will create an indisputable competence for the Union in the field of criminal law, some reflections on the previous regime are relevant. Although all pre-Lisbon acts will come within the competences of the Commission and the Court, the standard to assess whether a Member State has complied with its obligations under Union law cannot be altered after the fact, and must be based upon the obligations applicable at the time that the Union act was adopted. The rest of this section will, therefore, follow the old pillar structure in discussing the competences of the Community and the Union, and the resulting obligations for the Member States.

---

[593]   Court of First Instance, 11 July 2007, T-47/03, *Sison v. Council* [2007] ECR II-2047, par. 101.

[594]   17 December 1970, Case 11–70, *Internationale Handelsgesellschaft mbH* v. *Einfuhr- und Vorratsstelle für Getreide und Futtermittel* [1970] ECR 1125; 18 November 1987, Case 137/85, *Gesellschaft mbH and others, Bundesanstalt für landwirtschaftliche Marktordnung (BALM)* [1987] ECR 4587.

[595]   However, this amounts to treatment of competition law *as* criminal law, without formally stating that it *is* criminal law.

First Pillar

In September 2005, a matter that had seemed to be clear for decades was revised by the Court.[596] From the early days of the European Communities, it had been clear that criminal law belonged to the exclusive competence of the Member States. The latter were bound by the obligation to enforce Community law,[597] but had freedom with regard to the choice of the national means. Although the Court had recognised that the Community had the power to impose the penalties necessary for the effective application of the rules in the sphere of the Common Agricultural Policy already in 1992,[598] it had never stated that the Community legislature could impose that these penalties be criminal penalties and nothing else.[599] Occasionally, some exceptions were voluntarily accepted by the Member States, such as in the case of money laundering and EC fraud,[600] but this formally kept the exclusivity of the area of criminal law to the Member States.

Article 325 TFEU (formerly Article 280 TEC) provides for a unique reference in the Treaty with regard to one specific crime: "fraud and any other illegal activities affecting the financial interests of the Union." In Article 325 TFEU, the Treaty creates a special obligation, on top of the obligation of sincere co-operation of Article 4, paragraph 3 TEU, to counter fraud. Member States will have to do this in the light of the assimilation principle (Article 325, paragraph 2 TFEU). Paragraph 3 of Article 325 TFEU gives the European Parliament and the Council the mandate to adopt the necessary measures in the fields of the prevention of, and the fight against, fraud.

In two cases of the Commission against the Council, decided in 2005 and 2007, the Court completely changed the perspective that the implementation into criminal law would not have to be obligatory. Both cases dealt with the question of whether the competence of the Community in a specific area (for example, C-176/03 and C-440/05) provided by the TEC limited the competence of the Council to legislate criminal law upon the basis of the EU. The Commission

---

[596] In hindsight, there are other instruments and decisions that provide the Community with powers in the field of criminal law. See, for instance, Regulation 2241/87 (replaced by *Regulation 2847/93 establishing a Control System applicable to the Common Fisheries Policy*) establishing certain control measures for fishing activities and 27 March 1990, Case C-9/89, in *Spain* v. *Council* [1990] ECR I-1383.

[597] The phrase "Community law" has been kept in this section because it is relevant for understanding.

[598] 27 October 1992, Case C-240/90, *Germany* v. *Commission* [1992] ECR I-5383, par. 11.

[599] Advocate General Jacobs in his Opinion of 3 June 1992, Case C-240/90, *Germany* v. *Commission* [1992] ECR I-5383, point 12, did recognise Community power to harmonise the criminal laws of the Member States.

[600] In 8 July 1999, Case C-186/98, *criminal proceedings against Maria Amélia Nunes and Evangelina de Matos* [1999] ECR I-4883, the accused were prosecuted for forgery and corruption in relation to improper use of financial assistance granted from the European Social Fund. The Court held "that Community legislation does not classify the improper use of ESF assistance as a criminal offence". (par. 8).

challenged the Council's competence to adopt Framework Decisions containing provisions of criminal law in these areas. The Court first looked at the twin provisions of Article 47 EU and Article 29 EU. The first stated that none of the provisions of the TEC may be affected by a provision of the EU, the second that it is the task of the Court to ensure that acts that fall within the scope of Title VI do not encroach upon Community powers.[601]

In Case C-176/03, the Court re-iterates that, in principle, criminal law belongs to the competence of the Member States:

> "As a general rule, neither criminal law nor the rules of criminal procedure fall within the Community's competence. (...) However, the last-mentioned finding does not prevent the Community legislature, when the application of effective, proportionate and dissuasive criminal penalties by the competent national authorities is an essential measure for combating serious environmental offences, from taking measures which relate to the criminal law of the Member States which it considers necessary in order to ensure that the rules which it lays down an environmental protection are fully effective."[602]

The concluding step is that the Court examines whether the provisions of the Framework Decision "could have been properly adopted" by a Directive.[603] For example, given that Article 80, paragraph 2 TEC does not lay down any explicit limitations, the Community has broad legislative powers with regard to the whole transport sector.

In Case C-440/05, the Court repeats that, as a general rule, neither criminal law, nor the rules of criminal procedure fall within the Community's competence.[604] However, it then stipulates a revolutionary criterion:

> "the fact remains that when the application of effective, proportionate and dissuasive criminal penalties by the competent national authorities is an essential measure for combating serious environmental offences, the Community legislature may require the Member States to introduce such penalties in order to ensure that the rules which it lays down in that field are fully effective."[605]

---

[601]   In 20 May 2008, C-91/05, *Commission* v. *Council* [2008] ECR not yet reported, the Court took a similar decision regarding measures taken under Title V of the Treaty on European Union, and annulled a Decision in the field of the Common Foreign and Security Policy dealing with the non-proliferation of small arms and light weapons.

[602]   13 September 2005, Case C-176/03, *Commission* v. *Council* [2005] ECR I-7879, par. 47 and 48.

[603]   13 September 2005, Case C-176/03, *Commission* v. *Council* [2005] ECR I-7879, par. 51; 23 October 2007, Case C-440/05, *Commission* v. *Council* [2007] ECR I-9097, par. 54.

[604]   The Advocate General held that for a broader competence in the field of criminal law a specific legal basis would be desirable. See Opinion of Advocate General Mazák, 28 June 2007, in Case C-440/05, *Commission* v. *Council* [2007] ECR I-9097, par. 122.

[605]   23 October 2007, Case C-440/05, *Commission* v. *Council* [2007] ECR I-9097, par. 66.

In Case C-440/05, the Court further held that the "choice of the legal basis for a Community measure must rest on objective factors which are amenable to judicial review, including, in particular, the aim and the content of the measure".[606] This phrase relates to the principle of subsidiarity.

Several important questions arise. Which areas fall within the competence of the Community? This is important to know because the Community may have competence in the field of criminal law with regard to various topics.[607] In theory, under the influence of the new case law, all policy areas in which the Community has competence qualify for criminal legislation. However, given the fact that there is an impressive *acquis* of legislation in these areas, a justification for the need of further enforcement powers by means of criminal law may amount to proving why criminal law, as the last resort, would be able enforce what measures of another nature could not achieve. This comes down to a classical principle of criminal law, which affirms that, from the state perspective, criminal law is the last resort, the *ultimum remedium*, to make use of, when confronted with undesirable conduct. This would be in compliance with other case law in which the Court has stipulated that even in cases in which there is an obligation for Member States to enforce Community law, enforcement by means of criminal law is disproportional.[608] Proportionality has always been an overriding criterion in Union law. Harsher penalties may be used for more serious violations. Case law on the entitlement to aid provides cases that may be illustrating. There, the Court has consistently held "that the infringement of obligations whose observance is of fundamental importance to the proper functioning of a Community system may be penalized by forfeiture of a right conferred by Community legislation, such as entitlement to aid."[609]

A follow-up question then relates to the extent of this competence. Is this limited to the determination of the prohibited conduct, or does it also extend to determining the sanction that should be attached to it? The Court held that the competence of the Community to legislate in the field of criminal law is not unlimited. The determination of *the type and level of the criminal penalties* does not fall within the Community's sphere of competence.[610] This means that the competence is limited to defining criminal conduct and the mere indication that

---

[606]   23 October 2007, Case C-440/05, *Commission* v. *Council* [2007] ECR I-9097, par. 61.

[607]   The Commission proposed a Directive on criminal measures aimed at ensuring the enforcement of intellectual property rights, COM(2006) 168 final.

[608]   29 February 1996, Case C-193/94, *criminal proceedings against Sofia Skanavi and Konstantin Chryssanthakopoulos* [1996] ECR I-929.

[609]   See amongst other judgments: 12 October 1995, Case C-104/94, *Cereol Italia Srl* v. *Azienda Agricola Castello Sas.* [1995] ECR I-2983, par. 25.

[610]   23 October 2007, Case C-440/05, *Commission* v. *Council* [2007] ECR I-9097, par. 70. The Court follows the Advocate General here. See Opinion of Advocate General Mazák of 28 June 2007, Case C-440/05, *Commission* v. *Council* [2007] ECR I-9097, par. 111–112. That is different in competition law. There, the Treaty provides for sanctions (Articles 101–106 TFEU).

criminal sanctions should be provided. It would then be for the Member State to decide what sanction modality (imprisonment, fine, confiscation, *etc.*) it regards as the appropriate means, and with which intensity (duration of the penalty, level of the fine, *etc.*) they would impose the sanction on those convicted. The limitations formulated in this way will enable Member States to maintain the fundamental character of their criminal justice system. All other areas of substantive criminal and criminal procedure, such as the general part, the admissibility of evidence and fair trial rules, are not mentioned in this exclusion. Clearly, once again, the discretion of the Member States with regard to type and level of sanction is influenced by the general *Greek maize* criteria.

When is the use of criminal law necessary? The criterion of *necessity* raises many questions. How does the Court determine whether criminal penalties are fully effective?[611] What is the standard for fully effective? Is the question of whether an instrument complies with the necessity requirement subject to judicial review in a criminal trial?[612] Is the lack of necessity something that affects the legality of the legal instrument? With regard to effectiveness, Advocate General Mazák referred implicitly to the necessity of obtaining criminological insights: "It may be too simple to assume that criminal law is always the appropriate remedy for lack of effectiveness."[613] Accordingly, in Case C-440/05, the Court relied on the opinion of the Council with regard to the necessity of the use of criminal sanctions. The reasoning is, then, as follows: since the Council, which has direct competence in the field of the harmonisation of criminal law, took the decision in the Framework Decision that criminal sanctions are necessary, this is evidence of their necessity, as required under the necessity test. Thus, the Community was *entitled* to take these measures, because the sanctions *related* to an area in which the Community was competent. For the future, it may be expected that necessity will not simply derive from the intention of the Council and that a more materially-defined criterion will be developed.

Article 280 TEC provided the basis for the instruction that the Member States should take measures to combat fraud affecting the financial interests of the Community. This directly codified the principle of assimilation as formulated in

---

611   Did the Court intend to formulate a criterion similar to the statement of reasons, required by Article 235 TEC with regard to Directives, Regulations and Decisions?

612   In the slightly different context of the Common Agricultural Policy, the Court has held that the principle of legal certainty does not require "any measure adopted by the Community institutions to be founded on a rational and objective basis, judicial review must, (...) be limited to examining whether the measure in question is vitiated by a manifest error or misuse of powers, or whether the authority in question has manifestly exceeded the limits of its discretion." 13 November 1990, Case C-331/88, *The Queen* v. *Minister of Agriculture, Fisheries and Food and Secretary of State for Health, ex parte: Fedesa and others* [1990] ECR I-4023, par. 8. If this is the line of argumentation, the necessity requirement is quite easily fulfilled.

613   28 June 2007, Opinion of Advocate General Mazák, 23 October 2007, Case C-440/05, *Commission* v. *Council* [2007] ECR I-9097, par. 117.

the case law in the TEC. The measures should be based upon existing national measures.[614] However, paragraph 4 of Article 280 states that measures adopted by the Council are not to concern the application of national criminal law or the national administration of justice. Following up on the reasoning that the Court gave in Case C-440/05, this had the rather strange consequence that, in an area in which all the Member States had national criminal law legislation to combat violation of Community law (EC fraud), no competence would exist. However, the conclusion, that it was decisive whether legislative competence in the field of criminal law was excluded, finds support in the annulment of the Agreement with the United States on passenger name records by the Court. In this case, *Directive 95/46 on Data Protection* denied the Commission the competence to conclude agreements that aim at combating specific forms of crime with third states.[615]

Third Pillar

Although Articles 30 and 31 EU place all acts in the context of police co-operation and judicial co-operation in criminal matters, it has, in practice, been quite easy to establish such a link. Regardless of whether the principle aim of the drafters of the legal act was to facilitate co-operation or the harmonisation of national criminal law, an obligation concerning the definitions of offences will always have effects on co-operation. The Council has not followed a narrow interpretation of its competences in the area of freedom, security and justice. The same goes for the choice of the legal instrument. It is remarkable that, since the principle of mutual recognition was introduced in the legislation on co-operation in criminal matters, there have been fewer initiatives to harmonise or approximate substantive criminal law. However, this is logical from the perspective that mutual recognition can do without the harmonisation of substantive criminal law.

Although Article 34, paragraph 2 (c) EU allows for the adoption of Decisions for any other purpose than the approximation of the law and regulation of the Member States, some Decisions, nevertheless, clearly aim at approximation. One example of such an instrument is the *Decision 2000/375 on Internet Pornography*, which contains a number of obligations to criminalise certain conduct.

The Court, for its part, has certainly stimulated a quite liberal interpretation of the powers of the Union in the Third Pillar. Here, it is relevant to look at what Advocate General Kokott expressed in her Opinion of the *Pupino* case:

"The fields of common action expressly listed are not exhaustive, however, a fact which is most clearly apparent in the French version of the introductory sentence. Instead of 'shall include', in Article 31 EU the latter uses the phrase '*vise entre autres*'. The

---

[614] 21 September 1989, Case 68/88, *Commission* v. *Greece* [1989] ECR 2965.
[615] 30 May 2006, Case C-317/04, *European Parliament and European Data Protection Service (EDPS)* v. *Council, and European Parliament* v. *Commission* [2006] ECR I-4721.

individual policy fields therefore describe only potential legislative spheres, without thereby strictly delimiting the competence of the Union. That competence is to be determined in the light of the general objectives of police and judicial cooperation in criminal matters, as they are laid down in Article 29 EU. The principal objective under that article is to provide citizens with a high level of safety within an area of freedom, security and justice through, in particular, improved judicial co-operation."[616]

Before the Court gave the Community legislative powers in the field of criminal law in 2005, the lack of these criminal competences was compensated by using the so-called cross-reference technique, by which the prohibited conduct is found in one instrument (Directive) and the criminalisation of this conduct in another (Convention or Framework Decision). However, there are a few examples of this practice. Article 1 *Framework Decision 2002/946 on Unauthorised Entry* obliges Member States to provide for criminal penalties for infringements defined in Articles 1 and 2 of *Directive 2002/90 on Unauthorised Entry*. The rationale of this technique must be found in an attempt to combine the "best of both worlds". The Directive brings in the obligation to enforce, whereas the Framework Decision imposes the obligation to criminalise.[617] With the acceptance by the Court and the Treaty of Lisbon that a Directive may carry the obligation to use criminal penalties, this technique is no longer of further practical relevance.[618]

3.   GENERAL PART FRAGMENTS

Apart from the field of competition law, and before the European Public Prosecutor's Office becomes operative, there is no direct enforcement in the field of European criminal law, yet. However, this does not mean that Union law (both codified law and case law) does not stipulate rules that are applicable for criminal law. In this section, the rules on substantive criminal law will be deduced from the legal instruments already adopted by the Union, as well as from the limited number of Court cases rendered to date. The acts of the European Union contain elements of what belongs to the general part of criminal law in all criminal justice systems. However, since there has been no systematic thinking on this at Union level, there are a lot of *lacunae* and loose ends.

Despite its incompleteness, the visible fragments tell us something about what the Union regards as an offender, and how it sees complicity in an offence, as well

---

[616]   Opinion of Advocate General Kokott of 11 November 2004, Case C-105/03, *criminal proceedings against Maria Pupino* [2005] ECR I-5285, point 50.

[617]   Other examples include money laundering, EC fraud, unauthorised entry, environmental protection and ship-source pollution.

[618]   13 September 2005, Case C-176/03, *Commission v. Council* [2005] ECR I-7879; 23 October 2007, Case C-440/05, *Commission v. Council* [2007] ECR I-9097.

as what the definition of a criminal offence should look like. Although both the general part and the special part are fragmentary, they are growing by the day. Regardless of whether one day there will be direct criminal enforcement power for the European Union, the increasing influence of the criminal legislation of the European Union on national criminal law needs to be sketched into the structure of a criminal justice system. The very fact that both the European Union in its legislation, and the Court in its case law, respect the classical distinction between the general part and the special part is supportive to this approach.

The way in which the Union has legislated (from issue to issue) may raise some doubts as to the general part character of certain provisions. Each Joint Action or Framework Decision produces its own general part provisions with regard to a specific crime. Sometimes, these provisions on the general part are formulated in identical wording as the previous ones, while other provisions are unique and do not appear again. This raises the question of whether one can regard these provisions as being meant to be of a general nature. However, as in common law, the general part of European criminal law has not been codified, but is developed in practice, despite the fact that, occasionally, as a corollary to incidental legislation on individual offences, something of a general principle has been codified. It is for the judiciary to shape the system.

3.1. LEGALITY

Like all criminal justice systems governed by the rule of law, the legality principle is an inherent and key element under Union law. It has been recognised both in case law and in codification. It has the status of general principle of Union law. The legality principle was formulated in Article 49 Charter,[619] from which the following elements can be deduced: the classical safeguard of *nullum crimen sine lege* and *nulla poena sine lege*, the prohibition of retroactivity, the application of the *lex mitior* rule, the Nuremberg exception, and the requirement of proportional sentencing.

Starting in very early case law, the Court recognised the legality principle under various names. The Court referred to this principle as the principle that

---

[619] "1. No one shall be held guilty of any criminal offence on account of any act or omission which did not constitute a criminal offence under national law or international law at the time when it was committed. Nor shall a heavier penalty be imposed than that which was committed. If, subsequent to the commission of a criminal offence, the law provides for a lighter penalty, that penalty shall be applicable. 2. This Article shall not prejudice the trial and punishment of any person for any act or omission which, at the time when it was committed, was criminal according to the general principles recognised by the community of nations. 3. The severity of penalties must not be disproportionate to the criminal offence".

penalties must have a proper legal basis.[620] In *Kolpinghuis*, the Court stipulated that criminal liability cannot be based directly upon a Directive. Criminal liability for violations of Union law always requires implementation into national criminal law. In this sense, Union law is dependent on national law. The fact that Directives in criminal law require implementation into national law is fully in line with the legality principle thus formulated (Articles 83, 288 and 291 TFEU). The necessity of national implementation is not limited only to implementing legislation. The obligation to interpret in conformity with a Directive may not determine or aggravate criminal liability.[621] Thus, in *Milchwerke Köln*, the Court stated:

> "Notwithstanding the need to combat fraudulent transactions, a penalty consisting in the substitution of the purchaser for the producer pre-supposes the existence of a legal basis laying down the conditions for, and the scope of, that penalty."[622]

The same goes for obligations that result from a Framework Decision. Independently of an implementing law, they may neither determine nor aggravate criminal liability.[623]

In addition, a Regulation may not be the sole basis for criminal responsibility. The effects of a Regulation do not differ from those of the Directive in this respect. The national court is bound by an interpretation of the national law that is compatible with the Regulation.[624] If such a compatible interpretation is possible, the national court must do so. However, like the Directive,[625] a Regulation cannot, of itself and independently of implementing national law, determine or aggravate criminal liability.[626] In view of the differences between the two instruments, this is extraordinary, because, as the Court finds, a Regulation, by its very nature, does not require implementation. This exception can only be explained by the nature of criminal law,[627] as well as by the distinction of the legal effects of Directives and of Regulations that the Court wishes to uphold.

---

[620]   11 November 2004, Case C-457/02, *criminal proceedings against Antonio Niselli* [2004] ECR I-10853, par. 30.

[621]   12 December 1996, Joined Cases C-74/95 and C-129/95, *criminal proceedings against X* [1996] ECR I-6609, par. 24; 22 November 2005, Case C-384/02, *criminal proceedings against Knud Grøngaard and Allan Barg* [2005] ECR I-9939, par. 30.

[622]   14 July 1994, Case C-352/92, *Milchwerke Köln/Wuppertal eG v. Hauptzollamt Köln-Rheinau* [1994] ECR I-3385, par. 22.

[623]   16 June 2005, Case C-105/03, *criminal proceedings against Maria Pupino* [2005] ECR I-5285, par. 45.

[624]   7 January 2004, Case C-60/02, *criminal proceedings against X* [2004] ECR I-651, par. 59–63.

[625]   11 June 1987, Case 14/86, *Pretore di Salò v. Persons unknown* [1987] ECR 3969, par. 18; 26 September 1996, Case C-168/95, *criminal proceedings against Luciano Arcaro* [1996] ECR I-4705, par. 37 and 42.

[626]   7 January 2004, Case C-60/02, *criminal proceedings against X* [2004] ECR I-651, par. 60–62.

[627]   Article 2, paragraph 2 *Regulation 2988/95 on Protection of the Financial Interests* applies the legality principle also to administrative penalties.

Whereas an interpretation by analogy is prohibited, the *nullum crimen, nulla poena sine lege* principle does not prohibit "the gradual clarification of the rules of criminal liability".[628] With regard to the discretion of interpretation of what the offence is, the Court carefully follows the ECtHR case law in which the foreseeability is emphasised.[629] With regard to a provision of national criminal law that implemented a Directive on medicinal products, the ECtHR held that the categorisation of certain products as such was not a violation of Article 7 ECHR. It went on to admit that:

"... there will often be grey areas at the fringes of the definition. This penumbra of doubt in relation to borderline facts does not, in itself, make a provision incompatible with Article 7, provided that it proves to be sufficiently clear in the large majority of cases. The role of adjudication vested in the courts is precisely to dissipate such interpretational doubts as remain, taking into account the changes in everyday practice."[630]

Depending on their professional activity, individuals may have to proceed with a high degree of caution.[631] The Court held that the principle of legality is satisfied "where the individual can know from the wording of the relevant provision and, if need be, with the assistance of the courts' interpretation of it, what acts and omissions will make him criminally liable".[632]

The emphasis on *foreseeability*, makes it clear that the legality principle entails the element of *lex certa*. In criminal proceedings against *X*, the Court considered:

"the principle that a provision of the criminal law may not be interpreted extensively to the detriment of the defendant, which is the corollary of the principle of legality in

---

[628] 28 June 2005, Joined Cases C-189/02 P, C-202/02 P, C-205/02 P to C-208/02 P and C-213/02 P, *Dansk Rørindustri and Others* v. *Commission* [2005] ECR I-5425, par. 217.

[629] See ECtHR, 15 November 1996, *Cantoni* v. *France*, Application 17862/91. Foreseeability comes close to the common law notion of fair warning. See, also, 7 June 2007, Case C-76/06 P, *Britannia Alloys & Chemicals Ltd* v. *Commission* [2007] ECR I-4405, in which the Court adhered to the requirement of foreseeability. Advocate General Bot in his Opinion of 1 March 2007 in this case explicitly discussed the requirements of Article 7 ECHR.

[630] See ECtHR, 15 November 1996, *Cantoni* v. *France*, Application 17862/91, par. 32. The ECtHR cited a number of cases of the Court among which was 30 November 1983, Case 227/82, *criminal proceedings against Leendert van Bennekom* [1983] ECR 3883, in which the Court interpreted terms of the Directive. The ECtHR did not find a violation of Article 7 ECHR in the *Cantoni* case.

[631] 28 June 2005, Joined Cases C-189/02 P, C-202/02 P, C-205/02 P to C-208/02 P and C-213/02 P, *Dansk Rørindustri and Others* v. *Commission* [2005] ECR I-5425, par. 219.

[632] 3 June 2008, Case C-308/06, *The Queen on the application of: International Association of Independent Tanker Owners (Intertanko), International Association of Dry Cargo Ship owners (Intercargo), Greek Shipping Co-operation Committee, Lloyd's Register, International Salvage Union,* v. *Secretary of State for Transport* [2008] ECR, not yet reported, par. 71.

relation to crime and punishment and more generally of the principle of legal certainty precludes bringing criminal proceedings in respect of conduct not clearly defined as culpable in law."[633]

Thus, legal certainty is the broader concept, and legality and the prohibition of analogous interpretation must be regarded as sub-categories.

Union law adheres to the requirement of a penal provision in written national law. This becomes clear in the case law, which requires implementation into national law.[634] There is no indication at all in the case law that common law jurisdictions can escape the requirement of written penal provisions when implementing Union law. Advocate General Ruiz-Jarabo Colomer further distinguishes the *lex previa* and *lex certa* elements,[635] while Advocate General Kokott stated that:

> "This principle, which also prohibits interpreting criminal provisions broadly where that is to the disadvantage of the persons concerned, sets strict limits on interpreting provisions in conformity with a directive in criminal proceedings."[636]

However, the legality principle does not, in itself, require a specific interpretation of a Directive.[637] The Court confirmed this by stating that the criminal nature of the proceedings and the legality principle do not affect the strict interpretation:

> "The interpretation of a directive's scope cannot be dependent upon the civil, administrative or criminal nature of the proceedings in which it is invoked."[638]

---

[633] 12 December 1996, Joined Cases C-74/95 and C-129/95, *criminal proceedings against X* [1996] ECR I-6609, par. 25.

[634] The Court held that, outside the criminal sphere, a Community measure may exceptionally take effect from a point in time before its publication. Two conditions were raised in this respect: "where the purpose to be achieved so demands and where the legitimate expectations of those concerned are duly respected". 11 July 1991, Case C-368/89, *Antonio Crispoltoni* v. *Fattoria autonoma tabacchi di Città di Castelo* [1991] ECR I-3695, par. 17; 13 November 1990, Case C-331/88, *The Queen* v. *Minister of Agriculture, Fisheries and Food and Secretary of State for Health, ex parte: Fedesa and others* [1990] ECR I-4023, par. 45.

[635] Opinion of 18 June 1996, Joined Cases C-74/95 and C-129/95, *criminal proceedings against X* [1996] ECR I-6609, point 57.

[636] Opinion of Advocate General Kokott of 10 June 2004, Case C-457/02, *criminal proceedings against Antonio Niselli* [2004] ECR I-10853, point 54.

[637] Opinion of Advocate General Poiares Maduro of 24 May 2004, Case C-384/02, *criminal proceedings against Knud Grøngaard and Allan Barg* [2005] ECR I-9939, point 24.

[638] 22 November 2005, Case C-384/02, *criminal proceedings against Knud Grøngaard and Allan Barg* [2005] ECR I-9939, par. 28.

It is for the national court in interpreting the law to assess the compliance with the principle of legal certainty.[639] From this, it can be concluded that it is the national implementing criminal law which must comply with all the requirements of the principle, not the Union act that imposes the obligation to implement.

If a legal act is not available in the language version of the Member State, it cannot be held against an individual until the date in which the issue of the Official Journal was actually available.[640] In general, Union law is applicable from the moment that its text is available. Presumably, this is from the day the Official Journal was issued.[641] The case law on this point relates to hard copies of the Official Journal. When given the opportunity to answer the question of whether on-line publication counts as well, the Court did recognise that most users consult the EUR-Lex internet site. However, it re-iterated that the only version of Union law which is authentic is that which is published in the Official Journal of the European Union.[642] In its judgments, the Court has held that a condition cannot be relied on against economic operators, whether for purposes of criminal penalties or in civil proceedings, when it was not brought to their attention by adequate publicity in Union legislation.[643] In competition law, it has been accepted that the Commission may raise the level of fines. The Court considered this to be foreseeable,[644] and the Commission enjoys a wide discretion in setting fines.[645] The legal basis to impose fines is Article 23 Regulation 1/2003 (formerly Article 15, paragraph 2 of Regulation 17/62). The Guidelines of the Commission are not the legal basis for setting the amount of the fine, but merely clarify the application of the penalty provision of the competition Regulation.[646] In exercising their jurisdiction, both the Court of First Instance and the Court of Justice have the

---

[639]   22 November 2005, Case C-384/02, *criminal proceedings against Knud Grøngaard and Allan Barg* [2005] ECR I-9939, par. 29.

[640]   26 November 1998, Case C-370/96, *Covita AVE v. Elliniko Dimosio* [1998] ECR I-7711, par. 27; 8 November 2001, Case C-228/99, *Silos e Mangimi Martini SpA v. Ministero delle Finanze* [2001] ECR I-8401, par. 15–16; 25 January 1979, Case 98/78, *A. Racke v. Hauptzollamt Mainz* [1979] ECR 69, par. 15–17.

[641]   25 January 1979, Case 98/78, *A. Racke v. Hauptzollamt Mainz* [1979] ECR 69. In 31 March 1977, Case 88–76, *Société pour l'exportation des sucres SA v. Commission* [1977] ECR 709, it was published and distributed later because of a strike.

[642]   11 December 2007, Case C-161/06, *Skoma-Lux sro v. Celní ředitelství Olomouc* [2007] ECR I-10841.

[643]   20 May 2003, Case C-108/01, *Consorzio del Prosciutto di Parma and Salumificio S. Rita SpA v. Asda Stores and Hygrade Foods Ltd* [2003] ECR I-5121, par. 96–99.

[644]   28 June 2005, Joined Cases C-189/02 P, C-202/02 P, C-205/02 P to C-208/02 P and C-213/02 P, *Dansk Rørindustri and Others v. Commission* [2005] ECR I-5425, par. 232.

[645]   28 June 2005, Joined Cases C-189/02 P, C-202/02 P, C-205/02 P to C-208/02 P and C-213/02 P, *Dansk Rørindustri and Others v. Commission* [2005] ECR I-5425, par. 336. See, also, 7 June 1983, Joined Cases 100 to 103/80, *SA Musique Diffusion française and others v. Commission* [1983] ECR 1825, par. 105–108. 8 February 2007, Case C-3/06 P, *Groupe Danone* [2007] ECR I-1331, par. 90–92.

[646]   For example, 8 February 2007, Case C-3/06 P, *Groupe Danone* [2007] ECR I-1331, par. 28.

competence to cancel, reduce or increase the fine or penalty imposed by the Commission.[647] In other words, there is no maximum penalty in competition cases.[648] In *Ebony Maritime*, the Court held that the principle of *nulla poena sine culpa* did not require that the penalty for an infringement be specifically provided for in the Regulation.[649]

The conclusion that the legality principle, as understood in Union law, does not require that the penalty attached to an offence be provided, is relevant. Especially with regard to some *euro-crimes* the question that arises is whether their formulation is in compliance with the requirements of the legality principle. Other examples relate to a rather broad description of the criminalised conduct. Paragraphs 2 of both Article 2 and Article 3 *Joint Action 98/742 on Corruption in the Private Sector*, require the criminalisation of "such conduct which involves, or could involve, the distortion of competition, as a minimum within the common market, and which results, or might result, in economic damage to others by the improper award or improper execution of a contract". In particular, the element of "could involve distortion" has a highly speculative character and is far away from a clear description of the prohibited conduct. With effect from 31 July 2003, the Joint Action was replaced by a *Framework Decision 2003/568 on Corruption in the Private Sector*. Article 2, paragraph 3 of that Framework Decision does not seem to repair the objection mentioned with regard to the Joint Action: "A Member State may declare that it will limit the scope of paragraph 1 to such conduct which involves, or could involve, a distortion of competition in relation to the purchase of goods or commercial activities." These provisions make it extremely difficult for Member States to comply both with the legality principle and with their enforcement obligations.[650] It is questionable as to whether the somewhat vaguely phrased Article 1 *Common Position 2001/930 on Combating Terrorism* complies with the legality principle.[651] However, it will have its practical application not in prosecutions, but in freezing measures.

---

[647]   15 October 2001, Joined Cases C-238/99 P, C-244/99 P, C-245/99 P, C-247/99 P, C-250/99 P to C-252/99 P and C-254/99 P, *Limburgse Vinyl Maatschappij NV (LVM) (C-238/99 P), DSM NV and DSM Kunststoffen BV (C-244/99 P), Montedison SpA (C-245/99 P), Elf Atochem SA (C-247/99 P), Degussa AG (C-250/99 P), Enichem SpA (C-251/99 P), Wacker-Chemie GmbH and Hoechst AG (C-252/99 P) and Imperial Chemical Industries plc (ICI) (C-254/99 P)* v. *Commission* [2002] ECR I-8375.

[648]   See, further, Chapter 6, Section 3.

[649]   27 February 1997, Case C-177/95, *Ebony Maritime SA and Loten Navigator Co. Ltd* v. *Prefetto della Provincia di Brindisi and others* [1997] ECR I-1111, par. 35.

[650]   The only consequence of such an impossibility can be annulment of the relevant Union act, because the act requires Member States to violate a general principle of law when implementing the instrument.

[651]   "The *wilful* provision or collection, by any means, directly or indirectly, of funds by citizens or within the territory of each of the Member States of the European Union *with the intention* that the funds should be used, or *in the knowledge* that they are to be used, in order to carry out terrorist acts shall be criminalized." See Section 4.5 of this chapter.

The legality principle does not require double criminality in co-operation between the Member States. The abolition of the double criminality requirement in the so-called list of offences for which surrender between the Member States may take place does not infringe upon the principle of legality.[652] The Court's reasoning in *Advocaten voor de Wereld* is sound because the abolition of the double criminality requirement does not affect the legality. Alleged criminal liability will be based upon the applicable law of the Member State issuing the European Arrest Warrant.

Lex Mitior

In the *Berlusconi* case, the accused was charged that he had, between 1986 and 1989, drawn up false documents relating to the annual accounts of the company *Fininvest SpA* and of other companies in the group of that name in his capacity as chairman of *Fininvest* and reference shareholder in the companies belonging to this group. These false documents, it was claimed, had made it possible to increase hidden reserves earmarked for the financing of certain allegedly unlawful transactions.[653]

At the time of the commission of the offences, Article 2621 of the Italian Civil Code stipulated that the false notification and unlawful distribution of profits or dividends could be punished as a criminal offence and provided a term of imprisonment between one to five years and a fine between 1,032 Euro to 10,329 Euro. With effect of 16 April 2002, the relevant provisions of the Civil Code were amended by Legislative Decree 61/2002.[654] Both the penalty provided was reduced and the liability of both the managers and directors was formulated in a less strict manner. In addition, prosecution for the crimes was made conditional to the presence of a complaint. Before the amendment in 2002, the Italian legislation on company law was in compliance with the then applicable Directives on the annual accounts of companies. After the amendment, it was no longer in compliance with the Directives.

In the proceedings before the Court, the Commission argued that, given the fact that the national criminal law applicable at the time of the offences was in compliance with Union law, and with the obligation of the Member States to maintain this compliance, the effects of the national legislation applicable at the

---

[652] 3 May 2007, Case C-303/05, *Advocaten voor de Wereld VZW v. Leden van de Ministerraad* [2007] ECR I-3633, par. 54.

[653] 3 May 2005, C-387/02, C-391/02 and C-403/02, *criminal proceedings against Silvio Berlusconi (C-387/02), Sergio Adelchi (C-391/02), Marcello Dell'Utri and others (C-403/02)* [2005] ECR I-3565.

[654] At the time of the amendment, Silvio Berlusconi was prime minister of Italy. From 10 May 1994 – 17 January 1995, 11 June 2001 – 17 May 2006 and again since 8 May 2008. A circumstance that clearly lay at the basis of the reference. However, it was not mentioned by the referring national court, the Court, the Advocate General or any of the Member States in the proceedings before the Court.

time should be maintained.[655] The Court, however, did not follow the Commission in this and applied the general principles of Union law: "The principle of the retroactive application of the more lenient penalty forms part of the constitutional traditions common to the Member States."[656] With reference to its decision in *Kolpinghuis*, the Court held that:

> "… in a situation such as that in issue in the main proceedings, the First Companies Directive cannot be relied on as such against the accused persons by the authorities of a Member State within the context of criminal proceedings, in view of the fact that a directive cannot, of itself and independently of national legislation adopted by a Member State for its implementation, have the effect of determining or increasing the criminal liability of those accused persons."[657]

What, for instance, does the application of *lex mitior* mean for the fundamental freedoms which became effective for the new states with their accession to the European Union in 2004? Polish or Latvian workers without a national working permit could be punished before the accession of their states to the European Union. If such a case is still pending after accession, does this mean that the more favourable legislation (*i.e.*, full freedom) must be applied? *Skanavi* offers the answer to this question. The facts of the *Skanavi* case occurred three days before the Treaty of Maastricht entered into force, which stipulated the right of free movement in its Article 8A for the first time. The Court held:

> "The question submitted by the national court concerns the interpretation of the provisions of the EC Treaty, although the facts material to the main proceedings occurred on 28 October 1993, that is to say, three days before the Treaty on European Union entered into force. Although Article 6 of the EC Treaty substantially reproduces Article 7 of the EEC Treaty and Article 52 was not amended by the Treaty on European Union, Article 8a is a new provision which, in the view of the national court, may preclude application of the national rules at issue in the criminal proceedings which have been brought before it. It thus appears that the national court could apply the principle, recognized by its national law, that the more favourable rule of criminal law

---

655   3 May 2005, C-387/02, C-391/02 and C-403/02, *criminal proceedings against Silvio Berlusconi (C-387/02), Sergio Adelchi (C-391/02), Marcello Dell'Utri and others (C-403/02)* [2005] ECR I-3565, par. 49–50.

656   3 May 2005, C-387/02, C-391/02 and C-403/02, *criminal proceedings against Silvio Berlusconi (C-387/02), Sergio Adelchi (C-391/02), Marcello Dell'Utri and others (C-403/02)* [2005] ECR I-3565, par. 68.

657   3 May 2005, C-387/02, C-391/02 and C-403/02, *criminal proceedings against Silvio Berlusconi (C-387/02), Sergio Adelchi (C-391/02), Marcello Dell'Utri and others (C-403/02)* [2005] ECR I-3565, par. 78.

should take retroactive effect and, consequently, set aside national law to the extent to which it is contrary to the provisions of the Treaty."[658]

It follows from *Berlusconi*, that, even in cases in which the criminal law applicable at the time of the offences was in compliance with Union law, national law may not be applied if there was a subsequent change of the national legislation which was more favourable to the accused.[659] Advocate General Kokott presented – both in *Berlusconi* as in *Niselli* – an argumentation that goes contrary to what the Court later decided in *Berlusconi*:

> "There is therefore no reason for giving an individual the retroactive benefit of a change in the national legislature's opinion which runs counter to the unchanged prescriptions of Community law. On the contrary, the coherency of the legal system requires that Community law should be observed, since it has priority of application."[660]

The Court did not follow her opinion that Union law could require, even in situations as in the case at hand, the setting aside of national law that did not comply with Union law. Whilst, in general, the reasoning of the Court must be followed, the question must be raised as to whether the personal union of the principal accused and the premier may not lead to a different interpretation. If the accused himself brings about the change of law, one may doubt the objectiveness of the national legislature. Does not such an extraordinary situation fall under the Nuremberg exception, as formulated in Article 7, paragraph 2 ECHR?[661]

Notification of Draft National Legislation

While the *Berlusconi* case relates to the legality aspects of amendments to national criminal law that lead to a situation in which a Member State is no longer in compliance with Union law, notification requirements are more of a formal nature. Some Directives oblige states to notify the Commission of any draft

---

[658] 29 February 1996, Case C-193/94, *criminal proceedings against Sofia Skanavi and Konstantin Chryssanthakopoulos* [1996] ECR I-929, par. 16–17.

[659] In Muliez and others the Court repeated this view. See 4 May 2006, C-23/03, C-52/03, C-133/03, C-337/03 en C-473/03, *criminal proceedings against Michel Mulliez and others and Giuseppe Momblano (Joined Cases C-23/03 and C-52/03), Alessandro Nizza and Giacomo Pizzi (C-133/03), Fabrizio Barra (C-337/03), Adelio Aggio and Others (C-473/03)* [2006] ECR I-3923.

[660] Opinion of Advocate General Kokott of 10 June 2004, Case C-457/02, *criminal proceedings against Antonio Niselli* [2004] ECR I-10853, point 72. In other words, but with similar meaning Opinion of Advocate General Kokott of 14 October 2004, C-387/02, C-391/02 and C-403/02, *criminal proceedings against Silvio Berlusconi (C-387/02), Sergio Adelchi (C-391/02), Marcello Dell'Utri and others (C-403/02)* [2005] ECR I-3565, points 132–138 and 162.

[661] "This Article shall not prejudice the trial and punishment of any act or omission which, at the time it was committed, was criminal according to the general principles of law recognised by civilised nations".

legislation that falls within the scope of a Directive. This relates to Directives in which Member States may use their power to enact further legislation after the Directive has entered into force.[662] However, this national legislation may not be contrary to the Directive. The notification mechanism serves as a practical tool to deal with this issue. If a Member State notifies its draft to the Commission and the Commission does not object, the Member State may adopt its legislation. An important example of such a Directive is *Directive 83/189 on Technical Standards*,[663] and Commission Directive 88/301 of 16 May 1988 on Competition in the Market in Telecommunications Terminal Equipment. These Directives allow Member States to take further implementing measures.

What is the influence of the obligation for the Member States to notify certain draft legislation on the application of criminal law? The Court has held that a breach of this obligation to notify constitutes a substantial procedural defect, which makes the technical regulation inapplicable and thus unenforceable against individuals.[664] The accused in national criminal trials can directly invoke the notification Directive. In the context of criminal proceedings, the first issue is to determine whether the national legislation concerns a "technical regulation",[665] while the second is to determine against whom this technical regulation is addressed. Or, in other words, was the accused one of the addressees of the norm (technical regulation)? If the answer is "yes", then, the accused may not be convicted. In *CIA Security*, the Court held that a rule is classified as a technical regulation for the purposes of *Directive 83/189 on Technical Standards* if it has legal effects of its own.[666]

---

662   This special notification obligation must be distinguished from the regular obligation applicable in the process of implementation. Member States are then under the obligation to notify their draft legislation to the Commission. It enables the Commission to assist the Member States in the implementation, but also gives the Commission information as to situations in which Member States do not comply with their obligations by implementing incorrectly.

663   27 October 1993, C-69/91, *criminal proceedings against Francine Gillon, née Decoster* [1993] ECR I-5335.

664   30 April 1996, Case C-194/94, *CIA Security International SA v. Signalson SA and Securitel SPRL* [1996] ERC I-2201, par. 42; 16 June 1998, Case C-226/97, *criminal proceedings against Johannes Martinus Lemmens* [1998] ECR I-3711, par. 33.

665   It is often quite difficult for courts to do that themselves and they regularly refer to the Court with the question whether a specific national provision must be regarded as a technical regulation. See, for instance, 8 March 2001, Case C-278/99, *criminal proceedings against Georgius van der Burg* [2001] ECR I-2015; 21 April 2005, Case C-267/03, *criminal proceedings against Lars Erik Staffan Lindberg* [2005] ECR I-3247; 16 June 1998, Case C-226/97, *criminal proceedings against Johannes Martinus Lemmens* [1998] ECR I-3711.

666   30 April 1996, Case C-194/94, *CIA Security International SA v. Signalson SA and Securitel SPRL* [1996] ERC I-2201, par. 29 and 30.

Discrepancies Between Union and National Criminal Law

Discrepancies may exist between the applicable rule under Union law and the applicable national provision. In principle, the rule is that national criminal law is applicable unless Union law precludes the application of such a provision. Two issues relating to the principle of legality must be discussed here.

The first is whether Union law obligations to criminalise must be regarded as minimum provisions. This relates to the following: when implementing criminal provisions, the Member State may have criminalised more or broader conduct than stipulated in the Union act. Could an accused argue that the broader definition cannot be held against him because Union law required more limited criminalisation? The answer seems to be found in the spirit of the Union act. Was it intended to limit criminalisation or did it impose the obligation to criminalise *at least* the conduct described in the legal instrument upon the Member States? With the former, the accused was able to invoke the limited Union act and national law had to be set aside, with the latter, the Member States are left free. The Court held, in a case concerning insider dealing, that more stringent provisions in national criminal law may be applied, provided these provisions are of general applicability and do not single out a specific category of persons.[667] Looking at the text of Third Pillar legislation, the impression is that it is unlikely that the accused may be able to rely on the Union act. The acts can, to a certain degree, be characterised as minimum criminalisation. However, as expressed in Section 1, other rules such as the principle of proportionality may counter-balance broad definitions.

The second issue deals with the status of implementing national criminal law in a situation in which the original Union act is annulled. The annulment of the two Framework Decisions discussed earlier leads to the question of whether this affects the national criminal law implementing the Framework Decision. If it does not affect national criminal law, does this still force the national court to interpret national law in conformity with the Framework Decision? Are the Member States, with the annulment, also relieved of other obligations, such as the obligation to enforce? The answer to these questions must be that the annulment relates to the competence of the Council to adopt certain measures. The judgment of the Court does not annul the legislation of the Member States. In other words, the annulment does not affect national law. This may be explained by the fact that the competence to create substantive criminal law is exclusive to the Member States. It would be against legal certainty if the validity of national criminal law was dependent on the validity of Union law. National courts would then have to determine which part of the national legislation concerned the implementing legislation and which part did not.

---

[667]   3 May 2001, Case 28/99, *criminal proceedings against Jean Verdonck, Ronald Everaert and Edith de Baedts* [2001] ECR I-3399.

Implementation and application of national criminal law

Implementation period / (prohibited) conduct	Implementation period runs			Implementation period is over	
	Member State has not yet implemented	Member State has implemented incorrectly	Member State has implemented correctly or was already in compliance	Member State has implemented correctly	Member State should have implemented correctly
Violation of national law in conformity with Dir/FD (EU decriminalises conduct)	May be punished	May *not* be punished			May *not* be punished
Act in conformity with national law, in violation of Dir/FD (EU criminalises conduct)	May *not* be punished	May *not* be punished			May *not* be punished
Violation of national law and violation of Dir/FD	May be punished		May be punished	May be punished	

3.2. JURISDICTION

Jurisdiction can be defined as the power of the legislature to apply the law to certain forms of conduct. The relevant link to apply criminal law to conduct may relate to the place in which the conduct takes place. It may also relate to the person who performs the conduct or against whom certain behaviour took place. In this section, the various jurisdictional principles which can be found in Union law are discussed. As with criminalised conduct, jurisdictional principles must also be implemented. A Member State cannot claim jurisdiction upon a basis provided for in a Framework Decision, but not found in its national law. This would be contrary to the rule that direct application of a Union act may not establish or aggravate criminal responsibility.

3.2.1. Territorial Jurisdiction

In its views on jurisdictional principles, the Union follows, more or less, common avenues of jurisdictional principles. Like all criminal justice systems in the world,

Union law takes *territorial jurisdiction* as the basis of all other principles of jurisdiction. This means that crimes committed on the territory of the Member State fall within its jurisdiction. Article 8 *Framework Decision 2004/757 on Illicit Drug Trafficking* is an example of an obligation (sometimes permission) found in many other instruments to create jurisdiction over an "offence committed in whole or in part within its territory".[668] Thus, it basically requires a *nexus* with its territory, as determined by national law. Article 4 *Joint Action 98/733 on Participation in a Criminal Organisation* and several First Pillar legal acts, such as Article 1 *Regulation 2847/93 establishing a Control System applicable to the Common Fisheries Policy*, also determine obligations *vis-à-vis* jurisdiction.

Union law leaves theories of determining the *locus delicti* (the place where the crime has been committed) generally to national law. However, there are a few exceptions. Occasionally, legal acts stipulate an extension upon the basis of the means by which the offence is committed. Jurisdiction includes "situations where the offence is committed by means of a computer system accessed from its territory, whether or not the computer system is on its territory".[669] A similar extension, albeit in relation to the proceeds of the crime, can be found in Article 4, paragraph 1 of the *Financial Interests Convention*: "In whole or in part within its territory, including fraud for which the benefit was obtained in that territory."[670] Article 9, paragraph 4 *Framework Decision 2002/475 on Combating Terrorism* requires that jurisdiction be provided in cases in which any of the offences of a terrorist group "has been committed in whole or in part within its territory, wherever the terrorist group is based or pursues its criminal activities". Similarly, the provision of Article 8, paragraph 1 *Framework Decision 2003/80 on the Protection of the Environment* deviates from those regularly found, in that Member States should establish jurisdiction with regard to offences committed "fully or in part in its territory, even if the effects occur entirely elsewhere", There must be, in one way or another, a link with the territory. In competition law, the issue arose as to whether there is jurisdiction over undertakings that have their seat outside the Union, and the Court held that there is jurisdiction when the conduct has effects within the internal market.[671]

---

[668] Article 6 *First Protocol Financial Interests Convention*; Article 7 *Corruption Convention*; Article 7 *Joint Action 98/742 on Corruption in the Private Sector*; Article 9 *Framework Decision 2001/413 on Combating Fraud*; Article 9 *Framework Decision 2002/475 on Combating Terrorism*; Article 6 *Framework Decision 2002/629 on Combating Trafficking in Human Beings*; Article 4 *Framework Decision 2002/946 on Unauthorised Entry*; Article 7 *Framework Decision 2003/568 on Corruption in the Private Sector*; Article 8 *Framework Decision 2004/68 on Child Pornography*.

[669] Article 8, par. 5 *Framework Decision 2004/68 on Child Pornography*.

[670] See, also, Article 8, paragraph 1 sub c *Framework Decision 2003/80 on the Protection of the Environment*.

[671] 14 July 1972, Case 48–69, *Imperial Chemical Industries Ltd.* v. *Commission* [1972] ECR 619, par. 126. Advocate General Mayras in his Opinion of 2 May 1972 referred in detail to the 1927

Article 10, paragraph 2 *Framework Decision 2005/222 on Attacks against Information Systems* asks Member States to ensure that territorial jurisdiction covers both the situation in which the offender commits the offence when physically present on its territory, irrespective of whether or not the offence is against an information system on its territory, as well as the situation in which the offence is against an information system on its territory, irrespective of whether or not the offender commits the offence when physically present on its territory. In addition, Article 4, paragraph 1 *Financial Interests Convention* contains a very interesting provision which seems to adhere to the rule that participants have their own *locus*: "a person within its territory knowingly assists or induces the commission of such fraud within the territory of any other State". For the rest, there is no evidence that Union law determines anything on the *locus* of a crime.

Extra-territorial jurisdiction deals with jurisdiction over crimes committed outside the territory of the Member States. However, there is also good reason to distinguish between jurisdiction over crimes within and jurisdiction of crimes outside the European Union. As a preliminary issue, the Court has held that Union law does not require Member States "to extend their jurisdiction beyond the limits laid down by the generally accepted principles governing the distribution of criminal jurisdiction between States".[672] When it comes to the actual use of extra-territorial jurisdiction, the Union must respect international law in the exercise of its powers.[673] Article 7 *Framework Decision 2005/667 on Ship-source Pollution* refers to the Member States' exclusive economic zone or in an equivalent zone established in accordance with international law.

This necessary permission under international law to vest jurisdiction over crimes committed elsewhere in the Union can be found in the Union act. Article 9, paragraph 1 *Framework Decision 2002/475 on Combating Terrorism* allows for the extension of jurisdiction if the crimes are committed in the territory of another Member State. *Community territory* is defined as encompassing all territories of the Member States to which the Treaty is applicable.[674] In addition, there are provisions that apply to the nationals of the Member States and to the vessels registered in the Member States.

Lotus decision of the Permanent Court of Justice on jurisdiction in international criminal law. See [1972] ECR 694.

[672]   27 March 1990, Case C-9/89, *Spain* v. *Council* [1990] ECR I-1383, par. 27.

[673]   24 November 1992, Case C-286/90, *Anklagemyndigheden* v. *Peter Michael Poulsen and Diva Navigation Corp* [1992] ECR I-619.

[674]   7th recital of Regulation 2580/2001 of 27 December 2001 on specific restrictive measures directed against certain persons and entities with a view to combating terrorism, OJ 2001, L 344/70. Article 10 of this Regulation on the application of the Regulation may have resulted in the use of jurisdictional principles under national criminal law. See, further, 29 March 2007, Case C-111/05, *Aktiebolaget NN* v. *Skatteverket* [2007] ECR I-2697, par. 53–61.

3.2.2. The Flag Principle

The *flag principle* can be found in Article 9, paragraph 1 *Framework Decision 2002/475 on Combating Terrorism*, which states that: "the offence is committed on board a vessel flying its flag or an aircraft registered there."[675] The flag principle establishes jurisdiction over crimes committed on board a ship or aircraft that flies the flag of the Member State. The nationality of a vessel is determined under international law conditional to its registration in a specific state. As a consequence, European fishery legislation is not applicable to a vessel registered outside the European Union.[676] There is no dual nationality for vessels. This is the same even when the captain or even the whole crew has EU nationality. International law further allows for innocent passage in the territorial waters of a Member State. However, Union legislation may be applied when a vessel sails in the inland waters or is in a port of a Member State.[677]

3.2.3. The Active Nationality Principle

Active nationality is a jurisdictional principle that has found a place in many legal instruments. The term "active nationality" (also called "active personality"), means that a state has jurisdiction over crimes committed by its nationals. Article 8 *Framework Decision 2004/757 on Illicit Drug Trafficking* allows for extra-territorial jurisdiction over nationals and over legal persons established in its territory.[678] The Court has been given the opportunity to assess the compliance of the active nationality principle with the prohibition of discrimination on the basis of nationality. The Court held that the mere fact that a national of a Member State may be subjected to wider jurisdiction than non-nationals for offences committed abroad does not amount to discrimination upon the basis of nationality.[679] The

---

[675] Article 7, paragraph 1(c) *Framework Decision 2005/667 on Ship-source Pollution* for ships. Similarly, Article 8, paragraph 1 sub b *Framework Decision 2003/80 on the Protection of the Environment*.

[676] 24 November 1992, Case C-286/90, *Anklagemyndigheden* v. *Peter Michael Poulsen and Diva Navigation Corp* [1992] ECR I-619, par. 12–19.

[677] 24 November 1992, Case C-286/90, *Anklagemyndigheden* v. *Peter Michael Poulsen and Diva Navigation Corp* [1992] ECR I-619, par. 22–29.

[678] Article 7 *Joint Action 98/742 on Corruption in the Private Sector*; Article 9 *Framework Decision 2001/413 on Combating Fraud*; Article 9 *Framework Decision 2002/475 on Combating Terrorism*; Article 6 *Framework Decision 2002/629 on Combating Trafficking in Human Beings*; Article 4 *Framework Decision 2002/946 on Unauthorised Entry*; Article 7 *Framework Decision 2003/568 on Corruption in the Private Sector*; Article 8 *Framework Decision 2004/68 on Child Pornography*; Article 10 *Framework Decision 2005/222 on Attacks against Information Systems*; Article 7 *Framework Decision 2005/667 on Ship-source Pollution*.

[679] 14 July 1994, Case C-379/92, *criminal proceedings against Matteo Peralta* [1994] ECR I-3453.

decision is in-line with the case law, which allows for some disfavourable treatment of nationals by their own state.[680]

A special feature of the active nationality principle is the status of the perpetrator as an official. This can be found in provisions regarding *national officials* and *Community officials* in the *First Protocol Financial Interests Convention* and in the *Corruption Convention*.

Article 8, paragraph 1 sub b *Framework Decision 2003/80 on the Protection of the Environment* requires Member States to establish jurisdiction over their nationals "if the offence is punishable under criminal law where it was committed or if the place where it was committed does not fall under any territorial jurisdiction".[681] This relates to the fact that the definitions of many offences carry the element "unlawful". Lawfulness is, of course, determined by the law of the state in which the offence has been committed. This, however, becomes problematical if the offence is committed outside the territory or territorial waters of a state.

Generally speaking, and this, in comparison to national criminal justice systems, is quite astonishing, one can see that the active personality or nationality principle has not been made conditional on the criminalisation of the conduct in the *locus* state. A rare provision in this respect is the *double criminality* requirement that can be found in Article 4, paragraph 1 *Financial Interests Convention*.[682] Likewise, Article 9 *Framework Decision 2001/413 on Combating Fraud* also allows for such a condition with regard to the application of the active nationality principle. Furthermore, Article C of the repealed *Joint Action 97/154 on Trafficking in Human Beings*, required the Member States that maintain the double criminality requirement to review its necessity.

The *aut dedere, aut judicare* principle may often be found in the legal instruments.[683] This is an obligation which also has its origins in international criminal law. It imposes the obligation on the state which receives a request for extradition to choose between two options. Either to extradite (*aut dedere*) the requested person, or to try (*aut judicare*) the person. The possibility of opting for

---

680   See Chapter 3, Section 4.4.
681   Article 7, par. 1(d) *Framework Decision 2005/667 on Ship-source Pollution*.
682   See, also, Article B referring to Article A, sub F (ii) of the repealed *Joint Action 97/154 on Trafficking in Human Beings*.
683   See Article 5 *Financial Interests Convention*; Article 8 *Corruption Convention*; Article 7, par. 4 *Joint Action 98/742 on Corruption in the Private Sector*; Article 10 *Framework Decision 2001/413 on Combating Fraud*; Article 9, par. 4 *Framework Decision 2002/475 on Combating Terrorism*; Article 6, par. 3 *Framework Decision 2002/629 on Combating Trafficking in Human Beings*; Article 5 *Framework Decision 2002/946 on Unauthorised Entry*; Article 9 *Framework Decision 2003/80 on the Protection of the Environment*; Article 7, par. 3 *Framework Decision 2003/568 on Corruption in the Private Sector*; Article 8 *Framework Decision 2004/68 on Child Pornography*; Article 8, par. 3 *Framework Decision 2004/757 on Illicit Drug Trafficking*; Article 10, par. 3 *Framework Decision 2005/222 on Attacks against Information Systems*.

the latter presumes anterior jurisdiction over the crime. With the entering into force of *Framework Decision 2002/584 on the European Arrest Warrant*, these obligations have become inapplicable in the relationship between the Member States. Contrary to the international agreements and Union acts applicable before the *Framework Decision 2002/584 on the European Arrest Warrant* entered into force, Articles 4 and 5 of that Framework Decision no longer allow a refusal of the surrender of nationals and residents solely for the reason that the requested person is a national or resident. However, Member States may make the surrender conditional to the national or resident serving the sentence in his own Member State. Despite the fact that *aut dedere, aut judicare* principle is no longer applicable between Member States, it might have led to the implementation of various bases of extra-territorial jurisdiction in national criminal law in order to comply with the obligations set out in the instruments mentioned.

The *aut dedere, aut judicare* provision in *Framework Decision 2002/475 on Combating Terrorism* slightly differs from all other Framework Decisions and Joint Actions. Article 9, paragraph 3 reads:

> "Each Member State shall take the necessary measures also to establish its jurisdiction over the offences referred to in Articles 1 to 4 in cases where it refuses to hand over or extradite a person suspected or convicted of such an offence to another Member State or to a third country."

It deviates from the other legal instruments to the extent that it does away with the nationality requirement of the principle. This means that Member States must provide for a jurisdictional link for non-nationals who commit acts of terrorism.[684]

3.2.4. The Domicile Principle

The principle of *habitual residence,* also named the *domicile principle,* can be found in Article A, sub F (ii) of the repealed *Joint Action 97/154 on Trafficking in Human Beings.* This principle establishes jurisdiction over extra-territorial offences of non-nationals who are domiciled or have their habitual residence in the Member State. However, *Framework Decision 2004/68 on Child Pornography,* which replaced the Joint Action contains no reference to the domicile principle. Despite this, some Member States might, in the process of implementing the obligations from the Joint Action, have created this jurisdictional basis under national law. However, the only legal instrument that directly refers to the resident

---

[684]   Literally, the provision requires a Member State to establish jurisdiction over a convicted person.

or domicile principle is Article 9, paragraph 1, *Framework Decision 2002/475 on Combating Terrorism*.

In the context of the European Arrest Warrant, the Court defined habitual residence as "having either established his actual place of residence in the executing Member State or has acquired, following a stable period of presence in that State, certain connections with that State which are of a similar degree to those resulting from residence".[685] In the interpretation of this criterion, it is relevant whether the person's stay was (un)interrupted and whether he complied with the national legislation on the residence of foreign nationals. The fact that he systematically commits crimes in the country or has served a period of detention does not contribute to habitual residence.[686]

3.2.5. The Principle of Complementary Jurisdiction

Complementary jurisdiction denotes that a state may apply its own jurisdiction when another state having territorial jurisdiction cannot or does not use its own jurisdiction.[687] A state willing to apply jurisdiction may replace a more appropriate state. Article D of the repealed *Joint Action 97/154 on Trafficking in Human Beings* provides for a form of *complementary jurisdiction* in the cases of habitual residence as stipulated in Article A, sub F (ii), depending on unwillingness or inability of the state in which the offence was committed.

3.2.6. The Protective Principle

The *protective principle* can be found in an implicit manner in secondary legislation of the Union. With the protective principle, the relevant link for jurisdiction over the conduct committed abroad consists of the protection of the interests of the state. Its use relates to the idea that, otherwise, the enforcement of Union law could not be dealt with effectively. Regulation 990/93 concerning Trade between the EEC and the Federal Republic of Yugoslavia led to an interesting case in which the Court was able, albeit indirectly, to state its opinion on jurisdictional principles. From the wording of the Regulation, the Court concluded that a breach of the sanctions laid down by the Regulation may also result from conduct occurring in international waters.[688]

---

[685]   17 July 2008, C-66/08, *proceedings concerning the execution of a European arrest warrant issued against Szymon Kosłowski* [2008] ECR not yet reported, par. 46.

[686]   17 July 2008, C-66/08, *proceedings concerning the execution of a European arrest warrant issued against Szymon Kosłowski* [2008] ECR not yet reported, par. 46–51.

[687]   Most prominent example under international criminal law is the complementarity principle in Article 17 of the Statute of the International Criminal Court.

[688]   27 February 1997, Case C-177/95, *Ebony Maritime SA and Loten Navigator Co. Ltd* v. *Prefetto della Provincia di Brindisi and others* [1997] ECR I-1111, par. 25–27.

The protective principle is more clearly stated in Article 7, paragraph 1(f) *Framework Decision 2005/667 on Ship-source Pollution* when the offence has caused or is likely to cause pollution in its territory or its economic zone, and the ship is voluntarily within a port or, at an offshore terminal of a Member State. Likewise, *Framework Decision 2002/475 on Combating Terrorism* carries the protective principle: "the offence is committed against the institutions or people of the Member State in question or against an institution of the European Union or a body set up in accordance with the Treaty establishing the European Community or the Treaty on European Union and based in that Member State."[689]

The interpretative rule that an interpretation of a Union act which gives the instrument its useful effect must follow is conducive to the application of the protective principle regarding criminal jurisdiction. This appears from the *van Swieten* case, which concerned rest hours for drivers. The Court had to answer the question of whether the relevant Regulation, Regulation 3820/85 on the harmonisation of certain social legislation relating to road transport, should be interpreted in such a way as to take the time spent on journeys through third states also into account. The Court stated that:

> "The effectiveness of those rules would be compromised if the application of the Community system were dependent on the journeys made by vehicles registered in different Member States and if national laws continued to apply where the journeys were made only partly within the Community. It follows that Regulation No. 3820/85 covers all road transport services operated within the Community by vehicles registered in a Member State, even where the carriage takes place partly in non-member States."[690]

3.2.7. *The Principle of Universal Jurisdiction*

Universal jurisdiction denotes the application of national criminal law to criminal conduct regardless of where or by whom a crime may have been committed. The principle is rarely applied in Union law. Only *Framework Decision 2000/383 on the Introduction of the Euro* provides for the Member States that have introduced the euro as their currency in Article 7, paragraph 2 for jurisdiction independently of the nationality and the place where the offence has been committed. Similarly, Directive 2005/60 on Money Laundering specifies as money laundering "even

---

[689]   There is a proposal that aims at extending jurisdiction over incitement to terrorist offences of which the Union could become the victim. Proposal Framework Decision amending Framework Decision 2002/475/JHA on combating terrorism, Council Document 3 April 2008, 7785/2/08, Rev.2, CATS 24, DROIPEN 30.

[690]   2 June 1994, Case C-313/92, *criminal proceedings against Van Swieten BV* [1994] ECR I-2177, par. 17–18.

where the activities which generated the property to be laundered were carried out in the territory of another Member State or in that of a third country". (Article 1, paragraph 3 *Directive 2005/60 on Money Laundering*). Article 7, paragraph 1(g) *Framework Decision 2005/667 on Ship-source Pollution* creates jurisdiction over offences on the high seas. However, this is not an unlimited application of universal jurisdiction. The Framework Decision requires a link with the European Union, as jurisdiction may be conferred on condition that the ship is voluntarily within a port or at an offshore terminal of one of the Member States.

3.2.8. The Prevention of Conflicts of Jurisdiction

In Article 82 TFEU (formerly Article 31 EU), the European Union gave itself the obligation to strive for the prevention of conflicts of jurisdiction. To date, there has been no initiative at all to prevent conflicts of jurisdiction.[691] To the contrary, as described above, numerous legal instruments oblige Member States to confer extra-territorial jurisdiction. Thus, they automatically create overlapping jurisdiction. The forthcoming establishment of the European Public Prosecutor's Office will further demand the prevention of jurisdictional conflicts. However, some of the acts of the Union contain provisions that do aim at solving (but not at preventing) conflicts of jurisdiction.[692]

3.2.9. Jurisdictional Principles in the Union

As a concluding assessment, one can see that the European Union generally follows the principles of jurisdiction which are commonly provided in the law of civil law states. Notable exceptions include the complete absence of the principle of passive nationality (jurisdiction over the offence because of the fact that the victim is a national) and the principle of subsidiary jurisdiction (jurisdiction upon the basis of a request by another state).[693]

---

[691]   Contrary to private law, in which *Regulation 44/2001 on Jurisdiction and Recognition of Civil Judgments* strives for prevention of conflicts and "to avoid the risk of irreconcilable judgments resulting from separate proceedings". See 11 October 2007, Case C-98/06, *Freeport plc* v. *Olle Arnoldsson* [2007] ECR I-8319, par. 37.

[692]   However, the Union did take initiatives on solving conflicts of jurisdiction. The establishment of Eurojust contributes to regulating the effects of overlapping jurisdiction. This will be dealt with in Chapter 7, Section 4.3. It will be identified that some (vague) notions of a ranking order of jurisdictional principles do exist.

[693]   The principle of subsidiary or secondary jurisdiction is absent in the legal instruments of the European Union. Article 2 of the 1972 Council of Europe Convention on the Transfer of Proceedings in Criminal Matters provides that a Contracting State may prosecute any offence to which the law of another state is applicable, when this competence has been conferred pursuant to a request.

Notes

Kip

Session 1
  chap 1 + 2
  Chap 3   s 1 + 2

Session 2
Chap 4   s 1 + 2, 3.2 ✓
Chap 5   s 3 - 3.2

Session 3
Chap 7   s 1 - 3 + 4.4

Session 4
chap 7   s 1 - 3

Session 5
Chap 7   s 4.1, 5 + 6

Session 6
Chap 7   s 4.2, 4.3 + 4.5

Notes

Session 7
Chap 7 s6
Chap 8

The Union approach of jurisdictional principles is one that serves principally the interests of the individual Member State. There is no visible attempt to regard jurisdiction from the angle of a common European Union interest in combating crime. There is a remarkable difference between the generally limited focus on the internal market and the area of freedom, security and justice and the Union law provisions on jurisdiction. While most norms aim at application within the Union, the extra-territorial jurisdictional principles may also apply to conduct committed outside the Union. The idea that more extra-territorial jurisdiction for the Member States will be conducive to enforcement prevails over the task provided for in the TEU to prevent of conflicts of jurisdiction. In this context, one may doubt whether such a presumption can be upheld. It is more likely that it stimulates the adverse result and makes Member States passive: the job of everyone is the job of no one.

At this early stage, it is important to stress that the principle of mutual recognition as stipulated both in *ne bis in idem* rules and in forms of international co-operation may have an indirect effect of determining priority in cases of multiple jurisdiction. Article 54 *CISA* functions upon the basis of a "first come, first served" principle. The Member State that was the first to conclude criminal proceedings prevents all other Member States from exercising their jurisdiction. *De facto*, mutual recognition in co-operation in criminal matters may lead to a similar effect. The first Member State to issue a European Arrest Warrant with regard to a requested person and receive his surrender will make it *de facto* impossible for other (non-custodial) Member States to start or continue effective criminal proceedings with regard to the same set of facts at a later date.

'not twice for the same'

3.3. ACTUS REUS

Actus reus can be defined as the prohibited conduct. The legal instruments that define crimes predominantly refer to acts, action, behaviour or conduct. Omissions are criminalised only in the context of EC fraud. The Article 49 Charter refers, in the context of the requirements of the legality principle, to "act or omission". This establishes that both acts as well as omissions may constitute the basis for criminal liability.[694] However, none of the legal instruments actually defines acts and omissions. Nor has Union law formulated any conditions or criteria for the criminalisation of conduct.[695] There is no case law on the *actus reus*. The closest

---

[694] See, also, the definition of "victim" in Article 1 *Framework Decision 2001/220 on the Standing of Victims*: "'victim' shall mean a natural person who has suffered harm, including physical or mental injury, emotional suffering or economic loss, directly caused by *acts or omissions* that are in violation of the criminal law of a Member State".

[695] Only the requirement that the use of criminal law must be necessary comes close to this. See this chapter, Section 2.

would be *Skanavi*, in which the Court required the material conduct to be reviewed in a Union manner:

> "In the absence of Community rules governing the matter, the Member States remain competent to impose penalties for breach of such an obligation. However, it follows from settled case-law concerning non-compliance with formalities for establishing the right of residence of an individual enjoying the protection of Community law that Member States may not impose a penalty so disproportionate to the gravity of the infringement that this becomes an obstacle to the free movement of persons; this would be especially so if the penalty consisted of imprisonment (see, in particular, Case C-265/88 *Messner* [1989] ECR 4209, paragraph 14). In view of the effect which the right to drive a motor vehicle has on the actual exercise of the rights relating to the free movement of persons, the same considerations must apply with regard to breach of the obligation to exchange driving licences."[696]

Some Union acts provide for additional requirements on the definition of the offence, which shed a little more light on the values protected by criminalisation. Article 2, paragraph 1 *Framework Decision 2004/757 on Illicit Drug Trafficking* creates the category "without right" with regard to drug offences. This refers to the right that individuals involved in the very limited legal trade (for example, hospitals) in psychotropic substances have. Article 3 *Framework Decision 2001/413 on Combating Fraud* stipulates the same idea. Credit and financial institutions that disclose suspicious transactions in good faith, cannot be held liable for breach of confidentiality obligations (Article 26 *Directive 2005/60 on Money Laundering*). Article 1 sub (d) *Framework Decision 2005/222 on Attacks against Information Systems* defines "without right" to mean: "access or interference not authorised by the owner, other right holder of the system or part of it, or not permitted under the national legislation." Article 2, paragraph 2 further allows Member States to limit criminalisation to situations "infringing a security measure". The rationale is that the conduct may also appear in a form that it is definitely not illegal.

3.4. *MENS REA*, INTENT AND STRICT LIABILITY

With *mens rea* or the fault element it is expressed that in addition to the existence of prohibited conduct (*actus reus*) the perpetrator must be aware or must intend to behave in a certain manner. Criminal justice systems distinguish between various degrees of intent. Generally speaking, the legal instruments of the Union that criminalise conduct refer to "intentional conduct",[697] or to acts that have

---

[696] 29 February 1996, Case C-193/94, *criminal proceedings against Sofia Skanavi and Konstantin Chryssanthakopoulos* [1996] ECR I-929, par. 36.
[697] Article 2, paragraph 1 *Framework Decision 2004/757 on Illicit Drug Trafficking*.

been "intentionally" committed.[698] *Intent* is regarded in most criminal justice systems as the strongest indication that the *actus reus* was wanted. It seems fair to conclude that all Framework Decisions require intentional conduct.[699] *Joint Action 98/733 on Participation in a Criminal Organisation* cumulatively requires both intent and knowledge of the purposes of the organisation and active participation. The Joint Action requires a specific "further knowledge" of the perpetrator that his participation will contribute to the achievement of the organisation's criminal activities. In a competition law case, the Court has accepted, as a sufficient basis for a finding, that the undertaking acted intentionally, and that the undertaking "must have been fully aware that its conduct was of such a nature as to encourage restrictions on competition".[700]

Strict liability can be defined as the criminal liability which requires prohibited conduct only, irrespective of the *mens rea* of the perpetrator. The justification for strict liability can be found in the fact that the perpetrator was negligent in that he failed to prevent the harm from occurring. However, strict liability is not incompatible with Union law.[701] The first impression might be that Union law, with its emphasis on effective and dissuasive enforcement, is supportive of the use of strict liability. However, the Court is more lenient and holds that such a basis for liability must have consequences on the level of sanctions:

> "where national law contains, in penal matters, a general principle according to which everyone is presumed to know the law, Community law does not preclude that principle from being applied (...) None the less, in the light of the purpose of the directive, which is to promote the freedoms guaranteed by the Treaty, account must be taken of the good faith of the offender when determining the penalty imposed on him, (...)."[702]

Sanctions may not be imposed if the applicant for aid shows that he is not at fault in respect of irregularities.[703] In another competition law case, Advocate General Ruiz-Jarabo Colomer referred to the principle of culpability that limits the exercise of *ius puniendi*. This principle would make the system of objective responsibility (or strict responsibility) unacceptable. In the case of legal persons, the principle of

---

[698] *Directive 2002/90 on Unauthorised Entry.*

[699] See, also, *Framework Decision 2004/68 on Child Pornography* and Article 2 *Framework Decision 2003/568 on Ccorruption in the Private Sector.*

[700] 7 June 1983, Joined Cases 100 to 103/80, *SA Musique Diffusion française and others* v. *Commission* [1983] ECR 1825, par. 112.

[701] 10 July 1990, Case C-326/88, *Anklagemyndigheden* v. *Hansen and Søn I/S* [1990] ECR I-2911, par. 11–17.

[702] 12 July 2001, Case C-262/99, *Paraskevas Louloudakis* v. *Elliniko Dimosio* [2001] ECR I-5547, par. 76; 27 February 1997, Case C-177/95, *Ebony Maritime SA and Loten Navigator Co. Ltd* v. *Prefetto della Provincia di Brindisi and others* [1997] ECR I-1111, par. 37.

[703] 1 July 2004, Case C-295/02, *Gisela Gerken* v. *Amt für Agrarstruktur Verden* [2004] ECR I-6369, par. 60.

culpability must be applied in a different way, although there is no reason to abolish the subjective element of guilt.[704] The anti-competitive conduct of an undertaking can be attributed to another undertaking in cases in which the conduct of one undertaking on the market has not been decided upon independently and its conduct on the market was determined by instructions given to it by another undertaking.[705]

Negligent (or unintended) conduct is criminalised in the *Financial Interests Convention*, which also applies to omissions, in the *Framework Decision 2003/80 on the Protection of the Environment* and in the *Framework Decision 2005/667 on Ship-source Pollution*. In the criminal proceedings against *Rinkau*, the Court had the opportunity to interpret the concept of an "offence which was not intentionally committed" as it appeared in Article II *Protocol to the Brussels Convention*. The Court held that it must be regarded "as an independent concept which must be explained by reference, first, to the objectives and scheme of the Convention and, secondly, to the general principles which the national legal systems have in common".[706] It further held that:

> "It is therefore necessary to ascertain whether there is a criterion for classification which is common to the national legal systems of all the contracting states, by which offences may be distinguished according to their seriousness and on the basis of which most, if not all, of the offences connected with road accidents may be classified amongst the less serious offences. The national laws of most of the contracting states distinguish in one way or another between offences committed intentionally and those not so committed. Even though that distinction may lead to the classification of offences into categories of which the content may vary appreciably from one legal system to another, it still serves the aforementioned purpose. Whereas offences which were intentionally committed, if they are to be punishable, require an intent to commit them on the part of the person concerned, offences which were not intentionally committed may result from carelessness, negligence or even the mere objective breach of a legal provision. They are therefore, first, generally less serious in nature and, secondly, cover most offences connected with road accidents which are to be ascribed to carelessness, negligence or the mere actual breach of a legal provision. Consequently, the answer to the first question of the *Hoge Raad* must be that the expression 'an offence which was not intentionally committed' within the meaning of Article II of the Protocol annexed to the Convention of 27 September 1968 on jurisdiction and the enforcement of

---

704   Opinion of Advocate General Ruiz-Jarabo Colomer of 11 February 2003, Joined Cases C-204/00 P, C-205/00 P, C-211/00 P, C-213/00 P, C-217/00 P and C-219/00 P, *Aalborg Portland A/S and Others* v. *Commission* [2004] ECR I-123, points 63–65.

705   21 February 1973, Case 6–72, *Europemballage Corporation and Continental Can Company Inc.* v. *Commission* [1973] ECR 215, par. 15; 28 June 2005, Joined Cases C-189/02 P, C-202/02 P, C-205/02 P to C-208/02 P and C-213/02 P, *Dansk Rørindustri and Others* v. *Commission* [2005] ECR I-5425, par. 117.

706   26 May 1981, Case C-157/80, *criminal proceedings against Siegfried Ewald Rinkau* [1981] ECR 1395, par. 11.

judgments in civil and commercial matters should be understood as meaning any offence the legal definition of which does not require, either expressly or as appears from the nature of the offence defined, the existence of intent on the part of the accused to commit the punishable act or omission."[707]

It is clear that, in *Rinkau*, the Court distinguished between two main categories: intentional and non-intentional. The second category being sub-divided into lack of care, negligence, and objective responsibility. In Case C-308/06, the Court defined negligence as an "unintentional act or omission by which the person responsible commits a patent breach of his duty of care, which he should have and could have complied with in view of his attributes, knowledge, abilities and individual situation".[708]

The *Yonemoto* case is an interesting case with regard to negligent behaviour. In principle, manufacturers are responsible for the safety of machines. The importer is on the basis of *Directive 98/37 on the Approximation of the Laws of the Member States relating to Machinery* not obliged to check compliance with those rules. Thus, Union law may reduce the possibilities of negligent behaviour, because of the fact that the internal market requires Member States to refrain from checking whether goods have been placed legally on the market. An importer cannot be negligent in a task that he is not allowed to perform. However, some secondary obligations may be imposed on importers in a Member State.[709]

As an example of the fact that general substantive norms of Union law are applicable without distinction, a German case can be referred to, in which a distinction was made with regard to the requirement to be in possession of a valid identity document. In the case of a foreigner, negligence suffices to constitute an infringement, while, for Germans, intent or recklessness is necessary.[710] National criminal law may not treat nationals and EU nationals differently with regard to the degree of fault. This is an application of the general prohibition of non-discrimination.

---

[707] 26 May 1981, Case C-157/80, *criminal proceedings against Siegfried Ewald Rinkau* [1981] ECR 1395, par. 13–16.

[708] 3 June 2008, Case C-308/06, *The Queen on the application of: International Association of Independent Tanker Owners (Intertanko), International Association of Dry Cargo Shipowners (Intercargo), Greek Shipping Co-operation Committee, Lloyd's Register, International Salvage Union*, v. *Secretary of State for Transport* [2008] ECR, not yet reported, par. 77.

[709] 8 September 2005, Case C-40/04, *criminal proceedings against Syuichi Yonemoto* [2005] ECR I-7755, par. 45–55. See, further, Chapter 3, Section 4.6.2.

[710] 30 April 1998, Case C-24/97, *Commission v. Germany* [1998] ECR I-2133. Clearly, the same goes for providing different penalties. This would violate both the assimilation principle and the prohibition of discrimination.

3.5. PARTICIPATION AND INCHOATE OFFENCES

In a somewhat inconsistent manner, Third Pillar legal instruments carry obligations relating to participation. Under participation, criminal justice systems generally categorise all the other kinds of contributions to the offence from other persons than the principal. With the criminalisation of inchoate (incomplete) offences, the intention is to intervene before the undesirable harm materialises. However, none of this has been further defined by the specific legal instrument. Consequently, it is the responsibility of the Member States to lay down the conditions under which one of these forms of participation and inchoate offence are described.

3.5.1. Participation

Article A Title II *Joint Action 97/154 on Trafficking in Human Beings*, Article 4 *Framework Decision 2003/80 on the Protection of the Environment* and Article 1, paragraph 3 *Financial Interests Convention* require that *"participation in"* the offences should be covered by national criminal law. Article 2, paragraph 1, sub b *Joint Action 98/733 on Participation in a Criminal Organisation* provides the criminalisation of the "conduct of any person consisting in an agreement with one or more persons that an activity should be pursued". However, in this Joint Action, the participation in a criminal organisation is a separate crime and amounts to a conspiracy-like offence.

Instigation, aiding and abetting and attempt are found in various legal instruments. For example Article 3 *Framework Decision 2003/568 on Corruption in the Private Sector* requires Member States to criminalise these modalities of conduct without defining them.[711] Article 3 *Framework Decision 2005/667 on Ship-source Pollution* does the same, with the exception of "attempt". Article 3 *Framework Decision 2004/757 on Illicit Drug Trafficking* uses *"incitement"*, instead of "instigation", and further provides for exceptions for two types of attempts. Instigation is also criminalised under Article 4 *Framework Decision 2003/80 on the Protection of the Environment*. Another modality can be found in Article 4 *Joint Action 98/742 on Corruption in the Private Sector*, which requires the criminalisation of "the acting as an *accessory* in or instigator of such conduct". Article 5 *Framework Decision 2003/568 on Corruption in the Private Sector* implies the criminalisation of both instigators and accessories. Article 2 *Directive 2002/90 on Unauthorised Entry* stipulates that sanctions should be provided for "any

---

[711]   Similarly, Article 4 *Framework Decision 2002/475 on Combating Terrorism*; Article 2 *Framework Decision 2002/629 on Combating Trafficking in Human Beings*; Article 4 *Framework Decision 2004/68 on Child Pornography*; Article 5 *Framework Decision 2005/222 on Attacks against Information Systems*.

person who: (a) is the instigator of, (b) is an *accomplice* in, or (c) attempts to commit". Generally speaking, Union law leaves the definition of the modes of participation to the Member States.

Participation in anti-competitive conduct has led to some case law. It is sufficient for the Commission to show that the undertaking *participated* in meetings at which anti-competitive agreements were concluded, without manifestly opposing the conclusion thereof.[712] Where such participation is established, the undertaking must prove that it participated in an entirely different spirit.[713] Participation and complicity are, in competition law, more or less, two sides of the same coin:

> "A Party which tacitly approves an unlawful initiative, without publicly distancing itself from its content or reporting it to the administrative authorities, effectively encourages the continuation of the infringement and compromises its discovery. That complicity constitutes a passive mode of participation in the infringement which is therefore capable of rendering the undertaking liable in the context of a single agreement."[714]

In addition, the Court seems to require not only that a participant distanced himself from participation, but also requires the undertaking to report it to the authorities.

3.5.2. Inchoate Offences

Attempt can be found in Article A(a) Title II, 1997 *Joint Action 97/154 on Trafficking in Human Beings*. Article 5, paragraph 3 *Framework Decision 2005/222 on Attacks against Information Systems* allows Member States to apply "attempt" to the offences. A clue to the EU's understanding of when an attempt starts can be deduced from Article 4, paragraph 2 *Framework Decision 2002/475 on Combating Terrorism*. This paragraph excludes two acts mentioned in Article 1 from being criminalised in the modality of attempt. It concerns the attempt to possess weapons and the attempt to threaten to commit any of the offences listed in Article 1, paragraph 1(a) to (h). It further excludes offences relating to a terrorist group, as stipulated in Article 2, from being criminalised in the form of attempt. All the excluded offences are forms of preparatory offences. Conceptually, this

---

[712] 16 November 2000, Case C-291/98P, *Sarrió SA* v. *Commission* [2000] ECR I-9991, par. 50.

[713] 28 June 2005, Joined Cases C-189/02 P, C-202/02 P, C-205/02 P to C-208/02 P and C-213/02 P, *Dansk Rørindustri and Others* v. *Commission* [2005] ECR I-5425, par. 142.

[714] 28 June 2005, Joined Cases C-189/02 P, C-202/02 P, C-205/02 P to C-208/02 P and C-213/02 P, *Dansk Rørindustri and Others* v. *Commission* [2005] ECR I-5425, par. 143 (references omitted).

exclusion justifies the conclusion that, under Union law, attempt and preparatory offences must be regarded as being mutually exclusive.

The criminalisation of *preparatory offences* is also not a common feature. However, Article 1, paragraph 2 *Financial Interests Convention* requires that intentional preparation to commit EC fraud must constitute the principal offence if it is not already covered by other forms of participation. Although not characterised as such, Article 3, paragraph 1, sub d *Framework Decision 2000/383 on the Introduction of the Euro* criminalises preparatory acts.[715] A similar construction can be found with regard to Articles 3 and 4 *Framework Decision 2001/413 on Combating Fraud.*[716] Article 1 *Common Position 2001/930 on Combating Terrorism* is, in substance, a preparatory offence. However, it has been defined as an individual crime.

The overall picture with regard to participation and inchoate offences is one of confusing inconsistency. Some modalities appear in one instrument and not in another. It is unclear whether some terms should be regarded as interchangeable, such as accessory and accomplice, or incitement and instigation. The only picture that can be drawn here is that the Member States have full freedom in the definition of these specific modalities, as long as they can point at a modality that covers it in their criminal justice system. This is further enhanced by the fact that the legislation employs terminology that is well-known in criminal justice systems (participation, attempt). However, this will be conducive to attaching, to the terminology in the Union act, the interpretation that it already has under the national criminal justice system. Given the differences between the Member States on the general part of criminal law, it is predictable that it will maintain the existing disparities.

3.6. LEGAL ENTITIES

The first step, taken around 1995, to establishing criminal liability for legal entities did not go further than the criminalisation of the "heads of businesses or any persons having power to take decisions or exercise control within a business".[717] The second step, although still quite reluctant, was the introduction of liability for legal entities, which the Member States were left to create either in criminal law or on the basis of another liability.[718] It is clear that criminal liability for legal entities

---

[715]   This can also be concluded from the fact that Article 3, paragraph 2 excludes the attempt to prepare an offence.

[716]   Article 5 of that Framework Decision also excludes the criminalisation of the attempt to such preparatory conduct.

[717]   Article 3 *Financial Interests Convention*; Article 6 *Corruption Convention*.

[718]   See, for instance, Article 3 *Joint Action 98/733 on Participation in a Criminal Organisation* and the repealed *Joint Action 97/154 on Trafficking in Human Beings*.

was a sensitive issue for some Member States. At the time, Member States were not obliged to subject legal entities to criminal liability and still had the discretion to lay down conditions. However, if they would not opt for criminal liability, the Member States were obliged to look for another effective alternative. These instruments did not change the situation which was in place since the cases of *Hansen* and *Vandevenne*, in which the Court held "that when a Community regulation does not provide any specific penalty in case of breach, Member States retain a discretion as to the choices of penalties".[719] The relevant Regulation in the case of *Vandevenne* did not require Member States to introduce the principle of criminal liability of legal persons. However, it did not prohibit it, either.[720]

The freedom for hesitant Member States disappeared with the new generation of Union acts that unconditionally imposed criminal liability for legal persons. In Article 6, paragraph 1 *Framework Decision 2004/757 on Illicit Drug Trafficking*, a description of the attributive acts is given:

"legal persons can be held liable (…) committed for their benefit by any person, acting either individually or as a member of an organ of the legal person in question, who has a leading position within the legal person, based on one of the following: (a) a power of representation of the legal person (b) an authority to take decisions on behalf of the legal person (c) an authority to exercise control within the legal person."[721]

In addition, Article 6, paragraph 2 *Framework Decision 2004/757 on Illicit Drug Trafficking* provides for liability "where the lack of supervision or control by a person referred to in paragraph 1 has made the commission of any of the offence possible."[722]

---

[719]   10 July 1990, Case C-326/88, *Anklagemyndigheden* v. *Hansen and Søn I/S* [1990] ECR I-2911, par. 17; 2 October 1991, Case C-7/90, *criminal proceedings against Paul Vandevenne, Marc Willems, Jozef Mesotter and Wilms Transport NV*, [1991] ECR I-4371, par. 11.

[720]   The complaint of Hansen that the criminal liability rules amounted to a violation of Article 6, paragraphs 1 and 2 ECHR, ended with a friendly settlement. See ECtHR, 11 July 2000, *Hansen* v. *Denmark*, Application 28971/95.

[721]   Identical wording can be found in Article 3 *Second Protocol Financial Interests Convention*; Article 5 *Joint Action 98/742 on Corruption in the Private Sector*; Article 8 *Framework Decision 2000/383 on the Introduction of the Euro*; Article 7 *Framework Decision 2001/413 on Combating Fraud*; Article 7, par. 1 *Framework Decision 2002/475 on Combating Terrorism*; Article 4, par. 1 *Framework Decision 2002/629 on Combating Trafficking in Human Beings*; Article 2, par. 1 *Framework Decision 2002/946 on Unauthorised Entry*; Article 6 *Framework Decision 2003/80 on the Protection of the Environment*; Article 5 *Framework Decision 2003/568 on Corruption in the Private Sector*; Article 6, par. 1 *Framework Decision 2004/68 on Child Pornography*; Article 8 *Framework Decision 2005/222 on Attacks against Information Systems*; Article 5 *Framework Decision 2005/667 on Ship-source Pollution*.

[722]   Article 3 *Second Protocol Financial Interests Convention*; Article 5 *Joint Action 98/742 on Corruption in the Private Sector*; Article 8, par. 2 *Framework Decision 2000/383 on the Introduction of the Euro*; Article 7, par. 2 *Framework Decision 2002/475 on Combating Terrorism*; Article 4, par. 2 *Framework Decision 2002/629 on Combating Trafficking in Human Beings*; Article 6 *Framework Decision 2003/80 on the Protection of the Environment*; Article 6,

If this is taken as a factual issue, it will amount to strict liability: the occurrence of the offence being proof of lack of supervision. However, it is more likely that it was intended to criminalise negligent lack of control or supervision.

What the instruments that stipulate criminal liability for legal entities have in common is the provision that the criminal liability for legal entities is not exclusive, but additional to the individual criminal liability of natural persons.[723]

3.7. DEFENCES

Complete defences, which would justify or expunge the criminal character of an act have not been formulated at all at Union level. The closest the Union comes to this is the recognition of necessity as a justification of the infringement. In a competition law case, the Court did not reject the existence of necessity or self-protection which could have justified the infringements. However, in this specific case, the undertaking had not proved that its existence was threatened.[724] Article 12 of Regulation 3820/85 stipulates (in terms of what one would regard in criminal law as *necessity*) an exoneration of the provisions on daily rest hours in emergency situations. In a case in which the employer and the driver already planned this exoneration before the journey commenced, the character of this provision was discussed, and the Court held that derogation was only provided for events which were unforeseen.[725]

Despite the fact that, in both cases, the Court denied the existence of a necessity, it did accept that, in principle, the necessity could be a defence to the infringement. In the absence of any specific provision on defences in Union law, the defences available under national criminal law are fully applicable.

Member States may stipulate that the conduct does not fall within the scope of the Framework Decision "when it is committed by its perpetrators exclusively for their own *personal consumption* as defined by national law". This exception,

---

par. 2 *Framework Decision 2004/68 on Child Pornography*; Article 8, par. 2 *Framework Decision 2005/222 on Attacks against Information Systems*; Article 5 *Framework Decision 2005/667 on Ship-source Pollution*.

[723] Article 3 *Second Protocol Financial Interests Convention*; Article 5 *Joint Action 98/742 on Corruption in the Private Sector*; Article 7, par. 3 *Framework Decision 2002/475 on Combating Terrorism*; Article 2, par. 3 *Framework Decision 2002/946 on Unauthorised Entry*; Article 6 *Framework Decision 2003/80 on the Protection of the Environment*; Article 5 *Framework Decision 2003/568 on Corruption in the Private Sector*; Article 6, par. 3 *Framework Decision 2004/68 on Child Pornography*; Article 6, par. 3 *Framework Decision 2004/757 on Illicit Drug Trafficking*; Article 8, par. 3 *Framework Decision 2005/222 on Attacks against Information Systems*; Article 5 *Framework Decision 2005/667 on Ship-source Pollution*.

[724] 7 June 1983, Joined Cases 100 to 103/80, *SA Musique Diffusion française and others* v. *Commission* [1983] ECR 18250, par. 90.

[725] 9 November 1995, Case C-235/94, *criminal proceedings against Alan Jeffrey Bird* [1995] ECR I-3933.

related to small quantities of drugs for personal consumption can be found in Article 2, paragraph 2 *Framework Decision 2004/757 on Illicit Drug Trafficking.* Article 3, paragraph 2 sub b and c *Framework Decision 2004/68 on Child Pornography* creates similar categories. The rationale seems to be the harm principle, because, in the latter Framework Decision, it is limited to virtual child pornography[726] and images of children that have reached the age of *sexual consent* (Article 3, paragraph 2 (sub a and b)). While the consent of individuals of a certain age removes the criminal character of sexual conduct, the "consent of the victim" is specifically excluded as a justification in cases of trafficking in human beings (Article 1, paragraph 2 *Framework Decision 2002/629 on Combating Trafficking in Human Beings*).

A *humanitarian exception* has been allowed (not imposed) in *Directive 2002/90 on Unauthorised Entry*, in which Member States may decide not to impose sanctions "for cases where the aim of the behaviour is to provide humanitarian assistance to the person concerned".

4.   SPECIAL PART – EUROCRIMES

The contours of the special part of the crimes of the European Union are much clearer than its general part.[727] There are a number of instruments which criminalise, or at least prohibit – as a rule quite precisely – certain forms of conduct. Thus, a body of a special part of criminal law is gradually being built. In this section, the crimes under Union law are categorised with regard to the legal values that they protect.

4.1.   CRIMES AGAINST FAIR COMPETITION

Three categories can be depicted. First, *offences against competition law* stricto sensu. This refers to the conduct prohibited in Articles 101 and 102 TFEU (formerly Articles 81 and 82 TEC). The prevention, restriction or distortion of competition, as well as the abuse of a dominant position is incompatible with the internal market.[728]

Passive and active corruption in the private sector have been criminalised in Articles 1 and 2 of *Framework Decision 2003/568 on Corruption in the Private*

---

[726]   These are pictures that do not involve real children.

[727]   Various Resolutions exist that call for the criminalisation of conduct but which do not carry a clear obligation. They will not be discussed. An example is Resolution of 27 September 1996, on combating the illegal employment of third country nationals, OJ 1996, C 304/1.

[728]   See, further, Chapter 8, Section 3.4.

Sector.[729] The last category is the facilitation of unauthorised entry, transit and residence, prohibited in Article 1 of *Directive 2002/90 on Unauthorised Entry,* which, together with *Framework Decision 2002/946 on Unauthorised Entry* of the same date, provided for criminalisation. The Directive and the Framework Decision aim at two principal goals. One is to prevent and punish those who enter the European Union illegally. The other is to prevent illegally residing third state nationals from distorting the labour market. The protection of the internal market is even more apparent with the new Commission proposal.[730]

4.2. CRIMES AGAINST (THE INTEGRITY OF) THE FINANCIAL SECTOR

Money laundering was first prohibited in Article 1 of Directive 91/308. Although Article 2 of Directive 91/308 stipulates that money laundering as defined by Article 1 is to be "prohibited", and the Member States made a common statement that they would criminalise the conduct. In addition, the *Second Protocol Financial Interests Convention* criminalises the conduct defined in the Directive. The background of this lies in the division of powers as it was provided at the time. Directive 91/308 has been replaced by *Directive 2005/60 on Money Laundering.*[731]

Insider dealing was criminalised by the implementation of Articles 2 and 3 of Directive 89/592. In its judgment, in the criminal proceedings against *Grøngaard and Barg,* the Court interpreted the Directive and not the underlying law. However, it demonstrates that it is aware of the fact that enforcement takes place by use of criminal law. The Court looks at the larger context of the relevant Directive, and, in an actual case, it looks at the aims and means of the legislation. Since the prohibition of disclosing inside information is not absolute, the question of how restrictive the exception provided in Directive 89/592 actually is must be interpreted.[732]

---

729   The Framework Decision repealed its predecessor *Joint Action 98/742 on Corruption in the Private Sector.*

730   The Commission issued a Proposal for a Directive providing for sanctions against employers of illegally staying third-country nationals, 16.5.2007 SEC(2007) 603.

731   Quite a number of national and Union legal acts refer for the definition of money laundering to Directive 91/308. Article 44 of *Directive 2005/60 on Money Laundering* stipulates a transitionary provision: "Directive 91/308/EEC is hereby repealed. References made to the repealed Directive shall be construed as being made to this Directive and should be read in accordance with the correlation table set out in the Annex".

732   22 November 2005, Case C-384/02, *criminal proceedings against Knud Grøngaard and Allan Barg* [2005] ECR I-9939, par. 31–54. Another judgment interpreting *inside information* is 10 May 2007, Case C-391/04, *Ipourgos Ikonomikon Proistamenos DOI Amfissas* v. *Charilaos Georgakis* [2007] ECR I-3741.

Counterfeiting. Articles 3, 4 and 5 *Framework Decision 2000/383 on the Introduction of the Euro* provide for the criminalisation of all kinds of conduct relating to the counterfeiting of currency.

Offences related to Payment Instruments are criminalised by Articles 2, 3 and 4 *Framework Decision 2001/413 on Combating Fraud.*

4.3. CRIMES AGAINST THE FINANCIAL INTEREST OF THE UNION

EC Fraud was first criminalised by Article 1 *Financial Interests Convention*, although the conduct had been prohibited in other legal acts as "irregularity", such as *Regulation 2988/95 on Protection of the Financial Interests* which provides General Rules to Homogenous Checks and to Administrative Measures and Penalties concerning Irregularities with regard to Community law. Irregularity is defined in Article 1, paragraph 2, *Regulation 2988/95 on Protection of the Financial Interests* as:

> "any infringement of a provision of Community law resulting from an act or omission by an economic operator, which has, or would have, the effect of prejudicing the general budget of the Communities or budgets managed by them, either by reducing or losing revenue accruing from own resources collected directly on behalf of the Communities, or by an unjustified item of expenditure."

4.4. CRIMES AGAINST HUMAN DIGNITY

Racism and xenophobia have been prohibited by Article A of Title I *Joint Action 96/443 on Racism and Xenophobia.* This provision covers various forms of discrimination.

Trafficking in human beings has been criminalised in Article 1 *Framework Decision 2002/629 on Combating Trafficking in Human Beings.*

Sexual Exploitation of Children and Child Pornography Articles 1, 2 and 3 *Framework Decision 2004/68 on Child Pornography* impose upon the Member States to criminalise forms of sexual exploitation of minors.[733]

---

[733]   This Framework Decision repealed *Joint Action 97/154 on Trafficking in Human Beings*, which already covered the criminalisation of child pornography and other forms of sexual abuse of children.

4.5. CRIMES AGAINST THE DEMOCRATIC SOCIETY

Participation in a criminal organisation has separately been criminalised in *Joint Action 98/733 on Participation in a Criminal Organisation.*

Terrorist activities have led to an array of rather vaguely described offences. *Terrorist offences, participation in a terrorist group and offences linked to terrorist activities* have been criminalised in Articles 1, 2 and 3 *Framework Decision 2002/475 on Combating Terrorism. Common Position 2001/930 on Combating Terrorism* criminalises the financing of terrorism in Article 1. In addition, Article 14 *Common Position 2001/930 on Combating Terrorism* determines that Member States "shall become parties as soon as possible to the relevant international conventions and protocols relating to terrorism" listed in an Annex to the Common Position. What does this mean? First, it is clear that the European Union regards the behaviour criminalised in the 13 Conventions as terrorist acts that should be criminalised. Second, the margin for the Member States not to ratify the said Conventions is rather slim. The result is clear, they must ratify. However, the speed at which they do this is not fixed (as soon as possible). Its importance mainly lies in removing all possible impediments to smooth co-operation in criminal matters and not primarily in the field of substantive criminal law.[734] Does this bind the Member States? Does this make parliament superfluous? At the time of finalising the text of this book, negotiations were taking place on the criminalisation of the following three related offences: public provocation to commit a terrorist offence; recruitment for terrorism; and training for terrorism.[735]

Articles 2, 3 and 4 *Framework Decision 2005/222 on Attacks against Information Systems* stipulate the criminalisation of illegal access and interference with data and computer systems.

4.6. CRIMES AGAINST THE INTEGRITY OF PUBLIC ADMINISTRATION

Active and passive corruption is criminalised in Article 2 *Corruption Convention.* The criminalisation in the *First Protocol Financial Interests Convention* is limited to corruption which damages the financial interest of the Community.

---

[734] See, further, Chapter 7, Section 2.
[735] Proposal Framework Decision amending Framework Decision 2002/475/JHA on Combating Terrorism, Council Document 3 April 2008, 7785/2/08, Rev.2, CATS 24, DROIPEN 30.

Offences Against or by Officials During Operations in Another Member State
Article 15 *EU Mutual Assistance Convention* contains a more hidden criminalisation than is found in other legal instruments. It reads: "During the operation referred to in Articles 12, 13 and 14, officials from a Member State other than the Member State of operation shall be regarded as officials of the Member State of operations with respect of offences committed against them or by them."[736] Articles 12, 13 and 14 of the Convention deal with controlled deliveries, joint investigation teams and covert investigations. These are all forms of co-operation by which officials are allowed to operate in another Member State.

4.7. CRIMES AGAINST PUBLIC HEALTH

Drugs Offences
Various decisions of the Council call for the criminalisation, albeit without directly imposing it, of various synthetic substances.[737] The basis for this is to be found in Article 5, paragraph 1 of Joint Action 97/396 of 16 June 1997 concerning the information exchange, risk assessment and the control of new synthetic drugs.[738] Article 1, paragraph 1 *Framework Decision 2004/757 on Illicit Drug Trafficking*, also defines as "drugs" the substances that have been defined as new synthetic drugs by virtue of Joint Action 97/396.

4.8. CRIMES AGAINST THE FAIR ADMINISTRATION OF JUSTICE

Articles 27, 29 and 30 of the Statute of the Court relate to the obligation of witnesses and experts to appear before the Court and testify under oath. Defaulting witnesses may be fined by the Court directly. Regarding perjury, Article 30 provides for prosecution by the Member State concerned "as if the offence had been committed before one of its own courts".

A similar construction can be found with regard to false statements when testimony is taken by video conference. Article 6, paragraph 4 of the EU-USA

---

[736] Likewise Article 3a, paragraph 6 *Europol Convention* regarding Europol officials in joint investigation teams; Article 22 *Decision 2008/615 on Stepping up Cross-border Cooperation*.

[737] See, for instance, Decision 1999/615 of 13 September 1999 defining 4-MTA as a new synthetic drug which is to be made subject to control measures and criminal penalties, OJ 1999, L 244/1; Decision 2002/188 of 28 February 2002 concerning control measures and criminal sanction in respect of the new synthetic drug PMMA, OJ 2002, L 63/14; Decision 2003/847 of 27 November 2003 concerning control measures and criminal sanction in respect of the new synthetic drug 2C-I, 2C-T-2, 2C-T-7 and TMA-2, OJ 2003, L 321/64.

[738] OJ 1997, L 25/1.

Agreement on Mutual Assistance in Criminal Matters stipulates that "making an intentionally false statement or other misconduct of the witness or expert during the course of the video conference shall be punishable in the requested State in the same manner as if it had been committed in the course of its domestic proceedings". Both the crimes against the fair administration of justice and the offences concerning officials during operations in another Member State raise the question of whether specific national implementation or mere extensive interpretation is necessary to comply with these obligations.[739]

4.9. CRIMES AGAINST THE ENVIRONMENT

Crimes Against the Environment
The annulled *Framework Decision 2003/80 on the Protection of the Environment* creates intentional and negligent offences. This Framework Decision is mentioned, despite its annulment, because it has most likely led to national implementing legislation. The annulment took place on 13 September 2005, while the implementation period lapsed on 27 January 2005. It is likely that some Member States will have complied with their implementation obligations. In addition, Directive 2005/35 on Ship Pollution as well as the accompanying (and later annulled) *Framework Decision 2005/667 on Ship-source Pollution* must be mentioned.

5. A EUROPEAN CRIMINAL POLICY?

What kind of conclusions can be drawn from the legislative practice of the European Union regarding eurocrimes as described above? Does a certain legislative and practical criminal policy appear on the horizon? How are the topics for legislation selected? What are the underlying conditions for harmonisation? Given the lack of explanatory memoranda or statements of reasons, the intentions of the drafters must be deduced from the (preamble) of the legal act itself. On the basis of this, a predominant focus on financial crimes (money laundering, insider dealing, EC fraud, counterfeiting, all sorts of corruption and offences related to payment instruments) can be discovered. All of these aim to protect the undisturbed functioning of the internal market. With all of these crimes, there is an element of safeguarding the integrity of the sectors involved.

The other common element that can be found is that some crimes relate to a policy area of the Union (drugs, unlawful entry, environment, racism and

---

[739] See, further below, Section 6.

xenophobia). Other types of crime relate to the protection of vulnerable people: protecting children against sexual abuse and the combat against trafficking in human beings, as well as society as a whole against the dangers of terrorism.

Whilst the criminalisation of some forms of conduct may find its explanation in the link with a policy area, this cannot be said of others. In addition, there are numerous policy areas that have not led to any criminalisation of conduct. This raises the question of how the choices are made. Does the European Union look at serious offences only? The conditions for criminalisation are not made visible. In the 13th recital of *Framework Decision 2005/222 on Attacks against Information Systems*, it is stipulated that "there is a need to avoid over-criminalisation, particularly in minor cases, as well as a need to avoid criminalising right-holders and authorised persons".[740] Does the Union provide any research into the possible responses to undesirable conduct? And if conduct has been criminalised, are there mechanisms of impact assessment in place?

Earlier on, the question of criminal law as a means of enforcement was raised in the context of the competences of the Union.[741] With the entry into force of the Lisbon Treaty, the issue is no longer whether there is a competence for legislation in criminal law at all, but, given the fact that there is such a competence, why it should be used or not be used. What is apparent at this stage is that there is a presumption that the use of criminal law, because of its very nature, may contribute to better enforcement. Advocate General Ruiz-Jarabo Colomer, when giving his opinion in the case C-176/03, argued that some violations require:

> "punishment in the true meaning of the word, which must be more or less severe according to the importance of the legal interest under threat and the degree of social disapproval of the meaning of the infringing behaviour."[742]

There is an implicit presumption that a criminal penalty makes law effective.[743] On the other hand, there have also been cases in which certain restrictions to the fundamental freedoms under Union law have been admitted, but the use of criminal sanctions, notably a term of imprisonment, was regarded as disproportionate in view of the right to free movement.[744]

---

[740] See, also, the substantive provisions Article 2, 3 and 4 of the Framework Decision that stipulates obligations "at least for cases which are not minor".

[741] See Section 2.

[742] Opinion Advocate General Ruiz-Jarabo Colomer of 26 May 2005, Case C-176/03, *Commission v. Council* [2005] ECR I-7879, point 46. See, also, point 74.

[743] Opinion Advocate General Ruiz-Jarabo Colomer of 26 May 2005, Case C-176/03, *Commission v. Council* [2005] ECR I-7879, point 84.

[744] 3 July 1980, Case 157/79, *Regina* v. *Stanislaus Pieck* [1980] ECR 2171; 21 September 1989, Case C-378/97, *criminal proceedings against Floris Ariël Wijsenbeek* [1999] ECR I-6207, par. 44.

6.   IMPLEMENTATION INTO NATIONAL CRIMINAL LAW

At the beginning of this chapter, it was established that the principle of legality, being one of the general principles of law, requires that criminal liability finds its basis in national criminal law. Direct applicability of Union law, without national transposition, is prohibited. This leaves us with the question of what techniques the Member States use in practice when implementing the obligations to criminalise. Clearly, Member States will be guided by the principle of assimilation. This should bring Member States to criminalise eurocrimes in a similar manner as equivalent crimes under national law. With the exception of the new crimes of money laundering and insider dealing, it is most likely that the Member States already had national criminal provisions which dealt with the conduct described in Section 4 in one way or another. With regard to most crimes, the added value of the Union act has been to extend the existing national offences and to give a name to the conduct (for example, trafficking in human beings, terrorist activities, child pornography). From the description in the Union legal instrument, it must be assumed that the material implementation of the conduct is sufficient, and that Union law does not require the introduction of the formal name tag into national law. The legislative practice of Member States in implementation shows a wide variety of techniques, even within one Member State. Union law leaves Member States free in the use of these techniques. It is the result that counts. The standard phrase in Framework Decisions being: "Each Member State shall take the necessary measures to ensure that the following intentional conduct is punishable."

With the *copy and paste* method, the Member State copies the wording of the prohibited conduct into a provision of national criminal law. This seems to be a very safe method when a Member State wishes to live up to its obligations. It makes it quite easy to apply national legislation in conformity with the Union act. However, the dangers of such a method lie in the use of the terminology in the Union act which may not be compatible with the national criminal justice system and could thus lead to distortion.

Another safe method is the *reference* technique.[745] Here, a Member State will adopt national criminal legislation which states: "It is shall be a criminal offence to commit the conduct as described in Article xy of Framework Decision YZ." This method may be problematical with some national systems, because the Union instrument may use other terminology than the criminal justice system has used to date and this may lead to confusion. However, unlike the *copy and*

---

[745]   The obligation to refer to the Union legal instrument in the implementing legislation should be regarded as a way to recognise its European roots and corresponding connotations, not as an obligation to use direct reference in criminalisation. See Article 291, paragraph 4 TFEU.

paste method, the reference method may not oblige Member States to amend its legislation if there is an amendment of the European instrument. Naturally, this applies only if the amendment relates to the provisions referred to in the national criminal law alone. The latter method of implementation of Union law incorporates any changes to the Union legal instruments automatically. From a legislative perspective, this is primarily apparent with technical regulations to which frequent changes can be expected. The reference technique may come into conflict with the *lex certa* principle if the legality principle must be understood to require a national written norm that fully describes the prohibited conduct.

A more common technique is that of *translation*. By this method, the Member State translates the obligations deriving from the European instrument into its own words. A reason for this is that it allows the Member State to maintain the coherence of its national criminal justice system. But even when the Union legal instrument is adopted in every legal language, the terms under Union law may not fully correspond to the terminology used in national law. Apart from the fact that Union law is autonomously interpreted, this may find an explanation in the fact that a number of language versions cover more than one criminal justice system (Dutch, English, French, German, Greek and Swedish).

The last method found is not necessarily one of legislation, but one of application: the judicial *European interpretation* of the elements of the national definition of a crime. An example of the latter is that a national criminal court will interpret an existing provision of the national criminal code in the light of the existing Union legislation. In a situation in which the national provision is the product of the implementation of European obligations, this must already be done in the form of an interpretation that is in conformity with the Directive and Framework Decision. Additionally, there are also situations in which the significance of a term from the description of the offence is further defined by the underlying Union law. These can be either very broad terms, such as "unauthorised entry or residence", "unlawful" and "waste products", or very specific terms, such as "tethered".[746] National criminal courts will be legitimised to interpret the national terminology in a Union-minded manner without further implementation. The limits of the interpretation in conformity with Directives and Framework Decisions lie in the principle of legality.

The question arises as to whether the offences by and against officials during operations, and the crimes against the fair administration of justice require implementation, or whether the existing national criminal provisions on crimes committed by or against officials on duty may be interpreted in such a manner that they also cover foreign officials.[747] An interpretation *contra legem* is not

---

[746] 3 April 2008, Case C-187/07, *criminal proceedings against Dirk Endendijk* [2008] ECR not yet reported.

[747] See Sections 4.6 and 4.8 of this Chapter.

permitted under Union law.[748] Since Article 15 *EU Mutual Assistance Convention* is part of a Convention under international law, other rules of direct effect apply than those of the direct effect of Directives and Framework Decisions. The answer will depend both on the system of application of international law in the national legal order of the Member State (monistic or dualistic) and the concrete definition of the existing national crime.

The extremely detailed description of criminalised conduct in some of the Union legal acts raises the question of whether a Member State may subsume the conduct under a *chapeau* offence. Two examples may clarify the issue. Following a *Financial Interests Convention* on fraud, a Member State may incorporate a new crime of EU fraud into its Penal Code, which requires that the fraud be committed to the detriment of the European Union. This is an additional burden for the prosecution to prove in comparison to forgery, the provision previously used to combat EU fraud. The *lex generalis* can be proven more easily by the prosecution, because it consists of fewer elements. Does this entitle EU fraudsters to an indictment on the new (more complicated for the prosecution and more favourable to the perpetrator!) charge because it is a *lex specialis*? The other example relates to the *Framework Decision 2001/413 on Combating Fraud*. This Framework Decision, among other things, requires "theft of a payment instrument" to be criminalised. Does this require that, on top of the criminalisation of theft, the *lex generalis* which exists in all criminal justice systems, the Member States ought to introduce a *lex specialis* of theft of a credit card?

Another issue is where, in the national criminal legislation, the implementing legislation should find its place. It is apparent that Union law does not point Member States in any direction, and this is entirely left to the Member States. In the implementing legislation process, the national legislator must jump through all manner of hoops to maintain the existing system in place. Choices must be made. Will transposition be in the general Penal Code, or in a separate act? Member States may have all kinds of motives either to incorporate as much as possible into the existing system of a general code or into special criminal acts. The incorporation into the Penal Code may be more conducive to maintain the coherency of the national criminal justice system. However, the maintenance of this coherency could also provide good reason to do the opposite. Implementation of a Union norm can have a disruptive effect at the national level. On the other hand, adoption of a separate act may provide more recognition to the Union origins of this piece of legislation. Occasionally, one may have doubts as to whether the adoption of a separate act is not influenced by the desire to give its existence as little attention as possible.

---

[748]   See, further, Chapter 5, Section 8.2.

The lack of any case law on the compliance of the Member States with the obligation to criminalise behaviour originates from the fact that the Court did not have jurisdiction over such cases until the entry into force of the Treaty of Lisbon.

CHAPTER 5.
EUROPEAN CRIMINAL PROCEDURE

1. INTRODUCTION

The multi-level character of European criminal procedure is, generally speaking, more hidden than in the field of substantive criminal law. In the latter, Union law either requires a Member State to set aside national criminal law or asks a Member State to introduce new offences into national criminal law. In addition, regarding substantive criminal law, there is a grey zone in which mutual influence exists (for example, general principles, such as *nulla poena*). This ambiguous zone, or zone of mutual influence of Union law and national law, also exists in criminal procedure. However, in comparison to substantive criminal law, it is less concrete. For instance, there is only one Framework Decision that deals with criminal procedure. Here, its influence is exerted at the level of principles.

This chapter basically deals with three phenomena. Firstly, the mutual influence of Union law and national law on national criminal proceedings. Secondly, the procedures to be followed by the Commission when investigating infringements of Union law in general, and of competition law in particular. Thirdly, the influence of the general principles of Union law, especially human rights, on criminal procedure. Similar to Chapter 4, the integrative representation of this procedural law results in a picture of the current state of affairs of European criminal procedure.

Criminal procedure has not, with the exception of the *Framework Decision 2001/220 on the Standing of Victims*, been the central theme of a Union act.[749] The direct influence of Union law is, in comparison to the influence of substantive criminal law, much more limited. This certainly does not mean that there is no *acquis* of European criminal procedure. Procedural rules relating to evidence have been incorporated in Union acts in various policy fields of the "old Community": in the fisheries, and agricultural policy, for example. The general principles of Union law, as developed by the Court, are mainly of a procedural nature. The legislative competences of the Union in the field of criminal procedure

---

[749] There was a draft Framework Decision on Certain Procedural Rights of Persons Arrested in Connection with or Charged with a Criminal Offence, Council Document, 9937/07, 25 May 2007. However, it was never adopted.

are shaped similarly to substantive criminal law in Article 82 TFEU. On the basis of this provision, Directives establishing minimum rules should aim at facilitating mutual recognition of judgments and judicial decisions, and police and judicial co-operation in criminal matters. The rules should relate to mutual admissibility of evidence between Member States, the rights of individuals in criminal procedure, and the rights of victims of crime.[750] In other words, criminal procedure is fully within the competence of the Union.

Despite the similarities in the legislative competences created by the Treaty of Lisbon, the differences with substantive criminal law prevail and require a entirely different structure for Chapter 5 than that of the previous chapter. After this introductory section, a separate paragraph is dedicated to the general principles of the Union's law. This is justified, given the procedural nature of many of these principles. In Chapter 3, Section 5.3, the general principles were discussed from the viewpoint of the *sources* upon which the Court bases its interpretation of the law. In this chapter, all general principles of a procedural nature have been filtered out of the body of general principles, and are dealt with in more elaborate manner. The new approach aims to present the principles which are relevant in national criminal proceedings. In Section 2.3, both the necessity and the consequences of the European Union acceding to the ECHR will be dealt with. Section 3, entitled *The right to prosecute*, is almost completely dedicated to the principle of *ne bis in idem*. The focus on *ne bis in idem* can be explained by the fact that no other criminal topic has so often been the subject of the Court's judgment. Section 4 deals with an existential question of criminal procedure: *to prosecute or not to prosecute*, and will pay attention to the divergent national criminal justice systems of the Member States. Investigations, measures of coercion, and evidence are the topics of Section 6. The *sui generis* procedures of Section 6 relate to boycotts and anti-terrorism measures. The way criminal proceedings are conducted is the topic of Section 7, in which the position of the witness comes to the fore. In Section 8, the national implementation of Union law is discussed from the viewpoint of national criminal proceedings. Likewise, the reference for a preliminary ruling is also approached from the perspective of the national criminal court dealing with the matter. This section is of a very practical nature.

This chapter focuses on the aspects of criminal procedure that are influenced by Union law. Like substantive criminal law, criminal procedure also *"suffers"* from the general influence of Union law. In a similar vein as to substantive criminal law, it must be recalled that, when drafting Union law whose purpose is to take effect in the national legal order this is, by and large, done without taking either the consequences or the effects that it has for a specific field of law into account. However, despite the fact that Union law does not, in general, have a

---

750   Article 82 TFEU also stipulates the emergency-break procedure. See, further, Chapter 2, Section 4.6.

specific field of law in mind, it may have specific effects with regard to criminal procedure. In addition, there are procedural rules which are derived from Union legislation which clearly aim at exclusively influencing the rules of criminal procedure. This is, in short, the essence of this chapter.

As a result of the fact that the internal market creates freedoms, procedural national rules may also have to be set aside. Or, in the words of the Court:

> "Although in principle criminal legislation and the rules of criminal procedure, among which the national provision in issue is to be found, are matters for which the Member States are responsible, the Court has consistently held that Community law sets certain limits to their power. Such legislative powers may not discriminate against persons to whom Community law gives the right to equal treatment or restrict the fundamental freedoms guaranteed by Community law."[751]

Thus, in a similar manner as for substantive criminal law, even coercive measures of a procedural nature may also not restrict any of the freedoms recognised under the Treaties. In the *Rioglass* case, goods legally brought onto the market in Spain, were seized by the customs in France before they could leave France for a destination outside the European Union.[752] The French customs had seized the goods on suspicion that the goods in question were produced in violation of the rules on piracy. Even if the goods are in transit to a non-Member State, they still fall within the scope of Articles 34–36 TFEU (formerly Articles 28–30 TEC).[753] The exceptions under Article 36 TFEU (which allows for combating violations of trademarks) are not applicable because the goods are in transit and are, therefore, no longer on the market.[754]

The limitations of the four freedoms in criminal proceedings often relate to checks and control measures. The Court:

> "has consistently held that Community law sets certain limits in relation to the control measures which it permits the Member States to maintain in connection with the free movement of goods and persons. Administrative measures or penalties must not go beyond what is strictly necessary, and the control procedures must not be framed in such a way as to restrict the freedom."[755]

---

[751]   2 February 1989, Case 186/87, *Ian William Cowan* v. *Trésor Public* [1989] ECR 195, par. 19. 24 November 1998, Case C-274/96, *criminal proceedings against Horst Otto Bickel and Ulrich Franz* [1998] ECR I-7637, par. 17.

[752]   23 October 2003, Case C-115/02, *Administration des douanes et droits indirects* v. *Rioglass SA and Transremar SL* [2003] ECR I-12705.

[753]   23 October 2003, Case C-115/02, *Administration des douanes et droits indirects* v. *Rioglass SA and Transremar SL* [2003] ECR I-12705, par. 20.

[754]   23 October 2003, Case C-115/02, *Administration des douanes et droits indirects* v. *Rioglass SA and Transremar SL* [2003] ECR I-12705, par. 22–30.

[755]   14 December 1995, Case C-387/93, *criminal proceedings against Giorgio Domingo Banchero* [1995] ECR I-4663, par. 58.

Union law may lead to obligations and rights for individuals in the field of criminal procedure. Similar to other types of rules, obligations require implementation, the Court held that it is necessary to bear in mind that: "A Directive cannot by itself create obligations for a private individual and that a provision of a Directive may not therefore be relied upon as such against the latter."[756] However, there is also a striking difference with the application of Union rules that could be held against an individual. Unlike substantive rules, procedural rules may take immediate effect and may be applied to situations that date from a period before the Directive or Framework Decision entered into force.[757] In addition, they do not necessarily require implementation.

2.   THE GENERAL PRINCIPLES OF UNION LAW

In Chapter 3, the use which the Court makes of general principles of law common to the constitutional traditions of the Member States was discussed.[758] The Court uses these principles when interpreting the law. This often means that the direct effect of Union law is reduced slightly because of these overriding principles. Union law must not be applied at all costs! Its obligations on freedoms and enforcement rules are not purely instrumental. There is room for the safeguarding of the individuals involved. In this section, the detailed rights of the concepts of fair trial and the rights of the defence, both of which are recognised by the Court as part of the general principles of law, will be further elaborated on. The Court follows the case law of the ECtHR, which may lead us to reconsider its own case law upon the contents of a general principle.[759]

2.1.   FUNDAMENTAL RIGHTS

The Court has repeatedly held that fundamental rights form part of the general principles of law. Human rights obligations also form an integral part of the general principles of law, the observance of which the Court ensures. The ECHR has special significance in this respect. The Court also applies the International

---

[756]   26 May 2005, Case C-297/03, *Sozialhilfeverband Rohrbach* v. *Arbeitskammer Oberösterreich and Österreichischer Gewerkschaftsbund* [2005] ECR I-4305, par. 32.

[757]   16 June 2005, Case C-105/03, *criminal proceedings against Maria Pupino* [2005] ECR I-5285 par. 44–46; 28 June 2007, Case C-467/05, *criminal proceedings against Giovanni Dell'Orto* [2007] ECR I-5557, par. 48.

[758]   Chapter 3, Section 5.3.

[759]   22 October 2002, Case C-94/00, *Roquette Frères SA* v. *Directeur général de la concurrence, de la consommation et de la répression des fraudes and the Commission* [2002] ECR I-9011, on the question of whether business premises are protected like homes in the sense of Article 8 ECHR.

Covenant on Civil and Political Rights, the Convention on the Rights of the Child, and the Charter on Fundamental Rights as part of the general principles of community law.[760] Given the fact that the Court has given the ECHR a more prominent place, it is appropriate to deal with the relationship and rank of these legal instruments *vis-à-vis* national law. The ECHR has been explicitly referred to in Article 6, paragraph 3 TEU. This can be regarded as a codification of the Court's case law on the status of the ECHR as part of the general principles.[761]

The Charter of Fundamental Rights of the European Union (hereinafter: the Charter) is addressed to the institutions and bodies of the Union (Article 6, paragraph 1 TEU). In addition, it is addressed to the Member States when they are implementing Union law (Article 51, paragraph 1 Charter). Limitations of the rights and freedoms of the Charter can only be provided by law if they are necessary and genuinely meet the objectives of general interest recognised by the Union or the need to protect the rights and freedoms of others (Article 52, paragraph 1 Charter). The added value of the Charter is limited because it does not offer much more or different rights than those that were already protected under the ECHR. Advocate General Poiares Maduro states that the Charter "is nevertheless not without effect as a criterion for the interpretation of the instruments protecting the rights mentioned in Article 6(2) EU".[762] The relationship between the ECHR and the Charter is clarified in paragraph 3 of Article 52 of the Charter: rights corresponding to the rights guaranteed in the ECHR are to be considered as having the same meaning and scope. However, the Union may provide a more extensive protection.

Having clarified the relationship between the ECHR and the Charter, the question arises as to what the relation between the conglomerate of human rights (ECHR, Charter and other human rights treaties) and the fundamental freedoms under the Treaties actually is. Which right prevails in a situation in which there are competing rights? With regard to the obligations of the Member States, the Court weighed these against the rights of individuals under the ECHR. The basic

---

[760]   27 June 2006, Case C-540/03, *European Parliament* v. *Council* [2006] ECR I-5769, par. 33–39.

[761]   26 June 2007, Case C-305/05, *Ordre des barreaux francophones et germanophone, Ordre français des avocats du barreau de Bruxelles, Ordre des barreaux flamands, Ordre néerlandais des avocats du barreau de Bruxelles* v. *Conseil des Ministres* [2007] ECR I-535, par. 29; 18 October 2007, Case C-299/05, *Commission* v. *European Parliament and Council* [2007] ECR I-8695, par. 76; 14 December 2006, Case C-283/05, *ASML Netherlands BV* v. *Semicondutor Industry Services GmbH (SEMIS)* [2006] ECR I-12041, par. 26; 12 September 2006, Case C-479/04, *Laserdisken ApS* v. *Kulturministeret* [2006] ECR I-8089, par. 61. See, further, Chapter 3, Section 5.3.

[762]   Opinion of Advocate General Poiares Maduro of 14 December 2006, Case C-305/05, *Ordre des barreaux francophones et germanophone, Ordre français des avocats du barreau de Bruxelles, Ordre des barreaux flamands, Ordre néerlandais des avocats du barreau de Bruxelles* v. *Conseil des Ministres* [2007] ECR I-535, point 48; Opinion of Advocate General Poiares Maduro of 9 September 2008, Case C-465/07, *M. Elgafaji, N. Elgafaji* v. *Staatssecretaris van Justitie* ECR not yet reported, point 21.

---

line is that measures which are incompatible with the observance of human rights are not acceptable in the Community.[763] However, the Court also identified, in line with what is provided under the ECHR, that, apart from certain absolute rights (the right to life and the prohibition of torture), other rights may be restricted under certain circumstances.[764] The case of *Schmidberger*, a transporter who sued for damages caused by Austria having granted an environmental group permission to organise a demonstration on the Brenner motorway may serve as an example of the balance between a fundamental right and a fundamental freedom. This case dealt with restrictions on freedom of expression. The Court held that, in the light of the limited duration of the blockade of the Brenner motorway,[765] and the fact that the purpose of the public demonstration was not to restrict the trade in goods of a particular type or origin, there was no obligation for Austria to restrict the freedom of expression. More generally, it may be concluded that it is difficult to conceive of a situation in which Union law would prescribe or even tolerate a clear violation of a human rights obligation.[766]

Another question which must be dealt with here, is whether the Court may actually interpret the ECHR itself, or even state that the ECHR has been violated. Given the fact that the principal task of the Court is to interpret the Treaties, as well as secondary legislation, it has been reluctant in stating that a human rights violation has or has not occurred. Additionally, the Court can only deal with human rights obligations if the situation in question falls within the scope of the Treaties. In its interpretation of the ECHR, the Court follows the case law of the ECtHR. Similar remarks must be made with regard to the references made in the case law of the ECtHR to the Court's case law or to Union law. More so than the Court, the ECtHR has refrained from stating anything on Union law. This may be due to the more clearly-defined jurisdiction of the ECtHR, which exclusively deals with the interpretation of the ECHR. In comparison, the ECHR is part of the general principles which the Court has to interpret.

2.2. GENERAL PRINCIPLES OF CRIMINAL PROCEDURE

The Court has recognised an impressive catalogue of general principles that are applicable in criminal procedure. Some of these have their counterpart in the ECHR or in other human rights conventions, others have been independently developed. Most of the general principles of criminal procedure have been stated

---

[763]   12 June 2003, Case C-112/00, *Eugen Schmidberger, Internationale Transporte und Planzüge* v. *Republik Österreich* [2003] ECR I-5659, par. 73.

[764]   12 June 2003, Case C-112/00, *Eugen Schmidberger, Internationale Transporte und Planzüge* v. *Republik Österreich* [2003] ECR I-5659, par. 80.

[765]   This motorway links Germany with Italy through the Austrian Alps.

[766]   See, further, Chapter 3, Section 5.3.

in competition cases. In this sub-section all these principles and rights are discussed.

Fair Trial and the Rights of the Defence

The case law of the Court distinguishes between the general right to a fair trial, also known as the rights of the defence, and more specific rights.[767] Observance of the rights of the defence is a fundamental principle of Union law which must be complied with.[768] With regard to the rights of the defence, the leading Court cases are *Hoechst* and *Dow*, in which the obligations of the defendant to co-operate with the Commission during the investigations into competition law violations were discussed. Both companies applied to the Court, alleging that the Commission had violated their rights. The Court referred to the rights of the defence which had already been recognised in judgments prior to *Hoechst* and *Dow*, but then proceeded to elaborate the defence rights in much more detail,[769] in which it extended the scope of application of the rights of the defence under Union law to the stage of investigations:

> "it is also necessary to prevent those rights from being irremediably impaired during preliminary inquiry procedures including, in particular, investigations which may be decisive in providing evidence of the unlawful nature of conduct (…)."[770]

In a manner comparable to the ECtHR in its case law, the Court has held that the right to a fair trial or fair hearing is not a static right, but one that may be balanced with the rights and interests of others.[771] In *Pupino*, the Court emphasised the importance of both the ECHR and the fundamental rights that result from the constitutional traditions of the Member States.[772] The relevant Framework Decision also referred to the compatibility with the basic legal principles of the Member State concerned. The obligations deriving from Article 6 ECHR require that the accused's right to a fair trial be balanced with the rights of vulnerable victims.[773]

---

[767]   This case law has been codified in the Charter. Article 47 Charter stipulates the general right to a fair and public hearing. Article 48, paragraph 2, Charter, reads: "Respect for the rights of the defence of anyone who has been charged shall be guaranteed".

[768]   10 May 2007, Case C-328/05 P, *Appeal of SGL Carbon AG* [2007] ECR I-3921, par. 59.

[769]   7 June 1983, Joined Cases 100 to 103/80, *SA Musique Diffusion française and others* v. *Commission* [1983] ECR 1825, par. 10–11.

[770]   21 September 1989, Joined Cases 46/87 and 227/88, *Hoechst AG* v. *Commission* [1989] ECR 2859, par. 15; 17 October 1989, Case 85/87, *Dow Benelux NV* v. *Commission* [1989] ECR 3137, par. 26.

[771]   14 February 2008, Case C-450/06, *Varec SA* v. *Belgian State* [2008] ECR not yet reported.

[772]   16 June 2005, *criminal proceedings against Maria Pupino*, Case C-105/03 par. 57 and 58.

[773]   Opinion of Advocate General Kokott of 11 November 2004, Case C-105/03, *criminal proceedings against Maria Pupino* [2005] ECR I-5285, point 67.

The fact that oral evidence plays a minor role and written evidence a central role in competition law cases distinguishes competition from other criminal cases. As a result of this, the principle that everyone has a right to a fair trial cannot be interpreted as meaning that documents containing incriminating evidence must automatically be excluded as evidence when certain information must remain confidential.[774]

The specific rights that can be found in the case law or in the Charter include the right to be informed of the charge, the right of access to the file, the right to liberty and security, the right to privacy, the right to legal representation, the lawyer-client privilege, the right to be tried within reasonable time, the right to an effective remedy, the right to be tried by an impartial tribunal, and the presumption of innocence. This list may not be regarded as exhaustive.[775] It was drawn up upon the basis of the specific rights recognised in the case law of the Court and those stipulated in the Charter. However, it is conceivable that other rights recognised in the ECtHR case law will find their way into being applied as specific rights under the *chapeau* of a fair trial for the accused or under the rights of the defence.

Efforts to arrive at a Framework Decision on certain procedural rights of persons arrested in connection with, or charged with, a criminal offence have not led to the adoption of a Union act.[776] The Commission had initiated negotiations on such instruments in 2002 but the draft met with opposition from Member States on various points. One of the points of discussion was the question of whether the instrument should be applicable in all criminal proceedings or only in proceedings related to the European Arrest Warrant. By June 2007, the attempts to come to an agreement on this topic were abandoned. However, with the appearance of the "rights of individuals in criminal procedure" in Article 82, paragraph 2 TFEU, as one of the topics upon which the Union may adopt Directives, an instrument of this kind remains on the agenda.

Right to Be Informed of the Charge

In cases in which an indictment is sent to the accused, it must be written in a language which he can understand, and he must be clearly informed not only of the cause of the accusation against him, that is to say, the acts he is alleged to have committed and upon which the accusation is based, but also of the detailed legal character of those facts. The rights of the defence are not undermined by the mere fact that the indictment does not include the evidence which supports the facts

---

[774]   25 January 2007, Case C-411/04, *Salzgitter Mannesmann GmbH* v. *Commission* [2007] ECR I-959, par. 44.

[775]   21 September 1989, Joined Cases 46/87 and 227/88, *Hoechst AG* v. *Commission* [1989] ECR 2859, par. 16; 17 October 1989, Case 85/87, *Dow Benelux NV* v. *Commission* [1989] ECR 3137, par. 27; 18 May 1982, Case 155/79, *AM & S Europe Limited* v. *Commission* [1982] ECR 2033.

[776]   Council Document 9937/07, 25 May 2007.

upon which the accused stands charged.[777] In the competition law cases of *Hoechst* and *Dow*, the Court held that the Commission, when using coercive means, must inform the addressee of the nature of the charge:

> "Although the Commission is not required to communicate to the addressee of a decision ordering an investigation all the information at its disposal concerning the presumed infringements, or to make a precise legal analysis of those infringements, it must none the less clearly indicate the presumed facts which it intends to investigate."[778]

The right to be informed does not oblige the accused to respond to the information he receives. There is no obligation for the undertaking to reply to a statement of objectives issued by the Commission.[779] In *Roquette Frères*, the Court held that the requirement to inform about the measures is "designed not merely to show that the proposed entry onto the premises of the undertaking is justified, but also to enable those undertakings to assess the scope of their duty to co-operate whilst at the same time safeguarding their rights of defence".[780] The latter have been complied with if the defence has been granted the opportunity to comment upon the duration, the gravity and the nature of the infringement.[781]

Access to the File

In competition law cases, the Court has held that the right to access to the file means that the Commission must give the undertaking concerned an opportunity to examine all the documents in the investigation file which may be relevant for its defence.[782] This kind of disclosure obligation relates to both incriminating and exculpatory evidence. The failure to communicate a document constitutes a breach of the rights of the defence if the Commission relied upon that document to support the alleged infringement.[783] The Court held:

---

[777]   So the Court held, with reference to ECtHR case law in 8 May 2008, Case C-14/07, *Ingenieurbüro Michael Weiss und Partner GbR* v. *Industrie- und Handelskammer Berlin* [2008] ECR not yet reported, par. 70.

[778]   21 September 1989, Joined Cases 46/87 and 227/88, *Hoechst AG* v. *Commission* [1989] ECR 2859, par. 41; 17 October 1989, Case 85/87, *Dow Benelux NV* v. *Commission* [1989] ECR 3137, par. 9.

[779]   Court of First Instance, 12 December 1991, Case T-30/89, *Hilti AG* v. *Commission* [1991] ECR II-1439, par. 37–38.

[780]   22 October 2002, Case C-94/00, *Roquette Frères SA* v. *Directeur général de la concurrence, de la consommation et de la répression des fraudes and the Commission* [2002] ECR I-9011, par. 47.

[781]   10 May 2007, Case C-328/05 P, *Appeal of SGL Carbon AG* [2007] ECR I-3921, par. 58.

[782]   7 January 2004, Joined Cases C-204/00 P, C-205/00 P, C-211/00 P, C-213/00 P, C-217/00 P and C-219/00 P, *Aalborg Portland A/S and Others* v. *Commission* [2004] ECR I-123, par. 68.

[783]   7 June 1983, Joined Cases 100 to 103/80, *SA Musique Diffusion française and others* v. *Commission* [1983] ECR 1825, par. 36; Court of First Instance, 29 June 1995, Case T-30/91, *Solvay SA* v. *Commission* [1995] ECR II-1775; 15 October 2001, Joined Cases C-238/99 P, C-244/99 P, C-245/99 P, C-247/99 P, C-250/99 P to C-252/99 P and C-254/99 P, *Limburgse Vinyl*

"It is thus for the undertaking concerned to show that the result at which the Commission arrived in its decision would have been different if a document which was not communicated to that undertaking and on which the Commission relied to make a finding of infringement against it had to be disallowed as evidence. On the other hand, where an exculpatory document has not been communicated, the undertaking concerned must only establish that its non-disclosure was able to influence, to its disadvantage, the course of the proceedings and the content of the decisions of the Commission."[784]

The Right to Liberty and Security

The right to liberty and security is guaranteed in Article 6 Charter. Regarding the right to liberty, one may refer to the *acquis* that was developed under Article 5 ECHR by the ECtHR. The right to security is a new right on the horizon. It raises the question as to what its contents are, and to what extent it relates to the security that is offered to the citizens in the area of freedom, security and justice.[785]

The Presumption of Innocence

Article 48 Charter specifies the right to a fair trial in general, and the presumption of innocence in particular: "1. Everyone who has been charged shall be presumed innocent until proved guilty according to law."

Right to Remain Silent

The right to remain silent was acknowledged by the Court in *Orkem* and *Limburgse Vinyl Maatschappij*. Several companies had complained to the Court that the Commission had violated this right. In *Limburgse Vinyl Maatschappij*, the Court took the developments in the case law of the ECtHR into consideration.[786] The Court of First Instance held that the right to silence does not imply that the

---

Maatschappij NV (LVM) (C-238/99 P), DSM NV and DSM Kunststoffen BV (C-244/99 P), Montedison SpA (C-245/99 P), Elf Atochem SA (C-247/99 P), Degussa AG (C-250/99 P), Enichem SpA (C-251/99 P), Wacker-Chemie GmbH and Hoechst AG (C-252/99 P) and Imperial Chemical Industries plc (ICI) (C-254/99 P) v. *Commission* [2002] ECR I-8375, par. 315–317.

784   7 January 2004, Joined Cases C-204/00 P, C-205/00 P, C-211/00 P, C-213/00 P, C-217/00 P and C-219/00 P, *Aalborg Portland A/S and Others* v. *Commission* [2004] ECR I-123, par. 73–74. See, also, 2 October 2003, C-194/99 P, *Thyssen Stahl AG* v. *Commission* [2003] ECR I-10821, par. 30.

785   See, further, Chapter 9, Sections 3, 6 and 7.

786   15 October 2001, Joined Cases C-238/99 P, C-244/99 P, C-245/99 P, C-247/99 P, C-250/99 P to C-252/99 P and C-254/99 P, *Limburgse Vinyl Maatschappij NV (LVM) (C-238/99 P), DSM NV and DSM Kunststoffen BV (C-244/99 P), Montedison SpA (C-245/99 P), Elf Atochem SA (C-247/99 P), Degussa AG (C-250/99 P), Enichem SpA (C-251/99 P), Wacker-Chemie GmbH and Hoechst AG (C-252/99 P) and Imperial Chemical Industries plc (ICI) (C-254/99 P)* v. *Commission* [2002] ECR I-8375, par. 273–276.

defendant cannot be under an obligation to submit information to the Commission.[787]

The Right to Privacy – the Inviolability of the Home[788]

Articles 7 and 8 Charter ensure the respect for private and family life, as well as the protection of personal data. The fact that investigations into competition violations by the Commission find their basis in a competition Regulation complies with the requirements of Article 8, paragraph 2 ECHR, which states that any interference into private life must be in accordance with the law.[789]

In competition cases, the Commission may ask national authorities to use coercive measures which infringe upon fundamental rights. In order to comply with the requirements under the ECHR, the Court allows a national court to review whether a coercive measure requested by the Commission is arbitrary or disproportionate.[790] In this context, the Commission may be required to provide the national court with explanations to show that the Commission is in possession of information and evidence which provides reasonable grounds to suspect an infringement of the competition rules.[791] It is, however, not necessary for the national court to see or to test this evidence itself. It seems that the Court ensures that most possibilities for refusal exist in situations in which the proportionality requirement is not complied with.[792]

In *Hoechst* and in *Dow*, the Court held that the right to privacy is limited to natural persons, and that undertakings are not protected by it.[793] On this issue, the interpretation of the ECHR by the Court deviated from that of the ECtHR. A

---

[787]   Court of First Instance 20 February 2001, Case T-112/98, *Mannesmannröhren-Werke AG* v. *Commission* [2001] ECR II-729, par. 65–67. See, also: "The mere fact of being obliged to answer purely factual questions put by the Commission and to comply with its requests for the production of documents already in existence cannot constitute a breach of the principle of respect for the rights of defence or impair the right to a fair legal process." (par. 78).

[788]   In *Roquette Frères*, this right was named the Right to be Afforded Protection against Arbitrary or Disproportionate Intervention by Public Authorities in the Sphere of the Private Activities of any Person. 22 October 2002, Case C-94/00, *Roquette Frères SA* v. *Directeur général de la concurrence, de la consommation et de la répression des fraudes and the Commission* [2002] ECR I-9011.

[789]   26 June 1980, Case 136/79, *National Panasonic (UK) Limited* v. *Commission* [1980] ECR 2033, par. 19–20.

[790]   22 October 2002, Case C-94/00, *Roquette Frères SA* v. *Directeur général de la concurrence, de la consommation et de la répression des fraudes and the Commission* [2002] ECR I-9011, par. 52. In this decision the Court refers to case law of the ECtHR.

[791]   22 October 2002, Case C-94/00, *Roquette Frères SA* v. *Directeur général de la concurrence, de la consommation et de la répression des fraudes and the Commission* [2002] ECR I-9011, par. 61.

[792]   22 October 2002, Case C-94/00, *Roquette Frères SA* v. *Directeur général de la concurrence, de la consommation et de la répression des fraudes and the Commission* [2002] ECR I-9011, par. 80.

[793]   21 September 1989, Joined Cases 46/87 and 227/88, *Hoechst AG* v. *Commission* [1989] ECR 2859, par. 17–18; 17 October 1989, Case 85/87, *Dow Benelux NV* v. *Commission* [1989] ECR 3137, par. 28–29. However, Advocate General Mischo had advocated a fundamental right to the inviolability of business premises. See Joined Opinion of 21 February 1989, Joined Cases 46/87

few years after the Court had pronounced its judgments in *Hoechst* and in *Dow*, the ECtHR recognised the inviolability of non-private homes as a right under Article 8 ECHR.[794]

The Right to Be Present/Represented

It is national criminal procedure which determines whether the accused must be present at trial. Regardless of whether national law requires the presence of the accused, there is always a right to be present. In addition, there is the right to be represented. Article 47 of the Charter reads: "Everyone shall have the possibility of being advised, defended and represented". The right to legal presentation has been recognised by the Court as part of the rights of the defence.[795] Legal aid shall be made available to those who lack sufficient resources in so far as such aid is necessary to ensure effective access to justice. From this provision, a right to legal aid for EU-citizens can be deduced on the same conditions as those applicable to nationals. The simple statement made by a member of the bar of one of the Member States, who, as a barrister, is subject to a code of professional conduct, that he represents a client, is sufficient to determine that he has the power of attorney.[796]

Article II *Protocol to the Brussels Convention* (now replaced by *Regulation 44/2001 on Jurisdiction and Recognition of Civil Judgments*) entitled persons domiciled in another Member State, who are being prosecuted in a Member State of which they are not a national for an offence which was not intentionally committed to "be defended by persons qualified to do so, even if they do not appear in person."[797] This rule has been kept in Article 61 *Regulation 44/2001 on Jurisdiction and Recognition of Civil Judgments*. Article 61 reads:

"Without prejudice to any more favourable provisions of national laws, persons domiciled in a Member State who are being prosecuted in the criminal courts of another Member State of which they are not nationals for an offence which was not intentionally committed may be defended by persons qualified to do so, even if they do not appear in person. However, the court seized of the matter may order appearance in person; in the case of failure to appear, a judgment given in the civil action without the person concerned having had the opportunity to arrange for his defence need not be recognised or enforced in the other Member States."

---

and 227/88, *Hoechst AG v. Commission* [1989] ECR 2859, and Case 85/87, *Dow Benelux NV v. Commission* [1989] ECR 3137, point 103.

[794]   ECtHR, 16 December 1992, *Niemietz* v. *Germany*, Series A-251B.

[795]   22 October 2002, Case C-94/00, *Roquette Frères SA v. Directeur général de la concurrence, de la consommation et de la répression des fraudes and the Commission* [2002] ECR I-9011, par. 46.

[796]   18 January 2007, Case C-229/05, *Osman Ocalan (PKK) and Serif Valy (KNK) appellants, Council, defendant* [2007] ECR I-439, par. 116–122.

[797]   26 May 1981, Case C-157/80, *criminal proceedings against Siegfried Ewald Rinkau* [1981] ECR 1395, par. 5–9.

Free Choice of Defence Counsel

Accused persons are entitled to choose the lawyer of their own choice to represent them. In principle, all lawyers established in the Union may be chosen. It is therefore relevant to look at the applicable conditions for lawyers providing services in another Member State or for those who wish to establish themselves in another Member State. In the past, it was quite complicated for a lawyer to provide services or to establish himself in another Member State. For a long time, lawyers were generally excluded from the mutual recognition of their diplomas, certificates and other qualifications. This situation has come to an end for counsel as a result of the adoption of *Directive 77/249 on Lawyers' Freedom*. This Directive deals with the freedom to provide the service of legal counselling in another Member State than the one in which the lawyer is registered as a lawyer and where he is subject to a professional code of ethics. Member States must recognise all lawyers included in Article 1 of the Directive as lawyers empowered to pursue their activities on their territory. Before the Directive entered in to force, the Court had held that national law might require legal representatives to be permanently established for professional purposes within the jurisdiction of the court "where such requirement is objectively justified by the need to ensure observance of professional rules of conduct connected, in particular, with the administration of justice and with respect for professional ethics".[798] However, the place of establishment no longer plays a role in the observance of the rules of professional conduct. Article 4 *Directive 77/249 on Lawyers' Freedom* stipulates that a lawyer is under obligation to respect the rules of professional conduct of the host state, as well as those of his home state.

The Member States may, for the pursuit of activities relating to the representation of a client in legal proceedings, be required to work with a local lawyer (Article 5 *Directive 77/249 on Lawyers' Freedom*). This might result in a decision not to admit a lawyer qualified in another Member State. However, the Court has held that, in proceedings for which national legislation does not make representation by a lawyer mandatory, foreign lawyers may not be refused.[799] Although national law may (for security reasons) require that visits to persons in custody take place in conjunction with a local lawyer, other forms of corresponding with the person in custody may not be subject to restrictions.[800] The Court has held that the reference to "compliance with the rules relating to professional ethics of the host Member State" in *Directive 77/249 on Lawyers' Freedom* allows a Member State to refuse to permit a lawyer established in another Member State to pursue his activities "in another Member State where he had been barred from access to the legal profession

---

[798] 3 December 1974, Case 33–74, *Johannes Henricus Maria van Binsbergen* v. *Bestuur van de Bedrijfsvereniging voor de Metaalnijverheid* [1974] ECR 1299, par. 14.

[799] 25 February 1988, Case 427/85, *Commission* v. *Germany* [1988] ECR 1123.

[800] 25 February 1988, Case 427/85, *Commission* v. *Germany* [1988] ECR 1123, par. 29–32.

of the latter Member State for reasons relating to dignity, good repute and integrity".[801]

The Directive does not deal with the freedom of establishment. In the absence of specific Union legislation before *Directive 98/5 on Lawyers' Title* entered into force, the general rules on free movement applied. The case law of the Court in this area can be represented as follows: in the case of *Reyners*, the Court held that the exception to the freedom of establishment, based upon the fact that the activities related to "the exercise of official authority,"(now Article 51 TFEU), did not concern the activities of a lawyer "such as consultation and legal assistance or the representation and defence of parties in court, even if the performance of these activities is compulsory or there is a legal monopoly in respect of it".[802] The freedom to establish oneself as a lawyer in another Member State was the subject of the *Gebhard* case.[803] Gebhard, a qualified German lawyer, established himself and worked as a lawyer in Italy. When the local bar suspended him from exercising his functions, the question arose as to whether a Member State may impose conditions on the freedom of establishment of lawyers. The Court held that conditions may be provided by law, so that the "pursuit of a particular activity is restricted to holders of a diploma, certificate or other evidence of formal qualifications, to persons belonging to a professional body or to persons subject to particular rules or supervision. As the case may be, they may also lay down the conditions for the use of professional titles, such as *avvocato*".[804] Any prohibition on the establishment of chambers in more than one Member State is not compatible with the freedom of establishment.[805] Lawyers who wish to establish themselves in another Member State may not be refused solely because they do not possess the *national* diploma or because the host Member State does not recognise non-national qualifications.[806]

However, despite the fact that the Member State may apply national criteria, it must examine the knowledge and qualifications already acquired by the person in another Member State, and cannot disregard them because of their origin. The Court held in the case of *Vlassopoulou*:

---

[801] 19 January 1988, Case 292/86, *Claude Gullung* v. *Conseil de l'ordre des avocats du barreau de Colmar et de Saverne* [1988] ECR 111, par. 21–22.

[802] 21 June 1974, Case 2–74, *Jean Reyners* v. *Belgian State* [1974] ECR 631, par. 55.

[803] 30 November 1995, Case C-55/94, *Reinhard Gebhard* v. *Consiglio dell'Ordine degli Avvocati e Procuratori di Milano* [1995] ECR I-4165.

[804] 30 November 1995, Case C-55/94, *Reinhard Gebhard* v. *Consiglio dell'Ordine degli Avvocati e Procuratori di Milano* [1995] ECR I-4165, par. 35.

[805] 12 July 1984, Case 107/83, *Ordre des avocats au Barreau de Paris* v. *Onno Klopp* [1984] ECR 2971.

[806] 28 April 1977, Case 71–76, *Jean Thieffry* v. *Conseil de l'ordre des avocats à cour de Paris* [1977] ECR 765, par. 19.

"That examination procedure must enable the authorities of the host Member State to assure themselves, on an objective basis, that the foreign diploma certifies that its holder has knowledge and qualifications which are, if not identical, at least equivalent to those certified by the national diploma. That assessment of the equivalence of the foreign diploma must be carried out exclusively in the light of the level of knowledge and qualifications which its holder can be assumed to possess in the light of that diploma, having regard to the nature and duration of the studies and practical training to which the diploma relates (see the judgment in Case 222/86 *UNECTEF* v. *Heylens*, cited above, paragraph 13). In the course of that examination, a Member State may, however, take into consideration objective differences relating to both the legal framework of the profession in question in the Member State of origin and to its field of activity. In the case of the profession of lawyer, a Member State may therefore carry out a comparative examination of diplomas, taking account of the differences identified between the national legal systems concerned. If that comparative examination of diplomas results in the finding that the knowledge and qualifications certified by the foreign diploma correspond to those required by the national provisions, the Member State must recognize that diploma as fulfilling the requirements laid down by its national provisions. If, on the other hand, the comparison reveals that the knowledge and qualifications certified by the foreign diploma and those required by the national provisions correspond only partially, the host Member State is entitled to require the person concerned to show that he has acquired the knowledge and qualifications which are lacking. In this regard, the competent national authorities must assess whether the knowledge acquired in the host Member State, either during a course of study or by way of practical experience, is sufficient in order to prove possession of the knowledge which is lacking. If completion of a period of preparation or training for entry into the profession is required by the rules applying in the host Member State, those national authorities must determine whether professional experience acquired in the Member State of origin or in the host Member State may be regarded as satisfying that requirement in full or in part. Finally, it must be pointed out that the examination made to determine whether the knowledge and qualifications certified by the foreign diploma and those required by the legislation of the host Member State correspond must be carried out by the national authorities in accordance with a procedure which is in conformity with the requirements of Community law concerning the effective protection of the fundamental rights conferred by the Treaty on Community subjects. It follows that any decision taken must be capable of being made the subject of judicial proceedings in which its legality under Community law can be reviewed and that the person concerned must be able to ascertain the reasons for the decision taken in his regard (see the judgment in Case 222/86 *UNECTEF* v. *Heylens*, cited above, paragraph 17)."[807]

The purpose of *Directive 98/5 on Lawyers' Title,* is not only to enable lawyers to practice in another Member State under their home-country professional titles

---

[807]   7 May 1991, Case C-340/89, *Irène Vlassopoulou* v. *Ministerium für Justiz, Bundes- und Europaangelegenheiten Baden-Württemberg* [1991] ECR I-2357, par. 17–22.

but also to make it easier for them to obtain the professional title of the host Member State. Articles 6 and 7 *Directive 98/5 on Lawyers' Title* determine the applicability of rules of conduct and the disciplinary proceedings in cases in which these rules are violated. The conditions on which a lawyer may obtain the professional title of the host Member State are provided for in Article 10 *Directive 98/5 on Lawyers' Title*.

Lawyer-Client Privilege

The case in which the confidential relationship between lawyer and client was specifically dealt with was the case of various *Bar associations* versus the *Council of Ministers of Belgium*.[808] In his Opinion, Advocate General Poiares Maduro opined that the professional secrecy of lawyers has obtained a rank of fundamental status in the majority of Member States.[809] The Court subsequently acknowledged the special position of the lawyer in criminal matters.[810] Unlike the Commission, which wished to limit the exemption granted to lawyers to the stage of representation before courts, the Court also recognised that the lawyer-client privilege should be protected in the advice stage "as to the manner of instituting or avoiding judicial proceedings".[811]

In the *Akzo Nobel Chemicals* case, the Court of First Instance dealt at length with the principle of legal professional privilege.[812] Business records may be protected by the principle of legal professional privilege. The mere fact that an undertaking claims that a document is protected is not sufficient. An undertaking that claims that certain correspondence is protected by the principle must provide the Commission officials with relevant material which demonstrates that the communications fulfil the conditions for the granting of legal protection.[813] The Court held that an undertaking subject to an investigation regarding an alleged violation of competition rules is entitled to refuse to allow the Commission

---

[808]   26 June 2007, Case C-305/05, *Ordre des barreaux francophones et germanophone, Ordre français des avocats du barreau de Bruxelles, Ordre des barreaux flamands, Ordre néerlandais des avocats du barreau de Bruxelles* v. *Conseil des Ministres* [2007] ECR I-535.

[809]   Opinion of Advocate General Poiares Maduro, 14 December 2006, Case C-305/05, *Ordre des barreaux francophones et germanophone, Ordre français des avocats du barreau de Bruxelles, Ordre des barreaux flamands, Ordre néerlandais des avocats du barreau de Bruxelles* v. *Conseil des Ministres* [2007] ECR I-535, par. 39.

[810]   22 October 2002, Case C-94/00, *Roquette Frères SA* v. *Directeur général de la concurrence, de la consommation et de la répression des fraudes and the Commission* [2002] ECR I-9011, par. 46.

[811]   26 June 2007, Case C-305/05, *Ordre des barreaux francophones et germanophone, Ordre français des avocats du barreau de Bruxelles, Ordre des barreaux flamands, Ordre néerlandais des avocats du barreau de Bruxelles* v. *Conseil des Ministres* [2007] ECR I-535, par. 34.

[812]   Court of First Instance, 17 September 2007, Joined Cases T-125/03 and T-253/03, *Akzo Nobel Chemicals Ltd and Akcros Chemicals Ltd* v. *Commission* [2007] ECR II-3523.

[813]   Court of First Instance, 17 September 2007, Joined Cases T-125/03 and T-253/03, *Akzo Nobel Chemicals Ltd and Akcros Chemicals Ltd* v. *Commission* [2007] ECR II-3523, par. 79–80.

officials to take even a cursory look at one or more specific documents which it claims to be covered by the principle.[814]

The lawyer-client privilege embodies in the words of the Court:

"First, that protection seeks to safeguard the public interest in the proper administration of justice in ensuring that a client is free to consult his lawyer without fear that any confidences which he imparts may subsequently be disclosed. Secondly, its purpose is to avoid the harm which may be caused to the undertaking's rights of the defence as a result of the Commission reading the contents of a confidential document and improperly adding it to the investigation file. Therefore, even if that document is not used as evidence in a decision imposing a penalty under the competition rules, the undertaking may suffer harm which cannot be made good or can only be made good with great difficulty. Information covered by LPP might be used by the Commission, directly or indirectly, in order to obtain new information or new evidence without the undertaking in question always being able to identify or prevent such information or evidence from being used against it. Moreover, harm which the undertaking concerned would suffer as a result of disclosure to third parties of information covered by LPP could not be made good, for example if that information were used in a statement of objections in the course of the Commission's administrative procedure. The mere fact that the Commission cannot use privileged documents as evidence in a decision imposing a penalty is thus not sufficient to make good or eliminate the harm which resulted from the Commission's reading the content of the documents."[815]

Reasonable Time

Article 47 Charter entitles everyone to a fair and public hearing within a reasonable time by an independent and impartial tribunal. In various competition law cases the Court has dealt with the reasonableness of the period of the legal process. This must be assessed "in the light of the specific circumstances of each case and in particular, the importance of the case for the person concerned, its complexity and the conduct of the applicant and of the competent authorities."[816] In *Thyssen*, the Court attached a lot of weight to the fact that eleven undertakings had brought actions for the annulment of the Commission decision imposing a fine, and did so in four different languages of the procedure. This justified the long duration of the procedure.[817] By

---

[814]   Court of First Instance, 17 September 2007, Joined Cases T-125/03 and T-253/03, *Akzo Nobel Chemicals Ltd and Akcros Chemicals Ltd* v. *Commission* [2007] ECR II-3523, par. 82.

[815]   Court of First Instance, 17 September 2007, Joined Cases T-125/03 and T-253/03, *Akzo Nobel Chemicals Ltd and Akcros Chemicals Ltd* v. *Commission* [2007] ECR II-3523, par. 87.

[816]   2 October 2003, C-194/99 P, *Thyssen Stahl AG* v. *Commission* [2003] ECR I-10821, par. 155; 25 January 2007, Joined Cases C-403/04 P and C-405/04, *Sumitomo Metal Industries Ltd and Nippon Steel Corp.* v. *Commission* [2007] ECR I-729, p. 116–122.

[817]   See, also, 17 December 1998, Case C-185/95 P, *Baustahlgewebe GmbH* v. *Commission* [1998] ECR I-8417, par. 43. The Court acknowledged that the use of many languages is prescribed in the Rules of Procedure of the Court of First Instance.

emphasising these elements of complexity and the attitude of the defence during the proceedings, the Court follows the criteria stipulated by the ECtHR.[818] In cases in which the Court holds that there is a violation of the right to be tried within reasonable time, it may reduce the sentenced imposed.[819]

Effective Remedy

Article 47 Charter requires an effective remedy, as well as proceedings to be conducted before an impartial tribunal. The right to appeal or to lodge any other legal remedy must apply without discrimination. On the basis of the old *Directive 64/221 on Movement and Residence of Foreign Nationals*, the Court had already held that, even in cases in which Member States are fully justified to limit free movement rights because of criminal offences committed, the legal remedies against such decisions may "not be less than that which they make available to their own nationals".[820] Although the Court has recognised the principle of effective judicial protection as a general principle, it "does not require [it] to bring a free-standing action which seeks primarily to dispute the compatibility of national provisions with Community law".[821] The principle of effective judicial protection is violated when individuals seeking remedies have their vehicles impounded or have to opt to pay a standard fine in order to avoid criminal proceedings.[822]

Impartiality

The right to a fair trial embodies the right to an independent and impartial tribunal.[823] The Court has held that there are two aspects of impartiality: "(i) the members of the tribunal themselves must be impartial, that is, none of its members must show bias or personal prejudice, there being a presumption of personal impartiality in the absence of evidence to the contrary; and (ii) the tribunal must

---

[818]   15 October 2001, Joined Cases C-238/99 P, C-244/99 P, C-245/99 P, C-247/99 P, C-250/99 P to C-252/99 P and C-254/99 P, *Limburgse Vinyl Maatschappij NV (LVM) (C-238/99 P), DSM NV and DSM Kunststoffen BV (C-244/99 P), Montedison SpA (C-245/99 P), Elf Atochem SA (C-247/99 P), Degussa AG (C-250/99 P), Enichem SpA (C-251/99 P), Wacker-Chemie GmbH and Hoechst AG (C-252/99 P) and Imperial Chemical Industries plc (ICI) (C-254/99 P)* v. Commission [2002] ECR I-8375, par. 187.

[819]   17 December 1998, Case C-185/95 P, *Baustahlgewebe GmbH* v. *Commission* [1998] ECR I-8417.

[820]   5 March 1980, Case 98/79, *Josette Pecastaing* v. *Belgium* [1980] ECR 691, par. 13.

[821]   13 March 2007, Case C-432/05, *Unibet (London) Ltd, Unibet (International) Ltd* v. *Justitiekanselern* [2007] ECR I-2271, par. 47.

[822]   7 June 2007, Case C-156/04, *Commission* v. *Greece* [2007] ECR I-4129.

[823]   1 July 2008, Case C-341/06P and C-342/06P, *Chronopost SA (C-341/06 P), La Poste, (C-342/06 P), Union française de l'express (UFEX), established in Roissy-en-France (France), DHL Express (France) SAS, formerly DHL International SA, established in Roissy-en-France, Federal express international (France) SNC, established in Gennevilliers (France), CRIE SA, in liquidation, established in Asnières (France)* v. *Commission* [2008] ECR not yet reported.

be objectively impartial, that is to say, it must offer guarantees sufficient to exclude any legitimate doubt in this respect."[824] With reference to the ECtHR, the Court stated that this does not preclude the same Judge from sitting in two Chambers and hearing and determining the same case in succession.

The Reasoning of the Decision

According to the case law of the Court, the Court of First Instance must give its reasons for judgment. However, it is not required to provide an account that follows exhaustively and point by point all the reasoning articulated by the parties.[825] However, the reasoning must enable the persons concerned to know why the measures in question were taken. The other function of the reasoning is that it provides the reviewing court with sufficient material for it to exercise its power of review. These rules can be transplanted and applied in criminal proceedings as a specific right under the *chapeau* of a fair trial.

2.3. THE ACCESSION OF THE UNION TO THE ECHR

2.3.1. Complaints Against the Union

The consistent case law of the ECtHR and the now defunct European Commission of Human Rights (hereinafter EComHR) declared complaints against the EU or its organs inadmissible. In a decision in 1978, directed against the European Communities and their Member States, jointly and severally, the EComHR first found that the alleged violation took place under the responsibility of an organ of the European Communities that had legal personality.[826] It found that a complaint against the Member States jointly was equal to a complaint against the European Communities. However, the Member States severally was not equal to a complaint against the European Communities because "by taking part in the decisions of the Council of the European Communities (...) in the circumstances of the instant case [they] exercise their 'jurisdiction' within the meaning of Article 1 of the Convention". In a decision in 1989, the EComHR declared the application

---

[824] 1 July 2008, Case C-341/06P and C-342/06P, *Chronopost SA (C-341/06 P), La Poste, (C-342/06 P), Union française de l'express (UFEX), established in Roissy-en-France (France), DHL Express (France) SAS, formerly DHL International SA, established in Roissy-en-France, Federal express international (France) SNC, established in Gennevilliers (France), CRIE SA, in liquidation, established in Asnières (France)* v. *Commission* [2008] ECR not yet reported, par. 54 (references omitted).

[825] E.g. 8 February 2007, Case C-3/06 P, *Groupe Danone* [2007] ECR I-1331, par. 46.

[826] EComHR, 10 July 1978, *Confédération Française Démocratique du Travail* v. *the European Communities, their Member States, jointly and severally*, 8030/77, Decisions and Reports 13, 231.

inadmissible,[827] although it left the door open for a complaint against the Member States jointly, when all remedies that are provided by Community law have been exhausted, which the applicant in question had not done.[828]

One year later, the EComHR took a decision on a complaint directed against Germany that had enforced a decision of the Court which had found the applicant in violation of competition law and imposed a fine.[829] The EComHR first held that:

> "Under Article 1 of the Convention the Member States are responsible for all acts and omissions of their domestic organs allegedly violating the Convention regardless of whether the act or omission in question is a consequence of domestic law or regulations or of the necessity to comply with international obligations".

It then assumed that the competition proceedings in question would have fallen under Article 6, had they been conducted by German authorities and not by European judicial authorities.[830] It went on to state that:

> "It has next to be observed that the Convention does not prohibit a Member State from transferring powers to international organisations. Nonetheless, the Commission recalls that 'if a State contracts treaty obligations and subsequently concludes another international agreement which disables it from performing its obligations under the first treaty it will be answerable for any resulting breach of its obligations under the earlier treaty'. (cf., No. 235/56, Dec. 10.6.58, Yearbook 2, p. 256 (300)). The Commission considers that a transfer of powers does not necessarily exclude a State's responsibility under the Convention with regard to the exercise of the transferred powers. Otherwise the guarantees of the Convention could wantonly be limited or excluded and thus be deprived of their peremptory character. The object and purpose of the Convention as an instrument for the protection of individual human beings requires that its provisions be interpreted and applied so as to make its safeguards practical and effective (cf., Eur. Court H.R., *Soering* judgment of 7 July 1989, Series A no. 161, p. 34, para. 87). Therefore, the transfer of powers to an international organization is not incompatible with the Convention provided that within that international organization

---

827   EComHR, 19 January 1989, *Dufay* v. *les Communautés Européennes, subsidiairement, la collective de leur États Members et leurs États Membres pris individuellement*, 13539/88, unpublished.

828   See Court of First Instance 7 June 2004, Case T-338/02, *Segi, Araitz Zubimendi Izaga, Aritza Galarraga* v. *Council* [2004] ECR II-1647, par. 38: "Contrary to the Council's submissions, it would not be of any use for the applicants to seek to establish individual liability of each Member State for the national measure enacted pursuant to Common Position 2001/931, as a means to try to obtain compensation for the damage allegedly sustained.".

829   EComHR, 9 February 1990, *M. & Co.* v. *the Federal Republic of Germany*, 13258/87, Decisions and Reports 64, 138.

830   This case differs from *Tillack*, in which Belgium assumed full responsibility for investigations that Belgian authorities conducted on instigation from OLAF. See ECtHR, 27 novembre 2007, *Tillack contre Belgique*, Requête No. 20477/05.

fundamental rights will receive an equivalent protection. The Commission notes that the legal system of the European Communities not only secures fundamental rights but also provides for control of their observance."

For the Strasbourg judiciary, this *equivalent protection* test seems to be decisive in assessing the remedies available. This derives from the requirement that the ECHR must be interpreted and applied so as to make its safeguards both practical and effective. The EComHR is satisfied that the requirement is fulfilled, because the Court has developed a case law according to which it is called upon to control Union acts upon the basis of fundamental rights, including those enshrined in the ECHR.[831] More recently, the ECtHR has held that:

> "Where States establish international organisations, or *mutatis mutandis* international agreements, to pursue cooperation in certain fields of activities, there may be implications for the protection of fundamental rights. It would be incompatible with the purpose and object of the Convention if Contracting States were thereby absolved from their responsibility under the Convention in relation to the field of activity covered by such attribution."[832]

In the perspective of both this case law and the increasing role of the European Union in the direct enforcement of criminal law, it is necessary that complaints against the European Union or one of its bodies or offices are admissible. The activities of Europol and the future European Public Prosecutor's Office are briefly referred to at this stage.[833]

2.3.2. The Protocol on the Accession

Article 6, paragraph 2 TEU states that the Union "shall accede to the ECHR". That this will not be as simple as a mere ratification of a treaty becomes clear from Protocol No. 8 Relating to Article 6(2) of the Treaty on European Union on the Accession of the Union to the European Convention on the Protection of Human Rights and Fundamental Freedoms.[834] There is to be an agreement that will make provision for the specific characteristics of the Union with regard to the

---

[831] EComHR, 10 January 1994, *Heinz against the Contracting States party to the European Patent Convention in so far as they are High Contracting parties to the European Convention on Human Rights*, i.e., *Austria, Belgium, Denmark, France, Germany, Greece, Ireland, Italy, Liechtenstein, Luxembourg, Netherlands, Norway, Portugal, Spain, Sweden, Switzerland and the United Kingdom*, 21090/92, unpublished. The EComHR declared this complaint inadmissible on the same grounds as in the case of *M. & Co.* v. *Germany*. It examined the various procedural safeguards contained in the European Patent Convention.

[832] ECtHR, 7 March 2002, *T.I.* v. *United Kingdom*, Application 43844/98.

[833] See, further, Chapter 8, Sections 2.1.2 and 3.2.

[834] OJ 2007, C 306/155 and 156.

participation of the Union in the control bodies of the Convention, and, more importantly, for "the mechanisms necessary to ensure that proceedings by non-Member States and individual applications are correctly addressed to Member States and/or the Union as appropriate".[835] What are these specific characteristics that require special attention with regard to individual complaints?

The EU-ECHR Protocol can only be welcomed. It will bring an end to the undesirable situation in which more and more law is subtracted from the protection of the ECHR. Currently, citizens have less fundamental rights when confronted with the European Union and co-operating Member States, than when confronted with the acts of an individual Member State. With regard to competition law, the accession of the Union to the ECHR will have to result in a number of amendments of a procedural nature. In its current format, the Commission combines the roles of investigator, prosecutor and court.[836]

The EU-ECHR Protocol must deal with the accountability of the institutions of the Union and the bodies created by it. How should the exploration of national remedies be interpreted when a complaint is directed against an alleged violation committed by, for instance, Europol, the Commission in competition cases, or the European Public Prosecutor's Office? Does this require the proceedings used in one of the Member States, or does it require the proceedings used before the Court?

Specifically, issues that should further be dealt with relate to human rights protection in international co-operation in criminal matters.[837] The main issue is whether it should be the applicant's task to state at the time of the application to the ECtHR which Member State of the Union is responsible for the alleged violation. It may be too difficult for individual applicants to state with the application whether the responsibility lies with the Union or with one of its institutions, and/or with a number of Member States. Since the Union and its Member States have intensified their co-operation to such an extent that it raises the question of whether one can still speak of separate responsibilities under the ECHR, it should no longer be a relevant ground when deciding the admissibility of a complaint. The task of the applicant should be to state the facts that will pass the test of admissibility with regard to the alleged violation. When declared admissible, the division of responsibilities can be dealt with.

---

[835]   The Council of Europe carried out a Study of Technical and Legal Issues of a Possible EC/EU Accession to the European Convention on Human Rights, Report adopted by the Steering Committee for Human Rights (CDDH) at its 53rd meeting (25–28 June 2002), DG-II(2002)006, CDDH(2002)010 Addendum 2.

[836]   The Court, however, held that the Commission could not be classified as a tribunal within the meaning of Article 6 ECHR. See 29 October 1980, Joined Cases 209–215 and 218/78, *Heintz van Landewyck SARL and others* v. *Commission* [1980] ECR 3125, par. 81.

[837]   See Chapter 7, Section 6.4.

3.   THE RIGHT TO PROSECUTE

3.1. INTRODUCTION

In principle, the question of whether a Member State has the right to prosecute is decided upon the basis of its own national law, especially its provisions on jurisdiction. The various bases of jurisdiction have already been discussed in the previous chapter.[838] In this section, a great deal of attention is given to the loss of the right to prosecute, notably as a result of the application of the *ne bis in idem* principle, which prohibits a second prosecution if the accused has already been tried for the same facts by another state. This section ends with a look at some other reasons that bar a Member State from exerting its jurisdiction.

The right to prosecute is discussed here in the context of a chapter on criminal procedure. This may not be the choice of all the national criminal justice systems of the Member States. Some Member States regard the question of whether the state or the prosecution has the right or jurisdiction to prosecute as a preliminary issue and thus as an item of formal character. Other Member States may regard the right to prosecute as something relating to the question of whether criminal conduct has occurred and is thus related to issues of substantive criminal law. The consequences of such a division are visible in the procedural decision that follows the finding that the prosecution no longer has the right to prosecute. Member States arguing in the formal manner will take the decision that the case is inadmissible, that there is a finding of non-lieu or that there is no case to answer. For these Member States, there is no assessment of the merits of the case. Member States that categorise the right to prosecute as an issue under substantive law will simply acquit.

3.2. *NE BIS IN IDEM*

3.2.1. Article 54 CISA

The protection against a second prosecution has been regulated in Articles 54–58 of the Convention implementing the Schengen Agreement, which read:

> "Article 54
>
> A person whose trial has been finally disposed of in one Contracting Party may not be prosecuted in another Contracting Party for the same acts provided that, if a penalty

---

[838]   See Chapter 4, Section 3.2.

has been imposed, it has been enforced, is actually in the process of being enforced or can no longer be enforced under the laws of the sentencing Contracting Party."

Article 55

1. A Contracting Party may, when ratifying, accepting or approving this Convention, declare that it is not bound by Article 54 in one or more of the following cases:

(a) where the acts to which the foreign judgment relates took place in whole or in part in its own territory; in the latter case, however, this exception shall not apply if the acts took place in part in the territory of the Contracting Party where the judgment was delivered;

(b) where the acts to which the foreign judgment relates constitute an offence against national security or other equally essential interests of that Contracting Party;

(c) where the acts to which the foreign judgment relates were committed by officials of that Contracting Party in violation of the duties of their office.

2. A Contracting Party which has made a declaration regarding the exception referred to in paragraph 1(b) shall specify the categories of offences to which this exception may apply.

3. A Contracting Party may at any time withdraw a declaration relating to one or more of the exceptions referred to in paragraph 1.

4. The exceptions which were the subject of a declaration under paragraph 1 shall not apply where the Contracting Party concerned has, in connection with the same acts, requested the other Contracting Party to bring the prosecution or has granted extradition of the person concerned.

Article 56

If further proceedings are brought by a Contracting Party against a person who has been finally judged for the same offences by another Contracting Party, any period of deprivation of liberty served on the territory of the latter Contracting Party on account of the offences in question must be deducted from any sentence handed down. Account will also be taken, to the extent that national legislation permits, of sentences other than periods of imprisonment already undergone.

Article 57

1. Where a Contracting Party accuses an individual of an offence and the competent authorities of that Contracting Party have reason to believe that the accusation relates

to the same offences as those for which the individual has already been finally judged by another Contracting Party, these authorities shall, if they deem it necessary, request the relevant information from the competent authorities of the Contracting Party in whose territory judgment has already been delivered.

2. The information requested shall be provided as soon as possible and shall be taken into consideration as regards further action to be taken in the proceedings in progress.

3. At the time of ratification, acceptance or approval of this Convention, each Contracting Party will nominate the authorities which will be authorized to request and receive the information provided for in this Article.

Article 58

The above provisions shall not preclude the application of broader national provisions on the *ne bis in idem* principle with regard to judicial decisions taken abroad."

3.2.2. The Judgment in Gözütok and Brügge

No other provision of criminal law has triggered so many references for a preliminary ruling and enabled the Court to establish its case law on all the elements of the *ne bis in idem* principle. In each judgment, the Court further specifies the elements of the protection given by the Article. What is *ne*? Which new acts are prohibited? What is *bis*? Which act triggers the principle? What is *idem*? What is finally disposed of? What is the same fact? What jurisdictions are bound by the norm? Who is protected by the principle, and how? These are the questions that will be answered below.

In the first case dealing with Third Pillar legislation in the field of criminal law, the *Gözütok and Brügge* case, dating from 2003, the Court took a revolutionary decision with regard to the effects of *out-of-court settlements*. The ground breaking character of the decision justifies the integral reproduction of the relevant paragraphs here:

"23. Considering that an interpretation of Article 54 of the CISA was necessary in order to decide the case before it, the Rechtbank van eerste aanleg te Veurne decided to stay proceedings and refer the following question to the Court for a preliminary ruling:

Under Article 54 of the [CISA] is the Belgian Public Prosecutor's Office permitted to require a German national to appear before a Belgian criminal court and be convicted on the same facts as those in respect of which the German Public Prosecutor's Office has made him an offer, by way of a settlement, to discontinue the case after payment of a certain sum, which was paid by the accused?

24. The Court, after hearing the Advocate General, decided, on account of the connection between the cases, to join them for the purposes of the judgment, in accordance with Article 43 of the Rules of Procedure."

The questions referred for a preliminary ruling:

"25. By their questions, which it is appropriate to examine together, the national courts are essentially asking whether the *ne bis in idem* principle, laid down in Article 54 of the CISA, also applies to procedures whereby further prosecution is barred, such as those at issue in the main actions.

26. It is clear from the wording of Article 54 of the CISA that a person may not be prosecuted in a Member State for the same acts as those in respect of which his case has been finally disposed of in another Member State.

27. A procedure whereby further prosecution is barred, such as those at issue in the main actions, is a procedure by which the prosecuting authority, on which national law confers power for that purpose, decides to discontinue criminal proceedings against an accused once he has fulfilled certain obligations and, in particular, has paid a certain sum of money determined by the prosecuting authority.

28. Therefore, it should be noted, first, that in such procedures, the prosecution is discontinued by the decision of an authority required to play a part in the administration of criminal justice in the national legal system concerned.

29. Second, a procedure of this kind, whose effects as laid down by the applicable national law are dependent upon the accused's undertaking to perform certain obligations prescribed by the Public Prosecutor, penalises the unlawful conduct which the accused is alleged to have committed.

30. In those circumstances, the conclusion must be that, where, following such a procedure, further prosecution is definitively barred, the person concerned must be regarded as someone whose case has been finally disposed of for the purposes of Article 54 of the CISA in relation to the acts which he is alleged to have committed. In addition, once the accused has complied with his obligations, the penalty entailed in the procedure whereby further prosecution is barred must be regarded as having been enforced for the purposes of Article 54.

31. The fact that no court is involved in such a procedure and that the decision in which the procedure culminates does not take the form of a judicial decision does not cast doubt on that interpretation, since such matters of procedure and form do not

impinge on the effects of the procedure, as described at paragraphs 28 and 29 of this judgment, which, in the absence of an express indication to the contrary in Article 54 of the CISA, must be regarded as sufficient to allow the *ne bis in idem* principle laid down by that provision to apply.

32. Furthermore, it should be pointed out that nowhere in Title VI of the Treaty on European Union relating to police and judicial cooperation in criminal matters (Articles 34 and 31 of which were stated to be the legal basis for Articles 54 to 58 of the CISA), or in the Schengen Agreement or the CISA itself, is the application of Article 54 of the CISA made conditional upon harmonisation, or at the least approximation, of the criminal laws of the Member States relating to procedures whereby further prosecution is barred.

33. In those circumstances, whether the *ne bis in idem* principle enshrined in Article 54 of the CISA is applied to procedures whereby further prosecution is barred (regardless of whether a court is involved) or to judicial decisions, there is a necessary implication that the Member States have mutual trust in their criminal justice systems and that each of them recognises the criminal law in force in the other Member States even when the outcome would be different if its own national law were applied.

34. For the same reasons, the application by one Member State of the *ne bis in idem* principle, as set out in Article 54 of the CISA, to procedures whereby further prosecution is barred, which have taken place in another Member State without a court being involved, cannot be made subject to a condition that the first State's legal system does not require such judicial involvement either.

35. The aptness of that interpretation of Article 54 of the CISA is borne out by the fact that it is the only interpretation to give precedence to the object and purpose of the provision rather than to procedural or purely formal matters, which, after all, vary as between the Member States concerned, and to ensure that the principle has proper effect.

36. First, as is apparent from the fourth indent of the first paragraph of Article 2 EU, by the Treaty of Amsterdam the European Union set itself the objective of maintaining and developing the Union as an area of freedom, security and justice in which the free movement of persons is assured.

37. Furthermore, as the first paragraph of the preamble to the Protocol shows, the integration of the Schengen *acquis* (which includes Article 54 of the CISA) into the framework of the European Union is aimed at enhancing European integration and, in particular, at enabling the Union to become more rapidly the area of freedom, security and justice which it is its objective to maintain and develop.

38. Article 54 of the CISA, the objective of which is to ensure that no one is prosecuted on the same facts in several Member States on account of his having exercised his right to freedom of movement, cannot play a useful role in bringing about the full attainment of that objective unless it also applies to decisions definitively discontinuing prosecutions in a Member State, even where such decisions are adopted without the involvement of a court and do not take the form of a judicial decision.

39. Second, national legal systems which provide for procedures whereby further prosecution is barred do so only in certain circumstances or in respect of certain exhaustively listed or defined offences which, as a general rule, are not serious offences and are punishable only with relatively light penalties.

40. In those circumstances, if Article 54 of the CISA were to apply only to decisions discontinuing prosecutions which are taken by a court or take the form of a judicial decision, the consequence would be that the *ne bis in idem* principle laid down in that provision (and, thus, the freedom of movement which the latter seeks to facilitate) would be of benefit only to defendants who were guilty of offences which – on account of their seriousness or the penalties attaching to them – preclude use of a simplified method of disposing of certain criminal cases by a procedure whereby further prosecution is barred, such as the procedures at issue in the main actions.

41. The German, Belgian and French Governments none the less raise the objection that not only the wording of Article 54 of the CISA but also the general scheme of the provision and, in particular, its relationship with Articles 55 and 58 of the CISA, as well as the intentions of the Contracting Parties and certain other international provisions with a similar purpose, preclude Article 54 from being construed in such a way as to apply to procedures barring further prosecution in which no court is involved. The Belgian Government also adds that, for the purposes of applying Article 54, a decision taken on conclusion of a procedure such as that at issue in Mr Brügge's case does not amount to a case being finally disposed of unless the victim's rights have first been properly safeguarded.

42. As regards, in the first place, the wording of Article 54 of the CISA, it is appropriate to observe, as is apparent from paragraphs 26 to 38 of this judgment, that, given the object and purpose of Article 54, use of the term finally disposed of does not preclude the provision from being construed in such a way that it also applies to procedures whereby further prosecution is barred, such as the procedures at issue in the main actions, in which no court is involved.

43. In the second place, far from requiring that Article 54 of the CISA should apply solely to judgments or to procedures barring further prosecution in which a court is involved, Articles 55 and 58 of the CISA are consistent with the interpretation of Article 54 set out at paragraphs 26 to 38 of this judgment.

44. First, Article 55 of the CISA, in so far as it allows Member States to provide for exceptions from the *ne bis in idem* principle for certain exhaustively listed facts to which foreign judgments relate, must logically refer to the same acts and procedures as those by which, in relation to those facts, a case is likely to be finally disposed of for the purposes of Article 54 of the CISA. That is borne out by the fact that Articles 54 and 55 of the CISA use, in most of the language versions, the same term when referring to those acts and procedures.

45. In addition, applying Article 54 of the CISA to procedures whereby further prosecution is barred does not render Article 58 of the CISA nugatory. Under the terms of Article 58, it is possible for Member States to apply national provisions which are broader than those not only of Article 54 of the CISA but also all those of the CISA which relate to the *ne bis in idem* principle. Furthermore, it does not just allow them to apply that principle to judicial decisions other than those falling within Article 54 but acknowledges, more generally, their right to implement national provisions giving the principle a wider scope or to make its application subject to less restrictive conditions, regardless of the nature of the foreign decisions concerned.

46. In the third place, as regards the intention of the Contracting Parties, as revealed by certain national parliamentary documents relating to the ratification of the CISA or of the Convention between the Member States of the European Communities on Double Jeopardy of 25 May 1987, Article 1 of which contains a provision in essence identical to that in Article 54 of the CISA, it is sufficient to note that the documents predate the Treaty of Amsterdam's integration of the Schengen *acquis* into the framework of the European Union.

47. Finally, concerning the Belgian Government's contention that applying Article 54 of the CISA to settlements in criminal proceedings is likely to prejudice the rights of the victim, the Court observes that the only effect of the *ne bis in idem* principle, as set out in that provision, is to ensure that a person whose case has been finally disposed of in a Member State is not prosecuted again on the same facts in another Member State. The *ne bis in idem* principle does not preclude the victim or any other person harmed by the accused's conduct from bringing a civil action to seek compensation for the damage suffered.

48. In the light of the foregoing considerations, the answer to the questions must be that the *ne bis in idem* principle laid down in Article 54 of the CISA also applies to procedures whereby further prosecution is barred, such as the procedures at issue in the main actions, by which the Public Prosecutor in a Member State discontinues, without the involvement of a court, a prosecution brought in that State once the accused has fulfilled certain obligations and, in particular, has paid a certain sum of money determined by the Public Prosecutor."

The Court does not interpret the *ne bis in idem* principle of Article 54 *CISA* in isolation, but in the light of the right to free movement and in the context of the developments of European integration. This explains why the Court was able to give a finding that was so blatantly in contradiction of the legal history of the treaty.[839] Application of the principle to out-of-court settlements is regarded as being in line with free movement. As an argument *a contrario*, the Court held that, if it was not, perpetrators of serious crimes would profit from the principle, and those who committed minor offences would not. The Court thus extends the protection of Article 54 *CISA* to out-of-court settlements concluded by the prosecution. It does so because the effect of such a settlement is that further prosecution is definitively barred.[840] The Court emphasises that mutual recognition of foreign decisions is not made conditional to harmonisation. It is inherent that mutual recognition requires the recognition of the criminal law in the other Member State, "even when the outcome would be different if its own law were applied".[841] This is logical, because if recognition required harmonisation, it would not be an issue at all. Mutual recognition presumes the existence of differences. As a consequence, it rules out all relevance of the legal classification of the offence. If the legal qualification were relevant, there would never be a *ne bis in idem* case at all.[842] By definition, a legal classification of a crime and its formulation differs from Member State to Member State.

3.2.3. Finally Disposed of

The *Gözütok and Brügge* case already dealt with one aspect of the question of whether the case had been "finally disposed of". This aspect relates to the authority that took the first decision regarding the person involved. Later cases on Article 54 *CISA* dealt with another aspect of "finally disposed of": which kind of decisions qualify as "finally disposed of"? In *van Straaten*, the Court discussed the acquittal at length and held that:

---

[839]   Although it must also be re-iterated that the Court does not look at the legislative history when interpreting a provision. See, on the Court's rules of interpretation, Chapter 3, Section 5.3.

[840]   In Case C-491/07, *criminal proceedings against Vladimir Turansky*, the *Landesgericht für Strafsachen Wien* lodged a reference on 31 October 2007 with the question of whether Article 54 *CISA* is to be interpreted as precluding the prosecution of a suspect in the Republic of Austria for the same acts in respect of which criminal proceedings in the Slovak Republic were discontinued after its accession to the European Union by means of a binding order issued by a public authority suspending the proceedings without further sanction taken after examination of the merits of the case.

[841]   See, also, the Opinion of Advocate General Ruiz-Jarabo Colomer of 19 September 2002, Case C-187/01 and Case C-385/01, *criminal proceedings against Hüseyin Gözütok (C-187/01) and Klaus Brügge (C-385/01)* [2003] ECR I-1345, point 42: "the reply must be sought disregarding the pecularities of each system".

[842]   18 July 2007, Case C-288/05, *criminal proceedings against Jürgen Kretzinger* [2007] ECR I-6441, par. 33.

"In the event of an acquittal, any subsequent step is prohibited, provided the State monopoly on punishing crime has come into operation, in the form of an analysis of 'the merits'. That expression, coined in *Miraglia*, embraces several situations, depending on the grounds of the decision, some intrinsic to the defendant and others extrinsic. The intrinsic grounds include those for exonerating a defendant who lacks the indispensable requirements for accountability (grounds relating to lack of criminal responsibility, such as being under age or mental disorder). The extrinsic grounds cover factual situations, in which no other behaviour could be expected (justifying circumstances: self-protection, necessity or overwhelming fear) or in which the personal requirements of the offence (elements relating to the perpetrator of the crime) are not satisfied, and those relating to the passage of time and to the substantive truth of the facts under analysis. That latter group includes three types of acquittal, depending on whether: (1) the acts do not constitute a criminal offence, (2) the defendant did not commit them or (3) it is not proven that the defendant committed them; the question now referred concerns that third category."[843]

The Court simplifies the procedural consequences of final decisions to convictions and acquittals. For some national criminal justice systems, it will be somewhat strange to subsume all other decisions than a conviction under the heading of acquittal. This can only be understood when we recall that Union law has an autonomous meaning, not necessarily linked to the meaning of the same terminology as in a national criminal justice system.

In *Gözütok and Brügge*, the Court attached much weight to the question of whether the merits of the case had been dealt with. Advocate General Ruiz-Jarabo Colomer had already paved the way for the Court on this issue, when he opined that decisions in which the court decided as to the merits of the case qualify for a *ne bis*.[844] This corresponds to a judgment of the Court in the competition case of *Limburgse Vinyl Maatschappij*. With reference to the *ne bis in idem* provision of Article 4, paragraph 1 Protocol no. 7 to the ECHR, the Court then held:

"The application of that principle therefore presupposes that a ruling has been given on the question whether an offence has in fact been committed or that the legality of the assessment thereof has been reviewed. Thus, the principle of *non bis in idem* merely prohibits a fresh assessment in depth of the alleged commission of an offence which would result in the imposition of either a second penalty, in addition to the first, in the event that liability is established a second time, or a first penalty in the event that liability not established by the first decision is established by the second."[845]

---

[843] 28 September 2006, Case C-150/05, *van Straaten* v. *the Netherlands and Italy* [2006] ECR I-9327, par. 65–66 (footnotes omitted).

[844] Opinion of Advocate General Ruiz-Jarabo Colomer of 8 June 2006, Case C-150/05, *van Straaten* v. *the Netherlands and Italy* [2006] ECR I-9327, par. 67.

[845] 15 October 2001, Joined Cases C-238/99 P, C-244/99 P, C-245/99 P, C-247/99 P, C-250/99 P to C-252/99 P and C-254/99 P, *Limburgse Vinyl Maatschappij NV (LVM) (C-238/99 P), DSM NV and DSM Kunststoffen BV (C-244/99 P), Montedison SpA (C-245/99 P), Elf Atochem SA*

The fact that a court acquitted because of lack of evidence qualifies for the *ne bis in idem* protection.[846] In *Miraglia*, the Court also determined that a decision by the prosecution not to prosecute and to declare the case closed does not have such an effect. This is so because this is a decision "without any determination whatsoever as to the merits of the case". [847] In this case, the Public Prosecutor in the Netherlands had decided not to pursue prosecution on the sole ground that criminal proceedings concerning the same facts had been started in Italy. The prosecution did not make any determination whatsoever as to the merits of the case.[848] Since the decision of the Dutch prosecutor to terminate proceedings did not fulfil the other criteria mentioned in *Gözütok and Brügge*, there was no reason for the Court to give any further effect to it.

In the context of the previous case law, the Court's judgment in *Gasparini* is difficult to understand.[849] In *Gasparini*, the first chamber of the Court held that a court decision that the prosecution was time-barred would also trigger the application of the *ne bis in idem* principle. The Court stresses that, because of the implications of the principle of mutual trust, states should recognise each other's decisions even "when the outcome would be different if its own national law were applied".[850] It is submitted that the *Gasparini* case is conceptually wrong, because the decision that the prosecution is time-barred does not deal with an assessment of the merits of the case.[851] In addition, *Gasparini* seems to require the recognition of a decision from a state that has no (longer) jurisdiction over the matter. It is difficult to conceive how a state which has no jurisdiction to deal with the matter can determine that other states, which do have jurisdiction, may no longer use it. The jurisdictional question must be regarded as a preliminary question of a procedural nature which does not deal with the central question in a criminal trial:[852] whether the accused actually committed the alleged facts of which he is

---

(C-247/99 P), Degussa AG (C-250/99 P), Enichem SpA (C-251/99 P), Wacker-Chemie GmbH and Hoechst AG (C-252/99 P) and Imperial Chemical Industries plc (ICI) (C-254/99 P) v. Commission [2002] ECR I-8375.

846 28 September 2006, Case C-150/05, *van Straaten v. the Netherlands and Italy* [2006] ECR I-9327, par. 54–61.

847 28 September 2006, Case C-150/05, *van Straaten v. the Netherlands and Italy* [2006] ECR I-9327, par. 60.

848 10 March 2005, Case C-469/03, *criminal proceedings against Filomeno Mario Miraglia* [2005] ECR I-2009. Decided by the fifth chamber.

849 28 September 2006, Case C-467/04, *criminal proceedings against Gasparini and others* [2006] ECR I-9199.

850 28 September 2006, Case C-467/04, *criminal proceedings against Gasparini and others* [2006] ECR I-9199, par. 30.

851 See, also, Advocate General Sharpston who discusses this element at length, Opinion of Advocate General Sharpston of 15 June 2006, Case C-467/04, *criminal proceedings against Gasparini and others* [2006] ECR I-9199, points 92–124.

852 In his Opinion of 19 September 2002, Case C-187/01 and Case C-385/01, *criminal proceedings against Hüseyin Gözütok (C-187/01) and Klaus Brügge (C-385/01)* [2003] ECR I-1345, point 114,

accused. A national decision that a state has no jurisdiction is relevant for that state only and cannot bind others. Article 3, paragraph 1 *Framework Decision 2002/584 on the European Arrest Warrant* is an example of this inherent logic. A European Arrest Warrant must be refused when the offence is covered by amnesty in the executing Member State, *where that State had jurisdiction to prosecute the offence under its own criminal law.*[853]

Pursuing the line of thinking expressed in *Gasparini* only serves to underline further that its reasoning is unsound. To recognise the extraordinary decision that a Member State has no jurisdiction,[854] raises the question of whether mutual recognition only requires a decision by a court, or that, for instance, it would also be sufficient to trigger the *ne bis in idem* principle if a prosecutor of a Member State decided not to start proceedings because of the proceedings being time-barred.[855] This is the regular way in which these issues come up. When *ne bis in idem* requires recognition of the negative decisions not to exert jurisdiction, it would lead to a situation in which the Member State with the shortest period of the statute of limitations were to dictate non-prosecution to all other Member States that have jurisdiction.

Maybe the Court in *Gasparini* gives more weight to the element of the principle that a person enjoying the right of freedom of movement be left undisturbed after having already been involved as the accused in one Member State. However, this element is not recognised in the principle. Article 54, paragraph 2 *CISA*, for instance, does allow for a second prosecution if the sentence has not been completely served. However, the Court should revise this unjustified extensive protection and fully return to the requirement that the principle is only triggered after a judgment of the merits of the case. This interpretation is supported by the Convention relating to extradition between the Member States of the European Union, which explicitly stipulated in Article 8 that extradition may not be refused on the grounds that the prosecution or punishment of the person would be statute-barred according to the law of the requested Member State.[856]

---

[853] Advocate General Ruiz-Jarabo Colomer stated that the "*ne bis in idem* principle is not (...) a procedural rule, but a fundamental safeguard for citizens".

Similarly, the case law on the (non-) recognition of driving licences only requires recognition of driving licences issued by Member States having jurisdiction to issue such a document. 29 April 2004, Case C-476/01, *criminal proceedings against Felix Kapper* [2004] ECR I-5205; 6 April 2006, Case C-227/05, *Halbritter* v. *Freistaat Bayern* [2006] ECR I-49; 28 September 2006, Case C-340/05, *criminal proceedings against Stefan Kremer* [2006] ECR I-98.

[854] A criminal court finding that the prosecution is time-barred is extremely rare, because it can arise only after a wrong assessment of the prosecutor that his national law still actually allows for prosecution. Normally, prosecutors will themselves declare these kinds of cases closed, without involving a court.

[855] See Chapter 7, Section 3.2.3.

[856] Since 1 January 2004, this convention, together with other conventions on extradition, has been applicable in most exceptional cases and has been replaced by *Framework Decision 2002/584 on the European Arrest Warrant*, which does not have a similar provision.

Article 54 *CISA* is applicable for second prosecutions that took place after the entering into force of the convention between the two states involved.[857] Both the facts as well as the first decision may date from before the *CISA* entering into force. This might be regarded as an indication that the Court in *van Esbroeck* regarded the *ne bis in idem* principle as a procedural rule. The acquittal in *Gasparini* does not consist of one of the types of acquittal mentioned in *van Straaten*. Did the Court in *Gasparini* create a fourth category? *Gasparini* also conflicts with a much older decision involving the prosecution of certain French manufacturers of perfume, in which the Court held that the fact that the Commission had closed the file on the violation of Community rules on cartels because the Commission was of the opinion that the conduct did not fall under the prohibition of the Treaty would not preclude criminal prosecution for having violated stricter national competition rules.[858]

An interesting question was raised by the German *Bundesgerichtshof* with regard to suspended sentences. Has such a sentence been enforced or is it actually in the process of being enforced? The Court held that such a "penalty must be regarded as 'actually in the process of being enforced' as soon as the sentence has become enforceable and during the probation period. Subsequently, once the probation period has come to an end, the penalty must be regarded as 'having been enforced' within the meaning of that provision".[859] Periods of deprivation of liberty for the purpose of detention on remand do not qualify to trigger *ne bis in idem*.[860] Nor does the fact that the sentencing state could have asked for the surrender of the accused under the *Framework Decision 2002/584 on the European Arrest Warrant*, but did not do so, affect the notion of enforcement in Article 54.[861]

What amounts to "can no longer be enforced" is the question in the case of *Bourquain*.[862] The German national Bourquain had been convicted to death by a French criminal court for murder in 1961. Bourquain had managed to escape to the German Democratic Republic and the sentence was never executed. In 2002, the German prosecutor started criminal proceedings against him. Advocate General Ruiz-Jarabo Colomer opined that the fact that the sentence can no longer

---

[857]   9 March 2006, Case C-436/04, *criminal proceedings against van Esbroeck* [2006] ECR I-2333, par. 22–24.

[858]   19 July 1980, Joined Cases 253/78 and 1 to 3/79, *Procureur de la République and others* v. *Bruno Giry and Guerlain SA and others* [1980] ECR 2327.

[859]   18 July 2007, Case C-288/05, *criminal proceedings against Jürgen Kretzinger* [2007] ECR I-6441, par. 42.

[860]   18 July 2007, Case C-288/05, *criminal proceedings against Jürgen Kretzinger* [2007] ECR I-6441, par. 50–52.

[861]   18 July 2007, Case C-288/05, *criminal proceedings against Jürgen Kretzinger* [2007] ECR I-6441, par. 63.

[862]   Opinion of Advocate General Ruiz-Jarabo Colomer of 8 April 2008, Case C-297/07, *Staatsanwaltschaft Regensburg* v. *Klaus Bourquain*.

be enforced because of its nature, France no longer applies the death penalty, does not relieve the convicted person of protection under Article 54 *CISA*. In other words, the case must be regarded as being "finally disposed of".

3.2.4. The Same Act

The concept of the *same act* is an example of the use of principles that were developed over the years in the Court's case law on the general principle of law "*ne bis in idem*" in the field of competition law in a criminal setting.[863] When discussing this principle for use in competition law, however, the sources referred to originated from criminal law.[864] In competition law, the Court has applied the principle of *ne bis in idem* to situations in which the legal systems and competition authorities of non-Member States intervene within their jurisdiction dependent upon the identical nature of both the facts and the undertaking, as well as upon the nature of the alleged facts.[865] In the cases related to Article 54 *CISA*, the Court has further elaborated the competition case law.

The question of whether decisions of different courts relate to the same acts is of a highly practical nature. In *van Esbroeck*, the Court had to deal with a common situation in the adjudication of drug offences. Van Esbroeck had been convicted in Norway for importing drugs from Belgium.[866] Subsequently, he was prosecuted in Belgium for exporting the same drugs from Belgium to Norway. Should this be regarded as one set of facts, because importation into Norway and exportation from Belgium took place at the same time and location, and related to the same quantity? Or should this be regarded as two facts, because the legal qualification of importing drugs under Norwegian criminal law and exporting drugs under Belgian criminal law is quite different? The Court held that the only relevant criterion is the identity of the material acts, understood as the existence of a set of concrete circumstances which are inextricably linked together, and regarded the facts as the same.[867]

---

[863] See, for instance, the development of that case law in the Opinion of Advocate General Sharpston of 15 June 2006, C-467/04, *criminal proceedings against Gasparini and others* [2006] ECR I-9199, par. 57–58. See 14 December 1972, Case 7-72, *Boehringer Mannheim GmbH* v. *Commission* [1972] ECR 1281.

[864] See the most interesting Opinion of Advocate General Mayras of 29 November 1972, Case 7-72, *Boehringer Mannheim GmbH* v. *Commission* [1972] ECR 1281, who conducted an impressive comparative research into *ne bis in idem* in the criminal justice systems of the then six Member States.

[865] 29 June 2006, Case C-308/04P, *SGL Carbon AG* v. *Commission* [2006] ECR I-5977, par. 27. See, also, 10 May 2007, Case C-328/05 P, *Appeal of SGL Carbon AG* [2007] ECR I-3921, par. 28.

[866] Norway and Iceland are also a party to the Convention Implementing the Schengen Agreement. As a result, decisions of those states also trigger the *non bis in idem* effect. See 9 March 2006, Case C-436/04, *criminal proceedings against van Esbroeck* [2006] ECR I-2333.

[867] 18 July 2007, Case C-367/05, *criminal proceedings against Norma Kraaijenbrink* [2007] ECR I-6619, par. 26; 18 July 2007, Case C-288/05, *criminal proceedings against Jürgen Kretzinger*

The Court states that harmonisation is not a pre-requisite for recognition of foreign decisions.[868] The principle of *ne bis in idem* implies mutual trust, which means that states will have to recognise "even if the outcome would be different if its own national law were applied".[869] As in *Gözütok and Brügge*, the Court established a link with the fundamental freedoms under Union law when it states that:

> "[the] right of freedom of movement is effectively guaranteed only if the perpetrator of an act knows that, once he has been found guilty and served his sentence, or, where applicable, been acquitted by a final judgment in a Member State, he may travel within the Schengen territory without fear of prosecution in another Member State on the basis that the legal system of that Member State treats the act concerned as a separate offence."[870]

Thus, what matters is the *identity* of the material acts. This can be illustrated with the facts in the *van Straaten* case. Van Straaten was prosecuted in the Netherlands for (i) importing a quantity of approximately 5,500 grams of heroin from Italy into the Netherlands on or about 26 March 1983, together with A. Yilmaz; (ii) having a quantity of approximately 1,000 grams of heroin at his disposal in the Netherlands during or around the period from 27 to 30 March 1983; and (iii) possessing firearms and ammunition in the Netherlands in March 1983. By its judgment of 23 June 1983, the *Rechtbank 's-Hertogenbosch* ('s-Hertogenbosch District Court, the Netherlands) acquitted van Straaten on the charge of importing heroin, finding it not to have been legally and satisfactorily proved, but convicted him on the other two charges, sentencing him to a term of imprisonment of 20 months. In Italy, van Straaten was prosecuted along with other persons, for possessing on or about 27 March 1983, and exporting to the Netherlands on several occasions together with Karakus Coskun, a significant quantity of heroin, totalling approximately 5 kilograms. With the judgment delivered *in absentia* on 22 November 1999 by the *Tribunale ordinario di Milano* (District Court, Milan, Italy), van Straaten and two other persons were, upon conviction on the charges, sentenced to a term of imprisonment of 10 years, fined ITL 50,000,000 and ordered to pay the costs.[871] The Court referred to various considerations of the van Esbroeck decision, and further stipulated that "in the case of offences relating to

---

[2007] ECR I-6441, par. 29.

[868]   9 March 2006, Case C-436/04, *criminal proceedings against van Esbroeck* [2006] ECR I-2333, par. 25–42.

[869]   9 March 2006, Case C-436/04, *criminal proceedings against van Esbroeck* [2006] ECR I-2333, par. 30.

[870]   9 March 2006, Case C-436/04, *criminal proceedings against van Esbroeck* [2006] ECR I-2333, par. 34.

[871]   This description of the facts was copied from 28 September 2006, Case C-150/05, *van Straaten v. the Netherlands and Italy* [2006] ECR I-9327, par. 20–21.

narcotic drugs, the quantities of the drug that are at issue (...) are not required to be identical".[872]

Consistent case law requires identity of the material acts, understood as the existence of a set of concrete circumstances which are inextricably linked together. It is for the national court to judge whether this situation is present. The assessment that the facts must be considered as separable cannot be compensated by the accused having the same criminal intention with regard to both offences.[873] In *Kretzinger*, the question was whether the transportation of contraband cigarettes, involving successive crossings of internal Schengen area borders must be regarded as constituting a single act. The Court held that:

> "acts consisting in receiving contraband foreign tobacco in one Contracting State and of importing that tobacco into another Contracting State and being in possession of it there, characterised by the fact that the defendant, who was prosecuted in two Contracting States, had intended from the outset to transport the tobacco, after first taking possession of it, to a final destination, passing through several Contracting States in the process, constitute conduct which may be covered by the notion of 'same acts' within the meaning of Article 54. It is for the competent national courts to make the final assessment in that respect within the meaning of Article 54."[874]

The Charter has also incorporated a *ne bis in idem* provision. Article 50 Charter briefly states:

> "No one shall be liable to be tried or punished again in criminal proceedings for an offence for which he or she has already been finally acquitted or convicted within the Union in accordance with the law."

This provision is different from Articles 54–58 *CISA* in two aspects.[875] First, it is more general in the sense that it does not allow for all kinds of exceptions relating

---

872   28 September 2006, Case C-150/05, *van Straaten v. the Netherlands and Italy* [2006] ECR I-9327, par. 49–50.
873   18 July 2007, Case C-367/05, *criminal proceedings against Norma Kraaijenbrink* [2007] ECR I-6619, par. 29.
874   18 July 2007, Case C-288/05, *criminal proceedings against Jürgen Kretzinger* [2007] ECR I-6441, par. 37.
875   There are a few other European treaties in which a (similar) *ne bis in idem* provision appears. Articles 54–58 *CISA* give an identical protection as Articles 1–4 of the 25 May 1987 Convention between the Member States of the European Communities on double jeopardy (this Convention never entered into force). Similar provisions are to be found in Article 7 *Financial Interests Convention*. None of the provisions mentioned explicitly recognises any transnational protection based upon out-of-court settlements, nor does the much more recent Charter of Fundamental Rights. However, one of the preambular paragraphs of *Regulation 2988/95 on Financial Interests* reads: "Whereas, for the purposes of applying this Regulation, criminal proceedings may be regarded as having been completed where the competent national authority and the person concerned come to an arrangement".

to the place in which the crime was committed. Second, it is more limited because it does not mention the effect of out-of-court settlements. Both provisions are relevant within the European Union. On face value, the protection offered by Article 54 *CISA* is much broader than the protection provided by Article 50 of the Charter. Despite this, the reliance of the Court on principles, rather than on explicit reference in a legal instrument, supports the conclusion that the Article 54 *CISA* case law guides the interpretation of Article 50 Charter.

3.2.5. Two Types of Mutual Recognition

It is important to point out a number of differences with mutual recognition in international co-operation at this stage. In international co-operation mutual recognition requires another clearly-specified Member State to do something. If the executing state – for whatever reasons – does not execute the warrant, it is not essential to the proceedings in the issuing Member State, which may continue, although it might face practical difficulties because it lacks assistance. This form of mutual recognition serves the interests of the issuing Member State.[876] In most cases, the suspect, accused or convicted person will not be happy to bear the consequences of mutual recognition.

Ne bis in idem as stipulated in Article 54 *CISA* and Article 50 Charter is a form of recognition which, in principle, has no relation with co-operation in criminal matters (although it could). When a Member State "finally disposes" of a trial, it does not request any specific other Member State to do anything. It is only when another Member State takes a second initiative to prosecute that the first case is a *complete* impediment to the second case. This form of mutual recognition serves the interest of mainly the convicted or acquitted person, and, albeit to a lesser extent, the Member State which first prosecuted the case.

3.3. OTHER REASONS RESTRICTING THE RIGHT TO PROSECUTE

Apart from *ne bis in idem*, other reasons may cause a Member State not to have jurisdiction. These other reasons relate to time-bars, immunities and the lack of other formalities to be fulfilled.

3.3.1. Time-Bars to the Prosecution

Regulations may contain specific rules concerning the limitation period for proceedings, rules on interruption thereof, and on the period for implementing a

---

[876]   See, further, Chapter 7, Section 3.2.

decision establishing an administrative penalty.[877] The importance of mentioning this here basically lies in the fact that the limitation periods provided in Regulations are much shorter than those which national criminal law provides for corresponding criminal offences. Article 6 *Regulation 2988/95 on Protection of the Financial Interests* deals with the relationship of criminal proceedings and Community administrative measures, which may be suspended if criminal proceedings have been initiated (Article 6, paragraph 1). Administrative proceedings may be resumed when criminal proceedings are discontinued (Article 6, paragraph 2), or when they are concluded, unless this is precluded by general principles (Article 6, paragraph 3).

Article 8, paragraph 6 *Framework Decision 2004/68 on Child Pornography* has led to an extension of the period in which the prosecution has the right to prosecute. It requires Member States "to enable the prosecution, in accordance with national law, of at least the most serious of the offences referred to in Article 2 after the victim has reached the age of majority".

3.3.2. Immunity

Article 343 TFEU stipulates that the Union "shall enjoy immunity". The precise conditions are laid down in the Protocol No. 7 on the Privileges and Immunities of the European Union. Article 11 of that Protocol stipulates that officials and other servants of the European Union are to be immune from legal proceedings in respect of acts performed by them in their official capacity, including their words, both spoken and written.[878] This immunity continues after they cease to hold office. However, given that it is accorded solely in the interest of the Union, this immunity may be waived by the institution for which the official or other servant is working (Article 17 Protocol No. 7). On the basis of Articles 19 and 20, these rules apply to Commissioners, Judges, Advocates General, Registrars and the Assistant Rapporteurs of the Court. The same applies to the European Central Bank and the European Investment Bank.

Article 3 of the Statute of the Court of Justice of the European Union states that the Judges are to be immune from legal proceedings. Only the Court, sitting as a full Court, may waive this immunity. Article 3 further provides that:

---

[877] For instance, Article 3 *Regulation 2988/95 on Financial Interests*. See, further, Council Regulation 2988/74 of 26 November 1974 concerning limitation periods in proceedings and the enforcement of sanctions under the rules of the European Economic Community relating to transport and competition, OJ 1974, L 319/1.

[878] See on the immunity of Members of the European Parliament 21 October 2008, C-200/07 and C-201/07, *Marra v. de Gregorio (C-200/07) and Clemente (C-201/07)* [2008] ECR not yet reported.

"Where immunity has been waived and criminal proceedings are instituted against a Judge, he shall be tried, in any of the Member States, only by the court competent to judge the members of the highest national judiciary."

Article 1 Protocol No. 7 states that the premises and buildings of the Union are to be inviolable. They are to be exempt from search, requisition, confiscation or expropriation. Articles 8 and 9 govern the position of the Members of the European Parliament, who are not be subject to any form of inquiry, detention or legal proceedings in respect of opinions expressed or votes cast by them in the performance of their duties.[879]

Article 41 *Europol Convention* states that Europol, the members of its organs and the Deputy Directors and employees of Europol are to enjoy the privileges and immunities necessary for the performance of their task. This is further regulated in detail in a specific Protocol.[880] Article 2 of the said Protocol determines that the property, funds and assets of Europol, wherever located on the territories of the Member States, are to be immune from search, seizure, requisition, confiscation and any other form of interference. The archives of Europol are to be inviolable (Article 3 Protocol). Article 8 Protocol contains the personal immunity of Europol staff "from legal process of any kind in respect of words spoken or written, and of acts performed by them, in the exercise of their official functions". Article 12 Protocol deals with the conditions under which a waiver may take place. As referred to in Article 42, paragraph 2 *Europol Convention*, the Netherlands has concluded bilateral agreements with all Member States on the privileges and immunities of liaison officers. However, Europol officials participating in joint investigation teams are not to be granted immunity in respect of the official acts that they are required to undertake in the fulfilment of that task.[881]

---

[879] Articles 8 and 9 of Protocol No. 7 read:
"Article 8. Members of the European Parliament shall not be subject to any form of inquiry, detention or legal proceedings in respect of opinions expressed or votes cast by them in the performance of their duties.
Article 9. During the sessions of the European Parliament, its Members shall enjoy:
(a) in the territory of their own State, the immunities accorded to members of their parliament;
(b) in the territory of any other Member State, immunity from any measure of detention and from legal proceedings.
Immunity shall likewise apply to Members while they are travelling to and from the place of meeting of the European Parliament. Immunity cannot be claimed when a Member is found in the act of committing an offence and shall not prevent the European Parliament from exercising its right to waive the immunity of one of its Members".

[880] Protocol of 19 June 1997 on the privileges and immunities of Europol, the members of its organs, the Deputy Directors and employees of Europol, OJ 1997, C 221/2.

[881] Article 8, paragraph 4, inserted by Protocol of 28 November 2002, amending the Protocol on Immunities and Privileges.

Article 12 of the EU-ICC Agreement stipulates that if the International Criminal Court seeks to exercise jurisdiction over a person who enjoys any privilege or immunity as an EU official, the relevant institution is to waive these privileges in accordance with all relevant rules of international law.[882]

Two forms of a *temporary immunity* may result from international co-operation. The most important is the application of the *speciality rule*. A person surrendered from one Member State to another upon the basis of a European Arrest Warrant may not be prosecuted for offences other than that for which the surrender was obtained (Article 27, paragraph 2 *Framework Decision 2002/584 on the European Arrest Warrant*).[883] Another temporary immunity may result from an act of mutual assistance in criminal matters. Article 12 of the *1959 European Convention on Mutual Assistance in Criminal Matters* entitles the accused, witnesses or experts appearing on a summons before the judicial authorities of the requesting state to a so-called *safe conduct*. This means that a person appearing on a summons may "not be prosecuted or detained or subjected to any other restriction of his personal liberty in the territory of that Party in respect of acts or convictions anterior to his departure from the territory of the requested Party".[884] However, this safe conduct does not protect a person against measures in relation to new offences, notably perjury.

It is more difficult to place the exclusion of state organs for criminal liability in *Framework Decision 2001/413 on Combating Fraud* in the right perspective. Article 1 stipulates that Member States, or other public bodies in the exercise of Member State authority and public international organisations may not be regarded as legal persons under this Framework Decision. This provision, which confirms the immunity of state entities appears only once in the Third Pillar instruments. Given the general controversy in the Member States with regard to the criminal liability of (branches of) the state, it cannot be concluded from the absence – in all other legal instruments – that it was intended to subsume criminal liability for state organs under criminal liability for legal entities.

3.3.3. Other Formalities

The Accumulation of Administrative and Criminal Proceedings

In cases of irregularities that affect the financial interest of the Union, both administrative and criminal proceedings are possible. Article 6 *Regulation 2988/95 on Protection of the Financial Interests* more or less states that Member States must choose between the application of either one of the procedures. It is

---

[882]   Agreement of 10 April 2006 between the International Criminal Court and the European Union on cooperation and assistance, OJ 2006, L 115/50.

[883]   Article 27, paragraph 3 provides for exceptions.

[884]   See, further, Chapter 7, Section 4.1.3.

clear that the drafters do not regard it desirable for two different kind of proceedings relating to the same infringement to take place. On the other hand, Article 5, paragraph 2 *First Protocol Financial Interests Convention* does not prohibit the accumulation of disciplinary and criminal proceedings. A similar rule can be deduced from Article 2 *OLAF Regulation 1073/1999*. Investigations by OLAF do not affect the powers of the Member States to bring criminal proceedings.

Prosecution Conditional on Report of the Victim

Some Framework Decisions impose the obligation that investigations into, or prosecution of, offences shall not be dependent on the report or accusation made by the victim.[885] Other Framework Decisions generally abolish the requirement of a victim report or accusation, although they do leave Member States the discretion to continue to require this in cases of extra-territorial jurisdiction.[886]

4.   TO PROSECUTE OR NOT TO PROSECUTE?

The decision to prosecute is another issue where Member States practice entirely different systems. The dividing line here lies between the legality and the opportunity principles. In the criminal justice systems that apply the so-called *legality principle*, all offences that come to the attention of the police or the prosecution must be prosecuted. Although these systems allow for certain grounds that lead to a decision not to prosecute, the general picture is clear: prosecution is the rule, non-prosecution is the exception. In theory, the differences with the opposite system, which applies the *opportunity principle*, are very great. Here, prosecution does not take place automatically. The state may refrain from initiating a prosecution when the general interest requires it to do so. This may relate to, among others, the relative minor nature of the offence or the policy that the prosecution has decided to follow.

Although the basic concepts are traditionally diametrically opposed, it is questionable whether there is so much difference between the two systems in actual practice. Both systems, for instance, provide for out-of-court settlements and administrative sanctions. For Member States practising the *legality principle*, this finds its justification in the fact that prosecution takes place. For Member States practising the *opportunity principle*, it is argued that the general interest no longer requires prosecution, given the fact that there is a settlement or

---

[885]   See, to this extent, Article 7 *Framework Decision 2002/629 on Combating Trafficking in Human Beings* and Article 10, paragraph 1 *Framework Decision 2002/475 on Combating Terrorism*.

[886]   Article 7, paragraph 1 *Framework Decision 2002/629 on Combating Trafficking in Human Beings* and Article 9, paragraph 1 *Framework Decision 2004/68 on Child Pornography*.

administrative sanction. Furthermore, with the triggering mechanism (the establishment of facts that an offence has been committed), things might differ much more in theory than in practice. A *legality principle* Member State may argue that the facts are insufficient to prove the existence of an offence, and that, therefore, there is no obligation to prosecute. This is not much different from an *opportunity principle* Member State stating that it is not in the general interest to prosecute a case that offers no chance of obtaining a conviction. Additionally, both criminal justice systems provide for a correction mechanism, in the sense that the decision not to prosecute can be challenged before a court by interested parties. However, what remains clear is that the *opportunity principle* gives more discretion to refrain from prosecution than the *legality principle*. Criminal policy is a matter that basically concerns legislation in a *legality principle* Member State, while the *opportunity principle* Member State can additionally formulate an official policy for its prosecution.

In this section, the question of what the consequences of the use of a specific system are for the enforcement obligation that rests upon the Member States is dealt with. In this respect, regard must be paid to the enforcement criteria formulated by the Court in the *Greek maize* case. One could regard the requirements of effective and dissuasive enforcement as pointing more towards obligatory prosecution. On the other hand, the principle of same diligence could be read as allowing the *opportunity principle*.

The Court does not require Member States to opt for one system or another. It must be presumed that the Court was well aware of the diverging systems in the Member States when deciding the *Greek maize* case. Both systems will (and, indeed, must) be able to find a way to deal with the enforcement obligation, albeit with different justifications. The enforcement obligation does not require Member States to do the impossible. In other words, if the case has been seriously investigated and there is simply insufficient evidence to sustain a conviction, a Member State may refrain from bringing charges, on condition that it would do the same with regard to the enforcement of national law unrelated to Union law.[887] Both *legality principle* Member States and *opportunity principle* Member States would be in full compliance of their obligations under Union law, albeit with diverging justifications.

What, then, is the influence of the *Greek maize* case for the question of whether there is an obligation to prosecute? Whilst the judgment does not alter the foundations of the criminal justice system, it does require Member States to do something. An interesting case in this respect is the *French strawberries* case, in

---

[887] See, already in 21 September 1983, Joined Cases 205 to 215/82, *Deutsche Milchkontor GmbH and others* v. *Germany* [1983] ECR 2633, par. 23: "national authorities must act with the same degree of care as in comparable cases concerning solely the application of corresponding national legislation".

which the French authorities allegedly refrained from intervening in repetitive blockades of Spanish fruits and vegetables (mainly strawberries) through France for almost ten years. Both the strawberries and the trucks were vandalised by angry French farmers.[888] Despite the fact that criminal offences had very clearly been committed, the French authorities hardly intervened at all, very few investigations were carried out and only a handful of prosecutions took place.

The Court did not directly state that the French authorities should take measures of a criminal nature. First, the Court had to deal with the formal issue of whether acts of individuals could be attributed to the Member State. The case before the Court resulted from allegations by the Commission that France had violated its obligations under the Treaty. Since the enforcement obligation rests upon the Member States, it must clearly be established that there is an obligation to enforce in the given situation. The Court held:

"31. The fact that a Member State abstains from taking action or, as the case may be, fails to adopt adequate measures to prevent obstacles to the free movement of goods that are created, in particular, by actions by private individuals on its territory aimed at products originating in other Member States is just as likely to obstruct intra-Community trade as is a positive act.

32. Article 30 therefore requires the Member States not merely themselves to abstain from adopting measures or engaging in conduct liable to constitute an obstacle to trade but also, when read with Article 5 of the Treaty, to take all necessary and appropriate measures to ensure that that fundamental freedom is respected on their territory.

33. In the latter context, the Member States, which retain exclusive competence as regards the maintenance of public order and the safeguarding of internal security, unquestionably enjoy a margin of discretion in determining what measures are most appropriate to eliminate barriers to the importation of products in a given situation.

34. It is therefore not for the Community institutions to act in place of the Member States and to prescribe for them the measures which they must adopt and effectively apply in order to safeguard the free movement of goods on their territories.

65. Having regard to all the foregoing considerations, it must be concluded that in the present case the French Government has manifestly and persistently abstained from adopting appropriate and adequate measures to put an end to the acts of vandalism

---

[888]   More than a decade earlier, the Court had ruled that a threat to public order and security as a result of implementation of Community law does not constitute an exception to the obligation to enforce community law. See 29 January 1985, Case 231/83, *Henri Cullet and Chambre syndicale des réparateurs automobiles et détaillants de produits pétroliers* v. *Centre Leclerc à Toulouse and Centre Leclerc à Saint-Orens-de-Gameville* [1985] ECR 305, par. 32–33.

which jeopardize the free movement on its territory of certain agricultural products originating in other Member States and to prevent the recurrence of such acts.

66. Consequently, it must be held that, by failing to adopt all necessary and proportionate measures in order to prevent the free movement of fruit and vegetables from being obstructed by actions by private individuals, the French Government has failed to fulfil its obligations under Article 30, in conjunction with Article 5, of the Treaty and under the common organizations of the markets in agricultural products."[889]

Although the Court held the inevitability of measures of a *criminal* nature to be implicit, this reluctance could not be found in the Opinion of Advocate General Lenz: "The French authorities therefore also failed to prosecute those offences with the necessary vigour."[890] This case law constitutes an obligation to use criminal coercive measures.[891] Similarly, in the context of the lack of control measures in the fisheries legislation, the Court held that a Member State might violate its obligations "if the authorities of that Member State have failed either to initiate criminal or administrative proceedings or to transfer such proceedings to the Member State of registration".[892] The message of these cases is clear to the extent that Member States may not sit and watch when violations of Union law occur. They must, at the very least, investigate. The question of whether a prosecution must be initiated is a decision which has to be taken with the same diligence as in other national cases.

A decision not to investigate or not to prosecute because of the mere fact that EC fraud is time consuming, complicated and consumes a lot of resources is not in compliance with the enforcement obligation. But this is entirely different if there has been a serious effort. The enforcement obligation does not alter the priorities that Member States may pursue in prosecutions or in criminal policy.

Contrary to legal instruments of a criminal nature, Regulations dealing with any irregularities of various subsidy regimes contain all kinds of obligations to perform checks and to investigate. This can be seen in the general obligation of Article 8 *Regulation 2988/95 on Protection of the Financial Interests*, which requires them to take the necessary checks in order to prevent and detect irregularities. Member States genuinely complying with this obligation will have more information at their disposal. This may trigger more prosecutions than a

---

[889]   9 December 1997, Case C-265/95, *Commission v. France* [1997] ECR I-6959, par. 31–34 and 65–66.

[890]   Opinion of Advocate General Lenz of 9 July 1997, Case C-265/95, *Commission v. France* [1997] ECR I-6959, point 76.

[891]   Advocate General Jacobs seems to hint at that in his Opinion of 11 July 2002, Case C-112/00, *Eugen Schmidberger, Internationale Transporte und Planzüge v. Republik Österreich* [2003] ECR, I-5659, points 69–70.

[892]   27 March 1990, Case C-9/89, *Spain v. Council* [1990] ECR I-1383, par. 31.

situation in which there would only be the competence to investigate when there was reasonable suspicion. The Common Fisheries Policy has led to various regulations. The currently applicable *Regulation 2847/93 establishing a Control System applicable to the Common Fisheries Policy* imposes upon the Member States various obligations to ensure compliance with catch limitations. Article 31 states that, in the case of non-compliance with the applicable rules, the "Member States shall ensure that appropriate measures be taken, including of administrative action or criminal proceedings in conformity with their national law".

A Member State may not, therefore, be negligent in monitoring, or in conducting inspections and surveillance. The Court has held that the fact that this obligation to do something may lead to coercive measure of a criminal nature and to prosecution is not disproportional.[893] With regard to genocide, crimes against humanity and war crimes, a Council Decision requires Member States to take the necessary measures to create awareness "when facts are established which give rise to a suspicion" that these kinds of crimes have been committed.[894]

5. INVESTIGATIONS, COERCIVE MEASURES AND EVIDENTIARY MATTERS

In this paragraph, the mutual influence of Union law and national law on investigations, the collection, admission and weighing of evidence, as well as the use of coercive measures is discussed. In addition, the powers of the Commission will be identified.

5.1. INVESTIGATIONS

Various Union instruments require the Member States to provide for certain investigatory techniques in their national law. Examples of this include that Member States are required to provide for the confiscation, identification and tracing of the suspected proceeds from crime.[895] The Resolution of 17 January 1995 on the Lawful Interception of Telecommunications stipulates requirements that should be taken into account by the Member States when implementing measures relating to the interception of telecommunications.[896] Other instruments

---

[893] 27 March 1990, Case C-9/89, *Spain* v. *Council* [1990] ECR I-1383.

[894] Decision 2003/355 of 8 May 2003 on the investigation and prosecution of genocide, crimes against humanity and war crimes, OJ 2003, L 118/12.

[895] Article 1, paragraphs 2 and 3 *Joint Action 98/699 on Money Laundering* and Article B, Title I *Joint Action 96/443 on Racism and Xenophobia*.

[896] OJ 1996, C 329/1.

merely draw attention towards the relevance of a certain approach, such as targeting the assets of drug traffickers.[897] More practical effect can be expected from instruments that give guidelines for taking samples,[898] and describe the use of a specific method. Other Third Pillar instruments aim at facilitating and harmonising certain methods of criminal investigations and the building or concentration of expertise.[899] In one Recommendation, the Council invited the Member States to draw up terrorist profiles and to exchange information on this subject with both the other Member States and Europol.[900] The Schengen Executive Committee took a decision on general principles governing the payment of informers.[901] Occasionally, evaluation mechanisms on the implementation of certain techniques are provided.[902]

The influence of Regulations from the old Community has, in certain areas, been more consistent and structured. Several Regulations lay down the manner and the circumstances in which checks must be conducted.[903] The conditions are precisely formulated, and since a Regulation is directly applicable, these procedures must be followed. The accused is entitled to have the appropriate proceedings followed, as the Court held in the case of *Ohrt*. Finn Ohrt was accused of infringing the national provisions implementing Regulation 1382/87 Establishing Detailed Rules concerning the inspection of Fishing Vessels. Ohrt, the skipper of the

---

[897] Recommendation of 25 April 2002 on improving investigation methods in the fight against organised crime linked to organised drug trafficking: simultaneous investigations into drug trafficking by criminal organisations and their finances/ assets, OJ 2002, C 114/1. Joint Action 97/732 of 9 June 1997 for the Refining of Targeting Criteria, Selection Methods, etc., and Collection of Customs and Police Information, OJ 1997, L 159/1.

[898] Recommendation of 30 March 2004 regarding guidelines for taking samples of seized drugs, OJ 2004, C 38/1.

[899] Examples are Joint Action 96/747 of 29 November 1996 Concerning the Creation and Maintenance of a Directory of Specialized Competences, Skills and Expertise in the Fight against International Organized Crime, OJ 1996, L 342/2; Council Resolution of 9 June 1997 on the Exchange of DNA Analysis Results, which invites Member States to consider establishing national DNA databases, OJ 1997, C 193/2. See, also, Council Resolution of 25 June 2001 on the Exchange of DNA Analysis Results, OJ 2001, C 187/01; Decision 2001/887 of 6 December 2001 on the Protection of the Euro against Counterfeiting requires Member States to carry out the necessary expert analyses of suspected counterfeit notes and coins by a National Analysis Centre; Article 6 *Joint Action 98/699 on Money Laundering* requires adequate training and arrangements that enable authorities with best practice.

[900] Recommendation of 28 November 2002 on the Development of Terrorist Profiles, Doc. 11858/3/02 of 18 November 2002.

[901] Decision of 28 April 1999, OJ 2000, L 239/417.

[902] Decision 2002/996 of 28 November 2002 establishing a mechanism for evaluating the legal systems and their implementation at national level in the fight against terrorism, OJ 2002, L 349/1; Joint Action 97/827 of 5 December 1997 Establishing a Mechanism for Evaluating the Application and Implementation at National Level of International Undertakings in the Fight against Organized Crime, OJ 1997, L 344/7.

[903] See, for instance, Regulation 259/93 on the supervision and control of waste within, into and out the European Community; Regulation 386/90 on the monitoring carried out at the time of export of agricultural products receiving refunds or other amounts.

fishing vessel "Actinia", was sailing in the north Kattegat when he was approached by the inflatable boarding boat from the Danish inspection vessel "Nordjylland", which was carrying out a fisheries inspection. Ohrt did not change course and paid no attention to signals transmitted both by radio and signalling lamp ordering him to stop immediately. When prosecuted, he argued that the order to stop had not been given by an inspection vessel carrying the identification symbol required by the Regulation. The Court held that any vessel purporting to represent the competent inspecting authority must carry the symbol. If the symbols are not displayed,

> "it may be presumed that the skipper of a fishing vessel to be inspected is not aware that the order to stop is being given to him by the competent authority of a Member State. However, that presumption will be negated by proof that the skipper of the vessel to be inspected was aware of the status of the inspecting authority."[904]

Some Directives which allow for freedom of access to information for law enforcement authorities, provide for its refusal where it affects matters which are, or have been, *sub judice*, or which are the subject of preliminary investigation proceedings. In the case of *Wilhelm Mecklenburg*, the meaning of "preliminary investigation proceedings" in *Directive 90/313 on the Freedom of Access to Information on the Environment* had to be interpreted.[905] The Court held that "that exception covers exclusively proceedings of a judicial or quasi-judicial nature, or at least proceedings which will inevitably lead to the imposition of a penalty if the offence (administrative or criminal) is established".[906]

5.2. EVIDENCE COLLECTED BY NATIONAL AUTHORITIES

The previous section dealt with the normative influence of Union law on the way investigations are conducted. This, of course, also influences the way the results of such investigations are gathered, and may be decisive to answering the question of whether evidence is gathered lawfully. Generally speaking, if Union legislation applicable to the situation exists, the provisions of the relevant instruments should be followed. Respecting the procedures created by Union legislation has the almost automatic consequence that the evidence thus collected must be admissible in criminal proceedings. National criminal justice systems may not refuse

---

[904] 18 January 1996, Case C-276/94, *criminal proceedings against Finn Ohrt* [1996] ECR I-119, par. 13.

[905] 17 June 1998, Case C-321/96, *Wilhelm Mecklenburg v. Kreis Pinneberg – Der Landrat* [1998] ECR I-3809.

[906] 17 June 1998, Case C-321/96, *Wilhelm Mecklenburg v. Kreis Pinneberg – Der Landrat* [1998] ECR I-3809, par. 27.

admissibility for formal reasons.[907] This can be regarded as a form of mutual recognition of evidence. This will be rather problematical for those Member States whose procedural system attach more weight to orality of evidence and precludes the use of hearsay evidence. However, rules on admission do not state anything on the conclusion which may be attached to admissible evidence. This may "save" Member States applying the hearsay evidence rule in the sense that no weight is given to any hearsay evidence that they formally admit.

Directive 2005/60 on Money Laundering (formerly Directive 91/308) creates a mandatory system for reporting suspicious transactions. Credit and financial institutions are thereby under obligation to report all kinds of financial transactions. This information may later be used in criminal proceedings, but may also be exchanged with other Member States.[908]

A special position has been created for the submission of evidence by victims under the *Framework Decision 2001/220 on the Standing of Victims*, which stipulates in Article 3 that victims are to have the possibility of supplying evidence. The questioning of victims may only take place in so far as it is necessary for the purpose of criminal proceedings (Article 3). However, Article 8, paragraph 4 *Framework Decision 2001/220 on the Standing of Victims* provides for giving evidence in another manner than in open court, in cases in which there is a need to protect the victim. Article 1 of the same *Framework Decision* stipulates that Member States must do their utmost to enable victims residing in other states to give evidence by means of a video-conference. At the same time, it establishes the manner in which the evidence is collected and its admissibility as evidence. However, it does not lay down what weight should be attached to the evidence. Thus, this *Framework Decision* is an example by which citizens are entitled to invoke Union legislation, regardless of whether the Member State has implemented the Framework Decision or not. Moreover, legislation may subject the use of information as evidence to certain conditions. The use of evidence or information obtained via international co-operation may be precluded or may be subject to certain conditions which find a basis in the instrument governing mutual assistance.[909]

There is some case law regarding the applicable regime in the absence of Union legislation on the recognition of foreign evidence. In a case that dealt with conditions and procedures for the rectification of a date of birth, the Court allowed a German court not to recognise such a determination by a Greek authority. This was due to the fact that the Member States had neither harmonised

---

[907] For instance, Articles 12 and 16 Regulation 515/97 stipulate that all kinds of findings, certificates, information and documents obtained via mutual administrative assistance may be invoked as evidence.

[908] Likewise, information and evidence collected by OLAF, See, further, Section 5.3.

[909] See, for instance, Article 39, paragraph 2 *CISA*. Information given in the course of police co-operation may only be used as evidence after explicit permission granted.

the matter nor established a system of mutual recognition of such decisions.[910] With the further development of the principle of mutual recognition non-recognition will become the exception. The most drastic step that the Union is about to take lies in the mutual recognition of criminal evidence.[911]

The general rule concerning evidence of a violation of Union law is on a different footing, however, in such a case, rules of evidence may not be disfavourable to those which apply to similar domestic actions. National rules of evidence must not make it impossible or excessively difficult in practice for an individual to exercise rights conferred by Union law.[912]

5.3. EVIDENCE COLLECTED BY THE COMMISSION

The Commission has been entrusted with a number of competences to collect evidence directly itself. These competences have been established for various purposes. They must be seen firstly in relation to the Commission's task of supervising the enforcement of Union law by the Member States, and in relation to its power to bring a case against a Member State for violation of the Treaty before the Court upon the basis of Article 258 TFEU (formerly Article 226 TEC).[913] Secondly, the Commission has been charged with the task of combating EC fraud. Thirdly, it has specific competences in the field of competition law.[914] Information and evidence collected by the Commission for one of these purposes may be passed on to law enforcement authorities of the Member States. This section will deal with the Commission's competence to collect evidence directly

---

[910]   2 December 1997, Case C-336/94, *Eftalia Dafeki* v. *Landesversicherungsanstalt Württemberg* [1997] ECR I-6761, par. 16.

[911]   Framework Decision on the European Evidence Warrant, Council Document 13076/07, 21 December 2007.

[912]   3 February 2000, Case C-228/98, *Charalampos Dounias* v. *Ypourgio Oikonomikon* [2000] ECR I-577, par. 69–71.

[913]   See, for instance, the powers given to the Commission for on the spot checks in Articles 29–33 *Regulation 2847/93 establishing a Control System applicable to the Common Fisheries Policy*. Article 30, paragraph 3 of that Regulation states that in so far as national criminal procedure reserved certain acts to officials specifically designated by national law, Commission officials are not to take part in such actions. In particular, they are not to take part in searches or in the formal questioning of persons under national criminal law. However, they are to have access to the information thus obtained.

[914]   The Court rejected the claim that the Commission in competition law ought to be regarded as combining the functions of prosecutor and judge, being contrary to Article 6 ECHR. See 7 June 1983, Joined Cases 100 to 103/80, *SA Musique Diffusion française and others v. Commission* [1983] ECR 1825, par. 7–8. See, further, on the role of the Commission in competition law, Chapter 8, Section 3.1.

for purposes of the supervising and combating of EC fraud, and the provision of this evidence to the Member States for use in criminal proceedings.[915]

Upon the basis of Article 325 TFEU (formerly Article 280 TEC), a special Anti-fraud office named OLAF was set up by *OLAF Regulation 1073/1999*. The focus of the activities of OLAF lie with the safeguarding of Union interest against fraud, corruption and any other illegal activity (Article 1 *OLAF Regulation 1073/1999*). OLAF may conduct internal investigations in all the institutions, bodies, offices and agencies established by or upon the basis of the Treaties. The initiative to open an investigation may be taken by OLAF itself, but can also be triggered by a Member State (Article 5). It was envisaged at the time of the adoption of the Regulation that the investigations of OLAF could result in criminal proceedings (Article 1, paragraph 3 Regulation). The fact that OLAF has started administrative investigations does not affect the powers of the Member States to bring criminal proceedings (Article 2 *OLAF Regulation 1073/1999* and Article 1 *Regulation 2185/96 Concerning on-the-spot Checks*).

Internal (*i.e.*, within the institutions of the European Union) investigations are regulated in Article 4. OLAF has immediate and unannounced access to all and any information of the institutions. All officials of the institutions are under the obligation to cooperate with OLAF. This is further specified in the Inter-institutional Agreement of 25 May 1999 between the European Parliament, the Council of the European Union and the Commission of the European Communities concerning internal investigations by the European Anti-fraud Office (OLAF).[916] The Director of OLAF may forward the information obtained during internal investigations into matters liable to result in criminal proceedings to the judicial authorities of the Member States concerned (Article 10). If, after the internal investigation, no case can be made, the investigation is closed and the interested party is informed (Article 5 Inter-institutional Agreement OLAF).

On-the-spot checks with a view to investigating EC fraud are governed by the law of the Member States concerned (Article 6, paragraph 4). OLAF may carry out on-the-spot inspections at the premises of economic operators, and information forwarded or obtained in the course of internal investigations is subject to professional secrecy. It may only be used for purposes of preventing fraud, corruption or any other illegal activity (Article 8, paragraph 2). The investigation report drawn up by OLAF constitutes admissible evidence in proceedings in the Member States "in the same way and under the same conditions as administrative reports drawn up by national administrative inspectors. They shall be subject to the same evaluation rules as those applicable to administrative reports drawn up

---

[915]   In Chapter 7, the so-called vertical co-operation by which the law enforcement authorities of the Member States offer assistance to the Commission and *vice-versa* will be analysed, see Section 3.4.

[916]   OJ 1999, L 136/15.

by national administrative inspectors and shall be of identical value to such reports". (Article 9, paragraph 2).

The *Greek maize* criteria also apply to the checks of the Commission (Article 2, paragraph 1 *Regulation 2988/95 on Protection of the Financial Interests*), which stipulates that the Commission may carry out checks. The conditions under which Commission inspectors are to exercise their powers are found in *Regulation 2185/96 Concerning on-the-spot Checks*. Article 2 *Regulation 2988/95 on Protection of the Financial Interests* also stipulates that the Commission may carry out on-the-spot checks and inspections:

- "for the detection of serious transnational irregularities or irregularities that may involve economic operators acting in several Member States;
- where, for the detection of irregularities, the situation in a Member State requires on-the-spot checks and inspections to be strengthened in a particular case in order to improve the effectiveness of the protection of financial interests and so to ensure an equivalent level of protection within the Community;
- at the request of the Member State concerned."

The Commission may prepare and conduct the checks and inspections in close co-operation with the authorities of the Member States (Article 4 *Regulation 2185/96 Concerning on-the-spot Checks*). It may ensure that similar checks and inspections are not carried at the same time in respect of the same facts with regard to other regulations, or by the Member State upon the basis of its law (Article 3 *Regulation 2185/96 Concerning on-the-spot Checks*).

On-the-spot checks and inspections can be carried out on economic operators, who are required to grant access to premises, land, means of transport and other areas for business purposes (Article 5 *Regulation 2185/96 Concerning on-the-spot Checks*). In situations in which access is refused, the Member States are required to give the Commission inspectors the appropriate assistance (Article 9 *Regulation 2185/96 Concerning on-the-spot Checks*).[917] The Commission inspectors further enjoy the same access and facilities under the same conditions as national administrative inspectors in compliance with national law (Article 7 *Regulation 2185/96 Concerning on-the-spot Checks*).

Article 7, paragraph 1, *Regulation 2185/96 Concerning on-the-spot Checks* lists a series of examples to which on-the-spot checks and inspections may be related. It is the responsibility of the Member States to take the appropriate measures under national law to preserve evidence (Article 7, paragraph 2). The information collected in this manner falls under the professional secrecy legislation of the Member States concerned. The Commission is to report as soon as possible to the authorities of the Member States concerned "any fact or suspicion relating to an

---

[917] See, further, Chapter 7, Section 3.4.

irregularity" (Article 8, paragraph 2 *Regulation 2185/96 Concerning on-the-spot Checks*). The reports drawn up by the Commission upon the basis of this Regulation constitute admissible evidence, thus applying the assimilation principle once again (Article 8, paragraph 3 *Regulation 2185/96 Concerning on-the-spot Checks*). In order to facilitate this, Article 8, paragraph 3 of the same Regulation also stipulates that "Commission inspectors shall ensure that in drawing up their reports account is taken of the procedural requirements laid down in the national law of the Member States concerned".

The assimilation principle is also applied to the evaluation rules applicable to administrative reports (Article 8, paragraph 3 *Regulation 2185/96 Concerning on-the-spot Checks*). Furthermore, Article 8, paragraph 5 of the same Regulation allows Commission inspectors to carry out check and inspections outside Community territory. However, it does not state which law is applicable to these operations. It merely states that the reports are to be prepared "in conditions which would enable them to constitute admissible evidence in administrative or judicial proceedings of the Member States in which their use proves necessary".

5.4. WEIGHT OF EVIDENCE/ DEGREE OF PROOF

In the absence of Union legislation on the matter, it is for the national court to admit and assess the evidence before it.[918] However, the national court must take account of the right to a fair hearing. In the *Steffensen* case, the Court held:

> "It is for the national court to assess whether, in the light of all the factual and legal evidence available to it, the admission as evidence of the results of the analyses at issue in the main proceedings entails a risk of an infringement of the adversarial principle and, thus, of the right to a fair hearing. In the context of that assessment, the national court will have to examine, more specifically, whether the evidence at issue in the main proceedings pertains to a technical field of which the judges have no knowledge and is likely to have a preponderant influence on its assessment of the facts and, should this be case, whether Mr Steffensen still has a real opportunity to comment effectively on that evidence. If the national court decides that the admission as evidence of the results of the analyses at issue in the main proceedings is likely to give rise to an infringement of the adversarial principle and, thus, of the right to a fair hearing, it must exclude those results as evidence in order to avoid such an infringement."[919]

---

[918]   Some acts stipulate, in conformity with the assimilation principle, that the same rules should apply with regard to national reports. See Article 9, paragraph 2 *OLAF Regulation 1073/1999*.

[919]   10 April 2003, Case C-276/01, *Proceedings against Joachim Steffensen* [2003] ECR I-3735, par. 78–79: See, also, Advocate General Stix-Hackl in her Opinion to this case of 22 October 2002, point 68, relying on ECtHR case law: "a party to a criminal or civil trial must have the opportunity to have knowledge of and comment on all evidence adduced or observations filed with a view to influencing the court's decision; moreover, he must be able to present his case in

While the majority of rules applicable to evidence relate to the manner in which evidence is collected and require its admission as evidence, there are very few rules on the conclusions that should be drawn from it. Two instruments stipulate upon what basis the intent to commit the crime may be inferred. The first provision states that: "The intentional nature of an act or omission as referred to in paragraphs 1 and 3 may be inferred from objective, factual circumstances."[920] The second provision states that: "the knowledge, intent or purpose required as an element (…) may be inferred from objective factual circumstances."[921]

Article 2 of Regulation 1/2003 stipulates that the burden of proof "shall rest on the party or the authority alleging the infringement". It is sufficient for the Commission to prove that an undertaking has participated at a meeting during which agreements of an anti-competitive nature were concluded without publicly distancing itself from what was discussed.[922] Some Directives also refer to the burden of proof of certain allegations. This may have consequences for criminal proceedings unless criminal cases are explicitly excluded.[923]

5.5. DETENTION ON REMAND/ ELIGIBILITY FOR BAIL

As such, the national rules on which offences and what degree of suspicion qualifies for keeping a suspect in detention on remand also apply to other EU nationals. However, most Member States apply criteria that relate to the risk of absconding when provisionally or conditionally released. This risk is often regarded as higher when the suspect has no domicile in the country. Should a Member State, for instance, apply criteria that directly relate to nationality, or indirectly by using domicile as a relevant criterion, there is a fair risk that this would be incompatible with Union law (Article 18 TFEU).

This can be illustrated by the broad recognition of fundamental freedoms in the case of the British tourist *Cowan*. Cowan was regarded as a recipient of services, given the mere fact that he went to France as a tourist. After he had been the victim of a violent crime, Cowan unsuccessfully applied to the French victim

---

court in circumstances which do not put him at a significant disadvantage in relation to his adversary".

920   Article 1, par. 4 *Financial Interests Convention*.
921   Article 1, par. 4 *Directive 2005/60 on Money Laundering*.
922   25 January 2007, Joined Cases C-403/04 P and C-405/04, *Sumitomo Metal Industries Ltd and Nippon Steel Corp. v. Commission* [2007] ECR I-729.
923   See Article 8, paragraph 3 Directive 2000/43 of 29 June 2000 implementing the principle of equal treatment between persons irrespective of racial or ethnic origin, OJ 2000, L 180/22; Article 3, paragraph 2 Directive 97/80/EC of 15 December 1997 on the burden of proof in cases of discrimination based upon sex, OJ 1998, L 14/6; Article 10, paragraph 3 Directive 2000/78 of 27 November 2000 establishing a general framework for equal treatment in employment and occupation, OJ 2000, L 303/16.

compensation fund. His application was denied because he did not possess French nationality. The Court held that this was incompatible with Union law.[924] The more general rule which can be deduced from this is that measures that could affect non-nationals are prohibited, or, in the words of Advocate General Jacobs:

> "Although Cowan concerned a victim of criminal behaviour, the same principle must apply to the rights of an accused in criminal proceedings. Those rights are no less fundamental and must likewise be viewed as a corollary of the right to free movement."[925]

A national procedural rule may affect the free movement rights of non-nationals. The Court held in a civil procedure that "it is a corollary of those freedoms that they must be able, in order to resolve any disputes arising from their economic activities, to bring actions in the courts of a Member State in the same way as nationals of that State".[926] The consequences for EU nationals who are either suspected or convicted of having committed crimes in another Member State are that they may not receive disfavourable treatment because of their being non-national and/or non-resident.[927] All national authorities are under the obligation to give effect to this principle of equivalence.

The Court has held that:

> "The provisions of the Treaty on freedom of movement for persons are intended to facilitate the pursuit by Community nationals of occupational activities of all kinds throughout the Community, and preclude measures which might place Community nationals at a disadvantage when they wish to pursue an economic activity in the territory of another Member State."[928]

From the Court's case law, it becomes clear that EU nationals who make use of free movement rights, but, in addition, also commit crimes, may not be regarded as waiving their freedoms. Since none of the freedoms is absolute, EU nationals

---

[924] 2 February 1989, Case 186/87, *Ian William Cowan* v. *Trésor Public* [1989] ECR 195; 24 November 1998, Case C-274/96, *criminal proceedings against Horst Otto Bickel and Ulrich Franz* [1998] ECR I-7637.

[925] Opinion of Advocate General Jacobs of 19 March 1998, Case C-274/96, *criminal proceedings against Horst Otto Bickel and Ulrich Franz* [1998] ECR I-7637, point 18. The accused Bickel and Franz, as non-Italians, were not allowed to have their criminal procedure conducted in German, whilst German speakers of Italian nationality were entitled to that.

[926] 26 September 1996, Case C-43/95, *Data Delecta Aktiebolag and Ronny Forsberg* v. *MSL Dynamics Ltd* [1996] ECR I-4661, par. 13.

[927] It is also referred to the importance the Court has attributed to free movement in the context of recognition of *ne bis in idem* effect. See Chapter 5, Section 3.2 and in the context of the disproportionality of certain sanctions. See, further, Chapter 6, Section 3.

[928] 18 January 2007, Case C-104/06, *Commission* v. *Sweden* [2007] ECR I-671, par. 17. See, further, Chapter 7, Section 4.2.

may also be subjected to restrictions on suspicion or conviction of having committed offences. To both restrictions, the proportionality requirement applies. With regard to accused persons who are not finally convicted, the presumption of innocence also applies. This means that the offence and the facts supporting the suspicion must be very strong. In applying these criteria, EU nationals may not be placed at a less favourable position than nationals of the Member State where they find themselves with regard to provisional release and bail. In addition, the risk of not being available for trial has been seriously reduced by the establishment of the European Arrest Warrant mechanism. The risk will be further reduced when a *Framework Decision on the Mutual Recognition of Surveillance Orders* is adopted.[929] In comparison, it is useful to see how the Court rescinded a distinction under Italian criminal procedure regarding the language of the proceedings:

> "In those circumstances, it appears that German-speaking nationals of other Member States travelling or staying in the Province of Bolzano are at a disadvantage by comparison with Italian nationals resident there whose language is German. Whereas a member of the latter group may, if charged with an offence in the Province of Bolzano, have the proceedings conducted in German, a German-speaking national from another Member State, travelling in that province, is denied that right."[930]

This example illustrates that, for each and every aspect of the criminal proceedings, EU nationals may not be placed at a disadvantage with regard to the nationals of the Member State in which they find themselves.

5.6.   DATA PROTECTION

Article 16 TFEU stipulates that "Everyone has the right to the protection of personal data concerning them".[931] Rules laying down the protection of individuals with regard to the processing of personal data are to apply to the institutions,

---

[929]   However, Advocate General La Pergola took the view "that the principle of non-discrimination set forth in Article 6 is completely autonomous and does not need to be supported by conventions concluded by the Member States in the field of judicial cooperation in order to have effectiveness in its own right *vis-à-vis* national procedural rules". Opinion of Advocate General La Pergola of 23 May 1996, Case C-43/95, *Data Delecta Aktiebolag and Ronny Forsberg v. MSL Dynamics Ltd* [1996] ECR I-4661, point 17.

[930]   24 November 1998, Case C-274/96, *criminal proceedings against Horst Otto Bickel and Ulrich Franz* [1998] ECR I-7637, par. 24.

[931]   Declaration No. 20 on Article 16 of the Treaty on the Functioning of the European Union: the Conference declares that, whenever rules on the protection of personal data to be adopted upon the basis of Article 16 could have direct implications for national security, due account will have to be taken of the specific characteristics of the matter. It recalls that the legislation presently applicable (see, in particular, Directive 95/46/EC) includes specific derogations in this regard.

bodies, offices and agencies, and to the Member States when carrying out activities which fall within the scope of the Union.

Upon the basis of the 1981 *Council of Europe Convention for the Protection of Individuals with Regard to Automatic Processing of Personal Data*, several Directives have been adopted in which a balance is sought between the interests of the citizen in data protection, on the one hand, and the accessibility of data for the purpose of investigation, detection and the prosecution of crime, on the other.[932] *Directive 95/46 on Data Protection* is one of the few legal instruments in which rights are given to citizens. However, Article 13 of this Directive provides for exceptions in the interests of crime prevention. *Directive 2002/58 concerning the Processing of Personal Data and the Protection of Privacy in the Electronic Communications Sector* translates the principles set out in *Directive 95/46 on Data Protection* into specific rules for the electronic communications sector.[933]

6. *SUI GENERIS* MEASURES: FREEZING ORDERS, SANCTIONS AND BOYCOTTS

In this section, a series of measures that are related to criminal offences, but which cannot be regarded as being part of a proceeding that aims at a finding of guilt, have been grouped.[934] The measures discussed in this section aim at preventing certain goods or persons from crossing borders, and include freezing goods and property. The common element in all these measures is that they are not based upon a individual decision by a competent court or other law enforcement official, with regard to the reasonable grounds that a crime *might* have been (or *was*) committed, but upon the suspicion of the involvement in activities linked to terrorism, which is stipulated in the legal instrument itself. Article 75 TFEU entitles the Union to adopt administrative measures with regard to preventing and combating terrorism and related activities, such as the freezing of funds,

---

[932] See, on Data Protection in co-operation in criminal matters, Chapter 7, Section 4.1.1, and Chapter 8, Section 2.1.2.

[933] Amended by Directive 2006/24 on the retention of data generated or processed in connection with the provision of publicly available electronic communications services or of public communication networks, OJ 2006, L 105/54. Ireland has asked the Court to annul Directive 2006/24. Advocate General Bot concluded that the action should be dismissed. See Conclusion of Advocate General Bot of 14 October 2008, C-301/06, *Ireland* v. *European Parliament and Council of the European Union*, ECR not yet reported. See, on the relationship between the various Directives on data protection, 29 January 2008, Case C-275/06, *Productores de Música de España (Promusicae)* v. *Telefónica de España SAU* [2008] ECR not yet reported.

[934] AG Poiares Maduro referred to the fact that appellant claims that he would have been in a better position if criminal charges had been brought against him. See Opinion of 16 January 2008, Case 402/05 P, *Yassin Abdullah Kadi* v. *Council and Commission*, ECR, not yet reported, point 48.

financial assets or economic gains. In the light of the case law on pre-Lisbon freezing orders, the last sentence of Article 75 TFEU is interesting: "The acts referred to in this Article shall include necessary provisions on legal safeguards."[935]

At the time of the Yugoslav boycott, Regulation 990/93 provided that all Yugoslav aircraft were to be impounded. Turkish Bosphorus Airways had leased an aircraft from the Yugoslav company JAT. The aircraft was impounded at Dublin airport when it arrived for the purposes of having an overhaul and maintenance service there. The Court held that the fact that the aircraft was leased to a non-Yugoslav airline did not make it exempt from the scope of the Regulation. In rejecting the claim of violation of the principle of proportionality, the Court held, that compared to the interests of persons who were in no way responsible for the war with the aim pursued by the sanction mechanism in putting an end to the state of war in the region and the massive violations of human rights and humanitarian law.[936]

As part of a whole series of measures in response to the attacks of 11 September 2001, Regulation 2580/2001 lays down the conditions and circumstances under which measures which freeze the funds of persons and entities allegedly linked to terrorism may take place. These measures coincide with or are implemented by United Nations Security Council Resolutions in which the sanctions are announced. The person and entities on the list will have their funds and assets frozen (Article 2 Regulation 2580/2001). They may not receive financial services. The Regulation was adopted together with two Common Positions and by a subsequent Framework Decision. One Common Position criminalised acts of financing of terrorism and created a basis upon which to freeze funds and assets.[937] The other Common Position created a list of individuals and entities, to whom and to which the freezing measures were to be applied.[938] The Common Positions

---

[935] Declaration No. 25 on Articles 75 and 215 of the Treaty on the Functioning of the European Union: "The Conference recalls that the respect for fundamental rights and freedoms implies, in particular, that proper attention is given to the protection and observance of the due process rights of the individuals or entities concerned. For this purpose and in order to guarantee a thorough judicial review of decisions subjecting an individual or entity to restrictive measures, such decisions must be based on clear and distinct criteria. These criteria should be tailored to the specifics of each restrictive measure." Despite its general opt-out on measures in the area of freedom, security and justice, the United Kingdom has declared that it intends to participate in all proposals made under Article 75 TFEU. See Declaration 65 by the United Kingdom of Great Britain and Northern Ireland on Article 75 Treaty on the Functioning of the European Union.

[936] 30 July 1996, Case C-84/95, *Bosphorus Hava Yollari Turizm v e Ticaret AS v. Minister for Transport, Energy and Communications and others* [1996] ECR I-3953.

[937] OJ 2001, L 344/90.

[938] OJ 2001, L 344/93.

were adopted upon the basis of Article 23 EU in the framework of its Common Foreign and Security Policy.[939]

Since these measures do not relate to an actual finding of a criminal court that these individuals and entities are guilty of any crimes whatsoever, they must be regarded as provisional measures *vis-à-vis* accused persons to whom the presumption of innocence applies. The justifications of these measures, as well as the determination of criminal liability of the persons, groups and entities involved, may take place at a later moment.[940] The particularity, here, clearly lies in the fact that the question of whether the *suspicion* of criminal activity is strong enough to justify the measures is not decided by an impartial criminal court, but by the European legislature.[941]

Common Position 2001/931 on Specific Measures to Combat Terrorism is applicable to all persons, groups and entities involved in terrorist acts and listed in the Annex to the Common Position. Article 1, paragraphs 2 and 3 Common Position, define the terminology used. However, these provisions are relevant for the Council in order to place persons, groups or entities on the list. It does not give national authorities the possibility of considering whether certain individuals or entities comply with the criteria of Article 1, paragraphs 2 and 3.[942] The Council reviews whether the name of persons and entities should remain on the list every six months.[943]

It might have been expected that these measures would not meet much enthusiasm from those who were subjected to them. Apart from not being given a chance to express their views on the measures, it deprives individuals of financial

---

[939]   See Common Position 2004/694/CFSP on further measures in support of the effective implementation of the mandate of the International Criminal Tribunal for the Former Yugoslavia (ICTY), OJ 2004, L 315/52. The validity of the freezing measures was extended by Common Position 2006/671 of 5 October 2006, OJ 2006, L 275/66; Common Position 2007/635 of 1 October 2007, OJ 2007, L 256/30, amended by Decision 2008/613/CFSP of 24 July 2008, OJ 2008, L 197/63; in addition, Common Position 2008/614/CFSP of 24 July 2008 implementing Common Position 2004/293/CFSP renewing measures in support of the effective implementation of the mandate of the International Criminal Tribunal for the former Yugoslavia (ICTY), OJ 2008, L 197/65 lists persons who engaged in activities which help persons at large continue to evade justice for crimes for which the ICTY has indicted them.

[940]   Court of First Instance, 21 September 2005, Case T-315/01, *Yassin Abdullah Kadi* v. *Council and Commission* [2005] ECR II-3649, par. 248.

[941]   As a consequence, it is extremely difficult for those compromised by these instruments to find effective legal remedies.

[942]   Court of First Instance, 21 September 2005, Case T-306/01, *Ahmed Ali Yussuf, Al Barakaat International Foundation* v. *Council and Commission* [2005] ECR II-3533.

[943]   Common Position 2008/586/CFSP of 15 July 2008 was the most recent update, OJ 2008, L 188/71. The regular check of the necessity to maintain a name on the list will hopefully prevent embarrassing situations like the flagging of Nobel Peace Prize winner and former South African President Nelson Mandela on the United States terrorist watch list up to 2008. See USAToday: http://www.usatoday.com/news/world/2008-04-30-watchlist_N.htm (last accessed 21 August 2008).

means and makes their lives extremely difficult. Unexpectedly, the protection against freezing orders is quite problematical. The ECtHR declared the applications of applicants who had been deprived of their financial means because their names had appeared on the terrorist list to be inadmissible.[944] The Court held, upon the basis of an analysis of Article 34 ECHR, that it appeared that the applicants would not be able to establish that they had the status of a victim within the meaning of the selfsame Article.[945]

Thus, the Court offered the persons involved more protection than the ECtHR did under the ECHR. This is remarkable because the Court *had* taken note of the fact that the ECtHR had declined jurisdiction *ratione personae*. The Court regards it of particular importance that judicial protection is effective in view of the serious consequences of the measures laid down by Regulation 2580/2001.[946] The Council cannot, on the one hand, argue that the PKK lacks legal personality before the Court to complain about the measures taken, and, on the other, take decisions that subject it to restrictive measures.

Other politically active organisations, also affected by the Common Position because their names were on the list, applied for access to the documents upon which the Council based its placing on the terrorist list.[947] In both cases, the complainants argued that they had no means of challenging the inclusion on the list annexed to the Common Position and that their right to effective judicial protection was, therefore, prejudiced.[948] Although the Court admits that the system of the Union does not offer an extensive protection, the claimants were not, however, deprived of all protection. The Court also interprets Article 35 EU

---

[944]   ECtHR, 23 May 2002, *Segi and Gestoras Pro Amnistiá* v. *15 Member States of the European Union*, Application 6422/02 and 9916/02. The ECtHR held that "the mere fact that the name of two of the applicants appear in the list referred to (…) as groups or entities involved in terrorist acts may be embarrassing, but the link is much too tenuous to justify application of the convention". Subsequently, the ECtHR held that the applicant could not be regarded as a victim in the meaning of the ECHR.

[945]   18 January 2007, Case C-229/05, *Osman Ocalan (PKK) and Serif Valy (KNK) appellants, Council, defendant* [2007] ECR I-439, par. 79–83.

[946]   18 January 2007, Case C-229/05, *Osman Ocalan (PKK) and Serif Valy (KNK) appellants, Council, defendant* [2007] ECR I-439, par. 110.

[947]   See two identical decisions of 27 February 2007, Case C-354/04 P, *Gestoras Pro Amnistiá and others* [2007] ECR I-1579, par. 51 and 27 February 2007, Case C-355/04 P, *Segi and others* [2007] ECR I-1657, par. 51. These decisions build upon the Court's judgment in *Les verts*, in which the Court held that "the Treaty established a complete system of legal remedies and procedures designed to permit the Court of Justice to review the legality of measures adopted by the institutions. See 23 April 1986, Case 294/83, *Parti écologiste "Les Verts"* v. *European Parliament* [1986] ECR 1339, par. 23 and 1 February 2007, Case C-226/05P, *Jose Maria Sison* v. *Council* [2007] ECR I-103.

[948]   Maybe the inadmissibility of a complaint by a Member State against a decision of Eurojust is to be found in the element that it was not an individual who was affected but a Member State. The Court seems to hint at that. See 15 March 2005, Case C-160/03, *Spain* v. *Eurojust* [2005] ECR I-2077, par. 41–43.

(in the version before the Treaty of Lisbon) as limiting the jurisdiction of the Court to the interpretation of Framework Decisions and Decisions. However, Article 35, paragraph 1 EU, treats all measures adopted by the Council and intended to produce legal effects in relation to third parties as acts capable of being subject to a reference for a preliminary ruling. Because of the purpose of the legal instruments, the Court held that "it would run counter to that objective to interpret Article 35, paragraph 1 narrowly".[949] The Court thus allowed references for preliminary ruling related to Common Positions that were intended to produce legal effects.[950]

The Court additionally relied on Article 296 TFEU (formerly Article 253 TEC), which requires a statement of reasons for legal acts in which the Treaties do not specify how they are to be adopted. The statement of reasons must disclose in a clear and unequivocal fashion the reasoning followed by the institution which adopted the measure in question in such a way as to enable the persons concerned to ascertain the reasons for the measure and to enable the competent court to exercise its power of review of the lawfulness thereof.[951] In the *Al-Aqsa* case, the Court found that the decision to freeze the funds of applicant had to be annulled in the absence of "any indication of the actual and specific reasons justifying it, the applicant has not been placed in a position to avail itself of its right of action before the Court, given the connection between safeguarding of the obligation to state reasons and the safeguarding of the right to an effective remedy".[952] A failure to state reasons cannot be remedied by the fact that the person concerned learns the reasons for the act during the proceedings before the Union judicature.[953] With a comparable reasoning, the Court annulled the freezing Regulation which prohibited the exportation of certain goods and services to Afghanistan, because the institutions refused to grant the persons placed on the list an opportunity to dispute the grounds for their continued inclusion on the list. The Court held that, since the Council had, at no time, informed the appellants of the evidence allegedly adduced to them, in order to justify the inclusion of their names on the terrorist list, fundamental rights, including the right to an effective legal remedy, had been infringed.[954]

---

[949]   See two identical decisions of 27 February 2007, Case C-354/04 P, *Gestoras Pro Amnistiá and others* [2007] ECR I-1579, par. 53 and 27 February 2007, Case C-355/04 P, *Segi and others* [2007] ECR I-1657, par. 53.

[950]   AG Mengozzi rightly points out that the possibility for a preliminary ruling cannot be regarded as a remedy. See Opinion of 26 October 2006, Case C-354/04 P, *Gestoras Pro Amnistiá and others* [2007] ECR I-1579, par. 95.

[951]   11 July 2007, T-327/03, *Stichting Al-Aqsa* [2007] ECR II-79. See, also, Court of First Instance, 11 July 2007, T-47/03, *Sison v. Council* [2007] ECR II-2047.

[952]   11 July 2007, T-327/03, *Stichting Al-Aqsa* [2007] ECR II-79, par. 64.

[953]   Court of First Instance, 11 July 2007, T-47/03, *Sison v. Council* [2007] ECR II-2047, par. 186.

[954]   See 3 September 2008, Joined Cases 402/05 P and C-415/05 P, *Yassin Abdullah Kadi and Al Barakaat International Foundation v. Council and Commission* [2008] ECR, par. 345–353.

7.   THE SCOPE AND FORM OF THE CRIMINAL PROCEEDINGS

Some legal instruments contain provisions on the manner in which criminal proceedings must be conducted or what their scope and form should be. The case law may also have consequences on the way proceedings should be conducted. For instance, the Court has ruled that when national law entitles its own citizens to choose in which language proceedings will be conducted, this right must also be given to other EU nationals.[955] The most prominent and most detailed of the legal instrument is *Framework Decision 2001/220 on the Standing of Victims*,[956] which deals with requirements that aim at the protection of, and assistance to, victims.[957] Member States must ensure a suitable level of protection for victims, and, where appropriate, for their families and other related persons, where there is a serious risk of reprisals (Article 8, paragraph 1 *Framework Decision 2001/220 on the Standing of Victims*).[958]

The Framework Decision further provides for a series of measures that Member States must take in order to protect victims, as defined in Article 1 of the above-mentioned Framework Decision. They must be respected and treated with dignity, (Article 2, paragraph 1 Framework Decision) and secondary victimisation must be avoided (Article 15 Framework Decision). Specific treatment should be

---

[955]   11 July 1985, Case 137/84, *criminal proceedings against Robert Heinrich Maria Mutsch* [1985] ECR 2681. Belgian law provided for the German speaking part of the country that Belgian nationals could choose between German and French, and refused this to Mutsch, a worker from Luxembourg. In 24 November 1998, Case C-274/96, *criminal proceedings against Horst Otto Bickel and Ulrich Franz* [1998] ECR I-7637, the Court held that, if Italian law entitles German speaking Italians to have criminal proceedings conducted in German, this right should also be given to German speaking non-Italians.

[956]   Declaration 19 on Article 8 TFEU asks Member States to take all necessary measures to support and protect the victims of domestic violence.

[957]   In *Dell'Orto*, the *Tribunale di Milano* requested the court precisely who and what is attributed to the term "victim" as meant in the Framework Decision. 28 June 2007, Case C-467/05, *criminal proceedings against Giovanni Dell'Orto* [2007] ECR I-5557. Is the Framework Decision also applicable in a situation in which the victim is not a natural person but a legal person? The Court held that the Framework Decision only relates to natural persons.

[958]   Article 10, paragraph 2 *Framework Decision 2002/475 on Combating Terrorism* stipulates that, in addition to the measures laid down in the *Framework Decision 2001/220 on the Standing of Victims*, Member States are to "if necessary, take all measures possible to ensure appropriate assistance to victim's families". This provision of a general and binding application made other of a more limited scope without merit. Resolution of 23 November 1995 on the Protection of Witnesses in the Fight against international organised Crime calls on the Member States to guarantee proper protection of witnesses, OJ 1995, C 327/5. These witnesses and where necessary their relatives, must be protected against all forms of direct or indirect threat, pressure or intimidation. See, also, Resolution of 20 December 1996 on Individuals who co-operate with the Judicial Process in the Fight against International Organised Crime, OJ 1997 C 10/1. See, further, repealed *Joint Action 97/154 on Trafficking in Human Beings* contains a number of measures.

given to particularly vulnerable victims (Article 2, paragraph 2 Framework Decision), and children should be regarded as "particular vulnerable victims".[959] Child victims of trafficking in human beings and their families are entitled to appropriate assistance.[960] Article 3 Framework Decision, which stipulates that victims must have the possibility of being heard during proceedings, does not make it clear whether this right to be heard may serve other purposes than to give evidence.[961] Victims are entitled to receive information on a whole series of issues, as stipulated in Article 4 Framework Decision. Specific assistance and re-imbursement of expenses may be given (Articles 6 and 7 Framework Decision). Article 8, paragraphs 2–4 of this Framework Decision further stipulate that, in the appropriate cases, measures are to be taken to protect the privacy of the victims, to avoid their being put in contact with offenders and to create the possibility that testimony may be given in another manner than in open court.

The right to compensation for victims must be dealt with in the course of criminal proceedings (Article 9 Framework Decision). In 2004, a Directive relating to compensation of crime victims was adopted, which entitles victims of an intentional violent crime to apply for compensation in the state of residence (Article 1 *Directive 2004/80 on Crime Victims*). The Member States must designate one or several authorities to be responsible to receive applications.[962] A specialised service to victims must be set up and the involvement of victim support systems must be promoted (Article 13 Framework Decision), for which training must be provided (Article 14 Framework Decision). Finally, Member States are called upon to seek to promote "penal mediation" in Article 10 *Framework Decision on the Standing of Victims*. This, however, is not a direct obligation, but more soft law. The obligations of this procedural Framework Decision are of a mixed nature. Depending on the national legal system, some may require legislation, while others are of a practical nature and can be implemented directly without legislation.

---

[959]   Article 7, paragraph 2 *Framework Decision 2002/629 on Combating Trafficking in Human Beings*; Article 9, par. 2 *Framework Decision 2004/68 on Child Pornography*.

[960]   Article 7, par. 3 *Framework Decision 2002/629 on Combating Trafficking in Human Beings*; Article 9, par. 3 *Framework Decision 2004/68 on Child Pornography*.

[961]   The Court stated that a victim who has initiated a private prosecution must have the possibility of contributing to submitting evidence. This does not necessary require him to obtain the status of witness. See on a reference for a preliminary ruling from the *Fővárosi Bíróság*, Hungary, 9 October 2008, Case C-404/07, *criminal proceedings György Katz* v. *István Roland Sós*, ECR, not yet reported.

[962]   See, further, Chapter 7, Section 4.1.4.

8. NATIONAL IMPLEMENTATION AND PRELIMINARY REFERENCES

8.1. IMPLEMENTATION

From the moment that the implementation period is over, a rule that is unconditional and sufficiently precise can be invoked by the individual. As a consequence, Union law may not be relied on by individuals against the Member States before the expiry of this period.[963] Contrary to substantive criminal law, the application of procedural rules does not necessarily depend upon implementation of the Union instruments into the national legal system. This relates to the fact that quite some rules do not require a specific legal basis, but only a change in practice or in the case law. In addition, unlike substantive criminal law, which is bound by the *legality principle*, procedural rules may take immediate effect. However, this should not be interpreted to mean that procedural rules never require implementation. When it comes to the use of investigatory techniques, the collection and the use of evidence or, in other words: *measures of coercion* (or, in terms of Union law, obligations that can be held against a citizen), national criminal justice systems may require that certain measures find a basis under national law.[964] In such cases, the Member States will clearly have to provide for implementation. Article 291 TFEU requires Member States to adopt all measures *necessary* to implement legally binding Union acts.

As with substantive criminal law, when Member States must decide upon how to implement Union legislation, they have various options at their disposal.[965] They are free to make their choices, as long as they comply with the result. They may incorporate their obligations in the general Code of Criminal Procedure, or they may adopt a separate act or find another way.

8.2. INTERPRETATION IN CONFORMITY WITH THE DIRECTIVE OR FRAMEWORK DECISION

In Chapter 3, Section 5.3, the rules of interpretation of Union law were discussed. This is not the topic of this section. Here, the focus is on the interpretation of national law which implements Union law. Union law provides rules on how to

---

[963] 10 November 1992, Case C-156/91, *Hansa Fleisch Ernst Mundt GmbH & Co. KG v. Landrat des Kreises Schleswig–Flensburg* [1992] ECR I-5567, par. 20.

[964] This may also be required upon the basis of human rights obligations. The use of coercive measures may infringe upon human rights. In general, this is accepted only when provided by law.

[965] See Chapter 4, Section 6.

interpret national law in cases in which Union law is applicable. When applying national law,[966] whether it is adopted before or after the Directive, the national court has to interpret that law, and must do so, as far as possible, in the light of the wording and the purpose of the Directive in order to achieve the result it has in view.[967] In *Wagner Miret*, on a reference from the *Tribunal Superior de Justicia de Cataluña*, Spain, the Court held that:

> "The principle of interpretation in conformity with directives must be followed in particular where a national court considers, as in the present case, that the pre-existing provisions of its national law satisfy the requirements of the directive concerned."[968]

The interpretation of national law in conformity with Union law is facilitated by the obligation which can be found in many legal instruments for national measures to contain reference to the Union legal instrument that is being implemented.[969] In *Pfeifer*, the Court extended this rule also to national provisions that were not enacted as implementing legislation. The Court held that:

> "Although the principle that national law must be interpreted in conformity with Community law concerns chiefly domestic provisions enacted in order to implement the directive in question, it does not entail an interpretation merely of those provisions but requires the national court to consider national law as a whole in order to assess to what extent it may be applied so as not to produce a result contrary to that sought by the directive. In that context, if the application of interpretative methods recognised by national law enables, in certain circumstances, a provision of domestic law to be construed in such a way as to avoid conflict with another rule of domestic law or the scope of that provision to be restricted to that end by applying it only in so far as it is compatible with the rule concerned, the national court is bound to use those methods in order to achieve the result sought by the directive."[970]

This is a method already suggested by Advocate General Mischo in *Kolpinghuis*. However, the possibility of interpretation in conformity very much depends on

---

[966]   If the Member State complied with its obligations, the word "implementing" has been inserted in the title of the national implementing act. Compliance with this obligation under Article 291 TFEU will be of assistance to national authorities interpreting national implementing legislation.

[967]   16 December 1993, Case C-334/92, *Teodoro Wagner Miret* v. *Fondo de Garantía Salarial* [1993] ECR I-6911, par. 20; 14 September 2000, Case C-343/98, *Renato Collino, Luisella Chiappero* v. *Telecom Italia SpA* [2000] ECR I-6659, par. 21.

[968]   16 December 1993, Case C-334/92, *Teodoro Wagner Miret* v. *Fondo de Garantía Salarial* [1993] ECR I-6911, par. 21.

[969]   See, for instance, Article 4, paragraph 1 *Directive 2002/90 on Unauthorised Entry*.

[970]   5 October 2004, Joined Cases C-397/01 to C-403/01, *Bernhard Pfeiffer (Case C-397/01), Wilhelm Roith (Case C-398/01), Albert Süß (Case C-399/01), Michael Winter (Case C-400/01), Klaus Nestvogel (Case C-401/01), Roswitha Zeller (Case C-402/01), Matthias Döbele (Case C-403/01)* [2004] ECR I-8835, par. 115–116 (references omitted).

the definition of the offence under national law. In *Kolpinghuis*, the offence of "delivering water of unsound composition", offered a fair degree of discretion.[971] National courts must do whatever lies within their jurisdiction to ensure that the Directive is fully effected.[972]

The limitations on the obligation to interpret national law in conformity with a Directive or Framework Decision are twofold. One category relates to the national implementation law (or existing law) as such: the interpretation may not be *contra legem*.[973] Case law does not require courts to do the impossible.[974] The other category is of a specifically criminal nature: interpretation in conformity may not violate the general principles of law.[975] Advocate General Ruiz-Jarabo Colomer characterised the principle of legality in criminal law as "an inherent limit to the effectiveness of Community directives".[976] As a result, not only the determination of criminal liability as such, but also its aggravation may not rely solely on the extensive interpretation of the Directive.[977]

The Court has copied its rule of interpretation of national law in conformity with the Directive onto Framework Decisions in the *Pupino* case.[978] It did so by first looking at the fact that "the wording of Article 34(2)(b) EU is very closely inspired by the third paragraph of Article 249 EC". The binding character obliges courts to interpret national law in conformity with the Framework Decision. The fact that the Court's jurisdiction regarding Framework Decisions is not complete

---

[971] Opinion of Advocate General Mischo of 17 March 1987, Case 80/86, *criminal proceedings against Kolpinghuis Nijmegen B.V.* [1987] ECR 3969, points 25–27.

[972] In his Opinion of 27 April 2004, Joined Cases C-397/01 to C-403/01, *Bernhard Pfeiffer (Case C-397/01), Wilhelm Roith (Case C-398/01), Albert Süß (Case C-399/01), Michael Winter (Case C-400/01), Klaus Nestvogel (Case C-401/01), Roswitha Zeller (Case C-402/01), Matthias Döbele (Case C-403/01)* [2004] ECR I-8835, points 37–38, Advocate General Ruiz-Jarabo Colomer submits, with reference to the Court in *Arcaro*, that the principle of interpretation in conformity may not be used to create criminal liability.

[973] 16 June 2005, Case C-105/03, *criminal proceedings against Maria Pupino* [2005] ECR I-5285 par. 47 and Advocate General Elmer in his Opinion of 14 March 1996, Case C-168/95, *criminal proceedings against Luciano Arcaro* [1996] ECR I-4705, points 41–42.

[974] Opinion of Advocate General Kokott of 11 November 2004, Case C-105/03, *criminal proceedings against Maria Pupino* [2005] ECR I-5285, point 39.

[975] 16 June 2005, Case C-105/03, *criminal proceedings against Maria Pupino* [2005] ECR I-5285 par. 44, such as non-retroactivity and legal certainty. For the latter, see, also, 12 December 1996, Joined Cases C-74/95 and C-129/95, *criminal proceedings against X* [1996] ECR I-6609, par. 24 and 26.

[976] Opinion of 18 June 1996, Joined Cases C-74/95 and C-129/95, *criminal proceedings against X* [1996] ECR I-6609, point 54 and 73–76. See, also, 26 September 1996, Case C-168/95, *criminal proceedings against Luciano Arcaro* [1996] ECR I-4705, par. 42.

[977] Opinion of 18 June 1996, Joined Cases C-74/95 and C-129/95, *criminal proceedings against X* [1996] ECR I-6609, point 60 and 12 December 1996, Joined Cases C-74/95 and C-129/95, *criminal proceedings against X* [1996] ECR I-6609, par. 25.

[978] 16 June 2005, Case C-105/03, *criminal proceedings against Maria Pupino* [2005] ECR I-5285 par. 33–36.

(in the sense that not all national courts from all Member States may refer to the Court) does not invalidate this conclusion.

Specific attention should be paid to the situation when the implementation period is still running. During this period, in principle, the Member State is not under obligation to comply with the provisions of the Directive. However, what is the situation if a Member State does implement a Directive before the implementation period has lapsed? Is the standard by which the compliance of the national legislation with Union law is judged, the Directive, or is there still full freedom for the Member State to deviate from the provisions of the Directive? The answers to this question was given by the Court in *Inter-Environnement Wallonie*, in which the Court held that it is relevant to look at the purpose of the period of transposition, which is to give Member States the necessary time to comply with the result prescribed in the Directive.

Because of their clarity, the Court's considerations in *Inter-Environnement Wallonie* with regard to this issue are reproduced in full here:

"Although the Member States are not obliged to adopt those measures before the end of the period prescribed for transposition, it follows from the second paragraph of Article 5 (afterwards Article 10 TEC, now Article 4, paragraph 4 TEU: AHK) in conjunction with the third paragraph of Article 189 (afterwards Article 249 TEC, now 288 TFEU: AHK) of the Treaty and from the Directive itself that during that period they must refrain from taking any measures liable seriously to compromise the result prescribed.

46. It is for the national court to assess whether that is the case as regards the national provisions whose legality it is called upon to consider.

47. In making that assessment, the national court must consider, in particular, whether the provisions in issue purport to constitute full transposition of the Directive, as well as the effects in practice of applying those incompatible provisions and of their duration in time.

48. For example, if the provisions in issue are intended to constitute full and definitive transposition of the Directive, their incompatibility with the Directive might give rise to the presumption that the result prescribed by the Directive will not be achieved within the period prescribed if it is impossible to amend them in time.

49. Conversely, the national court could take into account the right of a Member State to adopt transitional measures or to implement the Directive in stages. In such cases, the incompatibility of the transitional national measures with the Directive, or the

non-transposition of certain of its provisions, would not necessarily compromise the result prescribed."[979]

In summary, if it appears that the Member State intended to implement the Directive fully, the question of whether the Member State meets its obligations under that Directive can already be assessed before the end of the period of implementation.

In cases in which the Commission has brought an action against a Member State for violation of Union law, the Court may, unlike when pronouncing preliminary rulings, hold that a specific national act violates Union law. This may have consequences for criminal proceedings as well. It follows from Article 260 TFEU (formerly 228 TEC) that:

> "All the institutions of the Member States concerned must in accordance with that provision, ensure within the fields covered by their respective powers, that judgments of the Court are complied with. If the judgment declares that certain legislative provisions of a Member State are contrary to the Treaty the authorities exercising legislative power are then under the duty to amend the provisions in question so as to make them conform with the requirements of Community law. For their part the courts of the Member States concerned have an obligation to ensure, when performing their duties, that the Court's judgment is complied with."[980]

How can the Union origin of national legislation be recognised? In practice, it may be difficult to discern that a national act is the implementation of a Union act. However, assistance to recognise the European origin is offered from various sources. First, there is the obligation for the national legislature to mention in the amending act that it is implementing Union legislation. However, Member States might not always comply with this obligation or it might no longer be visible in the final provision; for instance, if the implementing act amends a provision of a Penal Code, it is unlikely that the Union source will still be visible in the consolidated version of the Penal Code. Secondly, authorities and parties in criminal proceedings should be sensitive to situations that relate to the five freedoms. Secondary legislation, by and large, relates to these freedoms.

---

[979]   18 December 1997, Case C-129/96, *Inter-Environnement Wallonie ASBL* v. *Région Wallonne* [1997] ECR I-7411. See, also, the very interesting Opinion of Advocate General Jacobs of 24 April 1997 in this case, points 1–53.

[980]   14 December 1982, Joined Cases 314/81, 315/81, 316/81 and 83/82, *Procureur de la République and Comité national de défense contre l'alcoolisme* v. *Alex Waterkeyn and others*; *Procureur de la République* v. *Jean Cayard and others* [1982] ECR 4337.

8.3. THE PROCEDURAL CONSEQUENCES OF A FINDING THAT NATIONAL LAW MUST BE SET ASIDE

Union law does not stipulate what the decision, under national law, which the national court must take when it finds that national law must be set aside, must be. The Court does not instruct national courts what to do. It merely states:

> "that where criminal proceedings are brought by virtue of a national measure which is held to be contrary to community law, a conviction in those proceedings is likewise incompatible with community law."[981]

The national court will have to take the procedural decision that national law provides for these cases. It will be of no use to ask for assistance from the Court in this manner, because it may only supply the national court with an interpretation of Union law, not of national law. However, due to the fact that national law must be set aside, the national court may find itself in a situation in which national law does not provide for such an answer. It is then the task of the national court to be creative. This, however, will be difficult for the national court, because it must do something which national written law does not provide. It is, nevertheless, under obligation to achieve a result that is in compliance with Union law. The task of the national court will be further specified below, depending on the type of rule that may, or may not, be applied.

In situations in which Union law forces a national provision of substantive criminal law to be set aside, a conviction may not follow. The reason could be that the provision as such (for example, the transferring of goods to another Member State is prohibited) violates Union law, or that, in a specific case, (for example, foreigners who offer a specific service must apply for prior authorisation) the provision may not be applied. Whether the decision that should be taken is an acquittal (it cannot be proven that a criminal offence has been committed), or the alleged crime is not an offence,[982] a *non-lieu* (there is no real case), no case to answer (the allegations are not justified), dismissal of the charges (there is no legal basis to sustain the prosecution) or any other procedural decision a national system provides, depends upon the national system. Member States offer a wide variety of procedural consequences. Union law does not force Member States to take a specific decision, as long as they bring about a result that is in compliance with Union law.

---

[981]   16 December 1981, Case 269/80, *Regina* v. *Robert Tymen* [1981] ECR 3079, par. 16; 16 February 1978, Case 88/77, *Minister for Fisheries* v. *C.A. Schonenberg and others* [1978] ECR 473; 10 February 1982, Case 21/81, *criminal proceedings against Daniël Bout and BV, I. Bout en Zonen* [1982] ECR 381, par. 11.

[982]   This is the first category of acquittals mentioned in 28 September 2006, Case C-150/05, *van Straaten* v. *the Netherlands and Italy* [2006] ECR I-9327, par. 66.

Although non-compliance with procedural Union law is unlikely to lead to the termination of the criminal proceedings, this is certainly not impossible. As a general rule, one can presume that the violation of a procedural rule has consequences for the issue to which it relates. For instance, if rules on the collection of evidence have not been respected, the piece of evidence to which the violation relates may not be used. Other possibilities are that the accused receives a certain reduction of sentence if a sentence is imposed.[983] There is no indication that the Court follows the reasoning that failure to respect the rights of the defence with regard to one element of the procedure will have consequences for the entire proceedings in the sense that they may not be continued.

8.4. A QUESTION OF INTERPRETATION

This is the mirror section of Section 5 of Chapter 3, which dealt with the jurisdiction of the Court to hear preliminary references. The jurisdiction of the national court to refer is the topic of this paragraph. It is national law that determines which courts may refer to the Court, and the Court has held that:

> "it is for the legal system of each Member State to determine which court has jurisdiction to hear disputes involving individual rights derived from Community law, but at the same time the Member States are responsible for ensuring that those rights are effectively protected in each case. Subject to that reservation, it is not for the Court to intervene in order to resolve any questions of jurisdiction which may arise, within the national judicial system, as regards the definition of certain legal situations based on Community law."[984]

The accused is not entitled to a reference to the Court.[985] The national court decides whether questions should be raised at all,[986] and also decides which questions should be raised and when.

In *Peterbroeck*, national law limited the possibilities of raising an issue of Union law in a certain stage of the proceedings. Whatever the nature of such a procedural rule is, it must be set aside and the issue of interpretation of Union law

---

983 See Chapter 6, Section 3.

984 9 July 1985, Case 179/84, *Piercarlo Bozzetti* v. *Invernizzi SpA and Ministero del Tesoro* [1985] ECR 2301, par. 17; 16 December 1976, Case 33-76, *Rewe-Zentralfinanz eG and Rewe-Zentral AG* v. *Landwirtschaftskammer für das Saarland* [1976] ECR 1989, par. 5.

985 The ECtHR held that a decision not to refer to the Court does not amount to a violation of Article 6, par. 1 and 2 ECHR. See ECtHR, 7 septembre 1999, *Dotta c. Italie*, Requête No. 38399/97; ECtHR, 7 September 2006, *Grifhorst v. France*, Application 28336/02.

986 14 February 1984, Case 278/82, *Rewe Handelsgesellschaft Nord mbH und Rewe-Markt Herbert Kureit* v. *Hauptzollämter Flensburg, Itzehoe and Lübeck-West* [1984] ECR 721, par. 8.

must be dealt with in each stage of the proceedings. The Court held in *Peterbroeck*:

> "As regards the first part of the question, as thus reworded, the Court has consistently held that, under the principle of cooperation laid down in Article 5 of the Treaty, it is for the Member States to ensure the legal protection which individuals derive from the direct effect of Community law. In the absence of Community rules governing a matter, it is for the domestic legal system of each Member State to designate the courts and tribunals having jurisdiction and to lay down the detailed procedural rules governing actions for safeguarding rights which individuals derive from the direct effect of Community law. However, such rules must not be less favourable than those governing similar domestic actions nor render virtually impossible or excessively difficult the exercise of rights conferred by Community law. The Court has also held that a rule of national law preventing the procedure laid down in Article 177 of the Treaty from being followed must be set aside. For the purposes of applying those principles, each case which raises the question whether a national procedural provision renders application of Community law impossible or excessively difficult must be analysed by reference to the role of that provision in the procedure, its progress and its special features, viewed as a whole, before the various national instances. In the light of that analysis the basic principles of the domestic judicial system, such as protection of the rights of the defence, the principle of legal certainty and the proper conduct of procedure, must, where appropriate, be taken into consideration."[987]

Which court has the task to apply Union law directly? As was discussed in Chapter 3, with regard to the direct effect of Union law, it is for the national court before which a case is pending to apply Union law directly. It may not wait for other courts or bodies competent under national law to correct the violation of Union law,[988] and the order for reference is not subject to an interlocutory appeal under national law. Even when a lower court is generally bound under national law by decisions taken by the supreme court, the lower court remains free to refer to the Court.[989] Article 19, paragraph 1, third sentence TEU codifies the Court's case law:

> "Member States shall provide remedies sufficient to ensure effective legal protection in the fields covered by Union law."

Article 267 TFEU (formerly Article 234 TEC) reads:

---

[987]   14 December 1995, Case C-312/93, *Peterbroeck, Van Campenhout & Cie SCS* v. *Belgian State* [1995] ECR I-4599, par. 12–14 (references omitted).

[988]   9 March 1978, Case 106/77, *Amministrazione delle Finanze dello Stato* v. *Simmenthal SpA* [1978] ECR 629. See, further, Chapter 3, Section 3.1.

[989]   16 January 1974, Case 166–73, *Rheinmühlen-Düsseldorf* v. *Einfuhr- und Vorratsstelle für Getreide und Futtermittel* [1974] ECR 33.

"The Court of Justice of the European Union shall have jurisdiction to give preliminary rulings concerning:

(a) the interpretation of the Treaties;

(b) the validity and interpretation of acts of the institutions, bodies, offices or agencies of the Union;

Where such a question is raised before any court or tribunal of a Member State, that court or tribunal may, if it considers that a decision on the question is necessary to enable it to give judgment, request the Court to give a ruling thereon.

Where any such question is raised in a case pending before a court or tribunal of a Member State against whose decisions there is no judicial remedy under national law, that court or tribunal shall bring the matter before the Court.

If such a question is raised in a case pending before a court or tribunal of a Member State with regard to a person in custody, the Court of Justice of the European Union shall act with the minimum of delay."

On the question of when a question of interpretation of the law arises, the Court held in the famous *CILFIT* case:

"In this connection, it is necessary to define the meaning for the purposes of community law of the expression 'where any such question is raised' in order to determine the circumstances in which a national court or tribunal against whose decisions there is no judicial remedy under national law is obliged to bring a matter before the Court of Justice.

9 In this regard, it must in the first place be pointed out that Article 177 does not constitute a means of redress available to the parties to a case pending before a national court or tribunal. Therefore the mere fact that a party contends that the dispute gives rise to a question concerning the interpretation of community law does not mean that the court or tribunal concerned is compelled to consider that a question has been raised within the meaning of Article 177. On the other hand, a national court or tribunal may, in an appropriate case, refer a matter to the court of justice of its own motion.

10 Secondly, it follows from the relationship between the second and third paragraphs of Article 177 that the courts or tribunals referred to in the third paragraph have the same discretion as any other national court or tribunal to ascertain whether a decision on a question of community law is necessary to enable them to give judgment. Accordingly, those courts or tribunals are not obliged to refer to the court of justice a question concerning the interpretation of community law raised before them if that

question is not relevant, that is to say, if the answer to that question, regardless of what it may be, can in no way affect the outcome of the case.

11 If, however, those courts or tribunals consider that recourse to community law is necessary to enable them to decide a case, Article 177 imposes an obligation on them to refer to the court of justice any question of interpretation which may arise.

12 The question submitted by the *corte di cassazione* seeks to ascertain whether, in certain circumstances, the obligation laid down by the third paragraph of Article 177 might none the less be subject to certain restrictions.

13 It must be remembered in this connection that in its judgment of 27 March 1963 in joined cases 28 to 30/62 (*Da Costa* v. *Nederlandse Belastingadministratie* (1963) ECR 31) the Court ruled that: 'although the third paragraph of Article 177 unreservedly requires courts or tribunals of a member state against whose decisions there is no judicial remedy under national law ... to refer to the court every question of interpretation raised before them, the authority of an interpretation under Article 177 already given by the court may deprive the obligation of its purpose and thus empty it of its substance. Such is the case especially when the question raised is materially identical with a question which has already been the subject of a preliminary ruling in a similar case.'

14 The same effect, as regards the limits set to the obligation laid down by the third paragraph of Article 177, may be produced where previous decisions of the court have already dealt with the point of law in question, irrespective of the nature of the proceedings which led to those decisions, even though the questions at issue are not strictly identical.

15 However, it must not be forgotten that in all such circumstances national courts and tribunals, including those referred to in the third paragraph of Article 177, remain entirely at liberty to bring a matter before the court of justice if they consider it appropriate to do so.

16 Finally, the correct application of community law may be so obvious as to leave no scope for any reasonable doubt as to the manner in which the question raised is to be resolved. Before it comes to the conclusion that such is the case, the national court or tribunal must be convinced that the matter is equally obvious to the courts of the other member states and to the court of justice. Only if those conditions are satisfied, may the national court or tribunal refrain from submitting the question to the Court of Justice and take upon itself the responsibility for resolving it.

17 However, the existence of such a possibility must be assessed on the basis of the characteristic features of community law and the particular difficulties to which its interpretation gives rise.

18 To begin with, it must be borne in mind that community legislation is drafted in several languages and that the different language versions are all equally authentic. An interpretation of a provision of community law thus involves a comparison of the different language versions.

19 It must also be borne in mind, even where the different language versions are entirely in accord with one another, that community law uses terminology which is peculiar to it. Furthermore, it must be emphasized that legal concepts do not necessarily have the same meaning in community law and in the law of the various Member States.

20 Finally, every provision of community law must be placed in its context and interpreted in the light of the provisions of community law as a whole, regard being had to the objectives thereof and to its state of evolution at the date on which the provision in question is to be applied."[990]

This judgment still serves as a guideline for national courts on interpretation of Union law, as well as on assessing the necessity of referring to the Court. In addition, the Court issued an Information Notice on References from National Courts for a Preliminary Ruling.[991]

8.5. REFERENCE TO THE COURT

Generally speaking, national courts seem to be reluctant to refer to the Court. It is difficult to assess whether this relates to a lack of knowledge of Union law, a conviction that it is not their task, but that of the higher court, difficulties in formulating a question, the time-consuming prejudicial process, or to any other reason. Upon the basis of the case law, it is clear that all national courts and tribunals are also Union courts, and that all courts and tribunals are obliged to interpret Union law themselves. They cannot refer to a higher court or to a specialised court. The Court, however, demonstrates an open-mindedness in its willingness to assist national courts in cases in which, from the file submitted, it becomes clear that other issues of interpretation of Union law, not raised in the questions, are relevant as well.[992] Often, the Court re-formulates the question into the appropriate European dimensions. With regard to the European Arrest Warrant, Advocate General Ruiz-Jarabo Colomer expressed the "hope that other constitutional courts which are reluctant to accept their responsibilities as

---

[990]   6 October 1982, Case 283/81, *Srl CILFIT and Lanificio di Gavardo SpA* v. *Ministry of Health* [1982] ECR 3415, par. 8–20. See, also, 10 July 1997, Case C-261/95, *Rosalba Palmisani* v. *Istituto nazionale della previdenza sociale (INPS)* [1997] ECR I-4025, par. 20.

[991]   OJ 2005, C 143/1.

[992]   See Chapter 3, Section 5.2.

Community courts, will follow the example and enter into a dialogue with the Court of Justice which is essential for the purpose of building a united Europe".[993] A number of references have now been made on the European Arrest Warrant.[994]

References to the Court often take place with regard to the interpretation of a term that is part of the prohibited conduct as mentioned in the Directive.[995] A very popular word in this context is "*waste*", which has led to numerous references.[996] Another example is the term "material or equipment" in Regulation 3820/85 on the Harmonisation of Certain Social Legislation relating to Road Transport,[997] on the length of driving periods and breaks.[998]

Before referring to the Court, national courts and parties are advised to consult more than one of the language versions of the relevant legal instrument. This is especially important when the version in the national language is unclear. Arguments built only on the language version of the state in which the proceedings take place, may easily and successfully be contested if that version, either in detail or its entirety, does not reflect the real meaning of the instrument.[999]

National courts may refer to the Court *proprio motu*. The fact that the parties in the proceedings before it failed to raise a point of Union law does not preclude

---

[993] Opinion of Advocate General Ruiz-Jarabo Colomer of 12 September 2006, Case C-303/05, *Advocaten voor de Wereld VZW* v. *Leden van de Ministerraad* [2007] ECR I-3633, footnote 20.

[994] 3 May 2007, Case C-303/05, *Advocaten voor de Wereld VZW* v. *Leden van de Ministerraad* [2007] ECR I-3633; 17 July 2008, Case C-66/08, *proceedings concerning the execution of a European Arrest Warrant issued against Szymon Kosłowski* [2008] ECR not yet reported; Case C-123/08, criminal proceedings against D. Wolzenburg, reference of 21 March 2008 by the Amsterdam District Court ECR not yet reported; 12 August 2008, Case C-296/08 PPU, *Ignacio Pédro Santesteban Goicoechea* [2008] ECR not yet reported.

[995] For instance, when a calf is "tethered" in the meaning of Directive 91/629/EEC. See 3 April 2008, Case C-187/07, *criminal proceedings against Dirk Endendijk* [2008] ECR not yet reported. While the Dutch version of the relevant Directive refers to a tether which is metallic in nature, all other language versions refer to a general term. The Court held that also when the calf is tied with a rope, it is tethered within the meaning of Directive 91/629; 21 March 1996, Case C-39/95, *criminal proceedings against Pierre Goupil* [1996] ECR I-1601, on the words, "vehicles used in … refuse collection and disposal of" as meant in Regulation 3820/85.

[996] 25 June 1997, Joined Cases C-304/94, 330/94, 342/94, 224/95, *criminal proceedings against Euro Tombesi and Adino Tombesi, Roberto Santella, Giovanni Muri and others, and Anselmo Sanini* [1997] ECR I-3561; 15 January 2004, Case C-235/02, *criminal proceedings against Marco Antonio Saetti and Andrea Frediani* [2004] ECR I-1005; 7 September 2004, Case C-1/03, *criminal proceedings against Paul van de Walle, Daniël Laurent, Thiery Mensch and Texaco Belgium SA* [2004] ECR I-7613.

[997] 17 March 2005, Case C-128/04, *criminal proceedings against Annie Andréa Raemdonck and Raemdonck Janssens BVBA* [2005] ECR I-2445.

[998] 15 December 1993, Case C-116/92, *criminal proceedings against Kevin Albert Charlton, James Huyton and Raymond Edward William Wilson* [1993] ECR I-6775.

[999] One out of many examples is 22 March 1984, Case 90/83, *Michael Paterson and others* v. *W. Weddel & Company Limited and others* [1984] 1567, in which the accused relied on the ambiguous English version of the Regulation, while other language versions were worded in such a way as to exclude uncertainty. See, further, Chapter 3, Section 5.3.

---

the national court from bringing the matter before the Court.[1000] However, a national court is not obliged to raise a plea alleging infringement of the provisions of Union legislation on its own motion, as neither the principle of equivalence nor the principle of effectiveness require it to do so.[1001] As already stated, the parties in national (criminal) proceedings are not entitled to refer to the Court.[1002] This means that they have to convince the national court that such a reference is necessary. Convincing the national court to refer the matter to the Court may be difficult. If, however, a party takes the position that national law must be set aside in favour of overriding Union rules, it may force the national court to take a position. The same goes for a party stating that the Union legal act that lies at the basis of the criminal proceedings is invalid. The validity of this assertion may only be tested by the Court.[1003] National courts may not do this.[1004] If the Court judges the validity of a legal instruments, it does so upon the basis of Union law. In *Internationale Handelsgesellschaft*, the Court held that "the validity of a Community measure or its effect within a Member State cannot be affected by allegations that it runs counter to either fundamental rights as formulated by the Constitution of that state or the principles of a national constitutional structure".[1005]

The above considerations lead to the conclusion that, when the interpretation of Union law is in dispute, the national court has three options at its disposal:

– it may rule that there is no question of interpretation of Union law, things are crystal clear and national law is not in violation of Union law, and thus no reference to the Court is necessary;
– it may rule that there is no question of interpretation of Union law, it is absolutely clear that national law is in violation of Union law, that the national court has to set national law aside, and that thus no reference to the Court is necessary;

[1000]   16 June 1981, Case 126/80, *Maria Salonia* v. *Giorgio Poidomani and Franca Baglieri, née Giglio* [1981] ECR 1563, par. 7.
[1001]   7 June 2007, Joined Cases C-222/05 to C-225/05, *J. van der Weerd, Maatschap Van der Bijl, J.W. Schoonhoven (C-222/05), H. de Rooy, sen., H. de Rooy, jun. (C-223/05), Maatschap H. en J. van 't Oever, Maatschap F. van 't Oever en W. Fien, B. van 't Oever, Maatschap A. en J. Fien, Maatschap K. Koers en J. Stellingwerf, H. Koers, Maatschap K. en G. Polinder, G. van Wijhe (C-224/05), B.J. van Middendorp (C-225/05)*, v. *Minister van Landbouw, Natuur en Voedselkwaliteit* [2007] ECR I-4233, par. 42.
[1002]   See Article 267 TFEU and 6 October 1982, Case 283/81, *Srl CILFIT and Lanificio di Gavardo SpA* v. *Ministry of Health* [1982] ECR 3415, par. 9.
[1003]   13 December 1989, Case C-204/88, *Ministère public* v. *Jean-Jacques Paris* [1989] ECR 4361.
[1004]   However, Advocate General Mengozzi suggested that national courts might have that competence with regard to Third Pillar legislation. See, further, Chapter 3, Section 5.2.
[1005]   17 December 1970, Case 11–70, *Internationale Handelsgesellschaft mbH* v. *Einfuhr- und Vorratsstelle für Getreide und Futtermittel* [1970] ECR 1125, par. 3.

- the national court may hesitate on the interpretation of Union law and is unable to decide the matter before it without clarification. It will therefore refer to the Court.

In its effort to convince the national court that it should refer to the Court, it would help the defence if it were to submit evidence before the national court that, after it had informed the Commission of the difficulties the accused was experiencing with regard to enjoying fundamental freedoms, the Commission was examining the possibility of bringing an action against the Member State. Although the Commission clearly does not have the final say on Union law, its opinion is something which has to be taken into account. As a result, the national court may be far less reluctant.[1006] It is, therefore, tactically advantageous and potentially extremely efficient if the defence in criminal proceedings informs the Commission about the alleged violation of Union law.[1007] It frequently occurs that the Commission will then initiate infraction procedures and bring a case against the Member State in question to Court, and that the national court will refer for a preliminary ruling. Should the procedure of the Commission against the Member State result in a finding by the Court that national law is in violation of Union law, that judgment will influence any pending national proceedings.

Timing of the Reference

The Court has held that it is the national court which is in the best position to appreciate at what stage in the proceedings it requires a preliminary ruling from the Court. This decision of the national court must be dictated by considerations of procedural organisation and efficiency to be weighed by the national court.[1008] A combination of rules on the application of Directives and Framework Decisions, as well as the general principle of *lex mitior* require attention to be paid to the moment when a question is raised.[1009] While legal instruments may always be invoked when the implementation period is over,[1010] matters are slightly different during the period of implementation. A change of legislation will, naturally, influence the procedural attitude of those involved in a criminal trial. In more concrete terms, given the fact that Union law must be interpreted *ex nunc*, the defence in criminal proceedings has an interest to delay the proceedings when the new legislation is more favourable to the accused. Likewise, as follows from

---

[1006]   See, for instance, 16 January 2003, Case C-265/01, *criminal proceedings against Annie Pansard and others* [2003] ECR I-683, par. 16.

[1007]   This can be done by a simple letter to the European Commission, Wetstraat/Rue de la Loi 200, 1049 Brussel/Bruxelles, Belgium.

[1008]   10 March 1981, Joined Cases 36 and 71/80, *Irish Creamery Milk Suppliers Association and others v. Ireland* [1981] ECR 735, par. 7–8.

[1009]   See, further, Chapter 6, Section 3.

[1010]   5 April 1979, Case 148/78, *criminal proceedings against Tullio Ratti* [1979] ECR 1629, par. 24.

Skanavi, national courts may not neglect that new legislation will soon become effective even during the period of implementation.[1011] If, for instance, the new legislation creates more freedom, the application of a penalty during the implementation period might be regarded as disproportional, even when the Member State is still entitled to punish the behaviour in question.

Time line of application of a Directive with use of the *Skanavi* case

Directive 80/1263		28 October 1993 offence driving without licence committed	Directive 91/439
	29 July 1991 adoption of Directive 91/439 beginning of the implementation period		1 July 1996 end of the implemen- tation period

The Consequences of a Reference

When the national court refers to the Court, the first issue that it should take into consideration is that the procedure before the Court is generally time-consuming. The average duration of proceedings before the Court in 2006 and 2007 was 18 to 24 months. Since March 2008, however, the Rules of Procedure of the Court provide for a procedure with the minimum of delay when the reference relates to a person in custody. In the first case under this new rule, the reference for a preliminary ruling was received at the Court on 18 February 2008, judgment was rendered on 17 July 2008.[1012] Another case was lodged on 3 July 2008 and decided on 12 August 2008.[1013] If the accused is in detention, it is inevitable to consider, despite the urgent proceedings before the Court, whether the detention should be suspended or whether the accused should be released on bail. When the reason for the national court to refer relates to doubt as to whether the conduct may be regarded as criminal at all, release should follow. When such a basic doubt exists, the presumption of innocence requires that the accused await his trial in freedom.

[1011]   In *Skanavi* (29 February 1996, Case C-193/94, *criminal proceedings against Sofia Skanavi and Konstantin Chryssanthakopoulos* [1996] ECR I-929), the Court had used a conditional form regarding the application of lex mitior. The national court could apply the rule which finds a basis in national law. With the recognition of this rule in Article 49 Charter, this is no longer conditional.

[1012]   17 July 2008, C-66/08, *proceedings concerning the execution of a European arrest warrant issued against Szymon Kosłowski* [2008] ECR not yet reported.

[1013]   12 August 2008, Case C-296/08 PPU, *Ignacio Pédro Santesteban Goicoechea* [2008] ECR not yet reported.

8.6. THE PROCEEDINGS BEFORE THE COURT

Article 23 Protocol 3 on the Statute of the Court of Justice of the European Union determines that the decision of the national court which suspends its proceedings and refers a case to the Court is to be notified to the Court by the national court. The Registrar of the Court will notify the parties in the national proceedings, all Member States, the Commission and, where relevant, the institution, body, office or agency of the Union which adopted the act, of the validity or interpretation which is in dispute. All those notified are entitled to submit statements of case or written observations to the Court.

Despite the fact that the parties in the national proceedings are not entitled to refer to the Court, once such a decision has been taken, they may make observations to the Court. If a hearing is held, they may be present and address the Court. The Court finds that it is of the utmost importance that all parties to the dispute are given the opportunity to make observations. After all the observations have been made, the Advocate General will present his Opinion and the Court will give judgment.

As mentioned above, with effect of 1 March 2008, a new Article 23a has been inserted into the existing Protocol on the Statute of the Court, which mandates the Rules of Procedure, which provides for an expedited or accelerated procedure and for references for a preliminary ruling relating to the area of freedom, security and justice in *urgent procedures*.[1014] Article 104b of the Rules of Procedure of the Court of Justice provide for Third Pillar issues and asylum and urgent procedure which derogates from the normal procedure applicable to preliminary rulings. Furthermore, the Council has also called upon the Court to apply the urgent preliminary ruling procedure in situations involving deprivation of liberty.[1015] In cases in which a national court or tribunal applies for the urgent procedure, it has to set out, in its request, the matter of fact and law which establish the urgency and justify the application of the exceptional procedure. In addition, the referring court must, as much as possible, indicate the answer it proposes to the question referred.[1016]

8.7. THE ANSWER OF THE COURT

In principle, the national court determines, in its reference, which Union law provisions should come into consideration. However, the Court is not bound to

---

[1014] Council Decision 2008/79/EC, Euratom of 20 December 2007 amending the Protocol on the Statute of the Court of Justice, OJ 2008, L 24/42.
[1015] Statement by the Council, OJ 2008, L 24/44.
[1016] Rule 104b Rules of Procedure of the Court of Justice.

limit itself to the provisions referred to, if this is of assistance in adjudicating upon the case pending before the national court.[1017] The Court will declaratory state the law: "a preliminary ruling does not create or alter the law, but is purely declaratory, with the consequence that in principle it takes effect from the date on which the rule interpreted entered into force."[1018] The Court "classifies and defines the meaning and scope of a rule as it must be or ought to have been understood and applied from the time of its entry into force."[1019] After receiving the Court's judgment, the national court will interpret and apply its consequences to the national case. The national court may, however, depending on its national law, decide to give the parties the opportunity to state their views with regard to what the judgment means for the national criminal proceedings first. It may also, if it considers that there are further questions of interpretation, refer once again to the Court. Formally, there is no limit to referring to the Court in the same proceedings.

[1017] 25 January 2007, Case C-321/03, *Dyson Ltd* v. *Registrar of Trade Marks* [2007] ECR I-687, par. 24.

[1018] 12 February 2008, Case C-2/06, *Willy Kempter KG* v. *Hauptzollamt Hamburg-Jonas* [2008] ECR not yet reported, par. 35. See, further, Chapter 3, Section 5.3.

[1019] 6 March 2007, Case C-292/04, *Wienand Meilicke, Heidi Christa Weyde, Marina Stöffler* v. *Finanzamt Bonn-Innenstadt* [2007] ECR I-1835, par. 34.

CHAPTER 6.
EUROPEAN SENTENCING
AND PENITENTIARY LAW

1. INTRODUCTION

The shortness of this chapter should definitely be regarded as indicating that Union law only stands at the beginning of formulating detailed rules on sentencing and penitentiary law. Although there is a fair quantity of case law from the Court of First Instance and the Court on sentencing in competition law, not much more existed until the first Conventions and Joint Actions on criminal law were adopted after the conclusion of the Treaty of Maastricht. Since then, the Union has been quite influential on the legislation of the Member States regarding the sanctions provided for eurocrimes. However, this legislative development has not been accompanied with many judgments of the Court yet. This finds its explanation in the fact that the Commission did not have the competence to bring cases against a Member State to the Court.

The general rules on both the effects and the obligations deriving from Union law, which were discussed in Chapter 3, are also applicable on sentencing issues. The Court has held that:

> "where Community legislation does not specifically provide any penalty for an infringement or refers for that purpose to national legislation, Article 5 of the Treaty requires the Member States to take all measures necessary to guarantee the application and effectiveness of Community law. For that purpose, while the choice of penalties remains within their discretion, they must ensure in particular that infringements of Community law are penalized under conditions, both procedural and substantial, which are analogous to those applicable to infringements of national law of a similar nature and importance and which, in any event, make the penalty effective, proportionate and dissuasive."[1020]

Not only the *Greek maize* criteria, but also the non-discrimination rule has consequences with regard to the imposition of sentences. They may not be more severe for non-nationals as they are for nationals in similar situations. As a

---

[1020] 26 October 1995, Case C-36/94, *Siesse – Soluções Integrais em Sistemas Software e Aplicações Lda v. Director da Alfândega de Alcântara* [1995] ECR I-3573, par. 20.

consequence, a Member State may not give higher penalties to foreigners because of the fact that they are not eligible for re-habilitation programmes and will be expelled anyway after serving their sentence. Similarly, offences bearing an international element may not be punished more severely than those with only national elements. The Court held that it is incompatible with the Treaty to provide for higher penalties in situations of VAT evasion related to imported goods than to internal goods "in so far as that difference is disproportionate to the dissimilarity between the two categories of offences".[1021]

This chapter will first deal with the requirements on the sanctions which have to be provided in national criminal law (Section 2). Subsequently, the sentencing criteria are discussed (Section 3). Section 2 exclusively deals with the influence of Union law on legislation, while Section 3 deals with the rules that apply on the actual imposition of the sentence by the national court. The distinction drawn here between the sanctions that must be provided in the law and the application of Union law on concrete sentencing may be summarised as follows. Union law contains rules regarding the sanctions to be provided under national criminal law. These rules are addressed to the legislature of the Member State. Additionally, Union law gives indications of sentencing criteria for concrete cases. These are rules which may, albeit not necessarily, be addressed to the legislature, in the sense that national criminal law must allow these rules to be applied in court decisions. Union rules on sentencing are addressed to the national criminal court.

2.   PENALTIES TO BE PROVIDED UNDER NATIONAL LAW

It was established earlier that, in general, there is an obligation with regard to the results that the Member States must attain. In one way or another, Member States must achieve compliance with Union law. In the absence of a specific obligation to criminalise certain conduct, Member States may or may not criminalise infringements of Union law. However, the assimilation principle may force Member States to provide criminal sanctions. Whatever the sanction that Member States provide, it must comply with the enforcement of the *Greek maize* criteria.

Apart from instruments which leave it to the discretion of the Member States to provide criminal penalties,[1022] some Directives and Framework Decisions might require the criminalisation of certain conduct. As a rule, Framework

---

[1021]   25 February 1988, Case 299/86, *criminal proceedings against Rainer Drexl* [1988] ECR 1213, par. 23–25.

[1022]   In Chapter 4, paragraph 2, the question was raised what criminal sanctions are. See Chapter 4, Section 2.

Decisions codified the *Greek maize* criteria: "Each Member State shall take the measures necessary to ensure that the offences defined in Articles xy are punishable by effective, proportionate and dissuasive penalties," often adding that these measures are to involve "deprivation of liberty which may give rise to extradition".[1023]

The Greek *maize criteria* are additionally found in provisions that deal with the sanctions for legal persons.[1024] The standard phrase here is:

> "Member States shall take the necessary measures to ensure that a legal person held liable pursuant to Article xy is punishable by effective, proportionate and dissuasive sanctions."

The double appearance of the *Greek maize* criteria may be explained by the fact that the references serve distinct purposes. While the first reference points out that effective criminal penalties must be provided for natural persons, the second applies to sanctions both of a criminal and a non-criminal nature for legal persons. The latter allows Member States to provide for sanctions that are not of a criminal nature, whilst, at the same time, guaranteeing that all sanctions for legal persons are subject to the same criteria. In addition, the second reference to the *Greek maize* criteria underlines that specific penalties may have to be provided for legal persons.

Most references in the legal instruments to the criminal sanctions that national criminal law should provide, do not mention the assimilation principle.[1025] Since all general criteria that have normative influence on enforcement apply, the assimilation principle must be complied with. Occasionally, the principle is referred to. For instance, Article 5, paragraph 2 *Framework Decision 2002/475 on Combating Terrorism* imposes that the Member States ensure that terrorist offences "are punishable by custodial sentences heavier than those imposable under national law for such offences in the absence of the special intent". This provision should be regarded as a statement that the "special intent" of terrorism makes the offence not comparable (similar) to the existing national offences, as a

---

[1023]   Article 5 *First Protocol Financial Interests Convention*; Art. 5 *Corruption Convention*; Article 6, par. 1 *Framework Decision 2000/383 on the Introduction of the Euro*; Article 6 *Framework Decision 2001/413 on Combating Fraud*; Article 3 *Directive 2002/90 on Unauthorised Entry*; Article 5 *Framework Decision 2002/475 on Combating Terrorism*; Article 3, par. 1 *Framework Decision 2002/629 on Combating Trafficking in Human Beings*; Article 1 *Framework Decision 2002/946 on Unauthorised Entry*; Article 5 *Framework Decision 2003/80 on the Protection of the Environment*; Article 4, par. 1 *Framework Decision 2004/757 on Illicit Drug Trafficking*.

[1024]   Article 5 *Framework Decision 2002/629 on Combating Trafficking in Human Beings*; Article 3 *Framework Decision 2002/946 on Unauthorised Entry*; Article 7 *Framework Decision 2003/80 on the Protection of the Environment*; Article 6 *Framework Decision 2003/568 on Corruption in the Private Sector*; Article 7 *Framework Decision 2004/68 on Child Pornography*; Article 7 *Framework Decision 2004/757 on Illicit Drug Trafficking*.

[1025]   See, on the assimilation principle, Chapter 3, Section 3.2.

consequence of which different (higher) sanctions should be provided. The other reference found also confirms the general application of the assimilation principle:

> "Member States shall ensure that under their legal systems the penalties imposed for serious drug trafficking are among the most severe penalties available for crimes of comparable gravity."[1026]

Sanction Modalities

Union legislation provides for a panoply of sanction modalities. Clearly, the death penalty and executions are excluded in Article 2 of the Charter of Fundamental Rights of the European Union. A large number of other modalities are referred to in the legal instruments. The general impression is that there is a *lacuna* with regard to the sanction modalities by which the rehabilitative element is much stronger than the punitive element. For instance, community service or restorative justice have not been referred to in any of the legal instruments. However, this may relate to the seriousness of the crimes upon which the EU has legislated. A principled and fundamental approach to the purposes of sentencing cannot be identified. The same goes for the distinctions that some Member States make between the main penalties and accompanying penalties, and between sanctions and measures.

Imprisonment

Imprisonment as a sanction modality can be found in all Union legal instruments. In the early days of the Joint Actions, it was simply stipulated that, in serious cases, penalties involving the deprivation of liberty should "*at least*" be provided (Article 4 *Joint Action 98/742 on Corruption in the Private Sector*). Since then, obligations have become much more concrete.

Generally speaking, the European Union has refrained from giving Member States detailed instructions on the penalties that should be provided in their criminal laws. A notable exception is the so-called *minimum-maximum* penalty.[1027] This obligation is formulated as follows:

[1026]   Article 4 *Joint Action 96/750 on Illegal Drug Trafficking*, and, in a similar manner, Council Resolution of 20 December 1996 on sentencing for serious illicit drug-trafficking, OJ 1997, C 10/3.

[1027]   The obligation must be regarded as an exception to the general applicability of the principle of assimilation, because it requires the provision of a certain level of sanctions, regardless of what national criminal law stipulates regarding comparable infringements.

"Each Member State shall take the measures necessary to ensure that the offences defined in Articles xy are punishable by criminal penalties of: ..."

– a maximum of, at least, between one and three years;[1028]
– a maximum of, at least, between two and five years;[1029]
– a maximum of not less than four years;[1030]
– a maximum penalty of, at least, four years or a more serious penalty;[1031]
– a maximum of, at least, between 5 and 10 years;[1032]
– a maximum penalty that is not less than eight years;[1033]
– a maximum penalty of, at least, 10 years;[1034]
– a maximum penalty of no less than 15 years.[1035]

What is the obligation which derives from such a provision? The only obligation that derives from these provisions is that Member States must ensure that the maximum penalty provided under their legislation is equal or higher than the

---

[1028] Article 4, par. 2 *Framework Decision 2003/568 on Corruption in the Private Sector*; Article 5, par. 1 *Framework Decision 2004/68 on Child Pornography*; Article 4, par. 1 *Framework Decision 2004/757 on Illicit Drug Trafficking*; Article 6, par. 2 *Framework Decision 2005/222 on Attacks against Information Systems*; Article 4, par. 1 and 7 *Framework Decision 2005/667 on Ship-source Pollution*.

[1029] Article 7, par. 1 *Framework Decision 2005/222 on Attacks against Information Systems*; Article 4, par. 5 and Article 6 *Framework Decision 2005/667 on Ship-source pollution*.

[1030] See Article 2 *Framework Decision 2001/500 on Money Laundering*.

[1031] Article 1 *Joint Action 98/733 on Participation in a Criminal Organisation*.

[1032] Article 5, par. 2 *Framework Decision 2004/68 on Child Pornography*; Article 4, par. 2 and 4 *Framework Decision 2004/757 on Illicit Drug Trafficking*; Article 4, par. 4 *Framework Decision 2005/667 on Ship-source Pollution*.

[1033] Article 6, par. 2 *Framework Decision 2000/383 on the Introduction of the Euro*; Article 5, par. 3 *Framework Decision 2002/475 on Combating Terrorism*; Article 3, par. 2 *Framework Decision 2002/629 on Combating Trafficking in Human Beings*; Article 1, par. 3 *Framework Decision 2002/946 on Unauthorised Entry*.

[1034] Article 4, par. 3 *Framework Decision 2004/757 on Illicit Drug Trafficking*.

[1035] Article 5, par. 3 *Framework Decision 2002/475 on Combating Terrorism*. Dr. Pedro Caeiro of Coimbra University brought the following to the attention. The Portuguese version of the Framework Decision contains a mistake in Article 5, paragraph 3 and left out the word "maximum". The result is the formulation of a minimum penalty: "Cada Estado-Membro tomará as medidas necessárias para assegurar que as infracções referidas no artigo 2.o sejam passíveis de penas privativas de liberdade que não podem ser inferiores a quinze anos para a infracção prevista no n.o 2, alínea a), do artigo 2.o e a oito anos para as infracções previstas no n.o 2, alínea b), do artigo 2.o Na medida em que a infracção prevista no n.o 2, alínea a), do artigo 2.o apenas se refira ao acto previsto na alínea i) do n.o 1 do artigo 1.o, a pena máxima não pode ser inferior a oito anos.". Given the general rules of interpretation, which state that provisions must be read in the context of other language versions, Portugal (as any other Member State) is not obliged to introduce minimum penalties. See, further, Chapter 3, Section 5.3. The fact that Portugal apparently did introduce minimum penalties is founded on the misinterpretation that the language version in the national language is exclusively applicable.

penalty required in Union law.[1036] Literally, the minimum-maximum penalties in the list above could, respectively, be re-formulated to a maximum penalty of at least, one year, two years, four years, four years and so on, since everything equal or above that lowest number of years complies with the obligation. However, it does not oblige courts to impose the maximum penalty, nor does it force the Member States to introduce a system of mandatory or minimum penalties.[1037]

Despite the confusing name they were given, minimum-maximum penalties do not relate to mandatory penalties. Union law neither prescribes, nor prohibits minimum penalties.[1038] Member States are completely free to follow their own wishes here. In a Protocol attached to the Treaty of Amsterdam, this was expressed by allowing the Member States for whom the minimum sanctions were incompatible with the system, not to introduce them into their system. The Treaty of Lisbon no longer has such a Protocol, and Article 83 TFEU would definitely allow for minimum sanctions to be introduced. However, it is provided that a Member State which opines that this would affect fundamental aspects of its criminal justice system may prevent such a measure from being taken.

Some penalties are regarded as too severe. As part of her conviction for drug crimes, the Italian national *Donatella Calfa* was automatically banned from the territory of Greece for the rest of her life. The Court regarded the infringement on free movement unacceptable.[1039] This case law on expulsion orders raises the question of whether the application of the proportionality principle rules out minimum penalties. One reasoning by which minimum penalties could be saved under Union law is that the Court would accept that the proportionality requirement had already been fulfilled when the legislature decided that a minimum sentence would be proportionate for specific crimes.

Penalties other than the Deprivation of Liberty

These are provided for minor cases of active or passive corruption in the private sector (Article 4, paragraph 2 *Joint Action 98/742 on Corruption in the Private Sector*). *Framework Decision 2003/80 on the Protection of the Environment* suggests other penalties than deprivation of liberty:

[1036] See Chapter 2, Section 4.4, on the relatively moderate harmonising character of these kinds of obligations.

[1037] Some Regulations provide for minimum amounts to be retained. See, for instance, Commission Regulation 150/2001 of 25 January 2001 laying down detailed rules for the application of Council Regulation 104/2000 as regards the penalties to be applied to producer organisations in the fisheries sector for irregularity of the intervention mechanism and amending Regulation 142/98, OJ 2001, L 24/10. Article 3, paragraph 5 stipulates that the amounts retained and other sanctions provided shall not be regarded as criminal penalties.

[1038] However, there are some signals that fixed penalties could violate the principle of proportionality and the principle of guilt. See, further, Section 3 of this chapter.

[1039] 19 January 1999, Case C-348/96, *criminal proceedings against Donatella Calfa* [1999] ECR I-11.

"in particular the disqualification for a natural person from engaging in an activity requiring official authorisation or approval, or founding, managing or directing a company or a foundation, where the acts having led to his or her conviction show an obvious risk that the same kind of criminal activity may be pursued."[1040]

Fines

Fines are not mentioned in any of the provisions relating to natural persons. Neither as the single modality of a penalty provided, nor as an additional penalty besides other modalities. This raises the question of whether fines for eurocrimes is regarded as a measure that does not comply with the Greek *maize criteria*. Are fines regarded as ineffective, as not of a sufficiently dissuasive character, or as disproportionate to the gravity of the crimes on which the EU has legislated?

Confiscation

Article 4, paragraph 5 *Framework Decision 2004/757 on Illicit Drug Trafficking* requires Member States to provide for the confiscation of the substances, the instrumentalities and the proceeds or for the confiscation of property with corresponding value. Article 2, paragraph 2 *Framework Decision 2002/946 on Unauthorised Entry* stipulates that where appropriate confiscation of the means of transport should be provided for. In addition, Article 3 *Framework Decision 2001/500 on Money Laundering* requires Member States to provide for value confiscation in their legislation.

Temporary or Permanent Prevention from Exercising Professional Activities

Article 5, paragraph 3 *Framework Decision 2004/68 on Child Pornography* obliges Member States to ensure that natural persons convicted of the crimes mentioned in the Framework Decision, "if appropriate, be temporarily or permanently prevented from exercising professional activities related to the supervision of children".[1041] Article 4, paragraph 3 stipulates something similar relating to "business activity".

Deportation and Expulsion

In addition to criminal penalties, Member States should, "where appropriate", consider deportation from the Member State.[1042] However, with regard to EU nationals, Article 33, paragraph 1 *Directive 2004/38 Free Movement* stipulates that "Expulsion orders may not be used by the host Member State as a penalty or legal consequence of a custodial penalty, unless they conform to the requirements of

---

[1040]   Article 5, paragraph 2 *Framework Decision 2003/80 on the Protection of the Environment*; similarly, Article 4, par. 3 *Framework Decision 2005/667 on Ship-source Pollution.*
[1041]   Article 2, par. 2 *Framework Decision 2002/946 on Unauthorised Entry.*
[1042]   Article 2, par. 2 *Framework Decision 2002/946 on Unauthorised Entry.*

Articles 27, 28 and 29".[1043] In the context of automatic expulsion orders against EU nationals who have committed crimes, the Court has held that a decision to expel an EU national must be based upon personal conduct and may not be justified on the basis of previous convictions.[1044]

Sanctions for Legal Persons

In the first years of the Third Pillar, the obligations were quite hesitant: "Legal persons may be penalised in an effective, proportionate and dissuasive manner and (...) material and economic sanctions may be imposed on them." (Article 3 *Joint Action 98/733 on Participation in a Criminal Organisation*). But these are wordings that date from the days when the Member States could not reach agreement on the question of the principle of whether the criminal liability of legal persons should be obligatory or not.[1045] Since this step has been taken, the obligations with regard to the penalties that must be provided leave far less room for discretion. Article 6 *Framework Decision 2005/667 on Ship-source Pollution* provides minimum-maximum fines:

- a maximum of at least between EUR 150,000 and EUR 300,000;
- a maximum of at least between EUR 750,000 and EUR 1,500,000.

Article 6, paragraph 3 further stipulates that a Member State may apply a system whereby the fine is proportional to the turnover of the legal person. This is a system that has been applied for years in the field of competition law.

The legal instruments that provide for the criminal liability of legal entities also mention that Member States are to create possibilities for criminal or non-criminal fines and other sanctions, such as:

a. exclusion from entitlement to tax relief or other benefits or public aid;
b. temporary or permanent disqualification from pursuit of commercial activities;
c. placing under judicial supervision;
d. a judicial winding-up order;
e. temporary or permanent closure of establishments used for committing the offence;
f. confiscation.

[1043] These Articles deal with restrictions based upon public policy, public security or public health. See, further, Chapter 3, Section 4.6.1.

[1044] 7 June 2007, Case C-50/06, *Commission* v. *The Netherlands* [2007] ECR I-4383. See, further, Chapter 3, Section 4.4.

[1045] See Chapter 4, Section 3.6.

The large majority of instruments provide for categories a, b, c, and d.[1046] Categories e,[1047] and f,[1048] appear less often. Only the annulled *Framework Decision 2005/667 on Ship-source Pollution* provides for the obligation to adopt specific measures in order to eliminate the consequences of the offence which led to the liability of the legal person.

3.   SENTENCING CRITERIA

In comparison to the fact that there is hardly any case law on sentencing, the attention paid to sentencing by the Union legislature is astonishing. Member States are required to provide sanctions of a certain level. However, the imposition of sanctions in individual cases is left to the national criminal courts. Even in this area, Union law has produced rules which apply to sentencing. It is for the national court, in accordance with the Greek *maize criteria*, to determine the amount of the penalty.[1049] In general, the criteria which can be found are formulated along the lines of what can be found in the criminal justice systems of the Member States. For instance, Resolution of 20 December 1996 on sentencing for serious illicit drug-trafficking mentions the following sentencing factors:

– the extent of the trafficking;
– the extent to which the person concerned has profited from the illicit traffic;
– the involvement in the offence of an organized criminal group to which the offender belongs;
– the extent to which the offender has control of the drug-trafficking organisation;
– the victimisation or use of minors.

[1046]   Article 5 *Second Protocol Financial Interests Convention*; Article 8 *Framework Decision 2002/475 on Combating Terrorism*; Article 7 *Framework Decision 2003/80 on the Protection of the Environment*; Article 7 *Framework Decision 2004/68 on Child Pornography*; Article 7 *Framework Decision 2004/757 on Illicit Drug Trafficking*.

[1047]   Article 8 *Framework Decision 2002/475 on Combating Terrorism*; Article 7 *Framework Decision 2004/757 on Illicit Drug Trafficking*; Article 9 *Framework Decision 2005/222 on Attacks against Information systems*; Article 6 *Framework Decision 2005/667 on Ship-source Pollution*.

[1048]   *Second Protocol Financial Interests Convention*; *Joint Action 98/742 on Corruption in the Private Sector*; *Framework Decision 2000/383 on the Introduction of the Euro*; *Framework Decision 2002/629 on Combating Trafficking in Human Beings*; *Framework Decision 2002/946 on Unauthorised Entry*; *Framework Decision 2003/568 on Corruption in the Private Sector*; *Framework Decision 2004/68 on Child Pornography*; *Framework Decision 2004/757 on Illicit Drug Trafficking*.

[1049]   26 October 1995, Case C-36/94, *Siesse – Soluções Integrais em Sistemas Software e Aplicações Lda* v. *Director da Alfândega de Alcântara* [1995] ECR I-3573, par. 24.

The Principle of Proportionality

The factors mentioned are subsumed by the requirement that sanctions should be proportional. The principle of proportionality has obtained the status of a general principle of Union law and is found in the Charter: "the severity of penalties must not be disproportionate to the criminal offence." (Article 49, paragraph 3 Charter). However, the Charter is not the first instrument to stipulate the principle of proportionality. There is abundant case law on the application of this principle.[1050] Article 23, paragraph 3 Regulation 1/2003 reads: "In fixing the amount of the fine, regard shall be had both to the gravity and to the duration of the infringement." The size and economic power of the undertaking may also be taken into consideration, and, thus, the Commission may look at the overall turnover of an undertaking.[1051] The Court applies the proportionality principle concerning all kinds of penalties,[1052] including criminal penalties.[1053] There is case law in which fixed penalties have been found to be disproportional.[1054]

Proportionality, seen in relation to the gravity of the infringement, contains two elements. The first is related to the legislation. When criminalising and adopting the maximum or minimum penalties provided for the crime, the legislation of the Member States must take the requirement into consideration. The second element relates to the actual imposition of the penalty by the national court. When imposing sentence, the national court must again impose a penalty that is proportional to the offence actually committed. The Court held that "the question [of] whether the penalties applied are proportionate or disproportionate has to be assessed on the basis of the level of the penalties actually applied in the individual case".[1055] In a competition case, the Court has held:

> "For the purpose of determining the gravity of the infringement, it is necessary to take into consideration, in particular, the conduct of each of the undertakings, the role played by each of them in the establishment of the cartel and the profit which they were able to derive from it."[1056]

The elements that are relevant here include the character of the offence committed and the role of the accused in it. Earlier on, we identified that the imposition of

---

[1050]   12 July 2001, Case C-262/99, *Paraskevas Louloudakis* v. *Elliniko Dimosio* [2001] ECR I-5547, par. 67.
[1051]   29 June 2006, Case C-289/04 P, *Showa Denko KK* v. *Commission* [2006] ECR I-5859, par. 16–17.
[1052]   5 February 1987, Case 288/85, *Hauptzollamt Hamburg-Jonas* v. *Plange Kraftfutterwerke GmbH & Co* [1987] ECR 611, concerning a 20% increase of refunds unduly paid.
[1053]   31 March 1993, Case C-19/92, *Dieter Kraus* v. *Land Baden-Württemberg* [1993] ECR I-1663.
[1054]   20 February 1979, Case 122/78, *S.A. Buitoni* v. *Fonds d'Orientation et de Régularisation des Marchés Agricoles* [1979] ECR 677.
[1055]   7 June 2007, Case C-156/04, *Commission* v. *Greece* [2007] ECR I-4129, par. 72.
[1056]   See 10 May 2007, Case C-328/05 P, *Appeal of SGL Carbon AG* [2007] ECR I-3921, par. 44.

criminal penalties may, under some circumstances, be regarded as disproportional.[1057] In competition cases, the Court has accepted that in sentencing *equal treatment* should apply. This precludes different treatment of comparable situations and different situations being treated in the same way.[1058] However, the Court is not easily inclined to find a violation of the principle of equal treatment.

Lex Mitior

The principle of retroactive application of the more lenient penalty forms part of the constitutional traditions common to the Member States and is therefore part of the general principles of Union law.[1059] The Charter prohibits the application of a heavier penalty than that which was applicable at the time when the offence was committed. However, "if later legislation provides a lighter penalty, that penalty shall be applicable" (Article 49, paragraph 1, Charter). In Chapter 4, *lex mitior* was already discussed in the context of a more favourable description of the offence. In this chapter, the focus is only limited to a more favourable penalty, leaving the offences as such unaffected.

Deterrence

The Court has held, in a competition case, that deterrence is one of the factors to be taken into account in calculating the amount of the fine. Factors to be taken into consideration when determining the fines include, "*inter alia*, the particular circumstances of the case, its context and the dissuasive effect of fines".[1060]

Aggravating Circumstances

The terminology "aggravating circumstances" appears in Article 5 *Framework Decision 2004/68 on Child Pornography*, but other Framework Decisions mention circumstances which may be regarded as aggravating. Two categories of aggravation are mentioned in Article 4, paragraph 2 *Framework Decision 2004/757 on Illicit Drug Trafficking*:

–   the offence involves large quantities of drugs;
–   the offence either involves those drugs which cause the most harm to health, or has resulted in significant damage to the health of a number of persons.

[1057]   29 February 1996, Case C-193/94, *criminal proceedings against Sofia Skanavi and Konstantin Chryssanthakopoulos* [1996] ECR I-929. See, also, Chapter 4, Section 1.

[1058]   7 June 2007, Case C-76/06 P, *Britannia Alloys & Chemicals Ltd* v. *Commission* [2007] ECR I-4405.

[1059]   8 March 2007, Case C-45/06, *Campina* v. *Hauptzollamt Frankfurt Oder* [2007] ECR I-2089.

[1060]   E.g. 8 February 2007, Case C-3/06 P, *Groupe Danone* [2007] ECR I-1331, par. 37.

Some Framework Decisions use aggravating circumstances as elements for a more serious crime for purposes of qualification.[1061] The consequence is that the circumstances that were relevant for the qualification are used again in order to determine the gravity of the crime. It is questionable whether the dual use of aggravating circumstances, both for the qualification and for sentencing purposes, is in compliance with the proportionality principle.

Habitual Criminality/Recidivism

A specific Framework Decision of 6 December 2001 amended *Framework Decision 2000/383 on the Introduction of the Euro* and introduced a new Article 9A which imposed the obligation on Member States, for the purpose of establishing habitual criminality, to recognise "final sentences handed down in another Member State for the offences" of the decision of the Framework Decision.[1062] Repeated infringement has been recognised as an aggravating circumstance.[1063] The Court held that an irregularity is continuous or repeated where it is committed from a body of similar transactions which infringe the same provision of law.[1064]

The possibilities of obtaining a complete picture of the accused before the national court for the purpose of sentencing have been enlarged by the obligation to exchange information extracted from the criminal record.[1065] This will enable courts to take into consideration other convictions for similar offences, completely different offences, or to take note of the fact that the accused has never been convicted before. Article 6 Title III of the repealed *Joint Action 97/154 on Trafficking in Human Beings* provides accessibility of information concerning persons convicted of offences of child abuse for other Member States authorities.[1066] In *Sagulo*, the interesting issue arose as to whether a final conviction which was based upon national provisions not in accordance with Union law could be

---

[1061]   Article 3, par. 2 *Framework Decision 2002/629 on Combating Trafficking in Human Beings*; Article 1, par. 3 *Framework Decision 2002/946 on Unauthorised Entry*; Article 5, par. 2 sub b and c *Framework Decision 2004/68 on Child Pornography*.

[1062]   Framework Decision 2001/888 of 6 December 2001 amending Framework Decision 2000/383/ JHA on increasing protection by criminal penalties and other sanctions against counterfeiting in connection with the introduction of the euro, OJ 2001, 329/3.

[1063]   For example, 8 February 2007, Case C-3/06 P, *Groupe Danone* [2007] ECR I-1331, par. 10–11.

[1064]   11 January 2007, Case C-279/05, *Vonk Diary Products BV* v. *Produktschap Zuivel* [2007] ECR I-239.

[1065]   Council Decision 2005/876/JHA of 21 November 2005 on the exchange of information extracted from the criminal record, OJ 2005, L 322/33. Additionally, negotiations take place on a Framework Decision on the organisation and content of the exchange of information extracted from criminal records between the Member States.

[1066]   This specific obligation cannot be found in *Framework Decision 2004/68 on Child Pornography*.

regarded as an aggravating circumstance.[1067] The Court held that it could not, even though the principle of *res judicata* does not oppose this.

Mitigating Circumstances

Three mitigating circumstances can be found in the legal instruments of the Union:

- conduct that leads to co-operation with the authorities;
- the offender has already been punished;
- compensation for violation of the rights of the defence.

The Influence of Co-Operation

In order to encourage individuals who participate or have participated in criminal organisations to co-operate with the judicial process, Member States are called on to assess the possibility of granting benefits to individuals who break away from a criminal organisation.[1068]

In competition law, the Commission offers a reduction of fines for those who disclose prohibited activities.[1069] In this so-called *Leniency Notice*, the Commission sets out the conditions under which undertakings co-operating with it during its investigation into a cartel may be exempted from fines or may be granted a reduction. Subject to the moment when the undertaking discloses to the Commission, and to its involvement in the infringement, the co-operation with the Commission results in non-imposition of a fine, in substantial reduction or in significant reduction.

Article 6 *Framework Decision 2002/475 on Combating Terrorism* provides for the reduction of penalties in particular circumstances, although it leaves it to the discretion of the Member States, if the offender:

(a) renounces terrorist activity;[1070] and
(b) provides the administrative or judicial authorities with information which they would not otherwise have been able to obtain, helping them to:
   (i)   prevent or mitigate the effects of the offence;
   (ii) identify or bring to justice the other offenders;

[1067]   14 July 1977, Case 8–77, *Concetta Sagulo, Gennaro Brenca and Addelmadjid Bakhouche* [1977] ECR 1495.

[1068]   Resolution of 20 December 1996 on individuals who co-operate with the judicial process in the fight against international organised crime, OJ 1997, C 10/1.

[1069]   Commission Notice on the non-imposition or reduction of fines in cartel cases, OJ 1996, C 207/4.

[1070]   See, also, 5 *Framework Decision 2004/757 on Illicit Drug Trafficking* which is identical, except for the replacement of "terrorist activity" for "criminal activity relating to trafficking in drugs and precursors".

    (iii) find evidence; or

    (iv) prevent further offences referred to in Articles 2 and 3.

The provisions resemble much of what has been the practice in the field of competition law for years.

It is remarkable that the Framework Decisions that provide the severest minimum-maximum penalties, *Framework Decision 2002/475 on Combating Terrorism* and *Framework Decision 2004/757 on Illicit Drug trafficking*, are also the only two Framework Decision's that introduce reductions to the offenders who co-operate with the authorities.

Other Punishment

Article 5, paragraph 2 *First Protocol Financial Interests Convention* and Article 5, paragraph 2 *Corruption Convention* recommends that, in the case of cumulative disciplinary and criminal proceedings, "the national criminal courts may, in accordance with the principle of their national law, take into account any disciplinary penalty imposed on the same person for the same conduct".

Article 10, paragraph 3 *Corruption Convention* prescribes deduction of sentence in a Member State against a person whose trial, in respect of the same facts, has been finally disposed of in another Member State. Any agreement between the victim and the offender reached in mediation in criminal cases should be taken into account (Article 10, paragraph 2 *Framework Decision 2001/220 on the Standing of Victims*). Article 57 *CISA* carries a general obligation to consider information on proceedings in another Member State with regard to the same set of facts. Article 56 *CISA* obliges Member States which do not regard the final decisions of other Member States as an impediment to prosecution to deduct any period of deprivation of liberty served in the first Member State from any penalty imposed. Article 56 *CISA* concludes by suggesting: "To the extent permitted by national law, penalties not involving deprivation of liberty shall also be taken into account."

A person who has been brought to the issuing Member State on the basis of a European Arrest Warrant is entitled to the deduction of the period of detention that he underwent in the executing Member State (Article 26 *Framework Decision 2002/584 on the European Arrest Warrant*). Literally, this provision does not deal with taking other punishment(s) into account for the purposes of sentencing, because detention in relation to surrender proceedings must be regarded as being either part of the detention on remand, or part of the execution of the sentence. It is a provision to remind the executioner of the sentence that part of it has already been served.

Compensation for Violation of Defence Rights

The Court held, in a competition case in which violation of the duration of the proceedings took place, that a reduction of the fine from 3,000,000 to 2,950,000 Euro was reasonable. It also considered more drastic measures to compensate for the violation of the defence rights. However, "in the absence of any indication that the length of the proceedings affected their outcome in any way, to set aside the judgment in its entirety would not be appropriate".[1071]

4. THE CHARACTER OF PUNISHMENT AND THE TREATMENT OF SENTENCED PERSONS

There is a general normative influence of the Charter of Fundamental Rights of the European Union in the sense that its Article 4 prohibits torture and inhuman or degrading treatment or punishment. It may be assumed that the provisions of the United Nations Torture Convention, the European Convention against Torture, as well as the European Prison Rules, adopted under the *aegis* of the Council of Europe, will be regarded as general principles of Union law. Whilst Union law does not completely prohibit life imprisonment from being imposed, it attaches consequences to it in the field of surrender. Upon the basis of Article 5 *Framework Decision 2002/584 on the European Arrest Warrant*, a Member State may request that the issuing Member State guarantees that, in the event that life imprisonment is imposed, the law provides for a review of the penalty after 20 years, at the latest.

Review

Union law does not require a review of final decisions, even if this would enable it to remedy infringements of Union law.[1072] The Court seems to have retreated a little from the revolutionary decisions in *Kühne & Heitz NV,*[1073] in which it held that an administrative body which is competent to re-open a case which has become final may do so after a judgment of the Court has made it clear that the national decision was based upon a misinterpretation of Union law. The repetitive reference by the Court to administrative bodies in *Kühne & Heitz NV* must be interpreted as an effort to limit the effects of the Court's judgment to a review of decisions of administrative bodies and not to expand it to other courts, such as

---

[1071] 17 December 1998, Case C-185/95 P, *Baustahlgewebe GmbH* v. *Commission* [1998] ECR I-8417, par. 49.

[1072] 16 March 2006, Case C-234/04, *Rosemarie Kapferer* v. *Schlank & Schick GmbH* [2006] ECR I-2585.

[1073] 13 January 2004, Case C-453/00, *Kühne & Heitz NV* v. *Produktschap voor Pluimvee en Eieren* [2004] ECR I-837.

criminal courts. However, the ruling of *Kühne & Heitz NV* could play a role in applications for pardon. The principle of *res judicata* is a general principle of law. However, nothing precludes national authorities from applying review or pardon to cover the fact that, in hindsight, the conviction of an accused was (partly) based upon a misinterpretation of Union law.

Treatment of Prisoners

The manner in which prisoners are treated and how they are prepared for their return into society is hardly a matter of concern in Union law. This is in sharp contrast to the Council of Europe, which adopted conventions on the transfer of sentenced persons back to the state of nationality and residence.[1074] Only one single document relates to the treatment of drug abusers in prisons.[1075] Although the main approach remains reduction of the demand, the Resolution stipulates that adequate attention is to be paid to social and professional re-habilitation and re-integration of former addicts. It is interesting to see that the 7th recital of the Resolution requires "that in connection with the treatment of drug abusers in prisons due respect is given to the principles of patient's consent and medical confidentiality". This means that forcing addicts to dis-intoxicate themselves is not foreseen. In the 13th recital, Member States are called upon to introduce the possibility of sentencing drug abusers to serve sentences in ordinary treatment institutions, which demonstrates that drug abusers have not been given up because of their addiction. For the rest, there is very little attention to the fact that one day convicted persons will be released and will return into society. The obligation of Article 4, paragraph 3 *Framework Decision 2001/220 on the Standing of Victims* that "at least in cases where there might be danger to the victims, when a person prosecuted or sentenced for an offence is released", the victim will be notified of the release, which was certainly not written to further the integration of the accused in society.

[1074]   See Chapter 7, Section 4.5.
[1075]   Resolution of the Representatives of the Member States meeting within the Council on the treatment of drug abusers in prison, approved on 27 January and 8 February 2003, Doc. 10497/4/02 of 28 November 2002.

PART III.
EUROPEAN CO-OPERATION
AND EUROPEAN ENFORCEMENT

Part III deals with two issues: firstly, the co-operation of national and Union authorities with a view to assisting each other in criminal proceedings pending in a specific Member State; secondly, the development of common European Union mechanisms to deal with crime. Both may relate to all stages of the criminal proceedings: from the first investigations to the execution of a sentence.

Part III builds upon the first two parts. It makes use of the general notions described in Part I and the contextual approach in a criminal setting employed in Part II. Lastly, Part III discusses the conclusive step of the integrative approach of European criminal law, and the development of direct enforcement of criminal law by the European Union itself.

CHAPTER 7.
BILATERAL CO-OPERATION
IN CRIMINAL MATTERS

1. INTRODUCTION

This chapter deals with co-operation in criminal matters as it has developed between the Member States of the European Union. Two limitations immediately follow from this first sentence. The first limitation being that the focus of this chapter is on bilateral co-operation, or co-operation between the law enforcement authorities of two Member States (also called horizontal co-operation). In addition, attention will be paid to the bilateral co-operation between the Commission and an individual Member State (vertical co-operation). Multilateral forms of co-operation, such as Europol and the European Public Prosecutor's Office, will be dealt with in Chapter 8. The second limitation consists of an approach to co-operation between the law enforcement authorities of the Member States from a European Union angle. It is not intended to discuss at length the forms of co-operation that have been developed and are still in existence under the scheme of the Council of Europe.

The forms of co-operation developed in the Council of Europe network will be mentioned here, because much of the work of the European Union further elaborates the Conventions of the Council of Europe. Having said that, the focus here lies with what is specific for the European Union, as well as on the relationship in the current transitionary stage of Union law in which both Council of Europe rules and European Union rules apply to international co-operation. It will be seen that the Union is gradually legislating with regard to more modalities of international co-operation, which were previously, and exclusively, covered by the Council of Europe. The Council of Europe surpassed co-operation between two states. This was realised by the Union, which developed – and is still developing – co-operation between more than two Member States. Chapter 8 deals with the added dimension of the co-operation within the European Union: the emergence of multilateral co-operation.

Co-operation in criminal matters is an area in which the European Union has been an extremely active legislator. Since the Treaty on European Union paved the way for criminal legislation, hundreds of Conventions, Joint Actions, Common Positions, Recommendations, Resolutions, Decisions and Framework Decisions have been adopted. It is impossible to deal with all these instruments in detail here. The large majority of these instruments are of a programmatic character. They are evidence of political agreement that, on certain topics, legislation must follow.

The emphasis in this chapter is on the structure and character of the co-operation between the Member States of the European Union. Despite the impressive amount of legal instruments, the productive character of the European Union also recounts a story of failures, as many Conventions never entered into force as they failed to be ratified by all the Member States. In addition, since the European Union no longer uses the Convention as a legal instrument, problems arise with regard to draft Framework Decisions that never reach the stage of adoption,[1076] or are only adopted after a time consuming period of negotiation.

The fact that a Member State cannot comply with its obligations under the treaties without the co-operation of another Member State or of the Commission, does not release it from its obligations. The enforcement obligation can be fulfilled by seeking co-operation, or, when another Member State requests co-operation, by responding to that request or order. The principles identified in Part I, on enforcement, also apply to co-operation in criminal matters. Examples exist of transfers of proceedings under the First Pillar. For example, Article 31, paragraph 4 *Regulation 2847/93 establishing a Control System applicable to the Common Fisheries Policy*, provides for the transfer of criminal proceedings. It should be noted, in this connection, that the Court held in the case of *Spain v. Council*, that the Member States had a joint responsibility for monitoring the catch quota scheme.[1077]

[1076]   Two examples suffice: the draft *Framework Decision on Certain Procedural Rights of Persons Arrested in Connection with or Charged with a Criminal Offence*, Council Document, 9937/07, 25 May 2007; *Framework Decision on the European Evidence Warrant*, Council Document 13076/07, 21 December 2007. The former had been negotiated over several years and was finally abandoned, while, on the latter, political agreement had, apparently, been reached. However, it has not appeared in the OJ yet.

[1077]   27 March 1990, Case C-9/89, *Spain v. Council* [1990] ECR I-1383, Rep. 1990, I-1383. The duty of sincere co-operation is also imposed on Community institutions and is of particular importance in relation to the judicial authorities taking care of the enforcement of community law. See 13 July 1990 and 6 December 1990, Case C-2/88 Imm., *J.J. Zwartveld and others* [1990] ECR I-4405, par. 17–18.

2. THE HISTORICAL DEVELOPMENT OF CO-OPERATION IN CRIMINAL MATTERS

THE NETWORK OF MULTILATERAL TREATIES CREATED BY THE COUNCIL OF EUROPE

Since the 1950s, the Council of Europe has been concluding multilateral conventions with regard to all forms of international co-operation in criminal matters. The efforts of decades culminated in the completion of a network of treaties on international co-operation in criminal matters, which allowed the state parties to assist each other at each stage of the criminal proceedings. From the very first stages of a criminal investigation to the phase of execution of criminal judgments, state parties to the conventions can help each other. In 1957, the Council of Europe adopted the *European Convention on Extradition*,[1078] soon followed by the *1959 European Convention on Mutual Assistance in Criminal Matters*.[1079] Other major conventions were the 1972 European Convention on the Transfer of Proceedings in Criminal Matters,[1080] and the most popular Convention in numbers of ratification, the 1983 Convention on the Transfer of Sentenced Persons.[1081] Conventions drafted under the *aegis* of the Council of Europe are open for ratification for members of the Council and for other non-Member States which are invited to do so.[1082] From the moment that the European Union entered the playing field of international co-operation in criminal matters, in the mid 1980's, the network of the Council of Europe, more or less, covered all stages of criminal proceedings. However, not all Member States were a party to all the conventions. Whilst most Member States had ratified the conventions on extradition and mutual assistance, only a minority were a party to transfer of execution of judgments conventions. The least number of ratifications was obtained by the 1972 European Convention on the Transfer of Proceedings in Criminal Matters.

The European Union began its involvement with international co-operation in criminal matters in various ways. First, it adopted instruments that would build upon the work achieved by the Council of Europe. In addition, it allowed for forms of intensified co-operation. For the former, several conventions on extradition between the Member States, which all aimed at reducing formalities

---

[1078] European Treaty Series 24. As of 1 May 2004 no longer applicable between the Member States of the European Union due to the entering into force of *Framework Decision 2002/584 on the European Arrest Warrant*.

[1079] European Treaty Series 30, all Member States EU are a party.

[1080] European Treaty Series 73, as of 4 September 2008, 13 Member States EU are a party.

[1081] European Treaty Series 112, all Member States EU are a party. In total, as of 4 September 2008, 63 states ratified this Convention.

[1082] See, for instance, the 1983 *Convention on the Transfer of Sentenced Persons*.

and speeding up the process of extradition, can be referred to. Additionally, developments took place within a limited group of Member States, the most notable example being the *CISA*, which regulated certain forms of co-operation among themselves only.

With regard to the form of the legal instruments, an important revolution has taken place over the years. Initially, the European Communities and later the European Union had chosen to conclude conventions. This was, of course, the form in which agreements on international co-operation in criminal matters had always been created. Due to their character under international law, Conventions may only enter into force if all the states ratify them. It led to an incessant urging for full ratification or transposition of Third-Pillar instruments by the Commission. However, to the enormous frustration of the Commission, the Member States did not genuinely ratify the Conventions.

Another feature was that of consolidation of the previously-ratified legislation. EU instruments were accumulated into a new, all-encompassing instrument (see, for example, the *EU Mutual Assistance Convention*). After a few disappointing experiences with the (un)willingness of Member States to approve such instruments, the Union gradually changed its strategy. A system of "rolling ratification" was chosen, meaning that the Convention became effective for the Member States that ratified it, in other words, the Member States which ratified no longer needed to wait until the last Member State "got there". However, even with this method, it was still difficult to obtain a large number of ratifications, and it failed to speed up the ratification process. In order to combat these elements, a mechanism was developed that was no longer dependent on ratification: the Framework Decision, which was introduced in the Treaty of European Union by the Treaty of Amsterdam (1997). The use of the Framework Decision as the appropriate legal instrument rendered ratification unnecessary. This did not remove all the problems of Conventions, because Framework Decisions still require implementing legislation. However, unlike Conventions, Framework Decisions are applicable to all Member States without ratification. If a single Member State does not take the necessary implementing measures, it is not in compliance with its obligations.

Furthermore, when the choice for another legal instrument was made (from Convention to Framework Decision), the very character of co-operation was also changed. Since the first *Framework Decision 2002/584 on the European Arrest Warrant*, co-operation has rested strongly on the concept of *mutual recognition*. Member States are in agreement that they regard certain legal figures as equivalent in order to avoid creating obstacles to co-operation. These legal figures are not at all identical, but this difference is overlooked for the purposes of co-operation. Consider the list in Article 2, *Framework Decision 2002/584 on the European Arrest Warrant*, in which the differences between the Member States are abstracted. While, previously, the *double criminality* rule always had to be evaluated in the light of the entire complex of facts, now, the requesting state merely determines, by checking one of the offences on the list, whether the offence is one for which legal assistance must be given.

What has fundamentally changed, however, is the perspective on co-operation in criminal matters. The Union's vision is totally different from that of the Council of Europe. In the network of the Council of Europe, it is less important which state prosecutes, judges or enforces; what is important is that it happens. The objective was the fair administration of justice which responded to the requirements both to fight crime and to ensure legal certainty, and which takes all relevant interests (of the states, suspect, victims and witnesses) into account. The Council of Europe's network of Conventions offers an option for co-operation at every stage of criminal proceedings. It offers a wide range of alternatives, which allows for parallel use of co-operation, as well as for consecutive use of co-operation.

Three examples may demonstrate this. If a state is able to co-operate with regard to all forms of co-operation, a case in which it is impossible to act can hardly arise. If, for instance, Romania is unable to obtain the extradition or surrender of a suspect found in Estonia, it may request that the proceedings be transferred to Estonia. The second example is one from the Netherlands, which makes extradition or surrender conditional to the condemned serving his sentence in the state of his nationality. This means that after extradition to France, for example, takes place, the trial will be held in France, and subsequently the accused, if convicted, will be transferred back to the Netherlands. A third example relates to the situation in which two Member States, Spain and Italy, for example, are interested in the same accused person at the same time. Since most states cannot prosecute and render mutual assistance for the same case at the same time, both states cannot make use of the evidence collected by the other state and the accused faces two proceedings. Concerted action which leads to a determination of the most appropriate state for prosecution will enable fair proceedings to be held. If Italy then transfers proceedings to Spain, it will then be able to give mutual assistance to the prosecuting state. Thus, the accused will be confronted with only one trial, which will take place in Spain.

Originally, the focus of the European Union was limited to the area of co-operation in criminal matters, as was provided in the Treaty on European Union. However, the Union has, in practice, long since abandoned this restriction. Initiatives are also being developed in substantive criminal law and, to a lesser extent, in criminal procedure.[1083] In addition, another important development can be observed. Since the turn of the millennium most work has been focused on mutual recognition of the decisions and investigative methods of other

---

[1083]   See Chapters 4 and 5.

countries.[1084] The efforts in the Third Pillar are primarily oriented towards legislation, and only very minimally towards enforcement. Article 67 TFEU (formerly Article 29 EU) places the task of creating closer co-operation between *both* police authorities *and* judicial authorities, as well as other competent authorities in the context of achieving the Union's objective of a high level of security. Articles 82 TFEU (formerly Article 31 EU, albeit significantly different) and 87 TFEU (formerly Article 30 EU, albeit significantly different) can be regarded both as a formal mandate, as well as a legislative agenda for the European Union. They also testify to the development of the European Union, which no longer focuses exclusively on co-operation in criminal matters.

"Article 82 TFEU (formerly Article 31 EU)

1. Judicial cooperation in criminal matters in the Union shall be based on the principle of mutual recognition of judgments and judicial decisions and shall include the approximation of the laws and regulations of the Member States in the areas referred to in paragraph 2 and in Article 83.

The European Parliament and the Council, acting in accordance with the ordinary legislative procedure, shall adopt measures to:

(a) lay down rules and procedures for ensuring recognition throughout the Union of all forms of judgments and judicial decisions;

(b) prevent and settle conflicts of jurisdiction between Member States;

(c) support the training of the judiciary and judicial staff;

(d) facilitate co-operation between judicial or equivalent authorities of the Member States in relation to proceedings in criminal matters and the enforcement of decisions.

2. To the extent necessary to facilitate mutual recognition of judgments and judicial decisions and police and judicial cooperation in criminal matters having a cross-border dimension, the European Parliament and the Council may, by means of directives adopted in accordance with the ordinary legislative procedure, establish minimum rules. Such rules shall take into account the differences between the legal traditions and systems of the Member States.

[1084]   Two examples: *Framework Decision 2002/584 on the European Arrest Warrant* and *Framework Decision 2001/500 on Money Laundering.*

They shall concern:

(a) mutual admissibility of evidence between Member States;

(b) the rights of individuals in criminal procedure;

(c) the rights of victims of crime;

(d) any other specific aspects of criminal procedure which the Council has identified in advance by a decision; for the adoption of such a decision, the Council shall act unanimously after obtaining the consent of the European Parliament.

Adoption of the minimum rules referred to in this paragraph shall not prevent Member States from maintaining or introducing a higher level of protection for individuals.

3. Where a member of the Council considers that a draft directive as referred to in paragraph 2 would affect fundamental aspects of its criminal justice system, it may request that the draft directive be referred to the European Council. In that case, the ordinary legislative procedure shall be suspended. After discussion, and in case of a consensus, the European Council shall, within four months of this suspension, refer the draft back to the Council, which shall terminate the suspension of the ordinary legislative procedure.

Within the same timeframe, in case of disagreement, and if at least nine Member States wish to establish enhanced cooperation on the basis of the draft directive concerned, they shall notify the European Parliament, the Council and the Commission accordingly. In such a case, the authorisation to proceed with enhanced cooperation referred to in Article 20(2) of the Treaty on European Union and Article 329(1) of this Treaty shall be deemed to be granted and the provisions on enhanced cooperation shall apply."

"Article 83 TFEU (formerly Article 31 EU)

1. The European Parliament and the Council may, by means of directives adopted in accordance with the ordinary legislative procedure, establish minimum rules concerning the definition of criminal offences and sanctions in the areas of particularly serious crime with a cross-border dimension resulting from the nature or impact of such offences or from a special need to combat them on a common basis.

These areas of crime are the following: terrorism, trafficking in human beings and sexual exploitation of women and children, illicit drug trafficking, illicit arms trafficking, money laundering, corruption, counterfeiting of means of payment, computer crime and organised crime.

On the basis of developments in crime, the Council may adopt a decision identifying other areas of crime that meet the criteria specified in this paragraph. It shall act unanimously after obtaining the consent of the European Parliament.

2. If the approximation of criminal laws and regulations of the Member States proves essential to ensure the effective implementation of a Union policy in an area which has been subject to harmonisation measures, directives may establish minimum rules with regard to the definition of criminal offences and sanctions in the area concerned. Such directives shall be adopted by the same ordinary or special legislative procedure as was followed for the adoption of the harmonisation measures in question, without prejudice to Article 76.

3. Where a member of the Council considers that a draft directive as referred to in paragraph 1 or 2 would affect fundamental aspects of its criminal justice system, it may request that the draft directive be referred to the European Council. In that case, the ordinary legislative procedure shall be suspended. After discussion, and in case of a consensus, the European Council shall, within four months of this suspension, refer the draft back to the Council, which shall terminate the suspension of the ordinary legislative procedure.

Within the same timeframe, in case of disagreement, and if at least nine Member States wish to establish enhanced cooperation on the basis of the draft directive concerned, they shall notify the European Parliament, the Council and the Commission accordingly. In such a case, the authorisation to proceed with enhanced cooperation referred to in Article 20(2) of the Treaty on European Union and Article 329(1) of this Treaty shall be deemed to be granted and the provisions on enhanced cooperation shall apply."

"Article 87 TFEU (formerly Article 30 EU)

1. The Union shall establish police cooperation involving all the Member States' competent authorities, including police, customs and other specialised law enforcement services in relation to the prevention, detection and investigation of criminal offences.

2. For the purposes of paragraph 1, the European Parliament and the Council, acting in accordance with the ordinary legislative procedure, may establish measures concerning:

(a) the collection, storage, processing, analysis and exchange of relevant information;

(b) support for the training of staff, and cooperation on the exchange of staff, on equipment and on research into crime-detection;

(c) common investigative techniques in relation to the detection of serious forms of organised crime.

3. The Council, acting in accordance with a special legislative procedure, may establish measures concerning operational cooperation between the authorities referred to in this Article. The Council shall act unanimously after consulting the European Parliament.

In case of the absence of unanimity in the Council, a group of at least nine Member States may request that the draft measures be referred to the European Council. In that case, the procedure in the Council shall be suspended. After discussion, and in case of a consensus, the European Council shall, within four months of this suspension, refer the draft back to the Council for adoption.

Within the same timeframe, in case of disagreement, and if at least nine Member States wish to establish enhanced cooperation on the basis of the draft measures concerned, they shall notify the European Parliament, the Council and the Commission accordingly. In such a case, the authorisation to proceed with enhanced cooperation referred to in Article 20(2) of the Treaty on European Union and Article 329(1) of this Treaty shall be deemed to be granted and the provisions on enhanced cooperation shall apply.

The specific procedure provided for in the second and third subparagraphs shall not apply to acts which constitute a development of the Schengen *acquis*."

At this stage, it becomes apparent that the European Union is still in the process of constructing its own model of co-operation in criminal matters. This explains why certain forms of co-operation or certain stages of the criminal proceedings are not covered by Union legislation yet. However, the Union's system distinguishes itself from the Council of Europe network through the fact that it has not yet developed an overall goal of bilateral co-operation in criminal matters. Surprisingly, a European approach to international co-operation is still lacking. The mutual recognition model is more conducive to serving the interests of the Member State that takes the first initiative, than to serving the interests of accused and others involved as well as of other Member States. Mutual recognition has attributed an exclusive character to the initiative and does not, in principle, allow for alternatives or consultations. The dependence on the first Member State making an initiative makes the European Union scheme of international co-operation in criminal matters more vulnerable in the sense that, if the Member State cannot obtain the assistance it needs, there may not be any alternative option.

The Relationship Between European Union Instruments and Council of Europe Instruments

Since many legal instruments of the European Union build upon the existing *acquis* of the Council of Europe, to which, depending on the respective treaties, most or all Member States are a party, it is relevant to discuss the relationship of these legal instruments. As a principle rule, the instrument adopted later will contain a provision on the relationship of the Union instruments to Council of Europe instruments. Article 31, paragraph 1 *Framework Decision 2002/584 on the European Arrest Warrant* sets out that the Framework Decision is to replace the corresponding provisions of, for instance, the *European Convention on Extradition*.[1085] Article 1 *EU Mutual Assistance Convention* sets out the relationship with other Conventions on mutual assistance and makes it clear that it supplements these. Article 2, paragraph 2 of the same Convention repeats certain provisions of these earlier conventions because the matter has been regulated anew in the present convention. In some legal instruments, attention is paid to the relationship with other applicable legal instruments. The new instruments generally stipulate that they are not to affect the obligations of other international agreements.[1086]

Two issues deserve attention here. The first is of a practical nature. Apart from supplementing international co-operation conventions concluded by the Council of Europe, treaties of two other international organisations were amended and supplemented as well: the Benelux Economic Union, and the Nordic Council. In addition, Union legal instruments also supplemented conventions adopted between a limited number of Member States: for example, *CISA*. The other issue that must be mentioned is that it is not undisputed as to whether the Union has the competence under international law to determine that Council of Europe Conventions are no longer applicable in the bilateral relations of its Member

---

[1085]   In a Declaration to the Council of Europe, the EU Member States notified the Council of Europe of this change. The Declaration by Denmark is reproduced here as an example. All other Member States submitted similar declarations. The Danish declaration reads: "In accordance with Article 28, paragraph 3, of the European Convention on Extradition the Danish Government hereby notifies of the implementation in Danish legislation of the EU Framework Decision of 13 June 2002 on the European Arrest Warrant and the surrender procedures between Member States of the European Union (2002/584/JHA). The Framework Decision was implemented in Danish law by Act no. 443 of 10 June 2003. The Act will enter into force on 1 January 2004 and will be applicable to requests for surrender (extradition) made by Member States of the European Union as from that date. The provisions of the European arrest warrant will thereby replace corresponding provisions in the European Convention on Extradition of 13 December 1957 and its two Protocols of 15 October 1975 and 17 March 1978 in the mutual relationship between Denmark and the other Member States of the European Union".

[1086]   See Article 7, paragraph 4 *Financial Interests Convention*. Article 5 *Joint Action 98/733 on Participation in a Criminal Organisation*; Article 6 *Framework Decision 2002/946 on Unauthorised Entry* with reference to the 1951 Refugee Convention.

States. However, this question is of a purely international law character, and must be left unanswered here.

Closer and Enhanced Co-Operation

In 1985, the governments of the states of the Benelux Economic Union, Germany and France concluded the Schengen Agreement,[1087] which provided both political agreement on a wide range of issues following the principle decision of abolishing checks at their common borders, as well as a programmatic and legislative agenda to implement the agreement. This culminated in the *CISA*, which facilitated and simplified various forms of co-operation, such as police co-operation, mutual assistance, extradition and the transfer of the enforcement of criminal judgments. It set up the Schengen Information System. The Convention established a supervisory committee: the Schengen Executive Committee. Article 39, paragraph 4 *CISA* mandates the competent ministers to regulate co-operation in border areas by arrangements. Paragraph 5 of Article 39 *CISA* specifically allows for further bilateral agreements of Member States that have a common border. The Protocol Integrating the *Schengen Acquis* into the Framework of the European Union, which was added to the Treaty on European Union by the Treaty of Amsterdam, authorised this closer co-operation. The Protocol integrated the whole of the *Schengen acquis*, which incorporated numerous decisions of the Schengen Executive Committee into the Treaty on European Union.[1088]

The Bilateral Relations of Member States

Bilateral conventions and agreements between the Member States remain in existence unless they have been replaced completely and exclusively by a Union mechanism. This has only happened with the *Framework Decision 2002/584 on the European Arrest Warrant*. For all other areas, the existing bilateral (and multilateral) agreements remain in force. In addition, all Member States have their own set of bilateral and multilateral conventions with third states and international organisations, and in a Declaration attached to the Treaty of Lisbon, it is confirmed that Member States may negotiate and conclude agreements with third countries or international organisation regarding judicial co-operation in criminal matters and police co-operation.[1089]

[1087] OJ 2000, L 239/13.

[1088] See, also, Chapter 3, Section 2.4.

[1089] Declaration 36 on Article 218 of the Treaty on the Functioning of the European Union concerning the negotiation and conclusion of international agreements by Member States relating to the area of freedom, security and justice.

3.   MODELS OF CO-OPERATION

In the previous section, the fundamental change of the applicable models which took place with the appearance of the European Union as a legislator in the field of international co-operation in criminal matters was outlined. As a result of this, three different models currently exist: the *request* model, the *mutual recognition model*, and the *availability model*. The use of one model or another will depend on the material act which is needed. Some can be applied by one model exclusively, while, for others, a choice may be made by the Member State in need of a piece of evidence. For instance, in the case of surrender, a European Arrest Warrant will be issued and has to be recognised by all Member States. With confiscation and with the execution of financial penalties, the relevant Framework Decision applying mutual recognition did not replace the previous request model. The result is that both the mutual recognition and the request model may be applied. In the case of other forms of co-operation, such as of transfer of proceedings, only a request may be sent out to another Member State.

3.1. THE REQUEST MODEL

International Law – Treaty-Based and Treatyless Requests

The request model is based upon international law and gives full discretion to Member States to handle their relationships with other Member States in a manner that they can approve of in each and every case. This discretion is only limited to the extent that states have voluntarily accepted limitations of their sovereignty. In international co-operation, this is exemplified in the distinction between treaty-based requests for assistance, and requests for assistance which do not find a basis in a treaty. To start with the latter, if there is no treaty applicable for the request of assistance from one state to another, the requested state has full discretion to assist or to refuse on the grounds that it deems fit. The national law of the requested state may make certain modalities of international co-operation conditional upon the existence of a treaty,[1090] or on any other guarantee of reciprocity. International co-operation without a treaty is regarded as an act of comity between sovereign nations. Treaty-based co-operation is further focused on below.

In situations in which there is a treaty applicable, that treaty will, clearly determine the conditions under which mutual assistance may take place. The general characteristics of these treaties are that they carry a general obligation to assist each other.[1091] By ratifying the treaty, state parties have accepted a certain limitation of their sovereign rights. If a request falls within the terms of the treaty,

---

[1090]   Most EU Member States did stipulate a treaty requirement with regard to extradition.
[1091]   With the notable exception of the 1983 Convention on the Transfer of Sentenced Persons.

it must, in principle, be complied with. However, in order to remove the absolute character of the obligations, all treaties of the Council of Europe contain a set of grounds for refusal.[1092] This allows (does not impose) the requested state to refuse the request without breaching its obligations under international law. Other general notions of treaties on international co-operation will be dealt with later. All Conventions of the Council of Europe, as well as all the Conventions of the European Union follow the request model. The last Convention of this type concluded by the European Union in criminal matters is the *EU Mutual Assistance Convention*.[1093]

The Transmission of the Request

Most treaties stipulate how requests should be transmitted from the requesting State to the requested State. In instruments adopted before the Second World War, the prevailing way of transmission was via the diplomatic channel. This meant that a request would be initiated in a Ministry of Justice of a requesting state and would then go to its Ministry of Foreign Affairs. The latter would bring it either to its own embassy in the requested state, or to the embassy of the requested state in its own capital. Within the requested state authorities, the request would follow the same echelon, from the Ministry of Foreign Affairs to the Ministry of Justice. On completion of the request, the same time-consuming road would be followed in reverse. The Council of Europe had already replaced this cumbersome procedure by creating *central authorities* as well as by allowing for direct communication between judicial authorities under certain circumstances. The introduction of central authorities basically meant that the Ministries of Justice became exclusively competent to deal with international co-operation. Later, the European Union also called for the creation of *contact points* with regard to specific requests.[1094] Generally speaking, one can say that the contribution of the Union has been one of widening and deepening classical

---

1092   With the notable exception of the 1983 Convention on the Transfer of Sentenced Persons.

1093   The Framework Decision was introduced by the Treaty of Amsterdam, which entered into force on 1 May 1999. The first Framework Decision to be adopted was *Framework Decision 2000/383 on the Introduction of the Euro*, adopted on 29 May 2000, the same day on which the last Convention was adopted.

1094   Article B, Title I *Joint Action 96/443 on Racism and Xenophobia*; Recommendation of 25 June 2001 on contact points maintaining a 24-hour service for combating high-tech crime, OJ 2001, C 187/5; Decision 2002/494 of 13 June 2002 setting up a European network of contact points in respect of persons responsible for genocide, crimes against humanity and war crimes, OJ 2002, L 167/1; Decision 2002/956 of 28 November 2002 setting up a European Network for the Protection of Public Figures, OJ 2002, L 333/1; Decision 2003/335 of 8 May 2003 on the investigation and prosecution of genocide, crimes against humanity and war crimes, OJ 2003, L 118/12; Article 9 *Framework Decision 2005/667 on Ship-source Pollution*; Decision of 22 December 2004 on tackling vehicle crime with cross-border implications, OJ 2004, L 389/28; Decision 2005/671/JHA of 20 September 2005 on the exchange of information and cooperation concerning terrorist offences, OJ 2005, L 253/22.

international co-operation: a severe increase in the number of authorities that may request or answer requests for assistance, as well as the establishment of direct communication channels between those authorities.[1095]

Double Criminality

The treaties determine the conditions under which they can be applied. They may stipulate formal and material requirements, and one of the most prominent conditions is the requirement of double criminality. Article 2 *European Convention on Extradition* stipulates for instance that:

> "Extradition shall be granted in respect of offences punishable under the laws of the requesting Party and of the requested Party by deprivation of liberty or under a detention order for a maximum period of at least one year or by a more severe penalty."

The applicability of the double criminality requirement means that the requested state will only give assistance for cases for which the underlying offence is both a crime under the law of the requesting state as well as under the law of the requested state.[1096] It is presumed that the requesting state has made this assessment before sending out the request. The requested state will, by its own procedures, determine whether the facts are also a criminal offence under the law of the requested state.

While double criminality was a requirement which regarded some forms of international co-operation, it had never obtained the status of being applicable to all forms of co-operation in criminal matters. To the contrary, for most treaties, the requirement that the request related exclusively to criminal proceedings, was fulfilled by the conviction of the authority from which it emanated, that it dealt with criminal matters. Criminal matters as meant by the conventions has never been defined.[1097] As a result, there is no assessment of the character of the offence, neither on the law of the requested state, nor on the law of the requesting state. However, for some forms of international co-operation, which infringe more

---

[1095]   An example is found in Article 4 *Joint Action 98/699 on Money Laundering* encouraging Member States to allow for direct contacts between law enforcement authorities. A standard form to be used when exchanging information regarding terrorism has been recommended. Council Recommendation of 14 November 2002 on the introduction of a standard form of exchanging information on terrorists, Doc. 5712/6/02 of 29 May 2002. A state may also request that the assistance is urgently given. The urgency of a request requires an explanation (Article 4, paragraph 3 *Joint Action 98/699 on Money Laundering*).

[1096]   The origin of the double criminality requirement goes back to the first extradition treaties which were concluded around 1800. It was felt at the time that a state could not be requested to co-operate in the execution of a norm it would not recognise in its own criminal justice system.

[1097]   See Article 3, paragraph 1 *1959 European Convention on Mutual Assistance in Criminal Matters* "relating to a criminal matter". In practice, this means that the requesting state determines whether the underlying events fall within the notion criminal offence.

upon the rights of individuals, the treaties stipulate a requirement of double criminality. Traditionally, this concerned all forms of extradition, transfer of judgments, and transfer of proceedings. In addition, double criminality is often required with regard to requests for mutual assistance for which coercive powers must be used, such as searches, seizures[1098] and cross-border pursuit. Double criminality has never been required for forms of exchange of information and other forms of mutual assistance, which may take place without infringing upon the rights of individuals (for example, service of summons, and the interrogation of persons with their consent).

The general approach of Union instruments is aimed at making assistance less and less dependant on the fulfilment of conditions such as double criminality.[1099] Article 49 *CISA*, for instance, widened the proceedings to which the *1959 European Convention on Mutual Assistance in Criminal Matters* and the 1962 Benelux Treaty concerning extradition and mutual assistance could be applied. Articles 50 and 51 *CISA* limited the use of grounds of refusal.[1100] Likewise, Article 5 *EU Mutual Assistance Convention* reduces the number of instances in which the authorities of another Member State must be involved when documents are sent to a person on that state's territory. Article 6 of the same Convention allows for much more informal lines of communication between the various authorities.

The Commission has always regarded double criminality as a serious impediment to swift co-operation. It has continuously attacked the principle and declared it as problematical in each of its proposals for new instruments. The Commission has been successful in its struggle to reduce the application of double criminality. A most revolutionary step has been taken with regard to extradition, as *Framework Decision 2002/584 on the European Arrest Warrant* stipulates that double criminality is not required for a certain number of offences.[1101]

Despite this success, one may question whether double criminality was (and is), in practice, such an impediment to international co-operation. Apart from the fact that the claim was never substantiated with empirical evidence,[1102] the principle has a function in limiting serious forms of co-operation (which infringe upon the rights of the accused) to serious cases. In addition, the fact that extradition could not be obtained for all the offences charged, did not prevent extradition for those offences that did comply with the double requirement.

[1098] See, for instance, Article 5 *1959 European Convention on Mutual Assistance in Criminal Matters*.

[1099] Article 3 *EU Mutual Assistance Convention* determines that mutual assistance must also be afforded in certain administrative proceedings.

[1100] See, also, Article 1 *Framework Decision 2001/500 on Money Laundering*.

[1101] See, further, Section 3.2.2 in this chapter.

[1102] Such as numbers of refusals of extradition because of lack of double criminality in relation to the total number of (granted) extraditions.

Other Grounds of Refusal

Most grounds of refusal have been developed in extradition law and were later incorporated into treaties on mutual assistance and transfer of judgments. Classical grounds that entitle a state not to give the assistance requested are the *political nature of the offence* (Article 3 *European Convention on Extradition* and Article 2 *1959 European Convention on Mutual Assistance in Criminal Matters*); the *military nature* of the offence (Article 4 *European Convention on Extradition* and Article 1, paragraph 2 *1959 European Convention on Mutual Assistance in Criminal Matters*); the *fiscal nature* of the offence (Article 5 *European Convention on Extradition* and Article 2 *1959 European Convention on Mutual Assistance in Criminal Matters*); and, in cases of extradition, the *nationality* of the requested person. Article 6 *European Convention on Extradition* allows states to refuse the extradition of their own nationals. By virtue of *Framework Decision 2002/584 on the European Arrest Warrant*, nationals now must be extradited; however, Member States may make extradition conditional to a guarantee that the national, if convicted, may serve his sentence in his own state.

With regard to extradition, a state may also refuse to extradite when the crime was committed on his own territory (Article 7 *European Convention on Extradition*), or when the death penalty may be imposed (Article 11 *European Convention on Extradition* and Article 19 Charter). Extradition may also be refused if the requested state is already conducting proceedings against the requested person (Article 8 *European Convention on Extradition*). Assistance may also be refused when the *ne bis in idem* principle applies (Article 9 *European Convention on Extradition*), or when the case is time barred (Article 10 *European Convention on Extradition*). Apart from the grounds for refusal that can be found in the treaty itself, which are briefly referred to above, other grounds for refusal may find their basis in a reservation made to the convention.[1103]

With regard to the grounds of refusal, the contribution of the European Union has been to reduce the number of grounds or to remove them. The 1996 Convention relating to extradition between the Member State of the European Union,[1104] stipulated, in Articles 5, 6 and 7, the abolition of the political offence exception, the fiscal offence exception, and the facilitation of the extradition of nationals. Articles 7, 8 and 9 *Protocol to the EU Mutual Assistance Convention* abolished the banking secrecy, the fiscal and the political exception. Article 10 of the Protocol

---

[1103] See, for instance, the reservation of Belgium to Article 1: "Extradition will not be granted when the surrender might have consequences of an exceptional gravity for the person claimed, in particular on account of his or her age or health".

[1104] Convention of 27 September 1996, OJ 1996, C 313/11. Now replaced for the Member States of the European Union by *Framework Decision 2002/584 on the European Arrest Warrant*. The Convention has not been repealed. On its basis, an Agreement between the European Union and the Republic of Iceland and the Kingdom of Norway has been concluded, OJ 2006, L 292/2.

makes it clear, by referring to a special procedure involving Eurojust, that refusals are not meant to occur. As Article 5, paragraph 3 *Financial Interests Convention* stipulates:

"A Member State may not refuse extradition in the event of fraud affecting the European Communities' financial interests for the sole reason that it concerns a tax or custom duty offence."[1105]

Member States which made a reservation to Article 5 *1959 European Convention on Mutual Assistance in Criminal Matters* should review the necessity of maintaining the reservation.[1106] Article 1 *Joint Action 98/699 on Money Laundering* urges Member States that reservations should not be upheld. Article B, Title I *Joint Action 96/443 on Racism and Xenophobia* stipulates that the conduct may not be regarded as a political offence which justifies refusal of mutual assistance.

The Extent of the Obligation

The treaties also determine the extent of the obligations which derive from it. To which forms of co-operation does the obligation to assist apply? With most forms of co-operation, there is hardly any discussion about the question of whether the modality has been stipulated in the treaty.[1107] Extradition treaties deal with extradition, while transfer of judgments treaties deal with the transfer of judgments and nothing else. Conventions on mutual assistance raise more questions, which relate to the fact that these Conventions contain a general obligation to give mutual assistance and then stipulate specific forms. For instance, the *1959 European Convention on Mutual Assistance in Criminal Matters* provides, in a very general manner, for letters rogatory (Article 3) and is much more specific about summons (Article 7) and the transfer of a detained witness (Article 11). The *1959 European Convention on Mutual Assistance in Criminal Matters*, for instance, does not provide in the interrogation by video-link. Does this mean that a request for an interrogation by video-link by which the witness remains in the residing state also falls within the application of the Convention? The answer to this question is that there is no obligation for the requested state to co-operate in this manner. However, with mutual consent, state parties are free to apply forms not included in the treaty. Thus, the effect of explicitly regulating a specific material act lies in the creation of an obligation for the requested state to provide this modality. With regard to the example given, the hearing of persons

---

[1105] An identical provision is Article 6 *Second Protocol Financial Interests Convention*.

[1106] Article B, Title III, *Joint Action 97/154 on Trafficking in Human Beings*.

[1107] Articles 82 and 83 TFEU must be regarded as mandating the EU to legislate in the field of police co-operation and judicial co-operation, not as creating a direct basis upon which concrete acts of co-operation may take place.

by use of a video-link is now provided in Article 10 *EU Mutual Assistance Convention*.

Article 2, paragraph 2 *Joint Action 98/733 on Participation in a Criminal Organisation* stipulates that:

> "Member States will afford one another the most comprehensive assistance possible in respect of the offences covered by this Article, as well as those covered by Article 3(4) of the Convention relating to extradition between the Member States of the European Union drawn up by the Council on 27 September 1996."[1108]

The question is one of what the purposes of such a broad provision actually are.[1109] For the first category, the offences of the Joint Action, it seems superfluous, since Member States are already bound to provide mutual assistance upon the basis of other agreements. For the second category, things are slightly different, the provision may both be understood as a stimulus to ratify the convention referred to, as well as to furnish a basis for assistance in problematical situations.

The Applicable Law When Executing a Request

With regard to the collection of evidence, in particular, the question of which law is applicable is highly relevant. Is the evidence to be collected according to the law of the requesting state or in compliance with the law of the requested state? A state may request that certain formalities be applied in order to enable that state to admit the evidence collected in the proceedings. Gradually, the practice of international co-operation moved from applying the so-called *locus regit actum* rule to the *forum regit actum* rule.[1110] The *locus regit actum* rule means that a state executing a request for assistance will apply its own legislation. This rule finds its basis in a certain understanding of the sovereignty of the state. The advantage of this is that the requested authorities know the law that they will have to apply very well, and that, as a consequence, the chances for misapplication of the law are slim. The disadvantage is that it is precisely the application of rules of the requested state that may make the piece of evidence inadmissible in the requesting state.

[1108]   See, also, Article 6 *Financial Interests Convention* dealing with fraud cases that concern more than one Member State, they "shall co-operate effectively in the investigation, the prosecution and in carrying out the punishment imposed by means, for example, of mutual legal assistance, extradition, transfer of proceedings or enforcement of sentences passed in another Member State". *Common Position 2001/930 on Combating Terrorism* also carries a general obligation to afford mutual assistance. An interesting provision can be found in Article 3 *Joint Action 98/699 on Money Laundering*, which imposes upon the Member States the obligation to give the same priority to requests from other Member States as to domestic requests. This can be regarded as a form of assimilation on the practical level.

[1109]   In particular, this should be done "in accordance with the applicable conventions, multilateral or bilateral agreements or arrangements". Article 11 *Framework Decision 2001/413 on Combating Fraud*.

[1110]   See Article 4 *1959 European Convention on Mutual Assistance in Criminal Matters*.

This is the main reason why, in more recent treaties, the system has been switched to the application of the *forum regit actum* rule. This means that the requesting state will stipulate which formalities must be complied with (the use of certain seals, interrogation in the presence of defence counsel, the right to cross-examination, *etc.*), which will result in admissible evidence in the forum, to wit, the state in which the criminal proceedings are pending.

Modern legal instruments already start from the presumption that Member States will execute requests in the manner expected by the requesting state.[1111] In the unlikely event that this is not possible, they must provide for an alternative way. Certain measures should be taken by the requested state "where it is not contrary to its law" (Article 5 *Joint Action 98/699 on Money Laundering*). The most extreme modality is that the requesting state will, through its own authorities, perform the collection of evidence itself in the requested state. Although, in the European Union, this did not find a place in a Convention, it is practised with mutual consent with regard to some forms of mutual assistance, such as the voluntary interrogation of persons.[1112] With regard to some forms of co-operation, the assistance of the requesting authorities is no longer necessary. This, for instance, is the case with the sending and service of procedural documents, which may be done directly by post, without involvement of the authorities of the state where the addressee resides (Article 5 *EU Mutual Assistance Convention*). A third, and not very common mechanism to prevent inadmissibility of evidence, is to harmonise its collection and transmission. An example relates to transmission of samples of controlled substances.[1113] Article 1 Decision on the transmission of samples of controlled substances determines that the transmission of samples of controlled substances is lawful in all Member States when it is conducted in accordance with the Decision.

Police Co-Operation and Judicial Co-Operation

Chapters 4 (Articles 82–86) and 5 (Articles 87–89) of Title V of Part III TFEU (formerly Articles 30 and 31 EU) distinguish between police co-operation and judicial co-operation. Police co-operation relates to all kinds of co-operation between police authorities. Judicial co-operation can be defined as co-operation between judicial authorities, customs authorities and other specialised law enforcement services (Article 87 TFEU). The distinction relates to an organic element from which the request emanates and to whom it is directed. Although the term "police co-operation" has also been used in Chapter I of Title III *CISA*

[1111]　See, for example, Article 4, paragraph 2 *Joint Action 98/699 on Money Laundering*.

[1112]　It is interesting to see that there is no evidence that the EU has developed any initiative in the direction of self-help. See, further, Section 5 of this chapter.

[1113]　Council Decision 2001/419 of 28 May 2001 on the transmission of samples of controlled substances, OJ 2001, L 150/1.

(Articles 39–47), other Union legal instruments seem to favour the general term of mutual assistance. As such, the terms do not tell us anything with regard to the material acts of co-operation. Exchange of information, for instance, might take place both between police and judicial authorities. However, with regard to other modalities, exclusiveness does exist: cross border pursuit can only be performed by police authorities, and not by judges. On the other hand, a transfer of a judgment will take place without any involvement of the police. However, the organic criterion will not be explored in this book, because there are many modalities of co-operation which are not limited to certain categories of officials. Thus, only mutual assistance which encompasses a wide variety of modalities of co-operation, which may be used by either police authorities, judicial authorities or both, is explored. Generally speaking, mutual assistance relates to the investigation, prosecution, adjudication and execution of crimes already committed. However, under the terms of Article 87, paragraph 1 TFEU, police co-operation may also relate to the *prevention* of criminal offences.[1114]

Administrative Co-Operation and Customs Co-Operation

Two other related forms of co-operation must be mentioned: *administrative co-operation* and *customs co-operation*. Theoretically, they must be distinguished from co-operation in criminal matters, in the sense that they relate to co-operation that is not primarily aimed at criminal investigation and prosecution. However, the results of administrative or customs co-operation may lead to the suspicion that a criminal offence has been committed. The same goes for the authorities which have the right to request and respond to administrative co-operation or customs co-operation. Their principal tasks do not include the investigation and prosecution of crime.[1115]

Administrative co-operation may find its basis in a Directive or in a Regulation. Article 74 TFEU gives the Council competence to adopt measures that regard administrative co-operation. Council Directive 77/799 of 19 December 1977 Concerning Mutual Assistance by the Competent Authorities of the Member States in the Field of Direct Taxation is an example of a Directive that obliges the Member States to exchange information that may enable them to effect a correct assessment of taxes on income and on capital.[1116] Another example is Regulation 1798/2003 of 7 October 2003 on Administrative Cooperation in the Field of Value

---

[1114]   See specifically Decision 2008/617 of 23 June 2008 on the improvement of cooperation between the special intervention units of the Member States of the European Union in crisis situations, OJ 2008, L 210/73, as well as Articles 16 and 17 *Decision 2008/615 on Stepping up Cross-border Cooperation*.

[1115]   However, Article 23, paragraph 2 Regulation 515/97, as amended by Regulation 766/2008, states that its aim is "to assist in preventing, investigating and prosecuting".

[1116]   OJ 1977, L 336/15.

Added Tax and repealing Regulation (EEC) No. 218/92.[1117] Whilst its purpose does not primarily relate to criminal proceedings, it is clear that its application might result in the suspicion that criminal offences have been committed. Article 41, paragraph 1 Regulation 1798/2003 provides that the information communicated under the Regulation may be used for judicial proceedings, which may take all kinds of forms. In some legal instruments, the relationship with co-operation in criminal matters has been clearly defined,[1118] while, in others, it is not mentioned at all.

The main task of customs authorities is to apply Union customs rules. As a result of their position at the external border of the European Union, they may obtain information on criminal offences. The competences of customs authorities are different from criminal law enforcement authorities, in the sense that they may be applied without a reasonable suspicion of a crime being committed; the external borders allows for control checks. The two most important general instruments are the *Convention on Mutual Assistance between Customs Administrations* and Regulation 515/97 of 13 March 1997 on Mutual Assistance between the Administrative Authorities of the Member States and co-operation between the latter and the Commission to ensure the correct application of the law on customs and agricultural matters.[1119] Article 33 TFEU creates a legal basis for the Union to take measures with regard to customs co-operation between the Member States.

The European Union has concluded treaties on customs co-operation with various states.[1120] The existence of other channels of co-operation, which are of the utmost relevance for criminal matters, raises two important questions. The first is whether the existence of various legal instruments, both of a criminal and an administrative nature, require the authorities to use one or the other. This is clearly a question which is relevant only in situations in which a criminal case already exists, that is to say, there is the suspicion that a crime has been committed, because it is only then that the instruments of criminal co-operation may be used. The second question relates to the use of information and evidence obtained under administrative co-operation in criminal proceedings.

[1117] OJ 2003, L 264/1. Regulation 218/92 of 27 January 1992 on administrative co-operation in the field of indirect taxation (VAT), OJ 1992, L 24/1; Directive 76/308 of 15 March 1976 on mutual assistance for the recovery of claims relating to certain levies, duties, taxes and other measures, OJ 1976, L 73/18.

[1118] See, for instance, Article 7 Regulation (EC) No 1338/2001 of 28 June 2001 laying down measures necessary for the protection of the euro against counterfeiting, OJ 2001, L 181/6.

[1119] OJ 1998, C 24/1.

[1120] Agreements on customs co-operation and co-operation in customs matters with Norway, OJ 1997, L 105/13; Korea, OJ 1997, L 121/13; United States of America, OJ 1997, L 222/16, an additional agreement with the USA on container security, OJ 2004, L 304/32; Canada, OJ 1998, L 7/37; Hong Kong, OJ 1999, L 151/20. Additional Protocol on mutual administrative assistance in customs matters to the Framework Co-operation Agreement with Chile OJ 2001, L 167/21.

Article 1, paragraph 3 *Convention on Mutual Assistance between Customs Administrations* stipulates that the Convention "shall not affect the provisions applicable regarding mutual assistance in criminal matters" or any other more favourable provision. Article 3, paragraph 2 of the same Convention gives the judicial authority the choice regarding upon which basis a request will be submitted if both the *Convention on Mutual Assistance between Customs Administrations* and instruments on mutual assistance in criminal matters are applicable. The results of the mutual assistance under the Convention may be used as evidence (Articles 14 and 18 *Convention on Mutual Assistance between Customs Administrations*).[1121] Information exchanged by Financial Intelligence Units established upon the basis of Directive 91/308 may,[1122] in principle, be used for criminal purposes.[1123] The extent to which information obtained by customs or administrative authorities may be used in a criminal setting depends upon the question of whether the rights of the accused are compromised. One principal distinction between administrative and customs law, on the one hand, and criminal law, on the other, is that, with the former, there is an obligation to co-operate and to supply information, whereas, with the latter, individuals are entitled not to be forced to incriminate themselves. Administrative or customs measures implicating the self-incrimination of a person whom the authorities already regarded as the accused are unlawful.

International Agreements
The European Union and the United States of America concluded an Agreement that provides enhancement of the co-operation already covered by bilateral treaties on mutual legal assistance between individual Member States and the United States.[1124] Article 4 of this agreement provides for exchange of bank information. Article 5 creates the possibility of joint investigation teams between one or more Member States and the United States. Article 6 shapes the possibility of taking testimony by making use of video conferencing. Article 9 stipulates for which purposes evidence or information obtained from the requested state may or may not be used.

Article 8, paragraph 1 of the EU-USA Agreement on Mutual Assistance in Criminal Matters authorises mutual legal assistance "to a national administrative authority, investigating conduct with a view to a criminal prosecution of the conduct, or referral of the conduct to criminal investigation or prosecution

---

[1121]   Similarly, Article 45, paragraph 3 Regulation 515/97.

[1122]   Directive 91/308 is now replaced by *Directive 2005/60 on Money Laundering.*

[1123]   See Decision 2000/624 of 17 October 2000 concerning arrangements for co-operation between financial intelligence units of the Member States in respect of exchanging information, OJ 2000, L 271/4.

[1124]   Agreement on Mutual Legal Assistance between the European Union and the United States of America, OJ 2003, L 181/41.

authorities". Thus, at a very early stage of criminal activity, data may be exchanged between the European Union and the United States of America of the so-called Passenger Name Record, with a view to preventing and combating terrorism and transnational crime.[1125] A similar agreement has been concluded with Australia and the EU.[1126]

Notwithstanding the fact that the European Union does not, as an international organisation, extradite, only the Member States can do that, it has also concluded its first extradition treaty with the United States.[1127] The Agreement follows the classical model of extradition treaties under international law, and its function is to provide for enhancement to co-operation upon the basis of the existing bilateral treaties that individual Member States have. Its features are that Article 4 is to be applied instead of bilateral treaties which contain a list of offences. Article 4, paragraph 1 requires qualified double criminality. The offence must be punishable by deprivation of liberty for a maximum period of more than one year. Extradition of sentenced persons may take place for extraditable offences and the remaining sentence to be served must be of at least four months. Article 10 resolves problems arising from competing requests for extradition and European Arrest Warrants. Article 11 provides simplified extradition on consent of the requested person, and Article 13 provides for a refusal of extradition in cases in which the requesting state does not guarantee that the death penalty, if imposed, will not be carried out.

Co-Operation Between the European Union and the International Criminal Court (ICC)

An agreement concluded in 2006 obliges the EU and the ICC to co-operate mutually and assist each other.[1128] One of the obligations relates to the exchange of information (Article 7 Agreement), which is to be in compliance with the ICC Statute and its Rules of Procedure and Evidence. The Union's assistance may

---

[1125] Agreement of 23 and 27 July 2007 between the European Union and the United States of America on the processing and transfer of passenger name record (PNR) data by air carriers to the United States Department of Homeland Security, OJ 2007, L 204/18, which succeeds an earlier agreement which was annulled by the Court, as well as a provisional agreement of 16 and 19 October 2006, OJ 2006, L 298/29. See 30 May 2006, Case C-317/04, *European Parliament and European Data Protection Service (EDPS)* v. *Council, and European Parliament* v. *Commission* [2006] ECR I-4721. See, further, Agreement of 30 April 2007 between the European Union and the United States of America on the security of classified information, OJ 2007, L 115/30.

[1126] Agreement of 30 June 2008 between the European Union and Australia on the processing and transfer of European-Union sourced passenger name record (PNR) data by air carriers to the Australian customs service, OJ 2008, L 213/49.

[1127] Agreement on Extradition between the European Union and the United States of America, OJ 2003, L 181/27.

[1128] Agreement of 10 April 2006 between the International Criminal Court and the European Union on cooperation and assistance, OJ 2006, L 115/50.

amount to giving information and evidence, but also to measures of protection for current or former Union staff (Article 8). The Agreement also establishes co-operation between the Union and the Prosecutor of the ICC. On a regular basis, the Union also assists other international criminal tribunals. In 2000, the International Criminal Tribunal for the former Yugoslavia requested the European Community/European Union to "consider a Defence Application before the Tribunal and to disclose a series of documents",[1129] in order to help the defence with the collection of evidence which it could not obtain of its own. In addition, the European Union has lifted travel restrictions for any witnesses whose presence at a trial before the Special Court for Sierra Leone, which also holds hearings in The Hague, is required.[1130]

3.2. THE MUTUAL RECOGNITION MODEL (ORDER MODEL)

3.2.1. The Origins of Mutual Recognition

Mutual recognition was formulated by the Tampere Council of 1999 as a cornerstone principle for co-operation in civil and criminal matters. It has obtained a status in the TFEU which goes beyond application in the context of co-operation in criminal matters alone. Article 70 TFEU states that the Union shall strive for "full application of mutual recognition". Article 82, paragraph 1 TFEU emphasises that "judicial cooperation in criminal matters in the Union shall be based on the principle of mutual recognition of *judgments* and *judicial decisions*". It requires, in principle, a decision or order by the competent authorities of one Member State to be recognised and executed in another. Mutual recognition is inspired by internal market principles. The parallel with the internal market is apparent, also with regard to goods legally obtained and placed on the market in one Member State, a second check on the question of whether these goods are in compliance with the conditions in another Member State may not take place.[1131] The free flow of arrest warrants, confiscation orders, financial penalties and evidence warrants should result in a situation in which the role of the executing state is limited to mere execution.[1132] The conditions applicable to

---

[1129]   International Criminal Tribunal for the former Yugoslavia, Decision on Ex Parte Application for the Issuance of an Order to the European Community Monitoring Mission, *Prosecutor* v. *Kordić and Čerkez*, Case No. IT-95–14/2-T, T. Ch. III, 3 May 2000, André Klip and Göran Sluiter, Annotated Leading Cases of International Criminal Tribunals-IV-221.

[1130]   See Common Position 2008/81 (CFSP) of 28 January 2008, amending Common Position 98/409/CFSP concerning Sierra Leone, OJ 2008, L 24/54.

[1131]   See Chapter 3, Section 4.5.

[1132]   The terminology in the civil counterpart *Regulation 44/2001 on Jurisdiction and Recognition of Civil Judgments*, is "free movement of judgments in civil and commercial matters".

issuing these warrants and orders are defined by the issuing Member State. The expectations of the legislature are that such a system will work faster and thus be more efficient than assistance under the request model. In order to attain this, strict time-limits for execution have been set, legal remedies have been severely reduced, and postponement of the execution is conditional to the grounds provided for in the Framework Decision.

3.2.2. What Does Mutual Recognition Mean?

Despite its status as one of the cornerstones of the area of freedom, security and justice since the Tampere Council in 1999, the concept of mutual recognition has not been defined. It is built upon mutual trust and mutual confidence, and an understanding that the rules and legal protection in other Member States is more or less at an equivalent level. The rule is that there "shall be" mutual trust among the Member States. A second check as to whether all the relevant conditions have been fulfilled is then regarded as a signal of distrust and is, as such, unacceptable.[1133] In the driving licence case law, the Court held that:

> "as soon, therefore, as the authorities of one Member State have issued a driving licence (…) the other Member States are not entitled to investigate whether the conditions for issue laid down by that directive have been observed."[1134]

Stated simply, the message of a mutual recognition instrument is loud and clear: it should be complied with, and as soon as possible. The role of the executing authority is limited to execution. There is neither need, nor time to (re)consider anything. The executing authority must trust that the issuing authority is in compliance with the applicable law and that it respects the rights of the individual.

It is important to identify here that the meaning of mutual recognition is limited to recognition of formal acts in specific cases. In other words, the obligation to recognise a European Arrest Warrant mutually does not oblige

---

[1133] 26 June 2008, Joined Cases C-329/06 and C-343/06, *Arthur Wiedemann (C-329/06) v. Land Baden-Württemberg and Peter Funk (C-334/06) v. Stadt Chemnitz* [2008] ECR not yet reported, par. 51; 26 June 2008, Joined Cases C-334/06 to C-336/06, *Matthias Zerche (C-334/06), Manfred Seuke (C-336/06) v. Landkreis Mittweida and Steffen Schubert (C-335/06) v. Landkreis Mittlerer Erzgebirgskreis* [2008] ECR not yet reported, par. 48. See, similarly, Chapter 3, Section 3.2. Member States must have confidence that other Member States comply with their obligations. 14 January 1997, Case C-124/95, *The Queen, ex parte Centro-Com Srl v. HM Treasury and Bank of England* [1997] ECR I-81.

[1134] 26 June 2008, Joined Cases C-329/06 and C-343/06, *Arthur Wiedemann (C-329/06) v. Land Baden-Württemberg and Peter Funk (C-334/06) v. Stadt Chemnitz* [2008] ECR not yet reported, par. 53; 26 June 2008, Joined Cases C-334/06 to C-336/06, *Matthias Zerche (C-334/06), Manfred Seuke (C-336/06) v. Landkreis Mittweida and Steffen Schubert (C-335/06) v. Landkreis Mittlerer Erzgebirgskreis* [2008] ECR not yet reported, par. 51.

Germany to adopt the French definition of a crime into its national Penal Code. It only requires that, for the purposes of the surrender of a person to France, the differences in substantive criminal law do not represent an impediment to the surrender. As the Court held in *Advocaten voor de Wereld*:

> "(...) that nothing in Title VI of the EU Treaty, Articles 34 and 31 of which were indicated as forming the legal basis of the Framework Decision, makes the application of the European Arrest Warrant conditional on harmonisation of the criminal laws of the Member States."[1135]

On a similar footing, mutual recognition does not depend on harmonised procedural rules. However, to a certain extent, one can regard the mutual recognition mechanism itself as a harmonised system for providing and requesting assistance. Among the Member States, mutual recognition is limited to the context of international co-operation, it does not require Member States to change procedures in areas which do not relate to co-operation between Member States. Furthermore, the Court recognised that, in the context of arrest warrants, mutual recognition "requires approximation of the laws and regulations of the Member States with regard to judicial co-operation in criminal matters".[1136]

Mutual recognition is not a completely new concept in international co-operation. Traditional mutual assistance also recognises the decisions of others. However, the dimensions are different, and, unlike European Union mutual recognition, requested states cannot execute a foreign decision directly without transformation. Various Conventions of the Council of Europe on the transfer of execution of judgments create possibilities of executing foreign sentences after the conversion of the decision of the sentencing state into a decision of the administrating state. The 1983 Convention on the Transfer of Sentenced Persons creates two models of recognition. The first is the conversion of the sentence following procedures of the administrating state (Article 11). The second, which comes very close to mutual recognition as applied in Union law, is the continued enforcement of sentences of the sentencing state (Article 10).

Mutual recognition acknowledges or assumes differences, allows them to exist, but writes these differences off as an impediment to co-operation. It unilaterally imposes a normative standard by the Member State issuing the warrant, order or licence. The executing Member State may use a different definition of the offence or another criterion of suspicion. The authority competent to take the decision or to collect the evidence might be of an entirely different

---

[1135] 3 May 2007, Case C-303/05, *Advocaten voor de Wereld VZW v. Leden van de Ministerraad* [2007] ECR I-3633, par. 59.
[1136] 3 May 2007, Case C-303/05, *Advocaten voor de Wereld VZW v. Leden van de Ministerraad* [2007] ECR I-3633, par. 29.

status in another Member State. However, these differences may not stand in the way of recognition.

Earlier, the aim pursued by the European Union in order to strive for co-operation without applicable conditions was mentioned. The fifth preambular paragraph of *Framework Decision 2002/584 on the European Arrest Warrant* refers to a "system of free movement of judicial decisions in criminal matters". This *Framework Decision* was able, to a large extent, to abolish conditions. However, the Union has been unable to abolish the double criminality requirement completely, and, consequently, it remains there for the non-list offences (Article 2, paragraph 4 *Framework Decision 2002/584 on the European Arrest Warrant*). Given that this *Framework Decision* has been a model for other forms of co-operation, it will be the subject of an in-depth analysis.[1137] The European Arrest Warrant model has been copied into other Framework Decisions, such as *Framework Decision 2003/577 on Freezing Orders, Framework Decision 2005/214 on Financial Penalties* and *Framework Decision 2006/783 on Confiscation Orders*.

Article 2, paragraph 2 *Framework Decision 2002/584 on the European Arrest Warrant* lists 32 offences for which no "verification of the act" by the executing Member State may take place. In order to fall within this regime, the offences listed must be punishable in the issuing Member State by a custodial sentence or a detention order for a maximum period of at least three years as they are defined by the law of the issuing Member State. Most of the crimes on the list refer to offences criminalised by Union acts or other international obligations. This will be covered in the footnotes. Under the terms of the Framework Decision and without verification of the double criminality of the act, the following offences give rise to surrender pursuant to a European Arrest Warrant:

- participation in a criminal organisation;[1138]
- terrorism;[1139]
- trafficking in human beings;[1140]
- sexual exploitation of children and child pornography;[1141]

[1137] It is even the model on which surrender with Iceland and Norway takes place. See Agreement of 28 June 2006 between the European Union and the Republic of Iceland and the Kingdom of Norway on the surrender procedure between the Member States of the European Union and Iceland and Norway, OJ 2006, L 292/2.

[1138] *Joint Action 98/733 on Participation in a Criminal Organisation.*

[1139] *Common Position 2001/931 on Specific Measures to Combat Terrorism* and *Framework Decision 2002/475 on Combating Terrorism.*

[1140] *Joint Action 97/154 on Trafficking in Human Beings* and *Framework Decision 2002/629 on Combating Trafficking in Human Beings.*

[1141] *Decision 2000/375 on Internet Pornography* and *Framework Decision 2004/68 on Child Pornography.*

- illicit trafficking in narcotic drugs and psychotropic substances;[1142]
- illicit trafficking in weapons, munitions and explosives;
- corruption;[1143]
- fraud, including that affecting the financial interests of the European Communities within the meaning of the Convention of 26 July 1995 on the Protection of the European Communities' Financial Interests;[1144]
- laundering of the proceeds of crime;[1145]
- counterfeiting currency, including of the euro;[1146]
- computer-related crime;[1147]
- environmental crime, including illicit trafficking in endangered animal species and in endangered plant species and varieties;[1148]
- facilitation of unauthorised entry and residence;[1149]
- murder, grievous bodily injury;
- illicit trade in human organs and tissue;
- kidnapping, illegal restraint and hostage-taking;
- racism and xenophobia;[1150]
- organised or armed robbery;
- illicit trafficking in cultural goods, including antiques and works of art;
- swindling;
- racketeering and extortion;
- counterfeiting and piracy of products;
- forgery of administrative documents and trafficking therein;
- forgery of means of payment;[1151]
- illicit trafficking in hormonal substances and other growth promoters;
- illicit trafficking in nuclear or radioactive materials;[1152]
- trafficking in stolen vehicles;[1153]
- rape;

[1142] *Joint Action 96/750 on Illegal Drug Trafficking* and *Framework Decision 2004/757 on Illicit Drug Trafficking.*

[1143] *Corruption Convention, Joint Action 98/742 on Corruption in the Private Sector* and *Framework Decision 2003/568 on Corruption in the Private Sector.*

[1144] *Financial Interests Convention.*

[1145] *Joint Action 98/699 on Money Laundering* and *Framework Decision 2001/500 on Money Laundering.*

[1146] *Framework Decision 2000/383 on the Introduction of the Euro.*

[1147] Convention of 23 November 2001 on cybercrime.

[1148] *Framework Decision 2003/80 on the Protection of the Environment* and *Framework Decision 2005/667 on Ship-source Pollution.*

[1149] *Framework Decision 2002/946 on Unauthorised Entry.*

[1150] *Joint Action 96/443 on Racism and Xenophobia.*

[1151] *Framework Decision 2001/413 on Combating Fraud.*

[1152] Convention of 3 March 1980 on the Physical Protection of Nuclear Material.

[1153] Up to and including trafficking in stolen vehicles, the offences are included in the competence for Europol in the *Europol Convention.* See, further, Chapter 8, Section 2.1.2.

- arson;
- crimes within the jurisdiction of the International Criminal Court;[1154]
- unlawful seizure of aircraft/ships;[1155]
- sabotage.[1156]

In addition to the offences mentioned above, Article 5 *Framework Decision 2005/214 on Financial Penalties* has included the following offences on the list:
- "conduct which infringes road traffic regulations, including breaches of regulations pertaining to driving hours and rest periods and regulations on hazardous goods;
- smuggling of goods;
- infringements of intellectual property rights;
- threats and acts of violence against persons, including violence during sport events;
- criminal damage;
- theft;
- offences established by the issuing State and serving the purpose of implementing obligations arising from instruments adopted under the EC Treaty or under Title VI of the EU Treaty."

The revolutionary character of the change to the list of offences system is more a matter of principle than of substance. The practical influence of the abolition of the double criminality requirement is, at this stage, minimal. The reason for this is that the vast majority of offences on the list are offences which are criminal in all Member States, anyway. This is because there is an obligation for the Member States upon the basis of a separate legal instrument (Convention, Framework Decision) that these offences should be criminalised, as is evidenced in the accompanying footnotes. A more cynical vision would be that the list does not eliminate the double criminality requirement. What the list does is establish a number of offences for which, by definition, this condition is met. The remaining crimes are serious ordinary crimes common to all criminal justice systems of the Member States. A handful of the crimes does not immediately appeal to commonly accepted offences. This accounts for swindling, sabotage and criminal damage.

[1154] Statute of the International Criminal Court of 17 July 1998.

[1155] For example, among many other treaties: Convention of 10 March 1988 for the Suppression of Unlawful Acts against the Safety of Maritime Navigation.

[1156] Identical lists can be found in Article 3, paragraph 2 *Framework Decision 2003/577 on Freezing Orders*; Article 6, paragraph 1 *Framework Decision 2006/783 on Confiscation Orders*. The list has also been copied into the Agreement of 28 June 2006 between the European Union and the Republic of Iceland and the Kingdom of Norway on the surrender procedure between the Member States of the European Union and Iceland and Norway, OJ 2006, L 292/2.

Especially with regard to the crimes for which there is a common obligation to criminalise, it may be assumed that Member States have criminalised the conduct. However, this does not mean that they have implemented it in an identical manner. The issuing Member State determines on its national definition – not on the definition in the Union legal act – whether there is a list offence. The Court recognised, in *Advocaten voor de Wereld*, that the:

> "list of the categories of offences set out in Article 2(2) of the Framework Decision for the purposes of its implementation, the actual definition of those offences and the penalties applicable are those which follow from the law of 'the issuing Member State'. The Framework Decision does not seek to harmonise the criminal offences in question in respect of their constituent elements or of the penalties which they attract."[1157]

The Court also recognised that "the lack of provision in the definition of the categories of offences in question risks giving rise to disparate implementation of the Framework Decision within the various national legal orders".[1158] In addition, for the offences on the list, for which there is no common legal instrument, there is an assumption of double criminality. This is, after all, only about the name of the offence: the same label need not necessarily comprise the same message. In addition, Member States may change their legislation. It would appear to be more important to note that such a system must not change the substantive criminal law of the Member States, but only regulate (or make uniform) the co-operation between the Member States. However, this will not happen systematically, as the following example shows: because of the fact that, in surrender procedures, the guarantee of repatriation to serve out the sentence in the perpetrator's own country is required, another form of international co-operation must also be used, the transfer of the execution of a sentence. Consequently, the compliance with the conditions for the transfer of the execution of the sentence must be tested, and one of the most important of these conditions is the double criminality rule.

It is interesting to see that, with the list of offences, the European Union returned to a practice that used to be used in extradition treaties, since these treaties came into being around 1800. Extradition treaties contained a list of offences for which extradition was to be granted. The 1957 *European Convention on Extradition* broke with that system because it was felt that the list was inflexible and required regular amendments due to new circumstances or legislation. The parties then preferred a criterion which would not have to be amended by international legislation each time that changes were felt to be necessary. The European Union has returned to a more inflexible system.

[1157]   3 May 2007, Case C-303/05, *Advocaten voor de Wereld VZW v. Leden van de Ministerraad* [2007] ECR I-3633, par. 52.

[1158]   3 May 2007, Case C-303/05, *Advocaten voor de Wereld VZW v. Leden van de Ministerraad* [2007] ECR I-3633, par. 59.

3.2.3. What Triggers Mutual Recognition?

There must be a decision which falls under one of the Framework Decisions or other acts in which mutual recognition has been stipulated. Despite its status under the Treaties, mutual recognition is not a concept generally applicable to all acts, decisions and judgments of authorities of the Member States. It must find its basis in one of the legal instruments.

The fact that a competent authority of a Member State issues a European Arrest Warrant to another Member State triggers the obligation for those authorities to comply with it. The European Arrest Warrant or other order is notified to the executing authority in another Member State, which is subsequently obliged to execute it. Mutual recognition thus provides all the parties involved with a fair deal of clarity, as there is a *positive and notified decision* which requires another Member State to do something, which must be recognised.

The situation in which a national decision to refrain from ordering certain measures is taken, not to order a search or seizure, or not to confiscate a piece of evidence is more problematical. Making the order within the national setting, but refraining from issuing a European Arrest Warrant or order for whatever reason is equally problematical. This raises the question of whether a positive decision is the only *modus* that triggers mutual recognition.

The question raised here relates to *ne bis in idem*.[1159] On this subject, it was established that the protection against a second trial should not only be given to those who had committed serious offences, but also to those that had committed less serious offences, which would not lead to imprisonment. The Court placed this in the context of the freedoms under the Treaty. Does this imply that decisions not to take action bring their effect in another Member State? From the case law on Article 54 *CISA*, it is difficult to discern material justifications for different treatment of positive and negative decisions. In Chapter 5, the distinction that must be made to mutual recognition in and out of international co-operation situations were referred to. While decisions triggering a *ne bis in idem* effect are not communicated to the Member State that should respect these decisions,[1160] decisions triggering mutual recognition in international co-operation are addressed exclusively to a specific Member State.

In the *Gözütok and Brügge* case, Advocate General Ruiz-Jarabo Colomer did not rely on the requirement of a formal decision in a specific form. With regard to the restriction on the right to prosecute, he stated that:

[1159] See Chapter 5, Section 3.2.

[1160] This is logical from the perspective of the sentencing Member State; when a state *finally disposes* of a trial, it requires other Member States to do nothing.

"The extent of this restriction must be defined from the citizen's point of view, since it is one of his safeguards. If it means that once he has been prosecuted, judged and, if convicted, punished by the imposition of a penalty, the defendant has the right for no other signatory State to do the same. The form of the legal pronouncement and the manner in which it is given are of little importance provided that all the conditions and requirements fixed in the legal system under which the decision is delivered are fulfilled. It would be ludicrous to argue that Article 54 of the Convention can refer only to decisions taken by courts – that is to say, decisions delivered after proceedings conducted with all the safeguards –, and, precisely with that argument, to reduce the scope of application of one of those safeguards. Furthermore, a literal and strict interpretation of Article 54 of the Convention would have untoward consequences. Indeed, I have pointed out that the settlement procedure is a means of administering criminal justice in respect of minor or medium offences, but that it is not used in the field of more serious crimes. Therefore, the approach taken by the German, French and Belgian Governments would provide better treatment for the perpetrators of major offences, who would benefit from the *ne bis in idem* rule, than to the perpetrators of minor transgressions, which are less socially reprehensible. The perpetrator of a more serious crime, who may be convicted only by a final judgment, could not be judged again in another State signatory to the Convention, quite unlike the perpetrator of a petty offence who has accepted and completed the punishment suggested by the Prosecutor."[1161]

If the recognition were extended to decisions not to prosecute, it could create practical problems. How can the authorities of the Member States recognise (non-)decisions that have not been brought to their attention? With reference to Article 54 *CISA*, it must be established that mutual recognition does not, as a matter of principle, require that Member States be notified of relevant decisions. However, Article 54 *CISA* deals with a situation that is not necessarily related to international co-operation. Is it possible to transplant the fact that mutual recognition is not conditional upon a formal notification of the decision to apply international co-operation? This requires further elaboration of the principle of *ne bis in idem*.

3.2.4 *The Absolute Character of the Obligation to Recognise*

The principle of mutual recognition raises the question of whether the obligation to recognise is of an absolute character. Must Member States always comply with the decisions of other Member States, even if the circumstances differ greatly? Is there any room for the executing Member State to assess whether the issuing Member State has correctly issued the warrant or order? The abolition of the

---

[1161]   Opinion of Advocate General Ruiz-Jarabo Colomer of 19 September 2002, Case C-187/01 and Case C-385/01, *criminal proceedings against Hüseyin Gözütok (C-187/01) and Klaus Brügge (C-385/01)* [2003] ECR I-1345, point 115–116.

double criminality requirement was shaped in the form of the list of offences for which this requirement is no longer applicable. Which state determines whether a crime is a crime on the list? Is it the issuing state that ticks the box,[1162] or is it the executing state? To begin with the latter, if the opinion of the executing state were decisive, it could amount to an inquiry into the facts, as well as into the character of the offence. If the opinion of the issuing state is absolute, it could lead to a situation in which that Member State unjustifiably ticks a box (regardless of whether this was on purpose or by mistake), the executing Member State is still under obligation to comply.

In principle, Union law does not allow for double checks. This is expressed in the Framework Decisions on mutual recognition which provide, in an article on recognition and execution, that "the competent authorities in the executing State shall without further formality recognise …".[1163] Advocate General Ruiz-Jarabo Colomer stated that any assessment of opportuneness is irrelevant.[1164] The prohibition to make a new assessment does have consequences which carry practical and legal components. The first component is that the other Member State's decision is the decision to work with. An *exequatur*, a transmission into a national decision, is not necessary. The second component is that double criminality does not need to be tested. Before mutual recognition was introduced as a concept applicable to co-operation in criminal matters, it had already led to case law under Union law. Since the origin of the principle lies in the law of the former First Pillar, it is most relevant to analyse this case law.

An interesting case is *Centro*, which relates to the boycott of Yugoslavia during the Yugoslav war. In this case, the United Kingdom did not release Serbian and Montenegrin funds in exchange for exports to these republics unless the United Kingdom authorities had previously checked the nature of the goods, which were in Italy. The Italian company argued that the check as to whether the goods fell under the exception to the general ban on trade with Serbia and Montenegro could also be performed by the Italian authorities. The Court shared this view:

"effective application of the sanctions can only be ensured by other Member States' authorization procedures, as provided for in the Sanctions Regulation, in particular the procedure of the Member State of exportation. In that respect, the Member States must place trust in each other as far as concerns the checks made by the competent

---

[1162] This refers to the Model for the European Arrest Warrant on which the issuing Member State must tick the box of the applicable offence.

[1163] See Article 7 *Framework Decision 2006/783 on Confiscation Orders* and Article 5 *Framework Decision 2003/577 on Freezing Orders* and *Framework Decision 2005/214 on Financial Penalties*. N.B.: a notable exception is the *Framework Decision 2002/584 on the European Arrest Warrant*, which, indeed, does allow for some formalities.

[1164] Opinion of Advocate General Ruiz-Jarabo Colomer of 12 September 2006, Case C-303/05, *Advocaten voor de Wereld VZW v. Leden van de Ministerraad*, [2007] ECR I-3633, points 45 and 105.

authorities of the Member State from which the products in question are dispatched."[1165]

In *Hoffmann* v. *Krieg*, a civil case based upon mutual recognition under the *Brussels Convention*,[1166] the Court referred to "free movement of judgments", from which it follows "that a foreign judgment which has been recognised must in principle have the same effects in the state in which enforcement is sought as it does in the state in which judgment was given".[1167] The extent to which the court of the Member State in which enforcement is sought has discretion to refuse, is rather limited. In the *Krombach* v. *Bamberski* case, a case which, like *Hoffmann* v. *Krieg*, related to the interpretation of the *Brussels Convention*, the Court interpreted Article 28 of the said convention as such that recognition is required "even where the court of the State of origin wrongly founded its jurisdiction".[1168] In principle, a state may not refuse to enforce "solely on the ground that there is a discrepancy between the legal rule applied by the court of the State of origin and that of which would have been applied by the court of the State in which enforcement is sought had it been seised in the dispute".[1169]

In this context, the question is raised to what extent a Member State may correct the non-compliance of another Member State with Union law. In *Hedley Lomas*, the Court held that "a Member State may not unilaterally adopt, on its own authority, corrective or protective measures designed to obviate any breach by another Member State of rules of Community law".[1170] In a case against France, the Court held:

> "A Member State cannot under any circumstances unilaterally adopt, on its own authority, corrective measures or measures to protect trade designed to prevent any failure on the part of another Member State to comply with the rules laid down by the Treaty."[1171]

[1165] 14 January 1997, Case C-124/95, *The Queen, ex parte Centro-Com Srl* v. *HM Treasury and Bank of England* [1997] ECR I-81, par. 48 and 49.

[1166] As of 1 March 2002, replaced by *Regulation 44/2001 on Jurisdiction and Recognition of Civil Judgments*.

[1167] 4 February 1988, Case 145/86, *Horst Ludwig Martin Hoffmann* v. *Adelheid Krieg* [1988] ECR 645, par. 11.

[1168] 28 March 2000, Case C-7/98, *Dieter Krombach* v. *André Bamberski* [2000] ECR I-1935, par. 33.

[1169] 28 March 2000, Case C-7/98, *Dieter Krombach* v. *André Bamberski* [2000] ECR I-1935, par. 36.

[1170] 23 May 1996, Case C-5/94, *The Queen* v. *Ministry of Agriculture, Fisheries and Food, ex parte: Hedley Lomas (Ireland) Ltd.* [1996] ECR I-2553, par. 20.

[1171] 25 September 1979, Case 232/78, *Commission* v. *France* [1979] ECR 2729, par. 9.

Or to put it in the even stronger words of Advocate General Léger:

> "Nothing is more alien to Community law than the idea of a measure of retaliation or reciprocity proper to classical public international law. A Member State paralyses the free movement of goods on the ground that the higher interest of the protection of animals has allegedly been violated in another Member State. (...) A Member State cannot take unilateral action against defaults by other Member States."[1172]

Exceptions to Mutual Recognition

From the application of the principle in the internal market in general and from specific acts thereof in particular, notably the *Brussels Convention*,[1173] and *Directive 91/439 on Driving Licences*, as well as *Framework Decision 2002/584 on the European Arrest Warrant*, the following four categories of exceptions to mutual recognition emerge:
- prevailing obligations;
- clear shortcomings;
- applicable grounds for refusal;
- irreconcilable decisions.

Prevailing Obligations

Some international obligations of the European Union and international obligations to which a Member State is bound prevail over the obligation to recognise. Article 351 TFEU (formerly Article 307 TEC) refers to the treaty obligations of Member States, which were already in existence before the Treaty on the establishment of the European Community entered into force on 1 January 1958. Although this category diminishes by the day, they may still be influential: indeed, importantly enough, the ECHR of 1950 falls under this category.

What is the position of a Member State that receives a European Arrest Warrant or other order upon the basis of mutual recognition that has serious concerns on the respect for human rights in the other Member State? What is the meaning of Article 19 Charter, which stipulates that extradition may not take place where there is a serious risk that the death penalty, torture or other inhuman or degrading treatment or punishment may follow. Is the same mechanism applicable, as discussed earlier, in the sense that Member States must, in principle, place trust in other Member States when enforcing Union law? With regard to the ECHR, it is relevant to see that this is a Convention that dates from before 1 January 1958 for the founding states (and for acceding states at a later moment).

[1172] Opinion of Advocate General Léger of 20 June 1995, Case C-5/94, *The Queen* v. *Ministry of Agriculture, Fisheries and Food, ex parte: Hedley Lomas (Ireland) Ltd.* [1996] ECR I-2553, point 27. See, also, 25 January 1977, Case 46–76, *W.J.G. Bauhuis* v. *the Netherlands State* [1977] ECR 5.

[1173] As well as its successor *Regulation 44/2001 on Jurisdiction and Recognition of Civil Judgments.*

Application of Article 351 TFEU implies that the rights and obligations from these older agreements are not to be affected by the Treaties. This would indicate that ECHR obligations, for all the Member States that were bound by that Convention before they were bound to the Treaties, would prevail. In Centro, the Court stipulated the criterion that was relevant in these type of cases: Does the previous agreement impose obligations on the Member State whose performance may still be required by non-Member States which are parties to it?[1174]

The Court held:

> "If the agreement allows but does not require to adopt a measure to be contrary to Community law, the Member State must refrain from adopting such a measure."[1175]

If it is possible to reconcile the obligations from both treaties, the Member States must do so.[1176] It is for the national court to determine whether this is possible.

In the *Krombach* case, Bamberski, the father of a daughter unintentionally killed by Krombach in Germany, had successfully initiated criminal proceedings against Krombach in France. The proceedings in France were conducted *in absentia*. After convicting Krombach, the French authorities requested Germany to recognise the conviction to civil damages that was part of the sentence. The Court, relying partly on the public policy clause of Article 27 *Brussels Convention*, accepted that a Member State may refuse mutual recognition if it infringes a fundamental principle which constitutes a manifest breach of a rule of law regarded as essential in the legal order of the executing state.[1177] The right to be

---

[1174]   14 January 1997, Case C-124/95, *The Queen, ex parte Centro-Com Srl* v. *HM Treasury and Bank of England* [1997] ECR I-81, par. 57.

[1175]   14 January 1997, Case C-124/95, *The Queen, ex parte Centro-Com Srl* v. *HM Treasury and Bank of England* [1997] ECR I-81, par. 60.

[1176]   Case C-324/93, *The Queen* v. *Secretary of State for Home Department, ex parte Evans Medical Ltd and Macfarlan Smith Ltd* [1995] ECR I-563, par. 27–33. In point 20 of his Opinion of 4 October 1994 to this case, Advocate General Lenz even argued that: "the United Kingdom might even be under an obligation to denounce the Convention". See, also, 27 February 1962, Case 10–61, *Commission* v. *Italy* [1962] ECR English Special Edition 1.

[1177]   Article 27 *Brussels Convention* reads:
"A judgment shall not be recognized:
1. if such recognition is contrary to public policy in the State in which recognition is sought;
2. where it was given in default of appearance, if the defendant was not duly served with the document which instituted the proceedings or with an equivalent document in sufficient time to enable him to arrange for his defence;
3. if the judgment is irreconcilable with a judgment given in a dispute between the same parties in the State in which recognition is sought;
4. if the court of the State of origin, in order to arrive at its judgment, has decided a preliminary question concerning the status or legal capacity of natural persons, rights in property arising out of a matrimonial relationship, wills or succession in a way that conflicts with a rule of the private international law of the State in which the recognition is sought, unless the same result would have been reached by the application of the rules of private international law of that State;

---

defended *is* such a principle because it derives from the constitutional traditions that are common to the Member States.[1178] The Court also held that:

> "even though the Convention is intended to secure the simplification of formalities governing the reciprocal recognition and enforcement of judgments of courts or tribunals, it is not permissible to achieve that aim by undermining the right to a fair hearing."[1179]

Such a fundamental principle would not be infringed if it were decided to conduct the criminal trial in the presence of the accused. If the accused was there with counsel, there would be nothing to preclude recognition, including the civil claim which was dealt with by the criminal court.[1180]

In *Minalmet* v. *Brandeis* the Court held that:

> "a decision given in default of appearance in a contracting State must not be recognized in another contracting State if the document instituting proceedings was not duly served on the defaulting defendant. That interpretation is not invalidated by the fact that the defendant had notice of the judgment given in default and did not avail himself of the remedies provided for under the procedure of the State were it was delivered."[1181]

In addition to the requirement of "duly served", the service must take place at a moment that allows the defendant sufficient time to prepare his defence.[1182] The question of whether the service was "duly" or not may not be decided upon the

---

5. if the judgment is irreconcilable with an earlier judgment given in a non-contracting State involving the same cause of action and between the same parties, provided that this latter judgment fulfils the conditions necessary for its recognition in the State addressed".

[1178]   28 March 2000, Case C-7/98, *Dieter Krombach* v. *André Bamberski* [2000] ECR I-1935, par. 37–40. The ECtHR held in its judgment that there was a violation of a fair trial. See ECtHR13 February 2001, *Krombach* v. *France*, Application 29731/96.

[1179]   28 March 2000, Case C-7/98, *Dieter Krombach* v. *André Bamberski* [2000] ECR I-1935, par. 43.

[1180]   21 April 1993, Case C-172/91, *Volker Sonntag* v. *Hans Waidmann, Elisabeth Waidmann and Stefan Waidmann* [1993] ECR I-1963. Clearly, the lawyer present must act with the explicit authority of the defendant, see 10 October 1996, Case C-78/95, *Bernardus Hendrikman and Maria Feijen* v. *Magenta Druck & Verlag GmbH* [1996] ECR I-4943.

[1181]   12 November 1992, Case C-123/91, *Minalmet GmbH* v. *Brandeis Ltd* [1992] ECR I-5661, par. 14–15.

[1182]   11 June 1985, Case 49/84, *Leon Emile Gaston Carlos Debaecker and Berthe Plouvier* v. *Cornelis Gerrit Bouwman* [1985] ECR 1779. Similarly, even if the court that gave judgment has held that service was duly effected, the court in which enforcement is sought is required to examine whether service was effected in sufficient time to enable the defendant to arrange his defence. See 16 June 1981, Case 166/80, *Peter Klomps* v. *Karl Michel* [1981] ECR 1593, par. 16. The same goes for the situation in which the defendant was not served in due form, even though he was served in sufficient time to enable him to arrange for his defence. See 3 July 1990, Case C-305/88, *Isabelle Lancray SA* v. *Peters und Sickert KG* [1990] ECR I-2725.

basis of national law, but upon the international rules applicable between the two Member States.[1183]

The reference to the fair trial principle deriving from the constitutional traditions common to the Member States hints at the application of general principles, but is also linked to a discretionary ground for refusal in the Convention. Article 34 *Regulation 44/2001 on Jurisdiction and Recognition of Civil Judgments*, which replaced the *Brussels Convention* also gives room for respect for the rights of the defence. With regard to the application of Article 27, paragraph 2 *Brussels Convention*, the Court also held that, even if the court that gave judgment held that the defendant had sufficient time for the preparation of his defence, the executing court may give its own assessment.[1184] In contrast to Article 27, paragraph 2 *Brussels Convention*, which attaches much weight to duly served, Article 34, paragraph 2 *Regulation 44/2001 on Jurisdiction and Recognition of Civil Judgments* requires more generally that the rights of the defence are effectively protected.[1185]

Clear Shortcomings

The acceptation of clear shortcomings as an exception to mutual recognition, in essence, undermines the prescription of mutual trust, which implies that Member States trust that other Member States grant sufficient protection with regard to fundamental freedoms and fundamental rights. The shortcomings must be clear and based upon information that is submitted by the issuing Member State. Again, this is a phenomenon that was already developed in the internal market. This may be illustrated as follows. Houtwipper was prosecuted for not having fixed hallmarks for gold and silver with national indications, although the hallmarks of another Member State were already there. The Court held that the affixation of a second hallmark could not be required in situations where the products were provided with the hallmark of another Member State and legally marketed and "where the information provided by the hallmark, in whatever form, is equivalent to that prescribed by the Member State of importation and

---

[1183]   13 October 2005, Case C-522/03, *Scania Finance France SA* v. *Rockinger Spezialfabrik für Anhängerkupplungen GmbH & Co* [2005] ECR I-8639.
[1184]   15 July 1982, Case 228/81, *Pendy Plastics Products BV* v. *Pluspunkt Handelsgesellschaft mbH* [1982] ECR 2723.
[1185]   14 December 2006, Case C-283/05, *ASML Netherlands BV* v. *Semicondutor Industry Services GmbH (SEMIS)* [2006] ECR I-12041, par. 18–19.

intelligible to consumers of that State".[1186] The national court should determine whether such equivalence exists:

"The existence of double controls in the State of exportation and in the State of importation cannot be justified if the results of the control carried out in the Member State of origin satisfy the requirements of the Member State of importation."[1187]

The rule that can be deduced from this case law is that, in principle, second checks are prohibited, unless information is brought to the attention of the Member State that trust is, in the individual case in question, unjustified. This was confirmed in *Centro*, in which the Court took note of the fact that there was no indication that the system provided by the Sanctions Regulation had not functioned properly. This implies that mutual trust is not absolute. The Court, therefore, indicates that, if a Member State has serious doubts about the accuracy of the information submitted, it may ask the authorities of the Member State for further information.[1188]

At first sight, the judgments in *Houtwipper* and *Centro* seem to be in conflict with another Court case. In *Commission v. Spain*, the Court held that Spain could not refuse a visa to a third country national who was the spouse of an EU national, simply because another Member State, Germany, had provided an alert into the Schengen Information System that entry should be refused. The Court held that an automatic refusal conflicts with the rights embodied in *Directive 64/221 on Movement and Residence of Foreign Nationals* to the spouses of EU nationals. The Spanish authorities should have consulted Germany in order to verify whether the grounds for alert constituted a serious threat to society in Spain.[1189] To allow verification is problematical for the general rules of Union law: Member States may not correct or anticipate the shortcomings of another Member State. However, the interests at stake are different now. Although the information supplied by the German authorities should raise doubt in Spain, the person concerned is still entitled to certain rights. In the driving licence cases, the Court held that, in cases where a Member State has good reason to doubt the validity, it must inform the issuing Member State.[1190]

[1186]   15 September 1994, Case C-293/93, *criminal proceedings against Ludomira Neeltje Barbara Houtwipper* [1994] ECR I-4249, par. 15; 22 June 1982, Case 220/81, *criminal proceedings against Timothy Frederick Robertson and others* [1982] ECR 2349, par. 12.

[1187]   15 September 1994, Case C-293/93, *criminal proceedings against Ludomira Neeltje Barbara Houtwipper* [1994] ECR I-4249, par. 19.

[1188]   14 January 1997, Case C-124/95, *The Queen, ex parte Centro-Com Srl v. HM Treasury and Bank of England* [1997] ECR I-81, par. 50–52.

[1189]   31 January 2006, Case C-503/03, *Commission v. Spain* [2006] ECR I-1097.

[1190]   26 June 2008, Joined Cases C-329/06 and C-343/06, *Arthur Wiedemann (C-329/06) v. Land Baden-Württemberg and Peter Funk (C-334/06) v. Stadt Chemnitz* [2008] ECR not yet reported, par. 37; 26 June 2008, Joined Cases C-334/06 to C-336/06, *Matthias Zerche (C-334/06), Manfred*

The fact that the form of the European Arrest Warrant must contain, according to Article 8 *Framework Decision 2002/584 on the European Arrest Warrant*, "the nature and legal classification of the offence, particularly in respect of Article 2", and "a description of the circumstances in which the offence was committed, including the time, place and degree of participation in the offence by the requested person", does raise questions. Why is it necessary to furnish this information? This is information that the issuing authority is more than aware of itself. If it is addressed to the executing Member State, the question arises as to whether the executing authority may assess the information given and test whether the warrant complies with all conditions. Could this be regarded as an indication that a marginal test of compliance with the proportionality principle, which is a general principle of law, is admissible?[1191] At first sight, applying proportionality would not be alien to the system of surrender. Surrender is a serious measure and is, therefore, only applicable to serious cases. A justification for exceptions to absolute mutual recognition could lie in the fact that the liberty of persons is at stake, many of whom have not been convicted, and, are, therefore, presumed to be innocent. These are interests of a fundamentally different character than, for instance, with the mutual recognition of the placement of goods on the market, regardless of their size or value. In addition, the instrument of mutual recognition, *Framework Decision 2002/584 on the European Arrest Warrant* has limited the arrest warrants that qualify for mutual recognition to those of a certain degree of seriousness: list offences, which are punishable with at least three years imprisonment.

Applicable Grounds for Refusal

Naturally, where the Framework Decision or other Union act contains grounds for refusal, a Member State is entitled to invoke these. On this issue, too, the question must be raised as to whether the assessment of a (non-)executing Member State that a ground for refusal is applicable, is also subject to the mechanism of mutual recognition? These kinds of questions will have to be answered by the Court.

Seuke (C-336/06) v. *Landkreis Mittweida and Steffen Schubert (C-335/06)* v. *Landkreis Mittlerer Erzgebirgskreis* [2008] ECR not yet reported, par. 54.

[1191]   Again, a comparison with mutual recognition of civil judgments is relevant. The seventeenth preambular paragraph of *Regulation 44/2001 on Jurisdiction and Recognition of Civil Judgments* states that by virtue of the principle of mutual trust a declaration that a judgment is enforceable should be issued "virtually automatically after purely formal checks of the documents supplied, without there being any possibility for the court to raise of its own motion any of the grounds for non-enforcement provided for by this Regulation". Article 36 of the Regulation states very clearly: "Under no circumstance may a foreign judgment be reviewed as to its substance".

Framework Decision 2002/584 on the European Arrest Warrant formulates three mandatory grounds for the non-execution of the warrant (Article 3):

- the offence is covered by an amnesty in the executing Member State;
- *ne bis in idem* in one of the Member States applies;[1192]
- the accused has not reached the age of criminal responsibility according to the law of the executing state.

Apart from these mandatory grounds, Article 4 provides grounds for optional non-execution:

- lack of double criminality;[1193]
- pending prosecution in the executing Member State for the same acts;
- judicial authorities of the executing Member State have decided not to prosecute;
- prosecution or punishment is statute barred;
- *ne bis in idem* in a third state applies;
- the surrender of a convicted national or resident or person staying in the executing Member State undertakes to execute the sentence itself;[1194]
- the warrant relates to offences committed in whole or in part in the territory of the executing Member State;
- the warrant relates to offences committed outside the territory of the issuing Member State and the law of the executing Member State would not allow prosecution in a similar situation.[1195]

[1192]   Although the Framework Decision does not state so, the mandatory use of this ground by the executing authority should also lead to an end of the proceedings in the issuing Member State. Similarly, application of Article 7, paragraph 1 (c) *Framework Decision 2003/577 on Freezing Orders*.

[1193]   Clearly, this may relate only to crimes other than those on the list of Article 2, paragraph 2 *Framework Decision 2002/584 on the European Arrest Warrant*.

[1194]   "Staying" is not an independent category, but complementary to resident. The Court held that such a person must have "his actual place of residence in the executing Member State or has acquired, following a stable period of presence in that State, certain connections with that State which are of a similar degree to those resulting from residence." See 17 July 2008, C-66/08, *proceedings concerning the execution of a European arrest warrant issued against Szymon Kosłowski* [2008] ECR not yet reported, par. 46.

[1195]   A much more limited list of grounds of non-execution can be found in Article 7 *Framework Decision 2003/577 on Freezing Orders*, as well as in Article 8 *Framework Decision 2006/783 on Confiscation Orders*.

In fact, the guarantees which an executing Member State might require from the issuing Member State on the basis of Article 5 Framework Decision also function, if they are not complied with, as grounds for refusal:

- the guarantee of a re-trial for *in absentia* convictions if the person has not been summoned in person or otherwise informed of the hearing;[1196]
- the guarantee that, in cases of a conviction to life imprisonment, the issuing Member State provides for a review of the penalty at the latest after 20 years;
- the guarantee that the nationals or residents of the executing Member State will be returned to that state in order to serve the sentence there.

Irreconcilable Decisions

Whilst the system of mutual recognition is based upon the recognition and execution of a decision taken by one Member State originating from another Member State, it does not automatically give an answer to the question of how to deal with irreconcilable or competing decisions.[1197] Since the mutual recognition model is built upon the independent initiative of a Member State, Member States may take initiatives without knowing of the steps taken by others. Earlier, it was established that mutual recognition does not require a general notice to be given of a decision taken by a Member State authority. Decisions independently taken by Member States thus raise the question of who recognises whom?

Outside the field of criminal law, the issue appeared in the case law. The driving licence cases offer some examples here. Does the Member State that annulled the driving licence of a driving licence holder have to recognise a new driving licence obtained in another Member State or *vice versa*? And what are the consequences for third Member States which did not take any decision at all, but may have to

---

[1196] The impossibility of giving a guarantee that is regarded as sufficient leads to a significant number of non-executions of European Arrest Warrants. As a consequence, negotiations were initiated on amending the Framework Decision with the aim of clarifying the definition of *in absentia* convictions. Initiative of the Republic of Slovenia, the French Republic, the Czech Republic, the Kingdom of Sweden, the Slovak Republic, the United Kingdom and the Federal Republic of Germany with a view of adopting a Council Framework Decision on the enforcement of decisions rendered *in absentia* and amending Framework Decision 2002/584/JHA on the European Arrest Warrant and the surrender proceedings between the Member States, Framework Decision 2005/214/JHA on the application of the principle of mutual recognition to financial penalties, Framework Decision 2006/783/JHA on the application of the principle of mutual recognition to confiscation orders and Framework Decision on the application of the principle of mutual recognition to judgments in criminal matters imposing custodial sentences or measures involving deprivation of liberty for the purpose of their enforcement in the European Union, Council Document 11309/08, 2 July 2008, COPEN132.

[1197] "Irreconcilable" is the term used in Article 34 *Regulation 44/2001 on Jurisdiction and Recognition of Civil Judgments*.

answer the simple question of whether the driving licence is valid, because it finds the holder of such a licence driving through its territory?[1198]

A Member State that has withdrawn a driving licence may only refuse to recognise a new one obtained in another Member State if the new driving licence was issued within the period that the person in question was not entitled to a new driving licence.[1199] By its judgments of 26 June 2008, the Court does allow a Member State which has withdrawn the driving licence of a holder and finds that person on its territory with a new driving licence from another Member State to refuse to recognise the decision, but only:

"if it is possible to determine, not in light of information supplied by the host Member State, but on the basis of entries appearing in the driving licence itself or of other incontestable information supplied by the Member State of issue, that the condition of residence laid down by Article 7(1)(b) of Directive 91/439 had not been satisfied."[1200]

In *Hoffmann* v. *Krieg*, concerning divorce and maintenance proceedings, the Court dealt with the consequences of the obligation to recognise when the second state was confronted with a new set of facts that made it impossible to comply with the obligation. Such an exceptional case might justify the public policy clause being invoked. The Court held:

"that a foreign judgment whose enforcement has been ordered in a contracting state pursuant to Article 31 of the Convention and which remains enforceable in the state

---

[1198]   Some of these questions could have been answered by the Convention on Driving Disqualifications, Convention of 17 June 1998, OJ 1998, C 216/2, as of 6 September 2008 ratified by Bulgaria, Cyprus, Romania, Slovakia and Spain. Given the developments in the case law on driving licences, it is doubtful whether it will ever enter into force. The mechanism provided in the Convention, though, seems to be more of a preventive nature than that of mutual recognition. The Convention provides a notification of a decision by the state of the offence imposing disqualification to the state of residence. However, this would only be of partial help. It would cover situations in which a driving licence holder can be found in a state of residence. It would not cover cases of driving licence holders who make use of their free movement rights and leave their state of residence and of those who apply for a new driving licence in a third Member State.

[1199]   29 April 2004, Case C-476/01, *criminal proceedings against Felix Kapper* [2004] ECR I-5205; 6 April 2006, Case C-227/05, *Halbritter* v. *Freistaat Bayern* [2006] ECR I-49; 28 September 2006, Case C-340/05, *criminal proceedings against Stefan Kremer* [2006] ECR I-98.

[1200]   26 June 2008, Joined Cases C-329/06 and C-343/06, *Arthur Wiedemann (C-329/06)* v. *Land Baden-Württemberg and Peter Funk (C-334/06)* v. *Stadt Chemnitz* [2008] ECR not yet reported, par. 72; 26 June 2008, Joined Cases C-334/06 to C-336/06, *Matthias Zerche (C-334/06), Manfred Seuke (C-336/06)* v. *Landkreis Mittweida and Steffen Schubert (C-335/06)* v. *Landkreis Mittlerer Erzgebirgskreis* [2008] ECR not yet reported, par. 69. See, also, 11 December 2003, Case C-408/02, *criminal proceedings against José Antonio da Silva Carvalho*, not reported in the ECR; Opinion of 17 July 2008 of Advocate General Bot, Case C-1/07, *Staatsanwaltschaft Siegen* v. *Frank Weber* ECR not yet reported; 3 July 2008, C-225/07, *criminal proceedings against Rainer Günther Möginger* [2008] ECR not yet reported.

in which it was given must not continue to be enforced in the state where enforcement is sought when, under the law of the latter state, it ceases to be enforceable for reasons which are outside the scope of the Convention."[1201]

In the process of mutual recognition, Member States are not required to do the impossible. In the case in question, there were two judgments from two different states which had legal consequences which were mutually exclusive.[1202]

It is not difficult to imagine competing decisions in a purely criminal setting. A decision to seize the goods of one Member State may conflict with a decision by a court of another Member State to return the goods to a third party. A European Arrest Warrant issued by one Member State may conflict with an order to execute a judgment by another. Although some Framework Decisions provide for rules on competing decisions,[1203] not all problems can be solved. The observation must be made that, for both examples of a non-criminal nature, to wit, driving licences and civil judgments, the act that stipulates mutual recognition *also* determines rules of jurisdiction. Both acts aim to create exclusive jurisdiction for only one Member State. In the case of driving licences, only the Member State of residence is competent to issue a driving licence. In the case of civil judgments, more complicated rules which determine jurisdiction apply. None of the legal instruments on mutual recognition in criminal matters provide rules on the allocation of jurisdiction. The complete absence of rules on jurisdiction in a criminal setting creates the possibilities for competing decisions. At the same time, it must also be acknowledged that the very fact that Union acts based upon the principle of mutual recognition in criminal law do not regulate jurisdiction would be an argument to deviate from absolute recognition. The claim for mutual recognition is stronger when it is based upon allocation of jurisdiction.

3.2.5. The Consequences of Mutual Recognition

Mutual recognition is not yet completely adapted to the needs of criminal law. It is, of course, possible to transfer a piece of evidence from one Member State to another, but it derives its existential status from the legal context in the first Member State. Requiring the second Member State to accept the evidence blindly could have a harmonising effect if the second Member State took no more than

---

[1201] 4 February 1988, Case 145/86, *Horst Ludwig Martin Hoffmann v. Adelheid Krieg* [1988] ECR 645, par. 18.

[1202] The Court followed Advocate General Darmon, who expressed in his interesting Opinion of 9 July 1987, Case 145/86, *Horst Ludwig Martin Hoffmann v. Adelheid Krieg* [1988] ECR 645, that the irreconcilability of judgments should be sought at the level of the legal effects which recognition of the judgment would produce in the state of enforcement.

[1203] For example, the grounds for refusal of Article 3 *Framework Decision 2002/584 on the European Arrest Warrant* and some of those mentioned in Article 4 regulate competing decisions.

just the first Member State into account. However, this is not the case: there are 25 other Member States, each with totally different formalities. Mutual recognition cannot contribute to harmonisation this way, but may even have the opposite effect: anarchy or a "wild west" scenario, in which *any* piece of evidence *must* be admitted as long as it comes from abroad.

The other fundamental difference with the Council of Europe's model is that EU co-operation begins to look decidedly egocentrically mandatory. The emergence of all manner of orders (arrest, evidence, execution) rides roughshod over consultation with other parties. The recognition of orders and pieces of evidence originating from 27 Member States may lead to a panoply of applicable rules, forms and differences of all kind. It undermines equal treatment, because the applicable standards differ with each piece. Thus, it seems that neither the Union, nor the Member States are keeping sight of the big picture. Union legal instruments do not require to look at the larger whole, but only at the needs of the requesting Member State. The interests of the requested state and those of the suspect or of the victims do not count. National law enforcement authorities only execute without being in a position to have any control or make any choices of prioritisation. Although the 9th recital of *Framework Decision 2006/783 on Confiscation Orders* states that mutual recognition pre-supposes confidence that decisions will be taken in compliance with the principles of legality, subsidiarity and proportionality, no mechanism has been put in place to safeguard these principles.

Is mutual recognition of criminal law products problematical, then? Firstly, it is important to consider the types of "products" to which it refers. These products may be an order for arrest and surrender, evidence or a judgment, but may also be legislation and competent authorities. Each of these products form a legal fiction which represents no economic value. The Italian order for arrest and surrender is, in a manner of speaking, composed solely of Italian legal rules. Without this composition and its Italian context, it would simply not exist. Context, is everything: who may issue an order, under what circumstances, and what legal consequences the order has. If such an order goes across the border, then (unlike the beer), it is no longer the same product; more to the point, it is no longer a product at all. It has become a legal fiction, lacking the context that it requires to exist. The product "Italian order" does not exist outside of Italy. Foreign law will prescribe other authorities, other circumstances and other legal consequences and modalities. In addition, most coercive measures are not taken on a "once for ever" decision. The necessity of provisional detention is tested regularly in view of the suspicion, the charge and the lapse of time. What mutual recognition does, is transform the Italian order into a Union order, to which effect must be given.

Mutual recognition in the internal market requires unconditional admission to the market. But there can be no such thing with regard to criminal law. This is not because the Member States in question would not want to help each other, but because there is no Italian product on the Slovenian market. The criminal law markets are not competitive markets but *state monopolies*, as are the other core tasks of the government: national administration, foreign policy and defence. The criminal law markets do not live by supply and demand and do not follow any economic law. Even more importantly, the product "criminal law" is, by definition, non-economic: it produces no durable goods or consumer goods, and it restricts trade commerce and the five freedoms by its very definition. These discrepancies make the using of economic concepts, in the absence of any conversion into criminal law terms, extremely difficult. This relates to the fact that the "product" in criminal proceedings will very often be the accused, a human being who is entitled to a catalogue of rights and freedoms which might oppose mutual recognition. A balance between all the rights and interests involved needs to be found.[1204]

At a more practical level, the consequences of the absence of a grand design behind mutual recognition also make themselves felt. The limited scope of the material acts to be recognised may make some instruments somewhat useless. Take, for example, *Framework Decision 2001/500 on Money Laundering*. This Framework Decision contains a "mutual recognition, without further questions" of decisions for freezing objects, modelled on the form of the European Arrest Warrant. Freezing, in this case, is intended to prevent the destruction, processing, relocation, transfer or alienation of objects which are subject to confiscation or which may serve as evidence. In so far as measures other than those for seizure are required (for example, searches or orders to hand over), which is extremely likely, these will fall outside of the scope of the order, and traditional international judicial assistance must be requested. This means that, along with the order based upon mutual recognition, a second request will have to be made. Whilst *Framework Decision 2003/577 on Freezing Orders* applies the principle of mutual recognition to orders freezing property and evidence, it is, in many situations, almost inevitable that other coercive measures will have to be performed. In most situations, private homes need to be entered and searched. Since these measures are not covered by the freezing order, they must be requested via the ordinary means of international judicial assistance. In addition, the results of the freezing order can also only be transmitted in accordance with the rules applicable to international assistance in criminal matters (Article 10, paragraph 2 *Framework Decision 2003/577 on Freezing Orders*). This has led to a situation in which two requests based upon different legal bases must be made, instead of one. This is impractical and explains why this Framework Decision is not often used in practice. By the same token, confiscation requires yet another request for

---

[1204]   See Chapter 9.

international judicial assistance. Whereas "in the old days" only one request was needed, now, the practice (requesting and requested parties) must strictly distinguish the element under which the request is being made, as well as the elements that fall outside of the scope of this request and thus require a different basis. One does not need to be a clairvoyant to predict that this will result in protracted head-scratching and error.

The Abuse of Mutual Recognition

The very fact that the contents of the list of offences can be influenced by individual Member States raises the question of whether a Member State can abuse mutual recognition. There is some concern that the system behind the list of offences may invite Member States to be creative with regard to the name tag of an offence. This might prove problematical in view of the proportionality of a surrender for a minor offence. Imagine the hypothetical example in which a Member State brings all its criminal offences under the overall crime of, for instance, sabotage. Formally, this would comply with the Framework Decision, which stipulates that the requirements under the law of the issuing Member State must be fulfilled. However, materially, this would be in conflict with the clear intention of the Framework decision to limit the abolition of the double criminality requirement and not remove that requirement completely.[1205] While the example given of a Member State bringing *all* its offences under a list-crime might remain theoretical, it is predictable that border-line discussions will arise. It is most likely that Member States, when legislating in criminal law, will also take the consequences of one label of a crime over the other for international co-operation into consideration. In other words, the mechanism of mutual recognition might influence the number of crimes that will qualify as list offences under national criminal law. The fact that the abuse of mutual recognition by individuals in driving licence cases led to a fair number of disputes must give rise to this expectation. These are situations by which the state which, or the individual who, has an interest in recognition is in a position to influence the substance of what ought to be recognised.

3.3. THE AVAILABILITY MODEL

A new mode of international co-operation has come into existence with the application of the principle of availability. This means that information contained by national law enforcement agencies is directly accessible in an automated manner for the law enforcement authorities of another Member State. The first

---

[1205]   Please note that the intention of the drafters might *not* prevail when the Court will interpret the meaning of an instrument. See Chapter 3, Section 5.3.

treaty to apply this principle was the Prüm Treaty, which was concluded between a limited number of Member States.[1206] These states have been successful in transposing some provisions from the treaty into *Decision 2008/615 on Stepping up Cross-border Cooperation*. The fourth recital of the Decision contains a good definition of the principle of availability:

> "This means that a law enforcement officer in one Member State of the Union who needs information in order to carry out his duties can obtain it from another Member State and that the law enforcement authorities in the Member State that holds this information will make it available for the declared purpose."

The availability model performs an on-line check in databases upon the basis of a comparison of DNA material, fingerprints and the like. The importance for investigatory purposes should not be under-estimated, because the requesting party determines unilaterally whether and when the comparison takes place. Article 1 *Decision 2008/615 on Stepping up Cross-border Cooperation* exhaustively mentions the areas for which on-line access will be available: automated transfer of DNA profiles, dactyloscopic (fingerprint) data and vehicle registration data; data in connection with major events; information to prevent terrorist offences; and the stepping up of cross-border police co-operation. Information obtained may be immediately used for investigatory purposes. The advantages of the system are obvious, it can work much quicker than the current system. Requests are not necessary, and there is no need to wait for an answer. The weaker point of the above-mentioned *Decision 2008/615 on Stepping up Cross-border Cooperation* is that of certainly data protection. Since the transfer of data is automated, no check of the conditions under which data are transferred is performed by the state offering the data. The availability model is vulnerable when it comes to the protection of the rights of the individuals whose data it transfers. Grounds for refusal no longer apply, and legal remedies are not provided.

3.4. VERTICAL CO-OPERATION

The bilateral cooperation discussed in this chapter predominantly deals with co-operation between states. This section, however, focuses on the bilateral co-operation between Member States and the Commission. While the co-operation between the authorities of the Member States is called horizontal co-operation, which expresses their equality, the co-operation between national authorities and the Commission is defined as vertical co-operation. There is an element of hierarchy involved in this form of co-operation, to the extent that the Commission

---

[1206] The Treaty is also referred to as Schengen-II or SIS-II. See, further, Chapter 3, Section 2.4.

is entitled to certain information and assistance upon the basis of specific legislation. In addition, the general supervising task of the Commission with regard to the enforcement of Union law entitles it to certain information and co-operation. If the Commission is not satisfied with the co-operation offered, it may bring a case before the Court for violation of the obligations under the Treaties.

In the context of this book, the area that leads to most vertical co-operation is EC fraud. Article 325 TFEU (formerly Article 280 TEC) creates a specific obligation for both the Union and the Member States to co-operate in combating fraud that affects the financial interests of the Union. Upon the basis of this treaty provision, Regulations have attributed additional powers to the Commission, as well as more obligations to assist each other mutually.

The OLAF-Regulation states that OLAF "shall provide the Member States with assistance from the Commission in organising close and regular cooperation between their competent authorities" (Article 1, paragraph 2). Member States must allow that Commission inspectors carry out on-the-spot checks and inspections and are to co-operate in these tasks (Articles 3 and 4 *Regulation 2185/96 Concerning on-the-spot Checks*). Officials of the Member States may participate or, if they wish, carry out the checks and inspections jointly with the Commission. If the Commission inspectors find, as a result of the on-the-spot checks or inspections, "any fact or suspicion relating to an irregularity", they are to report to the competent authorities of the Member States (Article 8, paragraph 2 *Regulation 2185/96 Concerning on-the-spot Checks*).

Provisions on the co-operation between the Commission and the Member States are rarely found in Conventions. Article 7 *Second Protocol Financial Interests Convention*, is among the few that mentions co-operation, which is "to make it easier to establish the facts and to ensure effective action against fraud, active and passive corruption and money laundering". Article 8 of the Protocol subjects the Commission to *Directive 95/46 on Data Protection*.[1207] Article 10 of the Protocol entitles the Commission, subject to the relevant conditions, to transfer data to other Member States and to third countries.[1208]

The emphasis of the co-operation discussed so far in this section has been on the assistance that has to be given to the Commission by the Member States. All these obligations must also be understood in the context of the Commission's task of supervising the respect for Union law. All Member States and institutions are obliged to give the Commission the relevant and requested information. However, a similar obligation exists for the Commission itself. The Court has held that the obligation to give assistance also exist for the Commission, when Member States

---

[1207] Article 15 gives the Court competences on any claim of infringements of Article 8 by the Commission.

[1208] For the rest, the Commission has been largely kept out of Third Pillar instruments.

authorities are enforcing Union law. This became apparent in the rather strange *Zwartveld* case. A Dutch examining magistrate, investigating a criminal charge relating to violations of national criminal provisions implementing Community legislation on fishing quotas, requested co-operation from the Commission. The request related *inter alia* to reports drawn up by the Commission regarding inspections in the Netherlands and the authorisation of its officials to be examined before the examining magistrate (*rechter-commissaris*). With reference to its privileges and immunities, the Commission refused to give the assistance requested. The Court held that *both* the Member States *and* the institutions are subject to the obligation of sincere co-operation:

> "This duty of sincere cooperation imposed on Community institutions is of particular importance vis-à-vis the judicial authorities of the Member States, who are responsible for ensuring that Community law is applied and respected in the national legal system."[1209]

The Court, however, left open the possibility of refusal by the Commission in two situations: the protection of the rights of third parties, or where the disclosure of the information would be capable of interfering with the functioning and independence of the Community.[1210]

The obligation to supply the Commission with information is almost absolute. In the case law of the Court, only temporary postponement because of other interests has been accepted, such as the fact that disclosure of the information might interfere with the functioning and independence of the criminal investigations. This could justify a refusal to supply the Commission with information.[1211] With regard to this, the Court held that:

> "Rules which in the national systems of criminal law prevent the communication to certain persons of documents in the criminal proceedings may therefore be relied upon against the Commission in so far as the same restrictions may be relied upon against the national authorities."[1212]

Thus, the Court pronounced itself contrary to the position of the Advocate General who opined that national rules on the confidentiality of criminal investigations may not be invoked against the Commission.[1213]

[1209]   13 July 1990 and 6 December 1990, Case C-2/88 Imm., *J.J. Zwartveld and others* [1990] ECR I-4405, par. 18.

[1210]   13 July 1990 and 6 December 1990, Case C-2/88 Imm., *J.J. Zwartveld and others* [1990] ECR I-4405, par. 18, par. 11.

[1211]   10 January 1980, Case 267/78, *Commission v. Italy* [1980] ECR 31.

[1212]   10 January 1980, Case 267/78, *Commission v. Italy* [1980] ECR 31, par. 22.

[1213]   See Opinion of Advocate General Warner of 7 November 1979, Case 267/78, *Commission v. Italy* [1980] ECR 31.

4.   FORMS OF INTERNATIONAL CO-OPERATION

The previous section described the underlying principles of the three existing models of co-operation. In this section, an overview will be given of all the concrete material acts of co-operation which exist in the *acquis* of the European Union. The intention here is not to deal in depth with practical issues with limited dimensions,[1214] but to focus attention on the legal issues that relate to co-operation. The emphasis is on the particularities of co-operation within in the European Union, not on describing the existing mechanisms of the Council of Europe. Consecutively, mutual assistance, the supervision of pre-trial orders, the transfer of proceedings, and the extradition and the transfer of the execution of judgments are dealt with.

4.1.   MUTUAL ASSISTANCE

By and large, mutual assistance concerns, in terms of the numbers of requests and responses, the most voluminous form of international co-operation within the European Union, as well as elsewhere. The various acts can be categorised as aiming at the following six purposes: the exchange of information; the collection of evidence; the facilitation of the proceedings; serving the interests of third parties; the building of skills and expertise; and, the building of liaisons.

4.1.1. *The Exchange of Information*

A general obligation to assist each other has been provided for police authorities in Article 39 *CISA*. Paragraph 2 of Article 39 *CISA* provides a common rule with regard to the use of information as evidence. This may only take place with the consent of the judicial authorities. Exchange of information may also take place in the preventive stage, as a form of spontaneous information (Article 7 *EU Mutual Assistance Convention* and Article 46 *CISA*): "any information which may be important in helping to combat future crime and prevent offences against or threats to public policy and public security."[1215] With regard to the maintenance of law and order relating to events at which sizeable groups may participate, Member States may inform each other on the groups and their composition.[1216] An obligation to inform spontaneously both other Member States and the

---

[1214]   Such as the way the request is transmitted. This may vary from instrument to instrument and can easily be found in the respective instrument.

[1215]   See, also, Articles 15–18 *Convention on Mutual Assistance between Customs Administrations*.

[1216]   Joint Action of 26 May 1997 with regard to cooperation on law and order and security, OJ 1997, L 147/1. See, also, *Decision 2008/615 on Stepping up Cross-border Cooperation*.

Commission of the actual commission of an offence or of the risk of the commission of such an offence which causes, or is likely to cause, imminent pollution, is stipulated in Article 8, paragraph *Framework Decision 2005/667 on Ship-source Pollution.*

Various instruments exist which refer to the exchange of a particular type of information. Examples include information on bank accounts, transactions and the like (Articles 1–5 *Protocol to the EU Mutual Assistance Convention*), or the exchange of information on genocide, crimes against humanity and war crimes.[1217] Upon the basis of a specific Decision information from criminal records can be exchanged.[1218] *Decision 2008/615 on Stepping up Cross-border Cooperation,* which provides assistance upon the basis of the principle of availability has already been mentioned. It enables Member States to consult their respective databases on-line. The data to which this relates include DNA-data, dactyloscopical data, and vehicle registration data. No topic has led to the adoption of so many instruments as the combating of terrorism. The vast majority of these instruments do no more than recalling the importance of adequate and prompt exchange of information, or draw attention to a specific technique to be used. There are also instruments that relate to the combating of the financing of terrorist groups.[1219]

Data Protection

Mutual assistance relates to very sensitive information, and may infringe upon the right to privacy.[1220] Most European Union instruments demonstrate the concern that co-operation must be subject to the data protection rules.[1221] Article 23 *EU Mutual Assistance Convention,* for instance, formulates criteria for the use and communication of personal data. Similarly, Article 25 *Convention on Mutual Assistance between Customs Administrations* obliges Member States to comply

---

1217   Decision 2003/335 of 8 May 2003 on the investigation and prosecution of genocide, crimes against humanity and war crimes, OJ 2003, L 118/12.

1218   See Decision 2005/876 of 21 November 2005 on the exchange of information extracted from the criminal record, OJ 2005, L 322/33. This is also stipulated in Article 13 *1959 European Convention on Mutual Assistance in Criminal Matters.* Upon the basis of the principle of availability, the Commission proposed a Decision on the establishment of a European Criminal Record Information System, COM(2008) 332, 27 May 2008.

1219   Recommendation of 9 December 1999 on Cooperation in Combating the Financing of Terrorist Groups, OJ 1999, C 373/1.

1220   Declaration No. 21 on Protection of Personal Data in the Fields of Judicial Cooperation in Criminal Matters and Police Cooperation: "The Conference acknowledges that specific rules on the protection of personal data and the free movement of such data in the fields of judicial cooperation in criminal matters and police cooperation based on Article 16 of the Treaty on the Functioning of the European Union may prove necessary because of the specific nature of these fields".

1221   The Council is discussing a Proposal for a Framework Decision on the Protection of Personal Data Processed in the Framework of Police and Judicial Cooperation in Criminal Matters, Council Document 23 October 2007, 14119/07 LIMITE.

with the requirements of data protection. Article 25 refers to the respect that Member States must pay to the Council of Europe Convention of 28 January 1981 for the protection of individuals with regard to automatic processing of personal data. The obligation for Member States to fulfil their obligations does not depend upon this Convention being mentioned in an EU instrument, but is called to life by that state's own ratification of the 1981 Convention.

4.1.2. The Collection of Evidence

Upon the basis of the general provision of Article 3 *1959 European Convention on Mutual Assistance in Criminal Matters*, all sorts of evidence may be procured. This may relate to the hearing of witnesses or experts, for which Article 10 *EU Mutual Assistance Convention* provides for the hearing by video conference. The temporary transfer of a detained person to another Member State is provided for in Article 11 *1959 European Convention on Mutual Assistance in Criminal Matters*. It is, however, limited to witnesses, but Article 9 *EU Mutual Assistance Convention* extends these possibilities to any person held in custody, which includes the accused.

Evidence may be frozen or seized upon the basis of *Framework Decision 2003/577 on Freezing Orders*. The executing Member State must execute "without any further formality be[ing] required" (Article 5, paragraph 1, same *Framework Decision*). The issuing Member State may indicate the formalities and procedures that will be conducive to the taking of valid evidence (Article 5, paragraph 2, same *Framework Decision*). The freezing of property which constitutes the proceeds or the instrumentalities of crime may also be ordered. The freezing order will facilitate subsequent confiscation of this property. The property remains frozen until a request for confiscation has been made (Articles 6 and 10, same *Framework Decision*). In addition, Article 29 *Framework Decision 2002/584 on the European Arrest Warrant* provides that property which may be used as evidence, or may be subject to confiscation or seizure, may be handed over.

On the model of *Framework Decision 2002/584 on the European Arrest Warrant*, a Framework Decision on the European Evidence Warrant is being negotiated.[1222] This proposal relates to existing evidence, objects, documents and information which may subject to a warrant. Similar to the European Arrest Warrant, the issuing Member State orders the executing Member State to provide

---

[1222]   Framework Decision on the European Evidence Warrant, Council Document 13076/07, 21 December 2007. A new request for consultation of the European Parliament has been send on 10 July 2008. See Council Document 11725/08.

it with the requested evidence. The proposed warrant is not intended to be used to gather fresh evidence.[1223]

The interception of telecommunications is provided in Articles 17–21 *EU Mutual Assistance Convention*, in which all modalities created by modern techniques of telecommunication have been taken into consideration. While with wired telecommunications not that many States might be involved in the request, things are rather complicated with wireless connections. For instance, the user of a mobile phone on the Greek network might be in Italy and take up a satellite connection with a person using a German network in the United Kingdom. Thus, a simple international phone call might easily involve four or five states. Neither classical requests for assistance, nor modern EU-orders to execute will be able to meet all the necessary requests on a bilateral basis.

Thus, it is especially for the police and customs authorities that cross-border surveillance, covert investigation, controlled deliveries and *joint investigation teams* have been regulated.[1224]

Article 40 *CISA* allows the officers of one state who are keeping a person under surveillance to continue their surveillance on the territory of another state.[1225] Two situations are provided for: the first is on request and after authorisation;[1226] the second is without prior request and authorisation.[1227] In the second – and urgent – case, the officers must inform the local authorities immediately. Further conditions are stipulated in Article 40 for both situations. From the conditions, as well as from its twin provision on hot pursuit (Article 41 *CISA*), it is clear that this cross-border competence is designed to fill a factual *lacuna* in law enforcement. Although, in principle, the local authorities are competent – because of the fact that they are not there – foreign authorities may act because, because, if they did not, evidence would get lost or the suspect might abscond. The fact that the cross-border observation must cease after five hours (Article 40, paragraph 2 *CISA*) or if the local authorities so request, is evidence of this. Foreign officers may not enter private homes or carry out any other coercive measures.

[1223]   Since the Framework Decision has not been adopted and published in the Official Journal, it has refrained from further discussing the proposal.

[1224]   This is regulated in Article 13 *EU Mutual Assistance Convention* and will be dealt with further in Chapter 8, Section 2.1.3. The joint investigation teams should be distinguished from the joint patrols and other joint operations regulated in *Decision 2008/615 on Stepping up Cross-border Cooperation*. The latter have a clear preventive function.

[1225]   Article 21 *Convention on Mutual Assistance between Customs Administrations* stipulates the same for customs officials.

[1226]   Since the replacement of the extradition conventions by *Framework Decision 2002/584 on the European Arrest Warrant*, the condition of "extraditable offence" must also be interpreted as an "offence giving rise to surrender".

[1227]   Article 40, paragraph 7 limits this competence to a list of crimes. Article 40, paragraphs 1 and 7 *CISA* have been amended by Council Decision of 2 October 2003 amending the provisions of Article 40 (1) and (7) of the Convention implementing the Schengen Agreement of 14 June 1985 on the gradual abolition of checks at common borders, OJ 2003, L 260/37.

By a *covert investigation*, officers may act under cover of a false identity.[1228] The *controlled delivery* is regulated in Article 12 *EU Mutual Assistance Convention*.[1229] With this form of co-operation law enforcement officials try to follow the path of transportation and the delivery of a certain criminal activity, for instance, trafficking in illegal drugs or stolen goods.

4.1.3. The Facilitation of Criminal Proceedings

Article 5 *EU Mutual Assistance Convention* regulates the sending and service of procedural documents. This may take place without the involvement of the authorities of the Member States of the addressee. In addition, Articles 7–10 *1959 European Convention on Mutual Assistance in Criminal Matters* remain applicable for more complicated cases. The temporary transfer of the accused may take place upon the basis of Articles 18 and 19 *Framework Decision 2002/584 on the European Arrest Warrant*, which will enable the accused to make use of his right to be present during his trial.

The *cross border pursuit* is a form of co-operation that aims at apprehending a suspect or the accused who tries to abscond by making use of the border. Article 41 *CISA* entitles the law enforcement authorities of one state who are already pursuing an individual in their own country to continue the pursuit on the territory of another state.[1230] The pursuit relates to individuals caught in the act or those who have escaped from detention. The pursuing officers may detain the person until the local authorities arrive on the spot (Article 41, paragraph 2 *CISA*). This competence may be used for offences mentioned on the list of paragraph 4, as well as for extraditable offences.[1231]

4.1.4. Serving the Interests of Third Parties

Restitution of articles to *bona fide* third parties has been regulated in Article 8 *EU Mutual Assistance Convention*. *Directive 2004/80 on Crime Victims* entitles victims to apply for compensation in the Member State of residence.[1232] The Member State of residence must co-operate with the Member State in which the

---

[1228] See Article 14 *EU Mutual Assistance Convention* and Article 23 *Convention on Mutual Assistance between Customs Administrations*.

[1229] Article 2, paragraph 2 *EU Mutual Assistance Convention* repealed the earlier provision of this kind of Article 73 *CISA*. Article 22 *Convention on Mutual Assistance between Customs Administrations* provides this form of co-operation for customs authorities.

[1230] Article 20 *Convention on Mutual Assistance between Customs Administrations* stipulates the same for customs officers.

[1231] Since the replacement of the extradition conventions by *Framework Decision 2002/584 on the European arrest warrant*, the condition of "extraditable offence" must also be interpreted as an "offence giving rise to surrender".

[1232] *Directive 2004/80 on Crime Victims*. See, further, Chapter 5, Section 7.

crime was committed in order to facilitate access to compensation. Furthermore, the *Framework Decision 2001/220 on the Standing of Victims* provides for a whole series of measures that should protect the interests of victims. Article 12 of that Framework Decision obliges Member States to "foster, develop and improve co-operation between the Member States". Other instruments focus on the protection of witnesses in the fight against organised crime.[1233]

4.1.5. The Building of Skills and Expertise

Joint Action 96/747 of 29 November 1996 regulates the creation and maintenance of a directory of specialised competences, skills and expertise in the fight against organised crime.[1234] Joint Action 96/699 further intends to establish a cohesive mechanism for the transmission and dissemination of the results of drug profiling in the Member States.[1235]

4.1.6. The Building of Liaisons

The secondment of *liaison officers* to the authorities of another Member State serves the purpose of facilitating co-operation and the building of trust among the authorities. A liaison officer must establish and maintain direct contact with the competent authorities in the host state. Article 47 *CISA* mandates States to conclude bilateral agreements on this.[1236] Joint Action 96/602 has established a reference framework for the development of concerted initiatives regarding liaison officers.[1237] Decision 2003/170 further specifies the use of liaison officers, with specific attention to the common use of liaison officers in third states.[1238]

Similar to the framework for liaison officers, Joint Action 96/277 concerning a framework for the exchange of *liaison magistrates* to improve judicial co-operation between the Member States of the European Union[1239] serves the

---

[1233]   Resolution of 23 November 1995 calls on Member States to facilitate assistance in this field, OJ 1995, C 327/5; See, also, Resolution of 20 December 1996 on individuals who cooperate with the judicial process in the fight against international organized crime, OJ 1997, C 10/1.

[1234]   OJ 1996, L 342/2; Joint Action 96/610 of 15 October 1996 concerning the creation and maintenance of a Directory of Specialized Counter-terrorist Competences, Skills and Expertise to Facilitate Counter-terrorist Cooperation between the Member States of the European Union, OJ 1996, L 273/1.

[1235]   Joint Action 96/699 of 29 November 1996 concerning the exchange of information on the chemical profiling of drugs to facilitate improved co-operation between Member States in combating illicit drug trafficking, OJ 1996, L 322/5.

[1236]   See, also, Article 6 *Convention on Mutual Assistance between Customs Administrations*.

[1237]   Joint Action 96/602 of 14 October 1996 providing for a common framework for the initiatives of the Member States concerning liaison officers, OJ 1996, L 268/2.

[1238]   Decision 2003/170 of 27 February 2003 on the common use of liaison officers posted abroad by the law enforcement agencies of the Member States, OJ 2003, L 67/27.

[1239]   OJ 1996, L 105/1.

aim of increasing the speed and effectiveness of judicial co-operation by encouraging and accelerating all forms of judicial co-operation in criminal matters. Due to their knowledge of both the law and the language of both Member State, they can be of valuable assistance in formulating successful requests and addressing it to the competent authority.

The lines of communication in all the modalities described above are bilateral, as every Member State communicates with other individual Member States. No centralisation takes place.

Lines of communication between a limited number of five Member States

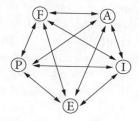

4.2. EUROPEAN SUPERVISION ORDER IN PRE-TRIAL PROCEDURES

The supervision of the compliance with the conditions for the release of the accused awaiting trial is difficult to realise for Member States outside their own borders. The Union is aware of this *lacuna* in international co-operation. The proposal of the Commission for a Framework Decision on the European Supervision Order in pre-trial procedures between the Member States of the European Union tries to fill this gap. It should establish a mechanism to report on non-compliance, which will be followed by a surrender to the Member State that conducts the criminal proceedings against the accused.[1240] It is unclear whether, and if so, when this legal instrument will be adopted.

4.3. THE TRANSFER OF PROCEEDINGS, THE SOLVING OF CONFLICTS OF JURISDICTION AND THE CONCENTRATION OF PROCEEDINGS

By transferring the proceedings, a state transfers its right to prosecute to another state. The latter subsequently has the exclusive right to deal with the case. It may convict, acquit or dismiss the case. Whatever it does, the transferring state has to

---

[1240]   Brussels 29.8.2006, COM(2006) 468 final.

recognise the decision. For a long time, the 1972 European Convention on Transfer of Proceedings was one of the most unpopular Conventions of the Council of Europe among the Member States of the European Union. With the enlargement of the European Union, the number of ratifications by Member States has increased, but some of the older Member States, in particular, are not a party to it. Whilst paying attention to the interest of the states that have jurisdiction, as well as to the accused, the victims, and the witnesses, the Convention provides for a consultation procedure in cases of plurality of criminal proceedings (Articles 30–34). The Convention further provides for *ne bis in idem* protection, and a rather broad recognition of foreign decisions after transfer. That this was a serious impediment to ratification is apparent from the attempt in the 1990s to adopt an Agreement between the Member States of the European Communities on the Transfer of Proceedings in Criminal Matters.[1241] This EC Convention did not require the absolute recognition provided in the Council of Europe Convention. In particular, it left more freedom for the requesting state to re-start proceedings in cases of discontinuance in the requested state. However, it never entered into force.

Given the developments in the European Union, the question of whether the objections to transfer of proceedings that were valid in the 1970s, 1980s and even in the 1990s are still applicable in the broad mechanism of mutual recognition of all kinds of criminal decisions is justified. Article 54 *CISA* now imposes upon the Member States an obligation to recognise foreign decisions, even if the result would have been different under their own law. The advantage of transfer of proceedings is that it may, unlike mutual recognition, take more interests involved into consideration than those of the requesting state alone.

Despite the absence of a generally applicable instrument governing the transfer of proceedings,[1242] some Union acts do refer to consultation which may result in a transfer of proceedings. Article 9, paragraph 2 *Framework Decision 2002/475 on Combating Terrorism* obliges Member States, in cases of a positive conflict of jurisdiction, to co-operate:

> "in order to decide which of them will prosecute the offender with the aim, if possible, of centralising proceedings in a single Member State. To this end, the Member States

---

1241   Agreement of 6 November 1990, apparently never published in the OJ.

1242   Although paragraph 49 (of the 1998 Action Plan of the Council and the Commission on how best to implement the provisions of the Treaty of Amsterdam on an area of freedom, security and justice, OJ 1997, C 19/1) mentions that "the feasibility of improved crossborder cooperation on the transfer of proceedings" should be examined, no initiative has become apparent. See, also, Resolution of 29 November 1996 on measures to address the drug tourism problem within the European Union, which under 2 sub (d) stimulates Member States "to make the operation of the transfer of proceedings as flexible and efficient as practicable so that, where this procedure is available to a Member State, it can be used effectively, to deal with a large number of relatively small offences". (OJ 1996, C 375/3).

may have recourse to any body or mechanism established within the European Union in order to facilitate cooperation between their judicial authorities and the coordination of their action."[1243]

This cryptic reference aims at Eurojust.[1244]

A special mechanism of co-ordination and periodic meetings was set up with regard to genocide, crimes against humanity and war crimes.[1245] For all these international crimes, there is, by definition, multiple jurisdiction; both for the Member States as well as for international criminal tribunals. Upon the basis of Article 5 of the above-mentioned Decision, the contact points for these crimes are to meet at regular intervals in order to co-ordinate ongoing efforts to investigate and to prosecute. These meetings may take place with representatives of the International Criminal Tribunal for the former Yugoslavia, the International Criminal Tribunal for Rwanda, the International Criminal Court and other relevant international bodies.

Article 7 *Framework Decision 2002/946 on Unauthorised Entry* entails an obligation that facilitates the transfer of proceedings. Member States are mutually obliged to inform each other of breaches of the law on the entry and residence of aliens in another Member State. Paragraph 2 of that Article stipulates that:

"Any Member State which requests another Member State to prosecute, on the grounds of a breach of its own laws on the entry and residence of aliens, infringements referred to in Article 1 (1) must specify, by means of an official report or a certificate from the competent authorities, the provisions of its law which have been breached."

Article 6, paragraph 2 *Financial Interests Convention* specifically calls for consultations in cases in which more than one Member State has jurisdiction:

"Member States involved shall cooperate in deciding which shall prosecute the offender or offenders with a view to centralizing the prosecution in a single Member State where possible."

An obligation to consult each other is found in Article 4 *Joint Action 98/733 on Participation in a Criminal Organisation*:

[1243] The Framework Decision further provides a ranking of jurisdictional principles. See Chapter 4, Section 3.2.

[1244] See, further, Chapter 8, Section 2.2.

[1245] Decision 2003/335 of 8 May 2003 on the investigation and prosecution of genocide, crimes against humanity and war crimes, OJ 2003, L 118/12.

"with a view to co-ordinating their action in order to prosecute effectively, taking account, in particular, of the location of the organisation's different components in the territory of the Member State concerned."[1246]

Article 7, paragraph 3 *Framework Decision 2000/383 on the Introduction of the Euro* is slightly more precise:

"Where more than one Member State has jurisdiction and has the possibility of viable prosecution of an offence based on the same facts, the Member States involved shall cooperate in deciding which Member State shall prosecute the offender or offenders with a view to centralising the prosecution in a single Member State where possible."

The solving of (possible) conflicts of jurisdiction by consultations was discussed above. Another way of solving, but not of preventing, conflicts of jurisdiction is by identifying a *ranking of jurisdictional principles*.[1247] However, a priority of jurisdictional principles can only be found in *Framework Decision 2002/475 on Combating Terrorism* and *Framework Decision 2005/222 on Attacks against Information Systems*.[1248] Article 9, paragraph 2 *Framework Decision 2002/475 on Combating Terrorism* creates a "sequential account" of factors to be taken into consideration when an offence falls within the jurisdiction of more than one Member State. The order presented is the following:

– the Member State in which territory the acts were committed;[1249]
– the Member State of which the perpetrator is a national or resident;
– the Member State of origin of the victims;
– the Member State in which the perpetrator was found.[1250]

In all the other instruments, the hierarchy between jurisdictional principles and the consequences thereof for a concentration of the proceedings is only discussed in an implicit way. Some instruments, for instance, give a certain discretion to Member States not to recognise foreign judgments relating to facts that occurred

---

[1246]   More or less, the same as in Article 10 *Framework Decision 2001/413 on Combating Fraud*.
[1247]   See, on principles of jurisdiction, Chapter 4, Section 3.2.
[1248]   See Article 10, paragraph 4, which is slightly different from Article 9, paragraph 2 *Framework Decision 2002/475 on Combating Terrorism*.
[1249]   The optional ground for non-execution of a European Arrest Warrant that the executing Member State regards the offence "as having been committed in whole or in part in the territory of the executing Member State or in a place treated as such" (Article 4, par. 7 *Framework Decision 2002/584 on the European Arrest Warrant*), must be regarded as underlining the predominance of the principle of territoriality. This is further substantiated by Article 55 CISA.
[1250]   A completely different but non sequential list of factors is found in Article 7, paragraph 5 *Framework Decision 2005/667 on Ship-source Pollution*.

on its own territory. This implies that territorial jurisdiction is regarded as stronger than extra-territorial jurisdiction.[1251]

The absence of a coherent approach to solving or reducing conflicts of jurisdiction is striking. A half-hearted attempt was made by the Commission in 2005, when it issued a Green Paper on Conflicts of Jurisdiction and the Principle of *ne bis in idem* in Criminal Proceedings.[1252] However, the proposal of the Commission did not entail any proposal on the reduction of conflicts of jurisdiction, but focused on solving the consequences of overlapping jurisdiction. The Commission gave no evidence that it regarded the area of freedom, security and justice as an area with a common European interest in combating crime. Thus, its behaviour strengthens the national claims for jurisdiction and stimulates the view that law enforcement is a purely national task. However, with a more modern approach regarding crime as a Union problem, one could also develop a system of allocation of European criminal jurisdiction to national criminal courts.[1253]

In this sense, the transfer of proceedings is certainly not a form of assistance that is alien to Union law. On the contrary, not only is there fragmentary Union legislation that calls for transfer of proceedings,[1254] there is also case law that underlines the concept that combating crime is a joint responsibility of the Member States. Moreover, a Member State may also fulfil its enforcement obligation by transferring proceedings to another Member State.[1255] However, it must be admitted that upgrading the transfer of proceedings also requires re-thinking of mutual recognition.[1256]

[1251]   See, for instance, Article 7 *Financial Interests Convention*; Article 10 *Corruption Convention*. In addition, the fact that the crime for which the requested person is sought is committed on the territory of the executing Member State is a optional ground for refusal of a European Arrest Warrant. See Article 4, paragraph 1 (7) *Framework Decision 2002/584 on the European Arrest Warrant*.

[1252]   COM(2005)696 of 23.12.2005.

[1253]   In civil law, *Regulation 44/2001 on Jurisdiction and Recognition of Civil Judgments* has allocated jurisdiction. The Court has recognised "that the courts of the Member States in which the defendant is domiciled are to have jurisdiction, constitutes the general principle". See 11 October 2007, Case C-98/06, *Freeport plc v. Olle Arnoldsson* [2007] ECR I-8319, par. 34.

[1254]   Article 31, paragraph 4 *Regulation 2847/93 establishing a Control System applicable to the Common Fisheries Policy* reads: "The provisions of this Article shall not prevent the Member State of landing or transshipment from transferring prosecution of an infringement to the competent authorities of the Member State of registration with the agreement of the latter and on condition that the transfer is more likely to achieve the result referred to in paragraph 2. The Commission shall be notified of any such transfer by the Member State of landing or transshipment".

[1255]   27 March 1990, Case C-9/89, *Spain v. Council* [1990] ECR I-1383, par. 24 and 31.

[1256]   See, further, Chapter 9, Section 5.

4.4. EXTRADITION OR SURRENDER OF PERSONS

Extradition is the assistance that states offer each other in order to surrender the accused or convicted person. The extradition of the accused will be followed by criminal proceedings in the requesting state, while that of a convicted person will lead to the execution of the judgment. Although *Framework Decision 2002/584 on the European Arrest Warrant* uses the term "surrender" instead of "extradition", the material act of surrender is no different from that of extradition. The requested person is arrested by the authorities of the requested state and brought to the custody of the authorities of the requesting state. This is not to say that there are no differences between surrender and extradition, but these relate to the conditions under which it may take place and the procedures to be followed, and not to the material act as such. Indeed, the use of the word "extradition" for the assistance given under *Framework Decision 2002/584 on the European Arrest Warrant* came in for criticism from Advocate General Ruiz-Jarabo Colomer, who argued, with reference to the new structure of assistance, which is not between hermetically sealed spaces but with someone with whom one shares principles, values and objectives, that extradition and surrender are something completely different.[1257]

The set of extradition treaties created by the Council of Europe is impressive. However, for the relations between the Member States, it has been completely replaced by *Framework Decision 2002/584 on the European Arrest Warrant*. Notwithstanding this, the *European Convention on Extradition* and its supplementary treaties remain the main basis for extradition for Member States with states that do not belong to the EU. Article 31 of the same *Framework Decision* stipulates that the Framework Decision is to replace the *European Convention on Extradition* and its two Protocols, as well as the 1977 *European Convention on the Suppression of Terrorism*, concluded under the *aegis* of the Council of Europe. Article 31 *Framework Decision 2002/584 on the European Arrest Warrant* also stipulates that it is to replace three EU Conventions on extradition.[1258] Article 31 of the same *Framework Decision* further replaces the provisions on extradition in the *CISA* (Articles 59–66).[1259]

[1257] Opinion of Advocate General Ruiz-Jarabo Colomer of 12 September 2006, Case C-303/05, *Advocaten voor de Wereld VZW* v. *Leden van de Ministerraad*, [2007] ECR I-3633, points 38–47.

[1258] Agreement of 26 May 1989 between the Member States of the European Communities on the simplification and modernisation of methods of transmitting extradition requests; Convention of 10 March 1995 on simplified extradition procedure between the Member States of the European Union, OJ 1995, C 78/2; Convention of 27 September 1996 relating to extradition between the Member State of the European Union, OJ 1996, C 313/11.

[1259] The old extradition scheme may exceptionally be used in the situations which fall under Article 32 *Framework Decision 2002/584 on the European Arrest Warrant*. See, for instance, 12 August

Extradition between the Member States of the European Union now takes place exclusively upon the basis of the *Framework Decision 2002/584 on the European Arrest Warrant*. The features of this mechanism were extensively dealt with in Section 3.2. on Mutual recognition. *Framework Decision 2002/584 on the European Arrest Warrant* has been a model for other Framework Decisions and is based upon the principle of mutual recognition, as a consequence of which, the differences between the various forms of co-operation diminish. This sub-section further concentrates on those issues which are of particular interest to surrender.

For the offences which are not on the list, paragraph 4 of Article 2 *Framework Decision 2002/584 on the European Arrest Warrant* stipulates that they may be subject to the requirement of double criminality. The Member States themselves determine the competent authorities for surrender cases (Article 6 of the above-mentioned *Framework Decision*) or will designate a central authority (Article 7 of same). The transmission of the warrants takes place directly between the issuing and the executing authority (Articles 9 and 10 of same). The executing authority informs the requested person of the warrant and the possibility that he may consent to surrender (Article 11). The requested person is entitled to legal counsel and an interpreter (Article 11) and the executing authority may decide to keep the requested person in detention (Article 12).

In cases of consent to surrender by the requested person, the *rule of speciality* does not apply. This means that the person surrendered may also be prosecuted for cases other than that for which he was surrendered (Articles 13 and 27).[1260] In cases of consent, there will not be a further hearing, and the requested person will be surrendered within 10 days. In cases where there is no consent, the requested person will be heard (Article 14). A decision to surrender should be taken within 60 days of the arrest of the requested person (Article 17). Finally, in cases in which the requested person does not consent to surrender, the *rule of speciality* will be upheld.[1261]

2008, Case C-296/08 PPU, *Ignacio Pédro Santesteban Goicoechea* [2008] ECR not yet reported.

[1260]   Subsequent surrender or extradition to third states requires consent of the executing Member States on conditions provided for in Article 28 *Framework Decision 2002/584 on the European Arrest Warrant*.

[1261]   This rule was developed in extradition law (Article 14 *European Convention on Extradition*) and kept for surrender proceedings.

4.5. THE TRANSFER OF THE EXECUTION OF JUDGMENTS[1262]

By transferring the execution of a judgment, states accept that the execution of a sentence in one Member State will be performed by another state. The reasons for doing this relate both to efficiency and to the creation of better opportunities for the rehabilitation of the offender. A convicted person who has fled from the state of conviction complicates the execution of the sentence. In this sense, the transfer of the execution to the state where he resides serves the good administration of justice. On the other hand, if a foreigner, convicted in another Member State serves his sentence there, rehabilitation is much more complicated in a state of which he is not a national and of which he may not speak the language. The transfer of sentenced persons may bring a convicted person to his home state, to serve a sentence pronounced elsewhere.

The most popular convention of the Council of Europe on international co-operation in criminal matters is the 1983 Convention on the Transfer of Sentenced Persons. Its popularity may be due to the fact that it does not oblige states to co-operate, but only provides a framework if both states want to transfer. The Convention is applicable only on the condition that the convicted person gives his consent to be transferred to his home state.[1263] Article 68 *CISA* widens the application of this convention by allowing for a transfer of a judgment regarding "a national of another Contracting Party who, by escaping to the national's own country, has avoided the enforcement of that penalty".

Two instruments lay down the application of the principle of mutual recognition in the execution of judgments. *Framework Decision 2006/783 on Confiscation Orders* lays down the conditions under which confiscation orders

---

[1262]   Negotiations on a Framework Decision on the mutual recognition of criminal judgments have not come to a conclusion yet. Similar to extradition, it is aimed at a system that should fully replace this currently existing system of the transfer of the execution of judgments. Likewise talks on a Framework Decision on the recognition and supervision of suspended sentences and conditional sentences are pending at the time of concluding this book. See 9 November 2007, Council Document 14759/07 LIMITE.

[1263]   The Agreement of 25 May 1987 on the application among the Member States of the European Communities of the Council of Europe Convention on transfer of sentenced persons and the Convention of 13 November 1991 between the Member States of the European Communities on the enforcement of foreign criminal sentences never entered into force. A special EU convention on transfer of judgments, the Convention of 17 June 1998 on Driving Disqualifications, OJ 1998, C 216/2, never entered into force. See, further, Section 3.2.5 in this chapter. Article 293 TEC, that provided that Member States enter into negotiations with each other with a view to securing for the benefit of their nationals: "the simplification of formalities governing the reciprocal recognition and enforcement of judgments of courts or tribunals", has never been used for criminal judgments. In view of the mutual recognition for both civil judgments (Article 81 TFEU) and criminal judgments (Article 82 TFEU), the provision is repealed by the Treaty of Lisbon.

will be executed throughout the European Union. Article 2 of this *Framework Decision* defines the confiscation order as a "final penalty or measure imposed by a court following proceedings in relation to a criminal offence or offences resulting in the definitive deprivation of property". The other instrument is *Framework Decision 2005/214 on Financial Penalties.* The *Framework Decision* enables Member States to execute a financial penalty of 70 euro or more in another Member State, and the decision of the issuing Member State may relate to both a natural person as to a legal person. Article 10 *Framework Decision 2005/214 on Financial Penalties* allows for imprisonment or other alternative sanctions where it is not possible to enforce the decision. Following the case law of the Court on the question of whether duties could be imposed on illegally imported drugs, customs fines for drugs cannot be transferred.[1264]

There is little case law on the transfer of the execution of judgments. By a judgment of 8 October 1970, two Greek nationals were sentenced to imprisonment and ordered to pay customs duties and other charges for having illegally imported tobacco into Italy. More than 30 years later, the question arose before a Greek court as to whether the enforcement of the Italian decision fell under Directive 76/308.[1265] The Court considered the provisions of the Directive to be of a procedural character and held that:

> "the Directive is to be interpreted as applying to customs claims which arose in one Member State under an instrument issued by that State before that directive entered into force in the other Member State, where the requested authority is situated."[1266]

5. EXTRA-TERRITORIAL INVESTIGATIONS AND SELF-HELP

Both the Council of Europe and the European Union have, to a limited extent, created possibilities for law enforcement officials to operate on the territory of another Member State. Both organisations have followed the same underlying principles based upon international law. The rules on extra-territorial operations are relatively simply and transparent. There is a general prohibition to operate on the territory of another state, as it is regarded as a violation of sovereignty when law enforcement officials enter the territory of another state. However, there are

---

[1264]   Chapter 3, Section 4.8.

[1265]   Directive 76/308 of 15 March 1976 on mutual assistance for the recovery of claims resulting from operations forming part of the system of financing the European Agricultural Guidance and Guarantee Fund, and of the agricultural levies and customs duties, and in respect of value added tax and certain excise duties.

[1266]   1 July 2004, Joined Cases C-361/02 and C-362/02, *Elliniko Dimisio* v. *Nikolaos Tsapalos (C-361/02), Konstantinos Diamantakis (C-362/02)* [2004] ECR I-6405, par. 23.

two exceptions which are fully in line with these sovereignty concerns. Firstly, states may agree to a general permission for certain operations and stipulate this in an agreement. The second exception is that, in the absence of a permanent international legal basis that governs the matter, states may grant *ad hoc* permission. In the past, these powers were provided in emergency situations. The hot pursuit and cross border surveillance of Articles 40 and 41 *CISA* are examples of this. Foreign officials may act and cross the border because the local authorities are not there (yet). These provisions filled penal enforcement *lacunae* until the moment in which the local authorities could take over.

A new generation of extra-territorial investigations which does not relate to emergency situations, but which was constructed in relation to specific cross border crime, has emerged. The controlled delivery, covert investigation and joint investigation teams (Articles 12–14 *EU Mutual Assistance Convention*), are examples of this. These investigative techniques are tailored for the type of crime for which it is most likely that offences have been committed in more than one state, and where there is a common interest to investigate. The foreign officials function under the supervision of the local authorities.

Free Flow of Law Enforcement Officials?

It is interesting to see that, with regard to law enforcement, there is no European Union initiative on the horizon that would allow for the free entry of law enforcement officials from one Member State to another, allowing them free investigations. Such powers have been given, though, to officials of the Commission. In the context of their general supervisory task or following specific Regulations, they may conduct on-site or on-the-spot inspections. The parallel with the principles of the market has not been followed up in this respect. This is surprising, given the weight that has been given to all sorts of free movement of orders, judgments and attempts to subject existing evidence and information to the principle of availability.[1267] However, all these examples of free flow of criminal products do not relate to the operational powers of foreign law enforcement officers. This may change in the future. Article 89 TFEU now creates the possibility of laying down the conditions and the limitations under which judicial authorities and police authorities may operate in the territory of another Member State.

[1267]   See *Decision 2008/615 on Stepping up Cross-border Cooperation.*

6. THE POSITION OF THE DEFENCE IN CO-OPERATION IN CRIMINAL MATTERS

6.1. THE POSSIBILITIES OF REQUESTING INTERNATIONAL CO-OPERATION

Generally speaking, the defence has no standing at all when it comes to requesting international co-operation. This can be explained by the fact that co-operation in criminal matters has been developed over the years as a matter of comity between sovereign nations. In addition, it has been shaped according to the needs of the criminal procedure of civil law states. Evidence in civil law states is collected by state authorities, and a private party, such as the defence, does not have a leading role to play. Both the Conventions of the Council of Europe and the instruments adopted by the European Union presume that international co-operation is an exclusive task for state authorities, and that the instruments are designed exclusively for these purposes. The defence in criminal proceedings may request that the prosecution or the court issues means of international co-operation, but it cannot send out a request itself. The Court has held, with regard to administrative co-operation, that individuals have no right to request mutual assistance from the authorities, even when the individual cannot obtain the evidence by himself.[1268] There is no obligation for the authorities of Member States to assist the defence in this respect.

This may be slightly different under national law in the few common law states which are members of the European Union, as, in common law states, the collection of evidence is a task for both parties, which have an equal position. Despite the fact that this may be so, within a national setting and within the national borders, there is no evidence that common law states have been able to grant the defence an independent position to request international co-operation in any of the instruments of the Council of Europe or of the European Union.

The only instrument that offers a convicted person the possibility of expressing his wish to be transferred to another state is the 1983 Convention on the Tranfer of Sentenced Prisoners, by which a convicted person can express this wish to the authorities of both the sentencing state and the state of which he is a national. However, there is no obligation for these states to comply with the wishes of the convicted person. Moreover, the opinion of the convicted person will become irrelevant when a new Framework Decision on the transfer of judgments has been adopted.

[1268] 27 September 2007, Case C-184/05, *Twoh International BV* v. *Staatssecretaris van Financiën* [2007] ECR I-7897, par. 30–34.

6.2. THE RIGHTS OF THE DEFENCE IN INTERNATIONAL CO-OPERATION

Despite the non-existent position of the defence in initiating international co-operation, described just above, some legal instruments do give the defence rights. These rights relate to the right to know the charge and to know of the procedure. Article 5, paragraph 3 *EU Mutual Assistance Convention* stipulates that:

> "Where there is reason to believe that the addressee does not understand the language in which the document is drawn up, the document, or at least the important passages thereof, must be translated into (one of) the language(s) of the Member State in the territory of which the addressee is staying. If the authority by which the procedural document was issued knows that the addressee understands only some other language, the document, or at least the important passages thereof, must be translated into that other language."

Articles 9–11 *EU Mutual Assistance Convention* may serve the interest of the defence.[1269] These articles deal with the temporary transfer of a detained person (Article 9), the hearing by video-conference (Article 10), and the hearing by telephone conference (Article 11). All of these modalities of international assistance may relate both to the accused as well as to witnesses and experts. Moreover, Article 10, paragraph 9 *EU Mutual Assistance Convention* and the Declaration attached to this convention both reiterate that the way they offer mutual assistance must respect the ECHR.

It is clear that these rights serve both the right to participate at the trial and the right to a fair trial as a whole. Furthermore, from the guarantee of a re-trial in cases of an *in absentia* conviction (*Framework Decision 2002/584 on the European Arrest Warrant*), it must be understood that the rule is "trial in the presence of the accused".

6.3. LEGAL REMEDIES AND THE RESPONSIBILITY OF CO-OPERATING MEMBER STATES

With reference to *Framework Decision 2002/584 on the European Arrest Warrant*, Advocate General Ruiz-Jarabo Colomer considered this to be "an example of a move towards cooperation in criminal matters which transcends the merely bilateral relationship between States and takes account of a third dimension,

---

[1269]   A right to be present at the execution of a request for assistance is stipulated in Article 4 *1959 European Convention on Mutual Assistance in Criminal Matters*.

namely, the rights of the individual concerned".[1270] Well, if there is one thing that is completely absent, it is a standing for the individual in surrender proceedings. It is mainly this abolition (less cynical commentators might say, "concentration") of legal remedies that has speeded up procedures. Most grounds for refusal which existed previously under the extradition scheme could be invoked by the requested person. A bilateral relationship no longer exists, nor does a three-dimensional one; the only thing in place is a unilateral determination of what ought to happen.

The introduction of mutual recognition in international co-operation has led to a severe reduction of legal remedies in the executing Member State (formerly the requested state). The almost absolute character of mutual recognition as well as the setting of time limits on its execution have led Member States to curtail legal remedies when executing on behalf of another Member State. In the implementation of *Framework Decision 2002/584 on the European Arrest Warrant*, for instance, Member States have abolished appeals. While concentration of legal remedies in the issuing Member State might, on the one hand, be a good thing, on the other hand, legal remedies might practically be inaccessible due to the distance of the relevant court in another Member State. The allocation of legal remedies is inconsistent and a bit confusing. Both *Framework Decision 2002/584 on the European Arrest Warrant* and *Framework Decision 2006/783 on Confiscation Orders* refer to legal remedies in the executing state. *Framework Decision 2003/577 on Freezing Orders* provides legal remedies in both the executing and issuing state. However, Article 11, paragraph 2 of that Framework Decision stipulates that:

> "The substantive reasons for issuing the freezing order can be challenged only in an action before a court in the issuing state."

All Framework Decisions on mutual recognition also apply to non-list offences. Whilst double criminality may be tested by the executing Member State and may lead to a refusal, the reduction of legal remedies also applies to the non-list offences. The legal remedies should be consistently allocated in order to maintain a transparent and predictable system, in compliance with the rule of law.

[1270]   Opinion of Advocate General Ruiz-Jarabo Colomer of 12 September 2006, Case C-303/05, *Advocaten voor de Wereld VZW* v. *Leden van de Ministerraad*, [2007] ECR I-3633, points 69.

6.4. HUMAN RIGHTS AND INTERNATIONAL CO-OPERATION IN CRIMINAL MATTERS

The development of international co-operation in criminal matters has resulted in a situation in which, in more and more criminal investigations, proceedings and executions of judgments, Member States offer each other assistance. Whereas, in 1950, the accused would be confronted with investigations and the collection of evidence in the trial state alone, almost 60 years later, in many serious criminal cases, the final criminal proceedings are the result of a collective effort of several Member States. This reversal of the responsibilities in criminal proceedings, from the exclusive responsibility of one state to shared responsibility with (an)other state(s) has not met with the corresponding protection under the ECHR. The ECtHR has continued to assess responsibilities under the ECHR in an exclusive relationship of one state versus an individual. This, however, no longer corresponds to the reality of many more serious criminal cases in the European Union, in which Member States co-operate and share responsibilities in investigation, conducting proceedings and execution.

The fact that international co-operation is increasingly used in criminal trials makes the direct application of human rights norms more difficult. For Member States, it might be unclear what their respective responsibility precisely is. The accused might be confronted with a situation in which he cannot invoke human rights norms because of the fact that the alleged violation relates to co-operation, where he *could* have invoked the human rights norms in each of the Member States involved, had every aspect of the criminal proceedings taken place within one state. These problems are highlighted in the cases in which evidence from Member States is necessary. The adjudicating state, which is responsible for the whole trial, defers one (or more) aspect(s) to the competence of another State, simply because the objects to be seized are not present in the adjudicating state or because the witness does not want to leave his state of residence.

Which state is responsible for a violation of the ECHR when a request for assistance is complied with? Firstly, the responsibilities of the adjudicating state will be examined. This state is responsible for the criminal trial, and subsequently for respecting the ECHR. Could this state be held responsible for the actions of the officials of another state directly? Direct responsibility for the adjudicating state only makes sense when this state has direct influence on the way in which foreign authorities respond to the request. However, requested states are quite free to decide in which manner to comply with a request for assistance. A direct responsibility for the adjudicating state is therefore limited to those actions in which it had direct influence.

Could the adjudicating state be held to be indirectly responsible for a violation of the ECHR at the execution of the request for assistance? The use of evidence obtained contrary to the provisions of the ECHR creates responsibilities under the ECHR. In a 1987 decision,[1271] the EComHR held:

> "Although this (the requesting state's) court was not responsible for the examination of C (the witness), on commission it is, in principle, conceivable that the use of the evidence thereby obtained could be contrary to that (Article 6 paragraph 1) provision."[1272]

In the light of ECtHR case law regarding the right to a fair trial and the hearing of witnesses, this is a logical consequence. The right to examine witnesses must be seen in the context of the proceedings as a whole, an overview of which is necessary to determine whether the right to a fair trial has been violated.[1273] This responsibility for the whole trial has been recognised in decisions of the EComHR regarding the right to be tried within a reasonable time.[1274]

Having dealt with the responsibilities of the state that requests assistance, it is necessary to deal with the responsibilities of the requested state which offers assistance. The EComHR has held, in the very few decisions that exist regarding requested states, that these states are responsible for that part of the trial which takes place on their territory, namely, the execution of the request for assistance.[1275] In a 1973 decision, the EComHR has held that the accused is not entitled to complain about a violation of Article 6, paragraph 1 ECHR on the part of the requested state, because there is no criminal charge against him in that state.[1276] However, the EComHR held that there could be a responsibility under Article 6, paragraph 3 sub d ECHR, which deals with the right to hear witnesses. It is very hard to determine the exact responsibility of the requested state. It must be remembered that in the context of the question of whether the accused could examine and interrogate the witnesses for the prosecution, the ECtHR requires

---

[1271] For instance, when evidence was collected by authorities of the adjudicating state abroad or at an embassy of the adjudicating state. See EComHR, 25 September 1965, *X* v. *Germany*, 1611/62, Collection of Decisions 17, 42.

[1272] EComHR, 13 July 1987, *X* v. *Germany*, 11853/85, European Human Rights Reports 1988, 521 and EComHR, 12 July 1978, *X* v. *Germany*, 7779/77, unpublished.

[1273] See ECtHR, 28 August 1992, *Artner* v. *Austria*, Series A-242 and ECtHR, 26 April 1991, *Asch* v. *Austria*, Series A-203.

[1274] EComHR, 7 May 1986, *Jesso* v. *Austria*, 9315/81, Decisions and Reports 50, 44 and EComHR, 10 September 1991, *X* v. *Switzerland*, 14379/88 unpublished.

[1275] EComHR, 5 February 1973, *X, Y and Z* v. *Austria*, 5049/71, Collection of Decisions 43, 38; EComHR, 12 October 1992, *Noviflora Sweden Aktiebolag* v. *Sweden*, 14369/88, unpublished; EComHR, 6 March 1989, *R.* v. *Austria*, 12592/86, Decisions and Reports 60, 201.

[1276] Or in a more recent variation: the proceedings before the requested courts did not involve the determination of a *new criminal charge* against applicant. See ECtHR 5 July 2007, *Saccoccia* v. *Austria*, Application 69917/01, p. 14.

that the question of whether the accused has had a fair trial must be based upon an assessment of the proceedings as a whole. This is problematical for the requested state, which does not have an overview over the entire proceedings, and cannot, in principle, foresee the consequences (for the trial) of what it does. A responsibility under Article 6 paragraph 3 sub d for the requested state is, therefore, hard to apply.

However, there is a third perspective from which international co-operation and the application of human rights norms must be viewed. This is the perspective of the individual accused, entitled to his rights under the ECHR. A case in point here is the ECtHR case of *Sari* against Denmark and Turkey.[1277] Before the criminal proceedings against Sari ended in Denmark with the transfer of the proceedings from Denmark to Turkey, five years had elapsed. Subsequently, the criminal proceedings in Turkey took another five years. The ECtHR looked at the individual responsibility of each state, not at the total with which the accused was confronted. Subsequently, it held that the five years for which Denmark was responsible did not amount to a violation, and held the same for Turkey.

Apart from these legal problems, practical problems may make it difficult for the accused to find the responsible Member State. In the context of the exchange of police information, for instance, it is very hard to determine which state is the requesting and which is the requested state. It seems fair to conclude that the more intensive international co-operation is, the more vague the respective responsibilities can become.[1278] Consequently, there is a serious risk of bringing a complaint forward against the wrong state. A case in point here is the complaint of *Chinoy* against the United Kingdom, which was declared inadmissible by the EComHR.[1279] Chinoy complained about the use of material (tape recordings) allegedly obtained illegally in France by United States' undercover agents in extradition proceedings in the United Kingdom. The EComHR emphasised that the United Kingdom authorities were not responsible for what had happened in France. The decision raises the question as to whether a complaint against France might have been more successful. It is, therefore, in the interest of the applicant to complain against all the possible states involved in the alleged violation. However, such a collective complaint may be declared inadmissible because the applicant might not have exhausted the national remedies in all states against which the complaint is directed.

[1277] ECtHR, 8 November 2001, *Sari v. Denmark and Turkey*, Application 21889/93.
[1278] With intensive co-operation it is meant, for instance, interrogation conducted by authorities of both states involved, spontaneous exchange of information, joint investigation teams and extra-territorial investigation.
[1279] EComHR, 4 September 1991, *Chinoy v. the United Kingdom*, 15199/89, unpublished.

The perspective of the accused on the responsibilities of states in co-operation may contribute to a sound reasoning. The fact that one state considers a person as a suspect or as the accused brings the protection of the ECHR into play. It is thereby irrelevant in which state or under which criminal justice system a person is regarded as a suspect or as the accused. There are basically two arguments for this: the *collective enforcement* argument, and the *practical and effective application* argument. The preamble of the Convention reveals that it was drafted "to take the first steps for the collective enforcement of certain of the Rights stated in the Universal Declaration", and that the states thereby established a supranational control mechanism with mutual obligations. Upon the basis of Article 1 ECHR, the ECtHR draws the following conclusion:

> "Unlike international treaties of the classic kind, the Convention comprises more than mere reciprocal engagements between contracting States. It creates, over and above a network of mutual, bilateral undertakings, objective obligations which, in the words of the preamble benefit from a 'collective enforcement'."[1280]

The similarity of this wording with that of the Court in *Costa* v. *E.N.E.L.* is striking. Both the ECtHR and the Court emphasise the unique character of the obligations, which is in marked contrast to the international law adopted previously.[1281]

In the *Soering* case, the Court dealt with this collective implementation of the Convention: In interpreting the Convention, regard must be given to its special character as a treaty for the collective enforcement of human rights and fundamental freedoms. Thus, the object and purpose of the Convention as an instrument for the protection of individual human beings require that its provisions be interpreted and applied so as to make its safeguards practical and effective.[1282] After all, the ECHR gives rights to human beings and not to states.

Under these circumstances, all the foreseeable consequences of executing a request for assistance in one way or another should have their impact on the requested state. With regard to extradition, the Court held in the *Soering* case:

> "In so far as a measure of extradition has consequences adversely affecting the enjoyment of a Convention right, it may, assuming that the consequences are not too

---

[1280]   ECtHR, 18 January 1978, *Ireland* v. *the United Kingdom*, Series A-25, par. 239.

[1281]   See Chapter 3, Section 3.1.

[1282]   ECtHR, 7 July 1989, *Soering* v. *the United Kingdom*, Series A-161, par. 87. See, also, two recommendations of the Committee of Ministers of the Council of Europe to the Member States. Recommendation R (80) 8 of 27 June 1980 Concerning the Practical Application of the European Convention on Mutual Assistance in Criminal Matters; Recommendation R (82) 1 of 15 January 1982 Concerning International Co-operation in the Prosecution and Punishment of Acts of Terrorism.

remote, attract the obligations of a Contracting State under the relevant Convention guarantee."[1283]

Co-operation can, therefore, bring about responsibility for the acts of others. States that are party to the ECHR are mutually "their brother's keeper". This is also expressed in Article 33 ECHR, which affirms that they can bring a complaint against each other for any alleged breach of the ECHR.

In a manner which is similar to direct enforcement by the European Union, multilateral co-operation also raises questions with regard to the responsibilities of the EU Member States under the ECHR. Which Member State is responsible when a joint investigation team is set up and a violation of the ECHR occurs? Against which Member State should a complaint be lodged when Eurojust or Europol allegedly violate human rights? Even without direct operational powers, Article 8 ECHR might easily be applicable to the activities of these offices since they might conduct investigations that touch upon the private sphere of individuals or make use of information that is privacy sensitive.

Scheme on initiatives for international co-operation

Member State in need of an "ingredient" for:	Member State in "possession" of:
– investigation; – trial; – execution.	– information; – evidence; – proceeds from crime; – persons; – proceedings; – final judgment.

1. Can you help me?

→

– exchange information;
– collect evidence;
– surrender of persons.

2. Would you like to transfer/accept proceedings?

←

[1283]   ECtHR, 7 July 1989, *Soering* v. *the United Kingdom*, Series A-161, par. 85.

Member State in need of an "ingredient" for:	Member State in "possession" of:
– investigation; – trial; – execution.	– information; – evidence; – proceeds from crime; – persons; – proceedings; – final judgment.

3. Would you like to transfer/accept judgments?

→

4. Do you know?

←

– spontaneous information and inserting information in an automated system.

5. Urgent, I cannot wait for you.

→

– cross border surveillance and cross border pursuit

6. Shall we do this together?

←→

– controlled delivery;
– covert investigation;
– joint investigation teams.

7. Silent co-operation

→

– sending documents by mail

8. Automated co-operation

←→

– Schengen Information System and other databases

9. Let me briefly check this

→

– automated comparison of data/availability principle

CHAPTER 8.
MULTI-LATERAL CO-OPERATION
AND DIRECT ENFORCEMENT

1. INTRODUCTION

This chapter deals with an area in which the European integration of investigation into crime, the analysis of criminal phenomena, operational powers and decision-making has progressed the most. It covers various forms of multi-lateral co-operation and direct enforcement performed by the European Union and its Member States. What these forms of co-operation and enforcement have in common is that their approach is *European*, and does not necessarily or exclusively serve the interest of a specific Member State. With bilateral co-operation between law enforcement authorities of the Member States, discussed in the previous chapter, the different roles in the process can easily be distinguished. One Member State is in need of something and another Member State is in a position to assist it in this matter. One Member State initiates international co-operation and maintains control over the process. However, this is not the case with *multi-lateral co-operation*. Often, it is not possible to see for which Member State's investigation or prosecution co-operation is provided. Clearly, the fact that these rules cannot easily be distinguished relates to the very early stage at which multi-lateral co-operation takes place. States may supply information at a stage in which it is not clear at all whether it will ever lead to a criminal case, and, if it does, in which Member State. In other situations, the fact that crimes have been committed is abundantly clear, multi-lateral co-operation then aims to clarify the roles of the individuals involved, as well as to create the possibility of taking a decision on the place of prosecution. Decisions within bodies of multi-lateral co-operation are taken by the relevant representatives of the Member States.

All the forms of co-operation and enforcement discussed so far in this book, as well as the multi-lateral co-operation to be discussed in Section 2 of this chapter, can be regarded as examples of indirect enforcement of Union law. Whilst the Union sets the norms, it leaves the enforcement to the Member States. However, this is different with direct enforcement, in which the Union sets the standards and norms and enforces these itself. *Direct enforcement* is defined as enforcement where a Union body has the power to make decisions on prosecution and/or on sentencing. The two relevant forms of direct enforcement mechanisms that will be dealt with are competition law and the European Public Prosecutor's Office. The Commission in competition law and the European Public Prosecutor's Office with regard to eurocrimes do not represent the Member States, but, instead, take decisions that are in the best interest of the European Union. Both the Commission and the European Public Prosecutor's Office co-operate with national authorities, but the latter work in a subordinate position. Decisions are taken at a European level.

Apart from competition law, the currently existing forms of multi-lateral co-operation are all of a relatively recent date. The "oldest" is Europol, which was established in 1995. This perspective leads one to the conclusion that revolutionary developments have taken place in less than fifteen years. It should be noted that multi-lateral co-operation has been developed at all relevant levels: at police level, at prosecutorial level, and even at the level of judges and courts, multi-lateral co-operation takes place.

Most developments, however, have taken place at police level, in which already three sub-categories can be identified, the first being co-operation in the form of automated computerised systems. The Schengen Information System and the Customs Information System will be discussed. The second form is the creation of an intelligence centre for strategical analysis: Europol. The third and most recent form is operational, in which joint investigation teams undertake multilateral operational actions. At prosecutorial level, Eurojust must be mentioned. Finally, the co-operation network for judges and courts, namely, the European Judicial Network, will be discussed.

2.   MULTI-LATERAL CO-OPERATION

2.1. POLICE LEVEL

2.1.1. Automated Computerised Systems: The Schengen Information System and the Customs Information System

The Schengen Information System
The *CISA* established the Schengen Information System (SIS) (Articles 92–119 *CISA*). This is a joint information system, which enables law enforcement authorities to have access to alerts on persons and property for the purposes of border checks and other police and customs checks carried out within the country by means of automated search procedures (Article 92). Access to the system exists exclusively for the authorities that are responsible for such checks. The purpose of the SIS is to maintain public order and public security.

The SIS may be used for various alerts. Article 95 provides that data on persons wanted for arrest for extradition are to be entered. Article 96 relates to alerts for the purpose of refusing entry. Article 97 contains alerts with regard to missing persons. Article 98 provides alerts for the purposes of determining the place of residence or domicile of witnesses and persons summoned before judicial authorities in connection with criminal proceedings in order to account for acts for which they are being prosecuted, or persons who are to be served with a criminal judgment or a summons to report in order to serve a penalty involving deprivation of liberty. Upon the basis of Article 99, data on persons and vehicles may be entered for the purposes of discreet surveillance or of specific checks. Article 100 deals with data on subjects sought for the purposes of seizure or use as evidence in criminal proceedings. Paragraph 3 of Article 100 limits the entry to certain categories of objects: motor vehicles, trailers and caravans, firearms, blank official documents, and issued identity papers, all of which might have been stolen or lost, as well as issued banknotes.

Articles 102–118 deal with both data protection rules and security protection rules. In addition, these provisions regulate how alerts are to be inserted and how they can be modified. Articles 109–111 regulate the right of access to the data of persons that are in the system, and the correction or deletion of incorrect or inaccurate data. Proceedings to correct or delete data may be brought before the courts of each state (Article 111, paragraph 1).[1284] Article 111, paragraph 2 provides that the states must "undertake mutually to enforce final decisions taken by the courts or authorities referred to in paragraph 1".

The Customs Information System

The Customs Information System was established by a Convention in 1995.[1285] It is a joint automated information system for customs purposes which aims to prevent, to investigate and to prosecute serious contraventions of national laws for which the customs administration has competence (Article 2). These national laws relate to the movement of goods subject to measures of prohibition, restriction or control, in particular to the measures covered by Articles 36 and 346 TFEU,[1286] as well as to the transfer, conversion, concealment or disguise of property or

---

[1284] The *van Straaten* case resulted from a request to delete data inserted in the SIS. 28 September 2006, Case C-150/05, *van Straaten v. the Netherlands and Italy* [2006] ECR I-9327.

[1285] Convention of 26 July 1995 on the use of information technology for customs purposes, OJ 1995, C 316/34. Amended by Protocol of 12 March 1999 on the scope of the laundering of proceeds in the Convention on the use of information technology for customs purposes, OJ 1999, C 91/2. Further amended by Protocol of 8 May 2003 amending, with regard to the creation of a customs files identification database, the Convention on the Use of Information Technology for Customs Purposes, OJ 2003, C 139/2.

[1286] In its preamble, the 1995 Customs Convention refers to three justifications for checks on goods in the TFEU: threat to public health, morality and security.

proceeds derived from, obtained directly or indirectly through, or used in, illicit international drug trafficking or any infringement of:

"(i) all laws, regulations and administrative provisions of a Member State the application of which comes wholly or partly within the jurisdiction of the customs administration of the Member State concerning cross-border traffic in goods subject to bans, restrictions or controls, in particular pursuant to Articles 36 and 223 of the Treaty establishing the European Community,[1287] and non-harmonised excise duties, or

(ii) the body of Community provisions and associated implementing provisions governing the import, export, transit and presence of goods traded between Member States and third countries, and between Member States in the case of goods that do not have Community status within the meaning of Article 9(2) of the Treaty establishing the European Community or goods subject to additional controls or investigations for the purposes of establishing their Community status, or

(iii) the body of provisions adopted at Community level under the common agricultural policy and the specific provisions adopted with regard to goods resulting from the processing of agricultural products, or

(iv) the body of provisions adopted at Community level for harmonised excise duties and for value-added tax on importation together with the national provisions implementing them."[1288]

The Customs Information System consists of a central database facility, and is accessible via terminals in each Member State. It contains certain categories of data, such as commodities, means of transport, business, persons, fraud trends and the availability of expertise (Article 3, paragraph 1). Article 5 provides which suggested actions can be entered, such as sighting and reporting, discreet surveillance or specific checks. In addition, Article 6 suggests the information which may be transmitted to the supplying state. Access to the Customs Information System is exclusive to customs authorities, subject to the conditions of Article 7.[1289] Member States may make use of the data retrieved only for the purposes stated in Article 2, paragraph 2 (Article 8). In order to create the possibility of exchanging information concerning the existence of investigations,

---

[1287] The reference is to the numbering of the TEC in the version applicable before the amendments of the Treaty of Amsterdam entered into force on 1 May 1999.

[1288] Article 1, paragraph 1 Convention of 26 July 1995 on the Use of Information Technology for Customs Purposes, as amended by Protocol of 12 March 1999.

[1289] See, further, Regulation 515/97 on mutual assistance between the administrative authorities of the Member States and co-operation between the latter and the Commission to ensure the correct application of the law on customs and agricultural matters.

or of files about ongoing or completed investigations, the Convention was again amended in 2003,[1290] and a new Chapter VA, which creates a Customs Files Identification Database (Articles 12A-12E), was inserted.[1291]

Amendment of the data supplied can only be done by the Member State that originally inserted the data, and the procedure for this has been laid down in Article 11. Data Protection is regulated in Articles 13 to 18 and is subject to the 1981 Council of Europe Convention on Data Protection. Individuals that make use of the right of access can do so with the authorities of each Member State (Article 15, paragraph 1). The same goes for actions for correction or deletion (Article 15, paragraphs 3 and 4). Identical to Article 111, paragraph 2 *CISA*, with regard to the SIS, Article 15, paragraph 4 1995 Customs Convention provides that states "undertake mutually to enforce final decisions taken by the courts or authorities" regarding corrections and deletions.

2.1.2. Europol: Intelligence Centre for Strategic Analysis[1292]

As a successor to the Europol Drugs Unit, the European Police Office, Europol, was established by a Convention in 1995,[1293] and has its seat in The Hague. Article 2 stipulates the objectives of Europol, which are to improve the effectiveness and co-operation of the competent authorities in combating serious forms of international crime:

> "where there are factual indications or reasonable grounds that an organized criminal structure is involved and two or more Member States are affected by the forms of crime in question in such a way as to require a common approach (...) owing to the scale, significance and consequences of the offences concerned."

[1290] Protocol of 8 May 2003 amending, with regard to the creation of a customs files identification database, the Convention on the Use of Information Technology for Customs Purposes, OJ 2003, C 139/2.

[1291] See, also, Regulation 766/2008 of 9 July 2008 amending Regulation 515/97 on mutual assistance between the administrative authorities of the Member States and co-operation between the latter and the Commission to ensure the correct application of the law on customs and agricultural matters.

[1292] Part of this sub-paragraph is taken from a letter of 10 January 1995 written by Monica den Boer, Bert Swart and the author on behalf of the Standing Committee of Experts on International Immigration, Refugee and Criminal Law to the European Communities Committee of the House of Lords. See House of Lords Session 1994–95, 10th report, HL Paper 51 Europol (with evidence).

[1293] Negotiations take place on the replacement of the Convention and all its protocols and other supplementary decisions by a Council Decision which should take effect in 2010. See Proposal for a Council Decision establishing the European Police Office (EUROPOL) – consolidated text, Council Document, 10 April 2008, 8296/08, EUROPOL 46.

In other words, Europol was not established to deal with local or minor offences, but was established to give a European dimension to the investigation of crime of a European dimension. Article 88 TFEU stipulates that a Regulation may further determine the structure, operation, field of action and tasks of Europol.[1294]

The crimes for which Europol is competent reflect this international and serious character. As the Convention stipulates in Article 2, paragraph 1, last sentence, the following crimes are to be regarded as having an international and serious character:

> "crimes committed or likely to be committed in the course of terrorist activities against life, limb, personal freedom or property,[1295] unlawful drug trafficking, illegal money-laundering activities, trafficking in nuclear and radio-active substances, illegal immigrant smuggling, trade in human beings and motor vehicle crime and the forms of crime listed in the Annex or specific manifestations thereof."

Paragraph 3 of Article 2 *Europol Convention* deals with the related crimes for which Europol is also competent. The following crimes are to be regarded as related:

- offences committed in order to procure the means for perpetrating acts within the sphere of competence of Europol;
- offences committed in order to facilitate or carry out acts within the sphere of competence of Europol;
- offences committed to ensure the impunity of acts within the sphere of competence of Europol.

Although Europol was initially only competent for the crimes listed in Article 2, paragraph 1 of the Convention itself, and could be made competent by special Decision by the Council for one or more of the crimes mentioned on the Annex to Article 2, a Council Decision of 6 December 2001 extended Europol's mandate to all the crimes included in the Annex.[1296] The crimes of paragraph 1 of Article 2 are defined in the Annex. The crimes of paragraph 2 are only mentioned.[1297] All

---

1294 At the time of concluding the manuscript, such a Regulation had not been adopted. The framework of Europol in the TFEU does not deviate much from the *Europol Convention*.

1295 Terrorist activities were already inserted by Council Decision of 3 December 1999, OJ 1999, C 26/22.

1296 Council Decision of 6 December 2001 extending Europol's mandate to deal with the serious forms of international crime listed in the Annex to the Europol Convention, OJ 2001, C 362/1.

1297 Annex referred to in Article 2
List of other serious forms of international crime which Europol could deal with in addition to those already provided for in Article 2(2) in compliance with Europol's objective as set out in Article 2(1).

the crimes for which Europol is competent, are also mentioned as list offences in Framework Decisions on mutual recognition for which double criminality does

Against life, limb or personal freedom:
- murder, grievous bodily injury
- illicit trade in human organs and tissue
- kidnapping, illegal restraint and hostage-taking
- racism and xenophobia

Against property or public goods including fraud:
- organized robbery
- illicit trafficking in cultural goods, including antiquities and works of art
- swindling and fraud
- racketeering and extortion
- counterfeiting and product piracy
- forgery of administrative documents and trafficking therein
- forgery of money and means of payment
- computer crime
- corruption

Illegal trading and harm to the environment:
- illicit trafficking in arms, ammunition and explosives
- illicit trafficking in endangered animal species
- illicit trafficking in endangered plant species and varieties
- environmental crime
- illicit trafficking in hormonal substances and other growth promoters

With regard to the forms of crime listed in Article 2(1) for the purposes of this Convention:
- 'crime connected with nuclear and radioactive substances' means the criminal offences listed in Article 7(1) of the Convention on the Physical Protection of Nuclear Material, signed at Vienna and New York on 3 March 1980, and relating to the nuclear and/or radioactive materials defined in Article 197 of the Euratom Treaty and Directive 80/836 Euratom of 15 July 1980,
- 'illegal immigrant smuggling' means activities intended deliberately to facilitate, for financial gain, the entry into, residence or employment in the territory of the Member States of the European Union, contrary to the rules and conditions applicable in the Member States,
- 'traffic in human beings' means subjection of a person to the real and illegal sway of other persons by using violence or menaces or by abuse of authority or intrigue, especially with a view to the exploitation of prostitution, forms of sexual exploitation and assault of minors or trade in abandoned children. These forms of exploitation also include the production, sale or distribution of child-pornography material.
- 'motor vehicle crime' means the theft or misappropriation of motor vehicles, lorries, semi-trailers, the loads of lorries or semi-trailers, buses, motorcycles, caravans and agricultural vehicles, works vehicles, and the spare parts for such vehicles, and the receiving and concealing of such objects,
- of the Council of Europe Convention on Laundering, Search, Seizure and Confiscation of the Proceeds from Crime, signed at Strasbourg on 8 November 1990,
- 'unlawful drug trafficking' means the criminal offences listed in Article 3(1) of the United Nations Convention of 20 December 1988 against Illicit Traffic in Narcotic Drugs and Psychotropic Substances and in the provisions amending or replacing that Convention.

The forms of crime referred to in Article 2 and in this Annex shall be assessed by the competent national authorities in accordance with the national law of the Member States to which they belong."

not apply, although the list offences applicable in mutual recognition is somewhat longer.[1298]

Unlike the list offences in mutual recognition, some of the crimes are defined in the *Europol Convention* by reference to certain international or European legal instruments which criminalise the conduct in question. Its rationale might lie in the fact that, unlike the authorities of the Member States, Europol does not work in the context of a national criminal justice system which has defined the conduct described. Europol does not have a similar frame of reference. In this perspective, reliance on a common binding instrument is a safe mechanism. However, with the entry into force of the Treaty of Lisbon, the crimes for which Europol is committed have been extended to serious crime which affects two or more Member States, terrorism, and forms of crime which affect a common interest covered by a Union policy.[1299]

The Director of Europol is responsible for the day-to-day activities of Europol (Article 29), and is assisted by a Management Board (Article 28). Article 31 obliges Europol to observe high standards of confidentiality and security, in order to prevent unauthorised persons gaining access to Europol information.[1300] Furthermore, Article 88 TFEU provides for a role of the national parliaments.

The Tasks of Europol

Article 3 of the Convention stipulates the principal tasks of Europol, which include facilitating exchanges of information between the Member States. In this respect, Europol might also improve the existing instruments of co-operation between police authorities by collecting, collating and analysing information and intelligence. It is to notify national authorities without delay of information concerning them, and of connections between criminal offences detected (Article 13), and gives support to national investigations by forwarding all relevant information to the national units. Furthermore, it may ask Member States to initiate investigations in specific cases.[1301] It is also to maintain three computerised collections of information containing data. Paragraphs 2 and 3 of Article 3 also entrust Europol with other tasks which concern mutual help on improving expertise and technical equipment, as well as assistance in the training of members of national police authorities.[1302]

[1298] See, further, Chapter 7, Section 3.2.2.

[1299] Article 88, paragraph 1 TFEU can be regarded as directly applicable even without the Regulations referred to in paragraph 2.

[1300] Council Act of 3 November 1998 adopting rules on the confidentiality of Europol information, OJ 1999, C 26/10, amended by Council Act of 5 June 2003, OJ 2003, C 152/1.

[1301] Member States are to give such a request due consideration and inform Europol on the follow up. See Recommendation of 28 September 2000 to Member States in respect of requests made by Europol to initiate criminal investigations in specific cases, OJ 2000, C 289/8.

[1302] European training of senior police officers is further facilitated through Decision 2005/681/ JHA of 20 September 2005 establishing the European Police College (CEPOL) and repealing

In order to improve efficiency, each Member State is to establish or to designate a national unit, which is to be the only liaison body between Europol and the competent authorities in the Member States (Article 4). In addition, Member States may allow direct contact between the designated national competent authorities and Europol (Article 4, paragraph 2). However, the lines of communication of Europol are restricted, and Europol will not contact the competent national authorities and the latter cannot contact them. National law enforcement authorities are only in contact with their national unit. The national units and Europol are to supply each other mutually with information and respond to requests. Paragraph 5 of Article 4 lists three grounds upon which a national unit may refuse to supply information and intelligence in a specific case.[1303] At its seat in The Hague, the liaison officers of every national unit represent the interests of the national unit within Europol (Article 5). Their task is to assist in the exchange of information between their national unit and Europol, and they must give advice with regard to the analysis of the information exchanged. To the extent necessary for the performance of their tasks, the liaison officers have access to the three information systems.

Lines of communication between Europol and national units

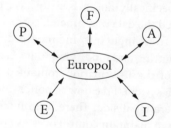

A Computerised System of Collected Information

Europol has set up a computerised system of collected information with three components: an *information system*, *work files* and an *index system* (Article 6). This requires some further explanation. The *information system* is the system in which national units and liaison officers can directly enter data and from which they can directly extract data (Article 7). In addition, Europol may enter the data supplied by third states and bodies, as well as analyse data. The direct access of national units to the information system is restricted to personal data as defined

---

Decision 2000/820/JHA, OJ 2005, L 256/63. CEPOL has its seat in Bramshill, United Kingdom.

[1303]   If this would mean: 1. Harming essential security interests; 2. Jeopardising the success of a current investigation or the safety of individuals; 3. Involving information pertaining to organisations or specific intelligence activities in the field of State security.

in Article 8, paragraph 2. The full range of data is only accessible via the liaison officers (Article 7, paragraph 1).

The contents of the information system are defined in Article 8. The system may store, modify and use data only for the performance of Europol's tasks. These data may relate to two categories of persons: the first being persons suspected of having committed a criminal offence for which Europol is competent, the second being persons for whom there are serious grounds under national law to believe that they will commit criminal offences which fall under the competence of Europol (Article 8, paragraph 1). The personal data include name, date and place of birth, nationality, sex and, when necessary, other characteristics likely to assist in identification, including particular physical characteristics that are not subject to change. In addition, the information system may include data linked to the particular criminal offence (and/or) miscellaneous data not necessarily personal (Article 8, paragraph 3). All data must contain a reference which indicates whether the data were provided by a third party or are the result of Europol's own analysis.

As mentioned above, not every competent police or other law enforcement authority of the Member States has access to the information system. Article 9 limits access to the national units, liaison officers, the director, the deputy-director and the Europol staff specifically authorised to have direct access. Only the national unit which entered the data may amend, correct or delete such data. The responsibility of retrieval from, input into and modifications of the system, all lie within the retrieving, inputting and modifying unit (Article 9, paragraph 3). It is basically the sensitivity of the information contained that prevented Europol from establishing an open system. Free flow of police information may cause too many dangers on the operational side. There is an interest for the police entity which submitted the data to maintain control over its operational use. The use of information elsewhere in the Union may be taken as a warning for other people involved in criminal activity and put promising further investigations at risk. In addition, the unexpected use of information may be dangerous to the physical integrity of undercover officials and witnesses. The principle of availability is definitively not applicable to the flow of information from Europol.

There is another element that explains, even under the current system of limited access, why Europol does not, by and large, obtain as much information as possible. This relates to a certain reluctance on the part of law enforcement officials to supply information, because it could lead to a situation in which other (foreign) entities might successfully terminate the operation. There is little enthusiasm to supply information which will lead to seizure, arrest and prosecution in another Member State, when most of the investigating work has been done at home. This phenomenon, of which the exact extent cannot be determined, is extremely detrimental to effective law enforcement. As a consequence, the potential of Europol is not fully used.

The second system of Europol contains *work files* for the purpose of analysis (Article 10).[1304] This not only brings together data concerning the persons mentioned in Article 8, but also persons who might serve as witnesses in any future criminal prosecution, persons who might be victims in the future, contacts and escorts, and persons who may provide information. The work files are established for the purpose of analysis. This may result in a general strategic analysis of certain types of crime. It may also concern an analysis of specific individual cases. Europol may request further data from various bodies in and outside the European Union (Article 10, paragraph 4) for information which might be useful to enter in the work files. Europol may also retrieve data from automated computerised information systems to which it has access, if this is necessary for the performance of its task(s) (paragraph 5 of Article 10).

The access of liaison officers to the work files is based upon the *need to know principle* (Article 10, paragraph 7). This means that the liaison officer of a Member State has to give sufficient reasons before being allowed to participate in the analysis. The liaison officer may have an interest because his Member State supplied certain information or because the information relates to his Member State. In this context, Article 10, paragraph 8, provides that the Member State that submitted the information "shall be the sole judge of the degree of its sensitivity". Any dissemination or operational use is to be decided in consultation with the analysis group. Article 10, paragraph 9, under the conditions stipulated in this provision, allows Europol to invite experts of third states or third bodies to be associated with the activities of the analysis group. The analysis system enables Europol to function as a criminal intelligence service at both a Union and an international level, the first of this kind ever to be created. The analysis is performed with the aim of taking operational measures. Europol, for instance, provides concrete and current threat assessments of certain organised crime groups, on cyber crime, on drug trafficking, on illegal immigration, and many others.[1305]

The third system is an *index to the analysis work files*. It is accessible to liaison officers who should be able to decide whether the case affects their country from the index description. Access by liaison officers should be designed in such a way that it is possible to establish both connections and draw further conclusions concerning the content of the files. But why does Article 11 limit free access to the index and not directly to the work files? The rationale behind this is to prevent

---

[1304]   Council Act of 3 November 1998 adopting rules applicable to Europol analysis files, OJ 1999, C 26/1, gives further rules which are applicable to the processing of data for analysis purposes as referred to in Article 10.

[1305]   Europol Work Programme 2009, Council Document 27 March 2008, 7801/08, EUROPOL 32.

Member States from using data for operational purposes in their own country, and, as a consequence of arrests, for instance, suspects in other countries are prevented from being warned. It thus provides co-ordination, and places Europol in a position to influence in which country operational steps should be taken. It is necessary to limit the output of data, because it would, otherwise, stop the flow of new data entering the system. No national unit is willing to supply important data when there is a major risk that it will no longer be able to use the data itself because another Member State has "spoiled" it. Eurojust is the prosecutorial platform both to make operational decisions and to solve problems.

The data, regardless of which data system from which it comes, may be used by the Member States in order to prevent and combat the crimes for which Europol is competent (Article 17, paragraph 1). Europol can use these data only for the performance of its tasks as referred to in Article 3. If a Member State or other supplier of information stipulates particular restrictions, these must be lived up to and communicated to those who retrieved the data. The use of such data may only take place after consultation (Article 17, paragraphs 2 and 3). Furthermore, Article 18 entitles Europol, under certain conditions, to communicate data to third states and third bodies.

Data Protection

The data in the data files is to be held by Europol only for as long as it is necessary for the performance of its tasks. The need for continued storage of data in data files is to be reviewed no later than three years after the input of the data (Article 21, paragraph 1). The need for continued storage of personal data relating to individuals is to be reviewed every year and the review documented (Article 21, paragraph 3). The activities of Europol are subject to the standardisation of data protection through the Council of Europe Convention for the Protection of Individuals with Regard to Automatic Processing of Personal Data (Article 14, paragraph 1 *Europol Convention*).[1306] Both the Data Protection Convention and Recommendation No. R (87) 15 of the Council of Europe are primarily restricted to information that is processed automatically.[1307] The responsibility for data protection matters is divided between the Member State which entered the data and Europol, in respect of data communicated by third parties or data which are the result of an analysis (Article 15, paragraph 1). The question is whether the reliance on national data protection provisions (see Article 15, paragraph 1 and Article 17 of the Convention) is satisfactory, given the variation between the standards of data protection in the absence of substantial and procedural harmonisation of data protection legislation. Some Member States have a special

---

[1306] Strasbourg, 28 January 1981, European Treaty Series 108.
[1307] Recommendation of 17 September 1987 of the Committee of Ministers of the Council of Europe to Member States Regulating the Use of Personal Data in the Police Sector.

Data Protection law for the exchange of police data, and, clearly, this may result in unequal protection of EU citizens.[1308]

Another problem concerns the exchange of data on persons for whom there are grounds for presuming that they *will* commit criminal offences (Article 8 *Europol Convention*). It is the question of when and how law enforcement agencies decide that this is the case, and whether the information processed by Europol results from pro-active (unregulated) policing methods. Principle 2.1 of the Recommendation on Police Data states that the collection of data on individuals for police purposes should be limited to that which is "necessary for the prevention of a *real danger* or the suppression of a specific criminal offence". There is a gap between Principle 2.1 and Article 10, paragraph 1, of the *Europol Convention*, which states the conditions upon which data may be stored "where this is necessary to achieve the objective laid down in Article 2(1) (…) on criminal offences for which Europol is competent under Article 2(2)". In this respect, the Recommendation is significantly more restrictive than the *Europol Convention*.

Questions also ought to be raised about the strictness of rules *vis-à-vis* the exchange of data between Europol and other international organisations, such as Interpol (Article 18 of the Convention), and the exchange of data between the Europol database and other international databases (Article 10, paragraph 5), and the data exchange with third countries, which will proceed bilaterally through a Member State and a third country (Article 10, paragraph 4, *sub* 4; Article 15, paragraph 2; Article 18). Data provided by non-Member States or third parties cannot be verified. These states are only expected to have an adequate level of data protection (Article 18, paragraph 1). Thus, Europol has a large margin of discretion in determining the level of adequate data protection in non-Member States. Both Europol and each Member State have to implement measures of data security (Article 25), which should prevent unauthorised persons from gaining access to data-processing equipment. Data protection and data security are also of considerable importance when Europol establishes co-operation relations with third states and units (Article 42).

Effective Remedies for Individuals

The Convention recognises several rights to individuals who may suffer because of inaccurate or unauthorised processing of personal data. The data subject must be given information upon his application concerning data relating to his person, including information relating to the source of the recipient of such data and the purpose of storage (Article 19). He has the right to the correction or the deletion of all data that are incorrect or have been received or stored by Europol in

---

[1308] *Directive 95/46 on Data Protection* is not applicable to Europol. Article 3, paragraph 2, explicitly excludes all activities within Title VI TEU as well as national activities in the criminal field from application.

contravention to the convention (Article 20), and has a similar right where data in paper files are concerned (Article 22).[1309] Finally, he may request the national supervisory body or the joint supervisory body to examine the permissibility of collection and entering of personal data, their retrieval, processing and utilisation (Articles 23 and 24).

The basic right, from which the other rights follow, is the right to information.[1310] How does an individual know whether Europol possesses any data on him? The exceptions to the right to information in paragraph 3 of Article 19, are very broad, indeed. They seem, however, to correspond to the exceptions mentioned in Article 9 of the Council of Europe Convention. However necessary these exceptions may be, they make it extremely difficult for an individual to obtain information. Article 10, paragraph 1, authorises Europol to store and utilise a number of personal data if it is to be expected that a person will commit criminal offences in the future. This expectation must be based upon "serious grounds under national law for believing (that they) will commit criminal offences for which Europol is competent" (Article 8).[1311] The fear exists that Europol will not often be in a position to verify that the data obtained from third units, especially non-Member States, are accurate, up-to-date and were lawfully obtained by these units. Moreover, there may be a danger that a third unit communicates data to national units which, in turn, communicate them to Europol. This process of information laundering may make the rights of the individual illusory.

Information requests should be addressed to the national competent authority, which will forward it to Europol (Article 19). Europol has to reply completely within three months of the receipt of the request from the national competent authority. Paragraph 5 of Article 19 shows that the range of the right to information may vary from state to state, depending on national law. It is unclear whether this means that the right to correction or deletion is a right *vis-à-vis* Europol or *vis-à-vis* the national competent authority. In this respect, it is rather strange that liability for unauthorised or incorrect data-processing lies with each Member State (Article 38).[1312] Claims for compensation can therefore not be directed against Europol. Each Member State in which the damage was caused, shall compensate the injured party, irrespective of whether the damage was due to

---

[1309] An example is that Europol maintains data on a person who has been acquitted by a final decision of the offence of which Europol has data. Article 8, paragraph 5, prescribes that the data concerning this final decision should be deleted.

[1310] See, also, Chapter 7, Section 6.

[1311] Germany and Austria attached a declaration to the Convention that such data may be stored "if there are reasons to suspect, because of the nature of the act or its perpetration, or any other intelligence, that criminal proceedings need to be taken against such persons for criminal offences for which Europol is competent under Article 2".

[1312] Does this determine responsibility under the ECHR? See, further, Chapter 7, Section 6.4.

another Member State or Europol. Article 32a creates the possibility to adopt rules on the right of access to Europol documents.

Europol Staff and Liaison Officers as Witnesses in Court

Article 32, paragraph 3 *Europol Convention* contains severe restrictions with regard to the possibilities of summoning Europol staff and liaison officers as witnesses in a national court. They must, according to the Convention, refer to the Director of Europol, when they receive a summons. The Director may even approach the judicial body that summons his staff in order to find a manner that would conceal the interests of Europol. Individual staff members are additionally subject to their own national legislation. If their own national law gives them the right to refuse to give evidence, they may only do so after authorisation from the Director. Article 32, paragraph 3, further states that:

> "Permission to give evidence may be refused only in so far as this is necessary to protect overriding interests of Europol or of a Member State or States that need protection."

Europol's Relations with Third States and Bodies

Upon the basis of Article 42 *Europol Convention*, co-operative relations are to be established and maintained with third states and third bodies with which exchange of information may take place.[1313] The exchange of information takes place for the purposes of investigation, prosecution and the prevention of criminal offences, and in all proceedings relating to criminal matters.[1314] Europol has concluded many agreements with third states[1315] with whom the Director was

---

[1313] Council Act of 3 November 1998 laying down rules concerning the receipt of information by Europol from third parties, OJ 1999, C 26/17, allows Europol to conclude agreements with third parties. See, further, Council Act of 3 November 1998 laying down rules governing Europol's external relations with third States and non-European Union related bodies, OJ 1999, C 26/19; Council Act of 12 March 1999 adopting the rules governing the transmission of personal data by Europol to third States and third bodies, OJ 1999, C 88/1, amended by Council Act of 28 February 2002, OJ 2002, C 76/1.

[1314] See Article 5, paragraph 3 Agreement of 6 December 2001 between the United States of America and the European Police Office.

[1315] Before they became a Member State of the European Union candidate states have concluded agreements which, as a result of their ratification of the *Europol Convention*, now have become obsolete: Estonia (2001); Hungary (2001); Poland (2001); Czech Republic (2001); Slovenia (2001); Cyprus (2002); Romania (2003); Slovakia (2003); Lithuania (2003); Latvia (2003); Bulgaria (2003); Malta (2004); With other states: Iceland (2001); Norway (2001); Switzerland (2001); United States of America (2001) and the Supplemental Agreement of 20 December 2002 between the United States of America and Europol on the exchange of personal data and related information; Colombia (2003); Turkey (2003); Russia (2003); Albania (2006); Moldavia (2006); Macedonia (2006).

authorised to conclude agreements.[1316] An agreement is essential to second liaison officers to Europol.[1317] As far as can be seen, none of these agreements have been published in the Official Journal. Their structure differs, and while the agreements with the candidate EU Member States, and Norway, Iceland and Switzerland, are, almost the same as the *Europol Convention* itself, the agreements with other states and bodies are of a more limited nature. Due to their status of not being a state, the agreements with other bodies have a very individual character.[1318]

Co-operation with Europol, Eurojust, and the European Judicial Network is provided for in many legal instruments on international co-operation between the Member States of the Union. An example is provided for with regard to the results of the analyses carried out by National Analysis Centres with regard to counterfeit banknotes and coins.[1319] Article 42, paragraph 3 *Europol Convention* states that Europol is to establish and maintain close co-operation with Eurojust, and to take the need to avoid the duplication of their efforts into account.[1320]

2.1.3. Multi-Lateral Investigations: Joint Investigations Teams

The first operational multi-lateral co-operation was established in Article 24 *Convention on Mutual Assistance between Customs Administrations*, soon followed by Article 13 *EU Mutual Assistance Convention*, in the form of a *joint investigation team*.[1321] This is a team that consists of law enforcement officials of two or more states. It may be set up by an agreement between the relevant authorities for a specific purpose and a limited period of time,[1322] which may be

---

[1316]   See Article 2 Council Decision of 27 March 2000 authorising the Director of Europol to enter into negotiations on agreements with third States and non-European related bodies, OJ 2000, C 106/1. See, also, Council Decision of 6 December 2001 amending Council Decision of 27 March 2000 authorising the Director of Europol to enter into negotiations on agreements with third States and non-European related bodies, OJ 2001, C 358/1. Further amended by Council Act of 13 June 2002, OJ 2002, C 150/1, and by Council Act of 25 October 2004, OJ 2004, L 342/27.

[1317]   See Article 2 Council Act of 3 November 1998 laying down rules governing Europol's external relations with third States and non-European Union related bodies, OJ 1999, C 26/19.

[1318]   Interpol (2001); World Customs Organisation (2002); European Central Bank, OJ 2002, C 23/9; United Nations Office for Drugs and Crime (2003); Eurojust (2003).

[1319]   Decision of 6 December 2001 on the protection of the euro against counterfeiting, OJ 2001, L 329/1.

[1320]   See mirror paragraph Article 26 *Eurojust Decision 2002/187*.

[1321]   *Framework Decision 2002/465 on Joint Investigation Teams*, is completely identical to Article 13 *EU Mutual Assistance Convention*. The only reason to adopt a Framework Decision was that the ratification of the *EU Mutual Assistance Convention* made little progress at the time. Article 5 of the Framework Decision stipulates that it shall cease to have effect when the *EU Mutual Assistance Convention* has entered into force in all Member States.

[1322]   See Council Recommendation of 8 May 2003 on a model agreement for setting up a joint investigation team (JIT), OJ 2003, C 121/1, which aims at providing a model for both the *EU Mutual Assistance Convention* as *Framework Decision 2002/465 on Joint Investigation Teams*.

extended by mutual consent. The agreement on the establishment of a joint investigation team determines the composition of the team. Such teams are set up when a Member State finds itself confronted with investigations which require difficult and demanding investigations with links to other Member States. Terrorist offences, especially, may offer a good reason for establishing a team.[1323] Another reason is that a number of Member States may be conducting an investigation the circumstance of which necessitate concerted action by the Member States. Europol officials,[1324] Eurojust officials, representatives of the Commission (for example, OLAF) may participate in the operations, as well as officials of third countries.[1325] Europol may, for instance, provide support through the national units by providing its knowledge and expertise, and by further analysing certain offences. For its part, Eurojust may propose that the relevant Member States set up a joint investigation team (Article 7 *Eurojust Decision 2002/187*).

The composition of a joint investigation team can be very mixed, and is certainly not restricted to police officials. The Council recommended the establishment of multi-national *ad hoc* teams for the gathering and exchanging of information on terrorists, with the involvement of Europol.[1326] The teams should have a flexible character and should be made up of officials of competent national authorities that are responsible for combating terrorism. A Protocol amending the *Europol Convention* inserted a new Article 3a, which deals with the participation of Europol in joint investigation teams.[1327] The Director may conclude agreements with national and other authorities on Europol's participation in a joint investigation team. It must be highlighted that Europol members cannot be involved in operational actions. Europol's task is merely "supportive". Article 3a, paragraph 1 states that "they shall not take part in any coercive measures". This corresponds with the more strategic and analytical role of Europol. For the rest, the inserted Article permits Europol members to be involved in all activities and exchange information with the members of a joint investigation team.

[1323]   See Article 3 Decision 2005/671/JHA of 20 September 2005 on the exchange of information and co-operation concerning terrorist offences, OJ 2005, L 253/22.

[1324]   See Recommendation of 30 November 2000 to Member States in respect of Europol's assistance to joint investigative teams set up by the Member States, OJ 2000, C 357/7.

[1325]   Article 5 of the Agreement on Mutual Legal Assistance between the European Union and the United States of America provide for the establishment of a joint investigation team between the United States and one or more Member States. It is further found in Article 19 United Nations Convention against Transnational Organized Crime of 15 November 2000 and the Second Protocol to the European Convention on Mutual Assistance in Criminal Matters of 8 November 2001.

[1326]   Recommendation of 25 April 2002, Doc. 5715/6/02 of 22 April 2002.

[1327]   Protocol of 28 November 2002 amending the Convention on the establishment of a European Police Office (Europol Convention) and the Protocol on the privileges and immunities of Europol, the members of its organs, the deputy directors and the employees of Europol, OJ 2002, C 312/2.

Europol officials may share information within the joint investigation team, and may, with the consent of, and under the responsibility of, the Member State which provided the information, add data to the computerised system (Article 3a, paragraphs 4 and 5).

One of the great advantages of a joint investigation team is that it may cross the borders of the participating Member States, depending on the necessities of its operations. It can move from one participating Member State to another when, for instance, the criminal organisation that it wishes to observe, does so. With regard to the applicable law and the question of which authority is to lead the joint investigation team, the Convention applies a kind of territoriality principle. Article 13, paragraph 3 (sub a) *EU Mutual Assistance Convention* determines that the leader should be a national of the Member State in which the team operates, and that the team must carry out its operations in accordance with the law of the Member State in which it operates (Article 13, paragraph 3 sub b). This means, of course, that, when the team moves from one Member State to another, both the leader and the applicable national legislation changes. Within the team, free exchange of information can take place. The various members of the joint investigation teams may request and obtain information from their own national authorities upon the basis of their national law. Requests for information and evidence upon the basis of the rules on mutual assistance do *not* have to be made, and the use of information is subject to certain conditions as mentioned in Article 13, paragraph 10. Members of the team, who are not of the Member State in which the operation takes place, may be entrusted with certain investigative measures when this has been approved by both national authorities (Article 13, paragraph 6).

Europol may request Member States to initiate criminal investigations (Article 88, paragraph 2 TFEU). Article 3b *Europol Convention* states that Member States should give due consideration to Europol requests. Europol should be informed as to whether the requested investigation will be initiated. Although the Convention does not state an obligation to initiate joint investigation teams, it becomes clear from paragraph 2 of Article 3b that the drafters did not like the possibility of Europol requests not being complied with. If a Member State fails to comply with the request, it must give reasons for doing so, unless national security interests or the interests of a pending investigation would otherwise be placed in jeopardy.

2.2. PROSECUTORIAL LEVEL: EUROJUST

Eurojust was established by a Decision in February 2002,[1328] as the successor of the Provisional Judicial Co-operation Unit.[1329] Article 2 *Eurojust Decision 2002/187* determines that Eurojust is composed of one national member seconded by each Member State.[1330] This member must be a prosecutor, a judge or a police officer. In practice, however, the majority of the members have had followed careers as prosecutors. The objectives of Eurojust are listed in Article 4, paragraph 1 Eurojust Decision; it is to:

- stimulate and improve co-ordination between the competent authorities of the Member States, of investigations and prosecutions;
- improve co-operation between the competent authorities of the Member States, in particular, by facilitating the execution of international mutual legal assistance and the implementation of extradition requests;[1331]
- support otherwise the competent authorities of the Member States in order to render their investigations and prosecutions more effective.

On condition that there is an agreement with a non-Member State, Eurojust may also assist investigations and prosecutions in non-Member States (Article 3, paragraph 2 *Eurojust Decision 2002/187*).

Article 4, paragraph 1 determines the crimes over which Eurojust has competence. These include those for which Europol is competent upon the basis of the *Europol Convention*, as well as other offences committed together with the offences mentioned above.[1332] For offences which do not fall into any of the previous categories, Eurojust has competence upon the request of a Member State (Article 4, paragraph 2 *Eurojust Decision 2002/187*). Article 85, paragraph 1 TFEU

[1328]   *Eurojust Decision 2002/187.* Article 85 TFEU provides a Regulation which will determine Eurojust's structure, operation, field of action and tasks. At the time of concluding the manuscript, such a Regulation, which should replace *Eurojust Decision 2002/187*, had not been adopted. Declaration 27 attached to the Treaty of Lisbon on Article 85(1), second sub-paragraph, of the TFEU states that the Regulations which will be drafted "should take into account national rules and practices relating to the initiation of criminal investigations".

[1329]   Decision 2000/799 of 14 December 2000 setting up a Provisional Judicial Cooperation Unit, OJ 2000, L 324/2. With the publication of *Eurojust Decision 2002/187* on 6 March 2002, the Provisional Judicial Co-operation Unit ceased to exist.

[1330]   In a Draft Council Decision on the strengthening of Eurojust amending Council Decision 2002/187/JHA of 28 February 2002, as amended by Council Decision 2003/659/JHA setting up Eurojust with a view to reinforcing the fight against serious crime, Council Document, 9980/08, 27 May 2008, it is proposed to set up a "on-call coordination" for urgent cases.

[1331]   See reference to Europol in Article 4 Decision 2001/887 of 6 December 2001 on the protection of the euro against counterfeiting.

[1332]   The reference to the offences mentioned in Article 2, par. 1(b) is now covered by the extension of Europol's competence under Article 2 *Europol Convention*.

extended Eurojust's competences to all "serious crime affecting two or more Member States or requiring a prosecution on common basis, on the basis of operations conducted and information supplied by the Member States' authorities and Europol".

Eurojust may act in two ways. The first way is to act through one or more members. The second way is that Eurojust acts as a College. When acting through a national member Eurojust may ask the competent authorities of the Member States all manner of questions. It may ask to start an investigation or a prosecution, it may ask a Member State to consider when another Member State may be in a better position to prosecute, or it may set up a joint investigation team and provide information (Article 6 *Eurojust Decision 2002/187*). Article 6 lists all kinds of initiatives which may be taken by Eurojust which aim to stimulate investigations and co-operation by the Member States and place emphasis on the co-ordination of prosecution.

The second manner in which Eurojust acts is as a College. The College of Eurojust is composed of all national members. One or more national members may request the College to act (Article 5, paragraph 1, sub (i)), when a case involves investigations or prosecutions which have repercussions at Union level, or which might affect Member States other than those directly involved (Article 5, paragraph 1, sub (ii)), when a general question relating to the achievement of its objectives is involved (Article 5, paragraph 1, sub (iii)), or when otherwise provided in the Decision (Article 5, paragraph 1, sub (iv)). Article 7 deals with Eurojust acting as a College, which can perform the tasks which may also be performed through a national member. In addition, the College may involve the assistance of Europol upon the basis of Europol's analysis. Article 8 makes it clear that, in principle, requests made by Eurojust when acting as a College should be complied with. A Member State that does not comply must state the reasons for doing so.[1333] Article 10 *Protocol to the EU Mutual Assistance Convention* gives Eurojust a role in solving problems relating to refusals of co-operation requests.

Contacts with national authorities and the Commission

The channel of communication between Eurojust and the Member States is exclusively through the national member (Article 9, paragraph 2 and Article 13). Article 9 further provides that a national member has the same access to all kinds of criminal records and other information as under national law. This means that the national member has no need of requests for mutual assistance. Access to personal data is limited to national members and their assistants (Article 18). Article 11 somewhat ambiguously determines that the Commission is to be fully associated with the work of Eurojust. The Decision stipulates that the legal basis for this association must be found in Article 36, paragraph 2 EU. In addition, the

---

[1333]   Article 8 provides two situations in which reasons need not be given.

Commission may be invited to provide its expertise, and Article 12 creates the possibility of appointing a national correspondent. However, the Decision does not specify what their tasks are, and merely states that it "shall be a matter of high priority to put in place a national correspondent for terrorism matters".

Article 14 empowers Eurojust to process the personal data of persons who, under the national legislation of a Member State, are the subject of a criminal investigation or prosecution for one of the crimes for which Eurojust is competent. Certain restrictions on data-processing are given upon the basis of Article 15 and all processing is subject to the regime provided by the 1981 Council of Europe Convention. In order to assist Eurojust in complying with data protection rules, a Data Protection Officer is appointed (Article 17). Article 16 stipulates that Eurojust may create an automated data file which constitutes an index of data relating to investigations, as well as structured manual files. The index contains references to temporary work files. Article 21 sets time-limits for the storage of personal data. The Eurojust Decision establishes a Joint Supervisory Body to monitor the activities of Eurojust with regard to personal data (Article 23).[1334]

Eurojust is to maintain close co-operation with Europol (Article 26, paragraph 1 *Eurojust Decision 2002/187*).[1335] One of the reasons for this is to avoid the duplication of effort. It is also to maintain relations with the European Judicial Network "based on consultation and complementarity". It is also to have access to all centralised information of the European Judicial Network (Article 26, paragraph 2). Further relations exists between Eurojust and OLAF.[1336] To this end, OLAF may contribute to Eurojust's work in order to co-ordinate investigations and prosecution procedures regarding the protection of the financial interests (Article 26, paragraph 3 and 4). However, OLAF does not have access to all or any of the information or evidence that has been collected by Eurojust (preambular paragraph 5). Article 27 further mandates Eurojust to exchange information with international organisations and bodies as well as with third states.[1337] However, in these cases, the national member of the Member State that submitted the information must give his consent to such an exchange.

Article 19 *Eurojust Decision 2002/187* grants the right to every individual to have access to all personal data concerning him that has been processed by Eurojust. Article 20 entitles every individual to request Eurojust to correct, block or delete data concerning him. Both the access and the correction and deletion

---

[1334] Act of the Joint Supervisory Body of Eurojust of 2 March 2004 laying down its rules of procedure, OJ 2004, C 86/1.

[1335] An agreement to this extent was concluded on 9 June 2004.

[1336] See Practical Agreement on arrangements of cooperation between Eurojust and OLAF, Council Document 9346/08, 14 May 2008.

[1337] There are agreements with Iceland (2005), Romania (2005), Norway (2006), the United States (2006), Croatia (2007). See Agreement between Eurojust and Switzerland, Council Document 9345/08, 14 May 2008.

are subject to several grounds of refusal. One of these being that access may jeopardise any national investigations which Eurojust is assisting. As with the other modes of co-operation discussed in this chapter, the basic question is: How does an individual know if Eurojust has data on him?

In the annual report to the Council and to the Parliament, Eurojust has to report on its activities and on any criminal policy problems within the European Union. It may also make proposals for the improvement of judicial co-operation in criminal matters (Article 32). Moreover, Article 85 TFEU provides a role for national parliaments in the evaluation of Eurojust's activities.

The improvement which the establishment of Eurojust has brought to international co-operation is twofold. First, it provides practical assistance at prosecutorial level for the transmission and execution of requests for international assistance. Second, it creates a forum in which decisions on the best place for the prosecution can be made. Eurojust does not have a formal competence to decide upon matters of plural jurisdiction. However, the very fact that prosecutors with expertise in the international co-operation of the relevant Member States can take up consultations on a specific case is *de facto* of enormous importance. The permanent structure should be conducive to the prevention of jurisdictional conflicts, and to multiple prosecutions and *ne bis in idem* problems.[1338]

2.3. JUDICIAL LEVEL: THE EUROPEAN JUDICIAL NETWORK

The European Judicial Network was created in 1998 upon the basis of a Joint Action.[1339] It consists of a network of contact points and central authorities responsible for international judicial co-operation. Article 3 of Joint Action 98/428 provides that the Network is to operate in particular by:

- facilitating the establishment of the appropriate contact points in the Member States;
- organising periodic meetings of the representatives of the Member States;
- providing up-to-date background information.

Through its task of facilitating judicial co-operation, the contact points are to serve as intermediaries. They should be available not only to local judicial authorities in their own country, but also to the contact points of other Member

---

[1338]   See Chapter 4, Section 3.2.8.

[1339]   Joint Action 98/428 on the European Judicial Network. There is a Draft Council Decision on the European Judicial Network, Council Document, 5039/08, 7 January 2008, of which a revised text was presented on 14 July 2008.

States and their local judicial authorities (Article 4 Joint Action). These contact points are to provide all Member States with the necessary legal and practical information in order to prepare an effective request for co-operation and to improve judicial co-operation in general. The purpose of the meetings of the European Judicial Network is, according to Article 5, to get to know each other and exchange experience, as well as to provide a forum for the discussion of practical and legal problems in the context of judicial co-operation. The European Judicial Network meets in Brussels (Article 7).

The information available within the European Judicial Network consists, upon the basis of Article 8 Joint Action 98/428, of the following:

- full details of the contact points;
- simplified list of judicial authorities in each Member State;
- concise legal and practical information on the judicial and procedural systems of the Member States;
- the texts of the relevant legal instruments.

In some legal instruments, reference is made to the European Judicial Network as a body that could be of assistance in the facilitation of requests for judicial assistance.[1340]

3.   DIRECT ENFORCEMENT

3.1.   COMPETITION LAW

The only area in which the Union currently has direct enforcement powers at its disposition is competition law. It has its origins in the internal market and was there from the very beginning of the European Communities. The substantive law of competition law is quite transparent. There are two prohibitions, which are clearly formulated in Articles 101 and 102 TFEU (formerly Articles 81 and 82 TEC): Article 101 prohibits price agreements, and Article 102 prohibits monopolies and abuse of a dominant position. Regulation 1/2003 further implements the rules on competition laid down in these two Treaty provisions.[1341]

[1340]   Article 2 *Joint Action 98/699 on Money Laundering*, Article 5 Decision 2003/335 of 8 May 2003 on the investigation and prosecution of genocide, crimes against humanity and war crimes, OJ 2003, L 118/12.

[1341]   Regulation 1/2003 repealed previous Regulation 17/62. It seems that the draft and the judgment of the Court in *Roquette Frères*, rendered only a few months before the adoption of the Regulation, mutually influenced each other. See 22 October 2002, Case C-94/00, *Roquette*

Regulation 1/2003 provides a system of de-centralised enforcement. Both the Commission and national competition authorities have the task of enforcing and applying Articles 101 and 102 TFEU directly. The Commission, acting on complaint or on its own initiative, may find that there has been an infringement of competition rules, and may impose behavioural and structural remedies (Article 7 Regulation 1/2003). Furthermore, in cases of urgency, the Commission may order interim measures (Article 8 Regulation 1/2003).

The powers of investigation which are given to the Commission are dealt with in Chapter V of Regulation 1/2003 (Articles 17–22). Article 18, paragraph 1 creates a general obligation for undertakings and associations of undertakings to provide all the necessary information when the Commission requires it. Non-compliance with this obligation may be subject to penalties as provided for in Articles 23 and 24. The Commission may interview any natural and legal person who consents to be interviewed for the purpose of collecting information (Article 19, paragraph 1 Regulation 1/2003). Article 20 provides the Commission with powers of inspection. Officials authorised by the Commission to conduct an inspection are empowered:

> "a. to enter any premises, land and means of transport of undertakings and associations of undertakings; b. to examine the books and other records related to the business, irrespective of the medium on which they are stored; c. to take or obtain in any form copies of or extracts from such books or records; d. to seal any business premises and books or records for the period and to the extent necessary for the inspection; e. to ask any representative or member of staff of the undertaking or association of undertakings for explanations on facts or documents relating to the subject-matter and purpose of the inspection and to record the answers."

On pain of penalties, undertakings are obliged to submit to inspections and to provide answers to the questions raised.

In addition, general principles of Union law may be influential. The accused may not be obliged to incriminate himself. The Court has held that any information that undertakings are obliged to give under the competition law Regulation may only be used in the context in which it has been furnished:

> "The purpose of the request for information is not to furnish evidence to be used by the Member States in proceedings governed by national law."[1342]

Frères SA v. Directeur général de la concurrence, de la consommation et de la répression des fraudes and the Commission [2002] ECR I-9011.

[1342]   16 July 1992, Case C-67/91, Dirección General de Defensa de la Competencia and eight Spanish banks [1992] ECR I-4085, par. 33.

Information that has been collected by the Commission through its own investigators may be used in national proceedings.[1343]

If the Commission encounters opposition from an undertaking with regard to an inspection, it may ask the authorities of the Member State in whose territory the inspection is conducted to offer the appropriate assistance of the police or of an equivalent authority (Article 20, paragraph 6). The competent national judicial authority will control the proportionality of the envisaged coercive measures (Article 20, paragraph 8). The Court has held that there is a reciprocal obligation for *both* the authorities of the Member States *and* the Commission to co-operate in good faith, this form of co-operation is regarded by the Court as being particularly crucial.[1344]

Other premises than those of the undertakings may be inspected if there is reasonable suspicion that the books or other records related to prohibited practices are kept there. Upon the basis of Article 21, paragraph 1, this may relate to "any other premises, land and means of transport, including the homes of directors, managers and other members of staff of the undertaking or associations concerned". This power of inspection is dependant on prior authorisation of the competent national judicial authority (Article 21, paragraph 3). Again, the judicial authority may test the proportionality of the inspection, but may not call the necessity for the inspection into question. The Court has ruled that the national court may examine whether the coercive measures requested by the Commission are arbitrary, whether they are proportionate to the subject-matter of the investigation, and whether a national court could examine the need for the investigation ordered by the Commission.[1345] All information collected pursuant to Articles 17 to 22 may only be used for the purpose for which it was acquired (Article 28, paragraph 1).

Article 22 empowers national competition authorities to carry out any inspection on their own territory or fact-finding measure under their own national law on the request of the competition authorities of other Member States or of the Commission. Article 11 Regulation 1/2003 contains a general and mutual obligation to co-operate with the Commission and the national competition authorities. This includes the transmission of documents, evidence and other information (Articles 11 and 12). Article 15 regulates the co-operation with national courts. Courts may ask the Commission to submit information that it

---

[1343]   23 November 1995, Case C-476/93 P, *Nutral SpA* v. *Commission* [1995] ECR I-4125, par. 20–22.

[1344]   22 October 2002, Case C-94/00, *Roquette Frères SA* v. *Directeur général de la concurrence, de la consommation et de la répression des fraudes and the Commission* [2002] ECR I-9011, par. 31 and 32.

[1345]   22 October 2002, Case C-94/00, *Roquette Frères SA* v. *Directeur général de la concurrence, de la consommation et de la répression des fraudes and the Commission* [2002] ECR I-9011, par. 34–40.

has in its possession, and competition authorities may submit written observations to national courts relating to the application of Articles 101 and 102 TFEU. Article 16 states that decisions of national courts may not run counter to the decisions taken by the Commission.

Article 13 deals with multiple proceedings and stipulates that where competition authorities of two or more Member States have received a complaint or are acting on their own initiative, the fact that one authority is dealing with the case represents sufficient grounds for the others to suspend their proceedings. The Commission may also reject a complaint on such grounds. Article 11, paragraph 6 affirms the primacy of the Commission. The initiation of proceedings by the Commission relieves the competition authorities of the Member States of their competence to apply Articles 101 and 102. If a national authority is already acting on a case, the Commission may only initiate proceedings after consultation with that authority. In order to facilitate this, an informal Network of Competition Authorities, which is made up of the national competition authorities and the Commission, has been set up.[1346]

The Commission has formulated allocation criteria to find the authority best-placed to deal with cases. The material link consists of three elements: 1. the practice has substantial direct effect on the territory of the Member State; 2. the local authority can effectively bring to an end the entire infringement; and 3. the local authority can gather the evidence required.[1347] The Commission is particularly well-placed if one or several agreements or practices have effect on competition in more than three Member States.[1348]

Undertakings will be given the opportunity to be heard before the Commission takes decisions on the question of whether there is a infringement or not (Article 27). The sentence that, "The Commission shall base its decisions only on objections on which the parties concerned have been able to comment", is procedurally of significant importance. Paragraph 2 of Article 27 states that the rights of the defence are to be fully respected in the proceedings. Article 27 provides for access to the file and an obligation to disclose, albeit with certain exceptions relating to internal documents. In addition to the undertakings concerned, the Commission may also hear other natural or legal persons (Article 27, paragraph 3).

Penalties for the various infringements are provided for in Articles 23 of Regulation 1/2003. All fines can be imposed by the Commission itself. Paragraph

---

[1346] See Commission Notice on cooperation within the Network of Competition Authorities, OJ 2004, C 101/43 and Joint Statement of the Council and the Commission on the functioning of the network of competition authorities, Council Document, 10 December 2002, 15435/02, Add. 1.

[1347] See Commission Notice on co-operation within the Network of Competition Authorities, OJ 2004, C 101/43, par. 8.

[1348] See Commission Notice on co-operation within the Network of Competition Authorities, OJ 2004, C 101/43, par. 11.

1 of Article 23 deals with a number of violations of the obligations to supply the Commission with (correct) information, to admit its officials to the premises of the undertaking, and so on. Paragraph 2 of Article 23 covers the penalties for the infringement of the hard core competition law obligations of Articles 101 and 102 TFEU. Article 24 gives the Commission the competence to impose periodic payments.

Article 25 stipulates a limitation period of three years for the imposition of penalties in cases of infringements of provisions concerning requests for information or the conduct of inspections. For all other infringements, the limitation period is five years. Article 25 further mentions a number of actions that have the effect of interrupting the period of limitation. The period of limitation for enforcement is five years for all decisions (Article 26). The Court has unlimited jurisdiction to review the decisions whereby the Commission has fixed a fine or periodic penalty payment. Furthermore, it may cancel, reduce or increase the fine or periodic penalty payment imposed (Article 31).

Article 23, paragraph 5 reads: "Decisions taken pursuant to paragraphs 1 and 2 shall not be of a criminal nature." In the eighth preambular of Regulation 1/2003, it is mentioned that:

"Furthermore, this Regulation does not apply to national laws which impose criminal sanctions on natural persons except to the extent that such sanctions are the means whereby competition rules applying to undertakings are enforced."

Despite these statements, competition law has been classified as criminal law upon the basis of an autonomous interpretation of the ECtHR of Article 6 ECHR.[1349]

In summary, competition law provides a micro criminal justice system at Union level. There is Union-wide applicable substantive law (Article 101 and 102 TFEU). There is a competent authority for investigation (the Commission), which follows common procedural rules (Regulation 1/2003). The Commission may impose fines, which are subject to appeal with the Court. There is jurisdiction both for national authorities and for the Commission. Although both apply the same substantive law, national authorities will follow national legislation. Regulation 1/2003 provides primacy of jurisdiction for the Commission. There are also points on which the current competition law scheme differs from criminal justice systems in the Member States. In particular, the combination of investigator, prosecutor and first instance judge does not exist in the criminal justice systems of the Member States for offences of such a serious nature that they incur drastic fines. Many countries provide for a similar accumulation of functions for the

---

[1349] See Chapter 1, and Chapter 4, Section 4.2.

public prosecution. This may lead to the imposition or conclusion of out-of-court settlements. However, such procedures are generally applied to minor cases.

3.2. THE EUROPEAN PUBLIC PROSECUTOR'S OFFICE

With the ratification of the Treaty of Lisbon a European Public Prosecutor's Office will not be immediately established from Eurojust. Further legislation will be necessary. Article 86 TFEU mandates the Council to establish a European Public Prosecutor's Office from Eurojust by means of a Regulation. The provision in the TFEU raises more questions than that it provides answers. Paragraphs 2, 3 and 4 of Article 86 stipulate the substantive jurisdiction of the European Public Prosecutor's Office:

"Article 86 TFEU

1. In order to combat crimes affecting the financial interests of the Union, the Council, by means of regulations adopted in accordance with a special legislative procedure, may establish a European Public Prosecutor's Office from Eurojust. The Council shall act unanimously after obtaining the consent of the European Parliament.

In the absence of unanimity in the Council, a group of at least nine Member States may request that the draft regulation be referred to the European Council. In that case, the procedure in the Council shall be suspended. After discussion, and in case of a consensus, the European Council shall, within four months of this suspension, refer the draft back to the Council for adoption.

Within the same timeframe, in case of disagreement, and if at least nine Member States wish to establish enhanced cooperation on the basis of the draft regulation concerned, they shall notify the European Parliament, the Council and the Commission accordingly. In such a case, the authorisation to proceed with enhanced cooperation referred to in Article 20(2) of the Treaty on European Union and Article 329(1) of this Treaty shall be deemed to be granted and the provisions on enhanced cooperation shall apply.

2. The European Public Prosecutor's Office shall be responsible for investigating, prosecuting and bringing to judgment, where appropriate in liaison with Europol, the perpetrators of, and accomplices in, offences against the Union's financial interests, as determined by the regulation provided for in paragraph 1. It shall exercise the functions of prosecutor in the competent courts of the Member States in relation to such offences.

3. The regulations referred to in paragraph 1 shall determine the general rules applicable to the European Public Prosecutor's Office, the conditions governing the performance of its functions, the rules of procedure applicable to its activities, as well as those governing the admissibility of evidence, and the rules applicable to the judicial review of procedural measures taken by it in the performance of its functions.

4. The European Council may, at the same time or subsequently, adopt a decision amending paragraph 1 in order to extend the powers of the European Public Prosecutor's Office to include serious crime having a cross-border dimension and amending accordingly paragraph 2 as regards the perpetrators of, and accomplices in, serious crimes affecting more than one Member State. The European Council shall act unanimously after obtaining the consent of the European Parliament and after consulting the Commission."

The crimes for which the European Public Prosecutor's Office is competent are offences against the Union's financial interests.[1350] Paragraph 4 allows for the extension of the list of crimes for which the European Public Prosecutor's Office is competent by decision by the European Council. This must relate to "the perpetrators of, and accomplices in, serious crimes affecting more than one Member State". Paragraph 4 is formulated somewhat ambiguously; it first refers to "serious crime having a cross-border dimension", which is distinct from crimes which affect more than one state. A Regulation will not only have to further determine the concrete offences, but also have to deal with offences that are committed in conjunction with offences for which there is no jurisdiction for the European Public Prosecutor's Office. Will the European Public Prosecutor's Office have exclusive jurisdiction, is its jurisdiction complementary to national jurisdiction, and, if so, under what conditions will the European Public Prosecutor's Office have primacy?

The group of suspects for which the European Public Prosecutor's Office is competent are the perpetrators of, and the accomplices in the offences, for which there is jurisdiction. The Regulations to be drafted will have to define who or what is considered to be a perpetrator or an accomplice at Union level. Does the European Public Prosecutor's Office base its assessment that it has jurisdiction upon Union criteria or does it do so upon the basis of the national rules of the Member State in which it wishes to bring the case to court? Does the national criminal court have to apply the provisions of the Regulation directly, for instance, as in competition law, or is the national implementing legislation the norm to assess criminal liability? These questions not only relate to the definition of the crime, but also to the penalties provided and the conditions under which the penalties imposed are executed.

[1350] The reference to the crimes in paragraph 2 differs from the wording in paragraph 1 "crimes affecting the financial interests of the Union".

The procedural tasks of the European Public Prosecutor's Office, given in paragraph 2 of Article 86, are threefold: it is to be responsible for investigating, prosecuting and bringing to judgment. The Treaty adds that, where appropriate, this is to be done in liaison with Europol. However, what has to be regulated is the (hierarchical) relationship with national police and prosecutorial authorities, as well as under which rules co-operation takes place. The last sentence of paragraph 2 of Article 86 is more than symbolic:

> "It shall exercise the functions of prosecutor in the competent courts of the Member States in relation to such offences."

This means that the European Public Prosecutor's Office not only decides upon which cases will be brought to a national criminal court, but also in which Member State they will take place.[1351] Does the possibility of out-of-court settlements exist? Or should Article 86 be read narrowly in the sense that it only envisages *prosecution* before court. However, what is self evident is that, if the case is brought to court, the European Public Prosecutor's Office will then also request the national court to impose a certain sanction. This is one of the most intriguing elements of the competence of the European Public Prosecutor's Office. Will European sentencing tariffs be formulated, or will the European Public Prosecutor's Office limit itself to the standards and customs of the relevant Member State?

The phrasing of paragraph 3 of Article 86 is rather broad:

> "the conditions governing the performance of its functions, the rules of procedure applicable to its activities, as well as those governing the admissibility of evidence, and the rules applicable to the judicial review of procedural measures taken by it in the performance of its functions."

Which court is to review? A national supreme court or the Court? There are some similarities with the structure of de-centralised enforcement of competition law which will require a role for the Court. But this will also depend on the scope of the review.

Article 86 TFEU does not mention the execution of the sentences or its termination. Since all other instances of the criminal proceedings are covered, it must be drawn from this that no role is provided for the European Public Prosecutor's Office in the execution of the sentences imposed by national criminal

---

[1351]   This requires full knowledge of the jurisdictional rules of the various Member States or to accept the risk of having to face a finding of incompetence by a national court that does not have jurisdiction.

courts. There is no competence under the current Article 86 to establish a European prison facility.

Article 86, paragraph 1, provides that the Regulation will be adopted by a special legislative procedure as provided in Article 289 TFEU. The Council must act unanimously after obtaining the consent of the European Parliament. In the absence of unanimity, which is, in the given political circumstances, most likely, a group of at least nine Member States may request a draft Regulation to be referred to the Council for discussion. Paragraph 1 further provides for different procedures in case of consensus or disagreement. What is more relevant for our topic, is that the Regulations on the establishment of a European Public Prosecutor's Office may be adopted and enter into force for a minimum of one third of the Member States (nine + x). Given the political situation of the day, it is most likely that the European Public Prosecutor's Office will initially start for a limited number of Member States.

When drafting the Regulation on the establishment of a European Public Prosecutor's Office, earlier attempts should be examined. The Commission presented a Green Paper on the Public Prosecutor,[1352] in 2001, after it had asked a group of experts to draft a number of guiding principles in relation to the protection, in criminal law, of the financial interests of the Union. It lead to the publication of the *Corpus Juris*, which introduced provisions for the purpose of protecting the financial interests of the European Union.[1353]

4.   THE POSITION OF THE DEFENCE IN MULTI-LATERAL CO-OPERATION AND DIRECT ENFORCEMENT

Earlier, in Chapter 7, the position of the defence in international co-operation in criminal matters was discussed.[1354] There are a number of aspects in multi-lateral co-operation which justify the conclusion that the position of the defence is worsened when it is confronted with multi-lateral co-operation. This first has to do with the very early stage of the criminal investigations in which the multi-lateral co-operation takes place. The (future) suspect might not be aware of the fact that he is already, or soon will be, suspected of having committed a crime. In addition to bilateral co-operation, it is even more difficult to find a court competent to complain to about violations of the law. Many cases in which investigations (and violations) have taken place, will not come to court. Complaints about

---

[1352]   COM(2001) 715, 11 December 2001.
[1353]   See M. Delmas-Marty & J.A.E. Vervaele, *The Implementation of the* Corpus Juris *in the Member States*, (Antwerp: Intersentia, 2000).
[1354]   See Chapter 7, Section 6.4.

infringements of rights for investigations which did not lead to criminal proceedings against the (former) suspect have difficulties in finding a court that can deal with the matter. This is not much better when (criminal) proceedings are brought against the person involved. Then, it will be both practically and legally most difficult to produce evidence of a violation which has been committed multi-laterally. The defence does not have access to the relevant information. This may be caused by the fact that law enforcement officials might be under an obligation not to testify, or might have an interest in not clarifying certain facts. All of this seriously undermines the possibilities for courts to check whether evidence, which has been collected as a result of multi-lateral co-operation was obtained lawfully or unlawfully. The Court is of no help in this respect, since Article 276 TFEU explicitly rules out any jurisdiction of the Court "to review the validity or proportionality of operations carried out by the police or other law-enforcement services of a Member State".[1355]

5.   THE EMERGENCE OF CO-ORDINATED EUROPEAN INVESTIGATIONS

The establishment of new bodies, such as Europol, Eurojust and the European Public Prosecutor's Office, represents something new, something pan-European. And because it does, this institutional integration has an effect which is different from that of normative harmonisation or integration, by virtue of more comprehensive co-operation. Where the normative harmonisation leads to changes in the national law of the Member States, but leaves the institutional structure in the Member States unaffected, institutional integration creates a European body which is there for all the Member States of the European Union. This, too, can have an integrative and harmonising effect. Clearly, some harmonising influence from the common body can be expected. But there is also another effect, in that all existing national structures remain in place (the national police forces have not, of course, been disbanded, and have not lost their authority).[1356] Prior to the foundation of Europol, all information exchange took place between the national police forces, as equals, and was always bilateral in nature. Now that Europol is operational, the horizontal-bilateral contacts are supplemented by a vertical line, with Europol.

[1355]   One may question whether this limitation, in view of the further integration since the provision first appeared in the Treaty of Amsterdam, should not be abolished.

[1356]   It seems that this effect is considered little, if at all, within the Union.

The lines of communication and the bodies involved in co-operation have multiplied

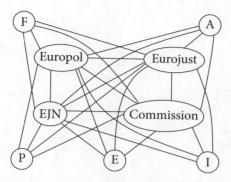

Progressively, the European Union covers more and more fields, and with bodies of its own. It started with Europol, but subsequently European bodies for prosecutors and judges have been created. The establishment of a European Public Prosecutor's Office is a logical next step if the European Union intends to create its own competences in the field of criminal law. At another level, more time and effort is dedicated to training. Article 3, paragraphs 2 and 3 *Europol Convention* give Europol the task of contributing to the building and improving of skills and expertise. The setting up of new bodies can be interpreted as steps that could ultimately lead to a European criminal justice system.

For the development of expertise in all the forms of crime that exist within the European Union, criminological research is important. The European crime prevention network aims to contribute to the development of crime prevention.[1357] This network does not relate to operational co-operation in concrete cases, but tries to improve the manner in which crime is prevented by exchange of experience and sharing of knowledge. Article 1, paragraph 3 of the Decision defines crime prevention as follows:

> "Crime prevention covers all measures that are intended to reduce or otherwise contribute to reducing crime and citizens' feeling of insecurity, both quantitatively and qualitatively, either through directly deterring criminal activities or through policies and interventions designed to reduce the potential for crime and the causes of crime. It includes work by government, competent authorities, criminal justice agencies, local authorities, and the specialist associations they have set up in Europe, the private and voluntary sectors, researchers and the public, supported by the media."

Insight into the reality of crime and criminal organisations may improve the quality of legislative initiatives.

[1357]   Decision of 28 May 2001 setting up a European Crime Prevention Network, OJ 2001, L 153/1.

PART IV.
THE CHALLENGES OF
EUROPEAN CRIMINAL LAW

The challenges for further development of European criminal law are numerous, and mainly relate to the merger of the internal market with the area of freedom, security and justice, as well as the embryonic stage in which a European criminal justice system entrenches itself. Part IV uses Parts I, II and III from the perspective of where the needs for a European criminal justice system actually lie. It pays particular attention to the person who is central to all criminal proceedings: the accused.

CHAPTER 9.
RETHINKING EUROPEAN
CRIMINAL LAW

1. INTRODUCTION

European criminal law deals with a multi-layered patchwork of legislation and case law in which both national courts, the Court, European and national legislatures, as well as other authorities and bodies play a role. It is a hybrid system with common notions and values, as well as individual particularities. This book has characterised European criminal law as a field of law in which the perspectives are changing. In other words, the European criminal justice system is in transition. In this concluding chapter, a number of changing perspectives will be further analysed, and are presented below as tendencies, and may, therefore, be generalisations to a certain extent.

2. THE CONVERGENCE OF THE INTERNAL MARKET AND THE AREA OF FREEDOM, SECURITY AND JUSTICE

Despite the complete merger of the internal market with the area of freedom, security and justice, the Court has interpreted notions of Third Pillar legal instruments in a predominantly internal market context. Thus, it has not completely given recognition of the changed character of the European Union after its coming into existence. However, from 1992 onwards, the Union is no longer a purely economic organisation. Although the four freedoms are unaffected by this development, in a relative way they have lost their paramount meaning in the sense that there are other dominant freedoms which Union law upholds. Thus, for the coming years, it may be expected that mutual recognition and the full abolition of discrimination between nationals will be the main themes in criminal law. This is explicitly stated, but vaguely described, in the goals of the area of freedom, security and justice: to provide citizens with a high level of safety.

To date, the Court has adjusted provisions of criminal legislation to the needs of the internal market. From the perspective of maintaining consistency and uniformity of the law in a fully-integrated European Union, this is logical.

However, more and more situations will arise in which internal market principles will need to be adjusted to the needs of criminal justice systems. The free flow of law enforcement officials, unconditional access to information and evidence, and unconditional recognition of decisions and judgments will simply frustrate effective law enforcement and will be detrimental to the rights of individuals. The main issue to be dealt with here is the translation of the concept of mutual recognition in a criminal setting. The current pre-dominant position of the Member State taking the first initiative stands in the way of the development of a Union approach to combating crime. As identified in Chapter 7, mutual recognition has been developed into a somewhat nationalistic, view on crime and the jurisdiction of Member States. In this view, the first Member State to positively act determines the course of proceedings. However, this may certainly come into conflict with the goal of the Union to provide its citizens with a high level of safety. A more European approach which corresponded much more to the goals of the internal market would not give priority to the self-defined interests of the individual Member State, but would, instead, establish criteria under which it would become irrelevant in which Member State a certain offence was dealt with, the prevailing notion being that, when crime is combated, the interests of everyone involved should be taken into consideration.[1358] After all, the area of freedom, security and justice has been declared to offer a high level of safety to the citizens of the Union as a whole, and not to serve the interests of a particular Member State alone.

In the context of the complex legal order in which the fundamental freedoms of the internal market are established, differences in legislation between the Member States are much more problematical than in the context of the high level of security ensured by the Union, which maintains 29 criminal justice systems. As long as individual Member State jurisdiction in criminal matters exists, there is more need for mutual recognition than for harmonisation. In this sense, the area of freedom, security and justice – unlike the internal market – maintains borders. By and large, Member States determine whether and where their national criminal law applies. A common European criminal justice area that directly determines the conduct that is criminal and enforces it itself, has not yet been proclaimed.

[1358]   The Member States involved, the Union, the accused, the victims and the witnesses.

3.   RIGHTS FOR CITIZENS AND RIGHTS FOR MEMBER STATES

While the internal market gives rights to the citizens of the European Union in the form of the five freedoms, the rights that are applicable in the area of freedom, security and justice are given to the Member States. The Member States profit directly from more flexibility with regard to all forms of international co-operation. Citizens, however, profit only in an indirect manner from the area of freedom, security and justice, because, although it does offer them a high level of security, it does so in the absence of a direct and concrete claim. A balance between economic interests and human rights, between the interests of the Union, the Member States and the citizens, which will also enable the citizen to profit directly from the achievements in this area, needs to be found.

The inclusion of non-economic fields into the Union legal order requires certain adjustments of long-standing principles because of a changed perspective in which the interests of EU citizens are central. These EU citizens have their own rights which may come into conflict with the rights of the Member States. The opposite perspectives of those who enjoy the rights of this area requires a balance to be found. While the internal market grants rights to citizens, the area of freedom, security and justice predominantly grants rights to the Member States. To apply the principles developed in the internal market in exactly the same manner in the latter context will lead to friction. The Court was implicitly confronted with this in the *ne bis in idem* cases. Both in *Gözütok* and in *Kretzinger*, the Court saw that the rights granted in Article 54 *CISA* could have a discriminating effect on the use of free movement rights. It was opposed to a situation in which those who had committed serious offences would benefit and those who had committed less serious offences would not.[1359] *Ne bis in idem* is, in this sense, an extraordinary phenomenon, because it offers rights both for a Member State (to have its decision recognised) as well as for the individual (not to be prosecuted again).

The case law on Article 54 *CISA* consists of promising steps towards the finding of an equilibrium between the values protected by both areas on the one hand, and between the rights of the individual citizen and the interests of the Member States on the other. The recognition of rights to EU nationals outside of the economic sphere will require the formulation of additional or new general principles of Union law. This may lead to principles that are much more fundamental rights-oriented than oriented towards the economic well being of the Union. Such principles may relate, for instance, to the relationship of the

---

[1359]   11 February 2003, Case C-187/01 and Case C-385/01, *criminal proceedings against Hüseyin Gözütok (C-187/01) and Klaus Brügge (C-385/01)* [2003] ECR I-1345, par. 38–40; 18 July 2007, Case C-288/05, *criminal proceedings against Jürgen Kretzinger* [2007] ECR I-6441, par. 43.

principle of proportionality and the principle of mutual recognition in surrender proceedings, or to the meaning of the rights of the defence in mutual recognition. It is useful to recall the words of the Court in *van Gend en Loos*, when it dealt with the new legal order that had come into being: The subjects of the new legal order is comprised not only of the Member States, but also of their nationals.[1360]

The principle of availability serves the exclusive interests of the law enforcement authorities. The exchange of privacy-sensitive data upon the basis of availability requires surveillance of data-protection rules. The fact that more and more mechanisms are constructed in which respect for data-protection rules is tested by those authorities that have an interest in gaining access to the information is not conducive to an objective approach. In a Union legal order which is striving for the free availability of all the information in the possession of all Member State authorities, data protection is essential.

4.   FREEDOM OF MOVEMENT AND EQUAL TREATMENT AS THE FIFTH FREEDOM

The development of free movement as a separate right (independent of the application of one of the other four freedoms) and the prohibition of discrimination upon the basis of nationality are of growing importance in the criminal justice system. The case law of the Court has virtually brought every EU-citizen in another Member State within the scope of the Treaties. Both suspects and the accused are notably included in the category of persons that are entitled to all Union freedoms. The combination of free movement and non-discrimination has also evolved a fifth freedom: within the Union, EU nationals may not be discriminated on grounds of nationality. This can also be regarded as an example of the principle of equivalence of conditions. For the coming years, this will have considerable impact on the practice of all national criminal justice systems, as many differences in the application of national criminal law and criminal procedure indirectly relate to differences founded upon the basis of nationality.

In situations before *Directive 2004/38 on Free Movement* became effective, the Court interpreted Article 18 TEC so that "a citizen of the Union must be granted in all Member States the same treatment in law as that accorded to the nationals of those Member State who find themselves in the same situation".[1361] Many Member States, when making decisions on either the continuation or the suspension of detention on remand, take into consideration whether the accused is domiciled within the country. In the past, this made sense, because if he was

---

[1360]   5 February 1963, Case 26-62, *Van Gend en Loos* [1963] ECR 1.
[1361]   29 April 2004, Case C-224/02, *Heikki Antero Pusa* v. *Osuuspankkien Keskinäinen Vakuutusyhtiö* [2004] ECR I-5763, par. 18.

not a domicile in the country, there would be an increased risk that he would abscond. Similar considerations are applied when decisions on early release or on conditional pardon are made. The fact that the convicted person may not stay in the country makes it almost impossible to supervise the conditions for his release or for his parole. Further discrimination may take place during detention when it comes to penitentiary programmes and vocational training. These may be structured towards the rehabilitation and re-integration of the convicted person into the Member State in which he was convicted, despite the fact that he will not stay there. The fifth freedom will have consequences in purely internal situations, but also in co-operation in criminal matters, both with Member States and with third states.[1362]

5. MUTUAL RECOGNITION: FROM A STATE APPROACH TO A UNION APPROACH

The understanding of mutual recognition as a mechanism by which the Member State taking the first initiative in a matter determines the conditions pertinent to the matter is not based upon an objective evaluation of all the interest involved. It has been characterised as a system with narcissistic elements, lacking a Union approach of combating crime. This Union approach only becomes possible when more interests are taken into consideration, but the mechanisms adopted by the Union in criminal law implicitly assume that the state taking the first initiative has exclusive jurisdiction. This can be deduced from the consequences that it attaches to the initiatives of the Member State in question. In the case of two prosecutions, the second Member State to prosecute, must terminate its proceedings when another Member State has finally disposed of the matter previously.

The exclusiveness of the jurisdiction of the Member State which takes the first initative is also implied in the principle of mutual recognition in international co-operation. In principle, the first Member State determines the conditions. The notion of exclusiveness, however, is in conflict with the, by and large, overlapping jurisdiction of the Member States in criminal matters. With regard to the special part of European criminal law, overlapping jurisdiction of the Member States exists by definition. As a consequence, the presumption of exclusive jurisdiction is unjustified and creates an undesired competitive element between Member States, and this situation jeopardises efficient action, because it diminishes the options for co-operation.

[1362] See Opinion of Advocate General Poiares Maduro of 9 September 2008, Case C-465/07, *M. Elgafaji, N. Elgafaji* v. *Staatssecretaris van Justitie* ECR not yet reported.

In the context of mutual recognition, there is a lot to learn from other fields of law. *Regulation 44/2001 on Jurisdiction and Recognition of Civil Judgments*, as well as *Directive 91/439 on Driving Licences* confers the exclusive competence to the issuing of driving licences,[1363] and Regulation 2201/2003 in Matrimonial Matters,[1364] first stipulate jurisdictional rules before they determine that decisions are to be mutually recognised. The advantages of this system are obvious: it reduces the possibility of competing decisions and it bases jurisdiction upon commonly accepted rules that contribute to recognition.

Such a severe reduction of competing decisions would be possible if the Union were to limit the criminal jurisdiction of the individual Member State to territorial jurisdiction. Other principles of jurisdiction would no longer apply to the *loci delicti* in the remaining 26 Member States. Thus, Germany would no longer be able to prosecute drug use in Spain by a German subject (or anyone else). But this would also mean that, if Greece deemed it necessary to make keeping notes of airplane registration numbers (plane-spotting) an offence, the Netherlands would have to help them in the investigation and prosecution. This would do justice to the principle of legality. It requires a great deal of trust, but offers advantages both for law enforcement as well as for the safeguards of the individual. It is also always clear which Member State is called upon to enforce, and this state is responsible if anything goes wrong and if fundamental rights are violated.

The abolition of the double criminality rule and restriction of jurisdiction to domestic territory, enables the Union to construct a better network of international co-operation in criminal matters. Legality does not play a role in international co-operation. As the Court held in *Advocaten voor de Wereld*, double criminality is not necessary to serve the needs of the legality principle. However, the reduction of overlapping jurisdiction may require the abolition of double criminality. But why would the substantive criminal law of a Member State that has no jurisdiction (or does not claim it) over the offence influence whether another Member State can be assisted or not?

[1363]   26 June 2008, Joined Cases C-329/06 and C-343/06, *Arthur Wiedemann (C-329/06)* v. *Land Baden-Württemberg and Peter Funk (C-334/06)* v. *Stadt Chemnitz* [2008] ECR not yet reported, par. 56; 26 June 2008, Joined Cases C-334/06 to C-336/06, *Matthias Zerche (C-334/06), Manfred Seuke (C-336/06)* v. *Landkreis Mittweida and Steffen Schubert (C-335/06)* v. *Landkreis Mittlerer Erzgebirgskreis* [2008] ECR not yet reported, par. 53.

[1364]   Regulation 2201/2003 of 27 November 2003 concerning jurisdiction and the recognition and enforcement of judgments in matrimonial matters and the matter of parental responsibility, repealing Regulation 1347/2000, OJ 2003, L 338/1.

6.   HUMAN RIGHTS IN THE UNION LEGAL ORDER

The impact of the accession of the Union to the ECHR cannot be overestimated. It makes the Union directly responsible for human rights violations. Complaints may be lodged against the Union itself. All of this will further contribute to the establishment of the Union legal order as a European criminal justice system.

The fact that the Union and the Member States share competences raises questions about the division of responsibilities under the ECHR. Is the enforcement obligation also applicable with regard to the rights embodied in the ECHR? Is there any hierarchy between fundamental freedoms and fundamental rights? What is the standing of the Charter where it offers rights other than those of the ECHR, such as the right to security (Article 6 Charter)? International co-operation, in particular, both under the request model, and under both the mutual recognition model and the availability model, requires a conceptualisation of the responsibility of the Member State and of the Union for human rights violations. Which Member State is responsible for the violations during the trial? The Member State that conducted the trial, or the Member State that executes the sentence after a transfer of execution based upon mutual recognition. A new perspective on human rights is necessary. Human rights must be ensured to individuals, regardless of whether it is a single Member State that violates human rights or whether two or more Member States or the Union commit the violations. Human rights must not be ensured within the jurisdiction of a single Member State, but within the area of freedom, security and justice as a whole.

7.   THE EMERGENCE OF A EUROPEAN CRIMINAL JUSTICE SYSTEM

The gradual establishment of Union bodies and offices in the field of criminal justice demonstrates that a European criminal justice system is emerging. This can be seen from the establishment of Europol, Eurojust, the European Judicial Network, and the European Public Prosecutor's Office. The merger of the two areas as provided by the Treaty of Lisbon will bring important changes to criminal justice. The Member States are under obligation to enforce Union law and the supervisory mechanism applies. All principles developed in the internal market will be applicable in the area of freedom, security and justice. In addition, the Union must accede to the European Convention on Human Rights. This results in a picture that allows the Union to be characterised as a criminal justice system *sui generis* that applies the rule of law.

With regard to criminal law, it raises, for instance, the question of whether codification of the general part is necessary. The developments to date have gone a different way and do not pay much attention to codification. The fragments of the general part which can be found on Union law are not codified. However, one must also realise that the existence of a general part does not depend upon codification. Common law systems are examples of this. For direct enforcement, it seems that codification is inevitable.

When looking back at the last fifty years of European integration, the process of integration can be characterised as a linear process. Gradually, steps towards further integration have been taken. Occasionally, these steps were taken by the Member States in the form of treaties or amendments to the existing treaties. This is not to say that there has never been a stand-still, but this was always of a rather temporary nature. Quite often, deadlock in the political process was opened up by decisions of the Court. It is astonishing that the Member States have never attempted to present legislation in order to restore the previous situation after any ground-breaking judgment of the Court. It demonstrates that the Court has obtained the respect of the Member States. In this sense, the Court fulfils the role of independent arbitrator in the political process. The Court has continuously been the driving engine behind the integration of all fields of law. For decades, the Court has proven to be averse to taking political considerations into account. Not only in preliminary decisions, but also infraction procedures, the Court has proven to be willing to break new ground in its decisions. In the cases *van Gend en Loos*,[1365] *Casati*,[1366] *Pretore di Salò*,[1367] *Kolpinghuis*,[1368] *Gözütok and Brügge*,[1369] *Pupino*,[1370] and *Commission* v. *the Council*,[1371] the Court has shown a considerable degree of creativity in the interpretation of *both* the significance of a Union without internal borders *and* its consequences for criminal law. In practice, the

---

[1365]   5 February 1963, Case 26-62, *Van Gend en Loos* [1963] ECR 1. In which the Court held that Union law creates a new legal order with direct applicable rights for individuals.

[1366]   11 November 1981, Case 203/80, *criminal proceedings against Guerrino Casati* [1981] ECR 2595. By holding that Union law may also influence criminal law and criminal procedure.

[1367]   11 June 1987, Case 14/86, *Pretore di Salò v. Persons unknown* [1987] ECR 3969. In which the Court admitted references for preliminary rulings during the investigatory stage of criminal proceedings.

[1368]   8 October 1987, Case 80/86, *criminal proceedings against Kolpinghuis Nijmegen B.V.* [1987] ECR 3969. In which the Court declared that Community legislation cannot – of itself – establish or aggravate criminal liability.

[1369]   11 February 2003, Case C-187/01 and Case C-385/01, *criminal proceedings against Hüseyin Gözütok (C-187/01) and Klaus Brügge (C-385/01)* [2003] ECR I-1345, For example, by giving an interpretation of the Schengen Convention which was explicitly rejected by the Contracting Parties at the time that the Convention was negotiated.

[1370]   16 June 2005, Case C-105/03, *criminal proceedings against Maria Pupino* [2005] ECR I-5285. In which the Court applied a Framework Decision de facto directly, even though Article 34, paragraph 2(b), EU Treaty, stipulates that Framework Decisions will not entail direct effect.

[1371]   13 September 2005, Case C-176/03, *Commission* v. *Council* [2005] ECR I-7879. In which the Court granted the Community the authority to execute its policy areas with criminal penalties, notwithstanding the explicit choice, from the founding of the European Communities, not to extend this authority to the Community and to leave it with the Member States.

Court has always kept the long-term goals of European integration in mind and has never limited its view to the text of legal instruments and the situations of the main proceedings. If the Court continues to execute its authority in a similar way, a further retreat of national criminal law autonomy and a greater degree of actual influence of Union law can be expected. Time and again, the Court has shown that it places a very high value on the concept of integration. The Court's challenge for the coming years will certainly be to establish the "rights" component of the area of freedom, security and justice.[1372]

Looking at the process of integration as a linear process, it might be expected that, one day, the Union will establish a European criminal court and that European prison facilities will have to be constructed. However, these are steps which are conditional on the political momentum of the day. Politicians may be inclined to symbolic gestures. Should, for instance, another terrorist attack like that of 11 September 2001 occur, the Union will be forced into a position from which it must demonstrate its power to react. If, by then, a European Public Prosecutor's Office already exists, it might emerge with something else, such as the European Criminal Court.

8. UNION LAW AS COMMON LAW

Union law requires from (the courts of) the Member States a different technique of interpretation than they might be used to in national law. The sharp distinction between national criminal law and Union law is gone and the new reality requires a multi-level approach. The postponement of the entry into force of the Treaty of Lisbon will not impede the further development of the law in the light of the lines defined by the Court. This is accompanied by much more reliance on a case law approach. The application of the law may, in practice, amount to a combination of national rules and Union law, with corresponding rules of interpretation. For instance, the literal and contextual interpretation of the Court is referred to here, and not the legal historical interpretation. Awareness of the Union origin of the law or of the fact that national law comes within the scope of Union law will provide a better interpretation of the law. Thus, the notion of regarding Union law as a form of common law may contribute to a better understanding of European criminal law.

[1372] Opinion of Advocate General D. Ruiz-Jarabo Colomer of 8 April 2008, Case C-297/07, *Staatsanwaltschaft Regensburg* v. *Klaus Bourquain*, points 47 and 48.

9. SINCERE CO-OPERATION AND ENFORCEMENT THROUGH CRIMINAL LAW

The merger of the pillars and the direct application of the obligation of sincere co-operation even in the field of criminal law, in combination with the abolition of the long-standing rule of freedom of the choice of means, introduces a new element into the assessment of the obligations of the Member States. In the past, the assessment of the compliance of the Member States with their Union obligations was always one based upon the results obtained. In what they actually do, the Member States must meet their Union obligations. How they get there, is much less of concern. With the abolition of the principle of freedom of choice of the means, by both the Court's case law and the TFEU, the Union may now impose that the Member States criminalise certain forms of conduct and introduce rules of criminal procedure. This implies that now the *means* to achieve a certain result may also be assessed, separately from the results of the implementation by the Member States. These developments require the conceptualisation of a Union law definition of *criminal law* and *criminal procedure.*

Other developments also require a re-evaluation of the obligation of sincere co-operation. This relates to the emergence of various forms of multi-lateral co-operation, some in a permanent structure (Europol, Eurojust) and others in an *ad hoc* form (joint investigation teams, for example). With regard to the institutions, the Court has, in consistent case law, held that the institutions are also, like the Member States, under the obligation of sincere co-operation. It would be logical to add that this is also so for the offices, bodies and agencies established in the field of criminal law. This may be more difficult with the non-permanent forms of multi-lateral co-operation, by which Member States co-operate together on an *ad hoc* basis. Here, the solution might be found by referring to the responsibilities of the Member States involved.

10. THE GENERAL PRINCIPLES OF THE UNION'S CRIMINAL LAW

Over the years, the Court has developed an impressive catalogue of general principles. As a result of the historic dimensions of the primarily economic-setting of the previous European Communities, there has hardly been a case in which the Court has had to deal with suspects, accused and convicted persons in detention and the specific legal questions that result from it. The full inclusion of criminal law will bring cases with questions of an entirely different nature to the Court. More prominently, the right to liberty will be of central focus. The Court has indicated that it has recognised the winds of change by the introduction of urgent procedures for cases that concern persons in detention and by reaching judgment within one or two months. However, this promising step relates to the formal side of the challenges for the Court.

The full inclusion of criminal law might lead to the elaboration of the existing general principles and to the recognition of new general principles, much more tailored towards the demands of criminal law. What, for instance, is the meaning of the proportionality requirement with regard to making arrests, to the warrant for surrender, and to the penalties imposed on EU nationals? A European Arrest Warrant is a severe instrument, which seriously infringes the rights and freedoms of EU nationals, and, therefore, we must ask ourselves if it is still proportional to use it if a Member State issues it for cases in which the accused are released soon after the surrender and the cases are never brought to court? It is a difficult task for the Court to reconcile the intentions of the Union legislature to view imprisonment as the appropriate sanction with the fundamental freedom of free movement and the fundamental right to liberty to which all EU citizens are entitled.[1373]

What is the influence of the general principle of *ne bis in idem* on the stage before final decisions are made? It does not seem logical for Union law to allow for double prosecution of the same individual for the same facts while no final decision has been taken, and to disqualify another Member State for slow procedures the moment the first Member State has finally disposed of the case. Should parallel prosecutions in two Member States concerning the same facts and the same accused be regarded as *proportional* under Union law? On a similar footing, the recognition of negative decisions requires further attention. In the present situation, the state making the first move determines that another state ought to acknowledge something. Why, in a system of mutual recognition, should a state that prosecutes be given priority over a state that has decided to attach no consequences to a certain act?

11. THE UNIFORM INTERPRETATION OF THE LAW AND THE DIVERGING APPLICATION OF THE LAW

It is the Court's task to ensure the uniform interpretation of the law. This task has been put under increasing pressure since the Treaty of Lisbon, which allows for

---

[1373] See the rhetorically formulated Proposed Solutions for the Future EU Justice Programme, Council Document 11549/08 LIMITE, 7 July 2008, p. 21: "We should determine concrete steps to strengthen citizen's rights at European level for 2010 and the following years – particularly following the adoption of the Lisbon Treaty. Otherwise, our citizens will often perceive the European Union only as an institution that curtails rather than guarantees rights".

various opt-outs and opt-ins, as well as for all forms of enhanced co-operation. It is inevitable that the Court, while interpreting a rule or provision of Union law which is applicable for all Member States, will have an impact on a rule or provision applicable to a limited number of Member States. *Vice versa*, it is also inevitable that the Court will interpret a rule or provision of an act adopted under enhanced co-operation that has implications for a rule or provision of Union law applicable to all Member States. But what, we must ask, is the balance that will be found here? Will the Court give the instrument an autonomous interpretation or will it take into consideration the fact that some Member States did not wish to be bound by it? The very fact that the Treaties allow for variable geometry undermines the uniformity of the law.

The Court is further handicapped by the fact that it does not have the jurisdiction to review the validity or proportionality of operations carried out by the police or other law-enforcement services of a Member State or the exercise of the responsibilities incumbent upon the Member States with regard to the maintenance of law and order and the safeguarding of internal security (Article 276 TFEU). Depending on how the Court interprets it, it has the potential of limiting the possibilities for citizens to invoke their freedoms and rights when confronted with restrictions by law enforcement authorities.

12. THE ADDED VALUE OF TRANSFER OF PROCEEDINGS

The failure of mutual recognition as a model that offers a one-sided view on the offence and the best way to deal with the matter, added to the subjective use of the "first come, first served" principle raises the question of whether there are alternatives. The failure of traditional international co-operation, in the sense that it was time-consuming and that there was uncertainty as to its result, since, in the end, there was no obligation to comply, also raises the question of whether there are no alternatives. On condition that a serious reduction of the overlapping jurisdiction of the Member States can be attained, the transfer of proceedings in criminal matters offers such a mechanism. In the past, it met objections that related to the sovereignty concerns of Member States which also had jurisdiction over the offence. Not all states that had jurisdiction were willing to recognise the (entirely different) outcome of criminal proceedings in another Member State. These objections have become without merit after the broad recognition of *ne bis in idem* upon the basis of the Article 54 *CISA* case law.

The growing influence of the principle of mutual trust stimulates the idea that it does not so much matter *which* Member State adjudicates the case, *as long as* the case is adjudicated. Member States must trust each other, and thus they must trust that the other Member State will also deal with the case in the appropriate manner, even if the outcome is different. To recognise that criminal jurisdiction is not exclusive to one Member State – if there is overlapping jurisdiction – would enable the Member States to use other factors that are indicative of the best place for the prosecution: for instance, the interests of the accused, the victims and the witnesses. A serious reduction of overlapping jurisdiction will make it easier to make decisions on the allocation of jurisdiction that are much closer to the interests of the citizens. If, in principle, it is possible to limit jurisdiction to territorial jurisdiction, a transfer of proceedings will be indicated when the accused is a resident of another Member State and it is not too complicated to produce the evidence against him in proceedings in his state of residence.

13. THE MODEL FOR THE EUROPEAN PUBLIC PROSECUTOR'S OFFICE

Of the many open questions regarding the European Public Prosecutor's Office, the relationship between European cases and Member State cases is prominent. How is the decision as to whether a case will be dealt with by the European Prosecutor, or whether it will be left to the Member States, to be taken? On these issues, there is a lot to learn from the experience that has been developed in competition law, including the mechanism of allocation of cases. This enables the Commission, in competition law, to supervise the enforcement by the authorities of the Member States and to take responsibility for cases which have overriding impact on the Union. However, in competition law, the substantive norms (what amounts to anti-competitive conduct) are uniformly applicable. Will this also be the case for the Regulations establishing the European Public Prosecutor's Office? The other model that could be used is the application of the principle of complementarity, in the form in which it is being used in the International Criminal Court. In this context, the Prosecutor for the ICC may step in if a state is unwilling or unable to prosecute. In the context of the Union, a lower threshold could be applied, which would allow the European Prosecutor to assume his responsibilities. If a Member State fails to investigate sufficiently or prosecute, in the view of the European Prosecutor, then the latter should assume primacy over the case.

14. FUNDAMENTAL ASPECTS OF THE NATIONAL CRIMINAL JUSTICE SYSTEM

The Treaty of Lisbon recognises the national identities of the Member States more than the previous treaties. It does so both in a symbolic way, by referring to the national identities and traditions of the Member States, and in a very practical manner, by creating the emergency-brake procedure in criminal law. When a Member State finds that a certain measure would affect the fundamental aspects of its criminal justice system, it may use the emergency-brake. On the other hand, the Treaty of Lisbon reduces the discretion of Member States to maintain their distinct criminal justice systems by introducing across the board competences for the Union to influence both national criminal law and criminal procedure. There is no aspect of criminal law that is excluded from the possible influence of Union law.

Both the Member States and the Union must formulate what they regard to be the tasks which belong to the Union and the tasks which should belong or remain with the Member States. The application of the principle of subsidiarity will serve to remind all negotiators of this necessity, as its interpretation is linked to the understanding of what affects the fundamental aspects of the criminal justice system. The formulation is inclined to allow a rather subjective interpretation, as it is the Member State itself that discovers that something affects its system. However, what is more interesting is whether it is possible to determine, upon a more objective basis, what affects the fundamental aspects of a national criminal justice system. Is this, for instance, the case when a Union act requires the abolition of lay judges or when it requires the opposite, the introduction of juries into all criminal justice systems? Are fundamental aspects endangered by the introduction of mandatory penalties or by their abolition? What about the criminalisation of abortion and euthanasia or their abolition? In essence, the whole catalogue of topics upon which Member States are in dispute could offer these kind of issues. In the context of the restrictions of the fundamental freedoms upon the basis of justifications provided in the Treaty, the Court has allowed the Member States a reasonable amount of discretion with regard to whether it is necessary to invoke the justification of public policy or public interest. However, it has subjected the application of justifications to more objective criteria, so as to ensure that the measure is not applied in a discriminatory way. The complete merger of the internal market and the area of freedom, security and justice might require a similar tolerant attitude on the part of the Court when it comes to the discretion of the Member States to go their own way in criminal law.

Intersentia

ANNEXES

TABLE OF CASES

COURT OF JUSTICE OF THE EUROPEAN COMMUNITIES (Including Court of First Instance)

Date	Parties	Case Number	Reference ECR	Page Number
27 February 1962	Commission v. Italy	10-61	[1962] ECR English Special Edition 1	342
5 February 1963	NV Algemene Transport- en Expeditie Onderneming van Gend & Loos v. Netherlands Inland Revenue Administration	26-62	[1963] ECR 1	15, 422 and 426
13 November 1964	Commission v. Luxembourg and Belgium	90-63 and 91-63	[1964] ECR 625	15
15 July 1964	Flaminio Costa v. E.N.E.L.	6-64	[1964] ECR 585	15 and 62
1 December 1965	Firma G. Schwarze v. Einfuhr- und Vorratsstelle für Getreide und Futtermittel	16-65	[1965] ECR English Special Edition 877	130
30 June 1966	G. Vaasse-Göbbels v. Management of the Beambtenfonds voor het Mijnbedrijf	61-65	[1966] ECR English Special Edition 261	134
5 December 1967	Bestuur der Sociale Verzekeringsbank v. J.H. van der Vecht	19-67	[1967] ECR English Special Edition 345	136
13 February 1969	Walt Wilhelm and others v. Bundeskartellamt	14-68	[1969] ECR 1	143
14 July 1972	Imperial Chemical Industries Ltd. v. Commission	48-69	[1972] ECR 619	179
17 December 1970	Internationale Handelsgesellschaft mbH v. Einfuhr- und Vorratsstelle für Getreide und Futtermittel	11-70	[1970] ECR 1125	16, 144, 145, 160 and 284
13 July 1972	Commission of the European Communities v. Italian Republic	48-71	[1972] ECR 527	43
21 March 1972	criminal proceedings against Società Agricola Industria Latte (SAIL)	82-71	[1972] ECR 119	49 and 126
17 May 1972	Orsolina Leonesio v. Ministero dell'agricoltura e foreste	93-71	[1972] ECR 287	50
21 February 1973	Europemballage Corporation and Continental Can Company Inc. v. Commission	6-72	[1973] ECR 215	147 and 190
14 December 1972	Boehringer Mannheim GmbH v. Commission	7-72	[1972] ECR 1281	243
7 February 1973	Commission of the European Communities v. Italian Republic (Premiums for slaughtering cows)	39-72	[1973] ECR 101	50
14 May 1974	J. Nold, Kohlen- und Baustoffgroßhandlung v. Commission	4-73	[1974] ECR 491	143

Date	Parties	Case Number	Reference ECR	Page Number
10 October 1973	Fratelli Variola S.p.A. v. Amministrazione italiana delle Finanze	34-73	[1973] ECR 981	50
16 January 1974	Rheinmühlen-Düsseldorf v. Einfuhr- und Vorratsstelle für Getreide und Futtermittel	166-73	[1974] ECR 33	279
30 October 1974	Officier van Justitie v. J.W.J. van Haaster	190-73	[1974] ECR 1123	81
21 June 1974	Jean Reyners v. Belgian State	2-74	[1974] ECR 631	222
11 July 1974	Procureur du Roi v. Benoît and Gustave Dassonville	8-74	[1974] ECR 837	79
3 December 1974	Johannes Henricus Maria van Binsbergen v. Bestuur van de Bedrijfsvereniging voor de Metaalnijverheid	33-74	[1974] ECR 1299	221
4 December 1974	Yvonne van Duyn v. Home Office	41-74	[1974] ECR 1337	97, 100 and 118
26 February 1975	Carmelo Angelo Bonsignore v. Oberstadtdirektor der Stadt Köln	67-74	[1975] ECR 297	87
8 July 1975	Rewe-Zentralfinanz eGmbH v. Landwirtschaftskammer	4-75	[1975] ECR 843	93
28 October 1975	Roland Rutili v. Ministre de l'intérieur	36-75	[1975] ECR 1219	86
26 February 1976	Commission v. Italy	52-75	[1976] ECR 277	64
3 February 1976	Pubblico Ministero v. Flavia Manghera and others	59-75	[1976] ECR 91	105
7 July 1976	Lynne Watson and Alessandro Belmann	118-75	[1976] ECR 1185	153
14 July 1976	Cornelis Kramer and others	3, 4 and 6-76	[1976] ECR 1279	33
16 December 1976	Rewe-Zentralfinanz eG et Rewe-Zentral AG v. Landwirtschaftskammer für das Saarland	33-76	[1976] ECR	278
15 December 1976	Suzanne Criel, née Donckerwolcke and Henri Schou v. Procureur de la République au tribunal de grande instance de Lille and Director General of Customs	41-76	[1976] ECR 1921	79 and 153
25 January 1977	W.J.G. Bauhuis v. The Netherlands State	46-76	[1977] ECR 5	341
2 February 1977	Amsterdam Bulb BV v. Produktschap voor Siergewassen	50-76	[1977] ECR 137	50 and 62
3 February 1977	Luigi Benedetti v. Munari F.lli s.a.s.	52-76	[1977] ECR 163	135
28 April 1977	Jean Thieffry v. Conseil de l'ordre des avocats à la cour de Paris	71-76	[1977] ECR 765	222
31 March 1977	Société pour l'exportation des sucres SA v. Commission	88-76	[1977] ECR 709	171
14 July 1977	Concetta Sagulo, Gennaro Brenca et Addelmadjid Bakhouche	8-77	[1977] ECR 1495	153 and 301
27 October 1977	Régina v. Pierre Bouchereau	30-77	[1977] ECR 1999	85
30 November 1977	Leonce Cayrol v. Giovanni Rivoira & Figli	52-77	[1977] ECR 2261	79

Date	Parties	Case Number	Reference ECR	Page Number
24 January 1978	Ministère public du Kingdom of the Netherlands v. Jacobus Philippus van Tiggele	82/77	[1978] ECR 25	81
16 February 1978	Minister for Fisheries v. C.A. Schonenberg and others	88/77	[1978] ECR 473	277
9 March 1978	Amministrazione delle Finanze dello Stato v. Simmenthal SpA.	106/77	[1978] ECR 629	63 and 279
28 November 1978	criminal proceedings against Michel Choquet	16/78	[1978] ECR 2293	94
29 November 1978	Pigs Marketing Board v. Raymond Redmond	83/78	[1978] ECR 2347	132
25 January 1979	A. Racke v. Hauptzollamt Mainz	98/78	[1979] ECR 69	171
20 February 1979	S.A. Buitoni v. Fonds d'Orientation et de Régularisation des Marchés Agricoles	122/78	[1979] ECR 677	298
7 February 1979	criminal proceedings against Vincent Auer	136/78	[1979] ECR 437	140
5 April 1979	criminal proceedings against Tullio Ratti	148/78	[1979] ECR 1629	49, 65 and 285
10 July 1980	Commission v. France	152/78	[1980] ECR 2299	96
28 March 1979	Regina v. Vera Ann Saunders	175/78	[1979] ECR 1129	87
28 March 1979	Procureur de la République v. Michelangelo Rivoira and others	179/78	[1979] ECR 1147	154
29 October 1980	Heintz van Landewyck SARL and others v. Commission	209 to 215/78 and 218/78	[1980] ECR ECR 3125	230
25 September 1979	Commission of the European Communities v. French Republic	232/78	[1979] ECR 2729	340
10 July 1980	Procureur de la République and others v. Bruno Giry and Guerlain SA and others	253/78 and 1 to 3/79	[1980] ECR 2327	242
5 March 1980	H. Ferwerda BV v. Produktschap voor Vee en Vlees	265/78	[1980] ECR 617	142
10 January 1980	Commission v. Italy	267/78	[1980] ECR 31	356
14 December 1979	Regina v. Maurice Donald Henn and John Frederick Ernest Darby	34/79	[1979] ECR 3795	97
13 December 1979	Liselotte Hauer v. Land Rheinland-Pfalz	44/79	[1979] ECR 3727	142, 144 and 145
18 March 1980	Procureur du Roi v. Marc J.V.C. Debauve and others	52/79	[1980] ECR 833	152
27 March 1980	Amministrazione delle finanze dello Stato v. Denkavit italiana Srl	61/79	[1980] ECR 1205	119
5 March 1980	Josette Pecastaing v. Belgium	98/79	[1980] ECR 691	226
6 May 1980	Commission v. Belgium	102/79	[1980] ECR 1473	68
11 March 1980	Pasquale Foglia v. Mariella Novello	104/79	[1980] ECR 745	132
26 June 1980	National Panasonic (UK) Limited v. Commission	136/79	[1980] ECR 2033	219
18 May 1982	AM & S Europe Limited v. Commission	155/79	[1982] ECR 2033	216
3 July 1980	Regina v. Stanislaus Pieck	157/79	[1980] ECR 2171	203
9 October 1980	criminal proceedings against Giovanni Carciati	823/79	[1980] ECR 2773	79

Date	Parties	Case Number	Reference ECR	Page Number
16 December 1980	criminal proceedings against Anton Adriaan Fietje	27/80	[1980] ECR 3839	79
10 March 1981	Creamery Milk Suppliers Association en anderen tegen Ierse Regering en anderen en Martin Doyle en anderen tegen An Taoiseach en anderen	36 and 71/80	[1981] ECR 735	285
5 February 1981	Joszef Horvath v. Hauptzollamt Hamburg-Jonas	50/80	[1981] ECR 385	112
5 February 1981	Officier van justitie v. Koninklijke Kaasfabriek Eyssen BV	53/80	[1981] ECR 409	102
13 May 1981	SpA International Chemical Corporation v. Amministrazione delle finanze dello Stato	66/80	[1981] ECR 1191	120
7 June 1983	SA Musique Diffusion française and others v. Commission	100 to 103/80	[1983] ECR 1825	171, 189, 196, 215, 217 and 258
5 February 1981	criminal proceedings against René Joseph Kugelmann	108/80	[1981] ECR 433	153
16 June 1981	Maria Salonia v. Giorgio Poidomani and Franca Baglieri, née Giglio	126/80	[1981] ECR 1563	284
18 June 1980	Jules Borker	138/80	[1980] ECR 1975	129
26 May 1981	criminal proceedings against Siegfried Ewald Rinkau	157/80	[1981] ECR 1395	139, 142, 190, 191 and 220
16 June 1981	Peter Klomps v. Karl Michel	166/80	[1981] ECR 1593	343
11 November 1981	criminal proceedings against Guerrino Casati	203/80	[1981] ECR 2595	81 and 426
16 February 1982	Procureur de la République and others v. Guy Vedel and others	204/80	[1982] ECR 465	109
12 November 1981	Amministrazione delle finanze dello Stato v. Srl Meridionale Industria Salumi and others; Ditta Italo Orlandi & Figlio and Ditta Vincenzo Divella v. Amministrazione delle finanze dello Stato	212 to 217/80	[1981] ECR 2735	142
16 December 1981	Regina v. Robert Tymen	269/80	[1981] ECR 3079	277
19 January 1982	Ursula Becker v. Finanzamt Münster-Innenstadt	8/81	[1982] ECR 53	48
10 February 1982	criminal proceedings against Daniël Bout and BV I. Bout en Zonen	21/81	[1982] ECR 381	277
6 May 1982	Firma Wilhelm Fromme v. Bundesanstalt für landwirtschaftliche Marktordnung	54/81	[1982] ECR 1449	155
26 October 1982	Hauptzollamt Mainz v. C.A. Kupferberg & Cie KG a.A.	104/81	[1982] ECR 3641	52 and 137
18 May 1982	Rezguia Adoui v. Belgian State and City of Liège; Dominique Cornuaille v. Belgian State	115 and 116/81	[1982] ECR 1665	98
1 April 1982	References for a preliminary ruling: Kantongerecht Apeldoorn - Netherlands	141 to 143/81	[1982] ECR 1299	132
22 June 1982	criminal proceedings against Timothy Frederick Robertson and others	220/81	[1982] ECR 2349	345

Date	Parties	Case Number	Reference ECR	Page Number
26 October 1982	Wilfried Wolf v. Hauptzollamt Düsseldorf	221/81	[1982] ECR 3681	112 and 114
15 July 1982	Pendy Plastic Products BV v. Pluspunkt Handelsgesellschaft mbH	228/81	[1982] ECR 2723	344
26 October 1982	Senta Einberger v. Hauptzollamt Freiburg	240/81	[1982] ECR 3699	112
6 October 1982	Srl CILFIT and Lanificio di Gavardo SpA v. Ministry of Health	283/81	[1982] ECR 3415	282 and 284
14 December 1982	Procureur de la République and Comité national de défense contre l'alcoolisme v. Alex Waterkeyn and others ; Procureur de la République v. Jean Cayard and others	314/81, 315/81, 316/81 and 83/82	[1982] ECR 4337	276
14 July 1983	criminal proceedings against Sandoz BV	174/82	[1983] ECR 2445	103
21 September 1983	Deutsche Milchkontor GmbH and others v. Federal Republic of Germany	205 to 215/82	[1983] ECR 2633	31 and 251
30 November 1983	criminal proceedings against Leendert van Bennekom	227/82	[1983] ECR 3883	169
22 September 1983	Vincent Rodolphe Auer v. Ministère public	271/82	[1983] ECR 2727	110
14 February 1984	Rewe Handelsgesellschaft Nord mbH und Rewe-Markt Herbert Kureit v. Hauptzollämter Flensburg, Itzehoe and Lübeck-West	278/82	[1984] ECR 721	278
31 January 1984	Graziana Luisi and Giuseppe Carbone v. Ministero del Tesero	286/82 and 26/83	[1984] ECR 377	83
28 February 1984	Senta Einberger v. Hauptzollamt Freiburg	294/82	[1984] ECR 1177	112
10 April 1984	Sabine von Colson and Elisabeth Kamann v. Land Nordrhein-Westfalen	14/83	[1984] ECR 1891	63 and 75
13 March 1984	criminal proceedings against Karl Prantl	16/83	[1984] ECR 1299	98
10 July 1984	Regina v. Kent Kirk	63/83	[1984] ECR 2689	142
22 March 1984	Michael Paterson and others v. W. Weddel & Company Limited and others	90/83	[1984] 1567	283
12 July 1984	Ordre des avocats au Barreau de Paris v. Onno Klopp	107/83	[1984] ECR 2971	222
6 November 1984	Th. Kohl KG v. Ringelhan & Rennett SA and Ringelhan Einrichtungs GmbH	177/83	[1984] ECR 3651	99
29 January 1985	Henri Cullet and Chambre syndicale des réparateurs automobiles et détaillants de produits pétroliers v. Centre Leclerc à Toulouse and Centre Leclerc à Saint-Orens-de-Gameville	231/83	[1985] ECR 305	252
23 April 1986	Parti écologiste "Les Verts" v. European Parliament	294/83	[1986] ECR 1339	268
23 May 1985	Commission v. Germany	29/84	[1985] ECR 1661	68

Date	Parties	Case Number	Reference ECR	Page Number
11 June 1985	Leon Emile Gaston Carlos Debaecker and Berthe Plouvier v. Cornelis Gerrit Bouwman	49/84	[1985] ECR 1779	343
5 June 1986	Commission v. Italy	103/84	[1986] ECR 1759	79
11 July 1985	criminal proceedings against Robert Heinrich Maria Mutsch	137/84	[1985] ECR 2681	270
12 March 1987	Commission v. Germany	178/84	[1987] ECR 1227	93
9 July 1985	Piercarlo Bozzetti v. Invernizzi SpA and Ministero del Tesoro	179/84	[1985] ECR 2301	278
15 May 1986	Marguerite Johnston v. Chief Constable of the Royal Ulster Constabulary	222/84	[1986] ECR 1651	62, 63, 64 and 143
27 February 1986	criminal proceedings against Hans Röser	238/84	[1986] ECR 795	136
10 December 1985	criminal proceedings against Léon Motte	247/84	[1985] ECR 3887	95 and 103
6 May 1986	criminal proceedings against Claude Muller and others	304/84	[1986] ECR 1511	103
5 March 1986	Wünsche Handelsgesellschaft GmbH & Co. v. Germany	69/85	[1986] ECR 947	131
12 June 1986	Michele Bertini and Giuseppe Bisignani and others v. Regione Lazio and Unità sanitare locali	98, 162 and 128/85	[1986] ECR 1885	132
11 March 1986	Conegate Limited v. HM Customs & Excise	121/85	[1986] ECR 17	97
18 November 1987	Maizena Gesellschaft mbH and others v. Bundesanstalt für landwirtschaftliche Marktordnung (BALM.)	137/85	[1987] ECR 4587	160
2 December 1986	Commission v. Belgium	239/85	[1986] ECR 3645	68
5 February 1987	Hauptzollamt Hamburg-Jonas v. Plange Kraftfutterwerke GmbH & Co	288/85	[1987] ECR 611	298
22 October 1987	Foto-Frost v. Hauptzollamt Lübeck-Ost	314/85	[1987] ECR 4199	130
21 April 1988	Fratelli Pardini SpA v. Ministero del Commercio con l'Estero and Banca Toscana (Lucca Branch)	338/85	[1988] ERC 2041	120, 126 and 129
25 February 1988	Commission v. Germany	427/85	[1988] ECR 1123	221
30 September 1987	Meryem Demirel v. Stadt Schwäbisch Gmünd	12/86	[1987] ECR 3719	144
11 June 1987	Pretore di Salò v. Persons unknown	14/86	[1987] ECR 3969	49, 125, 127, 128, 143, 168, 274 and 426
8 October 1987	criminal proceedings against Kolpinghuis Nijmegen BV	80/86	[1987] ECR 3969	49, 125, 127, 128, 142, 168, 274 and 426
24 March 1988	Commission v. Italy	104/86	[1988] ECR 1799	68
4 February 1988	Horst Ludwig Martin Hoffmann v. Adelheid Krieg	145/86	[1988] ECR 645	340 and 350
5 July 1988	W.J.R. Mol v. Inspecteur der Invoerrechten en Accijnzen	269/86	[1988] ECR 3627	112
22 September 1988	Ministère public v. Gérard Deserbais	286/86	[1975] ECR 843	93

Date	Parties	Case Number	Reference ECR	Page Number
5 July 1988	Vereniging Happy Family Rustenburgerstraat v. Inspecteur der Omzetbelasting	289/86	[1988] ECR 3655	112, 113 and 115
19 January 1988	Claude Gullung v. Conseil de l'ordre des avocats du barreau de Colmar et de Saverne	292/86	[1988] ECR 111	92 and 222
25 February 1988	criminal proceedings against Rainer Drexl	299/86	[1988] ECR 1213	290
8 December 1987	Ministère public v. André Gauchard	20/87	[1987] ECR 4879	88 and 132
21 September 1989	Hoechst AG v. Commission	46/87 and 227/88	[1989] ECR 2859	141, 142, 143, 145, 215, 216, 217, 219 and 220
17 October 1989	Dow Benelux NV v. Commission	85/87	[1989] ECR 3137	141, 145, 215, 216, 217, 219 and 220
2 February 1989	Ian William Cowan v. Trésor Public	186/87	[1989] ECR 195	91, 152, 211 and 263
20 September 1988	Oberkreisdirektor des Kreises, Borken and Vertreter des öffentlichen Interesses beim Oberverwaltungsgericht für das Land Nordrhein-Westfalen v. Handelsonderneming Moormann BV	190/87	[1988] ECR 4689	102
5 October 1988	Udo Steymann v. Staatssecretaris van Justitie	196/87	[1988] ECR 6159	78
22 September 1988	Pretura unificata di Torino v. X	228/87	[1988] ECR 5099	132
18 October 1989	Orkem v. Commission	374/87	[1989] ECR 3283	142 and 145
16 May 1989	R. Buet and Educational Business Services (EBS) v. Ministère Public	382/87	[1989] ECR 1235	99
6 December 1990	J.J. Zwartveld and others	2/88 Imm.	[1990] ECR I-4405	125, 308 and 356
13 July 1989	Hubert Wachauf v. Bundesamt für Ernährung und Forstwirtschaft	5/88	[1989] ECR 2609	143
11 May 1989	criminal proceedings against Esther Renée Bouchara, née Wurmser, and Norlaine SA	25/88	[1989] ECR 1105	79, 93 and 106
21 September 1989	Commission v. Greece	68/88	[1989] ECR 2965	68, 69, 70 and 165
13 December 1989	Ministère public v. Jean-Jacques Paris	204/88	[1989] ECR 4361	284
26 October 1989	criminal proceedings against F. Levy	212/88	[1989] ECR 3511	76 and 79
12 December 1989	criminal proceedings against Lothar Messner	265/88	[1989] ECR 4209	76 and 188
26 January 1990	Falciola Angelo SpA v. Comune di Pavia	286/88	[1990] ECR I-191	133
18 October 1990	Massam Dzodzi v. Belgium	C-297/88 and C-197/89	[1990] ECR I-3763	132 and 139
3 July 1990	Isabelle Lancray SA v. Peters und Sickert KG	305/88	[1990] ECR I-2725	343
13 December 1989	Salvatore Grimaldi v. Fonds des maladies professionnelles	322/88	[1989] ECR 4407	66

Date	Parties	Case Number	Reference ECR	Page Number
10 July 1990	Anklagemyndigheden v. Hansen & Soen I/S	326/88	[1990] ECR I-2911	71, 72, 76, 92, 142, 189 and 195
13 November 1990	The Queen v. Minister of Agriculture, Fisheries and Food and Secretary of State for Health, ex parte: Fedesa and others	331/88	[1990] ECR I-4023	142, 164 and 170
7 March 1990	GB-INNO-BM v. Confédération du commerce luxembourgeois	362/88	[1990] ECR I-667	80
27 March 1990	Milk Marketing Board of England and Wales v. Cricket St. Thomas Estate	372/88	[1990] ECR I-1345	136
27 March 1990	Spain v. Council	C-9/89	[1990] ECR I-1383	161, 180, 253, 254, 308 and 367
12 December 2001	Hilti AG v. Commission	T-30/89	[1991] ECR II-1439	217
11 January 1990	Ministère public v. Guy Blanguernon	C-38/89	[1990] ECR I-83	147
13 November 1990	Marleasing SA v. La Comercial Internacional de Alimentacion SA	C-106/89	[1990] ECR I-4135	67
23 May 1990	criminal proceedings against Gourmetterie Van den Burg	C-169/89	[1990] ECR I-2143	106
28 June 1990	Hoche GmbH v. Bundesanstalt für Landwirtschaftliche Marktordnung	C-174/89	[1990] ECR I-2681	145
8 November 1990	Krystyna Gmurzynska-Bscher v. Oberfinanzdirektion Köln	C-231/89	[1990] ECR I-4003	132
18 June 1991	Elliniki Radiophonia Tiléorassi AE and Panellinia Omospondia Syllogon Prossopikou v. Dimotiki Etairia Pliroforissis and Sotirios Kouvelas and Nicolaos Avdellas and others	C-260/89	[1991] ECR I-2925	144
7 May 1991	Irène Vlassopoulou v. Ministerium für Justiz, Bundes- und Europaangelegenheiten Baden-Württemberg	C-340/89	[1991] ECR I-2357	223
6 December 1990	Max Witzemann v. Hauptzollamt München-Mitte	C-343/89	[1990] ECR I-4477	112 and 114
5 February 1991	Danielle Roux v. Belgium	C-363/89	[1991] ECR I-273	78
4 October 1991	criminal proceedings against Aimé Richardt and Les Accessoires Scientifiques SNC	C-367/89	[1991] ECR I-4621	101
11 July 1991	Antonio Crispoltoni v. Fattoria autonoma tabacchi di Città di Castello	C-368/89	[1991] ECR I-3695	133 and 170
2 October 1991	criminal proceedings against Paul Vandevenne, Marc Wilms, Jozef Mesotten and Wilms Transport NV	C-7/90	[1991] ECR I-4371	195
23 April 1991	Klaus Höfner and Fritz Elser v. Macrotron GmbH	C-41/90	[1991] ECR I-1979	88
13 December 1990	criminal proceedings against Jean-Claude Bellon	C-42/90	[1990] ECR I-4863	88 and 103
11 July 1991	A. Verholen and others v. Sociale Verzekeringsbank Amsterdam	C-87/90, C-88/90 and C-89/90	[1991] ECR I- 3757	65

Date	Parties	Case Number	Reference ECR	Page Number
4 October 1991	The Society for the Protection of Unborn Children Ireland Ltd v. Stephen Grogan and others	C-159/90	[1991] ECR 4685	78, 115, 143 and 144
28 November 1991	Giacomo Durighello v. Istituto Nazionale Della Previdenza Sociale	C-186/90	[1991] ECR I-5773	119
27 October 1992	Germany v. Commission	C-240/90	[1992] ECR I-5383	158 and 161
27 November 1991	Meico-Fell v. Hauptzollamt Darmstadt	C-273/90	[1991] ECR I-5569	158 and 159
24 November 1992	Anklagemyndigheden v. Peter Michael Poulsen and Diva Navigation Corp.	C-286/90	[1992] ECR I-619	180 and 181
16 July 1992	Manuel José Lourenço Dias v. Director da Alfândega do Porto	C-343/90	[1992] ECR I-4673	128 and 132
7 July 1992	The Queen v. Immigration Appeal Tribunal et Surinder Singh, ex parte Secretary of State for Home Department	C-370/90	[1992] ECR I-4265	89
29 June 1995	Solvay SA v. Commission	T-30/91	[1995] ECR II-1775	217
16 July 1992	Dirección General de Defensa de la Competencia v. Asociación Española de Banca Privada and others	C-67/91	[1992] ECR I-4085	406
27 October 1993	criminal proceedings against Francine Gillon, née Decoster	C-69/91	[1993] ECR I-5335	176
16 July 1992	Wienand Meilicke v. ADV/ORGA F. A. Meyer AG	C-83/91	[1992] ECR I-4871	132
25 June 1992	Licensing Authority South Eastern Traffic Area v. British Gas plc.	C-116/91	[1992] ECR I-4071	49
12 November 1992	Minalmet GmbH v. Brandeis Ltd	C-123/91	[1992] ECR I-5661	343
10 November 1992	Hansa Fleisch Ernst Mundt GmbH & Co. KG v. Landrat des Kreises Schleswig-Flensburg	C-156/91	[1992] ECR I-5567	272
2 August 1993	criminal proceedings against Jean-Claude Levy	C-158/91	[1993] ECR I-4287	141
21 April 1993	Volker Sonntag tegen Hans Waidmann, Elisabeth Waidmann en Stefan Waidmann	C-172/91	[1993] ECR I-1963	343
25 January 1994	Angelopharm GmbH v. Freie Hansestadt Hamburg	C-212/91	[1994] ECR I-171	136
24 November 1993	criminal proceedings against Bernard Keck and Daniel Mithouard	C-267/91 and C-268/91	[1993] ECR I-6097	87
2 Augustus 1993	Commission v. France	C-276/91	[1993] ECR I-4413	80
1 July 1993	Procedural issue relating to a seizure of goods belonging to Metalsa Srl	C-312/91	[1993] ECR I-3751	137
31 March 1993	Dieter Kraus v. Land Baden-Württemberg	C-19/92	[1993] ECR I-1663	298
30 March 1993	Pierre Corbiau v. Administration des Contributions	C-24/92	[1993] ECR I-1277	126
12 October 1993	criminal proceedings against José Vanacker and André Lesage and SA Baudoux combustibles	C-37/92	[1993] ECR I-4947	95
2 August 1993	Wilfried Lange v. Finanzamt Fürstenfeldbruck	C-111/92	[1993] ECR I-4677	112

Date	Parties	Case Number	Reference ECR	Page Number
15 December 1993	criminal proceedings against Kevin Albert Charlton, James Huyton and Raymond Edward William Wilson	C-116/92	[1993] ECR I-6775	283
24 March 1994	Her Majesty's Customs and Excise v. Gerhart Schindler and Jörg Schindler	C-275/92	[1994] ECR I-1039	99, 115 and 116
2 June 1994	criminal proceedings against Van Swieten BV	C-313/92	[1994] ECR I-2177	185
16 December 1993	Teodoro Wagner Miret v. Fondo de Garantía Salarial	C-334/92	[1993] ECR I-6911	273
14 July 1994	Milchwerke Köln/Wuppertal eG v. Hauptzollamt Köln-Rheinau	C-352/92	[1994] ECR I-3385	74, 142 and 168
14 July 1994	criminal proceedings against Matteo Peralta	C-379/92	[1994] ECR I-3453	92, 138 and 181
10 February 1994	Mund & Fester v. Hatrex Internationaal Transport	C-398/92	[1994] ECR I-467	91
9 August 1995	Raymond Vander Elst v. Office des Migrations Internationales	C-43/93	[1994] ECR I-3803	89
5 October 1994	criminal proceedings against Johannes Gerrit Cornelis van Schaik	C-55/93	[1994] ECR I-4837	104 and 108
14 February 1995	Finanzamt Köln-Altstadt v. Roland Schumacker	C-279/93	[1995] ECR I-225	90
15 September 1994	criminal proceedings against Ludomira Neeltje Barbara Houtwipper	C-293/93	[1994] ECR I-4249	345
14 December 1995	Peterbroeck, Van Campenhout & Cie SCS v. Belgian State	C-312/93	[1995] ECR I-4599	128 and 279
28 March 1995	The Queen v. Secretary of State for Home Department, ex parte Evans Medical Ltd and Macfarlan Smith Ltd	C-324/93	[1995] ECR I-563	116 and 342
23 February 1995	criminal proceedings against Aldo Bordessa, Vicente Marí Mellado and Concepción Barbero Maestre	C-358/93 and C-416/93	[1995] ECR I-361	80 and 84
10 May 1995	Alpine Investments BV v. Minister van Financiën	C-384/93	[1995] ECR I-1141	98
14 December 1995	criminal proceedings against Giorgio Domingo Banchero	C-387/93	[1995] ECR I-4663	130 and 211
15 December 1995	Union royale belge des sociétés de football association ASBL v. Jean-Marc Bosman, Royal club liégeois SA v. Jean-Marc Bosman and others and Union des associations européennes de football (UEFA) v. Jean-Marc Bosman	C-415/93	[1995] ECR I-4921	88
14 December 1995	Jeroen van Schijndel and Johannes Nicolaas Cornelis van Veen v. Stichting Pensioenfonds voor Fysiotherapeuten	C-430/93 and C-431/93	[1995] ECR I-4705	64 and 128
23 March 1995	criminal proceedings against Mostafa Saddik	C-458/93	[1995] ECR I-511	130
23 November 1995	Nutral SpA v. Commission	C-476/93 P	[1995] ECR I-4125	407
23 May 1996	The Queen v. Ministry of Agriculture, Fisheries and Food, ex parte: Hedley Lomas (Ireland) Ltd.	C-5/94	[1996] ECR I-2553	340 and 341

Date	Parties	Case Number	Reference ECR	Page Number
7 December 1995	criminal proceedings against Denis Gervais, Jean-Louis Nougaillon, Christian Carrard and Bernard Horgue	C-17/94	[1995] ECR I-4353	128
16 February 1995	criminal proceedings against Jean-Louis Aubertin, Bernard Collignon, Guy Creusot, Isabelle Diblanc, Gilles Josse, Jacqueline Martin and Claudie Normand	C-29/94, C-30/94, C-31/94, C-32/94, C-33/94, C-34/94 and C-35/94	[1995] ECR I-301	87
26 October 1995	Siesse – Soluções Integrais em Sistemas Software e Aplicações Lda v. Director da Alfândega de Alcântara	C-36/94	[1995] ECR I-3573	289 and 297
5 July 1995	criminal proceedings against Michèle Voisine	C-46/94	[1995] ECR I-1859	134
30 November 1995	Reinhard Gebhard v. Consiglio dell'Ordine degli Avvocati e Procuratori di Milano	C-55/94	[1995] ECR I-4165	126 and 222
17 October 1995	Fritz Werner Industrie-Ausrüstungen GmbH v. Federal Republic of Germany	C-70/94	[1998] ECR I-3231	101
17 October 1995	criminal proceedings against Peter Leifer, Reinhold Otto Krauskopf and Otto Holzer	C-83/94	[1998] ECR I-3231	101
12 October 1995	Cereol Italia Srl v. Azienda Agricola Castello Sas	C-104/94	[1995] ECR I-2983	163
8 February 1996	criminal proceedings against Didier Vergy	C-149/94	[1996] ECR I-299	134
16 November 1995	criminal proceedings v. Geert Van Buynder	C-152/94	[1995] ECR I-3981	88
14 December 1995	criminal proceedings against Lucas Emilio Sanz de Lera, Raimundo Díaz Jiménez and Figen Kapanoglu	C-163/94, C-165/94 and C-250/94	[1995] ECR I-4821	84
7 April 1995	criminal proceedings against Juan Carlos Grau Gomis and others	C-167/94	[1995] ECR I-1023	122 and 131
1 February 1996	criminal proceedings against Gianfranco Perfili	C-177/94	[1996] ECR I-161	92
29 February 1996	criminal proceedings against Sofia Skanavi and Konstantin Chryssanthakopoulos	C-193/94	[1996] ECR I-929	20, 76, 153, 163, 175, 188, 286 and 299
24 October 1995	CIA Security International SA v. Signalson SA and Securitel SPRL	C-194/94	[1996] ERC I-2201	176
13 February 1996	Société Bautiaa v. Directeur des Services Fiscaux des Landes and Société Française Maritime v. Directeur des Services Fiscaux du Finistère	C-197/94 and C-252/94	[1996] ECR I-505	119 and 140
8 February 1996	criminal proceedings against Godefridus van der Feesten	C-202/94	[1996] ECR I-355	134
9 November 1995	criminal proceedings against Alan Jeffrey Bird	C-235/94	[1995] ECR I-3933	196

Date	Parties	Case Number	Reference ECR	Page Number
17 September 1996	Cooperativa Agricola Zootecnica S. Antonio and Others v. Amministrazione delle finanze dello Stato	C-246/94, C-247/94, C-248/94 and C-249/94	[1996] ECR I-4373	66
18 January 1995	criminal proceedings against Finn Ohrt	C-276/94	[1996] ECR I-119	256
25 June 1997	criminal proceedings against Euro Tombesi and Adino Tombesi and Others	C-304/94, C-330/94, C-342/94 and C-224/95	[1997] ECR I-3561	283
2 December 1997	Eftalia Dafeki v. Landesversicherungsanstalt Württemberg	C-336/94	[1997] ECR I-6761	258
26 September 1996	criminal proceedings against André Allain and Steel Trading France SARL, as a party liable at civil law	C-341/94	[1996] ECR I-4631	153
23 January 1997	Eckehard Pastoors and Trans-Cap GmbH v. Belgian State	C-29/95	[1997] ECR I-285	90
21 March 1996	criminal proceedings against Pierre Goupil. - Reference for a preliminary ruling: Tribunal de police de La Rochelle	C-39/95	[1996] ECR I-1601	283
26 September 1996	Data Delecta Aktiebolag and Ronny Forsberg v. MSL Dynamics Ltd	C-43/95	[1996] ECR I-4661	263 and 264
12 September 1996	criminal proceedings against Sandro Gallotti, Roberto Censi, Giuseppe Salmaggi, Salvatore Pasquire, Massimo Zappone, Francesco Segna and others, Cesare Cervetti, Mario Gasbarri, Isidoro Narducci and Fulvio Smaldone	C-58/95, C-75/95, C-112/95, C-119/95, C-123/95, C-135/95, C-140/95, C-141/95, C-154/95 and C-157/95	[1996] ECR I-4345	75 and 130
17 October 1996	Konservenfabrik Lubella Friedrich Büker GmbH & Co. KG v. Hauptzollamt Cottbus	C-64/95	[1996] ECR I-515	135
17 June 1997	Sodemare SA, Anni Azzurri Holding SpA and Anni Azzurri Rezzato Srl v. Regione Lombardia	C-70/95	[1997] ECR I-3395	88
24 October 1996	Aannemersbedrijf P.K. Kraaijeveld BV e.a. v. Gedeputeerde Staten van Zuid-Holland	C-72/95	[1996] ECR I-5403	136
12 December 1996	criminal proceedings against X	C-74/95 and C-129/95	[1996] ECR I-6609	125, 126, 127, 142, 168, 170 and 274
10 October 1996	Bernardus Hendrikman and Maria Feijen v. Magenta Druck & Verlag GmbH	C-78/95	[1996] ECR I-4943	343
30 July 1996	Bosphorus Hava Yollari Turizm v. e Ticaret AS v. Minister for Transport, Energy and Communications and others	C-84/95	[1996] ECR I-3953	266

Date	Parties	Case Number	Reference ECR	Page Number
14 January 1997	The Queen, ex parte Centro-Com Srl v. HM Treasury and Bank of England	C-124/95	[1997] ECR I-81	67, 101, 331, 340, 342 and 345
26 September 1996	criminal proceedings against Luciano Arcaro	C-168/95	[1996] ECR I-4705	132, 168 and 274
27 February 1997	Ebony Maritime SA and Loten Navigation Co. Ltd v. Prefetto della Provincia di Brindisi and others	C-177/95	[1997] ECR I-1111	135, 172, 184 and 189
17 December 1998	Baustahlgewebe GmbH v. Commission of the European Communities	C-185/95 P	[1998] ECR I-8417	2, 225, 226 and 303
23 October 1997	criminal proceedings against Harry Franzén	C-189/95	[1997] ECR I-5909	105
10 July 1997	Rosalba Palmisani v. Istituto nazionale della previdenza sociale (INPS).	C-261/95	[1997] ECR I-4025	282
9 December 1997	Commission v. France	C-265/95	[1997] ECR I-6959	253
11 June 1998	Karlheinz Fischer v. Finanzamt Donaueschingen	C-283/95	[1998] ECR I-3369	114
2 April 1998	The Queen v. Commissioners of Customs and Excise, ex parte EMU Tabac SARL, The Man in Black Ltd, John Cunningham	C-296/95	[1998] ECR I-1605	135 and 137
29 May 1997	Friedrich Kremzow v. Republik Österreich	C-299/95	[1997] ECR I-2629	87
29 May 1997	Administrative proceedings brought by VAG Sverige AB	C-329/95	[1997] ECR I-2675	140
26 June 1997	Vereinigte Familiapress Zeitungsverlags- und vertriebs GmbH v. Heinrich Bauer Verlag	C-368/95	[1997] ECR I-3689	97
20 March 1996	criminal proceedings against Carlo Sunino and Giancarlo Data	C-2/96	[1996] ECR I-1543	130
25 June 1996	criminal proceedings against Italia Testa	C-101/96	[1996] ECR I-3081	130
25 June 1997	criminal proceedings against René Kieffer and Romain Thill	C-114/96	[1997] ECR I-3629	107
18 December 1997	Inter-Environnement Wallonie ASBL v. Région Wallonne	C-129/96	[1997] ECR I-7411	276
16 June 1998	A. Racke GmbH & Co. v. Hauptzollamt Mainz	C-162/96	[1998] ECR I-3655	137 and 138
12 May 1998	Commission of the European Communities v. Council of the European Union	C-170/96	[1998] ECR I-2763	122
19 July 1996	criminal proceedings against Mario Modesti	C-191/96	[1996] ECR I-3937	130
24 November 1998	criminal proceedings against Horst Otto Bickel and Ulrich Franz	C-274/96	[1998] ECR I-7637	211, 263, 264 and 270
9 October 1997	criminal proceedings against Martino Grado and Shahid Bashir	C-291/96	[1997] ECR I-5531	129
17 June 1998	Wilhelm Mecklenburg v. Kreis Pinneberg - Der Landrat	C-321/96	[1998] ECR I-3809	136, 139 and 256

Date	Parties	Case Number	Reference ECR	Page Number
19 January 1999	criminal proceedings against Donatella Calfa	C-348/96	[1999] ECR I-11	86, 87 and 294
7 May 1998	Clean Car Autoservice v. Landeshauptmann von Wien	C-350/96	[1998] ECR I-2521	91
26 November 1998	Covita AVE v. Elliniko Dimosio (Greek State)	C-370/96	1998] ECR I-7711	171
28 May 1998	criminal proceedings against John Charles Goodwin and Edward Thomas Unstead	C-3/97	[1998] ECR I-3257	114
30 April 1998	Commission v. Germany	C-24/97	[1998] ECR I-2133	191
21 September 1999	Markku Juhani Läärä, Cotswold Microsystems Ltd and Oy Transatlantic Software Ltd v. Kihlakunnansyyttäjä (Jyväskylä) and Suomen valtio (Finnish State)	C-124/97	[1999] ECR I-6067	100, 101 and 118
30 April 1998	criminal proceedings against Italia Testa and Mario Modesti	C-128/97 and C-137/97	[1998] ECR I-2181	129
30 April 1998	Haydar Akman v. Oberkreisdirektor des Rheinisch-Bergischen-Kreises	C-210/97	[1998] ECR I-7519	135
9 March 1999	Centros Ltd v. Erhvervs- og Selskabsstyrelsen	C-212/97	[1999] ECR I-1459	104
29 April 1999	Erich Ciola v. Land Vorarlberg	C-224/97	[1999] ECR I-2517	88 and 91
16 June 1998	criminal proceedings against Johannes Martinus Lemmens	C-226/97	[1998] ECR I-3711	176
29 October 1998	criminal proceedings against Ibiyinka Awoyemi	C-230/97	[1998] ECR I-6781	109, 110 and 142
1 June 1999	Konle v. Austria	C-302/97	[1999] ECR I-3099	84
1 June 1999	criminal proceedings against Antoine Kortas	C-319/97	[1999] ECR I-3143	65, 67, 129 and 142
11 May 1999	Wilfried Monsees v. Unabhängiger Verwaltungssenat für Kärnten	C-350/97	[1999] ECR I-2921	108
21 September 1999	criminal proceedings against Florus Ariël Wijsenbeek	C-378/97	[1999] ECR I-6207	85, 137 and 203
28 March 2000	Dieter Krombach and André Bamberski	C-7/98	[2000] ECR I-1935	340 and 343
21 October 1999	Questore di Verona v. Diego Zenatti	C-67/98	[1999] ECR I-7289	98
20 February 2001	Mannesmannröhren-Werke AG v. Commission	T-112/98	[2001] ECR II-729	219
29 June 1999	Staatssecretaris van Financiën and Coffeeshop 'Siberië' vof	C-158/98	[1999] ECR I-3971	112 and 113
8 July 1999	criminal proceedings against Maria Amélia Nunes and Evangelina de Matos	C-186/98	[1999] ECR I-4883	72 and 161
3 February 2000	Charalampos Dounias v. Ypourgio Oikonomikon	C-228/98	[2000] ECR I-577	258
27 June 2000	Océano Grupo Editorial SA and Rocío Marciano Quintero and others	C-240/98 to C-244/98	[2000] ECR I-4941	67
16 November 2000	Sarrió SA v. Commission	C-291/98 P	[2000] ECR I-9991	193
14 September 2000	Renato Collino, Luisella Chiappero and Telecom Italia SpA	C-343/98	[2000] ECR I-6659	273
5 December 2000	criminal proceedings against Jean-Pierre Guimont	C-448/98	[2000] ECR I-10663	88

Date	Parties	Case Number	Reference ECR	Page Number
3 May 2001	criminal proceedings against Jean Verdonck, Ronald Everaert and Edith de Baedts	C-28/99	[2001] ECR I-3399	177
13 July 2000	Idéal Tourisme SA and Belgian State	C-36/99	[2000] ECR I-649	142
14 March 2000	Association Eglise de scientologie de Paris and Scientology International Reserves Trust v. The Prime Minister	C-54/99	[2000] ECR I-1335	84 and 96
27 September 2001	The Queen v. Secretary of State for the Home Department, ex parte Wieslaw Gloszczuk and Elzbieta Gloszczuk	C-63/99	[2001] ECR I-9565	137 and 145
2 October 2003	Thyssen Stahl AG v. Commission	C-194/99 P	[2003] ECR I-10821	218 and 225
2 October 2003	Corus UK Ltd v. Commission of the European Communities	C-199/99 P	[2003] ECR I-11177	2
8 November 2001	Silos e Mangimi Martini SpA v. Ministero delle Finanze	C-228/99	[2001] ECR I-8401	171
15 October 2002	Limburgse Vinyl Maatschappij NV (LVM) tegen Commissie van de Europese Gemeenschappen	C-238/99 P, C-244/99 P, C-245/99 P, C-247/99 P, C-250/99 P to C-252/99 P and C-254/99 P	[2002] ECR I-8375	172, 217, 218, 226, 239 and 240
12 July 2001	Paraskevas Louloudakis v. Elliniko Dimosio	C-262/99	[2001] ECR I-5547	189 and 298
6 March 2001	Bernard Connolly v. Commission	C-274/99 P	[2001] ECR I-1611	143
8 March 2001	criminal proceedings against Georgius van der Burg	C-278/99	[2001] ECR I-2015	176
18 October 2001	Commission v. Ireland	C-354/99	[2001] ECR I-7657	71 and 155
6 December 2001	Council of the European Union v. Heidi Hautala	C-353/99 P	[2001] ECR I-9565	137 and 145
22 January 2002	Canal Satélite Digital SL v. Administración General del Estado	C-390/99	[2002] ECR I-607	132
21 March 2002	Cura Anlagen GmbH v. Auto Service Leasing GmbH (ASL)	C-451/99	[2002] ECR I-3193	128 and 132
5 March 2002	Hans Reisch and Others (joined cases C-515/99 and C-527/99 to C-540/99) v. Bürgermeister der Landeshauptstadt Salzburg and Grundverkehrsbeauftragter des Landes Salzburg and Anton Lassacher and Others (joined cases C-519/99 to C-524/99 and C-526/99) v. Grundverkehrsbeauftragter des Landes Salzburg and Grundverkehrslandeskommission des Landes Salzburg	C-515/99, C-519/99 to C-524/99 and C-526/99 to C-540/99	[2002] ECR I-2157	131
11 July 2002	Mary Carpenter v. Secretary of State for the Home Department	C-60/00	[2002] ECR I-6279	89
22 October 2002	Roquette Frères SA v. Directeur général de la concurrence, de la consommation et de la répression des fraudes, and Commission of the European Communities	C-94/00	[2002] ECR I-9011	212, 217, 219, 220, 224, 405, 406 and 407

Date	Parties	Case Number	Reference ECR	Page Number
12 June 2003	Eugen Schmidberger, Internationale Transporte und Planzüge v. Republik Österreich	C-112/00	[2003] ECR I-5659	214 and 253
24 October 2002	criminal proceedings against Walter Hahn	C-121/00	[2002] ECR I-9193	103
10 December 2002	criminal proceedings against Paul der Weduwe	C-153/00	[2002] ECR I-11319	133
7 January 2004	Aalborg Portland A/S (C-204/00 P), Irish Cement Ltd (C-205/00 P), Ciments français SA (C-211/00 P), Italcementi - Fabbriche Riunite Cemento SpA (C-213/00 P), Buzzi Unicem SpA (C-217/00 P) and Cementir - Cementerie del Tirreno SpA (C-219/00 P) v. Commission of the European Communities	C-204/00 P, C-205/00 P, C-211/00 P, C-213/00 P, C-217/00 P and C-219/00 P	[2004] ECR I-123	190, 217 and 218
19 March 2002	Commission v. Italy	C-224/00	[2002] ECR I-2965	90 and 91
10 July 2003	Commission v. Netherlands	C-246/00	[2003] ECR I-7485	94
12 December 2002	F.W.L. de Groot v. Staatssecretaris van Financiën	C-385/00	[2002] ECR I-11819	88
21 January 2003	Commission v. Parliament and Council	C-378/00	[2003] ECR I-937	135
23 January 2003	criminal proceedings against Renate Sterbenz and Paul Dieter Haug	C-421/00, C-426/00 and C-16/01	[2003] ECR I-6445	106
13 January 2004	Kühne & Heitz NV v. Produktschap voor Pluimvee en Eieren	C-453/00	[2004] ECR I-837	303
20 May 2003	Rechnungshof v. Österreichischer Rundfunk and Others and Christa Neukomm and Joseph Lauermann v. Österreichischer Rundfunk	C-465/00, C-138/01 and C-139/01	[2003] ECR I-4989	97, 110 and 144
11 September 2003	Associação Nacional de Operadores de Máquinas Recreativas (Anomar) and Others v. Estado Português	C-6/01	[2003] ECR I-8621	97 and 128
5 February 2004	criminal proceedings against Greenham and Abel	C-95/01	[2004] ECR I-1333	103
24 October 2002	criminal proceedings against Gottfried Linkart and Hans Biffl	C-99/01	[2002] ECR I-9375	104 and 106
26 November 2002	Ministre de l'Intérieur v. Autor Oteiza Olazabal	C-100/01	[2002] ECR I-10981	86
6 November 2003	criminal proceedings against Bodil Lindqvist	C-101/01	[2003] ECR I-12971	110
20 May 2003	Consorzio del Prosciutto di Parma and Salumificio S. Rita SpA v. Asda Stores Ltd and Hygrade Foods Ltd	C-108/01	[2003] ECR I-5121	171
11 February 2003	criminal proceedings against Gözütok and Brügge	C-187/01 and C-385/01	[2003] ECR I-1345	122, 127, 139, 140, 238, 240, 338, 421 and 426

Date	Parties	Case Number	Reference ECR	Page Number
12 July 2001	H. Jippes, Afdeling Groningen van de Nederlandse Vereniging tot Bescherming van Dieren and Afdeling Assen van de Nederlandse Vereniging tot Bescherming van Dieren v. Minister van Landbouw, Natuurbeheer en Visserij	C-189/01	[2001] ECR I-5689	145
2 October 2003	criminal proceedings against Hans van Lent	C-232/01	[2003] ECR I-11525	82
6 November 2003	criminal proceedings against Piergiorgio Gambelli and Others	C-243/01	[2003] ECR I-13031	76, 82, 83 and 98
29 January 2004	S.A. Krüger v. Directie van de rechtspersoonlijkheid bezittende Dienst Wegverkeer	C-253/01	[2004] ECR I-1191	92 and 94
16 January 2003	criminal proceedings against Pansard and Others	C-265/01	[2003] ECR I-683	106 and 285
10 April 2003	Proceedings against Joachim Steffensen	C-276/01	[2003] ECR I-3735	261
21 September 2005	Ahmed Ali Yussuf, Al Barakaat International Foundation v. Council and Commission	T-306/01	[2005] ECR II-3533	267
21 September 2005	Yassin Abdullah Kadi v. Council and Commission	T-315/01	[2005] ECR II-3649	267
11 December 2003	Deutscher Apothekerverband eV v. 0800 DocMorris NV and Jacques Waterval	C-322/01	[2003] ECR I-14887	103
5 October 2004	Bernhard Pfeiffer (C-397/01), Wilhelm Roith (C-398/01), Albert Süß (C-399/01), Michael Winter (C-400/01), Klaus Nestvogel (C-401/01), Roswitha Zeller (C-402/01) and Matthias Döbele (C-403/01) v. Deutsches Rotes Kreuz, Kreisverband Waldshut eV.	C-397/01 to C-403/01	[2004] ECR I-8835	273 and 274
16 January 2003	criminal proceedings against Ulf Hammarsten	C-462/01	[2003] ECR I-781	106
29 April 2004	criminal proceedings against Felix Kapper	C-476/01	[2004] ECR I-5205	93, 94, 241 and 349
29 April 2004	Proceedings related to Georgios Orfanopoulou and Raffaele Oliveri	C-482/01 and C-493/01	[2004] ECR I-5257	86
2 October 2003	criminal proceedings against Marco Grilli	C-12/02	[2003] ECR I-11585	76 and 106
14 October 2004	Omega Spielhallen- und Automatenaufstellungs-GmbH v. Oberbürgermeisterin der Bundesstadt Bonn	C-36/02	[2004] ECR I-9609	98, 104 and 146
7 January 2004	criminal proceedings against X	C-60/02	[2004] ECR I-651	76, 127, 142 and 168
23 October 2003	Administration des douanes et droits indirects v. Rioglass SA and Transremar SL	C-115/02	[2003] ECR I-12705	137 and 211
23 October 2003	criminal proceedings against Jan Nilsson	C-154/02	[2003] ECR I-12733	49 and 133

Date	Parties	Case Number	Reference ECR	Page Number
28 June 2005	Dansk Rørindustri A/S (C-189/02 P), Isoplus Fernwärmetechnik Vertriebsgesellschaft mbH and Others (C-202/02 P), KE KELIT Kunststoffwerk GmbH (C-205/02 P), LR af 1998 A/S (C-206/02 P), Brugg Rohrsysteme GmbH (C-207/02 P), LR af 1998 (Deutschland) GmbH (C-208/02 P) and ABB Asea Brown Boveri Ltd (C-213/02 P) v. Commission of the European Communities	C-189/02 P, C-202/02 P, C-205/02 P to C-208/02 P and C-213/02 P	[2005] ECR I-5425	169, 171, 190 and 193
29 April 2004	Heikki Antero Pusa v. Osuuspankkien Keskinäinen Vakuutusyhtiö	C-224/02	[2004] ECR I-5763	422
15 January 2004	criminal proceedings before that court against Marco Antonio Saetti and Andrea Frediani	C-235/02	[2004] ECR I-1005	125 and 283
21 February 2006	Halifax plc, Leeds Permanent Development Services Ltd and County Wide Property Investments Ltd v. Commissioners of Customs & Excise	C-255/02	[2006] ECR I-1609	104
1 July 2004	Gisela Gerken v. Amt für Agrarstruktur Verden	C-295/02	[2004] ECR I-6369	142 and 189
7 June 2004	Segi, Araitz Zubimendi Izaga, Aritza Galarraga v. Council	T-338/02	[2004] ECR II-1647	228
1 July 2004	Elliniko Dimosio v. Nikolaos Tsapalos (C-361/02) and Konstantinos Diamantakis (C-362/02)	C-361/02 and C-362/02	[2004] ECR I-6405	371
22 November 2005	criminal proceedings against Knud Grøngaard, Allan Bang	C-384/02	[2005] ECR I-9939	77, 141, 168, 170, 171 and 198
3 May 2005	criminal proceedings against Silvio Berlusconi and Others	C-387/02, C-391/02 and C-403/02	[2005] ECR I-3565	49, 72, 142, 173, 174 and 175
11 December 2003	criminal proceedings against José Antonio da Silva Carvalho	C-408/02	not reported in the ECR	349
31 May 2005	criminal proceedings against Krister Hanner	C-438/02	[2005] ECR I-4551	105
27 April 2006	Commission v. Germany	C-441/02	[2006] ECR I-3449	85
15 July 2004	criminal proceedings against Nicolas Schreiber	C-443/02	[2004] ECR I-7275	96 and 102
11 November 2004	criminal proceedings against Antonio Niselli	C-457/02	[2004] ECR I-10853	168, 170 and 175
7 September 2004	criminal proceedings against Van de Walle and Others	C-1/03	[2004] ECR I-7613	283
26 May 2005	criminal proceedings against Marcel Burmanjer, René Alexander Van Der Linden, Anthony De Jong	C-20/03	[2005] ECR I-4133	81

Date	Parties	Case Number	Reference ECR	Page Number
4 May 2006	criminal proceedings against Michel Mulliez and Others and Giuseppe Momblano (joined cases C-23/03 and C-52/03), Alessandro Nizza and Giacomo Pizzi (C-133/03), Fabrizio Barra (C-337/03) and Adelio Aggio and Others (C-473/03)	C-23/03, C-52/03, C-133/03, C-337/03 and C-473/03	[2006] ECR I-3923	175
11 July 2007	Sison v. Council	T-47/03	[2007] ECR II-2047	160 and 269
31 May 2005	Synetairismos Farmakopoion Aitolias & Akarnanias (Syfait) and Others v. GlaxoSmithKline plc and GlaxoSmithKline AEVE	C-53/03	[2005] ECR I-4609	126
16 June 2005	criminal proceedings against Maria Pupino	C-105/03	[2005] ECR I-5285	18, 53, 65, 123, 125, 128, 166, 168, 212, 215, 274 and 426
17 September 2007	Akzo Nobel Chemicals Ltd and Akcros Chemicals Ltd v. Commission	T-125/03 and T-253/03	[2007] ECR II-3523	224 and 225
15 March 2005	Spain v. Eurojust	C-160/03	[2005] ECR I-2077	268
13 September 2005	Commission v. Council	C-176/03	[2005] ECR I-7879	17, 56, 76, 122, 162, 166, 203 and 426
21 April 2005	criminal proceedings against Lars Erik Staffan Lindberg	C-267/03	[2005] ECR I-3247	176
26 May 2005	Sozialhilfeverband Rohrbach v. Arbeiterkammer Oberösterreich and Österreichischer Gewerkschaftsbund	C-297/03	[2005] ECR I-4305	212
25 January 2007	Dyson Ltd v. Registrar of Trade Marks	C-321/03	[2007] ECR I-687	288
11 July 2007	Al-Aqsa v. Council	T-327/03	[2007] ECR II-79	269
16 September 2004	criminal proceedings against Olivier Dupuyand Hervé Rouvre	C-404/03	[2004] ECR I-8557	108
10 March 2005	criminal proceedings brought against Filomeno Mario Miraglia	C-469/03	[2005] ECR I-2009	240
26 May 2005	Kingscrest Associates Ltd, Montecello Ltd v. Commissioners of Customs and Excise	C-498/03	[2005] ECR I-4427	136
31 January 2006	Commission v. Spain	C-503/03	[2006] ECR I-1097	86 and 345
13 October 2005	Scania Finance France SA v. Rockinger Spezialfabrik für Anhängerkupplungen GmbH & Co	C-522/03	[2005] ECR I-8639	344
27 June 2006	European Parliament v. Council	C-540/03	[2006] ECR I-5769	143 and 213
8 September 2005	criminal proceedings against Syuichi Yonemoto	C-40/04	[2005] ECR I-7755	76, 107 and 191
17 March 2005	criminal proceedings against Annic Andréa Raemdonck, Raemdonck-Janssens BVBA	C-128/04	[2005] ECR I-2445	283
15 December 2005	criminal proceedings against Claude Nadin, Nadin-Lux SA (C-151/04) and Jean-Pascal Durré (C-152/04)	C-151/04 and C-152/04	[2005] ECR I-11203	105
7 June 2007	Commission v. Greece	C-156/04	[2007] ECR I-4129	226 and 298

Date	Parties	Case Number	Reference ECR	Page Number
5 June 2007	Klas Rosengren, Bengt Morelli, Hans Särman, Mats Åkerström, Åke Kempe, Anders Kempe, Mats Kempe, Björn Rosengren, Martin Lindberg, Jon Pierre, Tony Staf, v. Riksåklagaren	C-170/04	[2007] ECR I-4071	100
16 March 2006	Rosmarie Kapferer v. Schlank & Schick GmbH	C-234/04	[2006] ECR I-2585	142 and 303
12 January 2006	Turn- und Sportunion Waldburg v. Finanzlandesdirektion für Oberösterreich	C-246/04	[2006] ECR I-589	128
29 June 2006	Showa Denko KK v. Commission	C-289/04 P	[2006] ECR I-5859	298
6 March 2007	Wienand Meilicke, Heidi Christa Weyde, Marina Stöffler v. Finanzamt Bonn-Innenstadt	C-292/04	[2007] ECR I-1835	288
29 June 2006	SGL Carbon AG v. Commission	C-308/04 P	[2006] ECR I-5977	243
30 May 2006	European Parliament and European Data Protection Service (EDPS) v. Council, and European Parliament v. Commission	C-317/04	[2006] ECR I-4721	165 and 329
6 March 2007	criminal proceedings against Placanica, Palazzese and Sorricchio	C-338/04, C-359/04, C-360/04	[2007] ECR I-1891	82, 129, 131, 134, 135, 152 and 153
27 February 2007	Gestoras Pro Amnistía and Others v. Council	C-354/04 P	[2007] ECR I-1579	131, 268 and 269
27 February 2007	Segi and Others v. Council	C-355/04 P	[2007] ECR I-1657	268 and 269
24 November 2005	Georg Schwarz v. Bürgermeister der Landeshauptstadt Salzburg	C-366/04	[2005] ECR I-10139	102
10 May 2007	Ipourgos Ikonomikon Proistamenos DOI Amfissas v. Charilaos Georgakis	C-391/04	[2007] ECR I-3741	198
25 January 2007	Sumitomo Metal Industries Ltd and Nippon Steel Corp. v. Commission	C-403/04 P and C-405/04	[2007] ECR I-729	225 and 262
25 January 2007	Salzgitter Mannesmann GmbH v. Commission	C-411/04	[2007] ECR I-959	216
28 September 2006	criminal proceedings against Jan-Erik Anders Ahokainen, Mati Leppik	C-434/04	[2006] ECR I-9171	99 and 100
9 March 2006	criminal proceedings against Leopold Henri Van Esbroeck	C-436/04	[2006] ECR I-2333	139, 242, 243 and 244
23 February 2006	A-Punkt Schmuckhandels GmbH v. Claudia Schmidt	C-441/04	[2006] ECR I-2093	81
28 September 2006	Gasparini and Others	C-467/04	[2006] ECR I-9199	132, 138, 139, 240 and 243
12 September 2006	Laserdisken ApS v. Kulturministeriet	C-479/04	[2006] ECR I-8089	213
11 September 2007	Herbert Schwarz, Marga Gootjes Schwarz v. Finanzamt Bergisch Gladbach	C-76/05	[2007] ECR I-6849	84 and 85
18 December 2007	United Kingdom v. Council	C-77/05	[2007] ECR I-11459	57 and 59
20 May 2008	Commission v. Council	C-91/05	OJ 2008, C 183/2	162
29 March 2007	Aktiebolaget NN v. Skatteverket	C-111/05	[2007] ECR I-2697	180
18 July 2007	Commission against Italian Republic	C-134/05	[2007] ECR I-6251	83
28 September 2006	Jean Leon Van Straaten v. Staat der Nederlanden, Republiek Italië	C-150/05	[2006] ECR I-9327	139, 239, 240, 244, 245, 277 and 385

Date	Parties	Case Number	Reference ECR	Page Number
27 September 2007	Twoh International BV v. Staatssecretaris van Financiën	C-184/05	[2007] ECR I-7897	373
7 June 2007	J. van der Weerd and Others (C-222/05), H. de Rooy sr. and H. de Rooy jr. (C-223/05), Maatschap H. en J. van 't Oever and Others (C-224/05) and B. J. van Middendorp (C-225/05) v. Minister van Landbouw, Natuur en Voedselkwaliteit	C-222/05 to C-225/05	[2007] ECR I-4233	64 and 284
1 February 2007	Jose Maria Sison v. Council	C-226/05 P	[2007] ECR I-103	268
6 April 2006	Halbritter v. Freistaat Bayern	C-227/05	[2006] ECR I-49	241 and 349
18 January 2007	Osman Ocalan (PKK) and Serif Valy (KNK) appellants, Council, defendant	C-229/05	[2007] ECR I-439	139, 220 and 268
21 June 2007	criminal proceedings against Omni Metal Service	C-259/05	[2007] ECR I-4945	134
11 January 2007	Vonk Diary Products BV v. Produktschap Zuivel	C-279/05	[2007] ECR I-239	300
14 December 2006	ASML Netherlands BV v. Semiconductor Industry Services GmbH (SEMIS)	C-283/05	[2006] ECR I-12041	213 and 344
18 July 2007	criminal proceedings against Jürgen Kretzinger	C-288/05	[2007] ECR I-6441	61, 238, 242, 243, 244, 245 and 421
18 October 2007	Commission v. European Parliament and Council	C-299/05	[2007] ECR I-8695	213
3 May 2007	Advocaten voor de Wereld VZW v. Leden van de Ministerraad	C-303/05	[2007] ECR I-3633	53, 56, 133, 144, 173, 283, 332, 336, 339, 368 and 375
26 June 2007	Ordre des barreaux francophones et germanophone, Ordre français des avocats du barreau de Bruxelles, Ordre des barreaux flamands, Ordre néerlandais des avocats du barreau de Bruxelles v. Conseil des Ministres	C-305/05	[2007] ECR I-535	136, 143, 213 and 224
18 July 2007	Ismail Derin v. Landkreis Darmstadt-Dieburg	C-325/05	[2007] ECR I-6495	86
10 May 2007	SGL Carbon v. Commission	C-328/05 P	[2007] ECR I-3921	215, 217, 243 and 298
15 November 2007	criminal proceedings against Fredrik Granberg	C-330/05	[2007] ECR I-9871	80
28 September 2006	criminal proceedings against Stefan Kremer	C-340/05	[2006] ECR I-98	241 and 349
18 July 2007	criminal proceedings against Norma Kraaijenbrink	C-367/05	[2007] ECR I-6619	139, 143, 243 and 245
25 January 2007	criminal proceedings against Uwe Kay Festersen	C-370/05	[2007] ECR I-1129	82, 83, 97 and 144
16 January 2008	Yassin Abdullah Kadi v. Council and Commission	C-402/05 P	OJ 2006, C 36/19	265 and 269
4 October 2007	Max Rampion, Marie-Jeanne Rampion, née Godard v. Franfinance SA, K par K SAS	C-429/05	[2007] ECR I-8017	64

Date	Parties	Case Number	Reference ECR	Page Number
5 July 2007	Ntionik Anonymi Etaireia Emporias H/Y, Logismikou kai Paroxis Ypiresion Michanografisis and Ioannis Michail Pikoulas v. Epitropi Kefalaiagoras	C-430/05	[2007] ECR I-5853	76
13 March 2007	Unibet (London) Ltd, Unibet (International) Ltd v. Justitiekanselern	C-432/05	[2007] ECR I-2271	226
23 October 2007	Commission v. Council	C-440/05	[2007] ECR I-9097	17, 56, 122, 158, 162, 163, 164 and 166
19 April 2007	Velvet & Steel Immobilien und Handels GmbH v. Finanzamt Hamburg-Eimsbüttel	C-455/05	[2007] ECR I-3225	136
28 June 2007	criminal proceedings against Giovanni Dell'Orto, joined party: Saipem SpA	C-467/05	[2007] ECR I-5557	122, 128, 133, 135, 136, 138, 139, 212 and 270
12 February 2008	Willy Kempter KG v. Hauptzollamt Hamburg-Jonas	C-2/06	OJ 2008, C 79/3	14, 50, 267, 288
8 February 2007	Groupe Danone v. Commission	C-3/06 P	[2007] ECR I-1331	2, 142, 171, 227, 299 and 300
8 March 2007	Campina GmbH & Co., formerly TUFFI Campina emzett GmbH v. Hauptzollamt Frankfurt	C-45/06	[2007] ECR I-2089	299
7 June 2007	Commission v. Netherlands	C-50/06	[2007] ECR I-4383	85 and 296
18 December 2007	Fazenda Pública - Director Geral das Alfândegas v. ZF Zefeser - Importação e Exportação de Produtos Alimentares Lda.	C-62/06	[2007] ECR I-11995	159
14 June 2007	Telefónica O2 Czech Republic a.s. v. Czech On Line a.s.	C-64/06	[2007] ECR I-4887	65
7 June 2007	Britannia Alloys & Chemicals Ltd v. Commission	C-76/06 P	[2007] ECR I-4405	169 and 299
11 October 2007	Freeport plc v. Olle Arnoldsson	C-98/06	[2007] ECR I-8319	186 and 367
18 January 2007	Commission v. Sweden	C-104/06	[2007] ECR I-671	263
11 December 2007	Skoma-Lux sro v. Celní ředitelství Olomouc	C-161/06	[2007] ECR I-10841	171
6 March 2007	criminal proceedings against Gallo and Damonte	C-191/06	[2007] ECR I-30	131
21 June 2007	National Pensions Office v. Emilienne Jonkman (C-231/06), Hélène Vercheval (C-232/06) and Noëlle Permesaen (C-233/06) v. National Pensions Office	C-231/06 to 233/06	[2007] ECR I-5149	17
14 February 2008	Dynamic Medien Vertriebs GmbH v. Avides Media AG	C-244/06	OJ 2008, C 79/4	98
29 January 2008	Productores de Música de España (Promusicae) v. Telefónica de España SAU	C-275/06	OJ 2008, C 64/9	265
Pending Case	Ireland v. European Parliament and Council of the European Union	C-301/06	OJ 2006, C 237/5	138, 169 and 191

Date	Parties	Case Number	Reference ECR	Page Number
3 June 2008	The Queen on the application of: International Association of Independent Tanker Owners (Intertanko), International Association of Dry Cargo Shipowners (Intercargo), Greek Shipping Co-operation Committee, Lloyd's Register, International Salvage Union, v. Secretary of State for Transport	C-308/06	OJ 2008, C 183/2	265
26 June 2008	Arthur Wiedemann (C-329/06) v. Land Baden-Württemberg and Peter Funk (C-334/06) v. Stadt Chemnitz	C-329/06 and C-343/06	OJ 2008, C 209/5	94, 331, 345, 349 and 424
26 June 2008	Matthias Zerche (C-334/06), Manfred Seuke (C-336/06) v. Landkreis Mittweida and Steffen Schubert (C-335/06) v. Landkreis Mittlerer Erzgebirgskreis	C-334/06 to C-336/06	OJ 2008, C 209/6	94, 331, 345, 349 and 424
1 July 2008	Chronopost SA (C-341/06 P), La Poste, (C-342/06 P), Union française de l'express (UFEX), established in Roissy-en-France (France), DHL Express (France) SAS, formerly DHL International SA, established in Roissy-en-France, Federal express international (France) SNC, established in Gennevilliers (France), CRIE SA, in liquidation, established in Asnières (France) v. Commission	C-341/06 P and C-342/06 P	OJ 2008, C 209/7	226 and 227
4 October 2007	Murat Polat v. Stadt Rüsselsheim	C-349/06	[2007] ECR I-8167	118
14 February 2008	Varec SA v. Belgian State	C-450/06	OJ 2008, C 79/6	215
22 May 2008	Halina Nerkowska v. Zakład Ubezpieczeń Społecznych Oddział w Koszalinie	C-499/06	OJ 2008, C 171/7	91
Pending Case	Staatsanwaltschaft Siegen v. Frank Weber	C-1/07	OJ 2007, C 42/20	349
8 May 2008	Ingenieurbüro Michael Weiss und Partner GbR v. Industrie- und Handelskammer Berlin	C-14/07	OJ 2008, C 158/5	217
10 July 2008	Ministerul Administraţiei şi Internelor – Direcţia Generală de Paşapoarte Bucureşti v. Gheorghe Jipa	C-33/07	OJ 2008, C 223/11	89
Pending Case	Liga Portuguesa de Futebol Profissional (CA/LPFP) Baw International Ltd v. Departamento de Jogos da Santa Casa da Misericórdia de Lisboa	C-42/07	OJ 2007, C 69/9	79
5 June 2008	James Wood v. Fonds de garantie des victimes des actes de terrorisme et d'autres infractions	C-164/07	OJ 2008, C 183/3	91 and 126
3 April 2008	criminal proceedings against Dirk Endendijk	C-187/07	OJ 2007, C 129/9	205 and 283
21 October 2008	Marra v. De Gregorio (C-200/07) and Clemente (C-201/07)	C-200/07 and C-201/07	OJ 2007, C 129/13	247
3 July 2008	criminal proceedings against Rainer Günther Möginger	C-225/07	OJ 2007, C 183/17	349

Date	Parties	Case Number	Reference ECR	Page Number
Pending Case	Staatsanwaltschaft Regensburg v. Klaus Bourquain	C-297/07	OJ 2007, C 211/20	242 and 427
9 October 2008	criminal proceedings György Katz v. István Roland Sós	C-404/07	OJ 2007, C 283/13	125 and 271
Pending Case	M. Elgafaji, N. Elgafaji v. Staatssecretaris van Justitie	C-465/07	OJ 2008, C 8/5	213 and 423
Pending Case	criminal proceedings against Vladimir Turansky	C-491/07	OJ 2008, C 22/26	238
17 July 2008	Proceedings concerning the execution of a European arrest warrant issued against Szymon Kosłowski	C-66/08	OJ 2008, C 223/18	184, 283 and 286
Pending Case	criminal proceedings against D. Wolzenburg	C-123/08	OJ 2008, C 116/18	283
12 August 2008	Ignacio Pédro Santesteban Goicoechea	C-296/08 PPU	OJ 2008, C 260/4	283, 286 and 369

EUROPEAN COMMISSION OF HUMAN RIGHTS

Date	Parties	Application Number	Reference	Page Number
25 September 1965	X v. Germany	1611/62	Collection of Decisions 17, 42	377
5 February 1973	X, Y and Z v. Austria	5049/71	Collection of Decisions 43, 38	377
10 July 1978	Confédération Française Démocratique du Travail v. the European Communities, their member states, jointly and severally	8030/77	Decisions and Reports 13, 231	227
12 July 1978	X v. Germany	7779/77	Unpublished	377
7 May 1986	Jesso v. Austria	9315/81	Decisions and Reports 50, 44	377
13 July 1987	X v. Germany	11853/85	European Human Rights Reports 1988, 521	377
19 January 1989	Dufay v. les Communautés Européennes, subsidiairement, la collective de leur États Members et leurs États Membres pris individuellement	13539/88	Unpublished	228
6 March 1989	R. v. Austria	12592/86	Decisions and Reports 60, 201	377
9 February 1990	M. & Co. v. the Federal Republic of Germany	13258/87	Decisions and Reports 64, 138	228
4 September 1991	Chinoy v. the United Kingdom	15199/89	Unpublished	378
10 September 1991	X v. Switzerland	14379/88	Unpublished	377
10 January 1994	Heinz v. the Contracting States party to the European Patent Convention insofar as they are High Contracting parties to the European Convention on Human Rights, i.e. Austria, Belgium, Denmark, France, Germany, Greece, Ireland, Italy, Liechtenstein, Luxembourg, Netherlands, Norway, Portugal, Spain, Sweden, Switzerland and the United Kingdom	21090/92	Unpublished	229
12 October 1992	Noviflora Sweden Aktiebolag v. Sweden	14369/88	Unpublished	377

EUROPEAN COURT OF HUMAN RIGHTS

Date	Parties	Application Number	Reference	Page Number
18 January 1978	Ireland v. the United Kingdom		Series A-25	379
21 February 1984	Öztürk v. Germany	8544/79		2
7 July 1989	Soering v. the United Kingdom		Series A-161	379 and 380
26 April 1991	Asch v. Austria		Series A-203	377
16 December 1992	Niemietz v. Germany		Series A-251B	220
28 August 1992	Artner v. Austria		Series A-242	377
15 November 1996	Cantoni v. France	17862/91		169
7 septembre 1999	Dotta c. Italie	38399/97		278
11 July 2000	Hansen v. Denmark	28971/95		195
13 February 2001	Krombach v. France	29731/96		343
8 November 2001	Sari v. Denmark and Turkey	21889/93		378
7 March 2002	T.I. v. United Kingdom	43844/98		229
23 May 2002	Segi and Gestoras Pro Amnistiá v. 15 Member States of the European Union	6422/02 and 9916/02		268
7 September 2006	Grifhorst v. France	28336/02		278
5 July 2007	Saccoccia v. Austria	69917/01		377
27 novembre 2007	Tillack c. Belgique	20477/05		228

TABLE OF LEGISLATION

COMMON POSITIONS

of the International Criminal Tribunal for the former Yugoslavia (ICTY), OJ 2008, L 197/65   *267*

CONVENTIONS

DECISIONS

DIRECTIVES

FRAMEWORK DECISIONS

JOINT ACTIONS

JOINT POSITIONS

REGULATIONS

SELECTED BIBLIOGRAPHY ON EUROPEAN CRIMINAL LAW

Akehurst, M., The Application of General Principles of Law by the Court of Justice of the European Communities, 52 British Journal of International Law 1981, p. 29–51

Allen, C.G., Criminal offences against the law of the European Community, Common Market Law Review 1974, p. 183–190

Ambos, K., Internationales Strafrecht Strafanwendungsrecht Völkerstrafrecht Europäisches Strafrecht, Verlag C.H. Beck, 2nd Edition 2008

Armone, G.M. (ed.), Diritto Penale Europeo e Ordinamento Italiano, Giuffrè Editore 2006

Baker, E., Taking European Criminal Law Seriously, Criminal Law Review 1998, p. 361–380

Bassiouni, M. Ch., V. Militello and H. Satzger, European Cooperation in Penal Matters: Issues and Perspectives, Wolters Kluwer Italia 2008

Beken, T. Vander, Forumkeuze in het internationaal strafrecht, Maklu Antwerpen/ Apeldoorn 1999

Bennion, F.A.R., Understanding common law legislation, Oxford University Press 2001

Böse, M., Der Grundsatz der Verfügbarkeit von Informationen in der strafrechtlichen Zusammenarbeit der Europäischen Union, Bonn University Press 2007

Cadoppi, A., Towards a European Criminal Code, European Journal of Crime, Criminal law and Criminal Justice 1996, p. 2–17

Caeiro, P., Fundamento, conteúdo e limites da jurisdição penal do estado: o caso português, Dissertation University of Coimbra 2008

Cape, E. and J. Hodgson, T. Prakken and T. Spronken (eds.), Suspects in Europe, Intersentia 2007

Corstens, G. and J. Pradel, Het Europese strafrecht, Deventer, Kluwer 2003

Dannecker, G. and O. Jansen, Competition Law Sanctioning in the European Union, Kluwer Law International 2004

Delmas-Marty, M., Procédures pénales d'Europe, Presses universitaires de France 1995

Delmas-Marty, M., Quelle politique pénale pour l'Europe? Paris, Economica 1993

Delmas-Marty, M., The European Union and Penal Law, European Law Journal, 1998, p. 87–115

Delmas-Marty, M. and J.A.E. Vervaele, The Implementation of the Corpus Juris in the Member States, Intersentia 2000

Dijk, P. van, F. van Hoof, A. van Rijn and L. Zwaak (eds.), Theory and Practice of the European Convention on Human Rights, Intersentia Antwerpen-Oxford 2004, 4th edition

Droit pénal européen, Europees strafrecht, European Criminal Law, Presses universitaires de Bruxelles 1970

Droit pénal, droit européen, Mélanges offerts à G. Levasseur, Paris, 1992

Enschedé, Ch.J., Model Penal Code for Europe, Een uniform Europees strafrecht?, Gouda Quint Arnhem 1970, 1990

European Criminal Law, Special Issue of the Maastricht Journal of European and Comparative Law 2005, Vol. 12, number 2, p. 113–213

European Integration and Harmonisation and Criminal Law, Four Contributions on the Interplay between European Integration and European and National Law to celebrate the 25th Anniversary of Maastricht University's Faculty of Law 2006, p. 109–153

Europeanisering van het Nederlands recht, opstellen aangeboden aan Mr. W.E. Haak, (editors G.J.M. Corstens, W.J.M. Davids, M.I. Veldt-Foglia) Kluwer Deventer 2004

Fijnaut, C., De Europese Unie: een lusthof voor (strafrechtelijke) rechtsvergelijking, Gouda Quint Deventer 2001, inaugural lecture Tilburg University

Fijnaut, C., Rechtsvergelijking en strafrecht(swetenschap): enkele methodologische beschouwingen, Nederlandse Vereniging voor Rechtsvergelijking, Handelingen No. 61, Kluwer Deventer 2001

Fletcher, M. and R. Lööf, EU Criminal Law and Justice, Edward Elgar Publishing 2008

Grasso, G. and R. Sicurella, Lezioni di Diritto Penale Europeo, Giuffrè Editore 2007

Guerini, U., Il Diritto Penale dell'Unione Europea, G. Giappichelli Editore, Torino 2008

Harding, Chr. and B. Swart, Enforcing European Community Rules, Dartmouth 1996

Hecker, B., Europäisches Strafrecht, Springer Verlag 2005

Hendry, I.D., The third pillar of Maastricht, cooperation in the field of justice and home affairs, 36 German Yearbook of International Law 1993, p. 295–327

Henzelin, M., Le principe de l'universalité en droit pénal international, Collection Genevoise 2000

Hoecke, M. Van (ed.), Epistemology and Methodology of Comparative Law, Hart Publishing, Oxford and Portland Oregon 2004

Johannes, H., Le droit pénal et son harmonisation dans les Communautés Européenes, Revue trimestrielle de droit européen, 1971, p. 315–352

Jung, H., Criminal Justice – a European Perspective, Criminal Law Review 1993, p. 237–245

Kaiafa-Gbandi, M., The development towards Harmonization within Criminal Law in the European Union. A Citizen's Perspective, 9 European Journal of Crime, Criminal Law and Criminal Justice 2001, p. 239–263

Kerchove, G. De and A. Weyembergh, La reconnaissance mutuelle des décisions judiciaires pénales dans l'Union européenne, Bruxelles, Editions de l'Université de Bruxelles 2001

Kerchove, G. De and A. Weyembergh, L'espace pénal européen: enjeux et perspectives, Bruxelles, Editions de l'Université de Bruxelles 2002

Kerchove, G. De and A. Weyembergh, Quelles réformes pour l'espace pénal européen?, Bruxelles, Editions de l'Université de Bruxelles 2003

Kerchove, G. De and A. Weyembergh, Vers un espace judiciaire pénal européen, Towards a European Judicial Criminal Area, Bruxelles, Editions de l'Université de Bruxelles 2000

Klip, A.H., Conditions for a European Corpus Juris Criminalis, in: Michael Faure, Jan Smits en Hildegard Schneider (eds.), Towards a European Ius Commune in Legal Education and Research, Maastricht 2002, p. 109–123

Klip, A.H., Harmonisierung des Strafrechts – eine Idee fixe?, Neue Zeitschrift für Strafrecht 2000, p. 626–630

Klip, A.H., The Decrease of Protection under Human Rights Treaties in International Criminal Law, 68 Revue Internationale de Droit Pénal/ International Review of Penal Law 1997, p. 291–310

Klip, A.H., Uniestrafrecht/ Criminal Law of the European Union/ Le Droit Pénal de l'Union Européenne/ Strafrecht in der Europäischen Union, oratie/ inaugural lecture/ Antrittsrede/ discours inaugural, Maastricht University Kluwer 2005

Klip, A. and H. van der Wilt, Harmonisation and Harmonising Measures in Criminal Law, Royal Academy of Science/ Koninklijke Nederlandse Akademie van Wetenschappen, Verhandelingen, Afd. Letterkunde, Nieuwe Reeks, deel 186, Amsterdam 2002

Lawson, R.A., Het EVRM en de Europese Gmeenschappen, Kluwer Deventer 1999

Nelles, U., Europaïsierung des Strafverfahrensstrafprozessrecht für Europa, Zeitschrift für die gesamte Strafrechtswissenschaft 1997, p. 727–755

Nijboer, J.F. and W.J.J.M. Sprangers (eds.), Harmonisation in Forensic Expertise, An Inquiry into the Desirability of International Standards for Scientific Evidence, Thela Thesis, Amsterdam 2000

Peers, S., EU Justice and Home Affairs Law, Oxfor University Press, 2nd Edition 2007

Pradel, J. and G. Corstens, Droit Pénal Européen, 2e edition, Paris Dalloz 2002

Rodrigues, A.M., O Direito Penal Europeu Emergente, Coimbra Editora 2008

Roger France, E., The influence of European Community Law on the criminal law of the member states, European Journal of Crime, Criminal Law and Criminal Justice 1994, p. 324–358

Satzger, H., Internationales und Europäisches Strafrecht, Nomos 2005

Schünemann, B., Alternative-Project for a European Criminal Law and Procedure, Criminal Law Forum 2007, p. 227–251

Schünemann, B. and J. de Figueiredo Dias, Bausteine des europäischen Strafrechts, Coimbra-Symposium für Claus Roxin, Carl Heymanns Verlag KG 1995

Sevenster, H.G., Criminal law & EC Law, 29 Common Market Law Review 1992, p. 29–70

Sgubbi, F. and G. Insolera, L'interpretazione conforme al diritto comunitario in materia penale, Bononia University Press 2007

Sieber, U., European Unification and European Criminal Law, European Journal of Crime, Criminal Law and Criminal Justice 1994, p. 86–104

Sotis, C., Il Diritto Senza Codice, Uno studio sul sistema penale europeo vigente, Milano, Dott. A. Giuffrè Editore 2007

Spencer, J., The European Arrest Warrant, The Cambridge Yearbook on European Legal Studies 2004, p. 201–234

Spronken, T., A Place of Greater Safety, inaugural lecture Maastricht 2003

Spronken, T. and M. Attinger, Procedural Rights in Criminal Proceedings: Existing Level of Safeguards, Maastricht/ Brussel 2005

Strijards, G.A.M., Internationaal strafrecht, strafmachtsrecht, Gouda Quint Arnhem 1984

Swart, A.H.J., Een ware Europese rechtsruimte, Gouda Quint Deventer 2001, inaugural lecture University of Amsterdam

Swart, B. and A. Klip, International Criminal Law in the Netherlands, Beiträge und Materialien aus dem Max-Planck-Institut für internationales und ausländisches Strafrecht, Band S 66, Freiburg im Breisgau 1997

Vermeulen, G., Aspecten van Europees formeel strafrecht, Maklu Antwerpen/ Apeldoorn 2002

Vermeulen, G., Aspecten van Europees materieel strafrecht, Maklu Antwerpen/ Apeldoorn 2002

Vermeulen, G., Wederzijdse rechtshulp in strafzaken in de Europese Unie, Maklu Antwerpen/ Apeldoorn 1999

Vermeulen, G., T. Vander Beken, L. Van Puyenbroeck and S. Van Malderen, Availability of law enforcement information in the European Union, Maklu Antwerpen/ Apeldoorn 2005

Vervaele, J.A.E., El Derecho Penal Europeo, Del Derecho Penal Económico y Financiero a un Derecho Penal Federal, UBIJUS, Lima Peru 2006

Vervaele, J.A.E. (ed.), European Evidence Warrant, Intersentia 2005

Vervaele, J.A.E., Handen en tanden van het (gemeenschapsrecht), Inaugural lecture Utrecht University 1994, Kluwer Deventer 1994

Vervaele, J.A.E. (ed.), Transnational Enforcement of the Financial Interests of the European Union. Developments in the Treaty of Amsterdam and the Corpus Juris, Intersentia, Antwerpen 1999

Vervaele, J. and A. Klip, European Cooperation between Tax, Customs and Judicial Authorities, European Monographs 32, Kluwer Law International, The Hague, London, New York 2002

Verwey, D., The European Community, the European Union and the International Law of Treaties, TMC Asser Press, The Hague 2004

Vogel, J., Europäische Kriminalpolitik – europäische Strafrechtsdogmatik, Goltdammer's Archiv für Strafrecht 2002, p. 517–534

Weyembergh, A., L'harmonisation des législations: condition de l'espace pénal européen et révélateur des ses tensions, Editions de l'Université de Bruxelles 2004

Weyembergh, A. and S. de Biolley, Comment évaluer le droit pénal européen? Editions de l'Université de Bruxelles 2006

Wyngaert, Chr. Van den, Strafrecht, strafprocesrecht en internationaal strafrecht, Maklu Antwerpen/ Apeldoorn 2003

LITERATURE ON
EUROPEAN CRIMINAL LAW
IN THE MEMBER STATES

AUSTRIA[1]

Fuchs, H., Europäischer Haftbefehl und Staaten-Souveränität, Juristische Blätter 2003, p. 405 *et seq.*

Kert, R., Lebensmittelstrafrecht im Spannungsfeld des Gemeinschaftsrechts, Neuer Wissenschaftlicher Verlag, Wien 2004

Killmann, B.-R., Die rahmenbeschlusskonforme Auslegung im Strafrecht vor dem EuGH, Juristische Blätter 2005, p. 566 *et seq.*

Medigovic, U., Der Europäische Haftbefehl in Österreich, Juristische Blätter 2006, p. 627 *et seq.*

Medigovic, U., Die gegenseitige Anerkennung von vermögensrechtlichen Sanktionen innerhalb der EU und ihre Umsetzung im österreichischen Justizstrafrecht, Juristische Blätter 2008, p. 69 *et seq.*

Murschetz, V., Auslieferung und Europäischer Haftbefehl, Springer-Verlag, Wien – New York 2007

Reiter, S., Europäische Union und österreichisches Strafrecht: unter besonderer Berücksichtigung der Delikte gegen Menschenhandel und Schlepperei, Wien 2008

Schroeder, W., Der Rahmenbeschluss als Rechtssatzform in den Verträgen, in: Lagodny, Otto/ Wiederin, Ewald/ Winkler, Roland (Hrsg.), Probleme des Rahmenbeschlusses am Beispiel des Europäischen Haftbefehls – Ein neues Instrument der europäischen Integration aus Sicht von Europarecht, Strafrecht, Verfassungsrecht und Völkerrecht, Berlin/Graz 2007, p. 37–58

Schroeder, W., Die Durchführung von Gemeinschaftsrecht – einheitliche Wirkung versus nationale Verfahrensautonomie, in: Hummer, Waldemar (Hrsg.), Paradigmenwechsel im Europarecht zur Jahrtausendwende, Wien/New York 2004, p. 231–267

Schwaighofer, K., Die Neuordnung des Auslieferungsrechts durch den Europäischen Haftbefehl, in: Grafl/Medigovic (eds.), Festschrift für Manfred Burgstaller, Neuer Wissenschaftlicher Verlag, Wien – Graz 2004

Zeder, F., Der Europäische Haftbefehl in Österreich. Eine Analyse der materiellen Voraussetzungen für eine Übergabe nachdem EU-JZG, Juristische Blätter 2006, p. 627 *et seq.*

Zeder, F., Europastrafrecht – Aktueller Stand, in: Bundesministerium für Justiz (ed.), Vorarlberger Tage 2007, p. 51 *et seq.*

---

[1]   I thank Robert Kert and Johannes Keiler for providing me with this information.

BELGIUM[2]

Beken, T. Vander, From Brussels with love. Bespiegelingen over de invloed van de Europese Unie op het Belgisch strafrecht, T. Strafr. 2002, p. 2–26

Hert, P. de, Het einde van de Europese rechtshulp en de geboorte van een Europese horizontale strafprocesruimte, Justitiële Verkenningen, 2004, vol. 30, nr. 6, 96–118

Hert, P. de, Trends in de Europese politiële en justitiële informatiesamenwerking, Panopticon, Tijdschrift voor strafrecht, criminologie en forensisch welzijnswerk, 2004, vol. 25, nr. 1, 26–56

Kerckhove, G. De and A. Weyembergh (ed.), La confiance mutuelle dans l'espace pénal européen, Collection Études européennes, Université Libre de Bruxelles, Centre d'études européennes, Bruxelles, 2005, 261 p.

Stessens, G., De nationale en internationale bestrijding van het witwassen, Intersentia uitgevers 1997

Wyngaert, Chr. Van den, De internationale strafrechtelijke samenwerking bij de bestrijding van de EEG-Fraude, RW 1991–92, p. 417–424

Wyngaert, Chr. Van den, Droit pénal et communautés européenes, Revue de Droit Pénal et de Criminologie 1982, p. 837–862

Wyngaert, Chr. Van den, Kennismaking met het internationaal en Europees strafrecht, Maklu, Antwerpen, 2003

CYPRUS[3]

Tsadiras, A., National courts: Cyprus Supreme Court, Judgment of 7 November 2005 (Civil Appeal No. 294/2005) on the Cypriot European Arrest Warrant Law, 44 Common Market Law Review 2007, p. 1515 et seq.

DANMARK[4]

Cornils, K. and V. Greve, Dänemark. Organisierte Kriminalität und kriminelle Organisationen. Walter Gropp and Arndt Sinn (Hrsg.). Baden-Baden 2006, p. 31–71

Elholm, T., EU-konform fortolkning af national strafferet. In: Jurist uden omsvøb, Festskrift til Gorm Toftegaard Nielsen. Annette Møller-Sørensen et al. (eds.). Christian Ejlers Forlag. København, 2007, p. 97–116

Elholm, T., Strafrechtliche Maßnahmen der EU – verstärkte Repression in den nordischen Ländern? Müller-Dietz et al. (eds.): Festschrift für Heike Jung, 2007, p. 135–152

---

2   I thank Karin Weis for providing me with this information.
3   I thank Christina Peristeridou for providing me with this information.
4   I thank Jørn Vestergaard for providing me with this information.

Gade, I. et al., Det politimæssige og strafferetlige samarbejde i Den Europæiske Union. Jurist- og Økonomforbundets Forlag, 2005

Holst Christensen, N., Mens vi venter på Godot. In: Ikke kun straf... Festskrift til Vagn Greve. Thomas Elholm et al. (eds.). Jurist- og Økonomforbundets Forlag, 2008, p. 243–253

Vestergaard, J., Dansk lovgivning om bekæmpelse af terrorisme. In: Enhver stats pligt... International strafferet og dansk ret. Lars Plum & Andreas Laursen (eds.). DJØFs Forlag, 2007, p. 391–424

Vestergaard, J., Det strafferetlige værn mod terrorisme – nye konventionsforpligtelser mv. Tidsskrift for Kriminalret 4/2006, pp. 246–260

Vestergaard, J., Udlevering til strafforfølgning m.v. – den europæiske arrestordre som udtryk for gensidig anerkendelse. In: Festskrift til Hans Gammeltoft-Hansen. Arne Fliflet et al. (eds.). Jurist- og Økonomforbundets Forlag 2004, p. 627–653

FINLAND[5]

Frände, D., Om att frysa i EU- några iakttagelser. Rikosoikeudellisia kirjoituksia VIII Raimo Lahdelle omistettu. Suomalainen Lakimiesyhdistys, Helsinki 2006, p. 19–29

Frände, D., Om bevisupptagning inom EU. Juha Lappalaisen juhlakirja. COMI, Helsinki s. 69–83

Jahkola, K., Rikosasioita koskeva keskinäinen oikeusapu Euroopan Unionissa. Lakimies 2000/4 p. 506–536

Lahti, R., Harmonisering av den straffrättsliga lagstiftningen och konsekvenser för den nationella lagstiftningen. Materiella och rättskipningsrelaterade stötestenar. Juridiska Föreningens Tidsskrift 3–4/2004 p. 377–385

Lahti, R., Straffrättsligt samarbete i EU:s tredje pelare – något att sträva efter? – Förhandlingarna vid Det 36 nordiska juristmötet i Helsingfors 15–17 augusti 2002. Del I. Utgivna av lokalstyrelsen för Finland. Jyväskylä 2002, p. 431–444

Melander, S., Rangaistusten yhdenmukaistamisesta Euroopan unionissa. Defensor legis 2002/6 p. 966–973

Nuotio, K., Eurooppalaistuva rikosoikeus. EU-oikeuden perusteita II – aineellinen EU-oikeuden aloja ja ulottuvuuksia – teoksessa (toim. Ojanen and Haapea) Edita 2007 p. 375–411

Sihto, J., Den europeiska arresteringsordern. Juridiska Föreningens Tidsskrift 4–5/2003, p. 502–531

Suominen, A., Om giltigheten av ett rambeslut i europeisk straffrätt samt Lissabonfördragets inverkan på området för den europeiska straffrätten. Nordisk Tidsskrift for Kriminalvidenskap 2/2008, p. 130–150

Suominen, A., The past, present and the future of Eurojust. Maastricht Journal of European and Comparative Law, Volume 15, 2/2008 p. 217–234

---

5   I thank Annika Suominen for providing me with this information.

FRANCE[6]

Badinter, R., L'Europe judiciaire, Recueil Dalloz 2007 p. 208 *et seq.*

Bernardi, A., Le rôle du troisième pilier dans l'européanisation du droit pénal. Un bilan synthétique à la veille de la réforme des traités Revue de science criminelle 2007 p. 713 *et seq.*

Labayle, H., Architecte ou spectatrice? La Cour de justice dans l'Espace de liberté, sécurité et justice, RTDE 2006 n°1 p. 3 *et seq.*

Labayle, H., Instruments et procédures de l'espace de liberté, de sécurité et de justice: quelques réflexions critiques, Europe 2003 n° p. 3 *et seq.*

Labayle, H., La coopération dans le domaine de la justice et des affaires intérieures, Répertoire Dalloz de droit communautaire, 1998

Labayle, H., La politique extérieure de l'Union européenne en matière de Justice et d'affaires intérieures: chimère ou réalité?, Mélanges en l'honneur de JC Gautron, Pédone, 2004, p. 681 *et seq.*

Manacorda, S., La consolidation de l'Espace de liberté, de sécurité et de justice: vers une "mise à l'écart" du rapprochement pénal? Revue de science criminelle 2007 p. 899 *et seq.*

Meeusen, J., L'Europe entre unité et diversité: du marché intérieur à l'ELSJ, in Trajectoires de l'Europe, unie dans la diversité depuis 50 ans, sous la direction de S. Poillot-Peruzzetto, Dalloz 2008

Montain-Domenah, J., Le droit de l'espace judiciaire pénal européen: un nouveau modèle juridique?, Cultures & Conflits, n°62 (2/2006) p. 149–168

GERMANY[7]

Commentaries on Cooperation in Criminal Law (including a part on European Union Law and its implementation, e.g. the European Arrest Warrant and its implementation in §§78 et seq. IRG): Heinrich Grützner/ Paul-Günter Pötz/ Claus Kreß (ed.), Internationaler Rechtshilfeverkehr in Strafsachen, third edition, Heidelberg 2007 et seq. Schomburg, Wolfgang/ Lagodny, Otto/ Gleß, Sabine/ Hackner, Thomas, Internationale Rechtshilfe in Strafsachen, fourth edition, München 2006

Commentary on the Law of the European Union (with regard to Art. 29 to Art. 42 TEU): Jürgen Schwarze (ed.), EU-Kommentar, second edition, August 2008

Proposals on the reform of European Criminal Law: Bernd Schünemann (ed.), Ein Gesamtkonzept für die europäische Strafrechtspflege, Köln 2007; Jürgen Wolter/ Wolf-Rüdiger Schenke/Hans Hilger/Josef Ruthig/Mark A. Zöller (ed.), Alternativ-Entwurf Europol und europäischer Datenschutz, Heidelberg 2008

---

[6]   I thank Maitena Poelmans for providing me with this information.
[7]   I thank Martin Böse for providing me with this information.

GREECE[8]

Αναγνωστόπουλου H., 'Απάτη και κοινοτική απάτη', Ποινικά Χρονικά 2001, σ. 759 επ. (*Anagnostopoulou I.,* 'Apati kai koinotiki apati, Penal Chronicles', 2001, p. 759 *et seq.*)

[Anagnostopoulou I., 'Fraud and Community fraud', Penal Chronicles, 2001, p. 759 *et seq.*]

Ζημιανίτη Δ., Δικαστική Συνεργασία σε ποινικές υποθέσεις στην Ευρωπαϊκή Ένωση – Θεσμικό πλαίσιο, κεκτημένο, προοπτικές', Αθήνα 2007 (*Zimianitis D.,* 'Dikastiki sinergasia se poinikes ipotheseis stin Evropaiki Enosi – Thesmiko plaisio, kektimeno, prooptikes', Athens 2007)

[Zimianitis D., 'Judicial cooperation in criminal matters in the European Union-Institutional framework, *acquis*, prospective', Athens 2007]

Καϊάφα-Γκμπάντι M., 'Κοινές δικονομικές αρχές ως βάση μιας διακρατικής ποινικής καταστολής', Ποινικά Χρονικά 2007, σ. 673 επ. (*Kaiafa-Gbandi M.,* 'Koines dikonomikes arches os vasi mias diakratikis poinikis katastolis', Penal Chronicles 2007, p. 673 *et seq.*)

[*Kaiafa-Gbandi M.,* 'Common procedural principles as the basis for an inter-state criminal repression', Penal Chronicles 2007, p. 673 *et seq.*]

Καϊάφα-Γκμπάντι M., Γιαννακούλα A., 'Ποινική νομοθεσία της Ευρωπαϊκής Ένωσης και ελληνική νομοθεσία ενσωμάτωσης', Θεσσαλονίκη 2008 (*Kaiafa-Gbandi M., Giannakoula A.,* 'Poiniki nomothesia tis Evropaikis Enosis kai elliniki nomothsia ensomatosis', Thessaloniki 2008)

[Kaiafa-Gbandi M.; Giannakoula A., 'Penal legislation in the European Union and Greek Legislation of Implementation', Thessaloniki 2008]

Καλφέλη Γ., 'Το Ευρωπαϊκό ένταλμα σύλληψης – Μονοδιάστατη ενοποίηση των ευρωπαϊκών κατασταλτικών μηχανισμών;' σε *I. Μανωλεδάκη* Τιμητικό τόμο II: Μελέτες Ποινικού δικαίου – Εγκληματολογίας – Ιστορίας του εγκλήματος, Θεσσαλονίκη 2007, σ. 799 επ. (*Kalfelis G.,* 'To Evropaiko entalma sillipsis – Monodiastati enopoiisi ton evropaikon katastaltikon michanismon?' in *I. Manoledakis* Timitikos Tomos II: Meletes Poinikou Dikaiou – Eglimatologias – Istoria tou eglimatos, Thessaloniki 2007, p. 799 *et seq.*)

[*Kalfelis G.,* 'The European Arrest Warrant: One-dimensional unification of European repressive mechanisms?' in *I. Manoledakis* Honorary Volume II: Studies of Criminal Law- Criminology – History of crime, Thessaloniki 2007, p. 799 *et seq.*]

Μανωλεδάκη I., ' Μπορεί να επιβιώσει το Ποινικό Δίκαιο – όπως διαμορφώθηκε μέχρι σήμερα στον ευρωπαϊκό χώρο – και στο νέο αιώνα;', Υπεράσπιση 2000, σ. 15 επ. (*Manoledakis I.,* 'Borei na epiviosei to Poiniko Dikaio – opos diamorfothike mechri simera ston evropaiko choro – kai to neo aiona?', Yperaspisi 2000, p. 15 *et seq.*)

[*Manoledakis I.,* 'Can Penal law survive –as it has been shaped to date in the European Area and in the new century?', Yperaspisi 2000, p. 15 *et seq.*)

---

[8] I thank Maria Kaiafa-Gbandi and Christina Peristeridou for providing me with this information.

Μυλωνόπουλου Χ., 'Η επίδραση του κοινοτικού δικαίου στο ελληνικό ποινικό δίκαιο', Υπεράσπιση 1991, σ. 1061 επ. (*Milonopoulou Ch.,*' I epidrasi tou koinotikou dikaiou sto elliniko poiniko dikaio', Yperaspisi 1991, p. 1061 *et seq.*)
[*Milonopoulou Ch.,* 'The influence of Community law on Greek Penal law', Yperaspisi 1991, p. 1061 *et seq.*]

Παύλου Σ., Το ποινικό δίκαιο και οι «αποφάσεις-πλαίσιο» της ΕΕ – μια ακόμη (επικίνδυνη) πύλη εισόδου του ευρωπαϊκού ποινικού δικαίου στο ελληνικό, Ποινικά Χρονικά 2004, σ. 961 επ. (*Pavlou S.,* 'To poiniko dikaio kai oi "apofaseis-plaisio" tis EE – mia akomi (epikindini) pili eisodou tou evropaikou poinikou dikaiou sto elliniko', Penal Chronicles 2004, p. 961 *et seq.*)
[Pavlou S., 'Penal law and the framework decisions of the EU-yet another (dangerous) gate for European Criminal into Greek Criminal law', Penal Chronicles 2004, p. 961 *et seq.*]

Περράκη Σ., Ο χώρος ελευθερίας, ασφάλειας και δικαιοσύνης της ΕΕ. Από το Τάμπερε στη Χάγη και επέκεινα', 2008 (*Perrakis S.,*'O choros eleftherias, asfaleias kai dikaiosinis tis EE. Apo to Tampere sti Chagi kai epekeina', 2008)
[Perrakis S., 'The Area of Freedom, Security and Justice of the EU. From Tampere to The Hague and onwards', 2008]

Συμεωνίδου-Καστανίδου Ε., Για ένα νέο ορισμό του οργανωμένου εγκλήματος στην Ευρωπαϊκή Ένωση', Ποινικά Χρονικά 2006, σ. 865 επ. (*Symeonidou-Kastanidou E.,* 'Gia ena neo orismo tou organomenou eglimatos stin Evropaiki Enosi', Penal Chronicles 2006, p. 865 *et seq.*)
[*Symeonidou-Kastanidou E.,* 'Towards a new definition of organized crime within the European Union', Penal Chronicles 2006, p. 865 *et seq.*]

Τσόλκα Ό., 'Η πορεία προς το Corpus Juris: παράγοντας διαμόρφωσης της δικονομικής προστασίας του κατηγορουμένου', σε Δ. *Σπινέλλη* Τιμητικό Τόμο: Οι ποινικές επιστήμες στον 21ο αιώνα, Αθήνα 2001, σ. 1167 επ. (*Tsolka O.,* 'I poreia pros to Corpus Juris: paragontas diamorfosis tis dikonomikis prostasias tou katigoroumenou', in D. *Spinellis* Timitikos Tomos: Oi poinikes epistimes ston 21o aiona, Athens 2001, p. 1167 *et seq.*)
[Tsolka, O. 'The way towards the Corpus Juris: factor for shaping the procedural protection of the accused', in D. Spinellis Honorary Volume: The Penal Studies in the 21st century, Athens 2001, p. 1167 *et seq.*]

HUNGARY[9]

Karsai, K., Az Európai Bíróság büntetőjogi ítélkezése (Criminal law adjudication by the ECJ). Szeged 2007
Karsai, K., Az európai büntetőjogi integráció alapkérdései (Basic issues of European criminal law integration). KJK, Budapest 2004

---

9   I thank Katalin Ligeti for providing me with this information.

Kondorosi, F. and Ligeti, K. (ed.), Európai Büntetőjog Kézikönyve (Handbook on European Criminal Law), MHK, Budapest 2008

Ligeti, K., Az európai büntetőjog legitimációja (Legitimacy of European criminal law), in: Gellér Balázs (ed.): Festschrift for Kálmán Györgyi. KJK, Budapest 2004, 373–389 p.

Ligeti, K., Büntetőjog és bűnügyi együttműködés az Európai Unióban (Criminal law and Cooperation in Criminal Matters in the European Union). KJK, Budapest 2004.

M. Nyitrai, P., Nemzetközi és Európai büntetőjog (International and European Criminal Law), Osiris, Budapest 2006

IRELAND[10]

Bacik, I., Criminal law, in U. Kilkelly (ed.), ECHR and Irish Law (Bristol: Jordan Publishing 2004)

Conway, G., Judicial Interpretation and the Third Pillar: Ireland's Acceptance of the European Arrest Warrant and the Gözütok and Brügge Case, 13 European Journal of Crime, Criminal Law & Criminal Justice 2005, p. 255–283

Fennelly, N., The European Arrest Warrant – Recent Developments, ERA Forum Vol. 4, 2007

Hamilton, J., Mutual Assistance in Criminal Matters in Ireland and the Proposed European Evidence Warrant, ERA Forum – Special Issue on European Evidence 2005

Hamilton, J., The Interplay between EU and Irish Domestic Counter-Terrorism Laws, ERA Forum Vol. 4, 2007

Ni Raifeartaigh, U., The European Convention on Human Rights and the Irish Criminal Justice System, 7 Bar Review 2001, p. 111–121

Ni Raifeartaigh, U., The European Convention on Human Rights and the Criminal Justice System, 7 Judicial Studies Institute Journal 2007, p. 18–49

Peers, S., The European Union and Criminal Law: An Overview, 12 Irish Criminal Law Journal 2002, p. 2–6

Regan, E., Irish Criminal Law and the Convention on the Future of Europe, 8 Bar Review 2003, p. 161–166

Ryan, A., The European Evidence Warrant: The Emergence of a European Law of Evidence?, 16 Irish Criminal Law Journal 2006, p. 8–14

Walsh, D., The Democratic Deficit in Criminal Law and Criminal Justice in Title VI of the Treaty on European Union, 12 Irish Criminal Law Journal 2002, p. 7–16

---

[10]   I thank Gerard Conway for providing me with this information.

ITALY[11]

Aa.Vv., La lotta contro la frode agli interessi finanziari della Comunità europea tra prevenzione e repressione, a cura di Grasso, ed. Giuffrè, Milano, 2000, p. 414

Aa.Vv., Profili del processo penale nella Costituzione europea, a cura di Coppetta, ed. Giappichelli, Torino, 2005, p. 259

Musacchio, Diritto penale dell'Unione europea, ed. CEDAM, Padova, 2005, p. 153

Picotti, L. (ed.), Il Corpus Juris 2000. Nuova formulazione e prospettive di attuazione, Cedam, Padova 2004, p. XI-292, ed ivi: Picotti, Lorenzo, Il Corpus Juris 2000. Profili di diritto penale sostanziale e prospettive d'attuazione alla luce del Progetto di Costituzione per l'Europa, p. 3–91

Picotti, L. (ed.), Prospettive e limiti di un diritto penale dell'Unione europea, Giuffré, Milano 1999, p. XX-214

Picotti, L., Diritto penale comunitario e Costituzione europea, in Canestrari S., Foffani L. (ed.), Il diritto penale nella prospettiva europea. Quali politiche criminali per quale Europa? Giuffré, Milano 2005, p. 325–376

Picotti, L., Il campo di applicazione del mandato d'arresto europeo: i reati "in lista" e "fuori lista"e la disciplina della legge italiana di attuazione, in Bargis M., Selvaggi E. (ed.), Mandato d'arresto europeo. Dall'estradizione alle procedura di consegna, Giappichelli, Torino, 2005, p. 127–152

Picotti, L., Il mandato d'arresto europeo fra principio di legalità e doppia incriminazione, in Bargis M. and E. Selvaggi (ed.), Mandato d'arresto europeo. Dall'estradizione alle procedura di consegna, Giappichelli, Torino, 2005, p. 33–69

Picotti, L., L'attuazione in Italia degli strumenti dell'Unione europea per la protezione penale degli interessi finanziari comunitari, in Rivista trimestrale di diritto penale dell'economia, 2006, n. 3, p. 615–671

Picotti, L., Le fattispecie della "parte speciale" del Corpus Juris. Profili sistematici, in Bargis M., Nosengo S. (ed.), Corpus Juris, pubblico ministero europeo e cooperazione internazionale (Atti del Convegno di Alessandria, 19–21 ottobre 2001), Milano 2003, p. 237–268

Picotti, L., Presupposti e prospettive di un "sistema" di diritto penale comunitario. Aspetti sostanziali, in Bargis M., Nosengo S. (ed.), Corpus Juris, pubblico ministero europeo e cooperazione internazionale (Atti del Convegno di Alessandria, 19–21 ottobre 2001), Milano 2003, p. 95–129

Picotti, L., Ragioni politiche e "principi generali" nel sindacato di adeguatezza della lex mitior a tutela di precetti comunitari, in Bin R., Brunelli G., Pugiotto A., Veronesi P. (ed.), Ai confini del "favor rei". Il falso in bilancio davanti alle Corti costituzionale e di giustizia (Atti del Seminario di Ferrara, 6 maggio 2005), Giappichelli, Torino, 2005, p. 311–318

Rafaraci, T. (ed.), L'area di libertà, sicurezza e giustizia: alla ricerca di un equilibrio fra priorità repressive ed esigenze di garanzia, Giuffrè, 2007

---

11   I thank Lorenzo Picotti, Tommaso Rafaraci and Antonio Del Sole for providing me with this information.

Rafaraci, T., Ne bis in idem e conflitti di giuridizione in materia penale nello spazio di libertà sicurezza e giustizia dell'Unione europea, in Rivista di Diritto Processuale (RDP), 2007, p. 621–642

Sicurella, R., Diritto penale e competenze dell'Unione europea, ed. Giuffrè, Milano, 2005

LITHUANIA[12]

Abramavičius, A., D. Mickevičius and G. Švedas, Europos Sąjungos teisės aktų įgyvendinimas Lietuvos baudžiamojoje teisėje. – Vilnius, TIC, 2005

Abramavičius, A., Lietuvos Respublikos Baudžiamojo Kodekso Specialiosios dalies europeizacijos problemos // Mokslo darbai, „Teisė", 2005, Nr. 54

Burda, R., E. Gruodytė and R. Kriščiūnas, Prekybos žmonėmis tyrimo bei teisminio nagrinėjimo problemos Lietuvoje. – Vilnius, 2006

Čaikovski, A., Tarptautinės ir Europos Sąjungos teisės reikšmė reglamentuojant ir aiškinant nacionalinėje teisėje baudžiamąją atsakomybę už piktnaudžiavimą tarnyba // Mokslo darbai, „Teisė", 2005, Nr. 54

Čepas, A. and G. Švedas, Tarptautinė teisinė pagalba baudžiamosiose bylose. Asmenų, įtariamų padarius nusikalstamą veiką, išdavimas baudžiamajam persekiojimui (ekstradicija, perdavimas Tarptautiniam baudžiamajam teismui arba pagal Europos arešto orderį). – Vilnius, TIC. 2008

Fedosiuk, O., Prekyba žmonėmis baudžiamojoje teisėje ir teismų praktikoje // Mokslo darbai, „Teisė", 2005, Nr. 54

Gutauskas, A., Terorizmo baudžiamasis teisinis vertinimas pagal naująjį Lietuvos Respublikos Baudžiamąjį Kodeksą // Mokslo darbai, „Teisė", 2005, Nr. 54

Mickevičius, D., Kai kurie prekybos žmonėmis ir vaiko pirkimo arba pardavimo sampratų Lietuvos Respublikos BK suderinamumo su Lietuvos Respublikos tarptautinėmis sutartimis ir ES teisės aktais aspektai // Mokslo darbai, „Teisė", 2005, Nr. 54

Soloveičikas, D., Juridinių asmenų baudžiamoji atsakomybė: lyginamieji aspektai. – Vilnius, Justitia, 2006

Švedas, G., Kai kurios asmens perdavimo pagal Europos arešto orderį baudžiamajam persekiojimui teorinės ir praktinės problemos // Mokslo darbai, "Teisė", Nr. 66(1), 2008

Švedas, G., Tarptautinė teisinė pagalba baudžiamosiose bylose. Nuteistųjų laisvės atėmimu perdavimas tolesniam bausmės atlikimui. – Vilnius, TIC, 2007

THE NETHERLANDS

Borgers, M.J., (ed.), Implementatie van kaderbesluiten, Wolf Nijmegen 2006

Europese integratie, preadviezen van Curtin, Smits, Klip en McCahery, Handelingen Nederlandse Juristen-Vereniging 136ᵉ jaargang 2006-I, Kluwer Deventer 2006

---

[12]   I thank G. Švedas for providing me with this information.

Glerum, V. and K. Rozemond, Overlevering van Nederlanders, copernicaanse revolutie of uitlevering in overgang? Delikt en Delinkwent 2008, p. 816–848

Glerum, V. and V. Koppe, De Overleveringswet, Sdu, Den Haag 2005

Klip, A.H., Wederzijdse erkenning, Delikt en Delinkwent 2008, p. 671–684

Kristen, F., Misbruik van voorwetenschap naar Europees recht, Wolf Legal Publishers, Nijmegen 2004

Nelemans, M., Het verbod van marktmanipulatie, Dissertation University of Tilburg 2007

Sanders, H., Het Europees aanhoudingsbevel, Nederlands en Belgisch overleveringsrecht in hoofdlijnen, Intersentia Antwerpen 2007

Strijards, G.A.M., Het Europees Openbaar Ministerie, Delikt en Delinkwent 2008, p. 603–626

Verheijen, E.A.M., Nederlandse strafrechtelijke waarden in de context van de Europese Unie, Wolf Nijmegen 2006, Dissertation Tilburg University

POLAND[13]

Banach-Gutierrez, J., Ochrona Praw Człowieka w Prawie Karnym Unii Europejskiej (Protection of Human Rights in the European Union Criminal Law), [in]: Prokuratura i Prawo nr 1/2007

Banach-Gutierrez, J., Pomoc prawna państw Unii Europejskiej w sprawach karnych (Mutual Legal Assistance of the European Union Member States in criminal matters), [in]: Magazyn Prawniczy „ Jurysta" nr 5/2005

Banach-Gutierrez, J., Rozwój III filaru Unii Europejskiej: od ekstradycji do europejskiego nakazu aresztowania (Development of the Third Pillar of the European Union: from extradition to the European Arrest Warrant, [in]: Nowa Kodyfikacja Prawa Karnego, tom XVII, red. Leszek Bogunia, Wrocław 2005

Banach-Gutierrez, J., Wpływ prawa Unii Europejskiej na krajowe prawo karne – w kierunku zbliżonych czy identycznych przepisów? (The Impact of European Union Law on National Criminal Law – towards harmonised or unified (identical) regulations?), [in]: Księga Pamiatkowa Profesor Genowefy Grabowskiej, Katowice 2008. Forthcoming

Banach-Gutierrez, J., Wspólne zespoły śledcze jako nowa forma współpracy państw w sprawach karnych (JIT' s as a new form of states's cooperation in criminal matters), [in]: Nowa Kodyfikacja Prawa Karnego, tom XVIII, red., Leszek Bogunia, Wrocław 2005

Banach-Gutierrez, J., Współpraca policyjna na podstawie acquis Schengen (Police co-operation based on the Schengen acquis), [in]: Przegląd Policyjny Nr 2 (82)/2006 – The Police Review 82 (2006)

Banach-Gutierrez, J., Zamrażanie i konfiskata środków pochodzących z przestępstwa-regulacje europejskie a prawo krajowe (Freezing and confiscating crime proceeds –

---

13   I thank Joanna Banach-Gutierrez for providing me with this information.

European regulations and national law, [in]: Nowa Kodyfikacja Prawa Karnego, tom XX, red. Leszek Bogunia, Wrocław 2006

Banach-Gutierrez, J., Zasada Ne bis In idem w Prawie Karnym Unii Europejskiej (Ne bis In idem principle in the European Union Criminal Law), [in]: Magazyn Prawniczy „Jurysta" nr 11–12/2004

Hudzik, M., Przejęcie skazania w ramach europejskiego nakazu aresztowania - zagadnienia podstawowe, [in]: Palestra 2006, nr 11–12

Lach, A., Europejska pomoc prawna w sprawach karnych, Toruń 2007

Lach, A., Problemy funkcjonowania europejskiego nakazu aresztowania, [in]: Europejski Przegląd Sądowy 2006, nr 11

Lahti, R. and J. Banach-Gutierrez, Prawo karne europejskie i jego stosunek do prawa krajowego (European criminal law and its relation to national law), [in]: „Jurysta" nr 4/2008

Ostropolski, T., Problemy konstytucyjne państw członkowskich Unii Europejskiej w związku z Europejskim Nakazem Aresztowania, [in]: Prokuratura i Prawo 2006, nr 5

PORTUGAL[14]

Almeida, L. Duarte d', Direito Penal e Direito Comunitário. O Ordenamento Comunitário e os Sistemas Juscriminais dos Estados-Membros, Almedina: 2001

Caeiro, P., Perspectives de formation d'un droit pénal de l'Union Européenne (Rapport du Portugal, in: VIèmes Journées Gréco-latines de Défense Sociale. Perspectives de formation d'un droit pénal de l'Union Européenne, Publications de la Section Hellénique da la Société de Internationale de Défense Sociale, [9] 1996

Dias, J. de Figueiredo and P. Caeiro, A Lei de Combate ao Terrorismo (Lei n° 52/2003, de 22 de Agosto). Sobre a transposição, para o direito português, da Decisão-quadro do Conselho, de 13 de Junho de 2002, relativa à luta contra o terrorismo", Revista de Legislação e Jurisprudência 135 (2005), p. 70 *et seq.*

Duarte, M.L., Tomemos a sério os limites de competência da União Europeia – a propósito do Acórdão do Tribunal de Justiça de 13 de Setembro de 2005, Revista da Faculdade de Direito da Universidade de Lisboa 46–1 (2005), p. 341 *et seq.*

Lemos, M.Â. Loureiro Manero de, O Défice Democrático na União Europeia e o Direito Penal, 2006 (publication forthcoming; available at <http://www.fd.uc.pt/ma/doc1.pdf>)

Piçarra, N., O espaço de liberdade, segurança e justiça após a assinatura do Tratado que estabelece uma Constituição para a Europa: unificação e aprofundamento, O Direito 137 (4–5) (2005), p. 967 *et seq.*

Rodrigues, A.M. and Mota, J.L. Lopes da, Para uma Política Criminal Europeia, Coimbra Editora: 2002

---

14   I thank Pedro Caeiro for providing me with this information.

Sousa, C.U. de, O 'novo' Terceiro Pilar da União Europeia: a cooperação policial e judiciária em matéria penal, in: Jorge de Figueiredo Dias / Ireneu Cabral Barreto / *Teresa Pizarro Beleza / Eduardo Paz Ferreira* (org.), Estudos em Homenagem a Cunha Rodrigues, Vol. I, Coimbra Editora: 2001, p. 867 *et seq.*

Tenreiro, M.P., Crime de aborto e direito comunitário, Revista Portuguesa de Ciência Criminal 2 (1992), p. 353 *et seq.*

ROMANIA[15]

Antoniu, G., Activitatea normativă penală a Uniunii Europene (I), Revista de Drept Penal nr. 1/2007

Antoniu, G., Activitatea normativă penală a Uniunii Europene (II), Revista de Drept Penal nr. 2/2007

Banu, M., Perspectiva includerii în primul pilon al Uniunii Europene a unui drept penal comunitar, Revista Română de Drept Comunitar nr. 3/2006

Beatrice, A.G. and S. Tudorel, Drept comunitar, Ed. C.H. Beck, Bucharest, 2007

Costaş, C.F., Directiva 91/308/CEE. Prevenirea folosirii sistemului financiar în scopul spălării banilor. Obligaţia impusă avocaţilor de a informa autorităţile competente despre orice fapt care ar putea indica o spălare de bani. Dreptul la un proces echitabil. Secretul profesional şi independenţa avocaţilor [Curtea de Justiţie Europeană (Marea Cameră), hotărârea din 26 iunie 2007, cauza C-305/05, Ordre des barreaux francophones et germanophone, Ordre français des avocats du barreau de Bruxelles, Ordre des barreaux flamands, Ordre néerlandais des avocats du barreau de Bruxelles c. Consiliu, cu participarea Consiliului Barourilor din Uniunea Europeană, Ordre des avocats du barreau de Liège, acţiune preliminară formulată de Cour d'arbitrage (în prezent Cour constitutionnelle), Belgia], Caiete de Drept Penal nr. 4/2007

Deleanu, I., Obligativitatea hotărârilor Curţii Europene a Drepturilor Omului şi ale Curţii de Justiţie a Comunităţilor Europene, Dreptul nr. 2/2007

Dobozi, V., Cooperarea judiciară în materie penală în Uniunea Europeană şi limitele sale, Dreptul nr. 10/2006

Drăghici C. et al., Aspecte teoretice şi practice referitoare la procedura executării mandatului european de arestare, Dreptul nr. 10/2007

Fabian, G., Cooperarea judiciară şi poliţienească în materie penală, (chapitre en Gyula *Fabian*, Drept instituţional comunitar, Ed. Sfera Juridică, Cluj-Napoca, 2006)

Muntean, C.S., Mandatul european de arestare. Un instrument juridic apt să înlocuiască extrădarea, Caiete de Drept Penal nr. 1/2007

Octavian, M., Tratat de drept comunitar, Ed. C.H. Beck, Bucharest, 2006

Radu, F.R., Cooperarea în domeniul justiţiei şi al afacerilor interne în cadrul Uniunii Europene, Dreptul nr. 6/2007

---

15   I thank Florin Streteanu for providing me with this information.

Radu, F.R., De la extrădare la mandatul european de arestare. O privire istorică și juridică, Dreptul nr. 2/2006

Radu, F.R., Principalele instrumente juridice ale Uniunii Europene în domeniul extrădării și predării infractorilor, Dreptul nr. 9/2007

Raluca, B., Drept comunitar. Principii, Ed. C.H. Beck, Bucharest, 2007

Streteanu, F., Câteva considerații privind mandatul european de arestare, Caiete de Drept Penal nr. 1/2008

Streteanu, F., Normele adoptate la nivelul Uniunii Europene – izvoare de drept penal (chapitre en, Florin Streteanu, Tratat de drept penal. Partea generală, Ed. C.H. Beck, Bucharest, 2008)

Truichici, A., Lupta împotriva corupției la nivelul Uniunii Europene, Revista de Drept Penal, nr. 4/2007

Udroiu, M. and O. Predescu, Jurisprudența instanțelor europene privind principiul ne bis in idem, Dreptul nr. 6/2008

SLOVENIA[16]

Bavcon, L. and D. Korošec, International Criminal Law, Pravna fakulteta (Ljubljana, 2003) (the textbook is in Slovene language. Original title is Mednarodno kazensko pravo)

Bavcon, L., Okvirni sklep sveta Evropske unije o boju proti terorizmu. Pravosod. bilt., 2006, letn. 27, 1, str. 105–116

Bavcon, L., The Position of Criminal Law in Legal Order of European Union, Zbornik na trudovi na Pravniot fakultet "Justinijan Prvi" vo Skopje (Skopje – Zagreb, 2007), p. 47–60, (the article is in Slovene language. Original title is Status kazenskega prava v pravnem redu Evropske unije)

Bošnjak, M., Novelties in EU Criminal Law according to Lisbon Treaty, Pravna praksa (Ljubljana), No. 27/2008, p. 19–21 (the article is in Slovene language. Original title is Novosti v kazenskem pravu EU po Lizbonski pogodbi)

Korošec, D., Slovene Substantive Criminal Law in the View of (rising) Common Criminal Law of EU, Zbornik znanstvenih razprav Pravne fakultete v Ljubljani (Ljubljana), No. 61 (2001), p. 59–79 (the article is in Slovene language. Original title is Slovensko materialno kazensko pravo v luči (nastajajočega) skupnega kazenskega prava EU)

Ribičič, C., Uveljavljanje evropskih standardov v praksi slovenskega Ustavnega sodišča, Revus, 2004, V. 2, 2, p. 69–83

Šelih, A., Razširitev Evropske unije in problemi kriminalitetne politike. In: Štiblar, Franjo (ed.), Kranjc, Janez (ed.). Pravni vidiki slovenske samobitnosti leto po vstopu v EU, (Littera Scripta Manet, Zbirka Littera, 5). Ljubljana: Pravna fakulteta, 2005, pp. 221–230

---

[16]   I thank Katja Šugman and Liljana Selinšek for providing me with this information.

Selinšek, L., European Dimension of Ne Bis In Idem Principle, Pravna praksa (Ljubljana), No. 22/2003, p. 9–12 (the article is in Slovene language. Original title is Evropske razsežnosti načela ne bis in idem)

Selinšek, L., Expansion of EU Competences within Substantive Criminal Law, Pravna praksa (Ljubljana), No. 39–40/2006, p. 30–32 (the article is in Slovene language. Original title is Širjenje pristojnosti EU v kazenskem materialnem pravu)

Selinšek, L., Framework Decisions from the Field of Police and Judicial Co-operation, Pravna praksa (Ljubljana), No. 39–40/2005, p. 25–27 (the article is in Slovene language. Original title is Okvirni sklepi s področja policijskega in pravosodnega sodelovanja)

Šugman, K. and D. Petrovec, The European criminal record in Slovenia. In: Stefanou, Constantin (ed.). Towards a European criminal record. Cambridge; New York: Cambridge University Press, cop. 2008, pp. 226–241

Šugman, K., EU Criminal Law, Pravna praksa (Ljubljana), No. 25/2005, p. II-VII (the article is in Slovene language. Original title is Kazensko pravo Evropske unije)

Šugman, K., European Arrest Warrant, Pravna praksa (Ljubljana), No. 14/2004, p. IV-VII (the article is in Slovene language. Original title is Evropski nalog za prijetje in predajo)

Šugman, K., Kazensko pravo Evropske unije. PP, Prav. praksa (Ljubl.), 2005, V. 24, št. 25, pril. str. II-VII

Šugman, K., The Implementation of the European Arrest Warrant in the Republic of Slovenia. Eucrim, 2007, issue 3/4, pp. 133–137

Šugman, K., The Reconciliation of Slovene Criminal Procedure-Law Legislation with rising Criminal Law of European Union (Corpus Juris), Zbornik znanstvenih razprav Pravne fakultete v Ljubljani (Ljubljana), No. 61 (2001), p. 265–287 (the article is in Slovene language. Original title is Usklajenost slovenske kazenskoprocesne zakonodaje z nastajajočim kazenskim pravom Evropske unije (Corpus Juris)

SPAIN[17]

Arangüena Fanego, C. (ed.), Coperación judicial penal en la Unión Europea: la orden europea de detención y entrega (Valladolid: Lex Nova 2005)

Arangüena Fanego, C. (ed.), Garantías procesales en los procesos penales en la Unión Europea/Procedural safeguards in criminal proceedings throughout the European Union (Valladolid: Lex Nova, 2007)

Armenta Deu, T., El Derecho Procesal Penal en la Unión Europea. Tendencias actuales y perspectivas de futuro (Madrid: Colex, 2006)

Bujosa Vadell, L., Ejecución en la Union Europea de las resoluciones de embargo preventivo de bienes y de aseguramiento de pruebas. Comentrio a la decision marco 2003/577/JAI, del consejo, de 22 de julio de 2003, Revista General de Derecho Europeo

---

17   I thank Fernando Martin Diz, Coral Arangüena Fanego, Montserrat de Hoyos and Mar Jimeno-Bulnes for providing me with this information.

Bujosa Vadell, L., Reconocimiento y ejecucion de resoluciones judiciales penales; estado de la cuestión en la Union Europea, Cuadernos de Derecho Judicial, ISSN 1134–9670, N°. 13, 2003 (erecho penal supranacional y cooperación jurídica internacional, Angel Galgo Peco (dir.), p. 449–504

De Hoyos Sancho, M. (ed.), El proceso penal en la Unión Euroepa: garantías esenciales/ Criminal proceedings in the European Union: essential safeguards (Valladolid: Lex Nova, 2008, forthcoming)

De Hoyos Sancho, M., Causas de denegación de la euroorden, en la obra" Cooperación judicial penal en la Unión Europea: la orden europea de detención y entrega", Coord.: C. Arangüena Fanego, Editorial Lex Nova, Valladolid, 2005. Páginas 211 a 315

De Hoyos Sancho, M., El principio de reconocimiento mutuo de resoluciones penales en la Unión Europea: ¿Asimilación automática o corresponsabilidad?, Revista de Derecho Comunitario Europeo, editada por el Centro de Estudios Políticos y Constitucionales. Núm. 22, Madrid, sept.-dic. 2005, pp. 807 a 841

De la Oliva Santos, A., T. Armenta Deu and M.P. Calderón Cuadrado (eds.), Garantías fundamentales del proceso penal en el espacio judicial europeo (Madrid: Colex, 2007

Martín Diz, F. (ed.), Constitución Europea: aspectos históricos, administrativos y procesales (Santiago de Compostela: Tórculo, 2006

Martín Diz, F., Conflictos entre jurisdicciones nacionales concurrentes y delincuencia organizada transfronteriza en la Unión Europea: problemas y soluciones procesales, Revista Justicia, núm. I-II, Barcelona, 2008

Ormazábal Sáncehz, G., Espacio penal europeo y mutuo reconocimIEnto (perspectivas alemán y española), Madrid: Akal 2006

SWEDEN[18]

Asp, P., EG:s sanktionsrätt; Uppsala 1998
Asp, P., EU & straffrätten; Uppsala 2002
Gröning, L., EU, staten och rätten att straffa; Lund 2008
Påle, K., Villkor för utlämning; Uppsala 2003
Persson, G., Gamla och nya lagstiftare – om EU och straffrätt; rep. 2005:2
Persson, G., Gränslös straffrätt; rep. 2007:4
Thunberg Schunke, M., Internationell rättslig hjälp i brottmål inom EU; Uppsala 2004
Träskman, P.O., Strafflagen för Europeiska Unionen – fakta och fiktion; Svensk Juristtidning 2002, p. 345–362
Träskman, P.O., Vad gör vi med den europeiska kriminalpolitiken?; Svensk Juristtidning 2005, p. 859–875
Wersäll, F., EU och straffrätten; Svensk Juristtidning 2004 p. 665–675

---

18 I thank Petter Asp for providing me with this information.

RELEVANT WEBSITES

http://curia.europa.eu/jurisp/cgi-bin/form.pl?lang=en
    Court of Justice case law

http://eur-lex.europa.eu/JOIndex.do?ihmlang=en
    Official Journal of the European Union

http://eur-lex.europa.eu/en/legis/avis_consolidation.htm
    All Union legislation in a consolidated form

http://www.eurojust.europa.eu/
    Eurojust

http://www.ejn-crimjust.europa.eu/
    European Judicial Network

http://www.europol.europa.eu/
    Europol-site

http://ec.europa.eu/index_en.htm
    Commission

http://europa.eu/documents/eu_council/index_en.htm
    Council

http://www.eurowarrant.net/
    European Arrest Warrant project

http://conventions.coe.int/
    Treaty site of the Council of Europe

http://www.echr.coe.int/echr/index.htm
    European Court of Human Rights

TABLES OF EQUIVALENCES*

TREATY ON EUROPEAN UNION

Old numbering of the Treaty on European Union	New numbering of the Treaty on European Union
TITLE I – COMMON PROVISIONS	TITLE I – COMMON PROVISIONS
Article 1	Article 1
	Article 2
Article 2	Article 3
Article 3 (repealed)[1]	
	Article 4
	Article 5[2]
Article 4 (repealed)[3]	
Article 5 (repealed)[4]	
Article 6	Article 6
Article 7	Article 7
	Article 8

---

*   Tables of equivalences as referred to in Article 5 of the Treaty of Lisbon. The original centre column, which set out the intermediate numbering as used in that Treaty, has been omitted. OJ 2008, C 115/361.

[1]   Replaced, in substance, by Article 7 of the Treaty on the Functioning of the European Union ("TFEU") and by Articles 13(1) and 21, paragraph 3, second subparagraph of the Treaty on European Union ("TEU").

[2]   Replaces Article 5 of the Treaty establishing the European Community ("TEC").

[3]   Replaced, in substance, by Article 15.

[4]   Replaced, in substance, by Article 13, paragraph 2.

Old numbering of the Treaty on European Union	New numbering of the Treaty on European Union
TITLE II – PROVISIONS AMENDING THE TREATY ESTABLISHING THE EUROPEAN ECONOMIC COMMUNITY WITH A VIEW TO ESTABLISHING THE EUROPEAN COMMUNITY	TITLE II – PROVISIONS ON DEMOCRATIC PRINCIPLES
Article 8 (repealed)[5]	Article 9
	Article 10[6]
	Article 11
	Article 12
TITLE III – PROVISIONS AMENDING THE TREATY ESTABLISHING THE EUROPEAN COAL AND STEEL COMMUNITY	TITLE III – PROVISIONS ON THE INSTITUTIONS
Article 9 (repealed)[7]	Article 13
	Article 14[8]
	Article 15[9]
	Article 16[10]
	Article 17[11]
	Article 18
	Article 19[12]

[5] Article 8 TEU, which was in force until the entry into force of the Treaty of Lisbon (hereinafter "current"), amended the TEC. Those amendments are incorporated into the latter Treaty and Article 8 is repealed. Its number is used to insert a new provision.

[6] Paragraph 4 replaces, in substance, the first subparagraph of Article 191 TEC.

[7] The current Article 9 TEU amended the Treaty establishing the European Coal and Steel Community. This latter expired on 23 July 2002. Article 9 is repealed and the number thereof is used to insert another provision.

[8] – Paragraphs 1 and 2 replace, in substance, Article 189 TEC;
   – paragraphs 1 to 3 replace, in substance, paragraphs 1 to 3 of Article 190 TEC;
   – paragraph 1 replaces, in substance, the first subparagraph of Article 192 TEC;
   – paragraph 4 replaces, in substance, the first subparagraph of Article 197 TEC.

[9] Replaces, in substance, Article 4.

[10] – Paragraph 1 replaces, in substance, the first and second indents of Article 202 TEC;
   – paragraphs 2 and 9 replace, in substance, Article 203 TEC;
   – paragraphs 4 and 5 replace, in substance, paragraphs 2 and 4 of Article 205 TEC.

[11] – Paragraph 1 replaces, in substance, Article 211 TEC;
   – paragraphs 3 and 7 replace, in substance, Article 214 TEC.
   – paragraph 6 replaces, in substance, paragraphs 1, 3 and 4 of Article 217 TEC.

[12] – Replaces, in substance, Article 220 TEC.
   – the second subparagraph of paragraph 2 replaces, in substance, the first subparagraph of Article 221 TEC.

Old numbering of the Treaty on European Union	New numbering of the Treaty on European Union
TITLE IV – PROVISIONS AMENDING THE TREATY ESTABLISHING THE EUROPEAN ATOMIC ENERGY COMMUNITY	TITLE IV – PROVISIONS ON ENHANCED COOPERATION
Article 10 (repealed)[13] *Articles 27a to 27e (replaced)* *Articles 40 to 40b (replaced)* *Articles 43 to 45 (replaced)*	Article 20[14]
TITLE V – PROVISIONS ON A COMMON FOREIGN AND SECURITY POLICY	TITLE V – GENERAL PROVISIONS ON THE UNION'S EXTERNAL ACTION AND SPECIFIC PROVISIONS ON THE COMMON FOREIGN AND SECURITY POLICY
	Chapter 1 – General provisions on the Union's external action
	Article 21
	Article 22
	Chapter 2 – Specific provisions on the common foreign and security policy
	Section 1 – Common provisions
	Article 23
Article 11	Article 24
Article 12	Article 25
Article 13	Article 26
	Article 27
Article 14	Article 28
Article 15	Article 29
Article 22 (moved)	Article 30
Article 23 (moved)	Article 31
Article 16	Article 32
Article 17 (moved)	Article 42
Article 18	Article 33

[13] The current Article 10 TEU amended the Treaty establishing the European Atomic Energy Community. Those amendments are incorporated into the Treaty of Lisbon. Article 10 is repealed and the number thereof is used to insert another provision.

[14] Also replaces Articles 11 and 11a TEC.

Old numbering of the Treaty on European Union	New numbering of the Treaty on European Union
Article 19	Article 34
Article 20	Article 35
Article 21	Article 36
Article 22 (moved)	*Article 30*
Article 23 (moved)	*Article 31*
Article 24	Article 37
Article 25	Article 38
	Article 39
Article 47 (moved)	Article 40
Article 26 (repealed)	
Article 27 (repealed)	
Article 27a (replaced)[15]	*Article 20*
Article 27b (replaced)[15]	*Article 20*
Article 27c (replaced)[15]	*Article 20*
Article 27d (replaced)[15]	*Article 20*
Article 27e (replaced)[15]	*Article 20*
Article 28	Article 41
	Section 2 – Provisions on the common security and defence policy
Article 17 (moved)	Article 42
	Article 43
	Article 44
	Article 45
	Article 46

---

15   The current Articles 27a to 27e, on enhanced cooperation, are also replaced by Articles 326 to 334 TFEU.

Old numbering of the Treaty on European Union	New numbering of the Treaty on European Union
TITLE VI – PROVISIONS ON POLICE AND JUDICIAL COOPERATION IN CRIMINAL MATTERS (repealed)[16]	
Article 29 (replaced)[17]	
Article 30 (replaced)[18]	
Article 31 (replaced)[19]	
Article 32 (replaced)[20]	
Article 33 (replaced)[21]	
Article 34 (repealed)	
Article 35 (repealed)	
Article 36 (replaced)[22]	
Article 37 (repealed)	
Article 38 (repealed)	
Article 39 (repealed)	
Article 40 (replaced)[23]	*Article 20*
Article 40 A (replaced)[23]	*Article 20*
Article 40 B (replaced)[23]	*Article 20*
Article 41 (repealed)	
Article 42 (repealed)	

[16] The current provisions of Title VI of the TEU, on police and judicial cooperation in criminal matters, are replaced by the provisions of Chapters 1, 5 and 5 of Title IV of Part Three of the TFEU.
[17] Replaced by Article 67 TFEU.
[18] Replaced by Articles 87 and 88 TFEU.
[19] Replaced by Articles 82, 83 and 85 TFEU.
[20] Replaced by Article 89 TFEU.
[21] Replaced by Article 72 TFEU.
[22] Replaced by Article 71 TFEU.
[23] The current Articles 40 to 40 B TEU, on enhanced cooperation, are also replaced by Articles 326 to 334 TFEU.

Old numbering of the Treaty on European Union	New numbering of the Treaty on European Union
TITLE VII – PROVISIONS ON ENHANCED COOPERATION (replaced)[24]	*TITLE IV – PROVISIONS ON ENHANCED COOPERATION*
Article 43 (replaced)[24]	*Article 20*
Article 43 A (replaced)[24]	*Article 20*
Article 43 B (replaced)[24]	*Article 20*
Article 44 (replaced)[24]	*Article 20*
Article 44 A (replaced)[24]	*Article 20*
Article 45 (replaced)[24]	Article 20
TITRE VIII – FINAL PROVISIONS	TITLE VI – FINAL PROVISIONS
Article 46 (repealed)	
	Article 47
Article 47 (replaced)	*Article 40*
Article 48	Article 48
Article 49	Article 49
	Article 50
	Article 51
	Article 52
Article 50 (repealed)	
Article 51	Article 53
Article 52	Article 54
Article 53	Article 55

[24] The current Articles 43 to 45 and Title VII of the TEU, on enhanced cooperation, are also replaced by Articles 326 to 334 TFEU.

TREATY ON THE FUNCTIONING
OF THE EUROPEAN UNION

Old numbering of the Treaty establishing the European Community	New numbering of the Treaty on the Functioning of the European Union
PART ONE – PRINCIPLES	PART ONE – PRINCIPLES
Article 1 (repealed)	
	Article 1
Article 2 (repealed)[25]	
	Title I – Categories and areas of union competence
	Article 2
	Article 3
	Article 4
	Article 5
	Article 6
	Title II – Provisions having general application
	Article 7
Article 3, paragraph 1 (repealed)[26]	
Article 3, paragraph 2	Article 8
Article 4 (moved)	*Article 119*
Article 5 (replaced)[27]	
	Article 9
	Article 10
Article 6	Article 11
Article 153, paragraph 2 (moved)	Article 12
	Article 13[28]
Article 7 (repealed)[29]	

---

[25] Replaced, in substance, by Article 3 TEU.
[26] Replaced, in substance, by Articles 3 to 6 TFEU.
[27] Replaced, in substance, by Article 5 TEU.
[28] Insertion of the operative part of the protocol on protection and welfare of animals.
[29] Replaced, in substance, by Article 13 TEU.

Old numbering of the Treaty establishing the European Community	New numbering of the Treaty on the Functioning of the European Union
Article 8 (repealed)[30]	
Article 9 (repealed)	
Article 10 (repealed)[31]	
Article 11 (replaced)[32]	*Articles 326 to 334*
Article 11a (replaced)[32]	*Articles 326 to 334*
Article 12 (repealed)	*Article 18*
Article 13 (moved)	*Article 19*
Article 14 (moved)	*Article 26*
Article 15 (moved)	*Article 27*
Article 16	Article 14
Article 255 (moved)	Article 15
Article 286 (moved)	Article 16
	Article 17
PART TWO – CITIZENSHIP OF THE UNION	PART TWO – NON-DISCRIMINATION AND CITIZENSHIP OF THE UNION
Article 12 (moved)	Article 18
Article 13 (moved)	Article 19
Article 17	Article 20
Article 18	Article 21
Article 19	Article 22
Article 20	Article 23
Article 21	Article 24
Article 22	Article 25
PART THREE – COMMUNITY POLICIES	PART THREE – POLICIES AND INTERNAL ACTIONS OF THE UNION
	Title I – The internal market
Article 14 (moved)	Article 26

[30] Replaced, in substance, by Article 13 TEU and Article 282, paragraph 1, TFEU.
[31] Replaced, in substance, by Article 4, paragraph 3, TEU.
[32] Also replaced by Article 20 TEU.

Old numbering of the Treaty establishing the European Community	New numbering of the Treaty on the Functioning of the European Union
Article 15 (moved)	Article 27
Title I – Free movement of goods	Title II – Free movement of goods
Article 23	Article 28
Article 24	Article 29
Chapter 1 – The customs union	Chapter 1 – The customs union
Article 25	Article 30
Article 26	Article 31
Article 27	Article 32
Part Three, Title X, Customs cooperation (moved)	Chapter 2 – Customs cooperation
Article 135 (moved)	Article 33
Chapter 2 – Prohibition of quantitative restrictions between Member States	Chapter 3 – Prohibition of quantitative restrictions between Member States
Article 28	Article 34
Article 29	Article 35
Article 30	Article 36
Article 31	Article 37
Title II – Agriculture	Title III – Agriculture and fisheries
Article 32	Article 38
Article 33	Article 39
Article 34	Article 40
Article 35	Article 41
Article 36	Article 42
Article 37	Article 43
Article 38	Article 44
Title III – Free movement of persons, services and capital	Title IV – Free movement of persons, services and capital
Chapter 1 – Workers	Chapter 1 – Workers
Article 39	Article 45
Article 40	Article 46
Article 41	Article 47

Old numbering of the Treaty establishing the European Community	New numbering of the Treaty on the Functioning of the European Union
Article 42	Article 48
Chapter 2 – Right of establishment	Chapter 2 – Right of establishment
Article 43	Article 49
Article 44	Article 50
Article 45	Article 51
Article 46	Article 52
Article 47	Article 53
Article 48	Article 54
Article 294 (moved)	Article 55
Chapter 3 – Services	Chapter 3 – Services
Article 49	Article 56
Article 50	Article 57
Article 51	Article 58
Article 52	Article 59
Article 53	Article 60
Article 54	Article 61
Article 55	Article 62
Chapter 4 – Capital and payments	Chapter 4 – Capital and payments
Article 56	Article 63
Article 57	Article 64
Article 58	Article 65
Article 59	Article 66
Article 60 (moved)	Article 75
Title IV – Visas, asylum, immigration and other policies related to free movement of persons	Title V – Area of freedom, security and justice
	Chapter 1 – General provisions
Article 61	Article 67[33]
	Article 68

[33] Also replaces the current Article 29 TEU.

Old numbering of the Treaty establishing the European Community	New numbering of the Treaty on the Functioning of the European Union
	Article 69
	Article 70
	Article 71[34]
Article 64, paragraph 1 (replaced)	Article 72[35]
	Article 73
Article 66 (replaced)	Article 74
Article 60 (moved)	Article 75
	Article 76
	Chapter 2 – Policies on border checks, asylum and immigration
Article 62	Article 77
Article 63, points 1 et 2, and Article 64, paragraph 2[36]	Article 78
Article 63, points 3 and 4	Article 79
	Article 80
Article 64, paragraph 1 (replaced)	*Article 72*
	Chapter 3 – Judicial cooperation in civil matters
Article 65	Article 81
Article 66 (replaced)	*Article 74*
Article 67 (repealed)	
Article 68 (repealed)	
Article 69 (repealed)	
	Chapter 4 – Judicial cooperation in criminal matters
	Article 82[37]
	Article 83[37]

---

[34] Also replaces the current Article 36 TEU.
[35] Also replaces the current Article 33 TEU.
[36] Points 1 and 2 of Article 63 EC are replaced by paragraphs 1 and 2 of Article 78 TFEU, and paragraph 2 of Article 64 is replaced by paragraph 3 of Article 78 TFEU.
[37] Replaces the current Article 31 TEU.

Old numbering of the Treaty establishing the European Community	New numbering of the Treaty on the Functioning of the European Union
	Article 84
	Article 85[37]
	Article 86
	Chapter 5 – Police cooperation
	Article 87[38]
	Article 88[38]
	Article 89[39]
Title V – Transport	Title VI – Transport
Article 70	Article 90
Article 71	Article 91
Article 72	Article 92
Article 73	Article 93
Article 74	Article 94
Article 75	Article 95
Article 76	Article 96
Article 77	Article 97
Article 78	Article 98
Article 79	Article 99
Article 80	Article 100
Title VI – Common rules on competition, taxation and approximation of laws	Title VII – Common rules on competition, taxation and approximation of laws
Chapter 1 – Rules on competition	Chapter 1 – Rules on competition
Section 1 – Rules applying to undertakings	Section 1 – Rules applying to undertakings
Article 81	Article 101
Article 82	Article 102
Article 83	Article 103
Article 84	Article 104
Article 85	Article 105

38   Replaces the current Article 30 TEU.
39   Replaces the current Article 32 TEU.

Old numbering of the Treaty establishing the European Community	New numbering of the Treaty on the Functioning of the European Union
Article 86	Article 106
Section 2 – Aids granted by States	Section 2 – Aids granted by States
Article 87	Article 107
Article 88	Article 108
Article 89	Article 109
Chapter 2 – Tax provisions	Chapter 2 – Tax provisions
Article 90	Article 110
Article 91	Article 111
Article 92	Article 112
Article 93	Article 113
Chapter 3 – Approximation of laws	Chapter 3 – Approximation of laws
Article 95 (moved)	Article 114
Article 94 (moved)	Article 115
Article 96	Article 116
Article 97	Article 117
	Article 118
Title VII – Economic and monetary policy	Title VIII – Economic and monetary policy
Article 4 (moved)	Article 119
Chapter 1 – Economic policy	Chapter 1 – Economic policy
Article 98	Article 120
Article 99	Article 121
Article 100	Article 122
Article 101	Article 123
Article 102	Article 124
Article 103	Article 125
Article 104	Article 126
Chapter 2 – Monetary policy	Chapter 2 – Monetary policy
Article 105	Article 127
Article 106	Article 128

Old numbering of the Treaty establishing the European Community	New numbering of the Treaty on the Functioning of the European Union
Article 107	Article 129
Article 108	Article 130
Article 109	Article 131
Article 110	Article 132
Article 111, paragraphs 1 to 3 and 5 (moved)	Article 219
Article 111, paragraph 4 (moved)	Article 138
	Article 133
Chapter 3 – Institutional provisions	Chapter 3 – Institutional provisions
Article 112 (moved)	*Article 283*
Article 113 (moved)	*Article 284*
Article 114	Article 134
Article 115	Article 135
	Chapter 4 – Provisions specific to Member States whose currency is the euro
	Article 136
	Article 137
Article 111, paragraph 4 (moved)	Article 138
Chapter 4 – Transitional provisions	Chapter 5 – Transitional provisions
Article 116 (repealed)	
	Article 139
Article 117, paragraphs 1, 2, sixth indent, and 3 to 9 (repealed)	
Article 117, paragraph 2, first five indents (moved)	*Article 141, paragraph 2*
Article 121, paragraph 1 (moved) *Article 122, paragraph 2, second sentence (moved)* *Article 123, paragraph 5 (moved)*	Article 140[40]
Article 118 (repealed)	

[40] – Article 140, paragraph 1 takes over the wording of paragraph 1 of Article 121.
– Article 140, paragraph 2 takes over the second sentence of paragraph 2 of Article 122.
– Article 140, paragraph 3 takes over paragraph 5 of Article 123.

Old numbering of the Treaty establishing the European Community	New numbering of the Treaty on the Functioning of the European Union
Article 123, paragraph 3 (moved) *Article 117, paragraph 2, first five indents (moved)*	Article 141[41]
Article 124, paragraph 1 (moved)	Article 142
Article 119	Article 143
Article 120	Article 144
Article 121, paragraph 1 (moved)	Article 140, paragraph 1
Article 121, paragraphs 2 to 4 (repealed)	
Article 122, paragraphs 1, 2, first sentence, 3, 4, 5 and 6 (repealed)	
Article 122, paragraph 2, second sentence (moved)	*Article 140, paragraph 2, first subparagraph*
Article 123, paragraphs 1, 2 and 4 (repealed)	
Article 123, paragraph 3 (moved)	*Article 141, paragraph 1*
Article 123, paragraph 5 (moved)	*Article 140, paragraph 3*
Article 124, paragraph 1 (moved)	*Article 142*
Article 124, paragraph 2 (repealed)	
Title VIII – Employment	Title IX – Employment
Article 125	Article 145
Article 126	Article 146
Article 127	Article 147
Article 128	Article 148
Article 129	Article 149
Article 130	Article 150
Title IX – Common commercial policy (moved)	*Part Five, Title II, common commercial policy*
Article 131 (moved)	*Article 206*
Article 132 (repealed)	
Article 133 (moved)	*Article 207*
Article 134 (repealed)	

[41]   – Article 141, paragraph 1 takes over paragraph 3 of Article 123.
     – Article 141, paragraph 2 takes over the first five indents of paragraph 2 of Article 117.

Old numbering of the Treaty establishing the European Community	New numbering of the Treaty on the Functioning of the European Union
Title X – Customs cooperation (moved)	*Part Three, Title II, Chapter 2, Customs cooperation*
Article 135 (moved)	*Article 33*
Title XI – Social policy, education, vocational training and youth	Title X – Social policy
Chapter 1 – Social provisions (repealed)	
Article 136	Article 151
	Article 152
Article 137	Article 153
Article 138	Article 154
Article 139	Article 155
Article 140	Article 156
Article 141	Article 157
Article 142	Article 158
Article 143	Article 159
Article 144	Article 160
Article 145	Article 161
Chapter 2 – The European Social Fund	Title XI – The European Social Fund
Article 146	Article 162
Article 147	Article 163
Article 148	Article 164
Chapter 3 – Education, vocational training and youth	Title XII – Education, vocational training, youth and sport
Article 149	Article 165
Article 150	Article 166
Title XII – Culture	Title XIII – Culture
Article 151	Article 167
Title XIII – Public health	Title XIV – Public health
Article 152	Article 168
Title XIV – Consumer protection	Title XV – Consumer protection
Article 153, paragraphs 1, 3, 4 and 5	Article 169

Old numbering of the Treaty establishing the European Community	New numbering of the Treaty on the Functioning of the European Union
Article 153, paragraph 2 (moved)	*Article 12*
Title XV – Trans–European networks	Title XVI – Trans–European networks
Article 154	Article 170
Article 155	Article 171
Article 156	Article 172
Title XVI – Industry	Title XVII – Industry
Article 157	Article 173
Title XVII – Economic and social cohesion	Title XVIII – Economic, social and territorial cohesion
Article 158	Article 174
Article 159	Article 175
Article 160	Article 176
Article 161	Article 177
Article 162	Article 178
Title XVIII – Research and technological development	Title XIX – Research and technological development and space
Article 163	Article 179
Article 164	Article 180
Article 165	Article 181
Article 166	Article 182
Article 167	Article 183
Article 168	Article 184
Article 169	Article 185
Article 170	Article 186
Article 171	Article 187
Article 172	Article 188
	Article 189
Article 173	Article 190
Title XIX – Environment	Title XX – Environment
Article 174	Article 191

Old numbering of the Treaty establishing the European Community	New numbering of the Treaty on the Functioning of the European Union
Article 175	Article 192
Article 176	Article 193
	Titre XXI – Energy
	Article 194
	Title XXII – Tourism
	Article 195
	Title XXIII – Civil protection
	Article 196
	Title XXIV – Administrative cooperation
	Article 197
Title XX – Development cooperation (moved)	*Part Five, Title III, Chapter 1, Development cooperation*
Article 177 (moved)	*Article 208*
Article 178 (repealed)[42]	
Article 179 (moved)	*Article 209*
Article 180 (moved)	*Article 210*
Article 181 (moved)	*Article 211*
Title XXI – Economic, financial and technical cooperation with third countries (moved)	*Part Five, Title III, Chapter 2, Economic, financial and technical cooperation with third countries*
Article 181a (moved)	*Article 212*
PART FOUR – ASSOCIATION OF THE OVERSEAS COUNTRIES AND TERRITORIES	PART FOUR – ASSOCIATION OF THE OVERSEAS COUNTRIES AND TERRITORIES
Article 182	Article 198
Article 183	Article 199
Article 184	Article 200
Article 185	Article 201
Article 186	Article 202
Article 187	Article 203

---

42   Replaced, in substance, by the second sentence of the second subparagraph of paragraph 1 of Article 208 TFUE.

Old numbering of the Treaty establishing the European Community	New numbering of the Treaty on the Functioning of the European Union
Article 188	Article 204
	PART FIVE – EXTERNAL ACTION BY THE UNION
	Title I – General provisions on the union's external action
	Article 205
Part Three, Title IX, Common commercial policy (moved)	Title II – Common commercial policy
Article 131 (moved)	Article 206
Article 133 (moved)	Article 207
	Title III – Cooperation with third countries and humanitarian aid
Part Three, Title XX, Development cooperation (moved)	Chapter 1 – Development cooperation
Article 177 (moved)	Article 208[43]
Article 179 (moved)	Article 209
Article 180 (moved)	Article 210
Article 181 (moved)	Article 211
Part Three, Title XXI, Economic, financial and technical cooperation with third countries (moved)	Chapter 2 – Economic, financial and technical cooperation with third countries
Article 181a (moved)	Article 212
	Article 213
	Chapter 3 – Humanitarian aid
	Article 214
	Title IV – Restrictive measures
Article 301 (replaced)	Article 215
	Title V – International agreements
	Article 216
Article 310 (moved)	Article 217
Article 300 (replaced)	Article 218

[43] The second sentence of the second subparagraph of paragraph 1 replaces, in substance, Article 178 TEC.

Old numbering of the Treaty establishing the European Community	New numbering of the Treaty on the Functioning of the European Union
Article 111, paragraphs 1 to 3 and 5 (moved)	Article 219
	Title VI – The Union's relations with international organisations and third countries and the Union delegations
Articles 302 to 304 (replaced)	Article 220
	Article 221
	Title VII – Solidarity clause
	Article 222
PART FIVE – INSTITUTIONS OF THE COMMUNITY	PART SIX – INSTITUTIONAL AND FINANCIAL PROVISIONS
Title I – Institutional provisions	Title I – Institutional provisions
Chapter 1 – The institutions	Chapter 1 – The institutions
Section 1 – The European Parliament	Section 1 – The European Parliament
Article 189 (repealed)[44]	
Article 190, paragraphs 1 to 3 (repealed)[45]	
Article 190, paragraphs 4 and 5	Article 223
Article 191, first paragraph (repealed)[46]	
Article 191, second paragraph	Article 224
Article 192, first paragraph (repealed)[47]	
Article 192, second paragraph	Article 225
Article 193	Article 226
Article 194	Article 227
Article 195	Article 228
Article 196	Article 229
Article 197, first paragraph (repealed)[48]	
Article 197, second, third and fourth paragraphs	Article 230
Article 198	Article 231

[44]   Replaced, in substance, by Article 14, paragraphs 1 and 2, TEU.
[45]   Replaced, in substance, by Article 14, paragraphs 1 to 3, TEU.
[46]   Replaced, in substance, by Article 11, paragraph 4, TEU.
[47]   Replaced, in substance, by Article 14, paragraph 1, TEU.
[48]   Replaced, in substance, by Article 14, paragraph 4, TEU.

Old numbering of the Treaty establishing the European Community	New numbering of the Treaty on the Functioning of the European Union
Article 199	Article 232
Article 200	Article 233
Article 201	Article 234
	Section 2 – The European Council
	Article 235
	Article 236
Section 2 – The Council	Section 3 – The Council
Article 202 (repealed)[49]	
Article 203 (repealed)[50]	
Article 204	Article 237
Article 205, paragraphs 2 and 4 (repealed)[51]	
Article 205, paragraphs 1 and 3	Article 238
Article 206	Article 239
Article 207	Article 240
Article 208	Article 241
Article 209	Article 242
Article 210	Article 243
Section 3 – The Commission	Section 4 – The Commission
Article 211 (repealed)[53]	
	Article 244
Article 212 (moved)	*Article 249, paragraph 2*
Article 213	Article 245
Article 214 (repealed)[55]	
Article 215	Article 246

[49] Replaced, in substance, by Article 16, paragraph 1, TEU and by Articles 290 and 291 TFEU.
[50] Replaced, in substance, by Article 16, paragraphs 2 and 9 TEU.
[51] Replaced, in substance, by Article 16, paragraphs 4 and 5 TEU.
[52] Replaced, in substance, by Article 295 TFEU.
[53] Replaced, in substance, by Article 17, paragraph 1 TEU.
[54] Replaced, in substance, by Article 19, paragraph 2, first subparagraph, of the TEU.
[55] Replaced, in substance, by Article 17, paragraphs 3 and 7 TEU.

Old numbering of the Treaty establishing the European Community	New numbering of the Treaty on the Functioning of the European Union
Article 216	Article 247
Article 217, paragraphs 1, 3 and 4 (repealed)[56]	
Article 217, paragraph 2	Article 248
Article 218, paragraph 1 (repealed)[57]	
Article 218, paragraph 2	Article 249
Article 219	Article 250
Section 4 – The Court of Justice	Section 5 – The Court of Justice of the European Union
Article 220 (repealed)[58]	
Article 221, first paragraph (repealed)[59]	
Article 221, second and third paragraphs	Article 251
Article 222	Article 252
Article 223	Article 253
Article 224[60]	Article 254
	Article 255
Article 225	Article 256
Article 225a	Article 257
Article 226	Article 258
Article 227	Article 259
Article 228	Article 260
Article 229	Article 261
Article 229a	Article 262
Article 230	Article 263
Article 231	Article 264
Article 232	Article 265

[56] Replaced, in substance, by Article 17, paragraph 6, TEU.
[57] Replaced, in substance, by Article 295 TFEU.
[58] Replaced, in substance, by Article 19 TEU.
[59] Replaced, in substance, by Article 19, paragraph 2, first subparagraph, of the TEU.
[60] The first sentence of the first subparagraph is replaced, in substance, by Article 19, paragraph 2, second subparagraph of the TEU.

Old numbering of the Treaty establishing the European Community	New numbering of the Treaty on the Functioning of the European Union
Article 233	Article 266
Article 234	Article 267
Article 235	Article 268
	Article 269
Article 236	Article 270
Article 237	Article 271
Article 238	Article 272
Article 239	Article 273
Article 240	Article 274
	Article 275
	Article 276
Article 241	Article 277
Article 242	Article 278
Article 243	Article 279
Article 244	Article 280
Article 245	Article 281
	Section 6 – The European Central Bank
	Article 282
Article 112 (moved)	Article 283
Article 113 (moved)	Article 284
Section 5 – The Court of Auditors	Section 7 – The Court of Auditors
Article 246	Article 285
Article 247	Article 286
Article 248	Article 287
Chapter 2 – Provisions common to several institutions	Chapter 2 – Legal acts of the Union, adoption procedures and other provisions
	Section 1 – The legal acts of the Union
Article 249	Article 288

Old numbering of the Treaty establishing the European Community	New numbering of the Treaty on the Functioning of the European Union
	Article 289
	Article 290[61]
	Article 291[61]
	Article 292
	Section 2 – Procedures for the adoption of acts and other provisions
Article 250	Article 293
Article 251	Article 294
Article 252 (repealed)	
	Article 295
Article 253	Article 296
Article 254	Article 297
	Article 298
Article 255 (moved)	Article 15
Article 256	Article 299
	Chapter 3 – The Union's advisory bodies
	Article 300
Chapter 3 – The Economic and Social Committee	Section 1 – The Economic and Social Committee
Article 257 (repealed)[62]	
Article 258, first, second and fourth paragraphs	Article 301
Article 258, third paragraph (repealed)[63]	
Article 259	Article 302
Article 260	Article 303
Article 261 (repealed)	
Article 262	Article 304

[61] Replaces, in substance, the third indent of Article 202 TEC.
[62] Replaced, in substance, by Article 300, paragraph 2 of the TFEU.
[63] Replaced, in substance, by Article 300, paragraph 4 of the TFEU.

Old numbering of the Treaty establishing the European Community	New numbering of the Treaty on the Functioning of the European Union
Chapter 4 – The Committee of the Regions	Section 2 – The Committee of the Regions
Article 263, first and fifth paragraphs (repealed)[64]	
Article 263, second to fourth paragraphs	Article 305
Article 264	Article 306
Article 265	Article 307
Chapter 5 – The European Investment Bank	Chapter 4 – The European Investment Bank
Article 266	Article 308
Article 267	Article 309
Title II – Financial provisions	Title II – Financial provisions
Article 268	Article 310
	Chapter 1 – The Union's own resources
Article 269	Article 311
Article 270 (repealed)[65]	
	Chapter 2 – The multiannual financial framework
	Article 312
	Chapter 3 – The Union's annual budget
Article 272, paragraph 1 (moved)	Article 313
Article 271 (moved)	*Article 316*
Article 272, paragraph 1 (moved)	*Article 313*
Article 272, paragraphs 2 to 10	Article 314
Article 273	Article 315
Article 271 (moved)	Article 316
	Chapter 4 – Implementation of the budget and discharge
Article 274	Article 317
Article 275	Article 318

[64] Replaced, in substance, by Article 300, paragraphs 3 and 4, TFEU.
[65] Replaced, in substance, by Article 310, paragraph 4, TFEU.

Old numbering of the Treaty establishing the European Community	New numbering of the Treaty on the Functioning of the European Union
Article 276	Article 319
	Chapter 5 – Common provisions
Article 277	Article 320
Article 278	Article 321
Article 279	Article 322
	Article 323
	Article 324
	Chapter 6 – Combating fraud
Article 280	Article 325
	Title III – Enhanced cooperation
Articles 11 and 11a (replaced)	Article 326[66]
Articles 11 and 11a (replaced)	Article 327[66]
Articles 11 and 11a (replaced)	Article 328[66]
Articles 11 and 11a (replaced)	Article 329[66]
Articles 11 and 11a (replaced)	Article 330[66]
Articles 11 and 11a (replaced)	Article 331[66]
Articles 11 and 11a (replaced)	Article 332[66]
Articles 11 and 11a (replaced)	Article 333[66]
Articles 11 and 11a (replaced)	Article 334[66]
PART SIX – GENERAL AND FINAL PROVISIONS	PART SEVEN – GENERAL AND FINAL PROVISIONS
Article 281 (repealed)[67]	
Article 282	Article 335
Article 283	Article 336
Article 284	Article 337
Article 285	Article 338
Article 286 (replaced)	*Article 16*
Article 287	Article 339

[66]   Also replaces the current Articles 27a to 27e, 40 to 40b, and 43 to 45 TEU.
[67]   Replaced, in substance, by Article 47 TEU.

Old numbering of the Treaty establishing the European Community	New numbering of the Treaty on the Functioning of the European Union
Article 288	Article 340
Article 289	Article 341
Article 290	Article 342
Article 291	Article 343
Article 292	Article 344
Article 293 (repealed)	
Article 294 (moved)	*Article 55*
Article 295	Article 345
Article 296	Article 346
Article 297	Article 347
Article 298	Article 348
Article 299, paragraph 1 (repealed)[68]	
Article 299, paragraph 2, second, third and fourth subparagraphs	Article 349
Article 299, paragraph 2, first subparagraph, and paragraphs 3 to 6 (moved)	Article 355
Article 300 (replaced)	Article 218
Article 301 (replaced)	Article 215
Article 302 (replaced)	Article 220
Article 303 (replaced)	Article 220
Article 304 (replaced)	Article 220
Article 305 (repealed)	
Article 306	Article 350
Article 307	Article 351
Article 308	Article 352
	Article 353
Article 309	Article 354
Article 310 (moved)	Article 217

---

[68]   Replaced, in substance by Article 52 TEU.

Old numbering of the Treaty establishing the European Community	New numbering of the Treaty on the Functioning of the European Union
Article 311 (repealed)[69]	
Article 299, paragraph 2, first subparagraph, and paragraphs 3 to 6 (moved)	Article 355
Article 312	Article 356
Final Provisions	
Article 313	Article 357
	Article 358
Article 314 (repealed)[70]	

---

[69]   Replaced, in substance by Article 51 TEU.
[70]   Replaced, in substance by Article 55 TEU.

INDEX

Intersentia

IUS COMMUNITATIS SERIES

Published titles within the series:

1. Stefan Grundmann, *European Company Law. Organization, Finance and Capital Markets*, Antwerp-Oxford, Intersentia, 2007
   ISBN 978-90-5095-641-3

2. André Klip, *European Criminal Law. An Integrative Approach*, Antwerp-Oxford-Portland, Intersentia, 2009
   ISBN 978-90-5095-772-4